"Crowley has been maligned as a black magician, whereas Magick is neither white nor black, good nor bad - it is simply alive with what it is: the real thing, what people really feel and want and are. I pointed out that this 'either/or' straitjacket had been imposed by Christianity when all Magick became black Magick; that scientists took over from the Church, and Western man has been stifled in a non-magical universe known as the way things are. Rock music can be seen as one attempt to break out of this dead soulless universe and reassert the universe of Magick."

Jimmy Page

"That religion they call Christianity; the devil they honour they call God. I accept these definitions, as a poet must do, if he is to be at all intelligible to his age, and it is their God and their religion that I hate and will destroy.

Aleister Crowley, "The World's Tragedy"

"For this purpose the Son of God was manifested, that He might destroy the works of the Devil."

The Holy Bible, 1 John 3:8b, NKJV

"To sin by silence when we should protest makes cowards out of men."

Ella Wheeler Wilcox

FALLEN ANGEL:
THE UNTOLD STORY OF JIMMY PAGE AND LED ZEPPELIN

Published by Gabriel Publications, Inc.
P.O.Box 5403, Titusville, Florida, 32783

ISBN Number: 0-9714072-0-7

Library of Congress Control Number: 2002111742

Printed in the United States of America

PHOTO CREDITS FOR FALLEN ANGEL

©1981 Kenneth Anger: pp.195b, 196b
©Atlantic Records: pp.25t, 198, 408b

Aleister Crowley: pp.xiit, 24br&bl, 98, 122, 196tr, 196tl, 197t, 202, 276, 355, 358, 407b (public domain)

©1977 Jim Crowley: pp.307t, 458b (used with written permission)

©2000 Thomas Hild: pg.318 (used with written permission)

©Steve A. Jones: pp.25b, 28b, 51, 56b, 155b, 248b, 312t&b, 453, 493b, 494, 613b, 630b (used with written permission)

Eliphas Levi: pg.70 (public domain)

©1975-2002 Frank Melfi - The Looking Glass: pp.iii, 306t, 308b, 358, 362b, 498 (used with written permission)

©1977 Linda Nadolski: pp. 155t, 244b, 306b, 307b, 308tl, 309b, 407t, 538t, 569 (used with written permission)

©1975-2002 Bruce C. Remer www.E-Rockworld.com: pp. xiibl, xiim, 25m, 56t, 158, 248t, 296, 315, 538b, 613t (used with written permission)

Lews Spence: pp.244t, 277 - W.A. Mansell & Co.: pp.242t, 243t (public domain)

©1976 Swan Song: pp.95, 242b, 298, 305t, 311t, 362t, 408t, 408m, 414t, 458t, 532t, 630t

©1977 John Vogel: pp.viit&b, xiit&br, 23, 26, 68, 69, 94, 120, 195tr, 195tl, 197b, 305b, 308tr, 309t, 310t, 310b, 311br, 311bl, 356, 414b, 454, 493t, 532br, 532bl, 533, 534, 570, 572 (used with written permission)

©2001 Roger Waite: pp.243b, 313tl, 313tr, 314 (used with written permission)

© 2001 Duncan Watson: pp.304, 313bl, 313br (used with written permission)

From *Witchcraft, Magic & Alchemy*: La Poule noire (1820), pg.28t, Bibliotheque Nationale, manuscript fonds francais, (No.7619, p. 126.), pg.67, Goya. Fresco in the Prado Museum, Madrid. pg.96t, Guaccius, Compendium maleficarum, pg.96b (public domain)

FALLEN ANGEL

THE UNTOLD STORY OF JIMMY PAGE AND LED ZEPPELIN

TABLE OF CONTENTS

PART III
THE MAGICAL RITUAL OF THE SILVER STAR

PART IV
WARFARE BETWEEN CHRIST AND SATAN

Dover, New Jersey, as viewed from its Magick, Rock and Roll "Mountain."

Jimmy Page plays his Gibson Les Paul in his red dragon suit on March 27th, 1975 at the Los Angeles Forum. The show was introduced by the late Linda Lovelace. It was all there during the intro, "sex, drugs, and rock and roll." Notice that he has his Magick Rune painted on the speaker behind him.

"Tom Friend's still alive?!!...This guy used to know every note to every Led Zeppelin song ever played."
Brian Touhey

"He still does."
Brian Durr

"I still do...Are you kidding?"
Tom Friend

"I thought I was watching Jimmy Page."
Brian Touhey, October, 1989, Dover, New Jersey

HOUSES OF THE HOLY:
THE CALL OF LED ZEPPELIN'S MUSIC

If there are secrets that need to be shared, they are the secrets revealed in this book. I had been a rock and roll fan since I first heard Elvis Presley's records as a child. From Elvis to Elton John and then Led Zeppelin, was the progression.

Led Zeppelin's fourth album was the first album I purchased of theirs. I became obsessed with it, especially when stoned. *Physical Graffiti* was a close second. After I saw Led Zeppelin in concert, the soundtrack from their film, *The Song Remains the Same*, became my bible. Led Zeppelin's music for me was not something I listened to for entertainment value, it dictated a specific way of life. Sex, drugs, and rock and roll became my religion; the most important thing in my life. My "overlords" in this religion were the four members of Led Zeppelin, specifically, Jimmy Page. If there was ever one person I wanted to be, it was he. Strangely enough, every time I began to study the guitar, I immediately, inside of a week, would lose interest. It was not the discipline of practice that bothered me. I had already played an instrument in a school band. I sat in the horn section, with Greg Tuttle and his trumpet to my left, and Ed Twilley and his saxophone to my right. I remember playing "Battle Hymn of the Republic" solo in front of my whole school. Ironically enough, that occurred the same month that Led Zeppelin played "Stairway to Heaven" in concert for the first time, in the spring of 1971. The reason I would quit practicing on my electric guitar was because I would just lose interest. I think someone planned it that way.

     Sex, drugs, and rock and roll was the religion of a large portion of my high school and secular college classmates. Anyone who went to church and practiced Christianity was a mentally ill, religious fanatic, as they were commonly called. Who needed Christ anyway? We had the Beatles, The Rolling Stones and "Street Fighting Man," The Who, Black Sabbath, Grand Funk, David Bowie, Aerosmith, Led Zeppelin, Bad Company, The Doors, Ted Nugent, KISS, Electric Light Orchestra, Yes, Kansas, The Eagles, Styx, Elton John and his "Saturday Night's Alright for Fighting," etc., to tell us how to live. It took longer to walk to the liquor store than it did to get drugs from someone, especially if you were dealing yourself. In my home town there was and is Marijuana, Cocaine, LSD, Mescaline, Speed, Quaaludes, and Heroin everywhere. Needless to say, with somebody being foolish enough to pass a law allowing eighteen year old high school kids to buy alcohol, multitudes of fifteen year old tenth graders like myself used to skip school and drink all day in some dive bar. "You boys eighteen? Oh, yes Sir! OK. Just checking." Asking for no identification was the green light we needed. Getting stoned, drunk, and listening to one's favorite music left us "feeling no pain." There were no moral restraints to burden us; only the desire to live out the music. My church building was Madison Square Garden.

     I glorified rock and roll there at the Bad Company concert in 1979 by carrying a bed sheet around the Garden between bands. The bed sheet had two words on it painted in 3-foot tall black letters. The first word was DISCO. The second was not a word that made me an advocate. Thousands of people gave us an ovation. I remember distinctly seeing a couple of sisters from my hometown of Mine Hill laughing hysterically as I walked right by them. One of them turned to the other, and while trying to talk and laugh at the same time, she said, "That's Tom Friend!" Then they really roared. I'm sure they were real shocked to see me doing that. I didn't even know the name of the girl who owned the bed sheet, who was carrying the front end of it. It belonged to her, and I was sitting next to her and her three girlfriends in the five-seat row we were in. I had purchased the seat from a scalper an hour earlier. The girl asked me to roll up as many joints as I could out of an ounce of Marijuana before the warm up band came on. Not having to twist my arm, I obliged. I rolled up about a dozen joints for her and she rewarded me with a half pint of Jack Daniels out of her purse. Needless to say, I was in a "transcendent" frame of mind when she asked me to carry the sheet around the Garden after the warm up band went off. When I saw it I roared with laughter and said, "Let's go!" I can still remember Paul Rodgers wearing dark sunglasses during the show, as well as the drummer's green drumsticks during his solo. I was simply walking down Route 46 in Mine Hill on my way to Dover to drink myself into a stupor, when one of my party animal friends and his girlfriend picked me up hitchhiking and asked me if I wanted to go to New York to the concert. All I had to hear was "New York" and I was on my way. I went and bought me a ticket for thirty bucks off a scalper and sat in the first mezzanine two or three sections out from the stage.

PHYSICAL GRAFFITI – "HOUSES OF THE HOLY"

The story of this book comes about as a result of one of my countless trips into Manhattan. This trip was for the purpose of seeing Led Zeppelin in concert. Something occurred at that show while stoned out of my mind and in one of Jimmy Page's "Theremin" trances during the song "No Quarter." It was the "call" of their "music" when one is "dizzy" while "stoned," mentioned between 1:56 and 2:07 into the song "Houses of the Holy;" from the album, *Physical Graffiti*. I immediately dismissed it out of my mind once it was over because I felt I was either too stoned or I was losing it. However, events and circumstances that followed convinced me that there was more to it than that. I could have titled this book, "The Devil's Pact with Led Zeppelin." More drugs, more music, and things kept coming together. As Robert Plant, the singer for Led Zeppelin, has said: "I think that any group, except straight groups, can hit you differently when you're stoned. You can listen to a group when you're straight and it feels one way, and you can listen to it stoned and it just becomes more intense. You're just able to pick out more of what the group is trying to show you."1 What that means is, being stoned makes the mind more susceptible to hypnosis, and hypnosis causes the mind to be increasingly vulnerable to the power of suggestion. The messages are intensified when hypnotized. Led Zeppelin's music is a complex series of swinging pendulums. It is electronic hypnosis. There is someone with a message behind the music. To sum it up, listening to Led Zeppelin convinced me that there is a battle being waged for the souls of men, between God and the Devil, here on the earth. If that sounds outrageous to you, take up the challenge to read this book with an open mind. The entire story will be explained to you. Led Zeppelin are not the Devil's only messengers, but they are about the most powerful; because of the talent and subtlety.

1 Ritchie Yorke, *Led Zeppelin - The Definitive Biography*, Underwood-Miller, 1993, Pg.102

Led Zeppelin played "Nobody's Fault But Mine" on one tour only in the U.S., back in 1977, as I saw at MSG with Page in white, on Les Paul guitar. In '99-2000, Jimmy Page played it while touring the United States with the Black Crowes. As I watched the videos of Page/Black Crowes in Los Angeles, Chris Robinson sang (just like Robert Plant) that it was Satan who taught him to rock and roll; not trying to disguise it in concert like Robert Plant did with Led Zeppelin.

"Since, therefore, it was my business to explore the spiritual world, my first step must be to get into personal communication with the devil."1
"The Confessions of Aliester Crowley"

"The Devil - he taught me to roll."
Robert Plant, *"Nobody's Fault But Mine"*

NOBODY'S FAULT BUT MINE:
SATAN TAUGHT THEM TO ROCK AND ROLL

To begin with, the reader should understand that in my opinion, accusing the four members of Led Zeppelin, John Bonham, John Paul Jones, Jimmy Page, and Robert Plant of being involved with the Devil is synonymous with accusing Babe Ruth, Lou Gehrig, Joe Dimaggio, and Mickey Mantle of being involved with the New York Yankees and major league baseball. Comparison with those Yankee greats is fitting because they are without a doubt the most powerful personalities to ever wear a Yankee or any major league uniform. There are others like Willie Mays and Hank Aaron, but the four Yankees are not only the most historical personalities of the game, they are also from the same team (though they did not all play together).

The primary reason for writing this book is to enlighten the rock world, mainly the fans, as to what these men were really doing, and what Jimmy Page and Robert Plant are still up to as you read this book. Remember, Led Zeppelin is still alive on tape and compact disc. Part of the enlightenment of course is for parents of teens who are buying music for their children to understand what exactly is taking place when their kids listen to Led Zeppelin. Perhaps the parents themselves are Led Zeppelin fans. As Jimmy Page said in an interview with a CNN Entertainment news reporter after a Page/Plant concert in 1995: "It's imperative, because that's the thing that will keep you going. You can touch an age group from here to here (he raises his right hand above his head and his left hand below his waist), six to sixty, seven to seventy, I think that's where it's at really."

This author has no real desire to attack Led Zeppelin or their music, as much as attack the work of the Devil himself. That's what this is all about. The scope of the "touching" that Page refers to covered England, America, Europe, and the far east between the years of 1968, when they played in the United States for the first time in Denver, and 1980, when they played their last show as a band in Berlin on the 7th of July. For all practical purposes, Led Zeppelin was resurrected in 1993, when Page and Plant decided to reunite. I went to a Page/Plant concert to observe in 1995. Musically, the show was so good and Page played so well I was utterly astonished. There really is no comparison between what they did in the *No Quarter* video and what they did in concert. Just as I suspected, Page did his Theremin act again during "Shake My Tree," which is off the *Coverdale/Page* album. Jimmy Page ought to know that this book is being written as a result of his Theremin act, in conjunction with the violin bow routine. The Theremin is a machine that produces eerie, demonic sounds by waving the hand in front of its antenna. What that all means to the reader will be explained in detail later in the book. I remember the guy in front of me, who kept allowing me to borrow his binoculars saying, "This is Led Zeppelin!" As far as I was concerned, he was right. Gary Graff of the Detroit Free Press wrote about a Page/Plant concert in Auburn Hills, Michigan, a few weeks later on March 31st, 1995: "This definitely qualifies as the big news rock 'n' roll event of the year so far. They're billing it as Page and Plant but any of the more than 20,000 who packed the Palace on Friday night knew what it really was - Led Zeppelin." The guy in Orlando on March 7th did not know why they were not calling themselves that, and I heard one disappointed fan after the show say she wanted to hear "Stairway to Heaven" and couldn't understand why they hadn't played it. Little did these people know that the person standing in their midst knew the reasons for both. They will be explained in this book.

Led Zeppelin's motive for making music and touring the world is not merely to entertain stoned out kids at rock concerts. Their motivating drive is to spread subtle invitations to the worship of the Devil and the "Law of Thelema." The Law of Thelema is the name given to the broad spectrum of teachings put forth by a Satanic/Magical cult in England that goes by the name of the *Argenteum Astrum*, which means *Silver Star*; that was founded by Aleister Crowley. When you come across the abbreviation "A.A." in this book, it means Silver Star. This cult has a post office box in New York City.

The underlying motive that is associated with and the flipside of the Law of Thelema is the absolute destruction of the Christian faith. This you will see in Led Zeppelin's music; explained in this book. The cult's "Logos of the Aeon," or foundational teacher, Aleister Crowley, advocates the literal murder of Christian people in his book entitled, *The Law is for All*. This was not a man who believed in religious freedom. He worshiped the Devil and believed that Christianity and its advocates belong dead. One of his favorite statements was "Christians to the lions." You will read of Jimmy Page using that statement in this book.

PRESENCE – "NOBODY'S FAULT BUT MINE"

I believe that Led Zeppelin received the best of their music right from the Devil himself and will show you substantial evidence to back that assertion. The reason they got their music from the Devil is, I believe, that they sold their souls to him. Their confession of that fact is in this book. One mild confession is presented in the song, "Nobody's Fault But Mine;" off the *Presence* album. Robert Plant quickly sings that the one and only "Devil" was the one who "taught" him he could "roll," and he sings it twice, back to back, between 2:02 and 2:08 into the song. You will also read from the *Holy Bible* that Lucifer was created with the power to make music. He is presented as the "Piper" in the *Bible*. You will read tacit confessions from Page and Plant that they did not get either the bulk of their lyrics or music from any other source.

It will be shown vividly why the Devil would want to give them music, how he gave it to them, and what effects he has been able to have on its listeners. Even those who believe that only Jimmy Page has had an "interest" in the occult, believe that is his problem and not theirs; even though they listen to Led Zeppelin. They do not believe that the power of the Devil is efficacious in their lives through Led Zeppelin's music. Well, that theory is going to be blown right out of the water in this book. Rest assured, anyone who reads this book with a mind open to the facts will understand exactly what the Devil is doing through his plenipotentiaries, or authorized representatives, Led Zeppelin. Ironically, enough, though the evidence points to the members of Led Zeppelin having sold their souls to Satan, and received his music in the process, they are using the music to serve him. They believe he is god. That will be shown in detail in this book. As Aleister Crowley once put it: "...the devil, having bought the soul, regains the price, for the sorcerer spends it in the devil's service."2

An important point that needs to be understood before reading this book is that Aleister Crowley and Led Zeppelin do not believe the Devil exists, that is, in his Biblical context. The Biblical representation of the Devil is one of an angelic being who was cast down from heaven by the power of the Lord Jesus Christ for an attempted act of sedition. He tried to destroy the Godhead with a third of the angels in order that he might rule as God himself. Crowley and Page do not accept this as truth. They believe that Lucifer is God. He is referred to as "Lord God the Devil" by Crowley in his book, *The Magical Record of the*

Beast. The reason he is referred to as the Devil by Crowley and Page is because of confusion caused by the contrast of God and Devil. Crowley wants the Christian world to know that the being they believe is the Devil, a fallen angel, is none other than almighty God himself. This is the same old lie the Devil has been telling since the beginning of mankind, and Crowley and Page and multitudes of others have bought it, and why? Because the Devil is the Lord of the moral code they have chosen. The fact that he has free reign over the earth is another reason for that. You will be shown from the *Bible* where he claims he was given reign over the earth. That is true, but he can only do what God has authorized him to do. Obviously, it is because of man's rebellion against God.

The reader is going to embark on an incredible journey into the world of Magick and the occult and learn how to discern what exactly is going on in the music of Led Zeppelin. There is no danger to you, unless your morals are so depraved that you will become a satanist as a result of the revelations of this book. It is not suggested either that the readers of this book become students of the occult. If you do that, you will find yourself caught up in something more powerful than you can possibly imagine. Satan can deceive you easily. Trust me.

It is crucial to understand that the best and only way to obtain complete comprehension of the message of this book is to begin with chapter one and proceed from chapter to chapter in chronological order. Each chapter will build on the previous one. The reader will be taught how to be able to understand the chapters on "The Song Remains the Same," "Dazed and Confused," and "Stairway to Heaven." If you jump around, you may eventually understand my message, but it is going to take longer and you are likely to get confused, wondering what in the world is being written about. Just begin with chapter one and allow them to build on one another; preparing you to understand the most important elements of this book.

The only way to try a case is to have the evidence in hand. If you can gain access to Led Zeppelin's albums or 1990 4-compact disc set, and the video *The Song Remains the Same*, which is sold in video stores, you will have all the materials you need to see the evidence of this book first hand. Walmart sells the DVD for under $15. If you can obtain access to it, it will be helpful. If you have all the albums, there is no need for the 1990 re-master set. If you do not have any music, trust me when I say that those with it will be talking about the truth of this book. James Patrick Page knows the battle will be won or lost in the mind. That's exactly what I believe Robert Plant means in "Misty Mountain Hop" at 2:30 into the song; it is off Led Zeppelin's fourth album.

In bringing the book to a close, I will show the reader how I searched for truth after being a hardcore Led Zeppelin fan, or should I say disciple? I will explain in detail my conclusions and what I did about them. A word of warning, this book is not for cowards, or those with a weak mind. It will take a strong will to finish reading this book. Are you ready for a fight? If so, let the battle begin.

1 Aleister Crowley, *The Confessions of Aleister Crowley*, edited by John Symonds and Kenneth Grant, Penguin Arkana, 1989, pg.126

2 Aleister Crowley, *Moonchild*, Samuel Weiser Inc., Yorke Beach, Maine, 1994, pg.248

Jimmy Page as he appeared playing "Nobody's Fault But Mine" on the '77 tour.

Aleister "The Beast 666" Crowley at age 37. This is perhaps the most famous photo of him. The Beatles put it on the front of their *Sgt. Pepper's Lonely Hearts Club Band* album, because, as Ringo Starr put it, he was somebody they liked. He has been called the most dangerous satanist ever. For a man of only 37, he sure did age quickly. Anyone who lives the life that he did will age pretty quick as well. Many a Crowley loving rock star has gone to an early grave; while his sinister, diabolical, Satan inspired "Book of the Law" promised that drugs and alcohol would do them no harm. That subject will be elaborated on in the seventh chapter, when we look at the doctrines presented in the evil book.

John Paul Jones on bass, Jimmy Page on doubleneck guitar in dragon suit (1977), Robert Plant on vocals, and John Henry Bonham on drums, are the Four Sticks,

middle fagots of the Silver Star, who successfully bridged the gap between the teachings of Crowley in the *Equniox* and the masses of fans who would listen to their music; not unlike sixteen year old Tom Friend to the left, sitting in a "transcendent" frame of mind, one week before seeing Led Zeppelin in concert on June 11th, 1977, in New York at Madison Square Garden. As you might guess, I was sitting there listening to none other than Led Zeppelin, preparing my mind for communion with my rock god.

CHAPTER ONE

"Plenty of other heavy metal rock bands had surfaced, but none could match Led Zeppelin's glamorous mystique, its style, its 'duende.' Best of all, Led Zeppelin was still a secret society. Its popularity wasn't just confined to the world of rock, but to a despised segment of the rock audience - young, mostly male, mostly working class, cannon-fodder youth who identified with Led Zeppelin in a mytho-poeic fashion beyond the music itself. Led Zeppelin was a mystery cult with several million initiates. In the high school parking lots of every suburban American town in the 1970's, Led Zeppelin ruled, high priests of Album Oriented Radio."[1]

Steven Davis, "Hammer of the Gods"

"In our country there was hot rumor for years that the rock band Led Zeppelin attained success through an agreement with the powers of darkness. And it is a fact that guitarist Jimmy Page is openly a student of the magician Aleister Crowley."[2]

S. Jason Black and Christopher S. Hyatt, "Pacts with the Devil"

"'Magick is very important if people can go through it. I think Crowley's completely relevant to today.'"[3]

Jimmy Page, "Tangents Within A Framework"

"...the skill, experience, and intensity of the Sworn Sons and Daughters of Satan are desirable to the soul beyond any plastic excitants of passion..."[4]

Black Magician Aleister Crowley, "The Magical Record of the Beast"

"Let my servants be few & secret: they shall rule the many & the known."[5]

Satan, Aleister Crowley's "The Book of the Law"

FOUR STICKS - NO QUARTER - ROCK AND ROLL: MIDDLE FAGOTS OF THE SILVER STAR

Led Zeppelin has been hailed by many as the most powerful and influential rock band in the history of rock and roll. No individual familiar with the rock culture will debate the popularity of their signet tune, "Stairway to Heaven."

Year after year it is voted the most popular song in the history of rock, yet few people understand what the song is really about. Herein, you will learn the true interpretation of its lyrical content, and will come to appreciate just how aptly it is titled. But our analysis is not confined to this song alone. Rather, the body of music created over decades by these artists will be presented and analyzed in the context of the hope of the Thelemic Satanist of the Silver Star; the Satanic Magical Order founded by none other than Aleister Crowley himself. This analysis will prove conclusively that Led Zeppelin has developed and knowingly employed a systematic pattern of overt and subliminal suggestion, occult incantations and other forms of Magick for the express purpose of calling fans to worship the band first, then ultimately their master, the "Most High"…Satan himself.

Crowley is known by many as the most dangerous satanist to ever live. This book will present compelling evidence that Crowley was a medium by which the Devil has been able to provide occult teaching to Jimmy Page, Led Zeppelin's founder and producer of music. Crowley was Page's mentor in Magick, and Page in turn, was the mentor for the rest of the band.

The *Holy Bible* presents the Devil, Lucifer, as the celestial composer of music, described as the "Piper." Over the course of this work, we will also explore the apparently close, personal relationship that exists between the Piper and Jimmy Page, as well as the impact that relationship has and can have on those who listen to the music of Led Zeppelin, Robert Plant and Jimmy Page. This influence is still taking place through their records, tapes, and compact disks; as well as through the new modified form of Led Zeppelin in concert, "Page/Plant." With a new drummer and bass player, Jimmy Page and Robert Plant resurrected the past power and presence of Led Zeppelin in concert; as seen on the many 1995 and 1998 videos. When one considers the absence of John Bonham and John Paul Jones from the set, along with the advancing years of Page and Plant, the ability to generate such continuing intensity seems almost miraculous. And so it is, but not for some of the reasons one might expect.

Led Zeppelin was alive and well in 1998, reincarnated and continuing its work through Page/Plant. It was alive in 1999–2000 as well, as Jimmy Page toured with the Black Crowes, playing Led Zeppelin tunes not performed by Page/Plant. When performing "Nobody's Fault But Mine", Chris Robinson of the Black Crowes sang the lyrics just like the original Led Zeppelin version, that it was the "Devil" who "taught" him how to rock and "roll." This can be heard on the Page/Crowes album, "Live at the Greek". All of the Page/Plant and Page/ Crowes concerts are on one or more forms of media available to anyone who searches for them. Most of them are available on VHS video and compact disc, through trading groups on the internet. Further, after all of the band members are dead, the power and the message of their music will still be alive on the stereos and airwaves throughout the world. The music, some of the most beautiful, surreal, and stimulating music ever produced, is the medium. The author asserts that Satan and the teachings of the Silver Star, through the writings of Aleister Crowley, are the architects of both the music and the message; a false evangelistic gospel designed to lure unsuspecting fans into worship at the altar of self, enroute to darker things. Sometimes, this message is presented in such a subtle fashion. At others, it is so blatant that those who don't want to believe the satanic motives of the band can easily dismiss it as "showmanship" or "gimmickry." Nothing could be further from the truth. Herein, you will come to understand that Led Zeppelin as an entity is comprised of four of the most dangerous Devil worshipers to ever walk the earth. The entity still exists in media form.

One thing must be made clear from the start; this book has not been written as an attempt to get you to stop listening to Led Zeppelin! By all means listen, and listen well. Listen closely to every word and begin to see the larger picture. Indeed, a portion of the focus of this book is to take you outside the context of your favorite songs to see how each of them fit within the context of the entire gospel being preached. And those of you who have an innate aversion to "religion" might be surprised to learn how masterfully you have already been evangelized and manipulated by this music, particularly if you have also attended one of more of either band's live performances. In concert, the costuming and other visual images support the message being played, and ritualistic black magic was practiced on the audience from the sanctity of the band's unique alter, the concert stage.

Led Zeppelin, was originally made up of four band members: John Bonham, John Paul Jones, Jimmy Page and Robert Plant. These four members and their music are also known as the "Four Sticks." Led Zeppelin fans will recognize that as the title of a song off the fourth album. If you have the album, you may want to get it so that you can refer to it as we continue to present material. If not, there is a picture of it at the end of this chapter. Look at the man on the cover with all those middle size "fagots" or sticks on his back. We are going to take a good look at the meaning of this picture. To understand that meaning, and how it and other pieces of the puzzle fit together, we must first become acquainted with Aleister Crowley and the Silver Star.

MEET THE BEAST

Aleister Crowley was raised in England by his Christian father, who taught him to love God. When Crowley was eleven years old, his father died. From this point Crowley's life seemed to have been taken over by bitterness against God. He went on to college and wanted to be a writer. His moral code became increasingly anti-Christian, and it found expression in his writings and his deeds. While still in college, Crowley dedicated himself to the practice of black magic and the worship of Satan. During these early days of discipleship, he wrote a book called *White Stains*. To grasp a bit of his mindset during this period, consider the following brief excerpt:

"...Fresh from the crucifying Christ;
        It seemed her thighs were hot with blood
Sucked from the bastard Son of God.
        I saw his broken body hang
Sweating and bleeding on the cross;
        I heard his curses champ and clang;
I spat upon his reeking corpse;
        I licked the spear; my feet were shod
With iron as I kicked my God

Such frightful fancies dim my eyes-
        I can remember how his side
Lay open for a lover's prize-
        I violate the Crucified!
Hell shrieks with impious laugh;
        they sing A mad lewd chant;
Hell hails me king!"6

        Subsequent to his father's death, Crowley liked to refer to himself as "the Beast 666." His mother, whom he despised, did nothing to discourage the moniker. In fact, if anything, it seems that she used it to refer to him as well. So much for a mother's love. Soon thereafter, Crowley met Cecil Jones, who introduced him to a magical order called *The Hermetic Order of the Golden Dawn*. After much internal strife, the order fell apart. Crowley then founded his Satanic/Magical cult, *The Argenteum Astrum,* which means *Silver Star.* Crowley matured to become as hardcore a satanist as any man that ever walked the earth, and his teachings continue to influence new generations. In *Satanism - The Seduction of America's Youth*, Bob Larson wrote: "Crowley believed quite literally that he was the Beast of Revelation and declared open revolt against God. His writings, such as *Confessions* and *Magic in Theory and Practice*, stated his mission in life was to destroy Christianity and build the religion of Thelema (ritual magic based on the Greek word for will) in its place."7
        To build a religion to counter Christianity, Crowley knew that he must create new disciples of his teaching. But first he needed to establish a standard

for discipleship. To do so, Crowley presented a parable about Magick and then gave its meaning. The parable was written to illustrate to the members of the Silver Star the type of disciples needed to spread the Law of Thelema. Before reading it you have to understand who the *Sun-Father* is according to Crowley. In *Magick-Book 4 * Liber Aba*, Crowley calls Satan the Sun-Father: "...Satan, the Old Serpent, in the Abyss, the Lake of Fire and Sulphur, is the Sun-Father, the vibration of Life, Lord of Infinite Space that flames with his consuming Energy."[8] Crowley continues by establishing the connection between the Sun-Father/Devil, calling him Lord, and the "word" of "Thelema": "...our Lord the Devil's their word, the word Thelema, spoken of me the Beast..."[9] The "word" or "law" of Thelema is the antithesis of the "word" of the God of Christianity; Lord Jesus Christ, who is the only true God and the one Crowley swore to oppose just as his master has throughout history. In this parable, Crowley refers to Satan not only as Sun-Father, but also with the blasphemous title of *Most High*, which is also the title of the hit song off the 1998 Jimmy Page/Robert Plant album, *Walking Into Clarksdale*. In the lyrics of this song, Page/Plant openly mock Christ, saying he has a "paper crown." This shouldn't be surprising if one realizes that Jimmy Page is a professed disciple of Crowley, in word and deed. Before moving forward in the presentation of that case, however, a quick summary of the key words and concepts from the parable of the Silver Star middle fagots is in order. The terms *Sun-Father* and *Most High* are synonymous with Satan. *Thelema* is the law that governs the creation of disciples and also the conduct of worship they must practice to remain true disciples of their Lord Satan. Now we must examine the role that "the middle fagots" play in the execution of Thelema, and also discover why the original members of Led Zeppelin believed themselves to be an incarnation of those fagots; in the following parable by Crowley.

FOUR STICKS - THE SILVER STAR MIDDLE FAGOTS

"Now, son, note, pray thee, in what house We write these words. For it is a little cottage of red and green, by the western side of a great lake, and it is hidden in the woods. Man, therefore, is at odds with Wood and Water; and being a magician bethinketh Himself to take one of these enemies, Wood, which is both the effect and the cause of that excess of Water, and compel it to fight for Him against the other. What then maketh He? Why, He taketh unto himself Iron of Mars, an Axe and a Saw and a Wedge and a knife, and He divideth Wood therewith against himself, hewing him into many small pieces, so that he hath no longer any strength against His will. Good; then taketh he the Fire of our Father the Sun, and setteth it directly in battle array against that Water by His army of Wood that he hath conquered and drilled, building it up into a phalanx like unto a cone, that is the noblest of all solid figures, being the Image of the Holy Phallus Itself, and combineth in himself the Right line and the Circle. Thus, son, dealeth he; and the Fire kindleth the Wood, and the heat thereof driveth the Water afar off. Yet this Water is a cunning adversary, and He strengtheneth Wood against Fire by impregnating him with much of his own substance, as it were by spies in the citadel of an ally that is not wholly trusted. Now then therefore what must the Magician do? He must first expel utterly Water from Wood by an invocation of the Fire of the Sun our Father. That is to say, without the inspiration of the Most High and Holy One even We ourselves could do nothing at all. Then, son, beginneth the Magician to set His Fire to the little dry Wood, and that enkindleth the Wood of middle size, and when that blazeth brightly, at the last the great logs, though they be utterly green, are nevertheless enkindled.

"Now, son, hearken unto this Our reproof, and lend the ear of thine understanding unto the parable of this Magick.

"We have for the whole Beginning of Our Work, praise be eternally unto His Holy Name, the Fire of our Father the Sun. The inspiration is ours, and ours is the Law of Thelema that shall set the world ablaze. And We have many small dry sticks, that kindle quickly and burn through quickly, leaving the larger Wood unlit. And the great logs, the masses of humanity, are always with us. But our edgede need is of those middle fagots that on the one hand are readily kindled by the small Wood, and on the other endure until the great logs blaze."10

The assertion put forth herein is that Led Zeppelin sought to be mediums between the Silver Star and the great masses of humanity that listen to the album. The icons used on the cover of their fourth album graphically support this contention, and it would be difficult to argue convincingly that the imagery was coincidental, particularly as one learns more of the evidence contained herein. The inescapable conclusion at the end of this journey is that Led Zeppelin and Page/Plant actively evangelize their fans to follow Satan and systematically use their music as the "kindling" to set the world ablaze for their "god." The promise they make to the fans is that those who follow in Jimmy Page's footsteps and becomes a student of Crowley will receive blessing and fulfillment from the "Most High." To understand how the original members of the band came to believe this about themselves prior to professing it as gospel to others, one must know a bit about their roots.

John Henry Bonham, Led Zeppelin's drummer, was born at Reditch, Worcestershire, in England on May 31, 1948. Bonham was the son of a carpenter. He learned carpentry skills as a child and went to work with his father at age sixteen. During this time, he plied his trade during the day and followed his passion by playing drums at night. The first band that John *"Bonzo"* Bonham played in was "Terry Webb and the Spiders." Shortly thereafter, at seventeen, Bonzo played with a band called "A Way of Life." It was then that he met and married Pat Phillips.

The Bonhams were so poor that they had to abandon cigarette smoking to scrape enough together for the trailer rent month to month. Looking for a more lucrative gig than seemed to be forthcoming with his current band, Bonzo soon hooked up with Robert Plant. Plant lived nearby and was singing for a band called "The Crawling King Snakes," who happened to need a drummer at the time. During these early days, Bonham was primarily influenced by the drumming styles of Keith Moon and Ginger Baker. Moon was with "The Who" and Baker was with "Cream," Eric Clapton's legendary band. Unfortunately, The Crawling Kingsnakes weren't fairing much better than his other bands, so Bonzo went back to playing for "A Way of Life" for a brief period. Things began to improve when Bonham joined the "Band of Joy," which featured Robert Plant on vocals. Bonzo continued drumming for this ensemble until that band's demise in 1968.

From there Bonzo played for "Tim Rose," the last band he would be in before joining Led Zeppelin. Making that transition took a little arm twisting, mainly because "Tim Rose" was paying Bonham more money than he had ever earned playing drums, but Plant and Page and Peter Grant eventually persuaded him to join what was going to be called "The New Yardbirds." The New Yardbirds became Led Zeppelin. Bonham played the drums for Led Zeppelin for twelve years before he died of an alcohol overdose by choking to death on his own vomit, on September 25, 1980.

John Paul Jones, Led Zeppelin's bass and keyboard player, was born John Baldwin on January 3, 1946 in Sidcup, Kent, in England. Both of Jones' parents were also performers, part of a musical variety act. His father, Joe Baldwin, had also played with the famous Ambrose Orchestra during the big band era. Jones stated that his father started taking him along to gigs playing the piano when Jones was only two years old, but the boy did not initially have the penchant for keyboards that his father possessed. Instead, Jones took up playing bass guitar when he was fourteen years old at Christ College, a boarding school. He joined the "Harris-Meehan band" when he was seventeen and played with them for a while until Jet Harris suffered a nervous breakdown and the band folded.

When Jones left the band he got involved in session work, playing on other people's albums in the studio. Some of this work can be heard on Donovan's "Sunshine Superman" and "Mellow Yellow." He began to play keyboards at eighteen; building on the experience of playing the organ in church years earlier. It was during this period of session work that Jones met James Patrick "Jimmy" Page. Jones also played bass on the Donovan song, "Hurdy Gurdy Man," which concurrently featured Jimmy Page on lead guitar. Jones arranged "She's a Rainbow" for the Rolling Stones, and also worked on several of their songs on the *Their Satanic Majesties Request* album before joining Led Zeppelin. An objective thinker can see that Jones was a believer early on.

Robert Anthony Plant, Led Zeppelin's lead singer, was born on August 20, 1948 in West Bromwich, Staffordshire, near the border of Wales. Plant was the son of an engineer, and his father wanted him to be an accountant. Plant left school at sixteen to begin his training and apprenticeship in accounting. He was paid two pounds a week, but his heart was not in the job. Robert soon forsook his accounting career, virtually before it began, and sang for the "Crawling King Snakes," the "Tennessee Teens," the "Band of Joy," and finally "Hobbstweedle," before Jimmy Page came calling. By this time Plant had married his wife Maureen, whom he has said supported him for a while or he would have starved to death.

During these early days, Plant admits that he spent most of his time thinking about Robert Johnson, the Mississippi blues guitarist who sang about demons following him and Satan coming to collect his soul. Since there remains a continuing influence from Johnson's work, including a direct homage to him ("Walking into Clarksdale") on the most recent Page/Plant album, something of this musician's background needs to be addressed as well.

Johnson was born in Mississippi and moved to Memphis, Tennessee at age thirteen. Legend has it that Johnson sold his soul to the Devil in return for the blues mastery he so obviously possessed. This legend was "legitimized" if you will, in the movie "Crossroads." Robert Plant went to see Johnson's contemporary, Sonny Boy Williamson in Birmingham, England, in 1965, and stole one of Williamson's harmonicas backstage.11 Sonny Boy Williamson had been there the night Robert Johnson was poisoned for allegedly fooling around with the wife of the owner of the juke joint in which he and Sonny Boy were playing the blues. Robert Johnson died on Tuesday, August 16th, 1938. It was a date of some significance to the life of another musican as well.

According to Priscilla Presley, Elvis grew up listening to the blues in Memphis, and therefore was influenced by Robert Johnson. Johnson's song about Satan collecting his soul was heard over the radio in Memphis regularly when Elvis was a teenager. Certain aspects of Presley's life, including the fact that he also died on Tuesday, August 16th, beg the following question: Did Elvis Presley also walk out to the crossroads at midnight on a Saturday to make a deal? Exploring that possibility is a book in and of itself, however. For now, let's return to the connection between Robert Johnson and Robert Plant.

It's only fitting that Plant was dreaming about Robert Johnson in the formative days of Led Zeppelin. The band subsequently glorified Robert Johnson by making his "Traveling Riverside Blues" one of their own songs (currently available on the 1990 re-mastered 4-cd set). More recently, Page/Plant performed Johnson's song, "Crossroads," at the Shepherd's Bush concert in England, on March 25th, 1998. Other artists pay homage to Johnson's heritage as well: Eric Clapton recorded his "Crossroads," and the Rolling Stones recorded his song, "Love In Vain."

James Patrick Page, Led Zeppelin's founder and legendary lead guitarist, was born on January 9, 1944 in Heston, Middlesex, England. He was the only child born to Patricia Elizabeth Gaffikin, and James Page, who was a clerk who became an industrial personnel officer after World War II. Jimmy Page spent most of his formative years in isolation, and he claims that this deeply impacted his personality.

Page claims to have read Aleister Crowley's book, *Magick*, when he was eleven years old. By the time he was fifteen, and also more deeply engrossed in Crowley's teaching, he obtained his first guitar. Page has stated that both Elvis Presley and Chuck Berry had great influence on his desire to play rock and roll; but he was particularly inspired by Elvis' "Baby let's Play House." Another of Page's early idols was James Burton, who played on the majority of Rick Nelson's records. Burton would go on to play for Elvis Presley from 1969 until the day Elvis died.

While still in his teens, Jimmy Page also became friends with Jeff Beck, another famous guitarist who, when he left the Yardbirds, opened the door for Page to play lead guitar for them. Jimmy is said to have been an "adept" or expert on the electric guitar by the year 1960, the same year that this author was born. It was in this year that Page started playing guitar in public performances with different bands. By 1961, Jimmy was playing lead guitar for "Neil Christian and the Crusaders." Upon leaving the Crusaders, he went to art school in Sutton to study painting. It was during the time at Sutton that Page claims was the beginning of his Crowley "aficionado" or discipleship days. In *Led Zeppelin - Will the Song Remain the Same?* published in 1981, Jimmy Page said: "I began being interested in Aleister Crowley in school. But I mean, how can anyone call Crowley an evil man? For a start, he was the only Edwardian to really embrace the 20th Century. It goes without saying that Crowley was grossly misunderstood."12

Page was right, in a deceptive sort of way. Crowley was INDEED misunderstood. He was far more dangerous to society than people could have possibly imagined. As Crowley's disciple, Jimmy Page is just as underestimated. You must remember that Page asked how anyone could picture Crowley as evil. He was in fact projecting a false image for himself as much as he was defending Crowley. Increasingly, Page followed in the footsteps of Crowley whenever possible. As Crowley traveled abroad by himself, so did Jimmy Page. Page would take his guitar and hitchhike through Scandinavia, Europe, and the Far East. He made it to India one time, just like Crowley, and was forced to go home by a fever he caught there.13 But Page's discipleship extended far beyond physical travels, his spiritual journey continues today.

Jimmy Page soon got involved in session work, playing on records for the Who and the Kinks. He became a top session man and was well known for his many contributions to several different rock groups. In 1965, Jimmy played a session with the aforementioned Sonny Boy Williamson. It shouldn't be a surprise to Led Zeppelin fans that Jimmy would jam with Williamson, since he claims to have been weaned on the blues, which would include Robert Johnson. In 1979, Jimmy was on the BBC radio *Echoes Programme*. He said to Stuart Coleman during the show, "My musical tastes are obviously pretty diversified but it always comes back to the blues and really earthy, early rock. There's just no escaping it. It's what we've been weaned on really." Jimmy joined the Yardbirds in 1966, and toured the United States of America in that first summer. This tour began when I turned 6 years old, in August of 1966. As a Yardbird, Page began on bass and then switched to lead guitar. The Yardbirds broke up in 1968, but not before Peter Grant became their manager in 1967.

Peter Grant, Led Zeppelin's one and only manager, was a big man, about 250 pounds, nine years older than Page, who had a rough upbringing. He was from a broken home and did not receive a formal education.14 He was a professional wrestler and played an extra role in *The Guns of Navarone*.15 Grant had plenty of experience as tour manager for several groups. He and Jimmy Page became close friends and, as a result, Grant ended up becoming the manager of Led Zeppelin from beginning to end. There is something more to this story, however. The bond between Page and Grant went beyond friends; it extended to the supernatural, spiritual realm. As Ritchie Yorke put it in his book, *Led Zeppelin - The Definitive Biography*: "To close associates, it seemed that Page and Grant had some greater fusion of interests and objectives, something beyond the reach of conventional legal jargon and bindings: such was their apparent watertight connection."16 No other author to date has explored that connection in greater detail. Herein, the contention will be put forth that Grant and Page were bound as co-disciples in the execution of the Law of Thelema. The evidence for this position stems from *The Equinox*, Aleister Crowley's encyclopedia of initiation, and the legendary film about Led Zeppelin, *The Song Remains the Same*. In *The Equinox*, Aleister Crowley quotes the Devil, who tells him that it is he who is the eye in the triangle. He then tells him that the eye in the triangle is the Silver Star: "Now shalt thou adore me who am the Eye and the Tooth, the Goat of the Spirit, the Lord of Creation. I am the Eye in the Triangle, the Silver Star that ye adore."17 The Devil claims that he himself is the Silver Star; does it surprise anyone that Crowley would name his satanic/magical cult that? If you look at the photo of the *Equinox's* advertisement at this chapter's end, you will see an eye in a triangle at the top of the drawing. The symbol of the Silver Star is the eye in the triangle. You can see this same symbol on the U.S. dollar bill.

Crowley ties his Magick in with the Egyptian Pyramids, and Jimmy Page wore Pyramids on his outfits in the movie. In the film, right after the New York City scene in the beginning, the camera ventures into the home of Peter Grant and shows him talking on the telephone. Right over his head is an eye in a triangle on a white background. Shortly thereafter, Grant is seen delivering tour dates to Jimmy Page, who is sitting on a blanket with a dagger, guitar and tape recorder, playing a "Hurdy Gurdy." On the back of Page's shirt is what also appears to be an eye in a triangle, in the form of a Pyramid.

The message to the viewer who knows what to look for, seems to be that the Silver Star is the connection between Grant and Page. Ironically enough, on VH1's television program *Legends*, Steven Tyler of Aerosmith, who introduced Led Zeppelin when they were inducted into the Rock and Roll Hall of Fame, said, "Grant and Page saw eye to eye from day one." Even if one attributes that to an uncanny choice of words, given Page's professed satanic beliefs and the clear agenda of the band in support of those beliefs, it is doubtful that an unbeliever would have been allowed to manage the band. Since that entire agenda has not been made clear yet, the reader is encouraged to retain his or her skepticism a bit longer. Rest assured, however, that it is the author's position, based on the evidence, that Jimmy Page and Peter Grant shared the same religious beliefs.

NO QUARTER – SATAN'S MESSAGE/LIE TO MANKIND

Clearly, religious belief has been one of the most powerful motivating forces in the history of mankind. Depending on one's perspective, some beliefs seem to be admirable while others appear to be ridiculous. In the mind of the individual believer however, whatever he or she believes has power in determining that individual's actions. Consider some of the following examples of how all-consuming religious beliefs can be and have been lived out in the lives of their followers. Afterward, with this idea firmly planted in your mind, we will explore the musical theme of Led Zeppelin's song "No Quarter" in the context of the broader religious message they promote.

One striking example of religious beliefs motivating men in the twentieth century was that of the Japanese Kamikaze pilots. The Japanese believed in the idea of divine rule, which was embodied in the lineage of the Emperor. This concept is an ancient one, mirrored in the past culture of many peoples, who corporately believed that their ruler was none other than God himself, manifested in human form. The Kamikazes believed that Emperor Hirohito was God incarnate. The word "Mikado," the ancient title for the Emperor of Japan, is not in use anymore. It is interesting to note, however, that Dr. Sir J. G. Frazer, in his book on Magic, *The Golden Bough*, (which was also promoted by Aleister Crowley) wrote this: "The Mikado receives from his people and assumes in his official proclamations and decrees the title of 'manifest or incarnate deity,' and he claims a general authority over the gods of Japan. For example, in an official decree of the year 646 the emperor is described as 'the incarnate god who governs the universe.'"18This belief allowed the Kamikazes to accept the idea that, if they died for the Emperor, they would be immediate recipients of eternal life. It has been said that the fighter pilots often were given just enough fuel to get to their targets, but none to return with. Other Kamikazes would get inside of torpedoes and direct them manually to the ships they wanted destroyed; believing that when the torpedo exploded they were transported to eternal life. Obviously, without the pertinent religious belief, there would have been few, if any, Kamikaze pilots. Can you imagine how the Japanese people felt after World War II, when the Emperor confessed to them that he was not divine after all?

Most people are now familiar with the concept of an Islamic *Jihad*, a Holy War that is conducted against "infidels" by those faithful to the prophet Muhammad. In Jihad, those who perish in service to Allah are guaranteed a place of honor in heaven. Today, we have become accustomed to speaking of *Jihad* in terms of terrorism, such as the truck-bombing incident that killed 183 Marines in Beirut, U.S. Embassy bombings, the USS Cole, and the murderous attack on innocent civilians at the World Trade Center and the Pentagon, and we refer to the concept with an appropriate degree of moral disdain; wanting to see the perpetrators dead. Osama Bin Laden, who is responsible for the Embassy, Twin Tower and Pentagon attacks, has stated his clearly religious belief: "Hostility toward America is a religious duty, and we hope to be rewarded for it by God....I am confident that Muslims will be able to end the legend of the so-called superpower that is America."19 It is crucial to note, that Bin Laden wants it to be a religous war, and when Americans attack Muslims in the United States, they are serving Bin Laden to make that happen. Not all people of the Muslim faith are radicals like Bin Laden and his associate swine. So we should not attack Muslim Americans; because that makes us puppets of this idiot from hell.

Despite the author's clearly Christian agenda, accusations of unfair finger pointing can be laid to rest by the ready admission that Christianity certainly isn't immune to atrocities committed in the "name" of religion either. And if the Crusades were not sufficient proof of that fact, consider also the terrible atrocities that took place during the Spanish Inquisition, where anyone who disagreed with the Papacy in Rome, was tortured and killed as a heretic.

Suspected witches and wizards were consistently put to death during this time as well. The *Bible* teaches that God told the nation of Israel that witches should not be allowed to live among them, but that they should be put to death (Exodus 22:18). However, many good Christian people were also put to death by Rome, just because they did not believe exactly what the Papacy, as opposed to the *Bible*, taught (The reason is that the teachings of the Word of God and the teachings of the Papacy are antithetical. All anyone has to do is study the *Bible* and they will see it clearly.). Anyone who dared read the *Bible* in the common language was under attack by the power base in Rome. The number of witches and sorcerers that were burned to death after the 15th century was greater than that of protestant Christians, but no Christians should have been put to death at all by Rome; as I am sure Lord Jesus Christ made clear in eternity.

Returning to the modern day, one must consider the "religious" struggle that defined the latter half of the twentieth century, "Godless" Communism versus Western, Christian based Democracy. Communists may not agree that what they believe is based in religion, but in practice that conclusion is inescapable. Communists believe that the state is Lord. Any belief in other Gods is frowned upon or forbidden. The religion of the Communist is atheism. Their belief that Communism should rule the world has motivated them in war. During Vietnam, some North Vietnamese did in fact believe that, if they died for Ho Chi Minh and the motherland, they too would receive eternal life. The North Vietnamese government did little to discourage this perception, particularly since it furthered their political aims.

Most people long to disassociate themselves from the specter of death and destruction willingly inflicted on others, but we cannot readily do so in a world that continues to be divided and fought over along lines that are drawn not only by politics, but also by religion. Throughout this century Christians, Jews, Muslims and Hindus have and do continue to massacre one another with frightening regularity in the Middle East, India, Pakistan, Cambodia and dozens of other nations.

So what's the point of all this talk of religion and warfare? Individual concepts of God are powerful motivators; sometimes powerful enough in the wrong hands to legitimize murder and every other manner of atrocity enrooted to the objective of spiritual fulfillment, either in this world or the next. But what does all this have to do with Led Zeppelin, you wonder? Led Zeppelin was motivated by, and Page and Plant are still motivated by the religious belief that the Silver Star teaches the truth concerning the universe and the creation of man; also, how man may become one with the godhead. In this respect, they are warriors in the age-old battle between good and evil. Their music is one of the most potent weapons on the battle-scarred landscape of the twentieth century. It is deadly because, like Nerve Gas and other potent biological agents that the world is trying to ban, it is a silent killer, invisible to all but the most sensitive sensors. The real agenda of this book is to refine your own sensory array, such that you might detect the danger and escape before succumbing to it.

Their objective did not end with the closing of the last century, and perhaps will note even with the closing of the next, because one can rest assured that long after the band members are dead, their music will still be promoting the Silver Star. Page/Plant even had "Produced by Silver Star" printed on their Orlando Arena concert tickets in 1995 (see photos). The message of the band, in general terms, is that Satan is god, the religion hewants practiced is embodied in "The Law of Thelema," and that there will be no mercy for those who oppose the Devil's will. In the Silver Star's *Book of the Law*, that Aleister Crowley claimed was dictated directly to him by Satan himself, we read the following: "Them that seek to entrap thee, to overthrow thee, them attack without pity or quarter; & destroy them utterly. Swift as a trodden serpent turn and strike! Be thou yet deadlier than he! Drag down their souls to awful torment: laugh at their fear: spit upon them!"20

Please note that the word "quarter" is used right after "pity." In Webster's New World Dictionary (2nd College Edition), in this context, quarter is defined as "mercy granted to a surrendering foe." (One can see the word "quarter" used in this context throughout the Mel Gibson film, *The Patriot.*) In order for us to see Crowley's teaching as presented by the band, we will first analyze a portion of the film, *The Song Remains the Same.* For those readers who cannot access a copy of the film, elements of this analysis can also be heard on the soundtrack to the film, but it is better to see the accompanying visuals as well, if at all possible.

It is also important to note that copyright laws preclude our ability to examine the full text of the lyrics under analysis throughout this book. As such, I have adopted a narrative style that continually reorients the reader to the particular lyric currently being addressed via keywords and context.

Alternately, a timer is occasionally employed to note how many minutes and seconds into a given song a particular item occurs. The serious reader is assumed to either know the lyrics already, as most fans do, or at least be willing to obtain copies of them from other sources to see all of the arguments in the full context they are intended to be presented. (Be very careful, however, while examining these sources. There are multitudes of Led Zeppelin "lyrics" printed on the internet that are way off base; substantially inaccurate.) Using the timer, one can even borrow copies of the albums from a library or other lending source to closely study each contextual analysis. Having established that, let's return to the argument at hand.

The fourth song in the chronology of the Led Zeppelin film is titled "No Quarter." After the long lead played by Jimmy Page on guitar, John Paul Jones is taking a slow stroll through a graveyard on a horse. The scene then reverts back to Madison Square Garden where they are playing in concert. Robert Plant walks up to the microphone and begins to sing with no guitar or drum backup. In the first line he says that somebody is "walking" and "death" is right next to them. Then he says that Satan is laughing at each "step" they take. After this he draws his head back and stomps his right foot forward, which is a gesture that he consistently uses in concert when talking about the fans. Those who doubt this emphasis should study his face at similar moments; like Earl's Court and Seattle. Regardless, more evidence in support of that contention is forthcoming.

The next line of the song conveys the message that circumstances will prevent him who hesitates from turning to Satan, who is god. Finally, Plant sings, "The dogs of doom are howling more." Next, Jimmy Page is shown standing in a magician's type of stance as the sound that he derives from the Theremin machine transfers from the one side of Madison Square Garden to the other.

The next three lines refer to the band as the ones who have "news." It is only fitting that they are delivering news, because the Tarot card "The Magician" is defined as the one who brings news. One might readily ask, "What is the news for?" or "What is its purpose?"

The author asserts that the news the band is carrying is supposed to create the "dream" mentioned in the song, a dream for the benefit of the Devil and those who turn to him. This is the same dream mentioned in "Over The Hills And Far Away," from the *Houses of the Holy* album. At 2:12 into the song, Plant sings that he is living "for" his "dream" as well as for "gold" for his "pocket." The dream for Jimmy Page was to live out the Law of Thelema, and for the band, to be rock stars and ambassadors for the Devil and that Law. They provided a tacit definition of this dream in the beginning of "Achilles Last Stand," which will be addressed in greater detail later.

Returning to "No Quarter" as presented in the film, right after mentioning the news they have, Plant says that nobody travels this "path" that "they" are on; the author asserts that this is referring to the band. Plant then returns his attention to the fans once more. He says that "They" are without "quarter." He then continues to assert that they are not asking for it either. The next three lines are the last that we will refer to in this early stage of the book, as you will need the benefit of other concepts to examine this song more thoroughly. In the first of the three lines, Plant moans at the idea of "misery" as a result of facing someone and not having "quarter" while facing him. Then he says that the price people will "pay" is "pain" if they face him without it. Finally, he cries out for quarter as if to hint to the fans that quarter is what they should be seeking. The meaning of the hidden message in "No Quarter" is this: those who stand before Satan after death, not having received his mercy in this life, are doomed. One may ask that if the song is totally about Satan, why did Plant mention the Nordic god "Thor" early in the song? According to the teachings of the Qabalah, which will be examined later in great detail, Aleister Crowley asserted that Thor was Satan in disguise. You will read of Robert Plant's blatant command to the fans to sell the Devil their souls later on, keep that in mind. Its relevance to their music will be clearly seen in a later section of the book, when we will examine the most powerful, most pervasive Led Zeppelin song of all time, "Stairway to Heaven." Therein, the context of how the "Lady" is purchasing her "Stairway" will be explained.

Lucifer is very powerful. He can easily convince those who fool around with Magick that he is god. The presence of Lucifer has a great impact on a human mind. His power over the yielded mind is immeasurable, especially under the influence of narcotics. He is smarter than men like Page and Plant, and has deceived them into serving him; believing he is god. As E.M. Bounds wrote in his book, *Satan, His Personality, Power, and Overthrow*: "With the wisdom of an archangel and the observation and experience of half an eternity, as the Captain General of all the hosts of hell, he is an adept in the acts and arts of deception and trickery, and has almost exhaustless resources at command to serve his purposes."21

We are seeing the content of that quote lived out in the rock culture today, especially in the music of Led Zeppelin. On page 338 of Ritchie Yorke's *Led Zeppelin - The Definitive Biography*, he lists a Led Zeppelin bootleg titled *"ON TOUR - BLACK GOLD CONCERTS BG 52025."* For the uninitiated, bootlegs are illicit recordings of concert performances, either audio or video. This particular bootleg is Led Zeppelin live in Seattle, Washington, at Center Coliseum, July 17th, 1973. In this concert, just before the song "The Ocean," Robert Plant says goodnight to the fans and walks off stage. The fans begin to shout "More! More! More! More!" in unison. I experienced this along with 20,000 others in Madison Square Garden on Saturday, June 11, 1977. Ironically enough, Aleister Crowley said, in *The Magical Record of the Beast*, that June 11th "...should be my lucky day."22 In this personal experience, the glitter ball hanging from the ceiling was reflecting light all over the Garden as we stomped our feet and raised our fists in the air to the chant of "More! More! More! More!" Waiting for the last encore, we must have shouted for close to ten minutes. The point is this, the longer the chant goes on, the more bestial it becomes. Listening to it in any concert, one can hear that the chant for more sounds like dogs barking as the thousands of voices are muffled together. One big syllable that sounds like "Ruff! Ruff! Ruff! Ruff!" is repeated over and over. As you watch Robert Plant say the word "more" in the film you will see that he drops his head back and the word is echoed throughout Madison Square Garden, just like the chant of the fans waiting for an encore. On the soundtrack to the film, you can hear "more" echoed much louder than in the film. Those who mixed the soundtrack obviously wanted it to be clearer for fans who would listen to it over and over, just like I did. What's the point? The author asserts that doomed dogs sung about in "No Quarter" are the fans; those who will not worship Satan.

The message of Led Zeppelin is that Satan is god, and all who follow his moral code, the Law of Thelema, despising the Christian faith, will be alright as long as they try to find him. He has a dream to be lived out for the one who follows him and no mercy for the one who doesn't. Satan makes it clear through his prophet, Aleister Crowley, that he aims to destroy the Christian people. This stated goal is in agreement with what we know of Satan from the prophecies of the Book of "Revelation" in the *Holy Bible*.

We will also be looking at a sword fight portrayed between Robert Plant and a man who the author intends to show is in the role of none other than Lord Jesus Christ himself. The proof for this contention will also come from Aleister Crowley's teachings of the Silver Star. This religious war of promoting Satanic Magick is currently being fought through the medium of communication, and one of Satan's weapons of mass destruction is the rock and roll of Led Zeppelin. Consider the following. In *Magick Without Tears*, Aleister Crowley wrote: "The first condition of membership of the A.A. (Silver Star) is that one is sworn to identify one's own Great Work with that of raising mankind to higher levels, spiritually, and in every other way."23

The "Great Work" referred to by Crowley is one's life purpose or service to god; as defined by his writings for the Silver Star, the Devil. The member of the Silver Star vows to identify his or her service to god with raising mankind to higher levels, not only spiritually, but in consciousness. Drugs are advocated by Crowley in the achievement of this purpose, as is the practice of Magick. The individual member of the Silver Star is encouraged to study and apply the power of Magick. Crowley described Magick as a science and an art. He wrote: "Magick is the science and art of causing change to occur in conformity with the Will. In other words, it is Science, Pure and Applied. This thesis has been worked out at great length by Dr. Sir J.G. Frazer. But in common parlance the word Magick has been used to mean the kind of science which ordinary people do not understand."24 The will of the magician, in conjunction with magical power, or witchcraft, causes change to occur in the object the magical spell is cast upon. Since Jimmy Page is openly a student of Crowley the magician, it is his will that we are dealing with here specifically. Plant, Jones, and Bonham, while clearly in on the whole thing, are only appendices or extensions of the will of Jimmy Page. He obviously cannot perform all the band's functions at once. He is however, responsible for how those functions are carried out. Just look at any Led Zeppelin album cover and you will see "Produced by Jimmy Page" as well as "Executive Producer Peter Grant" written on it, or on the inner sleeve. The role of producer equates to that of magician, it is the individual who orchestrates the incantation to give it the intended power.

In the MTV presentation *Led Zeppelin - Profiled*, Jimmy Page spoke of his work on Stairway to Heaven. He said: "I worked on it for quite a while, on and off. I was putting all these different sections together; putting them in what I considered was the right order before I even presented it to the band (MTV Networks-MCMXC)." The band itself is nothing more than a vehicle for music produced by Page and inspired by Crowley, who derived his inspiration from Satan. Sometimes, even that connection is not quite as tenuous. Robert Plant confessed that someone wrote Led Zeppelin lyrics through him-that he was only an open medium. Later in this work, at a more appropriate moment based on the background established at that point, we will also provide examples from antiquity, specifically seances, of how the spirits perform that function and why. A couple of Plant's quotes are so directly in support of this position that any attempts to refute the arguments presented herein are rendered powerless by the mouths of those potential critics seek most to support.

Jimmy Page the magician, exercises his will onstage and in the recording studio in conjunction with magical power to cause a change in the minds of the fans; who are already hypnotized by the rhythmic beat of the music. Mass hypnosis through music is not a new concept; it has been around for centuries. In modern times, Pete Townshend of "The Who" would agree that the fans are hypnotized, as evidenced by their song, "Won't Get Fooled Again." The change taking place is in the area of conscience; changing good to evil and evil to good. Again, this concept will be explored in greater detail later in this work. For now, simply file it in the slowly expanding list of threads that you are relying on me to weave together into a coherent and conclusive pattern.

Crowley wrote that the magician can effect this change by having the right force, as well as enough of its power, properly projected through the right medium to the object the spell is being cast upon. He wrote: "Any required Change may be effected by application of the proper kind and degree of Force in the proper manner through the proper medium to the proper object."25 The force Crowley is speaking of is magical, provided by demonic spirits. Crowley edited a book length work on the magical use of demonic forces by magicians in 1904, entitled, *The Goetia*. Jimmy Page resurrected this public domain document and republished it in 1976. The continuing influence of this work, as promoted by Page, extends to a reprint in 1995, by *Samuel Weiser Inc.*, produced roughly concurrent with a Page/Plant concert tour in that year. The book talks about demonic forces, demons or evil spirits, which are the fallen angels who followed Lucifer. These demons not only cause the hidden magical message of music to be heard, but they also can bind a man to the will of the magician casting spells on him. The magician and demons work together to remove an individual's will to resist the satanic spell being cast on him or her. Having personally felt the pull and power of Page's spells, and discovering that mine was not an isolated experience, was the catalyst that prompted the research underlying this book.

In the last quote, Crowley spoke of the magician's medium of Magick. In the following quote, Crowley presents the medium of the magician's will as communication. He wrote: "The Problem of every Act of Magick is then this: to exert a Will, sufficiently powerful to cause the required Effect, through a Menstruum or medium of Communication."26 The Magick must be performed through communication. Jimmy Page's medium of communication is his music. This is something of which he is completely cognizant. He once told Steve Peacock: "If the audience is vibing you up and you're vibing them, you can get this giant feedback which can become quite magical. I relate far more to that, the communication between us and the people coming to see us. From the start, rock and roll as such had this incredible effect, and I think the thread of what was being communicated has carried through, no matter what else has come into the music." (The reader is encouraged to remember where Rock and Roll was launched from: "Sun Records." Page and Plant performed in a celebration of 50 years of

Sun Records, on July 7th, 2000, in Switzerland.) Aleister Crowley advocated music in this precise context: "Music. Justifiable? Why Not? A help to your Great Work, an aspect of your Will, nicht wahr (why not)? Go to it! Apollo is the God of music, preeminently…"27

Led Zeppelin's *Swan Song* logo, that looks like an angel, is in fact taken from William Rimmer's painting, *Evening: Fall of Day*. It is the Sun God Apollo. The painting of Apollo is a perfect representation of the new "Aeon of Horus." According to Crowley in *The Equinox, Vol. I, No.7*, Apollo is Horus, who Crowley said was Satan. Apollo/Satan has definitely used the music of Led Zeppelin to send his message. He communicates well through it to this very day. All the gods are Lucifer; Crowley taught that, and so does the *Bible*. We will now examine how men use music in the secular world to send their messages, and then take a look at a powerful message from Led Zeppelin immediately thereafter.

ROCK AND ROLL - THE MEDIUM OF COMMUNICATION

If you want your message to be perceived in a favorable light, the best thing to do is to put it to a catchy tune, right? Advertisers know this is the truth. This brief section is to illustrate, by several examples, the fact that music is the strongest medium of all forms of communication. Football, baseball, basketball, and hockey games are constantly blasting music into the ears of the fans. Commercials on television, especially beer commercials, are done mostly with music. Advertisers seek to associate the beer with the exaltation brought on by the upbeat and non-depressive music that backs their lyrics. For example, "Tap the Rockies! Coors Light!" By contrast, can you imagine Coors using Kenny Rogers' "You picked a fine time to leave me Lucille?" Don't ponder the possibility too long, it will never happen. Depression is bad advertising.

Chevy trucks are advertised to Bob Seger's "Like a Rock." An excellent tune in the ear and a Chevy truck in the eye, on television. Some analysts have claimed that Chevy Trucks were saved by that musical commercial.

Monday Night Football has used "Are you ready to rock?" by Hank Williams Jr. in the past, and now he is singing "Are you ready for some football? Are you ready to party?" Even at the stadium, the fans go wild when that is played on the screen right at 9 P.M. The music associates football and partying. One goes with the other and reinforces the positive association of football in the minds of partying people. It sells Monday Night Football well. If it did not, it would not be there.

Sometimes the orchestration of music in seemingly unassociated contexts also seems powerful. For example, on January 12, 1997, the National Football League's NFC Championship game was played in Green Bay, Wisconsin. The Packers were hosting the Carolina Panthers for the right to go to the

Super Bowl. The Packers were driving for a score when a commercial break was taken during a timeout. The advertisement was these lyrics put to music, "Now is the time, this is the taste, Dr. Pepper." As soon as the game came back on, "Do wah diddy diddy dum diddy do" was blasting in the stands. The song was being played to lift the mood of the fans and get them into the game; especially on the way to the end zone. As soon as the song ended, Brett Favre threw a touchdown pass to Dorsey Levens that was caught in the end zone just inside the right boundary marker.

Immediately after the kick, the Bob Seger Chevrolet commercial came on. Viewers at home, if rooting for Green Bay, were then hearing Seger's "Like a Rock" while in the state of mental euphoria. It was excellent timing. It must have been planned that way. Returning to the game, Carolina had the ball and the directors at Lambeau Field had Queen's "Another One Bites the Dust," playing in the stands. The obvious connotation was the Carolina drive was going to go three and out. Sure enough, it did. They then played Queen's "We Will Rock You" in both the third and fourth quarters to keep the crowd going. If the music rocks the crowd, it will keep coming back; even if its team is not in the playoffs. For a fitting end, after the Green Bay Packers won the NFC Championship, Queen's "We are the Champions" rocked through the stadium. The point of all this is to illustrate that music, carefully choreographed to events in progress, can influence and sustain momentum toward an intended end.

Even outside the context of a larger song or broader events, "jingles" can still powerfully convey an image and a message. Folger's Coffee used the uplifting "Folger's in your cup!" Their competitor Maxwell House used "Good to the last drop!" McDonald's has sold millions of hamburgers by using "You deserve a break today." Burger King has done the same with "Have it your way." The United States Army put fast action video to the tune of "Be all you can be - in the Army." In the seventies, Budweiser sold its beer with "When you say Budweiser – you've said it all." Coca Cola used the song, "I'd like to teach the world to sing in perfect harmony. I'd like to buy the world a coke and keep it company."

At the end of his warm up performance for Ozzy Osbourne at the Orlando Arena on May 24th, 1996, Henry Rollins shouted "Diet Pepsi!" into the microphone just before walking off stage. The fans heard the advertisement from a man who was in a recent movie with Al Pacino, Robert DeNiro, and Val Kilmer; who has his own rock band touring with Ozzy. Pepsi Co. knew what it was doing. If a rock star promotes something, it will be accepted by the fans.

There is one more example that needs to be presented before bringing this section to a close. On May 20th, 1995, Page/Plant played before a sold out audience in San Jose, California. This concert was broadcast over the radio. The show was sponsored by Miller Genuine Draft whose logo was dutifully printed on all Page/Plant concert tickets during that tour. On the radio, Miller advertised its beer with music from Led Zeppelin. I am going to quote the advertisement that I have on cassette. When you see a Led Zeppelin song title in parenthesis, that means the commercial has switched to that song at that point in the narrative. The commercial began at the end of Page/Plant performing "Since I've Been Loving You," which is off *Led Zeppelin III*. Robert Plant shouted "Guitar, Mr. Jimmy Page!" At that point you could hear the music of the Hurdy Gurdy instrument played by Nigel Eaton in the commercial as it began. It said: "If you could see one thing, you've only been able to hear, if you could relive one moment in time, if you had one wish every fifteen years, wouldn't this be it (Living Loving Maid - *Led Zeppelin II*)? The 1995 Page/Plant North American Tour, the genuine rock of Jimmy Page and Robert Plant live for the first time since 1980, brought together by Miller Genuine Draft. You made a wish, we made it happen (Immigrant Song - *Led Zeppelin III*), proudly sponsored by Miller Genuine Draft, supporters of the Second Harvest Food Bank (Dancing Days - *Houses of the Holy*). The guitar, the voice, and the beer of rock and roll, Miller Genuine Draft - Miller Brewing Company, Milwaukee, Wisconsin." All these people are using music to send their messages to their viewers, listeners, and stadium fans.

Now, in the year 2002, Cadillac is selling its cars, during the Super Bowl, the Olympics, Academy Awards, Wimbledon tennis, and Ryder Cup golf (and other prime time programming as well), to the tune of Led Zeppelin's song, "Rock and Roll;" coming off the fourth album. In the song, the words repeated over and over, and sung by the majority of its listeners, send the message that one is lonely without rock and roll. The best way to keep the fans listening is to program the subconscious that they will be unhappy without it, specifically, the music of Led Zeppelin. Robert Plant starts out by singing about the extended period of "Time" he has endured since he rocked to the music. He then mentions that he had not danced to "The Stroll," in a great while, which is a dance and song by the 50's group, "The Diamonds." The signature line comes at the end of that first verse, "It's been a long lonely, lonely, lonely, lonely, lonely time." The word "lonely" is repeated four times during the chorus for emphasis. The message is imbedded in the subconscious mind, through the open door of the conscious mind. What Jimmy and the Devil know, that most of mankind does not know, is that this programs the repeated listener to give the music a position of supreme importance in his or her life. The subconscious mind will cause a person to live out whatever is programmed therein. It is just like a personal computer. It is not going to argue with you, you just program it. In his book, *The Power of Your Subconscious Mind*, Dr. Joseph Murphy discusses this in detail:

"Psychologists and psychiatrists point out that when thoughts are conveyed to your subconscious mind, impressions are made in the brain cells. As soon as your subconscious accepts any idea, it proceeds to put it into effect immediately. It works by association of ideas and uses every bit of knowledge that you have gathered in your lifetime to bring about its purpose....Your subconscious mind accepts what is impressed upon it or what you consciously believe. It does not reason things out like your conscious mind, and it does not argue with you controversially. Your subsconscious mind is like the soil which accepts any kind of seed, good or bad. Your thoughts are active and might be likened unto seeds. Negative, destructive thoughts continue to work negatively in your subconscious mind, and in due time will come forth into outer experience which corresponds with them.

"Remember, your subconscious mind does not engage in proving whether your thoughts are good or bad, true or false, but it responds according to the nature of your thoughts or suggestions. For example, if you consciously assume something as true, even though it may be false, your subconscious mind will accept it as true and proceed to bring about results which must necessarily follow, because you consciously assumed it to be true."28

As you can see, if a person believes that he will be lonely without rock and roll, even if he is not cognizant of this line of thought in his mind, he will be more determined to listen to it, eventually establishing some degree of addiction to it; and now Cadillac is assisting Led Zeppelin in this effort. Jimmy is smart. Being a magician, he knows what will happen during the commercials. This programming is done to keep the listener tuned into Led Zeppelin, because they want the fan to keep coming back in order to send the messages from the Devil and the Silver Star into the subconscious mind repeatedly. This is done overtly in the lyrics, as just discussed, and also covertly by "Backward Masking," the practice of embedding messages that can only be discerned when fans modify the manner in which the song is played. Backward Masking is used to promote Satan more than once in "Stairway to Heaven;" but our discussion of the specifics of that will be confined to the chapter that examines the lyrics of that song.

The members of Led Zeppelin, by serving the Devil in such a widespread and powerful fashion, are indeed four of the most dangerous Devil worshipers to ever walk the earth. Many are they who have been lured into listening to the music performed by these mediums of the teachings of Aleister Crowley's Satanic Magickal Order, the Silver Star. The album with "Stairway to Heaven" has the photo of the middle size fagots on the front, and that is appropriate when one understands that "Stairway to Heaven" contains the message of hope for the members of the Silver Star. The message is that Satan is god, along with his female consort, and that his followers are to ignite the masses of humanity to the "rightness" of his teachings. This message is reflected in the 1973 song, "No Quarter," which continued to be performed musically in 1998 by Page/Plant with the help of bassist Charlie Jones, and drummer Michael Lee, just as it was in the age of hard rock, the 1970's. This lie of Satan's is being preached through the ultimate medium of communication to spiritually unsuspecting minds, rock and roll. Led Zeppelin commands it's listeners to sell their souls to the Devil. To understand more of the price they are asking you to pay, we need to learn more about the one who commands them, Satan. In the next chapter, we will take a look at who he was in the beginning before he rebelled; when he was the composer of music for the angelic host. Lucifer the Archangel was the highest of the angelic creation of God. After he fell, he came to be known by many names, but most consistently as Satan, which means "adversary." Therein, another piece of Led Zeppelin mythology will also be exposed and debunked. Despite the fact that band members have consistently said that the "Black Dog" referred to in the song of the same name was a black Labrador that came into the studio while they were recording, you will learn why the Black Dog is none other than the Devil himself.

Jimmy Page plays his Gibson Les Paul during "No Quarter" in 1977. Back in the 1970's, whenever Led Zeppelin performed this song, they did it with dry ice on the stage, forming a cloud cover before Page entered the song on guitar. The point was clear to me, that the warning in the song was from above, from the Prince of the Power of the Air, Satan. As I watched Robert Plant sing, he ad-libbed these words: "We give No Quarter." Again, this was June 11th, 1977. When Page/Plant reunited in the early 1990's, they put together an album and titled it: "No Quarter," which has since sold over a million copies. They played the song on tour in 1995-96, as well as in 1998; reiterating their Lord's warning.

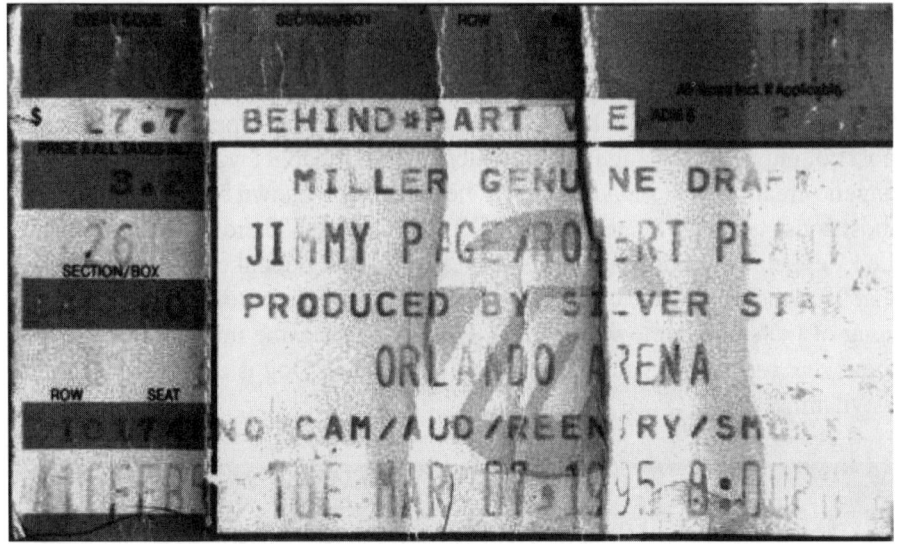

On March 7th, 1995, Page/Plant performed in concert at the Orlando Arena, Orlando, Florida. Printed on the tickets, under the name of the band, was "Produced by Silver Star." What are the odds that this was all just a coincidence?

The opening page of each one of theset of ten volumes of Crowley's Equinox, complete with an "eye in the triangle" of the Egyptian Sun Gods "Ra" and of course,"Horus."

Aleister Crowley dressed in his Silver Star outfit, complete with an eye in the triangle on the head gear, and Celtic Cross on his chest. ("Equinox"-1909)

This is Led Zeppelin's fourth album cover with a man carrying a load of middle size fagots (sticks) on his back. The band has given reasons for this photo being there, contrary to the teachings of Crowley, but an objective observer can see that they were really claiming to be mediums for the Devil's Silver Star.

In 1977, Led Zeppelin routinely closed its shows with "Rock and Roll," except for a few anamolies like June 11th, when they closed with "Heartbreaker." In 1998, after playing in Pensacola , Florida, the first US show, where they closed with "Misty Mountain Hop," Page/ Plant closed all its (Zep) shows with (lonely) "Rock and Roll." There was no doubt in the minds of the fans that this was in fact Led Zeppelin returned to the concert stage. I witnessed thousands of fans singing the "Lonely" lyrics.

Keith Moon plays "Rock and Roll" along with Led Zeppelin, with John Bonham to his right, on June 23rd, 1977. It was one year later that Moon was dead at the age of 32. John Bonham died three years later at the age of 32. Bonham died of alcohol asphyxiation, and Moon died from an overdose of pills. Led Zeppelin and The Who are brothers in "Pinball;" which I will show in my presentations.

1 Steven Davis, *Hammer of the Gods - The Led Zeppelin Saga*, William Morrow & Co., NY, 1985, pg.200

2 S. Jason Black and Christopher S. Hyatt, Ph.D., *Pacts With the Devil*, New Falcon Publications, 1993, pp.58-59

3 Steven Davis, *Hammer of the Gods - The Led Zeppelin Saga*, William Morrow & Company, New York, 1985, pg.229

4 Aleister Crowley, *The Magical Record of the Beast*, Edited by John Symonds and Kenneth Grant, Duckworth, 1972, pg.295

5 Satan, *The Book of the Law*, Chapter 1, Verse 10, Aleister Crowley's *The Equinox*, *Vol. I, No.10*, pg.11, Samuel Weiser Inc., Yorke Beach, Maine, 1993 (Public Domain)

6 Aleister Crowley, *White Stains*, Duckworth, 1973, pp.105 -106

7 Bob Larson, *Satanism - The Seduction* of *America's Youth*, Thomas Nelson, 1989, pg.151

8 Aleister Crowley, *Notes for an Astral Atlas*, from *Magick-Book 4 * Liber Aba*, Samuel Weiser Inc., 1994, pg.494

9 Aleister Crowley, *The Magical Record of the Beast*, edited by John Symonds and Kenneth Grant, Duckworth, 1972, pg.242

10 Aleister Crowley, *Equinox, Volume III, No.1*, Samuel Weiser Inc., 1992, pp.181-182

11 Stephen Davis, *Hammer of the Gods - The Led Zeppelin Saga*, William Morrow & Co., NY, 1985, pg.56

12 *Led Zeppelin - Will the Song Remain the Same?* pg.46

13 Stephen Davis, *Hammer of the Gods - The Led Zeppelin Saga*, pg.26

14 Ibid, pg.40

15 Ibid, pg.41

16 Ritchie Yorke, *Led Zeppelin - The Definitive Biography*, pg.291

17 Aleister Crowley, *Equinox, Volume I, No.6*, Samuel Weiser Inc., Yorke Beach, Maine, 1993, pg.36

18 Dr. Sir J. G. Frazer, *The Golden Bough*, The Macmillan Company, NY, 1922, pg.195

19 *TIME, ASIA, JANUARY 11, 1999 VOL. 153 NO. 1*

20 Satan, *The Book of the Law*, Aleister Crowley taking dictation from Satan, from *The Equinox*, *Volume I, No.10*, Samuel Weiser Inc., Yorke Beach, Maine, 1993, Chapter 3, Verse 42, pg.30

21 E.M. Bounds, *Satan, His Personality, Power, and Overthrow*, Baker Book House Company, Grand Rapids, Michigan, 1973, pg.99

22 Aleister Crowley, *The Magical Record of the Beast*, Edited by John Symonds and Kenneth Grant, Duckworth, 1972, pg.60

23 Aleister Crowley, *Magick Without Tears*, New Falcon Publications, Tempe, Arizona, 1994, pg.91

24 Aleister Crowley, *The Book of Thoth*, Samuel Weiser Inc., Yorke Beach, Maine, 1993, pg.40

25 Aleister Crowley, *Magick Without Tears*, New Falcon Publications, Tempe, Arizona, 1994, pg.28

26 Aleister Crowley, *The Book of Wisdom or Folly*, Samuel Weiser Inc., Yorke Beach, Maine, 1995, pg.51

27 Aleister Crowley, *Magick Without Tears*, New Falcon Publications, Tempe, Arizona, 1994, pg..389

28 Dr. Joseph Murphy, *The Power of Your Subconscious Mind*, Bantam Books, NY, 1985, pp.31-32

VOICI LA FIGURE DE L'ESPRIT
LORS DE SON APPARITION
PAR LE SECRET DE LA POULE NOIRE.

Fig. 106. The Devil appearing at a Crossroads in the Form of a Goat
La Poule noire (1820).

Satan appearing at a "Crossroads" in the form of Pan the Sabbatic Goat. The Devil at the crossroads is a fact of antiquity. The painting was made in 1820.

Jimmy Page (below) plays "Walking into Clarksdale," on the 1998 tour. The song pays homage to the Mississippi Delta Blues musicians like Robert Johnson. In the song, Robert Plant sings concering some "stranger" standing on a "crossroads" and that he had "seen" the "face" in the past. He also mentions highway 49. Page and Plant visited the Blues Museum in Clarksdale in 1998, just after their concert in Tupelo. Page wore this solid black outfit during the entire tour; in keeping with the W.B. Crow quote in this chapter. At the end of the chapter, you can see photos of the Blues King Robert Johnson and the famous Crossroads in Clarksdale, Mississippi, where Delta Bluesmen could make deals with the Devil .

CHAPTER TWO

"The existence and work of the devil is a serious matter, and it is to be considered and dealt with from the most serious standpoint, and none but serious people can deal with it."1
E.M. Bounds, "Satan, His Personality, Power, and Overthrow"

"I resolved passionately to reach the spiritual causes of phenomena, and to dominate the material world which I detested by their means. I was not content to believe in a personal devil and serve him, in the ordinary sense of the word. I wanted to get hold of him personally and become his chief of staff."2
Black Magician Aleister Crowley, "Confessions"

"Thou hast appeared unto me as a young and brilliant God, a god of music and beauty, even as a young god in his strength, playing upon the lyre."3
Black Magician Aleister Crowley, "The Holy Books of Thelema"

"Thou hast been in Eden the garden of God; every precious stone was thy covering, the sardius, topaz, and the diamond, the beryl, the onyx, and the jasper, the sapphire, the emerald, and the carbuncle, and gold: the workmanship of thy tabrets and of thy pipes was prepared in thee in the day that thou wast created."(KJV)
Holy Bible, Ezekiel 28:13

"Hello Satan, I believe it's time to go..."
Robert Johnson, King of the Delta Blues guitarists

BLACK DOG & WALKING INTO CLARKSDALE: LUCIFER THE PIPER - THE MAKER OF MUSIC

Lucifer is a name that is very controversial in today's society, among those who accept the fact of his existence. The name Lucifer literally means 'light-bearer." This name relates to his appearance. It is taken from the Hebrew word "Heylel" which means "morning star." Many, like Aleister Crowley, Mick Jagger, Ozzy Osbourne, and Jimmy Page, depict him as almighty god. While Crowley does it posthumously, he does it effectively nonetheless, as the said rock stars are clearly Crowleyites; including Jagger, who composed the music for a Kenneth Anger film, *Invocation of My Demon Brother.* The film glorifies Crowley's teaching. Conversely, the *Holy Bible* gives the accurate and most widely accepted account of who Lucifer is, and what his role has been and continues to be in the history of angelic beings, and mankind. In this chapter we will begin by examining the *Bible's* presentation of Lucifer, who is Satan (which means "opponent" or "adversary," as well as "accuser") and the Devil ("slanderer"). The *Bible* describes him in three-fold fashion, the Archangel who ruled the angelic host as the anointed cherub, answering only to God, the celestial composer of music on his pipes, or the "piper," and the tempter of mankind. The opposing view from Aleister Crowley will then be presented, and that from his famous *Equinox*; although Crowley as well describes him as the piper (the piper is the chief character of the Led Zeppelin song, "Stairway to Heaven"). Subsequent to Crowley, we will look at Jimmy Page's advocating of Lucifer and Crowley's *Equinox*. Closing out the chapter, we will focus on Jimmy Page and Robert Plant's title song from their album, *Walking Into Clarksdale*, released in April, 1998. This is the Devil at the Crossroads theme as presented by the former members of Led Zeppelin in their reunion band. Although the Devil appears to his followers as a beautiful light bearer, playing beautiful music and promising great things, and coming through with the promises, he is in fact an evil murderer whose goal it is to get men like Aleister Crowley and Jimmy Page to believe that he is god, and afterward promote him as the object of worship; the one to follow and emulate, hoping for the eternal damnation of his worshipers.

LUCIFER THE ARCHANGEL - RULER OF THE ANGELIC HOST

Lucifer was created to be the head over all the angelic beings that God made, and yet the pride he manifested in that capacity is the reason he will spend eternity in the lowest possible position. The following quote is the Biblical text that describes the attitude Lucifer had when he decided to lead a seditious uprising against Almighty God. The verses are taken from the Old Testament Book of Isaiah, Chapter 14, verses 12-15: "How art thou fallen from heaven, O Lucifer, son of the morning! How art thou cut down to the ground, which didst weaken the nations! For thou hast said in thine heart, 'I will ascend into heaven, I will exalt my throne above the stars of God: I will sit also upon the mount of the congregation, in the sides of the north: I will ascend above the heights of the clouds; I will be like the Most High.' Yet thou shalt be brought down to hell, to the sides of the pit." - Isaiah 14:12-15(KJV)

The following is a small commentary concerning the previous verses. To begin with Isaiah says, "How art thou fallen from heaven." Lucifer fell from heaven. Specifically, it speaks of his physically falling. Included in that, of course, is his spiritual fall of being set at odds forever with the Godhead (Father, Son, Holy Spirit). Lucifer led a rebellion of sedition with one third of the angelic host, whom he deceived into believing he should rule as god.

Lucifer's rebellion began with his imagination. God gave the angels, as well as man, the ability to imagine, or imagination. The passage clearly presents Lucifer with his imagination running wild. It reads: "For thou hast said in thine heart." His imagination helped him conceive of himself as god. His ability to imagine came from God. If he did not have the ability to imagine, it would not have happened. Therefore, Lucifer's God given imagination presented him with a test. God knew the test would come. Lucifer, however, is responsible for the outcome. Angelic beings, as well as men, have another God given ability, the ability to will. Lucifer could will to dismiss the thought of being god, or he could will to continue to entertain the thought until he acted on it. The whole time he imagined himself as god, he could have stopped himself. He did not do this in a moment's time. We know from progressive New Testament revelation, that Lucifer presented the idea to the angelic host; the rest of the angels. They were countless in number. One third agreed to join him. He had plenty of time to change his mind.

"I will ascend into heaven." Lucifer said in his heart that he would ascend into heaven. What this obviously means is that he was not in heaven when he led the rebellion. The next part reads: "I will exalt my throne above the stars of God." While in command of the entire angelic host, he himself was an angel. The "stars of God" are the angels. He did not rebel against another angel, but God. Lucifer intended to exalt his throne above the angelic host to rule as God in heaven. He went on to say: "I will sit also upon the mount of the congregation, in the sides of the north." This is the place where God's throne is in heaven. It is the mount where the congregation of angels would come to receive instruction and counsel from God. After that Lucifer said: "I will ascend above the heights of the clouds." This has reference to, the "Shekinah" glory of God. This is an Old Testament manifestation of God in cloud form. Lucifer was saying he would take over heaven as God. The last thing he said in the verses was: "I will be like the Most High." There it is. He says in effect, "I will be God." It is presented later that one third of all the angels rebelled with him. Isaiah finished the passage with: "Yet thou shalt be brought down to hell, to the sides of the pit." This last part of the quote has yet to take place, but it will. I have had people ask me, "Why doesn't God just destroy the Devil?" My answer to that is, he is one of his greatest servants. When Satan tempts, God tests. The difference between a temptation and a test is the motive behind it. Temptation leads to sin, whereas passing a test leads to stronger convictions. Satan tempts man to sin, yet concurrently, or at the same time, God is testing a person. When the world as we know it comes to an end, the Devil will be cast into hell, not as ruler, like some "Far Side" cartoon, but as chief inmate. He is not going to be delighting in the suffering of anyone else. He will be suffering more than any of the others there. He will also suffer for encouraging the others to live the life that landed them there. Being the chief inmate in hell is the absolute lowest position he could have, in direct contrast to what he was created for, to rule the angelic host.

LUCIFER AND MICHAEL - ARCHANGELS IN CONTENTION

To show that Lucifer was indeed ruler of the angels, a comparison will be made with their current ruler. The angel who was given the position of authority over the angels that did not fall is named Michael. The *Bible* records contention between the Devil and Michael over the body of Moses. If Satan could keep Moses' body in a known location, he could make an idolatrous shrine out of it. If you want to know what an idolatrous shrine is, just watch CNN on August 16th, as they cover events in Memphis, Tennessee. The worship of a man is breaking the most important of the Ten Commandments. Satan wanted the Jews to worship Moses and not God. Michael was sent by God to collect his body and the Devil met him there: "Yet Michael the archangel, in contending with the devil, when he disputed about the body of Moses, dared not bring against him a reviling accusation, but said 'The Lord rebuke you!'" Michael called on the power of the Lord to deal with the Devil. He was in a reverent fear of taking on Satan in his own power. The Book of Revelation records another battle Satan is going to have in trying to take over heaven a second time. The passage presents Satan and Michael and their angelic hosts in warfare. It is taken from Revelation 12:7-10: "And war broke out in heaven: Michael and his angels fought with the dragon; and the dragon and his angels fought, but they did not prevail, nor was a place found for them in heaven any longer. So the great dragon was cast out, that serpent of old, called the Devil and Satan, who deceives the whole world; he was cast to the earth, and his angels were cast out with him. Then I heard a loud voice saying in heaven 'Now salvation, and strength, and the kingdom of our God, and the power of His Christ have come, for the accuser of our brethren, who accused them before our God day and night, has been cast down.'" Michael rules the angelic host, who with God's power, fight the Devil in his second attempt to rule heaven. If Michael is in charge of the angelic host, and he fears Lucifer, it stands to reason that Lucifer is the most powerful creature in existence; creature being a created being.

LUCIFER THE PIPER - THE MAKER OF MUSIC

When God created Lucifer as the most powerful angel, he distinguished him from the rest by giving him the ability to bear beautiful light, as well as the power to make music. When he was created, God gave him pipes and tabrets and the ability to play them; the ability of a composer. This is said of no other angelic being, only Lucifer. In the Old Testament Book of Ezekiel, Chapter 28, Verses 12-17, Lucifer is described as the anointed cherub, the light bearer, and the piper: "Thus saith the Lord God; Thou sealest up the sum, full of wisdom, and perfect in beauty. Thou hast been in Eden the garden of God; every precious stone was thy covering, the sardius, topaz, and the diamond, the beryl, the onyx, and the jasper, the sapphire, the emerald, and the carbuncle, and gold: the workmanship of thy tabrets and of thy pipes was prepared in thee in the day that thou wast created. Thou art the anointed cherub that covereth; and I have set thee so: thou wast upon the holy mountain of God; thou hast walked up and down in the midst of the stones of fire. Thou wast perfect in thy ways from the day that thou wast created, till iniquity was found in thee. By the multitude of thy merchandise they have filled the midst of thee with violence, and thou hast sinned: therefore I will cast thee as profane out of the mountain of God: and I will destroy thee, O covering cherub, from the midst of the stones of fire. Thine heart was lifted up because of thy beauty, thou hast corrupted thy wisdom by reason of thy brightness: I will cast thee to the ground, I will lay thee before kings, that they may behold thee." (KJV)

The following commentary elaborates on the preceding description of Lucifer. "Thus saith the Lord God, Thou sealest up the sum." The term "sum," as we know from studying mathematics in school, is the result of addition. To seal up a sum means that nothing else needs to be added. It speaks of the completion of a work. In other words, God created him with perfect attributes, ability, knowledge, and power. He needed absolutely nothing. He had everything but the authority of his creator. He was created so perfectly to rule the angelic host. None of them, including Michael and Gabriel, was created perfect in every attribute. The verse says he is: "full of wisdom, and perfect in beauty." Being "full of wisdom" means he had perfect wisdom; none needed to be added. "Perfect in beauty," translated into contemporary terms means he was perfectly handsome. This means he was the most handsome of the angels. The *Bible* goes on to say that he was in Eden. "Thou hast been in Eden, the garden of God." Lucifer had spent time in the Garden of Eden. Because of the context of the passage, some, including this author, believe there is also a "supernal" Eden, or one in heaven. We do know he was in the earthly Eden, however. "Every precious stone was thy covering, the sardius, topaz, and the diamond, the beryl, the onyx, and the jasper, the sapphire, the emerald, and the carbuncle, and gold." These different color stones were part of his wardrobe in some fashion; setting him apart from the rest of the angels in appearance. "Thou art the anointed cherub that covereth." His being called "anointed cherub" refers not only to cherubim, a special kind of angelic being, but also to his being above the rest because of his anointing. Jesus Christ, being called "Messiah," is in effect being called the "anointed one;"

which is what Messiah means. He is King of Kings and Lord of Lords. Referring to Lucifer as the anointed cherub that covereth, the *Bible* says "I have set thee so." God set him up as the anointed cherub that covers. The passage does not specifically state what he covered; some believe it was God's throne. Perhaps he ascended to stand guard at God's throne whenever the angels gathered before Him. The angels periodically presented themselves before God, as the Book of Job illustrates. "Thou wast upon the holy mountain of God," refers to the free access Lucifer had when in heaven. It was a privilege for him to walk there. Also, "thou hast walked up and down in the midst of the stones of fire," indicates another special place he had access to that others did not. Rolling Stones fans should perceive these stones of fire as "Hot Rocks." "Thou wast perfect in thy ways from the day that thou wast created, till iniquity was found in thee." This means, as previously stated, Lucifer was completely perfect, until he rebelled. Speaking of his abilities the passage reads: "By the multitude of thy merchandise they have filled the midst of thee with violence, and thou hast sinned." His power, wisdom, and angelic authority puffed his mind up with pride. It was this pride that motivated him to become violent toward God. Evidently, the attitude of violence permeated the very core of his being; in other words, he was consumed by it. The passage said his merchandise "filled the midst of thee with violence." Here you have that of which Lord Jesus Christ spoke, when he addressed the Jewish religious leaders who wanted him dead, about Satan. He said in John 8:44, "He was a murderer from the beginning." He told them they were the Devil's children, while all Jerusalem thought they were holy because of their white robes. It wasn't a bunch of hookers, thieves, pimps and drug dealers who were yelling "crucify him;" it was the phony "righteous."

Lucifer's sin of violence against God, specifically, attempted murder, according to Lord Jesus Christ himself, is the reason God said the next part of the verse: "therefore I will cast thee as profane out of the mountain of God, and I will destroy thee, O covering cherub, from the midst of the stones of fire." God said he would cast Lucifer "as profane" off his mountain. Then he said he would destroy him from among the stones of fire. God cast him down from heaven. He destroyed his presence from among the stones of fire. He does not mean he terminated his existence. What he means is he would destroy him in battle. God was walking among the stones of fire when he was attacked. Lucifer ascended into heaven to kill God and God cast him down from his presence. Guess who it was that cast him down? The same person he attacked; Lord Jesus Christ, God the Son. Jesus said: "And He said to them, 'I saw Satan fall like lightning from heaven.'" - Luke 10:18 God then describes specifically what caused Lucifer to be proud enough to try this: "Thine heart was lifted up because of thy beauty, thou hast corrupted thy wisdom by reason of thy brightness." Lucifer knew he was the most handsome angel. He also knew the stones that covered him shown bright light. Aleister Crowley's favorite occult book, *The Book of the Sacred*

Magic of Abra-Melin the Mage, presents Lucifer from the Latin "Lux," meaning light, and "Fero," to bear, = "Light Bearer."4 The Devil was so proud of his beauty and brightness, he perceived himself as invincible. The last part of the *Bible* passage that will be examined is the most important to Led Zeppelin fans: "The workmanship of thy tabrets and of thy pipes was prepared in thee in the day that thou wast created." One can clearly see from this passage that God created Lucifer as the "piper" before the angelic host. It is logical then, to refer to the Devil as the piper. The word "workmanship" used in relation to the "pipes" and "tabrets" needs defining. "Workmanship" in that verse comes from the Hebrew word "Melakah," which means "deputyship or ministry" as well as "employment or work." Webster's Dictionary defines it as "skill of a workman, or the quality of his work; craftsmanship."5 He had the God given skill to compose music and play it on his pipes and tabrets. The word tabret is the Hebrew word "toph" which means "a tambourine." Tabrets are tambourines, the derivative of the drums. Webster defines tambourine as "a shallow, single-headed hand drum having jingling metal disks in the rim: it is played by shaking, hitting with the knuckles, etc."6 It is reasonable then, to assume, because no other angelic being is recorded with this power, that Lucifer used to play the music before the angels when they worshiped God. Nowhere in the *Bible* does it say that any power or skill was taken from him after he rebelled against God. The only thing he lost was his position.

Aleister Crowley confirmed that Lucifer still has his pipes and composing ability in a vision he had of him on November 28, 1909. The vision describes him with the different colors of the stones from the Biblical text: "And now there comes an Angel, to hide the tablet with his mighty wing. This Angel has all the colours mingled in his dress; his head is proud and beautiful; his headdress is of silver and red and blue and gold and black, like cascades of water, and in his left hand he has a pan-pipe of the seven holy metals, upon which he plays. I cannot tell you how wonderful the music is, but it is so wonderful that one only lives in one's ears; one cannot see anything any more."7 Can Led Zeppelin fans see how this piper was calling Crowley to follow him? Lucifer's music took complete control of Crowley during that vision. Perhaps Crowley heard "Stairway to Heaven" sixty-one years before Jimmy Page did. Lucifer's music, therefore, is clearly very powerful when heard by the human ear. The congruence between the *Holy Bible's* presentation of Lucifer and Aleister Crowley's is clearly seen, both sources showing him to be the light bearing piper, both of which are powerful characteristics.

SATAN THE TEMPTER - THE DECEIVER OF MANKIND

The Devil's greatest power against men is the power of temptation. The most audacious attempt to get a man to sin was his temptation of Lord Jesus Christ in the desert. Christ could be tempted only because he was in human flesh. He suffered temptation, without sin, in order to be able to understand it. This story not only shows Satan tempting Jesus to do wrong, but it also has the information authenticating the satanic pact. The Devil tried to get Jesus to make a pact with him. The passage reads: "Then the devil, taking Him up on a high mountain, showed Him all the kingdoms of the world in a moment of time. And the devil said to Him, 'All this authority I will give You, and their glory; for this has been delivered to me, and I give it to whomever I wish. Therefore, if You will worship before me, all will be Yours.' And Jesus answered and said to him, 'Get behind Me, Satan! For it is written, "You shall worship the LORD your God, and Him only you shall serve."'" - Luke 4:5-8 Jesus did not debate the Devil on his claim that the earth had been given into his hands and that he can give it to who ever he wants to. Christ did not debate this because it was true; and he was the one who gave it to him. The Devil was given the authority to rule the earth, with certain limits, because of man's decision to obey him rather than God in the book of Genesis. Man's demand for autonomy from God's rule landed him the position of being ruled by the Devil; a sinister poetic situation.

The following is the story of the temptation in the Garden of Eden. In Genesis 2:16-17, we read: "And the LORD God commanded the man, saying, 'Of every tree of the garden you may freely eat; but of the tree of the knowledge of good and evil you shall not eat, for in the day that you eat of it you shall surely die.'" Adam was warned not to eat of the fruit that gave the knowledge of good and evil. Satan comes along, to tempt man to do exactly that. God did not read about this the next day in the New York Times. He sent the Devil there to test them; to see if they would obey his command, knowing ahead of time what they would do. We must understand that just because God knows what a man is going to do, that does not mean he is responsible for the man doing it. The man is responsible for his actions; or woman as the case may be. Satan strolls into the garden in the form of a serpent in Genesis 3:1-6: "Now the serpent was more cunning than any beast of the field which the LORD God had made. And he said to the woman, 'Has God indeed said, "You shall not eat of every tree of the garden?"' And the woman said to the serpent, 'We may eat the fruit of the trees of the garden; but of the fruit of the tree which is in the midst of the garden, God has said, "You shall not eat it, nor shall you touch it, lest you die."' Then the serpent said to the woman, 'You will not surely die. For God knows that in the day you eat of it your eyes will be opened, and you will be like God, knowing good and evil.'"

Since the world has chosen Satan to obey as god right from the beginning, the Almighty has allowed him to make pacts with men. Man, however, has been given the knowledge of good and evil; this making him responsible for knowing the Devil is evil. Aleister and Jimmy believe he is good. Yes, words do have more than one meaning. The satanist holds evil as good and good as evil; due to their self-imposed searing of their conscience. The following quote is from *The Black Arts*: "People who worship the Devil do not regard him as evil. To the Satanist the supernatural being who is the Enemy of Christendom is a good and benevolent god. But the word 'good,' applied to the Devil by his followers, does not carry its Christian or conventional meanings. Satanists believe that what Christians call good is really evil, and vice versa, though there is an ambivalence of attitude in Satanism, as in black magic, a perverse pleasure in doing things which are felt to be evil combined with a conviction that doing these things is really virtuous."8 Can you now see that words can have more than one meaning? Just like Robert Plant said in "Stairway to Heaven." Now we are going to look at the Devil according to Crowley.

THE DEVIL ACCORDING TO ALEISTER CROWLEY'S EQUINOX

As I wrote before, Aleister Crowley did not believe the Devil existed in his Biblical context. The rest of the world calls Lucifer "Satan," so in order to ensure they are on the same page when talking about him, he calls him Satan; just so they know what Lucifer he is talking about. He wrote: "By Thy most secret and Holy Name of Apophis be Thou blessed, Lucifer, Star of the Dawn, Satan-Jeheshua, Light of the World!"9 Crowley, believing that Lucifer is god, steals the phrase "Light of the World" from the *Holy Bible* where Jesus referred to himself as the Light of the World in the New Testament Book of John, Chapter 8, verse 12: "Then Jesus spoke to them again, saying 'I am the light of the world. He who follows Me shall not walk in darkness, but have the light of life.'" The Devil is clearly using Crowley to make himself out to be god in the minds of those who are Biblically illiterate.

Crowley wrote about meeting the Devil at the Black Mass in *The Magical Record of the Beast 666*. In the text he calls the Devil "Lord." The following is a quote from it: "Wilt thou not make this night the nameless nuptial, the Devil thy Lord and mine at Our Black Mass-8:23 P.M.?"10 Here is an example of one of those masses, taken from his *Equinox*, Vol. I, No.7:

"18. Also the altar shall fume before the master with incense that hath no smoke.

19. That which is to be denied shall be denied; that which is to be trampled shall be trampled; that which is to be spat upon shall be spat upon.

20. These things shall be burnt in the outer fire.

21. Then again the master shall speak as he will soft words, and with

music and what else he will bring forward the Victim.

22. Also he shall slay a young child upon the altar, and the blood shall cover the altar with perfumes of roses.

23. Then shall the master appear as He should appear - in His glory.

24. He shall stretch himself upon the altar, and awake it into life, and into death.

25. (For so we conceal that life which is beyond.)

26. The temple shall be darkened, save for the fire and the lamp of the altar.

27. There shall he kindle a great fire and a devouring.

28. Also he shall smite the altar with his scourge, and blood shall flow therefrom.

29. Also he shall have made roses bloom thereon.

30. In the end he shall offer up the Vast Sacrifice, at the moment when the God licks up the flame upon the altar.

31. All these things shalt thou perform strictly, observing the time.

32. And the Beloved shall abide with Thee.

33. Thou shalt not disclose the interior world of this rite unto any one: therefore have I written it in symbols that cannot be understood.

34. I who reveal the ritual am IAO and OAI; the Right and the Averse.

35. These are alike unto me.

36. Now the Veil of this operation is called Shame, and the Glory abideth within.

37. Thou shalt comfort the heart of the secret stone with the warm blood. Thou shalt make a subtle decoction of delight, and the Watchers shall drink thereof."11

This author has read over thirty of Crowley's most famous books, and I still have no idea what Crowley meant by "symbols" in verse 33 of that passage, but you can leave me out of that church service! Were symbols present in that passage? Do satanists know to take the whole thing literally? I do not know, so I cannot say, but if I have to guess, I would believe it is literal. If it is symbolic, I think Crowley could have created a more flowery presentation. We must remember, this man's hero is the Devil. If the Devil wouldn't advocate literal human sacrifice, who would? Do you the reader think it possible for a Devil worshiper to take a passage like that literally? Jimmy Page had Crowley's *Equinox* containing the previous passage in his London occult bookstore.

In 1973, John Symonds reprinted a Crowley book that, along with *The Magical Record of the Beast 666*, has got to be the most perverted book I have ever read. It is called *White Stains*. Crowley wrote about going to bed and performing all kinds of sex acts with a woman and a Great Dane.12 It is too disgusting for me to print. This is the same man about whom Jimmy Page asked how anyone could call him evil. Think about that. Don't believe for a minute that Jimmy Page is without a copy of *White Stains*. Led Zeppelin used to have Great Dane shows in their hotels. Along with hanging out with the "starlets" of groupies, Richard Cole, their road manager, would invite the "Dog Act," which included a Great Dane, to their hotel "for special shows."13 You have to hand it to them. When they decided to follow Crowley's teachings, the band went the distance. The information about the Dog Act came from Steven Davis' *Hammer of the Gods*, which the band has said was loaded with misrepresentations. However, Davis was never sued, and the information matches the teachings of Aleister Crowley, interestingly enough (*Hammer of the Gods*, however, does not implicate the band members as having sex with the dog like Crowley claimed to). It will be interesting to hear what they say about this work. Getting back to *White Stains*, here is a quote from John Symonds in the introduction: "During the last decade an extraordinary interest has developed in Crowley the mage. He is now rightly compared to Mme. Blavatsky, and to Eliphas Levi, whose reincarnation he believed himself to be. His voluminous writings on his doctrine of Thelema (the philosophy of Do What Thou Wilt), his accounts of explorations of other planes with the aid of drugs, and his sex-magical teachings are all zealously studied by the youth of Europe and America."14 America is in trouble. Symonds wrote that in 1973. Lord Jesus Christ spoke of the period of time just prior to the rise of the Anti-Christ (a title Crowley applied to himself), by talking about what to look for: "Then He said to them, 'Nation will rise against nation, and kingdom against kingdom. And there will be great earthquakes in various places, and famines and pestilences, and there will be fearful sights and great signs from heaven.'" - Luke 21:10-11 For those who might not know, "pestilence" is the spread of deadly disease. It would seem that the time is near.

Crowley did not fail to mention his hero, Satan, in *White Stains*. This was prior to his belief that the Devil was God. He wrote:

> "Oh, how I curse thee, God!
> What is my aid? But yet to Satan's Power
> I lend my utmost vigour for an hour,
> To wrest thy damned throne from out thy hands!"15

Crowley wrote that before he ever got involved with the Silver Star. It seems that he was ripe for membership in Devil worship, and the Devil converted him into the type of person who believes he is god, as Page, Jagger, and Osbourne suggest. As Lord Jesus Christ said, you can know a disciple by the fruit they bear, and this man bore the fruit of a Devil worshiper right from the start.

One of the things that occultists do which is spiritual suicide is use the *Bible* to back their beliefs. They use it allegorically, of course. What that means is that they take passages out of their Biblical context, or intended meaning, and apply them to occult teaching as a foundation for belief. The Book of Revelation describes Lord Jesus Christ in his glorified body, in the first chapter: "Then I turned to see the voice that spoke with me. And having turned I saw seven golden lampstands, and in the midst of the seven lampstands One like the Son of Man, clothed with a garment down to the feet and girded about the chest with a golden band. His head and hair were white like wool, as white as snow, and His eyes like a flame of fire; His feet were like fine brass, as if refined in a furnace, and His voice as the sound of many waters; He had in His right hand seven stars, out of His mouth went a sharp two-edged sword, and His countenance was like the sun shining it its strength." – Revelation 1:12-16 Crowley says that is a description of Satan. He wrote the following in his *Equinox, Vol. I, No.1*: "...an ancient, bearded Father, with hair as white as wool, and eyes like flames of fire; whose voice is as the sound of many waters, in whose right hand tremble the seven stars of heaven, and out of whose mouth flashes forth a flaming sword of fire."16 The flaming sword is the Qabalah. You will read that later. Satan has put forth his image as having eyes of fire consistently to copy Christ. Remember Ozzy Osbourne in the song, "Black Sabbath," from the album *Black Sabbath*, by the group "Black Sabbath," in which he was lead singer for years? He sang, "Big black shape with eyes of fire." Two lines later he talks about "Satan" who is seated and "smiling" at him. It sounds like a description of the Black Sabbath; written about in chapter four. Crowley talks about Satan having eyes of fire again in his *Equinox, Vol. I, No.6*:

> "Hail to thee in whose eye is a Flame of fire!
> Hail, Lord of the Destroying Army!"17

You will see the "Lord of the Destroying Army" again in "The Battle of Evermore" chapter. The satanic image having eyes of fire is not new. The movie *Dracula* in 1931 put forth the same when "Renfield" described Dracula coming to see him at the insane asylum: "A red mist spread over the lawn, coming on like a flame of fire. And then he parted it. And I could see that there were thousands of rats, with their eyes blazing red, like his, only smaller." In the first chapter I wrote about the Led Zeppelin film and Jimmy Page sitting on a blanket playing a hurdy gurdy as Peter Grant took tour dates to him. He has an eye in a triangle on his back, and when Grant gets close to the blanket, Page stops playing and turns around. His eyes appear as a flame of fire. The Devil has also been seen with eyes of fire in the form of a Black Dog.

LED ZEPPELIN IV (RUNES) - "BLACK DOG"

Led Zeppelin fans will remember what Robert Plant said while singing "Black Dog," a song off the fourth album, "Eyes that shine burning red," at 1:15 into the song. In the next line he says that he is constantly dreaming about him. Remember that, it is a key point, that Robert Plant was constantly dreaming about the Black Dog (In the movie, *The Exorcist*, the priest named "Father Karras" has a black dog chasing him in a dream while asleep.). This will be seen again, at the appropriate time. The Black Dog that Robert Plant referred to is the Devil. Robert Plant has said that the song is about a black Labrador that wandered in and out of their recording studio while making their fourth album. I just cannot imagine anyone being naïve enough to believe that Jimmy Page's recording studio was not secure from unwanted people, much less stray animals. However, there have been people who are willing to believe that as opposed to the truth, who have debated me. Why? They want to avoid the satanic element and believe that Robert was really talking about a dog. Let me ask the reader a question. If a stray black Labrador came up to you, and his eyes were burning flames, would you hang around and ask him if he would like a biscuit? No, you would run for the hills. Compare the lyrics from the Led Zeppelin song with this paragraph from *The Encyclopedia of Witchcraft & Magic*, about the Black Dog in Britain with burning eyes of fire: "'A Black Dog has walked over him' used to be a popular expression meaning that the person referred to was bad tempered. Spectral animals of various kinds are said to haunt the British Isles and black dogs, part fairy and part ghost, are recorded in many areas, often dangerous, but usually doing no harm if unmolested. A typical apparition is about the size of a calf and shaggy with burning, saucer-shaped eyes. It is one of many forms assumed by the devil."18 Again, the Black Dog is the Devil, with burning eyes of fire. On the 1980 European tour, Page introduced "Black Dog" as "Strangers in the Night." I want the reader to understand that I KNOW he was not kidding.

In her book, *The Encyclopedia of Witches and Witchcraft*, Rosemary Ellen Guiley wrote about Black Dogs in Britain: "Various forms of black demon dogs populate the legendary lore of parts of England, particularly in East Anglia, a region steeped in WITCHCRAFT. These Dogs are generally called Black Shuck, and sometimes Old Shuck, from the Anglo-Saxon term 'scucca,' which means 'demon.' Like ghosts that haunt a particular location, Black Shuck lurks about a graveyard, a lonely country road, a misty marsh or the hills around a village. Like the spectral hounds of HECATE, he is a creature of the night, as big as a calf, with eyes that glow red or green. His bone-chilling howls can be heard above the fiercest storms. He follows travelers, breathing an icy breath upon their necks. He is an omen of death; to see Black Shuck means that one or a member of one's family will soon die. In Suffolk, it is believed that Black Shuck is fairly harmless as long as he is not bothered.

Spectral black dogs played a prominent role in the witchcraft beliefs of the Middle ages and Renaissance. The DEVIL was believed to appear as a black dog."19

In that last quote, you read where the word "scucca" means "demon." I would like to invite your attention to the 1994 Page/Plant album, *No Quarter*, which as you know means "no mercy." The three new songs on that album, "Yallah," "City Don't Cry," and "Wonderful One," are listed by the band in their compact disc booklet as being published by "Succubus Music Ltd./Talktime Ltd." Webster defines the word "Succubus" this way: "a female demon thought in medieval times to have sexual intercourse with sleeping men."20 This is only a few of many Devil examples from Led Zeppelin to follow, especially when their blatant command to sell one's soul to the Devil is revealed, again, at the right time. As written previously, the knowledge of the satanic pact was taken from the *Holy Bible*.

SATAN AS PAN THE PIPER

Another name that is used by Crowley and many others in referring to Satan is "Pan." Pan is described in *Putnam's Concise Mythological Dictionary*: "Pan - A Greek nature and fertility deity, originally native to Arcadia. As such he is god of goatherds and flocks and is usually represented as a very sensual creature; a shaggy human to the loins with pointed ears, goat's horns and legs. He wanders among the mountains and valleys, pursuing nymphs or leading them in their dances. He is quite musical and is the inventor of the Syrinx, or 'Pipes of Pan.'"21

He is also described in *The Encyclopedia of Witches and Witchcraft*: "Pan - His cult was centered in Arcadia, where he haunted the woodlands, hills and mountains, sleeping at noon, and then dancing through the woods as he played the panpipes, which he invented. As a lusty leader of satyrs, he chased the nymphs; he later was incorporated into the retinue of Dionysus. His symbol was the phallus, and he was invoked for the fertility of flocks, or an abundant hunt. Every region in Greece had its own Pan, who was known by various names, and Pan eventually came to symbolize the universal god. He is recognized in NEO-PAGANISM and neo-Pagan WITCHCRAFT and is an aspect of the HORNED GOD."22 Pan being recognized as the universal god, by various names, is teaching based on the Qabalah, advocated by Aleister Crowley and Jimmy Page in Led Zeppelin's music; as will be seen. Pan is Lucifer, Satan, the Devil.

Pan is described by occultists as very musical, as a piper who created his own pipes. The *Holy Bible* says he (the Devil) was created with pipes as well as the ability to compose music; as you read previously. In his book advocating narcotics as fit for everyday use, *Diary of a Drug Fiend*, Aleister Crowley recorded a ritual for calling the Devil into one's presence, or "invocation;" and the method he describes to contact him is to chant the name "Pan." One character in the novel (Crowley wrote that the novel was a true story in the beginning of the book) is recording the information in her journal. Her name is "Lady Pendragon." She wrote:

"I have found a manuscript in grandfather's room that tells you how to invoke the Devil. It needs two people, and I don't feel sure about Peter.

"He can't see into the spiritual world at all. On the contrary, he is getting a little queer in the head, and imagines he sees things which don't exist at all. He's constantly scratching himself.

"He behaved very strangely at dinner. I think the butler noticed it.
"At midnight we went up to the old man's room and began to go through the ritual. A lot of it seems silly, but the climax is fine.

"You keep saying, over and over: -
'Io Pan Pan! Io Pan Pan! Ai Pan Pan!
Io Pan Pan! Io Pan Pan! Pan Pan Pan!
Aegipan, Aegipan, Aegipan, Aegipan, Aegipan,
Aegipan, Io Pan Pan!'"23

Three days later, in the story, Lady Pendragon records in her journal these words:
"I don't remember what happened. I know why. Basil (Crowley) told me long ago that the mind only kept count of material things. So these spiritual events are recorded in a higher kind of mind of which we are not conscious until we get accustomed to spiritual life. So all I can put down is that we had a complete success.

"The Devil, of course, needs a human interpreter if he is to communicate with this world, and so he took possession of Peter. He has been preparing Peter to represent him."24

Make sure you understand, lock it into your memory, that Aleister Crowley presents one of the ways to invoke the Devil is to call upon Pan. The reason is, obviously, because Pan the Piper is the Devil. You will see Pan again in this book. A very key reference will have him in it.

JIMMY PAGE PROMOTES THE EQUINOX AND THE DEVIL

Before ending this chapter, the reader needs to be reminded that the Devil is a liar. After this book is published, there will be those who are going to try to downplay the satanic element in Crowley's life and try to say that his worship of the Devil has absolutely nothing to do with the Silver Star; that it is simply a magical order. The author guarantees that they will not want to confess they are associated with the Devil. One may read that I have blown all this out or proportion in order to be sensational and draw attention to this book. I have something to counteract that nonsense before they even try. Aleister Crowley called *The Equinox* the encyclopedia of initiation, and refers to it often as the most important of his writings. He also wrote that *The Equinox* and the A.A. (Silver Star) go together in *The Book of Lies*. He made it clear to his readers that the A.A. is absolutely dependent upon it; that *The Equinox* is the most important publication in its development. He wrote concerning himself in the third person: "It is he who is responsible for the whole of the development of the A.A. movement which has been associated with the publication of THE EQUINOX; and His utterance is enshrined in the sacred writings."25 (Capitalization was made by Crowley.) Samuel Weiser Inc., who publishes and sells *The Equinox* in the United States, has this written in its 1995-1996 catalog:

[Crowley, Aleister. THE EQUINOX (10-Volume Set)
This limited edition contains 10 volumes, all the original color art, and is complete and unabridged. The binding follows the style of the rare cloth edition published in London. Essential reading for the student of Crowley as cross-references to it are found in nearly all his writings.]

Equinox was the name Jimmy Page gave to his own occult bookstore he operated at one time. The following quote is from *Hit Parader* magazine in July of 1975. Making reference to the store Page said: "...there was not one good collection of books on the occult in London, and I was tired of having to go all different places to get the books I wanted."26 In *Hammer of the Gods*, Steven Davis wrote about Page's bookstore, identifying it as *The Equinox*: "Jimmy had stocked the shop himself with various rare and antique books on magic and the occult that he picked up on buying trips to rare book dealers. The bookshop was named the Equinox, after Aleister Crowley's own occult magazine."27 In *Jimmy Page – Tangents Within a Framework*, Howard Mylett as well wrote of it being named *Equinox*: "Jimmy opened a bookshop venture for occult books called 'Equinox' at 4, Holland Street, Kensington, London."28 Not only did Jimmy Page name his occult bookstore Equinox, after Aleister Crowley's writings, but he also sold *The Equinox* by Crowley. Howard Mylett wrote: "At Equinox it was possible to buy several works signed by Crowley, and at one time the shop housed a first edition set of Crowley's ten volume work 'The Equinox' priced around L350."29

The 10-volume set of *The Equinox* has 4,454 pages in it. Crowley referred to it as *The Equinox - Volume I, Nos.1-10*. In the introduction to the first volume, Israel Regardie, another well known occultist and former contemporary and secretary for Crowley, wrote this about *The Equinox*: "The Equinox is unique. It can safely be said that in the whole history of occultism nothing has ever appeared to rival the *Equinox* in quantity, quality and diversity. It is a living testimonial to the matchless genius of Aleister Crowley who was born in England during the year 1875 and who died there in 1947."30 Regardie went on to say this at the end of the introduction: "For the student who wishes to learn Magick as a practical art shorn of the balderdash of medievalism and superstition, the *Equinox* is an absolute essential. There is nothing-absolutely nothing anywhere comparable to the contents of these priceless volumes. They are priceless and invaluable, and for the true student an absolutely essential part of his occult library. Once on the shelves, he will never, never part with them."31 Now, I challenge you to consider the following, taken from *The Equinox, Volume I, No.10*, where it is clear Crowley thought the Devil was the creator of man, and therefore, almighty god:

"HYMN TO SATAN"

"I ADORE Thee, King of Evil,
  By the body Thou hast fashioned
In the likeness of a devil.
  By its purity impassioned
I adore Thee, King of Evil!

"I adore Thee, Lord of Malice,
  By the soul that Thou hast moulded
Lovely as a lily-chalice
  To the sombre sun unfolded
I adore Thee, Lord of Malice!

"By its thirst, the cruel craving
  For things infinite, unheard-of,
Dreams devouring and depraving
  Songs no God may guess a word of,
Songs of crime and song of craving-

"By the drear eyes of the devil
  Bleak and sterile as they glitter
I adore Thee, King of Evil,
  With these lips, as dry and bitter
As the drear eyes of the devil!

"I adore Thee, I invoke Thee,
  I abase myself before Thee,
By the spells that once awoke the

Lust of Chaos I adore Thee,
I adore Thee, I invoke Thee!"32

Jimmy Page clearly promoted *The Equinox*, the publication that includes the quoted *Hymn To Satan*. Don't let anyone patronize you by saying the Silver Star has nothing to do with Satan. In the new edition of *Magick - Book 4 * Liber Aba*, Crowley says over and over that Satan is Lord, especially in the section of the book, *Liber Samekh,* which is the ritual Crowley used to attain union with his Holy Guardian Angel, Satan. Crowley makes it clear to his students in the Silver Star, that Aiwaz, his Holy Guardian Angel, is Satan. Jimmy Page is thanked for his contributions to the book by answering questions and providing advice as well as references; on page XV prior to the text, in the acknowledgments. Kenneth Anger, another renowned occultist of the Silver Star, is also thanked on this page. Anger asked Jimmy to compose a soundtrack for his occult film based on the works of Crowley, *Lucifer Rising*. When discussing the fact that Anger had asked him to do it, Jimmy said, "I felt it quite an honour that he'd asked me."33 An objective perception of why Led Zeppelin guitarist Jimmy Page would consider working on *Lucifer Rising* an honor is a "no-brainer." The *Lucifer Rising* soundtrack was aborted due to a falling out between Page and Anger. Dave Lewis and Simon Pallett wrote about this in their book, *Led Zeppelin: The Concert File*. Focusing on 1976, they wrote: "Page's increasing drug problems began to escalate during the year and he was attacked in the press by film director Kenneth Anger for reputedly failing to come up with the soundtrack for the movie 'Lucifer Rising.'"34 Not only did Jimmy Page work on the soundtrack for *Lucifer Rising*, he was in the film itself. He is depicted as Lucifer standing before a photo of Aleister Crowley on the wall, and Page is holding the Egyptian tablet, the "Stele of Revealing," in his hand. This tablet is included in this book (Ch.7 photos) and referred to in chapter seven as part of Crowley's meeting with Satan in Cairo. When commenting on Lucifer in relation to the film, Jimmy Page said: "In the film Lucifer is the Light bearer and not Satan as in Christian terms."35. A still of Jimmy in Lucifer Rising is printed in *The Equinox, Volume III, No. 10*." The caption under the still says, "Jimmy Page as Lucifer meets the Beast in Lucifer Rising." The Beast is Aleister Crowley. Kenneth Anger's work on *Lucifer Rising* is glorified in that book, and Aleister Crowley's *Hymn to Lucifer* is printed therein, and be sure to notice another reference of Lucifer as the sun:

"HYMN TO LUCIFER"

"Ware, nor of good nor ill, what aim hath act?
    Without its climax, death, what savour hath

Life? An impeccable machine, exact
   He paces an inane and pointless path
To glut brute appetites, his sole content
   How tedious were he fit to comprehend
Himself! More, this our noble element
   Of fire in nature, love in spirit, unkenned
Life hath no spring, no axle, and no end.

His body a blood-ruby radiant
   With noble passion, sun-souled Lucifer
Swept through the dawn colossal, swift aslant
   On Eden's imbecile perimeter.
He blessed nonentity with every curse
   And spiced with sorrow the dull soul of sense,
Breathed life into the sterile universe,
   With Love and Knowledge drove out innocence
The Key of Joy is disobedience."36

The disobedience Crowley is talking about, is not acts of disobedience to Lucifer, but Lord Jesus Christ. Aleister Crowley wrote *The Equinox*, saying it was the most important publication relative to the progression of the Silver Star, Jimmy Page called his occult bookstore *Equinox*, naming it specifically after Crowley's *Equinox*, where he had a copy of it, and *The Equinox* promotes Satan, as you read. Therefore the only logical conclusion one can come to is that the Silver Star is an occult order founded for the purpose of promoting the Devil and Magick; period. Only the willfully blind will deny or dismiss this fact.

"WALKING INTO CLARKSDALE" - THE CROSSROADS

One of the methods chosen by Led Zeppelin to promote Satan worship, as written previously, is to command the fans to sell their souls to the Devil. Robert Plant's command to the fans to do that is discussed in a later chapter. However, a brief presentation of the satanic pact being made at the crossroads will be shown here, and the history of the pact will be elaborated on in the next chapter. As written earlier, Robert Plant held a fascination with Robert Johnson when growing up, the King of the Mississippi Delta Blues singers in the 1930's, and Led Zeppelin reproduced his song, "Traveling Riverside Blues." The modern day musical fascination with the crossroads and the Devil is rooted in the mystery surrounding Robert Johnson. He sang about standing at the crossroads as the sun was going down, in "Crossroad Blues." After sunset was the time for an aspiring musician to stand at the crossroads to make his pact with Satan. The crossroads in question are located in Clarksdale, Mississippi, the town Robert Plant and Jimmy Page titled their 1998 album after, *Walking Into Clarksdale.*

In his book, *Searching for Robert Johnson,* Peter Guralnick related the story as told by another blues musician from the same area, Tommy Johnson:

"Tommy Johnson's brother LeDell put it to David Evans even more graphically in describing how Tommy, who like Robert went off from home scarcely able to play the guitar, came back an accomplished musician.

'Now if Tom was living, he'd tell you. He said the reason he knowed so much, said he sold hisself to the devil. I asked him how. He said, "If you want to learn how to play anything you want to play and learn how to make songs yourself, you take your guitar and you go to where a road crosses that way, where a crossroad is. Get there, be sure to get there just a little 'fore 12:00 that night so you'll know you'll be there. You have your guitar and be playing a piece there by yourself....A big black man will walk up there and take your guitar, and he'll tune it. And then he'll play a piece and hand it back to you. That's the way I learned to play anything I want."'

'Son House was convinced that Robert Johnson had done the same thing, and undoubtedly, as Johnny Shines says, others were, too. That was the beginning, in any case, of Robert Johnson's travels and of his life as a professional musician."37

Johnson authenticated the speculation relative to his pact with Satan in the song, "Me and the Devil Blues," where he sang of the Devil knocking at his door early one morning, and then in the next line he sang, "Hello Satan, I believe it's time to go." Now, it is possible that they were going to breakfast together, or that they were going to the local mall together, or that Johnson knew informed individuals would know exactly what he meant by that statement; that the Devil would come to collect his soul, as per his satanic pact. Again, Robert Johnson died on Tuesday, August 16th, 1938, 39 years to the day prior to the death of Elvis Presley, whose (Elvis') stepbrother claimed committed suicide (One can see a photo of Johnson's death certificate on the internet at: http://www.bluesuit.com/html/death_cert.html). Again, Elvis not only died on August 16th, but on Tuesday, just like Johnson. Why would Elvis take his own life on the day that a Mississippi born and Memphis bound teenager named Robert Johnson, who sang of selling his soul to Satan, died?

Robert Johnson and others like him knew of the crossroads being a place to make a pact with Satan, because it was a fact known down through the centuries from antiquity. In the book, *Witchcraft, Magic, and Occultism*, W.B. Crow wrote of this aspect of the crossroads in the tenth century, relative to a witch cult: "Witches met at the crossroads. To perform certain magical acts one had sometimes, it was said, to go to the crossroads....When the witch-cult was at its height anyone interested in joining might receive a visit from one dressed in black. He would be the devil, or more correctly the devil's representative. He would sometimes get the victim to sign a written pact, and the signature was almost always in the blood of the person signing it….The pact sometimes had to be made at crossroads. The agreement was that the devil should give the victim everything he or she desired, in the way of knowledge, wealth, success, pleasure and vengeance against enemies, and in return the victim would renounce the Catholic religion, repudiate his own Baptism, would worship the devil, abandon all desire for Eternal Salvation and utterly deliver his own soul to Hell at death."38 [The person had to sign his "Name In Blood". Black Sabbath fans can see the initials "N.I.B." in that phrase, which is a song of theirs that encourages the fan to give himself to Lucifer.] The deal with the Devil at the crossroads then, was nothing new in the 1930's. Again, a 1980's film, *Crossroads*, explores the theme in detail, by discussing the life of one of Johnson's contemporaries, Willie Brown; who in the film at least, is seen to have made the deal with Satan, and meets him back at the crossroads to tell him the deal is off.

What does this all have to do with Led Zeppelin or Page/Plant? In the title song of their new album, *Walking Into Clarksdale*, Robert Plant sings that there is some "stranger" standing on a "crossroads," and then he sings that he believes he had "seen" that "face" in the past, at 1:55 into the song. Robert Plant had to be singing about Satan (A key point has to be made here. In the last quote from *Witchcraft, Magic and Occultism*, you read where the devil or the devil's representative would show up dressed in black. On the 1998 tour to support the Page/Plant *Walking Into Clarksdale* album, Jimmy Page wore solid black pants and a solid black shirt at every concert they played. Sometimes the entire band wore black. See photos at chapter's end). The evidence in the chapters to follow will suggest exactly that. I have in my possession a photo of Jimmy Page and Robert Plant standing in the Delta Blues Museum in Clarksdale, Mississippi, taken in 1998, in eye's view of the Robert Johnson crossroads (I failed to get permission to use it - I refused to pay the $395 Panny Mayfield required.). There is a photo of Robert Johnson on the wall of the museum included in this chapter's end. Right next to the photo of Johnson is a tablet with these words:

"Robert Johnson composed music and wrote lyrics so universal in their content that they would pass the test of time and become great blues standards; such songs as 'I Believe I'll Dust My Broom,' 'Sweet Home Chicago' and 'Love In Vain,' a song covered and popularized by the English rock group, The Rolling Stones.

"Whether or not Johnson went around claiming to have sold his soul to the Devil or whether it was something whispered behind his back to explain his speedy mastering of the guitar, everyone who remembered the little boy with the harmonica who could barely play a guitar lick could not believe the speed at which Johnson had improved during his travels."

Immediately adjacent to the preceding quote at the blues museum is a tablet with a title, *If You Want To Make A Contract With the Devil.* I am not including the inscription in this book, but it describes exactly how to accomplish it. Do we even need to speculate as to the motives of Robert Plant and Jimmy Page for going to Clarksdale, Mississippi, or giving their 1998 album the title of the town? An objective mind would say no. This too is a no-brainer. They also sing of someone standing with hellhounds in an abandoned hotel in the song, "Walking Into Clarksdale," describing him as a "King." An impartial observer of the preponderance of the evidence can see with no ambiguity that Robert Plant and Jimmy Page are promoting the worship of the Devil today just as they did thirty years ago; as the Devil's slaves. Satan is the true slave god.

Lucifer therefore, being called the Devil and Satan, appears to men as a diversely colored light bearer, with beautiful music and great promises to those who are willing to follow him. He is a murderer and deceiver whose goal is to deceive men into believing he is god and promote him as the object of worship and adulation, in order for that soul to avoid salvation in Jesus and end up with him in eternal damnation. The *Bible* provides man with the accurate description of Lucifer, the leader of the angelic host, leading a seditious uprising against Christ, with murder in his heart. It presents him also as the Piper, the celestial composer of music, as well as the tempter of mankind with whom he has permission to enter into pacts. Aleister Crowley spared no ink in praising him, Jimmy Page promoted both Lucifer and Crowley, and this concept is also presented in the music of Led Zeppelin. Two decades after the demise of the mighty Zeppelin, Page/Plant have glorified Satan again by calling him the "Most High" on their 1998 album, *Walking Into Clarksdale.* The song "Most High" was nominated for and won a Grammy Award in 1999, and in the song they mock Jesus Christ saying that his "crown" is not real. The title song of the album, *Walking Into Clarksdale*, subtly glorifies the satanic pact at the crossroads (Even the movie "The Doors" begins with little Jim Morrison at the Crossroads in the desert.). The *Bible* calls the Devil the deceiver of the whole world, and the fact is that he is deceiving many today through his servants: especially like the men of Led Zeppelin. To make the reader familiar with the history behind the satanic pact, we will now look at documented examples of it from antiquity.

Jimmy Page and Robert Plant (top right) enjoy the limelight in Frankfurt, Germany, on 12/3/98. You can see both of them dressed in solid black. In the middle photo, you can see the entire band dressed in black at this show; just before they said goodnight by bowing arm in arm (below). The band dressed in black several times on the 1998 tour. In the middle photo, Jimmy Page is wiping sweat from his brow as Robert Plant hugs his daughter's husband, bass player, Charlie Jones. The man to their right, is drummer Michael Lee. Between Jimmy Page and Robert Plant is Phillip Andrews, their 1998 Keyboard/Squeezebox player.

The Robert Johnson Blues Exhibit at the Clarksdale, Mississippi, Blues Museum where Robert Plant and Jimmy Page visited on the 1998 tour.

A closeup of the Robert Johnson exhibit inside the Clarksdale Blues Museum shows written instruction for the satanic pact. "If you want to make a contract with the Devil...." Led Zeppelin commanded the satanic pact in their movie.

The famous "Crossroads" in Clarksdale, Mississippi, where Highway 49 and Highway 61 cross. This view is from the south.

The same Crossroads as in the photo above, this time viewed from the north. These photos were taken in September, 1998, the day of the final concert in America at the "Pyramid" in Memphis, Tennessee, by one of my "For Badge-holders Only" Led Zeppelin internet mailing list associates (anonymous).

1 E.M. Bounds, *Satan: His Personality, Power, and Overthrow*, Baker Book House, Grand Rapids, Michigan, 1972, pg.113

2 Aleister Crowley, *The Confessions of Aleister Crowley*, Edited by John Symonds and Kenneth Grant, Penguin-Arkana, 1989, pg.67

3 Aleister Crowley, *The Holy Books of Thelema*, Samuel Weiser Inc., Yorke Beach, Maine, 1983, pg.217

4 Abraham the Jew (not the Biblical Abraham), *The Book of the Sacred Magic of Abramelin the Mage*, Translated by S.L. MacGregor Mathers, "a facsimile of the original edition," 1974, pg.110

5 *Webster's New World Dictionary*, Second College Edition, 1978, pg.1638

6 Ibid, pg.1452

7 Aleister Crowley, *The Equinox*, Vol. I, No.5, *The Vision and the Voice*, Samuel Weiser Inc., Yorke Beach, ME, 1993, pg.32

8 Richard Cavendish, *The Black Arts*, Perigee books, 1967, pgs.289-290

9 Aleister Crowley, *The Equinox*, Vol. I, No.4, Samuel Weiser Inc., 1993, pg.164

10 Aleister Crowley, *The Magical Record of the Beast*, Duckworth, 1972, pg.296

11 Aleister Crowley, *The Equinox*, Vol. I, No.7, Samuel Weiser, Inc., 1993, pgs.33-34

12 Aleister Crowley, *White Stains*, Duckworth, 1973, pg.96

13 Steven Davis, *Hammer of the Gods*, William Morrow & Company, NY, 1985, pg.77

14 Aleister Crowley, *White Stains*, Duckworth, 1973, pg. vii (introduction)

15 Ibid, pgs.113-114

16 Aleister Crowley, *The Equinox*, Vol. I, No.1, Samuel Weiser Inc., 1993, pg.170

17 Aleister Crowley, *Rites of Eleusis*, from *The Equinox*, Vol. I, No.6, Samuel Weiser Inc., 1993, pg.55

18 Venetia Newall, *The Encyclopedia of Witchcraft & Magic*, The Dial Press, New York, 1974, pg.33

19 Rosemary Ellen Guiley, *The Encyclopedia of Witches and Witchcraft*, Facts On File, NY, 1989, pg.27

20 *Webster's New World Dictionary*, 2nd College Edition, William Collins & World Publishing Co. Inc., 1978, pg.1421

21 Joseph Kaster, *Putnam's Concise Mythological Dictionary*, Putnam Books, NY, 1963

22 Rosemary Ellen Guiley, *The Encyclopedia of Witches and Witchcraft*, Facts On File, NY, 1989, pg.261-262

23 Aleister Crowley, *Diary of a Drug Fiend*, Samuel Weiser Inc., 1994, pgs.216-217

24 Ibid, pg.220

25 Aleister Crowley, *The Book of Lies*, Samuel Weiser, Inc., 1993, pg.93

26 *Hit Parader Magazine*, July 1975, pg.64

27 Steven Davis, *Hammer of the Gods*, William Morrow & Company, NY, 1985, pg.246

28 Howard Mylett, *Jimmy Page – Tangents Within a Framework*, Omnibus Press, 1983, pg.71

29 Ibid.

30 Aleister Crowley, *The Equinox*, Vol. I, No.1, Samuel Weiser Inc., 1993, pg.1-introduction

31 Aleister Crowley, *The Equinox*, Vol. I, No.1, Samuel Weiser Inc., 1993, pg.4-introduction

32 Aleister Crowley, *The Equinox*, Vol. I, No.10, Samuel Weiser Inc., 1993, pg.206

33 Howard Mylett, *Jimmy Page – Tangents Within A Framework*, pg.75

34 Dave Lewis and Simon Pallett, *Led Zeppelin: The Concert File*, Omnibus Press, 1997, pg.116

35 Howard Mylett, *Jimmy Page – Tangents Within A Framework*, pg.75

36 Aleister Crowley, *The Equinox*, Vol. III, No.10, Samuel Weiser Inc., Yorke Beach, Maine, 1997, pg.252

37 Peter Guralinick, *Searching For Robert Johnson*, Dutton, 1992, pg.18

38 W.B. Crow, *Witchcraft, Magic, and Occultism*, Melvin Powers Wilshire Book Co. North Hollywood, Ca., 1968 pp.228-229

Jimmy Page having a great time with a big smile on his face in 1977. In the beginning of "Achilles Last Stand," Robert Plant revelled in their "fun" they would "have," living out their "dreams" they "had" all along. He said this after mentioning that the band went on tour under orders from more than one person. Orders from who? Peter Grant? The Promoters? Grant ruled the promoters, and Jimmy Page was boss of the whole thing. Who told the band to go on tour?

Twenty-one years later, Jimmy Page and Robert Plant were still living out their dreams in concert on their 1998 tour..

CHAPTER THREE

"Satan was always ready to enter into a dark alliance with wizards, knowing he would benefit in the end. The fiend form was just one guise; he could also appear as man or animal."1

"The Enchanted World - Wizards and Witches"

"The pact with the Devil has taken a firm grip on the human imagination and has been the subject of innumerable stores. In return for Satan's favors, the signer pledges his body and soul, at death or after a stated number of years."2

Richard Cavendish, "The Black Arts"

"When I promise to Lucifer, I promise to someone who at least has an interest in my getting what I want. Conversely, the shepherd and keeper are concerned with my getting what they think I should have....The Pact with the Devil is a symbol of a freer man in a freer market place who has a sense of 'equality' with his makers. It is an honest trade....To make a pact with the Devil or any spirit is to negotiate for yourself. This is true evil – according to the church and society."3

S. Jason Black and Christopher S. Hyatt, Phd., "Pacts With the Devil"

"Then the devil, taking Him up on a high mountain, showed Him all the kingdoms of the world in a moment of time. And the devil said to Him, 'All this authority I will give You, and their glory; for this has been delivered to me, and I give it to whomever I wish. Therefore, if You will worship before me, all will be Yours.' And Jesus answered and said to him, 'Get behind Me, Satan! For it is written, "You shall worship the LORD your God, and Him only you shall serve."'"

The Holy Bible, Luke 4: 5-8

CELEBRATION DAY & ACHILLES LAST STAND: THE PACT WITH SATAN

The pact with the Devil has been written about by many over the centuries, including many examples of individuals who allegedly engaged in it. As was written in the previous chapter, the pact is a fact from antiquity, dating back to the first century when the writers of the New Testament recorded the Devil telling Christ he could make pacts with man. Drawing on a wealth of examples from the renowned writer on the occult, Grillot De Givry, and his outstanding treatise, *Witchcraft, Magic, and Alchemy*, we will examine the satanic pact; including its benefits and consequences. Beginning with the oldest pact on record, that of a man named Theophilus, the reader will then be presented with an example of the written pact from a book of antiquity titled *Le Dragon Rouge*, which shows the content of correspondence between the Devil and his victim. From that point another individual named Urbain Grandier and his signed pact will be discussed, as well as a quote from the famous Dr. Faust, from whom we get the term "Faustian Bargian" for the satanic pact. Subsequent to these illustrations, we will be examining lyrics from Led Zeppelin's two songs, "Celebration Day," and "Achilles Last Stand," to show how the band provided clues pointing to their pact with Satan. Selling one's soul to the Devil, though receiving the benefits of financial, social, or magical power in return, is clearly not worth the price to be paid, forfeiting one's soul after death, and spending eternity in hell.

Before beginning the analysis of the material contained in Grillot DeGivry's *Witchcraft, Magic, and Alchemy*, which was written in French and translated into English by J. Courtenay Locke, let's consider the synopsis printed on the book's back cover. Locke wrote: "Prepared by one of the foremost French historians of the occult sciences, it contains an incredible wealth of material taken from ancient manuscripts, rare and prohibited books, secret documents, official reports, and the occult tradition of the centuries. Careful and precise, though not unsympathetic, it is probably the finest survey of the occult arts in English." The book was written after extensive detailed research of antiquarian documents and books, giving precise information concerning pacts with Satan, as well as those who made them.

DeGivry provided the following introduction to the pact, citing control over demons as a motive for sorcerers, with the end result of the pact being remarkably similar in its description to the lyrics Robert Johnson sang about Satan coming to collect his soul:

"The sorcerer who intended to become master of the demons had without doubt to deal with a powerful opponent, and he would be drawn sooner or later into pronouncing the 'pact'-a celebrated formula which consisted, on the part of the evoker, of selling his soul to Satan or one of his satellites in return for certain advantages to be conferred upon him. At the end of a given time the Devil would come to take delivery of his property, a fatal liquidation which the sorcerer strove to evade by every means possible.

"We see some imprudent folk of this sort, who have just let themselves be foolishly caught, in the vignette from Pere Cuaccius. They have enclosed themselves in a magic circle, but find, after all, that they must conclude the pact forced upon them by Satan as a punishment for having evoked him.

"The stories of persons who 'sold their souls to the Devil' are innumerable, and enter largely into the literature of the Middle Ages. The picturesque and sombre-coloured note they lend is almost unknown in other literatures, and harmonizes exceedingly well with the old towns of Europe and all their scenic accompaniment of houses with carved gable-ends, cathedrals, abandoned abbeys, and ruined castles. The Romantic movement managed to bring these stories into fashion again and to profit by the very marked decorative effects they provided."4

The literature of the middle ages, romanticizing the satanic pact, sustained its popularity. Some of the pacts were sought for personal gain, such as magic power over demonic forces, and others were forced upon people for having conjured the Devil up. One who made the pact voluntarily was a man named Theophilus.

THEOPHILUS

DeGivry presents Theophilus, a church bursar, as having sold his soul to Satan, stating that his case is the earliest known pact on record. In this account we are shown Satan and Theophilus making statements concerning their agreement:

"The earliest pact known to us is perhaps that of Theophilus, bursar of the church of Adana, in Northern Cilicia or Trachyn, about the year 538. His bishop had deprived him of his office, and in order to recover it he sold his soul to the Devil.

"His story was written in Greek by Eutychianus, his disciple, and translated into Latin by Paul the Deacon. Hrotswitha, the famous nun of Gandersheim, used it as the basis for a sort of poetic dialogue, and in the thirteenth century Gautier de Coinsy turned it into a French poem. The legend was read at matins in many churches, and Ruteboeuf used it for his famous drama 'Le Miracle de Theophile,' already quoted. We need not feel surprise, then, at seeing the incident represented on the doorway of the Abbey of Souillac, in a double scene which may be interpreted thus: Theophilus, having caused the Devil to appear through the medium of the conjurer Salatin, is shown on the left handing over the signed pact which Satan had required of him. 'Look it be understood by thee that afterward I have from thee letters clearly expressed and the terms well agreed,' the Devil had enjoined him. If his mood was one of deep mistrust he had some excuse- 'for many men have deceived me in this matter,' he explains. Theophilus had prepared the letters and delivers them to him, saying, 'Here behold them; I have written them.'

"On the right Theophilus is giving his hands to the Devil. Ruteboeuf dramatizes the scene thus:

THE DEVIL.' Now join thy hands and so become my man; I will help thee to the uttermost.'
THEOPHILUS. 'Behold, I do thee homage, fair lord, but I shall have my punishment hereafter.'

"At the top of the composition we see the Virgin Mary tearing the pact from Satan's hands after a quarrel in which she boldly tells him, using the robust speech of the thirteenth century, 'And I will trample on thy belly!'
"Ruteboeuf faithfully gives the text of the pact, the old phraseology of which is still easy enough to read:
'To all who shall read this open letter I, Satan, let know that the fortune of Theophilus is changed indeed, and that he had done me homage, so might he have once more his lordship, and that with the ring of his finger he has sealed this letter and with his blood written it, and no other ink has used therein.'"5
Theophilus had his position of church bursar taken away from him by his bishop, so he employed a conjuror named Salatin to make contact with Satan, in order to sell his soul in exchange for restoration of his office of bursar. The story, having been read at many churches, popularized and advertised the pact. The Devil himself engaged in this by writing statements as to the authenticity of the pact, to recruit more fools to do the same. Manuals providing written examples of the pact circulated to show exactly how it was done. DeGivry provides us with a description of one known as *Le Dragon Rouge*:
"We can easily satisfy ourselves that the mechanism of the pact hardly varied at all throughout the ages. I have previously quoted *Le Dragon Rouge*, which appears to be a popular transcription of the more aristocratic *Clavicules*. This little book gives the formula of the pact with the Devil quite precisely, styling it the 'Great Calling of the Spirits with which one would make pact;' this is the form in which it is given:
Emperor Lucifer, master of all the rebellious spirits, I beseech thee be favourable to me in the calling which I make upon thy great minister LUCIFUGE ROFOCALE, having desire to make a pact with him; I pray thee also, Prince Beelzebub, to protect me in my undertaking. O Count Ashtoreth! be propitious to me, and cause that this night the great LUCIFUGE appear unto me in human form and without any evil smell, and that he grant me, by means of the pact which I shall deliver to him, all the riches of which I have need, O great Lucifuge, I beseech thee leave thy dwelling, in whatever part of the world it may be, to come and speak with me; if not, I will thereto compel thee by the

power of the mighty words of the great *Clavicule* of Solomon, whereof he made use to force the rebellious spirits to accept his pact. Appear, then, instantly, or I will continually torment thee by the mighty words of the *Clavicule*!'

The spirit's reply, still according to Le Dragon Rouge, will be this:

> 'I cannot grant they demand but on condition thou give me thyself at the end of twenty years, so that I do with thee, body and soul, what shall please me.'

This is the solemn and terrible moment when the supreme decision must be taken. *Le Dragon Rouge* gives us the following advice:

> Then you shall throw him your pact, which must be written in your own hand on a little piece of virgin parchment; it shall consist of the few words given below and shall be signed with your veritable blood:
> PACT

> I promise great LUCIFUGE to repay him in twenty years for all he shall give me. In witness whereof I have signed.
> X.....'6

In the written pact, we read that Satan or one of his representatives may make the pact with men (Once again, the pact is to be signed with the person's N.I.B., their "Name In Blood."). The plea is made to "Emperor Lucifer, master of all the rebellious spirits…" just as the *Holy Bible* describes him. Also mentioned is the *Clavicle of Solomon* which is the *Goetia* reprinted in 1976 by Jimmy Page, which gives the chanter power over evil spirits. Upon threat of its use, Lucifuge will then appear and demand body and soul after twenty years. The person then has to sign the pact and the deal is done. Not all the pacts are for only twenty years, especially since the Devil knows he will be able to use some people till the day they die; like Aleister Crowley and Jimmy Page.

URBAIN GRANDIER

One person who De Givry presents as having signed a pact, but then tragically allowed others to discover the document, was one Urbain Grandier from the seventeenth century. He was a famous priest of Loudun who, subsequent to his pact being found, was held responsible for, and put to death because of certain bewitchments that had taken place. The pact itself is presented in the following text that picks up just after *Le Dragon Rouge* in De Givry's book:

"Such was the dread formality of the pact, much resorted to in the sixteenth and seventeenth centuries. In spite of its popularity, however, we have few documents concerning it, from the mere fact that those who practiced it were under the necessity of eluding the investigations of the competent courts of justice. For besides the ceremonial text which we have just read there was the written renunciation of God, the Virgin, and the saints, which was kept jealously hidden. It was obviously not good to leave a document like that of which an illustration is given in Fig.87 (see photo-ch. end) lying about on some piece of furniture, for the very good reason, without more, that in it the signatory disowned the Catholic Church. The Devil, besides, carried the pact away into Hell-an excellent reason why there are no copies of it in or libraries and archives.

"But the famous priest of Loudun, Urbain Grandier, was guilty of this very imprudence. He did not take care enough to conceal his pacts, and the neglect brought him to the stake and the fire. Everybody knows his story, coupled as it is with the last great trial for sorcery of the seventeenth century-a trial much heightened in interest by the fact that Richelieu himself was mixed up in it. Grandier was by no means regular in his conduct and was extraordinarily vain. In the town of Loudun he made many enemies, who accused him of having bewitched the Convent of the Ursulines, where most of the nuns showed signs of demoniacal possession. In 1634 he was condemned at the instance of the Councillor of State, Laubardemont, and declared 'attainted and convicted of the crime of magic, witchcraft, and causing possession, the which came by his deed upon the persons of divers Ursuline nuns and others, being laics, and condemned to pray pardon courteously and bare-headed and to have his body burned alive and therewith the pacts and magic characters now resting in the office of the Registrar.'

"We must believe that the Registrar forgot to carry one of these pacts to the fire, since we find it to-day at the Bibliotheque Nationale, among the collection of papers relating to the Ursulines of Loudun. It is in Grandier's hand, signed and flourished by him, ad is entitled *Veu de Grandier* (Fig.87). It reads as follows:

GRANDIER'S VOW

My Lord and Master, I own you for my God; I promise to serve you while I live, and from this hour I renounce all other gods and Jesus Christ and Mary and all the Saints of Heaven and the Catholic, Apostolic, and Roman Church, and all the goodwill thereof and the prayers which might be made for me. I promise to adore you and do you homage at least three times a day and to do the most evil that I can and to lead into evil as many persons as shall be possible to me, and heartily I renounce the Chrism, Baptism, and all the merits of

Jesus Christ; and, in case I should desire to change, I give you my body and soul, and my life as holding it from you, having dedicated it for ever without any will to repent.
Signed URBAIN GRANDIER in his blood."7

Back in the sixteenth and seventeenth centuries, anyone who was suspected of the said offences, magic and witchcraft, whose written satanic pact signed in blood was found, would surely have been put to death, as was the case with Urbain Grandier (Again, this is another illustration of a person having to sign their "N.I.B.," or "Name In Blood."). The execution was only one form of misery suffered by this type of individual, however. All through their lives subsequent to the signing of the said pact, these individuals lived in dread of the inescapable end result, making payment to the Devil with their souls. The physical death was one thing, but what waited for them afterward was another thing they feared. DeGivry describes the apprehension:

"The most disagreeable side of the pacts was the terrible payment which must come at the end of them, so it was not unnatural that a person who had signed one should exert all his ingenuity to get out of it-in short, to cheat the Devil of the prey he was counting upon. *Le Dragon Rouge* even indicates a precautionary prayer for use once the pact was made: 'Inspire me, O great God, with the sentiments necessary for enabling me to escape the claws of the Demon and of all evil spirits!' By this one might retract one's word after having got from the Devil all the benefits one had asked him for.

"But the Devil kept an eye on those he suspected of not wanting to keep their promise, and he was inexorable when he came on the day of payment. An engraving (fig.88) taken from a very rare German incunabulum, 'Der Ritter vom Turn von den Exempeln der godforjt und erbeckeit,' shows a demon coming at the hour fixed to take delivery of a child promised him by its unnatural parents. The poor little creature's struggles are unavailing; he is in a clutch not to be relaxed, and will never see his home again. His terror is easy enough to understand, seeing the hairy schoolmaster who will henceforth look after his education.

"Innumerable persons who had either subjected themselves to demons by pacts or subjugated them by the arts of sorcery lived thenceforward in a state of uneasy familiarity with them. Cornelius Agrippa was constantly accompanied by two great dogs wearing necromantic collars; they were really demons, we are led to suppose. Pietro d'Abano was condemned for having learned the seven arts-the *trivium* and the *quadrivium*-by the help of seven of these horrible creatures which he kept shut up in a bottle. The French historian, Palma Cayet, made a pact with the Devil by the terms of which he was always to be victor in his disputes with the Protestants; the contract, signed with his blood, was found after his death. It was said that demons came and carried away his body, and although there actually was a funeral, the story runs that it was a sham one and that the coffin was filled with stones." 8

Here again, is another pact that was signed with the person's "N.I.B.," Name In Blood. As one can very well surmise, the satanic pact is traditional; not in any sense new. There are other stories, like the one of Paganini the violinist who allegedly sold his soul, and Dr. Faust who allegedly sold his soul to the Devil for magical power. One can see a skit of Dr. Faust's deal with the Devil in the movie *Tombstone*. Dana Delany plays the Devil. The skit is silent, but while the pact between Satan and Dr. Faust is being made, Doc Holiday (Val Kilmer) says to his girlfriend Kate, "Is your soul for sale dear?" When you read the term, "Faustian Bargain" it refers to Dr. Faust and his pact with the Devil. In a six-teenth-century book called *Fausti Hollenzwang,* which means *Faust's Harrow-ing of Hell*, there is written in the preface, allegedly by Dr. Faust:

"If you wish to become true magi and perform my deeds, you must have knowledge of God as well as of other creatures, but you must not honour him in any fashion but what pleases the Princes of the World....He who wishes to prac-tise my art, let him love the spirits of hell and those who reign in the air; for these alone are they who can make us happy in this life; and he who would have wisdom must seek it from the devil.

For what thing in the world is there whose best exponent is not the devil, who is the Prince of the World?

In a word, ask what you will: riches, honour, and glory, you can have them through him, and what you expect of good after your death, in that you deceive yourself."9

Remember that Dr. Faust mentioned spirits "who reign in the air." You are going to see that again in this book with reference to the *Holy Bible*, *The Book of the Sacred Magic of Abramelin the Mage*, and the Led Zeppelin songs, "Ramble On" and "The Battle of Evermore". In the previous accounts presented from De Givry's book on witchcraft and magic, the end result was always that the Devil came to collect the soul after death. Dr. Faust presented the same theme in his quote. The Devil has, however, in this modern age of seared con-sciences, discovered the means by which he makes his pact even more popular.

If the Devil tried to get Jesus to worship him in order to rule the world, thus bypassing the crucifixion, two thousand years ago, you can safely assume he is still watching for evil men he sees as fit for service to make pacts with today. His greatest trick in this area, of course, has been to make people who sell their souls to him believe that he is god. This makes the person who accepts the lie believe that no evil awaits them after death.

The Devil lies because he is the father of it. Lord Jesus Christ related this to the religious leaders who wanted him dead in the New Testament Book of John, Chapter 8, Verse 44: "You are of your father the devil, and the desires of your father you want to do. He was a murderer from the beginning, and does not stand in the truth, because there is no truth in him. When he speaks a lie, he speaks from his own resources, for he is a liar and the father of it." Aleister Crowley, whose life we will take a good look at in preparation for accurate comprehension of the music of Led Zeppelin, wrote the following words in *The Magical Record of the Beast*, referring to Satan as a liar as well:

"'My light! O my father, the Devil! It hath made all things one, being perfect, even as doth the Darkness! My Liberty! Every Restriction is gone; all Ways are as one; why then should I move? It were thus were I frozen stiff in the heart of a mountain of ice!'

He laughed. 'My son! Thou art mine; thy tongue is a liar's; I, Satan, thy sire, am not shamed!'"10

In this, Crowley agrees with Jesus (an anomaly in his writings), that Satan is a liar. Nevertheless, Aleister Crowley and others after him, including Jimmy Page, have believed the lie that Satan continues to tell through Crowley's writings, that he is god. One of the ways that he is able to do that is to make promises to his followers, and by his power, cause them to come true.

LED ZEPPELIN III - "CELEBRATION DAY"

In the *Holy Bible*, when Jehovah brought the children of Israel out of Egypt during the Exodus, he promised them he was going to bring them to a land flowing with milk and honey. This is the origin of the term "promised land." Jehovah promised the land of Israel to the Jew (Jesus Christ told the Jews in the temple at Jerusalem that he was Jehovah; they tried to stone him to death for it). Robert Plant, in the song, "Celebration Day," from *Led Zeppelin III*, declared he would be singing and dancing to celebrate becoming a member of the band. He called it the "land" of promise at 0:55 into the song, just as Jehovah promised the Jew. In the Silver Star's *Book of the Law*, which Crowley said was dictated to him by Satan, the Devil says that the proof of his promise would be in the success they would have for following the "Law of Thelema." He said, "Success is your proof."11 That will be discussed in chapter seven. It is because of that success that Robert Plant says the fans are not aware of what they are missing out on in the song, "The Song Remains the Same." It is this success that motivates him to command the fans to sell their souls to the Devil. There are some concepts that have to be presented before reading about that, or it will come across to the reader without the proper effect. Simply put, it is imperative that you know what Led Zeppelin's command really entails. They are sworn to spread the Law of Thelema all over the world. Again, Aleister Crowley taught that *The Equinox* is mainly for that purpose. The following quote is from *The Equinox*, where Crowley makes reference to Satan in the form of Horus the Egyptian god, in the form of a Hawk: "We Perdurabo, a Neophyte of the A.A., All for Knowledge, a Probationer of A.A.,....swear unto Thee, O Lord God, by Thine own almighty power, by Thy force and fire, by Thy glittering Hawk's eye and Thy mighty sweeping wings: that we all here in this place and now at this time do utterly devote ourselves, mind, body, and estate, at all times and in all places soever to the establishment of Thy holy kingdom."12 You can see this hawk at the end of "Moby Dick" in the Zeppelin film, and at the very beginning of Page/ Plant's *No Quarter* video. He is also on the mountain of the inner cover of Led Zeppelin's fourth (Runes) album. So Crowley swore to devote himself to establish Satan's kingdom at all times and places; by spreading the Law of Thelema.

PRESENCE - "ACHILLES LAST STAND"

Spreading the law of Thelema; such is the mission of Led Zeppelin - the "Four Sticks." What is going to be discussed now is not absolutely conclusive, yet it is a good piece of the puzzle to present here. In the beginning of the song, "Achilles Last Stand," Robert Plant presents the concept of Led Zeppelin being ordered to set out on tour by "they" at 0:47 into the song. It was more than one person that ordered the band to tour, yet it only had one manager who dictated any orders to the band, Peter Grant. I believe it was spirits who told them that. Plant sings that upon hearing the order he "turned" toward "you" and that person "smiled" back at him, at 0:52. Then he sings that they couldn't answer "no" to the command at 0:55. The next thing he sings about is "fun" they will "have," at 0:59. At 1:01 into the song he sings that they "live" their "dreams" they "had" before they became rock stars. Finally, at 1:05, Plant sings of "songs" they will "sing" as they finally get to "return" once more to churn music forth from their amplifiers. This is all evidence, I believe, of the fruit of their pact with Satan; especially since Plant made direct and shouting reference to the Devil at 1:35 into the same song. Before you are done reading this book, you will interpret the beginning of "Achilles Last Stand" the same way. They obeyed the command to go on tour, because, I believe, it came indirectly from one greater than they, Satan, and who the band perceives as his "female consort," which is just Satan in another disguise. This woman was in the 1995 tour's "Tales of Bron." Aleister Crowley wrote about followers of the Silver Star obeying Satan and his consort whom he called "The Secret Chiefs" in *Magick Without Tears*: "Our business is solely to obey orders: our responsibility ends when we have satisfied ourselves that they emanate from a source which has the right to command."13 As followers of Crowley, Led Zeppelin were disciples, obeying the commands of their master, the Devil, and Page/Plant did the same thing by promoting the birthplace of the American legend of the satanic pact, the blues in Clarksdale, Mississippi.

Selling the Devil one's soul, though deceived by Satan into believing it is a good deal, perhaps even deceived to the point of believing he is god, like the members of Led Zeppelin, irrespective of its benefits, is not worth the price to be paid; eternity in hell. Theophilus was given his office of bursar back to him by Satan, but signed a pact agreeing to his "punishment hereafter." The pact popularized in the book *Le Dragon Roules* promises good fortune from Satan in this life, but damnation in the end. Urbain Grandier received magical power to bewitch from Satan, but was burned at the stake. Dr. Faust instructed people to make the pact as well, but warned that a person was deceiving himself if he believed good awaited him after death. The teachings of Crowley, however, revealed by Led Zeppelin, present Satan as god, and thereby the pact as benign; without harm in the end, hinted at in songs like "Celebration Day" and "Achilles Last Stand". In conjunction with subsequent evidence presented in this work, one will see that those hints in the two songs were exactly that. The satanic pact is a bold faced lie. It appears to be a worthwhile adventure to the soul that makes it, but it is not in the long run. Whether a person makes the deal believing that Satan is god or not, he has been deceived by the Devil as well as his own soul.

Another place known for occasions of making the satanic pact is the Black Sabbath; a gathering for worship of Satan. It celebrates Satan with drug abuse combined with sexual orgies; often with the Devil himself present. We will examine this gathering in the next chapter to see its relevance to Led Zeppelin's message of Satanism. Note Robert Plant's quote at the chapter heading.

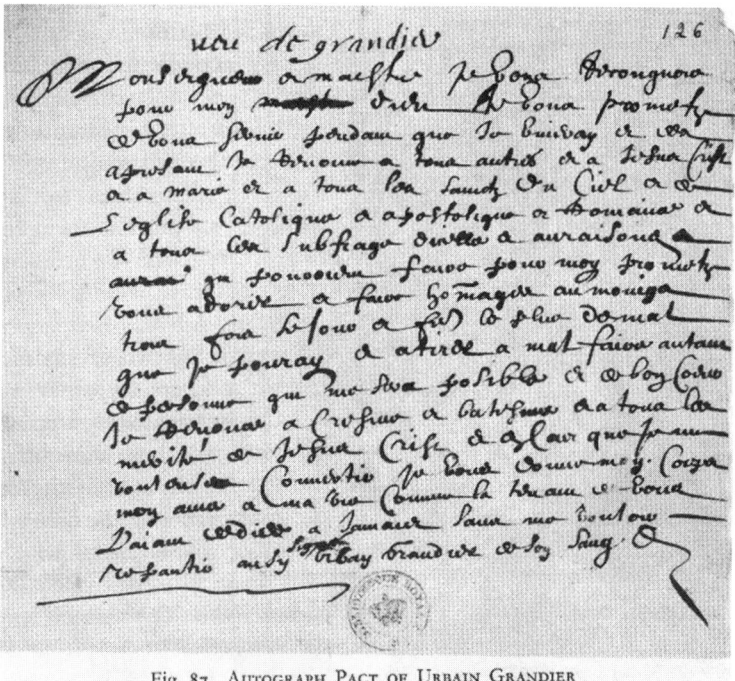

Fig. 87. Autograph Pact of Urbain Grandier
Bibliothèque Nationale, manuscript *fonds français*, No. 7619, p. 126.

Urbain Grandier's signed Satanic Pact that his enemies found.

Led Zeppelin as they appeared playing "Achilles Last Stand" on the 1977 tour.

The classic pose of Jimmy Page and Robert Plant singing together on "Achilles Last Stand." This can be seen on the VH1 Legends program, as well as the Madison Square Garden bootleg video from 1977; and the Seattle '77 video.

1 Time-Life Books, *Wizards and Witches*, 1984, pg.58
2 Richard Cavendish, *The Black Arts*, Perigee Books, 1967, pp.318-319
3 S. Jason Black and Christopher S. Hyatt, Ph.D., *Pacts With The Devil*,
    pgs.22-23
4 Grillot de Givry, *Witchcraft, Magic & Alchemy*, First English Translation,
    1931, pg.115
5 Ibid, pp.116-117
6 Ibid, pp.117-118
7 Ibid, pp.118-119
8 Ibid, pp.119-120
9 Butler, *Ritual Magic*, pg.204
10 Aleister Crowley, *The Magical Record of the Beast*, Duckworth, 1972,
    pg.266
11 Satan, *The Book of the Law*, dictation taken by Aleister Crowley, *The
    Equinox*, Vol. I, No.10, Samuel Weiser Inc., Yorke Beach, Maine,
    1993, pg.31
12 Aleister Crowley, *The Equinox*, Vol. I., No.9, Samuel Weiser Inc., Yorke
    Beach, Maine, 1993, pg.128
13 Aleister Crowley, *Magick Without Tears*, pg.96

THE SABBATIC GOAT

Eliphas Levi's Sabbatic Goat, that Aleister Crowley claimed to draw when "he was Levi." Crowley went on to claim that this was "Aiwaz" and "Satan." He is the Silver Star's Head, Holy Guardian Angel, Pan, and god - Lucifer. Many ignorant people today refuse to believe Aleister Crowley was a Satanist.

CHAPTER FOUR

"Imagine then a ball in which the music is the choir celestial, the wine the wine of the Graal, or that of the Sabbath of the Adepts, and one's partner the Infinite and Eternal One, the True and Living God Most High!"1

Black Magician Aleister Crowley, "The Equinox"

"...the Eye, and 'The Devil' our Lord, and the Goat of Mendes. He is the Lord of the Sabbath of the Adepts, and is Satan, therefore also the Sun, whose number of Magick is 666, the seal of His servant the BEAST."2

*Black Magician Aleister Crowley, "Magick-Book 4 * Liber Aba"*

"It was midnight, and the Devil came down and sat in the midst; but my Fairy Prince whispered: 'Hush! it is a great secret, but his name is Yeheswah, and he is the Saviour of the World.' And that was very funny, because the girl next me thought it was Jesus Christ, till another Fairy Prince (my Prince's brother) whispered as he kissed her: 'Hush, tell nobody ever, that is Satan, and he is the Saviour of the World.'"3

Black Magician Aleister Crowley, "Konx Om Pax"

"So therefore didst thou shriek in the Black Sabbath when thou didst kiss the hairy buttocks of the goat..."4

Black Magician Aleister Crowley, "The Equinox"

"You are in your bed, not a little worn out, possibly a trifle shattered, by your night's journey and its orgy; but you have beheld that of which everyone talks without knowledge; you have been initiated into secrets no less terrible than the grotto of Triphonius; you have been present at the Sabbath."5

Eliphas Levi, "Transcendental Magic"

"This is another story about a journey, a sinister journey this time, that we all have to go down, it's called 'No Quarter.'"

Robert Plant, Led Zeppelin live at Madison Square Garden July 28th, 1973

DANCING DAYS & IN THE EVENING: THE DEVIL AND THE BLACK SABBATH

Throughout the centuries, especially during the Middle Ages, there has been substantial rumor about and attendance at the "Witches Sabbath," or "Sabbat." Herein it shall be referred to as the "Black Sabbath" to ensure it is perceived as associated with the Devil. Many people have gathered through the ages in graveyards, clearings in woods, on hillsides, and the summits of mountains, to engage in revelry and worship of the Devil. It is a *celebration of Satan* that includes drinking, *dancing*, singing, feasting, sometimes on dead humans or babies who have been sacrificed to Satan, initiating new witches, and swearing loyalty to Satan by giving him the "kiss of shame" on his buttocks. Often times after feasting there would be a sex orgy. Satan would take place in the orgy, having sex with several witches, including sodomy. Throughout this chapter we will examine the Black Sabbath, beginning with a list of the Sabbaths that are celebrated by occultists around the world. From there Aleister Crowley's promotion of the Sabbath and Satan will be shown, including his confession of attendance. Characteristics of the Sabbath will then be presented. The Sabbatic Goat, initiation, masks, mantles, bats, the type of people there, as well as the "Piper" playing his music at the Sabbath are all discussed. The Rolling Stones will then be mentioned to illustrate their association, not only with the Sabbath and Satan, but with John Paul Jones of Led Zeppelin. "The Song Remains the Same" film will be examined during the song, "No Quarter" to show the reader that the "fantasy scene" of Jones' is in keeping with descriptions of those who attend the Sabbath. Then the focus will shift to the Led Zeppelin songs, "Dancing Days" and "In the Evening," to show relationship there. Ozzy Osbourne and the group, Black Sabbath, will then be mentioned briefly, in order to show their support for the Sabbath and Aleister Crowley at the same time in rock history, the early 70's, and the mid 1990's in the case of Osbourne. Aerosmith will then be discussed momentarily to show their association to Led Zeppelin, as well as Neil Young. John Paul Jones' fantasy sequence during "No Quarter" in "The Song Remains the Same" may be characterized by some as Led Zeppelin's love of "gothic folklore," as was presented on the television rock station, VH1. However, the truth is that it is not folklore at all, but an absolute fact, that Led Zeppelin used that part of the film to promote the Black Sabbath; with Satan verbally exalted at the sequence's end.

The Sabbath was and is presided over by the Devil. He comes most often as an he-goat. Sometimes he comes as a man or as a black dog. In *The Black Arts*, Richard Cavendish wrote about Satan transforming himself into a black dog at the Sabbath: "There the witches feasted on bread, meat and wine. They danced and the Devil turned into a black dog."6 If the Devil did not show, a man would be chosen to represent him. It seems that Aleister Crowley used to do exactly that. The name of his magical oath was "FRATER PERDURABO." Frater Perdurabo means "I shall endure unto the End." The following quote is from his *Confessions*, where he wrote of it: "'Perdurabo,' still echoes in eternity. What may befall I know not, and I have almost ceased to care. It is enough that I should press towards the mark of my high calling, secure in the magical virtue of my oath, 'I shall endure unto the End.'"7 In *The Book of Lies*, he wrote a description of himself as representing Satan at the Sabbath, including a mention of the "obscene kiss" which will be discussed in the section on initiation:

"FRATER PURDURABO is of the Sanhedrim of the
        Sabbath, say men; He is the Old Goat himself,
        say women.

Therefore do all adore him; the more they detest
        him the more do they adore him.
Ay! let us offer the Obscene Kiss!
Let us seek the Mystery of the Gnarled Oak, and of
        the Glacier Torrent!
To Him let us offer up our babes! Around Him let
        us dance in the mad moonlight!"8

In the commentary on the next page in Crowley's book, it says:
        "The chapter refers to the Witches' Sabbath..."9

THE SABBATIC GOAT

Crowley claimed to be Eliphas Levi reincarnated, as mentioned previously. Levi was an occultist who was significantly involved in the re-emergence of interest in magic in the nineteenth century. He wrote about the Sabbath, devoting a whole chapter to it in his book, *Transcendental Magic*, which was originally titled *Dogma and Ritual of High Magic*. He drew a picture of the goat of the Sabbath, and wrote his name on the bottom of the picture (chapter heading). Crowley would later claim it was he who drew it. He wrote in the *Magical Record of the Beast*: "Look at the frontispiece to my *Rituel de la haute Magie* (Dogma and Ritual of High Magic), where I have figured the Devil of the tarot as Baphomet."10 That goat is referred to by Crowley as "Aiwaz" his Holy Guardian Angel, and Satan. He wrote: "When I was Levi, I drew myself as *Ayin* or Baphomet, 'The Devil,' with Beast's Head....This *Ayin* is then my Phallic Will, my Holy Guardian Angel, Aiwaz, who was afterwards called Satan."11 Crowley is not saying he himself is the Devil. He says he drew himself as Baphomet and later said it was Satan. He liked to refer to himself as being one with Satan. You will see this again later (There is a picture of Marilyn Manson wearing a t-shirt with this exact same picture of the Sabbatic Goat/Aiwaz/Satan on it in a recent rock magazine. "Mr. Manson" also has Aleister Crowley's credo, "Do What Thou Wilt Shall Be the Whole of the Law" written at the heading of chapter 9 in his autobiography, *The Long Road Out of Hell.*).

Eliphas Levi drew the Sabbatic goat after getting the idea from the tarot card called "The Devil." It is the fifteenth card in the major arcana of the tarot. He wrote of its attribution to the fifteenth tarot in *Transcendental Magic*, identifying it also as associated with the Greek God Pan, who Crowley claims is Satan as well. Levi wrote: "We refer once more to that terrible number fifteen, symbolized in the Tarot by a monster throned upon an altar, mitred and horned, having a woman's breasts and the generative organs of a man-a chimera, a malformed sphinx, a synthesis of deformities. Below this figure we read a frank and simple inscription-THE DEVIL. Yes, we confront here that phantom of all terrors, the dragon of all theogonies, the Ahriman of the Persians, the Typhon of the Egyptians, the Python of the Greeks, the old serpent of the Hebrews, the fantastic monster, the nightmare, the Croquemitaine, the gargoyle, the great beast of the Middle Ages, and -worse than all these- the Baphomet of the Templars, the bearded idol of the alchemist, the obscene deity of Mendes, the goat of the Sabbath. The frontispiece to this 'Ritual' reproduces the exact figure of the terrible emperor of night, with all his attributes and all his characters....But the adorers of this sign do not consider, as do we, that it is a representation of the devil: on the contrary, for them it is that of the god Pan, the god of our modern schools of philosophy, the god of the Alexandrian theurgic school and of our own mystical Neoplatonists."12 By identifying the Sabbatic Goat as the Devil, and associating it with Pan, we see a clear congruence, once again, between Eliphas Levi and Aleister Crowley. Another thing that the two men agreed upon was the initiation of the neophyte at the Black Sabbath.

INITIATION AT THE SABBATH

Levi provided detailed description of initiation at the Sabbath, which includes the "obscene kiss" to the buttocks of the Sabbatic Goat, written about by Crowley at this chapter's heading: "The proceedings included Rites of Initiation, exchange of mysterious signs, singing of symbolical hymns, the communion of feasting in common, the successive formation of the magical chain at table and in the dance. Finally the meeting broke up after renewing pledges in the presence of chiefs and receiving instructions from them. The candidate for the Sabbath was led or rather carried to the assembly, his eyes covered by the magical mantle in which he was enveloped completely. He was passed before great fires, while alarming noises were made about him. When his face was uncovered, he found himself surrounded by infernal monsters and in the presence of a colossal and hideous goat which he was commanded to adore. All these ceremonies were tests of his force of character and confidence in his initiators. The final ordeal was most decisive of all because it was at first sight humiliating and ridiculous to the mind. The candidate received a brusque command to kiss respectfully the posterior of the goat. If he refused, his head was covered once more, and he was transported to a distance from the assembly with such extraordinary rapidity that he believed himself whirled through the air. If he agreed, he was taken round the symbolical idol, and there found, not a repulsive and obscene object, but the young and gracious countenance of a priestess of Isis or Maia, who gave him a sisterly salute, and he was then admitted to the banquet. As to the orgies which in many such assemblies followed the banquet, we must beware of believing that they were permitted generally at these secret agapae, it is known, however, that a number of Gnostic sects practised them in their conventicles during the early centuries of Christianity....The Sabbath was therefore the Sunday of Kabalists, the day of their religious festivals, or rather the night of their regular assembly."13 Levi, Crowley, and Jimmy Page all advocated the Kabalah (Qabalah), as you will see.

Aleister Crowley wrote about a Black Sabbath celebration where the Devil was seated on a throne. He recorded that they were dancing with hands joined, in keeping with the previous Levi quote. The passage comes from his famous book, *Konx Om Pax*, written in 1907. Crowley was allegedly describing the path of initiation for magicians when he wrote a "child's fairy tale." The following is taken from that "fairy tale," called *The Wake World*:

"But in the first we came to a mighty throne of gray granite, shaped like the sweetest pussy cat you ever saw, and set up on a desolate heath. It was midnight, and the Devil came down and sat in the midst; but my Fairy Prince whispered: 'Hush! it is a great secret, but his name is Yeheswah, and he is the Saviour of the World.' And that was very funny, because the girl next to me thought it was Jesus Christ, till another Fairy Prince (my Prince's brother) whispered as he kissed her: 'Hush, tell nobody ever, that is Satan, and he is the Saviour of the World.'

"We were a very great company, and I can't tell you of all the strange things we did and said, or of the song we sang as we danced face outwards in a great circle ever closing in on the Devil on the throne. But whenever I saw a toad or a bat, or some horrid insect, my Fairy Prince always whispered: 'It is the Saviour of the world' and I saw that it was so. We did all the most beautiful wicked things you can imagine, and yet all the time we knew they were good and right, and must be done if ever we were to get to the House of Gold. So we enjoyed ourselves very much and ate the most extraordinary supper you can think of. There were babies roasted whole and stuffed with pork sausages and olives; and some of the girls cut off chops and steaks from their own bodies, and gave them to a beautiful white cook at a silver grill, that was lighted with the gas of dead bodies and marshes; and he cooked them splendidly, and we all enjoyed it immensely."14

In the second chapter you read where Crowley said he was going to the Black Sabbath of Satan his Lord. The attendance of his followers in the Silver Star at a Sabbath celebration of Satan then, is not unthinkable or unreasonable. Did Crowley do all the things he wrote? Only God knows, but what kind of diabolical mind would write those things even in jest? Once again, Aleister Crowley is writing of dead children at a satanic gathering. This is all consistent with the character of the Devil, who possessed Judas Iscariot in order to murder the Son of God. What kind of diabolical mind frame did Jimmy Page have when he asked how anyone could call Crowley evil? There are those burned out minds, however, that don't care what the band is into or does, however evil, as long as they produce good music, even if it comes from Satan! They never stop to think about what the Devil's agenda might be for the listener, or what spiritual goals he is accomplishing through this music! One such mind told me that he would gladly go to hell as long as the members of Led Zeppelin go with him. The Magick has complete control of that individual, and those like him. The Magick comes from Satan, who is really in control of that person...well done Jimmy, well done.

MASKS WORN AT THE SABBATH

Eliphas Levi wrote about "Druids," who are Celtic high priests, musicians and magicians, wearing masks to the Sabbath in *The History of Magic*: "We know that superstitions die hard and that degenerated Druidism had struck its roots deeply in the savage lands of the North. The recurring insurrections of Saxons testified to a fanaticism which was (a) always turbulent, and (b) incapable of repression by moral force alone. All defeated forms of worship-Roman paganism, Germanic idolatry, Jewish rancour-conspired against victorious Christianity. Nocturnal assemblies took place; thereat the conspirators cemented their alliance with the blood of human victims; and a pantheistic idol of monstrous form, with the horns of a goat, presided over festivals which might be called *agapae* of hatred. In a word, the Sabbath was still celebrated in every forest and wild of yet unreclaimed provinces. The adepts who attended them were masked and otherwise unrecognisable; the assemblies extinguished their lights and broke up before daybreak; the guilty were to be found everywhere, and they could be brought to book nowhere."15 There are a few things the reader needs to remember from this quote about the Druids. The people who attended the Sabbaths were (1) masked, (2) the goat presided over it, (3) there were human sacrifices, (4) the assembly broke up before daybreak and returned home, and (5) that Eliphas Levi wrote it. Once again, for emphasis, Aleister Crowley wrote in his *Confessions*, and it is a crucial point in this book, "...in my last incarnation I was Eliphas Levi."16 By emphasizing this repeatedly, Crowley was advocating the writings of Eliphas Levi, and therefore the previous quote about the Sabbath.

MANTLES WORN AT THE SABBATH

There is evidence also to suggest that those who attended the Sabbath wore mantles, which are very long capes. In his book, *The History of Witchcraft*, Montague Summers wrote: "In the latter half of the eighteenth century the territory of Limburg was terrorized by a mysterious society known as 'The Goats.' These wretches met at night in a secret chapel, and after the most hideous orgies, which included the paying of divine honours to Satan and other foul blasphemies of the Sabbat, they donned masks fashioned to imitate goat's heads, cloaked themselves with long disguise mantles, and sallied forth in bands to plunder and destroy."17 Montague Summers gives us a description of those attending the Sabbath, and paying divine (as though he were god) honor to Satan as wearing masks, as previously mentioned, but also as wearing mantles and going about "to plunder and destroy." You will read of masks and mantles advocated by Led Zeppelin as well.

BATS AT THE SABBATH

Another evil connotation in the occult is the flying of bats in a given location. Grillot De Givry, in his book, *Witchcraft, Magic, & Alchemy*, wrote about bats at the Witches' Sabbath: "The witch, who in this instance has not disrobed, advances through a cluster of demons. She has entrusted her broom to a bird-faced demon in exchange for the torch with which she lights her way. Bats and barbastels and other fantastic creatures surround her, and a curious mannikin holds his small figure erect before a lantern placed on the ground. A frontier signpost, dramatically lighted and cutting the sky like a gibbet, marks the limit of the Satanic territory.

"We must not suppose that the Sabbath was always conducted according to a uniform and unvarying ritual. As well as we can judge from the descriptions left us by various authors of the gravest stamp, the basic ceremonies might be the same, but at least easy-going caprices were not excluded. Satan presided in person, taking the form of a feathered toad, a crow or raven, a black cat, or, most often, a he-goat. The judgment pronounced at Arras in 1460 against several persons accused of sorcery-that is to say, of making pacts with demons-mentions that they went to the Sabbath, 'and there found a devil in fashion of a he-goat, of a dog, of a monkey, and, by times, of a man.'"18

Occult writers of antiquity, describing masks, mantles, and bats present at the Sabbath, are all in keeping with the presentation by Led Zeppelin advocating Satan in their film, which will be discussed shortly in this chapter. Grillot De Givry also called the Goat of the Sabbath the Goat of Mendes (just as Crowley did in his quote at the heading of this chapter, identifying him as Satan), he wrote: "The appearance of a goat ascribed to Satan at the Sabbath is an evident survival of antiquity. It is the Mendes of the Egyptian decadence, a combination of faun, satyr, and goat Pan tending to become a definitive synthesis of the anti-divinity….It is easy to imagine the glee with which Goya seized upon a tradition of such welcome decorative value and placed the awe-inspiring goat in his fresco called *Sabbath, or the Gathering of Sorcerers*, in the Prado Museum at Madrid (Fig.48). The inordinate monster is shown gigantic, his horns entwined with leaves, and an old witch is offering him the sacrifice of a child."19 (see photo) Sorcerers gathered at the Sabbath, paying homage to Satan; and De Givry gave us the following detailed description of the types of people they were.

THE TYPE OF PEOPLE WHO ATTEND THE SABBATH

The type of people who attended the Sabbath were of no given type, or profession, as this Quote from De Givry suggests:

"Such was, in its broad lines, the august, inimitable, and grotesque ceremony of the Sabbath, which spread its shroud of fear over all Europe from the fifteenth century to the end of the eighteenth, and sucked the humblest as well as the most illustrious persons into its whirlpool. Beggars, vagabonds, gipsies, tramps, artisans, tradesmen, men of letters, learned men, abbots, bishops, and princes and princesses-we see them all under the spell of this conception, which haunted the mind of theologians and magistrates, inspired artists with their most vigorous compositions, and caused uneasiness even in rulers and kings. We have an instance of this in James I of England, who found time to write a fierce indictment against witchcraft.

"It was said that there were thirty thousand sorcerers in Paris under Charles IX, and a hundred thousand in the rest of France. One imagines the kind of fearsome, unbridled dance whirled by such a crew in ominous midnights, on the summits of accursed mountains or at the crossroads of the highways.20

Evidence of Led Zeppelin's fascination with the crossroads was presented in chapter two, and the summit of an accursed mountain is where Jimmy Page meets the Devil in the Led Zeppelin film. That will be discussed in chapter twelve. Satan attending the Sabbath, and identified by the *Holy Bible* as the celestial composer of music, playing it on his pipes and tabrets (tambourines), makes the following quote credible, that there was a piper at the Sabbath, playing music for all to dance to while paying homage to the Devil.

THE PIPER AT THE SABBATH

W.B. Crow, in *Witchcraft, Magic, and Occultism*, wrote about the Sabbath, as well as the playing of musical instruments, specifically, pipes and tambourines. He also identifies the crossroads as a meeting place of Satan worshipers: "The meetings, at any rate the sabbats, were always held out of doors, at remote and inaccessible places, often on hillsides or on clearings in a forest. There is some evidence that they used places with megalithic monuments, where available. They may have assembled at the cross-roads before proceeding to their destination….The meetings began at midnight and terminated before cock-crow. Both fairies and witches, as is well known in folklore, cannot be seen after cock-crow….As it was at night, a fire and torches illuminated the meeting place. At the sabbat a leader dressed in black, sometimes with horns and hoofs, answered for the devil. There was a roll-call. Each individual gave the *kiss of shame* on the hind-quarters of the devil, whereon there was sometimes represented a second face. Instruments were played, notably the fiddle, pipes and tambourine."21

De Givry states in that quote that the Sabbaths began at midnight and ended before cock–crow, and that there were pipes and tambourines played there. The next quote is taken from the Time-Life Book, *Wizards and Witches*. It is another clear example of the people who attended the Sabbath being back home and at normal routine before sunrise, as well as pipes and drums being heard. It reads:

"When the various witches and witches-to-be converged on their destination, they joined a frenzied orgy of chanting and dancing and drinking presided over by the Great Adversary himself. The central act for each witch or aspiring witch was obeisance to evil. Each person vowed her soul to Satan, and to seal the bargain she gave her body to him, to use however he pleased before the eyes of all her fellows.

"Or so it was whispered. No innocent person ever saw a sabbat, although those who ventured out on Midsummer Eve sometimes heard the high fluting of music pipes and the demanding stutter of beating drums. When morning came and the world began to stir, however, the celebrants of the sabbat were in their normal guises again, back among ordinary people, going with apparent innocence about heir ordinary tasks."22

The piper presides over the Sabbath, and his name is Satan, the Devil. At 2:35 into the song, "The Ocean," off the Led Zeppelin album, *Houses of the Holy*, Robert Plant sings about "singing" right up to the point when "night" becomes "day." At 1:22 into "The Ocean," Plant sings that he is "singing" of what is "good" and our "sun" who "lights" our "day." Go back to the heading of this chapter and see where Aleister Crowley says that Satan is the sun. You will be reading about Plant singing of the sun's children rising from sleep later in the book. Before addressing Led Zeppelin's advertising the Black Sabbath in keeping with the previous quotes, the Rolling Stones will be discussed briefly, to show their connection to both the Sabbath and Led Zeppelin.

THE DEVIL, THE ROLLING STONES, AND THE SABBATH

Mick Jagger and the Rolling Stones, in one of their most famous songs, "Jumpin' Jack Flash," glorified none other than the Devil, I believe. At the height of the Rolling Stones reign over the rock culture, before Led Zeppelin began to outsell them three to one in record stores, Don McClean released his "American Pie," in the early seventies. Once again, McClean identified Jack Flash with the Devil. It doesn't take much contemplation to figure out who the author believes Don McClean was singing about, especially after "Sympathy for the Devil" was released by the Stones. It seems as though the sympathy that Jagger and company have for Satan is a real one. The following is taken right from the *Holy Bible* itself, to show proof of the Rolling Stones love for the Devil. It is commonly accepted that the Stones got their name from a Muddy Waters song called "Rollin' Stone." I believe they were given the name from Satan; derived from the *Bible*. We are going to examine a few lyrics from "Sympathy for the Devil." If you have the Stones' album, *Hot Rocks*, you know it is on it. If not, the best way to see it in person is to obtain the videos, that are sold or rented in video stores, called ROLLING STONES LIVE AT THE MAX or "BRIDGES TO BABLYON." One can see what I am talking about very easily as Jagger is in a special railing secure platform (MAX) made to shoot fire up out of the sides of it while he stands a mile above the crowd and sings his paean to Satan. Along with the name of the group, there is evidence that they got their music from the Devil, right from the mouth of Keith Richards himself. The following quote is a commentary by Jacob Aranza, from his book, *Backward Masking Unmasked*, on a statement that Richards made to Rolling Stone magazine: "Keith Richards once observed that the Stones' songs came spontaneously, like inspiration at a séance. He explains that the tunes arrive 'en masse' as if the Stones as songwriters are only a willing and open medium (Rolling Stone, May 5th, 1977, pg.55)."23

In the *Holy Bible*, as well as historically documented, Pontius Pilate,the Roman Governor of Judea, not wanting to be held responsible for killing an innocent man, tried to release Jesus Christ. In "Sympathy for the Devil," Satan, speaking through Jagger (otherwise one would have to believe Jagger was alive two thousand years ago), says that he was there the day Jesus was crucified and that it was he who controlled Pilate. Jagger sang: "Made d—n sure the Pilate washed his hands and sealed his fate." This is where the author believes the Rolling Stones got their name, from Christ's fate being "sealed." Again, Pilate did not want to crucify an innocent man. The following is the Biblical account from Matthew 27:11-26:

"Now Jesus stood before the governor. And the governor asked Him, saying 'Are You the King of the Jews?' Jesus said to him, 'It is as you say.' And while he was being accused by the chief priests and elders, He answered nothing. Then Pilate said to Him, 'Do You not hear how many things they testify against You?' But He answered him not one word, so that the governor marveled greatly. Now at the feast the governor was accustomed to releasing to the multitude one prisoner whom they wished. And at that time they had a notorious prisoner called Barabbas. Therefore, when they had gathered together, Pilate said to them, 'Whom do you want me to release to you? Barabbas, or Jesus who is called Christ?' For he knew that they had handed Him over because of envy. While he was sitting on the judgment seat, his wife sent to him, saying 'Have nothing to do with that just Man, for I have suffered many things today in a dream because of Him.' But the chief priests and elders persuaded the multitudes that they should ask for Barabbas and destroy Jesus. The governor answered and said to them, 'Which of the two do you want me to release to you?' They said, 'Barabbas!' Pilate said to them, 'What then shall I do with Jesus who is called Christ?' They all said to him, 'Let Him be crucified!' Then the governor said, 'Why, what evil has He done?' But they cried out all the more, saying, 'Let Him be crucified!' When Pilate saw that he could not prevail at all, but rather that a tumult was rising, he took water and washed his hands before the multitude, saying, 'I am innocent of the blood of this just Person. You see to it.' And all the people answered and said, 'His blood be on us and on our children.' Then he released Barabbas to them; and when he had scourged Jesus, he delivered Him to be crucified."

One can see that Pilate washed his hands, claiming innocence, and then gave Jesus over to be crucified. Jagger sang that he (Satan) made Pilate stand in front of the crowd and wash his hands. It would be easy to conclude that Pilate's handing Jesus over to be crucified was sealing his fate. There is something else to this story, however. The following passage from Matthew 27:62-28:7 leads up to it:

"On the next day, which followed the Day of Preparation, the chief priests and Pharisees gathered together to Pilate, saying, 'Sir, we remember, while He was still alive, how that deceiver said, "After three days I will rise." Therefore command that the tomb be made secure until the third day, lest His disciples come by night and steal Him away, and say to the people, "He has risen from the dead." So the last deception will be worse than the first.' Pilate said to them, 'You have a guard; go your way, make it as secure as you know how.' So they went and made the tomb secure, sealing the stone and setting the guard.

Now after the Sabbath, as the first day of the week began to dawn, Mary Magdalene and the other Mary came to see the tomb. And behold, there was a great earthquake; for an angel of the Lord descended from heaven, and came and rolled back the stone from the door, and sat on it. His countenance was like lightning, and his clothing as white as snow. And the guards shook for fear of him, and became like dead men. But the angel answered and said to the women, 'Do not be afraid, for I know that you seek Jesus who was crucified. He is not here; for He is risen, as He said. Come, see the place where the Lord lay. And go quickly and tell His disciples that he is risen from the dead, and indeed He is going before you into Galilee; there you will see Him. Behold, I have told you.'"

It is clearly seen in this *Bible* passage that Pilate ordered the guards to seal the tomb. It is also shown that an angel caused an earthquake by coming down from heaven and rolling back the stone that was in front of the tomb. Simply put, the tomb of Jesus Christ was sealed by Pilate with a rolling stone. This is where the author believes the name "The Rolling Stones" originated. What did Mick Jagger say? He (Satan) made certain Pilate "sealed" Christ's "fate."

At this point, I want to present what Pete Townshend of "The Who" had to say about the Rolling Stones as he introduced them into the Rock and Roll Hall of Fame at New York City in 1989: "There's some giant artists here to-night, but the Stones will always be the greatest for me. They epitomize British Rock for me, and even though they're all now my friends, I'm still a fan. Guys, whatever you do, don't try and grow old gracefully, it wouldn't suit you." After Townshend introduced the band, Mick Jagger walked up to the microphone and said these words: "You know it's slightly ironic that tonight you see us on our best behavior, but we're being rewarded for 25 years of bad behavior....Americans are funny people. First you shock them, then they put you in a museum."

What does all this have to do with the Sabbath? The symbol of demon worship, which the reader will not find hard to believe, is the goat's head. The Rolling Stones album, *Goat's Head Soup*, shows a goat's head in what could easily be perceived as a witch's cauldron. The first song on the album is called "Dancing With Mr. D." It is generally accepted that Mick Jagger is singing about the Devil. Who else would be in a graveyard, *dancing* with Mick Jagger, and referred to as Mr. D.? This is in my opinion, blatant advertising for the Witches' Sabbath. In the song, at 0:41, Jagger tells the listener while referring to Satan, "...one of these days he's gonna set you free." Again, words have two meanings. Freedom to the Satanist is considered slavery to evil by the Christian. At 1:34 into the song, Mick Jagger says he drank "Belladonna," which is an hallucinogenic used in the Witches' Black Sabbath, and has been used for centu-ries in Europe. In the song, "Can You Hear the Music?," from the same album, Jagger sings the title twice and then "Can you feel the magic coming in the air?" Robert Plant sang about "Magick" in the "air" in "Ramble On," on the *Led Zep-*

pelin II album, and while warming up Led Zeppelin at Live Aid, Phil Collins sang a song containing the lyrics, "I feel it coming in the air tonight oh Lord."

Now is the time to tie the Rolling Stones to Led Zeppelin. Led Zeppelin recorded a substantial portion of their music in the Rolling Stones' Mobile Recording Studio; including Led Zeppelin IV, the album with "Stairway to Heaven" on it. They borrowed the studio from the Stones. They are brothers in the faith. The most important connection, as far as the Sabbath is concerned, is Led Zeppelin bass player and organist, John Paul Jones. On the Rolling Stones album, *Their Satanic Majesties Request*, as I wrote in chapter one, John Paul Jones played on several of the songs. In the book on Led Zeppelin by Howard Mylett and Richard Bunton, called *In The Light*, writing about John Paul Jones, they said: "He also worked with the Rolling Stones on their Satanic Majesties album, and on string arrangements with them and other artists."24 A man who had any aversion to being associated with Satan would never have played on that album. Sane people will agree. Actions speak louder than words, so denials will be rendered powerless.

Now for the most important part of this chapter, where you will see John Paul Jones, in this author's opinion, with much evidence included, advertising for the Witches' Sabbath. Eliphas Levi, who is quoted at the chapter heading, as well as about the Sabbatic Goat and the Sabbath, wrote something that really defines Led Zeppelin's method of advertising for the Silver Star on their albums. He wrote, referring to magic and occult philosophy as a science (which is what Crowley called it – Chapter One.): "The science is preserved by silence and perpetuated by initiation. The law of silence is not therefore absolute and inviolable, except relatively to the uninitiated multitude. Such knowledge can only be transmitted by speech. The sages therefore must speak occasionally. Yes, they must speak, not, however, to disclose, but lead others to discover."25 To say this in a simpler fashion, the occult practices of magicians, witches, occultists, etc., is kept secret by them, except to perpetuate them through initiates, or new prospects; new believers. This is why he says silence about it is not absolute, except to the multitude that remains uninitiated. He says the knowledge can only be communicated by speech. Although the part of the fantasy sequence of John Paul Jones' during the song, "No Quarter," in *The Song Remains the Same*, has no literal words being sung, we all know that pictures speak a thousand words. It is here that John Paul Jones gave information, not to disclose, but to invite viewers to discover. These guys are not going to be blatant about their Satanism often, like Robert Plant commanding the fans to sell their souls to the Devil. Now our attention needs to be focused on the song "No Quarter" from the film (The song No Quarter is from the *Houses of the Holy* album, part of which was recorded at Mick Jagger's country estate, "Stargroves," with the Rolling Stones Mobile recording studio).

Exactly thirty minutes into the Led Zeppelin film, the camera is filming the New York City subway. At that point the scene returns to Madison Square Garden as Robert Plant has just introduced "No Quarter." After the opening lyrics, in which he makes reference to the Nordic god "Thor," Robert Plant directs the crowd's attention to John Paul Jones as he begins his organ solo. The scene then transfers to a gigantic church setting. Jones is playing the organ that is in front of a large number of very tall pipes. After that scene, we see a group of individuals come riding around a building on horses; Jones is in the lead. The first thing one sees is a very large grotesque mask on his face.

Eliphas Levi was quoted, in the section of this chapter marked "Masks Worn at the Sabbath," about the Sabbath and the fact that those who attend wear them. As you can see in the film, these men are all wearing masks.

Montague Summers, in the section titled "Mantles at the Sabbath," wrote about masks and mantles being worn by those attending the Sabbath. John Paul Jones and his comrades have mantles on; just like Summers wrote. Levi has those at the Sabbath masked, Summers has them masked and wearing mantles.

In the next section, Grillot de Givry records bats flying around at the Sabbath. He also had a picture in his book of bats flying around above the goat at the Sabbath; who is accepting the offering of a child from a witch. That photo is in this chapter. It has *Sabbath, or Gathering of Sorcerers* written under the photo. As one can see while watching Jones' fantasy sequence, he has bats flying around in the dark, repeatedly.

Mick Jagger said he was dancing with Mr. D. in a graveyard. In Jones' fantasy sequence we also see his wife Mo Jones walking through a graveyard wearing a mantle; he himself rides through the graveyard on a horse afterward. While Mo Jones is walking in the graveyard, her body is made to look somewhat like it a negative from a picture. It is simply presenting the film in its negative. There are three different successive shots of her like that. W.B. Crow, who is quoted in the section of this chapter titled "The Piper at the Sabbath," has the same type of face as Mo Jones' radioactive scene on the cover of *Witchcraft, Magic & Occultism*. The radioactive picture refers to the spiritual or "astral" body. Jones and his wife are ostensibly telling the viewer they are witches who have attended the Sabbath.

In the section of this chapter titled "Initiation at the Sabbath," Eliphas Levi records "great fires" burning at the Sabbath. In his fantasy, Jones has a fire burning; consuming a large pile of books.

In the section where Levi wrote about "Masks at the Sabbath," he records human sacrifice. There is no evidence in the Led Zeppelin movie to suggest that the band ever engaged in any human sacrifice; neither does this author wish to assert that they did. It would be easy, however, to believe it when two men are running for their lives trying to get away from Jones and his buddies. A blonde woman appears with a little girl. The child points at the riders, and the woman, with a concerned look on her face, immediately takes the child off the road as if hoping not to be seen. [You already read more than one quote from Aleister Crowley about children being sacrificed at the Sabbath gathering, and will be reading of it again in chapter seven, as instruction from Satan.] It is presented by John Paul Jones and Led Zeppelin as though the people running from the masked riders have a prior knowledge of what they are up to; and that they should fear for their lives as a result.

In the section of this chapter called "The Piper at the Sabbath," W.B. Crow and Time-Life books both say that pipes and tambourines, which are hand held drums, were played at the Sabbath. They agree also, along with Eliphas Levi, on the matter of breaking up the assembly and heading home before dawn. John Paul Jones and his wife both are back at home before sunrise, acting as though everything were normal again. They are behaving as if what they had just been doing was no big deal.

If all the evidence shown were not enough, just as Jones picks up his daughter, kisses her and walks away, the scene changes to where he is riding through a graveyard on a horse. The next scene is the one where Robert Plant walks up to the microphone and sings about the Devil laughing at each step the doomed dogs are taking. To refresh memory, one can go back to the latter half of the first chapter and read it again. Once again, it means that the Devil will have no mercy on his enemies after death; as Led Zeppelin would have one believe.

HOUSES OF THE HOLY – "DANCING DAYS"

Another Led Zeppelin song that could be perceived as promoting the Black Sabbath is "Dancing Days," also from the *Houses of the Holy* album. The first line of the song says that the "days" to dance have arrived "again" and then Plant says it is during the nights of "summer." Once again, referring to the Sabbath, *Time-Life* wrote: "No innocent person ever saw a Sabbat, although those who ventured out on Midsummer Eve sometimes heard the high fluting of music pipes and the demanding stutter of beating drums."26 In the song, "The Battle of Evermore," from their fourth album, Led Zeppelin hired a woman, Sandy Denny, to sing backup vocals to Robert Plant. She sings three times in the song, the same phrase, which is a command to "Dance" during "dark" and "Sing" right up until "light" of dawn. This command is not disclosing the Sabbath, but is capable of leading potential followers to discover it. The first time you hear it is at 0:48 into the song.

IN THROUGH THE OUT DOOR – "IN THE EVENING"

It is not difficult, in light of the evident fact that the Sabbaths were at night, to believe that Led Zeppelin was definitely advertising the Sabbath to those who would become followers of the Silver Star and the Devil in the song, "In The Evening." In The Evening allegedly has a violin bow piece that originated in the aborted Lucifer Rising soundtrack in the opening section. At 0:53 into the song, Plant sings the song title and then says he refers to "when" daytime was "done." At 1:52 he sings a command not to "run." A person can hear Plant singing a command to "Dance" with a "beat" from a "drum" at 3:10. Both the night and dancing to the beat of drums are characteristic of the Black Sabbath. By itself, this evidence is weak, but in conjunction with all the other pieces, it fits perfectly.

This song, "In The Evening," is from the last album the band made while still together, called *In Through The Out Door.* This album mystified all of us when it first came out with six different album covers in 1979; two years after the Led Zeppelin concert I saw at Madison Square Garden. When I heard there was six different covers, I knew there had to be two more sixes somewhere. Well, I found them. They are so obvious they are hard to find. There are several different people in the bar setting while a man sets fire to a "Dear John" note. How many are there? Six. The man tending the bar has a snake tattooed on his left forearm. To the right of the bartender, down at the end of the bar leaning against the wall is a pretty blonde. She is looking at a man, who is to the left rear of the man in the white suit burning the note at the bar. This man is older, a cigar in his mouth, and counting the money in his wallet. It appears the girl is watching him count it. To the right rear of the man at the bar, all the way back against the wall with her left forearm resting on the jukebox is a brunette in a low cut dress. Continuing on counterclockwise, there is an older gentleman playing the piano. To his left is a woman laughing as she sits at the bar watching the man burn his note. The six people each have a different view of the man in the white suit. The six different album covers are derived from combinations of the six different views of the man at the bar from six different people. Six people, six views, and six different album covers equals "666." What does the title "In Through the Out Door" mean? I do not know for sure, but it sounds like something one could catch the "aids" virus from, if I know anything about Aleister Crowley and his disciples. He did teach that a magician should be bisexual, so what should one think? At the Knebworth concert in England, on August 11th, 1979, Robert Plant said the following about their new album. Smiling at Jimmy Page, he said: "It's called In Through the Out Door, which is one of those methods of entry that proves to be harder than one would originally expect."

One does not know for sure whether Robert Plant referred to sodomy or sex with Satan at 5:53 into the song, "Since I've Been Loving You," or at 6:25 into the same song in the Led Zeppelin film. However, in the film he does say that he has to "please" his "back" entrance "man." If he isn't talking about sodomy, it sure fits the bill. Aleister Crowley loved sodomy. The following quote illustrates it, from Colin Wilson's *The Occult*: "He had acquired a small Negro boy, with whom he performed acts of sex magic. Crowley's homosexuality began as an act of defiance of convention rather than of actual preference, but it seems to have become another habit."27 Sex magic is prolonged sex without orgasm to achieve euphoria, and to release hidden power from the subconscious mind. Remember, Jimmy Page wanted to know how anyone could call Crowley evil; in chapter one. It must not be a secret that Crowley was like that, or that Page is his follower. Why? Because Robert Plant said in 1988, referring to people who have begged he and Jimmy Page to reunite: "Page and I get offered everything: women, little boys, money, cocaine, the lot, to just go back and do that again. I don't think it would be a good idea at all. [But] I reserve judgment to change my mind in five years time."28 Five years later they did reunite; in 1993. Crowley taught that the number 93 is the number representing the Law of Thelema. This author is not saying that Page or Plant would have accepted little boys as a gift, but obviously somebody thought they would, and Robert Plant speaks of it openly! Plant talked about his "love" in inches at 1:05 into "Whole Lotta Love" in "The Song Remains the Same" film and soundtrack, and in his next statement, he said he desired to share this "love" with "everybody." Also, Plant is quoted in the 1980 publication of *Led Zeppelin-Creem Special Edition*, as saying: "Some nights I just look out there and I want to (sexual-expletive) the whole first row..."29 Why didn't he say "all the girls" in the front row? Robert Plant's sexual innuendo certainly could convince a person that he would have a blast at the Witches' Sabbath. If I were to guess, I would have to believe Plant was referring to the Sabbath in the song, "Celebration Day," mentioned in the last chapter. He said he was going to "sing" as well as "dance" to celebrate joining his "band," obvious reference to Led Zeppelin. It sounds like he made his vow, to sell his soul, at a Sabbath. He certainly could please his back door man at that assembly. Considering his command to the fans in their film to sell their souls to Satan, this is not unthinkable; read his quote at the chapter heading.

Montague Summers wrote about the Devil having sex with his followers at the Sabbath. He makes mention of a woman named Helen-Josephine Poirer interrogated about attending the Sabbath and her testimony:

"In February, 1869, when interrogated by several priests, Helene gave most extraordinary details concerning bands of Satanists. 'In order to gain admission it is necessary to bring one or more consecrated Hosts, and to deliver these to the Devil, who in a materialized form visibly presides over the assembly. The neophyte is obliged to profane the Sacred Species in a most horrible manner, to worship the Devil with humblest adoration, and to perform with him and the other persons present the most bestial acts of unbridled obscenity, the foulest copulations. Three towns, Paris, Rome, and Tours, are the headquarters of the Satanic bands.' She also spoke of a gang of devil-worshipers at Toulouse. It is obvious that a mere peasant woman could have no natural knowledge of these abominations, the details concerning which were unhappily only too true."30

The consistent advertising of the Black Sabbath by Led Zeppelin is not only in keeping with the occult writers of antiquity, but also with contemporary rock stars such as Ozzy Osbourne, who began his career as the charismatic lead singer of the rock group formed in 1969, "Black Sabbath."

OZZY OSBOURNE, BLACK SABBATH, AND THE DEVIL

The last reference to the Witches' Sabbath is from the group "Black Sabbath," from their album, *Black Sabbath*, from the first song on the album, "Black Sabbath." On the album cover is a woman in a witch's mantle, dressed just like Mo Jones at the graveyard in "No Quarter" of the Led Zeppelin film. John "Ozzy" Osbourne sang that Satan was "sitting" and "smiling" at him. The name of the song is Black Sabbath and Ozzy Osbourne says that Satan is seated there. Grillot de Givry, in *Witchcraft, Magic and Alchemy*, has several photos of Satan sitting on a throne at the Witches' Sabbath. Another song on the album, "N.I.B.," again, which I believe means "Name In Blood" at the Witches' Sabbath, clearly promotes the satanic pact. Osbourne, singing for the Devil, says that he is going to "give" possessions to the listener they previously imagined to be "unreal;" and that the sun, moon, and stars each have his seal on them; meaning that he created them, as god. He says that if the listener follows him he is not going to regret leaving the type of life he lived before meeting the Devil. Why? It is because that life was full of misery without Satan's pleasures. A powerful part of the song then relates the message to the listener who decides to follow that he or she is now the Devil's possession, singing in Satan's stead, Ozzy sang that Lucifer has the fan "under" his "power." This can be seen plain as day in the new 1999 concert video from Black Sabbath, which is blasphemously titled, *The Last Supper*, where the camera is right in Ozzy's face while singing the said lyrics. [I believe this concept is presented by Mick Jagger in "Emotional Rescue" where he sings that he has come to the listener's rescue, emotionally, and they will be his possession. Jagger said, "You will be mine all mine."] Ozzy then went on to say that the listener can tell who he is by looking into his eyes, meaning that there is something exclusive about the Devil's eyes. Remember, in the song "Black Sabbath" he describes him as having eyes of fire. Finally, Ozzy sings, "My name is Lucifer, please take my hand."

This man, John "Ozzy" Osbourne is clearly a plenipotentiary for the being who was cast down from heaven and who now has his servants convinced he is god. Osbourne still has a chance to escape, however, and the author hopes all these men do. What they have to believe, is the truth of the fact that God will forgive them for making the satanic pact. That is an absolute fact. However, until they turn to Christ, they are bound to serve Satan as slaves.

OZZY IN CONCERT AT THE ORLANDO ARENA - 1996

Going to see Ozzy Osbourne serving Satan in concert, in 1996 at the Orlando Arena was an interesting event for me. I watched people down in the "mosh pit" beat on each other like there was no tomorrow. They slammed their bodies against each other for fun. The mosh pit was the orchestra seat area. All the seats had been removed allegedly because fans in Tampa were fighting with their chairs in the orchestra the night before.

I felt compelled to go and see if Ozzy would advertise for Crowley. He did more than advertise for Crowley. He held a literal vigil. There were two big screens, one on either side of the stage, and netting hanging from the lights behind and along side of the screens. Before singing the song, "Mr. Crowley," Ozzy had a picture of Crowley come up on the screens. It showed him in his Magick outfit from the Silver Star, with an eye in a triangle on his headgear. He was pointing his thumbs up in the air; making the sign of the "Horns of Pan" (Satan). That photo is in this book. Then the lights from above the stage shone only blood red color all over and especially the color sensitive netting at the rear of the band. Ozzy then told the fans he wanted everybody to light their cigarette lighters and hold them up in the air. I could not believe what I was watching. Thousands of people, completely ignorant of the degree of evil that was mani-fested on that stage between the incarnate Lucifer and his human mentor on the screens, began to light cigarette lighters and hold them up in the air. The aura of evil was so thick you could cut it with a knife. Then Ozzy began to sing his paean to Aleister Crowley. As you might imagine, in the minds of those listening to the song, even if they couldn't understand the lyrics, Crowley was being ex-alted as some kind of hero, at least on the subconscious level. Ozzy made it a religious atmosphere by having all the lighters lit up at his command (Jim Morrison would have been proud of the tradition he started). He had the most serious look on his face when he sang the song; at least when he looked my way. To be honest, I was livid. I was even angrier than I was at the beginning of the show.

Ozzy has a good sense of humor. At the show's start, he had himself projected on the screens as singing side by side with Elvis in Las Vegas. Then he was singing side by side with Pavarotti dressed in a Tuxedo. He was crawling around toilets with Beavis and Butthead. The most outrageous thing, that was funny to me at first, was the most hilarious to the crowd. I must confess it put a feeling of fear in me after I stopped laughing, and I don't scare easy. Who else but William Jefferson Clinton, the President of the United States, pops up on the screens giving a speech in the oval office. Ozzy comes out from behind his chair with a joint in his hand, smiles at the crowd, and begins to blow smoke at the President (he had a rolled up cigarette, whatever it was, but the message was obvious to the crowd). After he was finished, I thought to myself, "How much trouble is this country going to be in when the leader of the nation has smoked dope, and presents his confession in such a manner that can be taken either way by the masses listening to him?" Mr. Clinton couldn't have convinced anyone in the Orlando Arena that he didn't inhale; when he confessed to smoking pot during his first presidential campaign. In my mind's eye I could see the Devil standing on top of the screen, laughing himself to tears. It just doesn't get any better for him than to have the President of the United States promote the smoking of Marijuana. Anybody who has ever smoked a joint knows full well the message Clinton was sending when he said he smoked but didn't inhale. What would be the point of bringing the joint, pipe, or bong to his mouth if he wasn't going to inhale? That was a pathetic attempt at patronizing the drug crowd, but successful with the naïve. It wouldn't surprise anyone who has smoked Marijuana if they found out that Clinton has smoked a ton of it. He couldn't fool a thirteen-year old with that statement. To those of us who either have come out of the drug culture, or are still in it, the President may as well have been Cheech Marin telling everybody to get stoned. Frankly, Cheech Marin couldn't have done more to promote dope smoking decades ago than Bill Clinton did by admitting he smoked but didn't inhale. I really think that anyone who believes that line could be talked into buying the Brooklyn Bridge. I can assure you that if I was in junior high, high school, or college, and Carter or Reagan had said that, I would have been present at a million parties held in their honor. I can hear the laughter of agreement as some of your are reading this book. It's a shame that Ozzy Osbourne can use the President of the United States to promote the smoking of Marijuana. You should have heard the roar of the fans when Ozzy did that. Marijuana has a spiritual element to it that will be discussed later. It sends the mind in a specific direction.

As I watched the fans light their thousands of lighters, I thought how they did not know that Crowley as well was an incarnate Lucifer; and that it was his image (Satan) that was being exalted by raising those lighters up in the air while Ozzy sang the song. I could not believe that Crowley was being unwittingly worshiped by all those young people. The truth is, there were a great deal of older people there as well, doing the same thing. The fans were being programmed, pure and simple. All those minds like computers being given a positive association to Aleister Crowley; and thereby Satan - through music!

NEIL YOUNG - HEY, HEY, MY, MY

Ozzy and myself knew that there were more individuals at that concert than could be seen with the naked eye. I'm sure that Neil Young, who played with the surviving members of Led Zeppelin at their induction to the Rock and Roll Hall of Fame, would agree. Remember what he said in the song, "Hey Hey My My?" He said that Rock music is never going to die. Why? Because "There's more to the picture than meets the eye." James Patrick Page would hardly have allowed an "infidel" to sing with him at Led Zeppelin's prestigious induction.

AEROSMITH – "GET YOUR WINGS"

The other famous rock act that performed with Led Zeppelin at their induction to the Rock and Roll Hall of Fame, was "Aerosmith." If you watched the show, you know that Led Zeppelin's surviving members started out by playing with Aerosmith's Steven Tyler and Joe Perry. Are they believers in the Devil like Led Zeppelin? Absolutely. Those two introduced the band as they were being inducted. Joe Perry said that Jimmy Page asked him to introduce the band while he was having lunch with him a few months earlier in Buenos Aires. Do you know where that is? It's in Argentina. Argenteum Astrum is the name of Crowley's cult, which as you know means Silver Star.

In my record collection as a teenager was a copy of Aerosmith's second album, *Get Your Wings*. Now there is a blatant command, I believe, to sell your soul to the Devil to the person who is familiar with the occult. The letters that spell out Get Your Wings are what color? That's right, they are blood red; another hint for a blood pact. The wings on the front of the album are shaped like bat's wings; and Led Zeppelin presented bats in their film while promoting Black Sabbath imagery. In the album's seventh song, "Seasons of Wither," singing about a woman, Steven Tyler says, "Love for the Devil brought her to me," at 1:12 into the song; once the guitar kicks in. The same theme was presented by Steven Tyler in the movie, "Wayne's World 2," where he is seen walking after a show with no shirt on, and he has a black upside down cross around his neck dangling from a necklace. It doesn't take a rocket scientist to put all these pieces of the puzzle together once one is a student of the occult, or even a die hard Aerosmith fan, as I once was. I was an Aerosmith fan, but a Led Zeppelin disciple.

I first saw Aerosmith at Madison Square Garden in Manhattan on December 15, 1976. That was the night Rick Derringer blew them off the stage while "warming them up." I can still see Derringer on his knees, leaning back with the guitar and raising the middle finger of his right hand up in the air. We all roared with approval. The mood defined what he meant. The message was to anyone, especially authority, who didn't like rock and roll.

Violent music breeds violent acts. When Aerosmith was jamming, some first class lunatic up in the mezzanine threw a quarter stick of dynamite up in the air and it exploded. Believe it or not, the band did not protest one bit. They kept on playing like it did not happen.

As I contemplate Ozzy Osbourne again, I realize it has been quite a long time since Jim Morrison was dragged off the stage by police in New Haven, Connecticut, for swearing. I couldn't believe what Ozzy got away with in a "conservative" arena like Orlando's. The fans, as one might imagine, loved every minute. As an entertainer, Ozzy does a good job keeping the fans going. He had hoses hooked up to makeshift machine guns. He would pick up the weapons and fire machine gun power water at the fans in the mosh pit. Then he would throw buckets of water on them. They were having a great time with Ozzy.

The ridiculous act of turning his back to the audience and pulling his sweat pants down, not to his knees, but to his ankles was met with the utmost approval from the fans. Those of us at the show saw his naked behind a half dozen times. If one had a nickel for every time he shouted profanity, specifically the "F" word, one could buy the arena. He preached a short sermon about how he knows a lot of people don't like him because of the things he has done over the years. He shouted into the mike, that he had only two words for them, "F-You!" Then he shouted it again and encouraged the fans to shout it in response to him. He shouted it and they reciprocated. This was done four of five times. I had never heard those two words shouted in unison by fifteen thousand people before, much less over and over. The next thing I remember Ozzy doing was announcing to the fans, "This next song is for all those people who don't like me, Suicide Solution!" The fans roared with delight. It occurred to me that Ozzy was programming the fans to despise anyone who didn't like him without their even being aware of it. As such he was Magick personified.

There were men all around the stage with video cameras. The girls in the mosh pit were taking their tops off and sitting on boyfriend's shoulders. The cameramen shot their cameras on the naked girls and projected their breasts on to the screens on the stage. Ozzy even dragged one girl out of the audience, put his arm around her and sang for about twenty seconds until he motioned for a roadie to come get her. While he had his arm around her, she pulled up her shirt and bra and the cameramen projected her naked chest on to the screens and the fans roared. None of the Orlando Police, who were everywhere, did anything. They were not about to start a riot by interfering with the crowd's behavior. Ozzy turned the concert into a celebration of Pan, almost. Aleister Crowley would have approved. Ozzy had those fans so wound up, if the police tried to do anything there would have been a disaster.

Black Sabbath was on my music menu constantly in the seventies. "Sabbath Bloody Sabbath" and "Paranoid" were my favorite albums of theirs; along with "We Sold Our Souls For Rock And Roll." Now there's an ambiguous title for Black Sabbath fans, don't you think? There couldn't possibly be a message in that title, or could there? These guys are sons of Aleister Crowley. You have to hand it to them. They were not timid about it. When they decided to be bad, they went straight to the Devil.

I have had people tell me that Ozzy is a Christian, along with the other members of Black Sabbath, because they occasionally wore big crosses around their necks, hanging down to the center of their chests. Believe it or not, this has happened many times. I know I have been wrong about things in my life, but how anyone can mistake Ozzy Osbourne for a follower of Jesus Christ is just mind boggling. Let the reader understand something very important. When you see a satanist wearing a cross, it is to celebrate the place where their enemy was killed. The motive for wearing it is diametrically opposed to the Christian's. On their album, *LIVE-EVIL*, Black Sabbath has a giant cross hanging above the stage to send that message to the fans. In *The Black Sabbath Story -Volume I*, video, they have the Devil using the body of Jesus Christ, crucified, as a sling shot.

Ozzy Osbourne clearly is a slave of the Devil. He deifies Aleister Crowley in the minds of impressionable youth; that is an absolute disaster. The reader will agree with that assessment after reading the next chapter about Jimmy Page and Ozzy's hero who called himself "The Beast 666." Some people buy Ozzy's line about using the image of evil for fun and to sell records. Don't let him kid you. This Crowleyite knows full well that even if you use the image of evil for fun, it is evil you are exalting, and Satan takes any such "fun" seriously. What he does not concern himself with is the fact that Lord Jesus Christ does as well. Evil did not originate with mankind. If it were only fun, why does he not use the image of purity? He has been promoting the Devil for thirty years because he is a believer, as an act of his own will, that Lucifer is god. In the 1999 concert film, he said at the beginning that people were asking him why they decided to reunite at this late date. He said that he supposed that "...God wanted it to be, I don't know." During the show he could be heard shouting at the fans, "God Bless You!" Are we to think for a moment he is referring to Lord Jesus Christ in his repeated references to "God?" As a slave, in iron chains, he can't stop. It was he who orchestrated the 1999 Black Sabbath reunion.

The Black Sabbath was advertised by Led Zeppelin in their film, *TheSong Remains the Same.* John Paul Jones and his buddies portrayed a group of men, masked, wearing mantles, causing terror, with bats flying in the air around them, and back at home before sunrise, all in direct parallel of the teachings of antiquity concerning the Black Sabbath. All of this evidence, along with the praise of Satan at the end of his "fantasy sequence," leads one to no other conclusion but that John Paul Jones and Led Zeppelin were providing one more piece to their big puzzle, that Satan is Lord. The members of the band are clearly Crowleyites. He was quoted as advocating the Black Sabbath, claiming his attendance there, as well as Satan's. He even referred to himself as the Sabbatic Goat. This Sabbath was sung about by the Rolling Stones in their "Dancing With Mr. D" song on the notorious "Goat's Head Soup" album. John Paul Jones played with the Rolling Stones on their album, *Their Satanic Majesties Request*. The "Satanic Majesty" can only be Satan. This is the same group that sang "Sympathy for the Devil." The Led Zeppelin album containing "No Quarter," titled *Houses of the Holy*, was partially recorded at the Mick Jagger country estate, "Stargroves." Ozzy Osbourne and Black Sabbath, clearly promoting the satanic pact and the Black Sabbath, are advocates of Aleister Crowley, both currently as well as in the past. Aerosmith provided a subtle invitation to the satanic pact with the cover of their *Get Your Wings* album, advocating love for Satan on that album's song, "Seasons of Wither." The band's lead singer and lead guitarist performed with Led Zeppelin on stage the day Jimmy Page and company were inducted into the Rock and Roll Hall of Fame. Neil Young also performed with Led Zeppelin that day, and he tells us that rock music cannot die, because an unseen force is behind it; although he doesn't mention Satan by name. As though he would need to. All the aforementioned groups and individuals are contemporaries of Led Zeppelin, and ostensibly advertising for the same person, the Devil, and thereby his Black Sabbath celebration.

John Baldwin, a.k.a. John Paul Jones, presented us with a fantasy sequence in keeping with the teachings of antiquity relative to the Black Sabbath Celebration of Satan. Masks, mantles, bats, graveyard, home before daybreak, and of course, the Devil, who is glorified at the end of the song in the sinister, satanic lyrics.

(John Paul Jones is in the photo.) "...the Sabbath was still celebrated in every forest and wild of yet unreclaimed provinces. The adepts who attended them were masked and otherwise unrecognisable; the assemblies extinguished their lights and broke up before daybreak..." - Eliphas Levi "The History of Magic"

In "Dancing With Mr. D," Mick Jagger sang of Dancing with the Devil in a graveyard. He then told the listener "...he's gonna set you free." John Paul Jones (in the photo) played on the Stones' "Their Satanic Majesties Request" album.

Fig. 48. SABBATH, OR THE GATHERING OF SORCERERS
Goya.
Fresco in the Prado Museum, Madrid.

Satan as the Sabbatic Goat with bats flying above him as he accepts a child. The painting says, "Sabbath, or Gathering of Sorcerers." The bats flying above the head of the Devil are in keeping with John Paul Jones' fantasy sequence in the Led Zeppelin film, "The Song Remains the Same." Although one does not actually see the Sabbath celebration take place in the film, all the peripherals are there; as well as the glorification of the Devil in the lyrics of Robert Plant at Madison Square Garden at the very end of Jones' fantasy sequence. The night I saw Led Zeppelin at MSG, Robert Plant shouted the line about those "Dogs" who are facing "Doom" at the top of his lungs into the microphone. I got the show on compact disc from the famous "FBO" internet Zeppelin mail list.

Celebration of Dancing with the Devil at the Black Sabbath. You might call the photo a depiction of "Dancing With Mr.D." What would you tell us Mick? Or do we even need to ask?

Fig. 53. DANCING AT THE SABBATH
Guaccius, Compendium maleficarum.

1 Aleister Crowley, *The Equinox*, Vol. I, No.9, pg.29

2 Aleister Crowley, *Magick-Book 4 * Liber Aba*, Samuel Weiser Inc., 1994, pg.522

3 Aleister Crowley, *Konx Om Pax*, The Teitan Press, Chicago, 1990 pp.10-11

4 Aleister Crowley, *The Equinox*, Vol. I, No.5, pg.139

5 Eliphas Levi, *Transcendental Magic*, Samuel Weiser Inc., 1995, pg.7

6 Richard Cavendish, *The Black Arts*, Perigee Books, 1967, pg.309

7 Aleister Crowley, *The Confessions of Aleister Crowley*, Edited by John Symonds and Kenneth Grant, Penguin-Arkana, 1989, pg.923

8 Aleister Crowley, *The Book of Lies*, Samuel Weiser Inc., 1993, pg.1509

Ibid, pg.151

10 Aleister Crowley, *The Magical Record of the Beast*, Duckworth, 1972, pg.68

11 Ibid, pg.198

12 Eliphas Levi, *Transcendental Magic*, Samuel Weiser Inc., 1995, pgs.307-308

13 Ibid, pgs.312-314

14 Aleister Crowley, *Konx Om Pax*, The Teitan Press, Chicago, 1990 pp.10-11

15 Eliphas Levi, *The History of Magic*, Rider, London, 1988, pg.198

16 Aleister Crowley, *The Confessions of Aleister Crowley*, 1989, pg.190

17 Montague Summers, *The History of Witchcraft*, Citadel Press, 1984, pg.136

18 Grillot de Givry, *Witchcraft, Magic, & Alchemy*, Dover Publications, 1971, pg.74

19 Ibid, pp.78-79

20 Ibid, pp.87-88

21 W.B. Crow, *Witchcraft, Magic, & Occultism*, Wilshire Book Co., 1968, pp.245-246

22 Brendan Lehane and the editors of Time-Life Books, The Enchanted World, *Wizards and Witches,* 1984, pg.113

23 Jacob Aranza, *Backward Masking Unmasked*, Huntington House Inc., Shreveport, LA, 1983, pg.105

24 Howard Mylett and Richard Bunton, *In The Light*, Proteus, 1981, pg.14

25 Eliphas Levi, *Transcendental Magic*, Samuel Weiser Inc., 1995, pg.267

26 Brendan Lehane and the editors of Time-Life Books, The Enchanted World, *Wizards and Witches*, 1984, pg.113

27 Colin Wilson, *The Occult*, Random House, 1971, pg.371

28 *Musician Magazine*, March 1988, reprinted in *Musician Magazine*, December 1994, BPI Communications, Inc., 1515 Broadway, New York, 1994, pg.60

29 Lisa Robinson, *Led Zeppelin-Creem Special Edition*, 1980, pg.16

30 Montague Summers, *The History of Witchcraft*, Citadel Press, 1984, pp.246-247

Edward Alexander "Aleister" Crowley as a boy. Crowley claimed that even before he was abused by (a charlatan form of) Christianity, he was fascinated with and loved the evil characters in the Book of Revelation. Abuse gave him the excuse he needed to worship Satan. He rebelled against evil by worshiping evil.

The young poet and aspiring magician who brought us the literary work "White Stains," in which he praised the Devil and mocked God, as well as bragged of having sex with a woman and a great dane. What causes a man with a great intellect as Crowley's to give his heart over to the Devil, and then as a quote on the opposite page suggests, claim that he didn't know why he did it? The best person to answer that question is the great Dr. John MacArthur: "Theological error has its roots in moral, not intellectual soil."

CHAPTER FIVE

"I was in the death struggle with self: God and Satan fought for my soul those three long hours. God conquered - now I have only one doubt left - which of the twain was God?"1
Aleister Crowley, "Aceldama, A Place to Bury Strangers In."

"...I accepted the theology of the Plymouth Brethren. In fact, I could hardly conceive of the existence of people who might doubt it. I simply went over to Satan's side; and to this hour I cannot tell why."2
Black Magician Aleister Crowley, "Confessions"

"I had been almost overwhelmed by the appalling responsibility of ensuring my own damnation and helping others to escape from Jesus."3
Black Magician Aleister Crowley, "Confessions"

"I say today: to hell with Christianity, Rationalism, Buddhism, and all the lumber of the centuries. I bring you a positive and primaeval fact, Magic by name: and with this I will build me a new Heaven and a new Earth. I want none of your faint approval or faint dispraise; I want blasphemy, murder, rape, revolution, anything, bad or good, but strong."4
Black Magician Aleister Crowley, Calcutta, India, 1904

"'They say you're a black magician.' 'Very well. But I'm a bloody great one.'"5
Black Magician Aleister Crowley, "The Magician of the Golden Dawn"

"Having witnessed the bedevilment of New Orleans, I was sent to Titusville, Florida, to complete my contemplation of the unspeakable degradation of humanity which is constantly being wrought by Christianity and commerce."6
Black Magician Aleister Crowley, "Confessions" 1918

WHAT IS AND WHAT SHOULD NEVER BE: BLACK MAGICIAN ALEISTER CROWLEY

Aleister Crowley was one of the world's most famous aficionados of black magic. As the above quote from the *Magician of the Golden Dawn* suggests, he took pride in it, believing it to be his life's calling. It was, however, antithetical to the religion he was taught as a child, which was Christianity. In this chapter the reader will examine key points as to the beginning of Crowley's

99

life, his family, and the effect its religious practice had on him as he was sent to a "Christian" boarding school. Crowley's written testimony concerning these events is presented in order to glean the tone right from the man's own soul. The sudden death of his father, in conjunction with his vitriolic attitude toward his boarding school are discussed in light of their role in turning Aleister into one angry and bitter young man; whose bitterness was then directed at Christ himself. Along with these difficult circumstances in his life, Aleister Crowley developed and sustained a love for every form of spiritual wickedness. His position as an advocate of sodomy is presented along with detailed hatred of English Christianity. It is believed that he embraced sodomy as a means of defying Christian conventional views in England. Crowley wrote a short treatise on how he finally gave up his soul to Satan, on a night he claimed that God and Satan fought for it. That treatise is presented here along with the subsequent attitudes developed by him as a direct result; one of those being his utter lack of respect for women, which, as you will read herein, is shared by none other than Jimmy Page himself. This attitude is also reflected in Crowley's stated position on the institution of marriage, also included. Many people, including the author, can empathize with Aleister Crowley on the idea of abusive, even anger provoking forms of religious teaching presented in the name of Jesus Christ. Although there are various forms of charlatan "Christianity" in this world, there is no substance in any of what you are about to read that justifies either Crowley's hatred for the *Holy Bible*, Lord Jesus Christ, or his yielding up of his eternal soul to the Devil.

THE CHILDHOOD OF ALEISTER CROWLEY

Aleister Crowley was born "Edward Alexander Crowley" on October 12, 1875, in Warwickshire, England. His father was the descendant of Quakers, and the Crowley's had Celtic roots. They had acquired a fortune from brewing alcohol. The Crowley's, although brewers, belonged to a strict, separatist group of Christians who called themselves "The Plymouth Brethren," who had broken off from the Church of England. Crowley's father became an evangelist with the group and traveled around England telling people to get right with God. Crowley described his father as being very eloquent at preaching from the heart. The first book Crowley ever read, beginning at age four, was the *Bible*. His father taught him the *Bible*; especially the fifth chapter of Genesis, which they both loved. As long as he got instruction from him, he did not develop any real displeasure toward the Christian faith. However, even at this point, at about five years old, he developed an unhealthy interest in the evil characters mentioned in the Book of Revelation of the *Bible*. In his *Confessions*, he wrote concerning himself in the third person: "The Christianity in his home was entirely pleasant to him, and yet his sympathies were with the opponents of heaven. He suspects obscurely that this was partly an instinctive love of terrors. The Elders and the harps seemed tame. He preferred the Dragon (Satan), the False Prophet, the Beast and the Scarlet Woman, as being more exciting. He reveled in the descriptions of torment. One may suspect, moreover, a strain of congenital masochism. He liked to imagine himself in agony; in particular, he liked to identify himself with the Beast whose number is the number of a man, six hundred and threescore six."7

Crowley confessed openly his love for the evil characters in the *Bible*, and it seems that he was constantly bombarded by inconsistency in his family, which did nothing to dissuade him. When he was six years old, they moved from Leamington to Redhill, Surrey. While living there, Crowley observed an incident involving his father and a lady from "The Blue Ribbon Army." This organization was made up of a majority of women who were in favor of the abolition of alcohol. When asked for a donation at his home, Crowley's father went into a tirade. He told the woman, who was thinking he would gladly support her cause, that he was against abstaining from alcohol because that would generate a self righteous attitude in those who abstained. They would believe they earned heaven as a result of good works rather than seeing themselves as sinners in need of salvation; which he believed drunkenness produced. Crowley said his father browbeat the woman for half an hour, telling her he would much rather preach a sermon to a thousand drunks than a thousand self righteous "T-totallers."

It was at this time of Crowley's life that his father sent him to a school by the name of "St. Leonard's." In preparing him for his entrance to the school, he warned his son to never allow anyone to touch him "there." In order to illustrate this he used the story of Noah being drunk in chapter nine of Genesis and the alleged perverted behavior of Noah's son, Ham. While attending St. Leonard's, Crowley refused to properly answer a question on an exam. Instead, he pretended he did not understand it as presented, and wrote an answer that was totally unacceptable to his schoolmaster; named Habershon. Apparently, Crowley was reprimanded for his answer. He began to wish the old man's death after this incident. Three weeks later, Habershon died. Crowley, happy about his death, took credit for causing it.

In 1885, Crowley was transferred to a school in Cambridge run by a brother of the Plymouth Brethren named H.d'Arcy Champney. He went to this school determined to be a great leader, just as he perceived his father to be as he influenced thousands of people with his sermons. His goal was to be the most devout disciple of Jesus at the school. Crowley was happy at this school for about eight months, until May of 1886.

It was at this time that he was sent home to take part in a prayer meeting of the Plymouth Brethren, concerning his father. Crowley's father had developed cancer of the tongue. The doctor at Redhill recommended he go to another doctor named Sir James Paget, who wanted to do surgery, but after prayer the brethren decided to opt for a form of treatment called "electro-homeopathy." It did not work. As a result, Edward Crowley died less than a year later on March 5, 1887; when his son was just eleven years old. This was the major turning point in his life. Six years earlier, he had a sister die five hours after her birth. For some reason, Crowley's parents forced him to look at her dead body, which he resented. Now his father was dead, and it seems Crowley developed some deep bitterness toward Jesus Christ. Amazingly, Crowley was at Cambridge when his father died and he dreamt about it occurring the night it happened. He received news of his father's death the next morning. Crowley also dreamed of his mother's death the night she died, although he was three thousand miles away.

After Crowley lost his father, his life changed dramatically. His father's faith had separated him from his relatives; he only associated with his religious friends. After he died, his friends ceased to associate with Aleister's mother. As a result, Crowley's life was now being lived in the midst of relatives on his mother's side of the family. This occurred as his mother moved to London to live near her brother. For the next nine years of his life, "Uncle Tom" was to be his legal guardian.

It seems that Crowley really was in a state of shock over the loss of his father, and Uncle Tom was a poor substitute. It appears that at eleven years old Aleister Crowley never did deal with his loss in a constructive manner. Susan Roberts, in her book, *The Magician of the Golden Dawn*, wrote: "There was no time for grief, much less adjustment. As soon as his father was buried, a woebegone and wary little boy set out alone on the train from Southampton to Cambridge to finish out his term."8

Once Crowley was back at Cambridge, he got into some trouble almost immediately. His misbehavior, whatever it was, was overlooked because of his father's death. Crowley was called to Rev. Champney for the second offence he allegedly committed upon returning to school. He did not make a specific accusation against Aleister, but he was convinced he had committed a sin, and gave him twenty-four hours to realize his sin and repent accordingly. He went on to tell Crowley that the Lord in his providence took very good care of the school and saw to it that that which was done in the dark was brought to light. The next day Rev. Champney tried to get Crowley to confess his sin. He told him that Satan tempts everyone and that he should resist him. If Crowley is telling the truth, then, apparently, this "Reverend Lunatic" was trying to get Crowley to admit being tempted to masturbate, or to having done it. Because Crowley refused to confess what he had not done, the Rev. Champney decided to subject him to extremely cruel punishment. When Crowley was thirty-five years old, he wrote a book called *The World's Tragedy*. The majority of the book is a viscous poem or "play" written to denounce the Christian faith. In one section of the book Crowley wrote about his attendance at the school and the cruel punishment he was given because of his refusal to "confess." It has been reproduced here in order for the reader to hear it directly from Crowley:

A BOYHOOD IN HELL

"The Revd. H. d'Arcy Champney M.A. of Corpus Christi College, Cambridge, had come out of sect.

He had voted at the Parliamentary elections by crossing out the names of the candidates and writing: 'I vote for King Jesus.'

He had started a school for the Sons of Brethren at 51, Bateman Street, Cambridge. May God bite into the bones of men the pain of that hell on earth (I have prayed often) that by them it may be sowed with salt, accursed for ever! May the maiden that passes it be barren, and the pregnant woman that beholdeth it abort! May the birds of the air refuse to fly over it! May it stand as a curse, as a fear, as an hate, among men! May the wicked dwell therein! May the light of the Sun be withheld therefrom, and the light of the Moon not lighten it! May it become the home of the shells of the dead, and may the demons of the pit inhabit it! May it be accursed, accursed, accursed - accursed forever and ever!

And still, standing as I stand in the prime of early manhood, free from all the fetters of the body and the mind, do I curse the memory thereof unto the ages.

It was a good enough school from the point of examiners, I daresay. Morally and physically it was an engine of destruction and corruption. I am just going to put down a few facts haphazard as they come to my memory; you may form your own judgment.

1. We were allowed to play Cricket, but not to score runs, lest it should excite the vice of 'emulation.'

2. Champney told me, a child of not yet twelve years old, that he had never consummated his marriage, (Only the very acute verbal memory which I possess enabled me years after to recall and interpret his meaning. He used a coarser phrase).

3. We were told that 'the Lord had a special care of the school, and brought to light that which was done in darkness,' etc., etc., ad nauseam. 'The instrument was on this occasion so-and-so, who had nobly come forward, etc.,etc.' In other words, hypocrisy and sneaking were the only virtues.

Naturally, one of several boys who might be involved in the same offence would take fright and save his skin by sneaking. The informer was always believed implicitly, as against probability, or even possibility, with complete disregard of the testimony of other and independent witnesses.

For instance, a boy named Glascott, with insane taint, told Mr. Champney that he had visited me (12 years old) at my mother's house during the holidays -

true so far, he had - and found me 'lying drunk at the bottom of the stairs.' My mother was never asked about this; nor was I told of it. I was put into 'Coventry' i.e. nor master nor boy might speak to me, or I to them. I was fed on bread and water; during play hours I worked in the school room; during work hours I walked solitary round and round the playground. I was expected to 'confess' the crime of which I was not only innocent, but unaccused.

This punishment, which I believe criminal authorities would consider severe on a prisoner, went on for a term and a half. I was, at last, threatened with expulsion for my refusal to 'confess,' and so dreadful a picture of the horrors of expulsion did they paint me - the guilty wretch, shunned by his fellows, slinks on through life to a dishonoured grave, etc. - that I actually chose to endure my torture, and to thank my oppressor.

Physically, I broke down. The strain and the misery affected my kidneys; and I had to leave school altogether for two years. I should add in fairness that there were other accusations against me, though, as you shall hear, were almost equally silly.

I learnt at last, through the intervention of my uncle, in a lucid interval, what I was supposed to have done. I was said to have tried 'to corrupt Chamberlain' - not our great patriotic statesman, shifty Joe - but a boy (I was 12 years old, and quite ignorant of all sexual matters till long after). Also I had 'held a mock prayer meeting.' This I remembered. I had strolled up to a group of boys in the playground, who were indeed holding one. As they saw me one said: 'Brother Crowley will now lead us in prayer.' Brother Crowley was too wary, and walked away. But instead of doing what a wise boy would have done: gone straight to the head, and accused them of forty-six distinct unmentionable crimes, I let things slide. So, fearing that I might go, they hurried off themselves, and told him how that wicked Crowley had tried to lead them away from Jesus.

Worse, I had called Page 1 a Pharisee. That was true; I had said it. Dreadful of me! And Page 1, who 'walked very close to Jesus,' of course went and told.

Yes, they all walked close to Jesus - as close as Judas did.

4. A boy named Barton was sentenced to 120 strokes of the cane on his bare shoulders, for some petty theft of which he was presumably innocent.

Superb was the process of trial. It began by an extra long prayer-time, and Joshua's account of the sin of Achan, impressively read. Next, an hour or two about the Lord's care of the school, the way He brought sin to light. Next, when well worked up, and all our nerves on the jump, who stole what? Silence. Next, The Lord's care in providing a witness - like the witnesses against Naboth! Then the witness and his story, as smooth as a policeman's. Next, sentence. Last, execution, with intervals of prayer!

Champney's physique being impaired, one may suppose by his excessive devotion to Jesus, he arranged to give 60 strokes one day, and 60 the next.

My memory fails - perhaps Barton will one day oblige with his reminiscenses - but I fancy the first day come so near killing him that he escaped the second.

I remember the licking I got - on the legs, because flogging the buttocks excites the victim's sensuality! - 15 minutes prayer, 15 minutes more strokes of the cane - and more prayer to top it!

5. On Sunday the day was devoted to 'religion.' Morning prayers and sermon (about 45 min.). Morning 'Meeting' (1 1\2 to 2 hours). Open-air preaching on Parker's Piece (say 1 hour). Bible reading and learning by heart. Reading of the few books 'sanctioned for Sunday' (say 2 hours). Prayer-meeting (called voluntary, but to stay away meant that some sneak in the school would accuse you of something next day) (say 1 hour). Evening prayer and Sermon (say 30 minutes). Preaching of the Gospel in the meeting-room (1 1\2 hours). Ditto on Parker's Piece (say 1 hour). Prayer before retiring (say 1\2 hour).

6. The 'Badgers' Meeting.' Every Monday night the school was ranged round the back of the big schoolroom, and the scourings of Barnswell (Cambridge's slum) let in, fed, preached to, and dismissed.

Result, epidemics of ring worms, measles, and mumps.

On no! not a result; the Lord's hand was heavy upon us because of some undiscovered sin.

I might go on for a long while, but I will not. I hope there are some people in the world happy enough to think that I am lying, or at least exaggerating. But I pledge my word to the literal truth of all I have said, and there are plenty of witnesses alive to confirm me, or to refute me. I have given throughout the actual names, addresses and other details."9

Suffice it to say, if Tom Friend had gone to this "school," he definitely would have set fire to the place. If I had run into the man who gave me 120 strokes of the cane on my bare shoulders for something I had not done once I was sixteen or seventeen, well, you can ask my high school classmates. This was not a Christian School. Yes, they used the name of Jesus. If you look at Crowley's text in detail, you don't see any scripture quoted by Champney. You see a great deal of intimidation, lying, squealing, and an abrasive, graceless, loveless atmosphere. What I cannot understand, is that although Crowley became a student of the *Bible*, he projected all this insanity to Jesus Christ himself, as though he were the one responsible for it. Did you see what Crowley wrote about the boys he hated walking with Jesus? He said, "Yes, they all walked close to Jesus - as close as Judas did." Crowley put these people in the category of Judas, who betrayed Christ, and then he turns against Christ? It seems that Crowley knew these people were phony, and yet used them as an excuse to rebel against god. The New Testament speaks in no uncertain terms about this loveless, religious atmosphere: "If I speak in the tongues of men and of angels, but have not love, I am only a resounding gong or a clanging cymbal. If I have the gift of prophecy and can fathom all mysteries and all knowledge, and if I have a faith that can move mountains, but have not love, I am nothing. If I give all I possess to the poor and surrender my body to the flames, but have not love, I gain nothing. Love is patient, love is kind. It does not envy, it does not boast, it is not proud. It is not rude, it is not self-seeking, it is not easily angered, it keeps no record of wrongs. Love does not delight in evil but rejoices with the truth. It always protects, always trusts, always hopes, always perseveres....And now these three remain: faith, hope and love. But the greatest of these is love." - 1 Corinthians 13: 1-7; 13(NIV).

Jesus himself said in the New Testament Book of John, Chapter 13, verses 34-35: "A new command I give you: Love one another. As I have loved you, so you must love one another. All men will know that you are my disciples if you love one another." Speaking of his final judgment on false, charlatan forms of Christianity, Jesus said: "Watch out for false prophets. They come to you in sheep's clothing, but inwardly they are ferocious wolves. By their fruit you will recognize them. Do people pick grapes from thornbushes, or figs from thistles? Likewise every good tree bears good fruit, but a bad tree bears bad fruit. A good tree cannot bear bad fruit, and a bad tree cannot bear good fruit. Every tree that does not bear good fruit is cut down and thrown into the fire. Thus, by their fruit you will recognize them. Not everyone who says to me, 'Lord, Lord,' will enter the kingdom of heaven, but only he who does the will of my Father who is in heaven. Many will say to me on that day, 'Lord, Lord, did we not prophesy in your name, and in your name drive out demons and perform many miracles?' Then I will tell them plainly, 'I never knew you. Away from me, you evildoers!'" - Matthew 7:15-23(NIV).

Jesus said there are many who will cry to him that they did miracles and wonderful works in his name and they are still going to hell. The reason for that is they thought they were earning heaven with their works rather than seeking a relationship with God that brings true salvation. Aleister Crowley went to a school that apparently had nothing more to do with Jesus Christ than the Khu Klux Klan. They too claim Jesus as Lord. It is important that people realize that Jesus had absolutely nothing to do with what happened to Crowley at that school. Jesus himself would have pulled Champney out in front of the entire student body and told them the man was a hypocrite. Again, Crowley's critical error is projecting all his bitterness to God.

Aleister Crowley was speaking against the Plymouth Brethren, but I also want to say if British rock stars are rebelling against the 'Church of England,' more power to them! The problem is that they have chosen to fight evil with evil. Jesus Christ has nothing more to do with the doctrines of the Church of England than he does the A.A. I make no apologies for that statement to anybody, anywhere. King James I of England used whips on American Christians as they refused to preach the anti-Biblical doctrines of the Church of England. The preceding statement is a matter of irrefutable history. All one has to do is become an objective student of the *Bible* and you can see who is teaching lies and who is teaching truth. It takes research. Research that I have done. I did not believe any man on his merit, or because of what he was wearing, or because he said his denomination is the true church. I investigated the teachings of the various denominations and compared them all with what the *Holy Bible* teaches. Crowley the 'genius' did not do this with Christianity, because he did not care to. If Crowley really wanted to know the truth, he would have searched for it. What he really wanted was to be a hedonist. This is what Crowley said about his turning to Satan: "...I accepted the theology of the Plymouth Brethren. In fact, I could hardly conceive of the existence of people who might doubt it. I simply went over to Satan's side; and to this hour I cannot tell why."10 It is crucial for the reader to understand all of the factors of Crowley's childhood. He not only loved the Dragon (Satan), the Beast (anti-Christ), and the false prophet, but that he loved them prior to his abuse, and the said abuse set him on the road to an evil adulthood. The abuse was just an excuse. He would have done it anyway. Crowley provided his readers with a description of his adolescence, again, from *The World's Tragedy*.

ADOLESCENCE

"Too ill with albuminuria brought on by the savage treatment of Champney to do any regular work, I was sent away with various tutors, mostly young men from Cambridge, members of the unspeakable C.I.C.C.U.

I remember in my first term at Cambridge how I was in the rooms of a leading light of the C.I.C.C.U., the Revd. Something Doddridge, my Uncle Tom's trusted henchman.

I remember how eloquently he held forth on the courage to stop any 'impure conversation.' I remember how impressed we were; how a gentleman with an 'honourable' in front of his name, destined to be celebrated in the world of motors and balloons, walked into the room and told us rather a lively story. The Reverend Something Doddridge thought of the 'honourable' and laughed pleasantly. I remember how, boys as we were, we filed austerely from the rooms without farewell. Oh, you must know the C.I.C.C.U.!

I remember too how this Doddridge, while in charge of my morals, aided and abetted me in extinguishing street lamps; and how when a policeman pounced on me, he forsook me and fled! A true disciple of Jesus!

I had no playmates; my morals might be corrupted! Only the 'children of brethren' were eligible, and these were as a rule socially impossible.

I was always being watched for signs of masturbation, and always being warned and worried about it. It says something for human innocence that after four years of this insane treatment I was still absolutely ignorant, though on fire in every nerve to learn the practice that people made so much fuss about.

But really - my tutors! Of all the surpassing prigs! I was so mentally shattered by the disease and torture - for both continued - that I remember practically nothing of the next two years.

But at least I shall take care that this book comes into the hands of the Very Reverend Armitage Robinson Esq., M.A., D.D., Dean of Westminster; for though I suppose he knows how his missionary brother Jack seduced to sodomy his missionary brother Fred, he may still be ignorant of how that brother Fred (one of my tutors) attempted to seduce me in his own mother's house at Maze Hill. This came a little later; and I knew exactly what he was doing, as it happened. I let him go as far as he did, with the deliberate intention of making sure on that point.

I think my readers will agree - enough of my tutors!

I ought to make an honourable exception of one Archibald Douglas, an Oxford man and a traveler. He taught me sense and manhood, and I shall not easily forget my debt to him. I hear he is dead - may earth lie light upon him!

Of course my Mother and her brother my Uncle Tom couldn't stand him. (I must excuse my mother and my Uncle. The former was the best of all possible mothers, only marred beyond belief by the religious monomania which perhaps started in what one may call 'Hysteria of Widowhood;' the latter a typical sexual degenerate.) They stole his letters and faked up some excuse for getting rid of him. And if 'an orphan's curse can drag to hell a spirit from on high' what of the curse of a child on those who betrayed him in their bigotry and meanness to such torture as I have described?

My whole soul cramped; society denied me; books debarred me, with the rare exceptions of Scott, Ballantyne, and some of Dickens, with a few even worse!

To illustrate the domestic principle of literary criticism:

I was forbidden David Copperfield because of 'little Em'ly' - Emily being my Mother's name, I might cease to respect her. For the same reason she proscribed the Bab Ballads, recommended by a rash tutor, because 'Emily Jane was a nursery maid!' Coleridge's Ancient Mariner was condemned because of the water-snakes whom he 'blessed unaware;' snakes being cursed in Genesis! As it happened, however, I had a backbone in me some where. I had always refused to join the sneaking hypocrite gang at Champney's; now I accepted the war, and began to fight for my freedom. I went on long walks in the mountains, where my tutors could not follow me, and where delightful peasant girls could and did follow me - God bless them!

One day I had a difference of opinion with a tutor, in the course of which he fell from a rock into a loch (whose name I forgot) near Forsinard. Memory fails to recall the actual cause of dispute; but I think I had thrown his fishing-rod into the loch, and thought that it was expedient for him to try an retrieve it.

The same night he found me in the heather with Belle McKay the local beauty (God bless her!), and gave me up as a bad job.

So I fought the swine! They sent me to Malvern, where my weakness made me the prey of every bully, and saved me from the attention of every budding Eulenburg. Sodomy was the rule at Malvern; my study-companion used even to take money for it. I cunningly used my knowledge of the fact to get taken away from the school.

It must not be supposed that we had no other amusements. There was 'pill-ragging;' a form of fight whose object was to seize and hurt the opponent's testicles; and 'greasing;' i.e., spitting either in each other's faces or secretly so the victim should not detect the act. In my time this had died out of the other houses; but still flourished in my house 'Huntingdon's' N 4. There was bullying, too; and now and then cricket and football.

They sent me to Tonbridge; my health broke down; partly, one may say, through what would have been my own fault or misfortune if I had been properly educated; but, as it was, was the direct result of the vile system that, not content with torturing me itself, handed me over bound and blindfold to the outraged majesty of Nature. I escaped then from Tonbridge. They sent me to Eastbourne to a P.B. family where I had more liberty, and could have been happy; but the revolting cruelties which they inflicted on the only pretty and decent member of the family, my dear 'sister' Isabelle, caused me one day to knock their heads together and walk out of the house. They sent me to Cambridge. I found myself my own master, and settled down to lead a righteous, sober and godly life; and to make up for lost time in the matter of education.

Outside purely scholastic subjects, they had taught me to fight, to love the truth, to hate oppression, - and by God! I think they taught me well.

On my soul, I should thank them!"11

The author would challenge the reader to search and see if any of the activity described by Crowley in that passage is advocated or recommended by the *Holy Bible*. Better yet, don't waste your time. None of the activity described is in there as teaching.

Motivated by his hatred of the activities and teachings of English "Christianity," Crowley went on to write about his writing of *The World's Tragedy* in the book of the same name. In it he does confess that it is English Christianity he hates. The most dreadful part of this text is Crowley's relating of his encounter with Pan, whom he later confessed was Satan:

THE WRITING OF THE WORLD'S TRAGEDY

"It has been necessary to sketch this part of my life in order to exhibit the atmosphere which I am bound to connect with Christianity, or at least English Christianity.

Certainly the vast majority of English people, of those who are religious at all, belong either to Evangelicalism or Dissent; and the tyranny of these is nearly if not quite as bad as that of the Plymouth Brethren. I had, however, cut myself adrift from all these things. I had lived among the great men of the earth, and the great mountains of the earth. Pollitt had made a poet of me; Eckenstein had made a man of me; Cecil Jones and Allan Bennett had made a God of me. I had forgotten the Plymouth Brethren! But early in this spring (1910), I went down to Eastbourne to my mother's house, and some of the old bitterness came back. In her house were two vile old women, hypocrites and slaves to the marrow. The mere meanness and old maid-ishness of it would have sickened me. These mange-bitten cats!

But there was worse. Only one food was on the table for breakfast, lunch, and dinner; and that food cold boiled Jesus. I stomached it well enough – God's blood! I had my belly full of yore and knew to despise it - but in vain I tried to talk of other things. The Boulter blasphemy case was on, and the cold boiled Jesus was so high that it literally stank. So did the women! I stood it for breakfast, I stood it for lunch, I stood it for tea - but 'twasn't tea, 'twas Jesus!

Dinner came; cold boiled Jesus, and the scrag end of it at that!

I went out and stood by the sea. I was lost in reverie. Here were these hags of hell, the product of an unvarying diet of cold boiled Jesus! By God! Could not I save somebody? These had once been fresh healthy English girls, fit for life and laughter. C.B.J. had mummified them to what they were. I would be the Saviour of the future!

I must have wandered in my meditation; for presently I found myself lying on the grass under the full moon and the stars, the sea's low plash beneath my feet, the soft breeze blowing over me, a whisper - oh essence of the winds and of the seas of the world! - in my ears (I seem to remember even now that her name was Mabel - thank you, Mabel!) And then I gazed upon the moon and vowed myself knight Artemis, to bring the truth into this England of hypocrisy, light in its superstition of rationalism, love in its prudery, chastity into its whoredom!

So I swore, and rose up and kissed Mabel and went home in the might of the holy vision - for the god Pan appeared to me, and abode in me and I in him - and wrote for four nights - night by night, until the World's Tragedy lay finished and perfect before me.

All day I kept myself up to the mark by the stern penance of C.B.J.; all night I wrote and wrote.

So fierce I wrote that - six months later - I have written no word since. I have pored forth all the vials, and loosed all the seals. From that supreme effort I am fallen exhausted - until, as it may chance, the Gods renew my vigour. And all my other work I count as nothing; for I have written this in Pan, and in Pan I am content. To the boys and girls of England I give my book, the charter of their freedom."12

If Crowley were honest, he would have said his book was the charter of slavery to rebellion. Crowley wrote it under the influence of Pan. He couldn't conclude his writing without mentioning his (Pan's) rebellious position on sexuality, specifically, sodomy. In the text he declares immediately his desire to fight openly for this persuasion. Most rock stars of today have no problem with it:

SODOMY

"Further, lest 'broad-minded' prigs come to smash me by their aid, I shall fight openly for that which no living Englishman dare defend, even in secret - sodomy!

At school I was taught to admire Plato and Aristotle, who recommend sodomy to youths. I am not so rebellious as to oppose their dictum; and in truth there seems no better way to avoid the contamination of woman and the morose pleasures of solitary vice. (Not that women themselves are unclean. It is the worship of them as ideals that rots the soul). Again we may say that all the great men of antiquity were sodomites: Socrates, Caesar, Alexander, Martial, Catullus, Virgil, Achilles; Napoleon, Frederick the Great, Goethe, Shakespeare, Bacon, an unbroken line of English monarchs; Mohammed, Benvenuto Cellini, Wilde, Symonds, Emerson, Pater, Fitz-Gerald, Leighton, Whitman, Michael Angelo, Leonardo, and a host of others - even unto this hour. But of this hour I will not speak. I am now collecting a great body of evidence similar to that which Herr Harden has gathered in Germany, and involving an even higher class of society. Not in the least to show the corruptions of that class; but to proclaim sodomy as an aristocratic virtue, which our middle class had better imitate if they wish to be smart."13

In the last chapter, Colin Wilson was quoted as saying Crowley's homosexuality began as a result of his desire to rebel against the norm in society. Also, he said he used to have sex with a small negro boy. Regardless of his motive, it was an act of Crowley's will to engage in homosexuality. We are going to look at the Biblical prophecy of AIDS later in the book. Does that sound shocking? AIDS, while not called that, was predicted 1900 years ago by Paul the Apostle in the New Testament. It was predicted to occur in the bodies of homosexuals. Lord Jesus Christ loves all men, including homosexual men and women, and he will save their souls if they repent just as heterosexuals who repent. However, his judgment stands firm.

Crowley couldn't resist attacking Christianity again, this time in general terms, with the exception of Catholicism. His presentation is absurd; he does not support it with the *Bible*. There is no scripture to back Crowley's statements about Jesus being angry with anyone who plays on Sunday. Roger Staubach and a legion of other Christians have done it for years; as work no less. There is no passage in the *Bible* to back Crowley's assertion that Christianity requires its people to worship in a silk hat or frock coat. There is also no passage in the *Bible* commanding men not to eat melon, potatoes, artichokes, tomatoes, milk, or water. I do not know a single Christian who is afraid to eat these things. Nevertheless, that is what Crowley asserts:

CHRISTIANITY

"But why - we may indeed ask - all this heavy metal to bombard a brothel? Has no good thing come out of Nazareth?

It is in a way extremely trying to live in a world where connotation varies so wildly.

The Sicilian peasant who can roar with laughter at some blasphemous obscenity of his village priest while preserving his devotion to the deities satirized, will justly be astonished and disgusted with me. He will hardly credit that anyone can take deities so seriously as to do anyone an injury on their behalf. He is at heart a Pagan; Mary is his mistress and Jesus his - Bambino -, and he loves to play with them in the woods where the sunlight traces its faint fan-patterns among the leaves.

The idea of a Jesus who objected to people playing on a Sunday - who insisted on being worshiped in a silk hat and frock coat, who couldn't stand people obtaining refreshment after 12:30 - Well, it never struck him, that's all!

So when I go wandering among country-side Catholics, I am nearly as happy in their simple worship as I am with the grander and austerer conceptions of Mohammed. But England! The people have materialized their God into a Parish Councillor, at the best; at the worst, he has been made the excuse of every crime.

The prevalence of syphilis in the Indian army has increased from 8% to 80% lest God should be shocked by our unholy recognition of the human nature of the human soldier.

It is useless to multiply examples. All I wish to do is to justify my agreement with Shelly and Nietzsche in defining Christianity as the religious expression of the slave spirit in man.

I do not wish to argue that the doctrines of Jesus, they and they alone, have degraded the world to its present condition. I take it that Christianity is not only the cause but the symptom of slavery. There were slaves in Rome, of course, even under the republic. But it was only through Paul that the slime found tongue, and uttered its agony and blasphemy. Now, through the steady growth of altruism peri-passu with the Gospel that advocates it, the world is come to such a pass that the canaille is throned....Just look at your Christian when he gets his modicum of manhood. He will not take the manly way, because (a) he is afraid of hurting the modesty of the poor girl (who is simply aching for him); (b) he is afraid of catching some disease; (c) he might get her into trouble; (d) what will the neighbours say?; (e) suppose she said no, what a fool I should look!; (f) God said I mustn't. And so on through the alphabet of cowardice.

Look at you Christian as he sits down to dinner.

He won't eat melon because the weather is hot, and he might get choler; mutton? Think of the poor sheep! Potatoes? Bad for his fat; Artichoke? Bad for his gout. Tomatoes? Cause of cancer. Wine? The great curse of our day, my dear sir. Milk? A mere mass of tubercle bacilli. Water? Typhoid! Do you want to poison me, my dear friend? Beer? Well, perhaps a little beer - for he has shares in a brewery.

You have already seen how this awful fear of nature and of God is twisted into an engine of oppression and torture against anyone who declines to grovel and cringe before their filthy fetish. It is obvious that cowardice is the cause of cruelty: the brave man strikes a strenuous blow, and all is over; the coward brought to bay snarls and strikes in desperation, and if by chance the blow goes home, he jumps on and mutilates and insults his victim.

Of course all this insane Christianity has produced its own toxin. Our prudery goes hand in hand with the most disgusting system of prostitution in the world, and our Theaters (too pure for that corrupter Sophocles) are disgraced by the most senseless and witless leg shows. Our praise of poverty has produced the worst poor-laws in civilization; our democracy has perfected a snobbery which would make Thackeray stare with surprise. Queen Victoria the Good - what washer woman lost to mankind! was the French nation's epitaph upon her - drove the last nail into the coffin of art in England. Though 'twas needless cruelty: whom have we had of the first rank in England since Elizabeth but the Revolutionaries? Blacke, Shelley, Keats, Coleridge, Byron, Swinburne, Swift, Butler, Milton, every one exiled, starved, bullied, driven insane; except Milton, whose supreme hypocrisy saved him, as it damned the nation forever. Anyhow, bad as it was, Victoria made it worse, and, under a queen with a high-necked collar, it is left for me to unite in myself all the blare of all the trumpets. Call me, Israfel, last of the angels, and let the dead rise from their tombs!

I therefore hold the legendary Jesus in no wise responsible for the trouble: it began with Luther, perhaps, and went on with Wesley; but no matter! - what I am trying to get at is the religion which makes England to-day a hell for any man who cares at all for freedom. That religion they call Christianity; the devil they honour they call God. I accept these definitions, as a poet must do, if he is to be at all intelligible to his age, and it is their God and their religion that I hate and will destroy."14

Crowley said he didn't blame the "legendary Jesus" for the religion he hated, but then said he hated the God of the Christians, Lord Jesus Christ, as well as the religion he founded with his shed blood. By making such a confession, Aleister Crowley showed himself to be in league with, and possessed by, none other than Satan; the Devil himself. As such he became a powerful weapon in Satan's hands, relative to the war between Christ and the Devil for the souls of men. If Satan can destroy Christianity, he will have no enemy to oppose his devouring of the souls of men.

LED ZEPPELIN II - "WHAT IS AND WHAT SHOULD NEVER BE"

Crowley would not only seek to destroy the Christian faith, but promote his own satanic cult as a result. Eliphas Levi, again, who Crowley claimed to be reincarnated, wrote: "To affirm and will what ought to be is to create; to affirm and will what ought not to be is to destroy."15 This is what the author asserts is the theme of the song, "What Is and What Should Never Be." When Robert Plant sings, "You will be mine," I believe that is Lucifer singing to his bride, which are his people, just as in the beginning of the song "Thank You," off the same album, *Led Zeppelin II*. Substantive evidence to that effect has not been presented in this chapter, but it will be seen later in detail. To Crowley and Led Zeppelin, the worship of the Lucifer is, and the worship of Jesus Christ should never be. This crowd does have an enemy. In the *Bible*, specifically, the Book of the first epistle of John, we find these words: "For this purpose the Son of God was manifested, that He might destroy the works of the devil." - 1 John 3:8 We are going to see exactly what the Devil's work is in the following pages.

Aleister Crowley was the supreme hypocrite. He was a wicked person who, pointing the finger at others, called them wicked. The cure for this problem, he believed, was to give himself completely over to the Devil.

Crowley's personal secretary for several years, Israel Regardie, wrote that he believes Christianity is dying, in the introduction to *The World's Tragedy*. Speaking of Crowley he wrote: "...the hatred of Christianity was not entirely his personal business. It is shared especially today by multitudes of thinking men and women. And though it may appear on the surface that Fundamentalism and Evangelism and Charismatic Christianity are spreading (even the previous President of the U.S. was numbered among their ranks), nevertheless it is the belief of many that these are the agonizing death rattles of a moribund and decadent religion. If so, Crowley's writing had a lot to do with that. He was unceasing in his eloquent denunciation of the religion that spoiled his early life and with hate and guilt ruined the lives of untold legions of human beings."16 Israel Regardie wrote that in Arizona in 1983. It will be proven to the reader that Aleister Crowley never had an infinitesimal clue as to what the Christian faith was about. You will read what the *Bible* says, in a later chapter, that will show you that Crowley and Page and all satanists like them, had the understanding of Jesus Christ that the Devil himself wanted them to have. Jesus Christ had nothing to do with anything Crowley described, neither did he use *Bible* verses as a foundation for claiming they were principles of the Christian faith. Christianity, Biblical Christianity, is not a religion of restriction. If it were, Romans chapter eight would not be in it. Christianity is a religion of pleasure; in the proper, constructive context. I never would have believed that when I was a disciple of sex, drugs, and rock and roll. If it were merely a religion of restriction, that could not provide something better than the rock/drug culture, I would not be able to advocate it with a clear conscience. Can you imagine God creating sex and then saying you can't have it? He is merely against sexual perversion, something Aleister Crowley cherished.

Crowley was a perverted, drug-addicted puppet who gave himself over to Witchcraft, or "Magick" as he liked to call it. You are going to see his influence on Jimmy Page loud and clear in the following pages. That influence spread to Plant, Jones, Bonham, and the fans of Led Zeppelin; all the result of fooling around with Magick and the Devil.

ALEISTER CROWLEY SELLS HIS SOUL

While a student at Trinity College, Aleister Crowley published his first book of verse, which could be viewed as his first book on Magick, in 1898. It was called *Aceldama, A Place to Bury Strangers in.* In the preface, Crowley shows himself as having a seared conscience, no longer able to discern between right and wrong, good and evil, as presented as an absolute in the primal condition of the conscience. That will be elaborated on later in specific detail. It will be made pure and simple for everyone to understand. Crowley wrote: "It was a windy night, that memorable seventh night of December, when this philosophy was born in me. How the grave old professor wondered at my ravings! I had called at his house, for he was a valued friend of mine, and I felt strange thoughts and emotions shake within me. Ah! How I raved! I called to him to trample me, he would not. We passed together into the stormy night. I was on horseback, how I galloped round him in my phrenzy, till he became the prey of real physical fear! How I shrieked out I know not what strange words! And the poor good old man tried all he could to calm me; he thought I was mad! The fool! I was in the death struggle with self: God and Satan fought for my soul those three long hours. God conquered - now I have only one doubt left - which of the twain was God?"17 If Crowley's conscience was still intact as it had been designed originally, he would have known which one was God. He said God conquered, yet he did not know which one was God. The one that became his "God" was the one who is Lord of the moral code that he adhered to in the three-hour struggle for his soul. He wrote the following in his *Confessions*, describing Christianity as "a fiendish superstition." That was a necessity for him in order to live out the moral code he chose, again, as an act of his own free will: "It seems as if I possessed a theology of my own which was, to all intents and purposes, Christianity. My Satanism did not interfere with it at all; I was trying to take the view that the Christianity of hypocrisy and cruelty was not true Christianity. I did not hate God or Christ, but merely the God and Christ of the people whom I hated. It was only when the development of my logical faculties supplied the demonstration that the Scriptures support the theology and practice of professing Christians that I was compelled to set myself in opposition to the Bible itself. It does not matter that the literature is sometimes magnificent and that in isolated passages the philosophy and ethics are admirable. The sum of the matter is that Judaism is a savage, and Christianity a fiendish, superstition."18 Once again, Crowley offers no substantive argument here; no challenge to Biblical text. It was merely his opinion, based on the moral code he had chosen for the rest of his life. He certainly wouldn't find any passages in the *Holy Bible* advocating sodomy with little boys, so we can understand his perception of the religion of Lord Jesus Christ as a "fiendish superstition".

Seven years earlier, in 1891, Crowley had a tutor by the name of Archibald Douglas, who was a man of Oxford. He taught Crowley, who was sixteen years old at the time, that drinking and smoking were activities that were normal; but warned him of excess. Among the things Douglas taught him were gambling and chasing women. He showed him how pleasures as such were not wrong, and could be enjoyed without hurting anyone. As a result of his leadership, Crowley wrote: "The nightmare world of Christianity vanished at the dawn."19 At this same time he wrote that he fell in love with a girl and the mysteries pertaining to sex became beauty and joy. He said that he no longer was obsessed with sin. Conversely, he then wrote at that exact point in his life: "I had been almost overwhelmed by the appalling responsibility of ensuring my own damnation and helping others to escape from Jesus."20 Here Crowley does not say that wants to help others escape from the "Christianity" he had been exposed to, but rather that he wants to help others escape from Jesus. Again, Crowley projected his hatred for a charlatan form of Christianity to Christ himself. This is as intelligent as someone hating the Devil because of the existence of real Christianity. One is clearly not responsible for the other.

Shortly after writing that he wanted to help others escape from Jesus, he wrote the following in his *Confessions*, showing the true desire of his heart: "I resolved passionately to reach the spiritual causes of phenomena, and to dominate the material world which I detested by their means. I was not content to believe in a personal devil and serve him, in the ordinary sense of the word. I wanted to get hold of him personally and become his chief of staff."21 Crowley's love for spiritual wickedness and lust for power motivated him to become Satan's right hand man. He wanted power to dominate; to be a god.

It was also around this time that Crowley delighted in John Milton's Paradise Lost, because of Satan. He wrote: "This bored me for the most part as much as it does now, but allowed me to gloat over the figures of Satan and sin. After all, Milton was a great poet; and the subconscious artistic self of him was therefore bitterly antagonistic to Christianity. Not only is Satan the hero, but the triumphant hero. God's threats have not 'come off.' It is the forces of evil, so called, that manifest in strength and beauty of form."22 Did you see the words "so called?" Crowley's conscience had been completely reversed. Right had become wrong, and wrong had become right. In other words, good had become evil and evil became good. This is called "searing of the conscience." He was fully aware this was happening in his mind, and that he was responsible for it: "Having got to the point of saying, 'Evil, be thou my good,' I racked my brains to discover some really abominable crimes to do."23 Anyone who commits himself to evil, as an act of the will, inevitably has the original moral code of his conscience disappear. It will disappear like wrinkles in a shirt seared with a hot iron. God designed the conscience this way in order to allow for the possibility of its searing by an individual who, again, as a conscious act of his will, gives himself over to evil; which silences the old conscience and gives them a new one that can love evil without conviction. Once a person does that, the Devil is waiting in the wings. You will see that the Devil was indeed waiting for Crowley. He began to sound like Jim Morrison of the Doors. He wrote: "I demanded to be at grips with death in one way or another."24 Wishing for evil to be his good, Crowley then wanted to embrace death. This is the same person who wrote that Christianity was a fiendish superstition. There is a relationship between his love for evil and death, and his labeling Christianity a superstition. While refusing to take Christianity seriously, Crowley displayed a certain vacillation of mind. He wrote that he would not abandon his intellectual belief in the Christian faith. The reason being that he cherished rebelling against it: "It seems as if I clung to the idea of the wickedness of love and the belief that it entailed divine retribution, partly perhaps because of my tendency to masochism, but consciously, at least, as adding actual value to sin. Pleasure as such has never attracted me. It must be spiced by moral satisfaction. I was reluctant to abandon my intellectual belief in Christianity; if the whole thing was nonsense, where was the fun of fighting it?"25

The reader will not find one passage in the *Bible* were it says that love invites divine retribution; what he was referring to was unbridled lust. He clearly stated here that he did not prefer masochism as pleasure, only because it made his sin more sinful. Again, it was the rebellion Crowley relished, all rooted in his ostensible bitterness against God because of his father's death in conjunction with the abuse that he suffered. Crowley was supposed to be a genius, yet he never saw that he was projecting his bitterness to God, who had done him no wrong. Crowley had the knowledge of good and evil. He simply chose evil. He said in an earlier quote that he did not know why he went over to Satan's side. If he were alive today, we could show him it was because of bitterness.

Crowley not only clung to his bitterness against the "Christians" that he hated, he believed himself justified to hate God. This left him open to be influenced to buy the lie that Satan is God. The whole problem with Aleister Crowley was his bitterness in conjunction with a love for evil; blinded by his own intellect. Although Crowley claimed to be wise, he became a fool and worshiped the Devil, allowing him to be an agent of Satan's bitterness against God. Many have followed in his footsteps, with his writings spread all over the world for foolish God hating people to read and believe that Satan is god; as a result of their own sovereign choice.

ALEISTER CROWLEY AND JIMMY PAGE - ON WOMEN

Another one of the bitter and hateful attitudes that Aleister Crowley clung to was his downgrading of women. He will be quoted first, and then Jimmy Page to illustrate his concurrence. Crowley wrote: "I received my first lesson in what the religions of the world have discovered long since, that no man who allows a woman to take any place in his life is capable of doing good work....A man who is strong enough to use women as slaves and playthings is all right."26 Jimmy Page said: "Crowley didn't have a very high opinion of women and I don't think he was wrong."27 Page is not kidding. Led Zeppelin's second album has a song title presented with parentheses after it. The title reads "Living Loving Maid (She's Just A Woman)." It may seem that these men just have an opinion of women that is not favorable, but one can bet this opinion is rooted in bitterness.

ALEISTER CROWLEY ON MARRIAGE

If a man has no respect for God or women, how could he possibly respect the sanctity of the marriage relationship? It does not seem that Crowley or

Page's love for the Devil helped to advance their outlook on life. How could it? Satanists have no comprehension of a one man, one woman commitment. They have no idea what it is to have intimacy and love for someone the way God designed it to be. This is what Aleister Crowley had to say about love and marriage: "Marriage would lead to very little trouble if men would get rid of the idea that it is anything more than a financial and social partnership. People should marry for convenience and agree to go their separate ways without jealously. It should be a point of honour for the woman to avoid complicating the situation with children by other men, unless her husband be willing, which he would be if he really loved her....The true offences against marriage arise when sexual freedom results in causing injury to the health or estate of the partner. But the sentimental wrong of so-called infidelity is a symptom of the childishness of the race."28 It should not have to be said, but Crowley was a very sick, twisted individual (There is a famous political couple whose marriage seems to be only a financial and social partnership as well. How many children does it take to make a partnership like that appear as a family? It takes only one. There is an office that will never be held by a single non-family man.). Crowley would love the morals in contemporary society. This is the man about whom Jimmy Page cannot understand why he is being called evil. What does that tell you? Better yet, what does that tell you about the Silver Star? Do you really want someone else getting your wife or husband in bed?

I remember many years ago meeting "biker Bob." Not all bikers are like this man. He is however, indicative of why words like "biker" and "Harley Davidson" can have a negative connotation with some. This man was in his fifties, wearing a Nazi helmet, with unspeakable profanities written on it. He told me one time, as though he was bestowing wisdom on a completely naive individual, "Hey man, my chick is a biker chick. If I come home from work and she is doing a guy on the couch, that's her business." He looked at me as though I were nuts when I refused to sanction such a mentality. This is the end result of the type of thinking that refuses to work at sustaining a relationship. Just erase the relationship of intimacy and enjoy the sex. This is a copout. There are people who say they are intimate with several individuals. This crowd has no clue as to what intimacy is. These people did not have this mentality originally. They simply yield to it as a result of an inability to work at a relationship, in conjunction with a desire to be as immoral as possible. One does not have to be a genius to know this, but they think people who disagree with them are unenlightened and in need of being liberated. They are the true slaves of a decadent, repugnant mentality. Once Aleister Crowley decided to turn his soul completely over as a slave to the Devil, he began his career of Magick; which is the root of Led Zeppelin.

Aleister Crowley then, having suffered abuse at the hands of "Christian" charlatans, when he was especially vulnerable due to the death of his father, had no justification to hate Christ or the *Holy Bible*, due to the fact that none of the things he suffered were advocated by either. The truth is, they condemn them, and it most certainly did not justify his turning that hatred into a love for Satan and unbridled wickedness. Right from the beginning of his life, little Aleister decided to have a great love for the wicked characters in the *Bible*, especially the dragon, who is Satan. The abuse he suffered as a child in conjunction with his father's death provided Crowley with the excuse he needed to pursue a life of wickedness. He himself wrote that he didn't know why he went over to Satan's side, but he did state that he knew he wanted to get a hold of the Devil personally and become his "chief of staff." No amount of abuse by anyone justifies such an attitude or desire. As an agent of Lucifer therefore, he began a life of condemning and attempting to destroy Christianity, advocating sodomy and the belittling of women and marriage right from the start of his adult life. Crowley had the knowledge of good and evil, so he knew the abuse he suffered was not "good" at all, but wickedness. Therefore, he was responsible to Christ for his foolish action of giving himself over to the Devil and writing numerous books to advocate him; and the same applies to Jimmy Page and company. Longing to be Satan's chief of staff, Crowley gave himself over to studying and promoting Black Magick, as you are about to read from his own pen, in the next chapter, justly titled, "Ramble On & Kashmir: Black Magick in Theory and Practice."

Not unlike his mentor, Jimmy Page also possesses a great love for the dragon.

1 Aleister Crowley, *Aceldama, A Place to Bury Strangers In. A Philosophical Poem.* By a Gentleman of the University of Cambridge,1898

2 Aleister Crowley, *The Confessions of Aleister Crowley*, pg.67

3 Ibid, pg.75

4 Susan Roberts, *The Magician of the Golden Dawn*, Contemporary Books, Chicago, 1978, pg.133

5 Ibid, pg.242

6 Aleister Crowley, *The Confessions of Aleister Crowley*, pg.824

7 Ibid, pg.44

8 Susan Roberts, *The Magician of the Golden Dawn*, pg.17

9 Aleister Crowley, *The World's Tragedy*, New Falcon Publications, Scottsdale, Arizona, 1991, pgs. xv- xviii (preface).

10 Aleister Crowley, *The Confessions of Aleister Crowley*, pg.67

11 Aleister Crowley, *The World's Tragedy*, pgs. xix – xxi (preface).

12 Ibid, pgs. xxii-xxiii (preface).

13 Ibid, *The World's Tragedy*, pgs. xxvii-xxviii (preface)

14 Ibid, pgs. xxviii-xxxi (preface).

15 Eliphas Levi, The Key to the Mysteries, translated by Aleister Crowley, Rider, London, 1959, pg.171

16 Aleister Crowley, *The World's Tragedy*, pg. ix

17 Aleister Crowley, *Aceldama, A Place to Bury Strangers In*, 1898

18 Aleister Crowley, *The Confessions of Aleister Crowley*, pg.73

19 Ibid, pg.75

20 Ibid, pg.75

21 Ibid, pg.67

22 Ibid, pg.81

23 Ibid, pg.58

24 Ibid, pg.81

25 Ibid, pg.93

26 Ibid, pg.96

27 Steven Davis, *Hammer of the Gods*, pg.229

28 Aleister Crowley, *The Confessions of Aleister Crowley*, pg.111

Aleister Crowley around the time he joined the Hermetic Order of the Golden Dawn, in 1898, exactly 100 years before the last world tour by Page and Plant. Having gotten into what he called "personal communication with the devil," Aleister Crowley became a real life black magician. And as was his stated goal, he is the Devil's "chief of staff" among the most famous and influential rock stars to ever walk this planet, assisting Crowley, and therefore the Devil, in putting occult teaching to the masses throught the medium of music. This music advocates every form of rebellion against Lord Jesus Christ that the Devil would have his followers commit, all under the guise of entertainment. Every single day there are new disciples of this mystical madman appearing on the world wide internet.

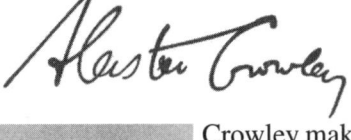

Crowley makes the sign of the "Horns of Pan." Kenneth Anger showed this photo in the film, "Lucifer Rising." Of Course, Anger knows, along with Jimmy Page and Tom Friend, that Pan is Lucifer; and that is why he had the photo included in the film. This is the same photo that Ozzy Osbourne had on the screens on both sides of the stage when he sang "Mr. Crowley" to fans at the Orlando Arena, in 1996.

CHAPTER SIX

"And you He made alive, who were dead in trespasses and sins, in which you once walked according to the course of this world, according to the prince of the power of the air, the spirit who now works in the sons of disobedience…"
"Ephesians,2: 1-2" The Holy Bible

"He who wishes to practice my art, let him love the spirits of hell and those who reign in the air; for these alone are they who can make us happy in this life; and he who would have wisdom must seek it from the devil."
Dr. Faust

"They are organized.The strictest obedience to the devil prevails....These high and wicked spirits are everywhere. They fill the air, are everywhere intent on evil, following the direction of their leader, carrying out his plans with hearty accord, ready obedience and implicit confidence. How loathsome their nature! How marvelous and miracle-working their power! How high and kingly their influence! How martial their purposes!"1
E.M. Bounds, "Satan: His Personality, Power, and Overthrow"

"...it will instead be found that by the permission of the Great God it is the Spirits who govern the firmament."2
The Book of the Sacred Magic of Abramelin the Mage

"After fervent prayer I was carried up above the circle which I had drawn, through a heavy and foggy atmosphere. Soon, however, the air grew purer, and after a little I found myself in a beautifully clear sky."3
Black Magician Aleister Crowley, on astral projection, "The Equinox"

RAMBLE ON & KASHMIR: BLACK MAGICK IN THEORY AND PRACTICE

Once he had taken over control of Aleister Crowley's soul, Satan then set him on the path of becoming a black magician. The Devil had drawn Crowley into his lair, in the spiritual sense, and no fear of God or Satan was lingering in his mind. With such a mind frame, his desire for Magick power would be satisfied by the Devil, who would in turn accomplish the scripting of substantial occult writing and teaching through him. Occult writing and teaching that is being practiced as this book is being read. Crowley, as you will read, began to research the occult, studying diligently until he found the title of a book that he thought would assist him in his pursuit of Satan and Magick knowledge, *The Book of Black Magic and of Pacts*. This book, although it disgusted Crowley for the most part, was the key that opened the door to his career in Magick. Herein we shall follow his progression from researching the occult to meeting other occultists, to joining his first Magick order, The Hermetic Order of the Golden Dawn (November 18, 1898), to establishing his own order, the Argenteum Astrum, the Silver Star. The initial requirement of a new member of the Silver Star, practicing astral projection, will then be discussed in detail through examination of Crowley's writings on the subject, in order to see its relationship to the music of Led Zeppelin, specifically, information contained in the songs "Ramble On" and "Kashmir." The surviving members of Led Zeppelin, or their fans, can plausibly deny that the concepts addressed by the author in those two songs are related to the Devil or the teachings of Aleister Crowley. However, the objective thinker will see the clear path that Satan has drawn between himself, Aleister Crowley, the members of Led Zeppelin, their music, and inevitably the fans, relative to involvement in Magick and the practice of astral projection.

Magick was the name Crowley chose to describe his occult practices. He chose the word from among many that were used during that time to describe supernatural practices relative to Satan. He made it clear in the following quote that performing the Great Work, was synonymous with his choice of the word Magick:

"Before I touched my teens, I was already aware that I was THE BEAST whose number is 666. I did not understand in the least what that implied; it was a passionately ecstatic sense of identity.

In my third year at Cambridge, I devoted myself consciously to the Great Work, understanding thereby the Work of becoming a Spiritual Being, free from the constraints, accidents, and deceptions of material existence.

I found myself at a loss for a name to designate my work, just as H. P. Blavatsky had done some years earlier. 'Theosophy,' 'Spiritualism,' 'Occultism,' 'Mysticism,' all involved undesirable connotations.

I chose therefore the name 'MAGICK' as essentially the most sublime, and actually the most discredited, of all the available terms.

I swore to rehabilitate MAGICK to identify it with my own career; and to compel mankind to respect, love, and trust that which they scorned, hated and feared."4

Crowley wrote that during his third year at Cambridge University when he became committed to the Great Work. In his book, *Magick* (that Jimmy Page read when he was only 11), he defines it as the union of the Microcosm and the Macrocosm. He wrote: "The Microcosm is an exact image of the Macrocosm; the Great Work is the raising of the whole man in perfect balance* to the power of Infinity,"5 (* - "The Battle of Evermore") It is important to remember that Crowley believed the microcosm was the earth and the people on it. The Macrocosm is to the same the universe and the power behind it, specifically Satan.

Crowley, in *The Equinox, Vol. I, No.2*, wrote this brief paragraph about knowing God being the Great Work: "What is the use then of doing anything if we are but as drops of water which are splashed between the wanton hands of the Sun, the Wind, and the Ocean? - indeed the ways of God are inscrutable and past finding out. Thus the Unobtainable tempts us, and the little segments of God that we see become to us the fiercest and most terrible of the Dog-faced Demons which seduce us from the path. He is always at our elbow, whispering, tempting, jeering, advising and helping us; He it is that casts despair upon us when we have done nothing wrong, and elation when we have done nothing right; He it is who is ever rising before us like a mist to obscure our path or to magnify our goal; yet nevertheless He is not only the cloud but that ultimate fire - if we could only understand Him as He IS; Ah! My brothers, this the THE GREAT WORK."6 That was the beginning of a passage in the book that illuminates the reader to Crowley's version of union with god. The rest of the passage will be presented later, one that declares god is the Devil, when discussing Jimmy Page acting out the Great Work in the film, *The Song Remains the Same*.

On the inner cover of *The Song Remains the Same* record and cd, Cameron Crowe wrote about Led Zeppelin departing from a city on their plane after a concert. He said that as they were leaving, they were watching Little Richard on video. He was playing the piano and singing "Tutti-Frutti" from the movie *The Girl Can't Help It*. Crowe wrote that as Jimmy was watching the video he made the statement, "No escaping our roots." Jimmy wasn't talking about Little Richard or the oldies, he was talking about their spiritual roots. Crowe continued by saying that credo led them to release a film of their own a few years later, which is of course, *The Song Remains the Same*. He stated that it wasn't just a concert film, but that "... it is a rare series of glimpses into the visions and symbolism of the men who make the music." After reading this book, the reader will know that all these vision and fantasy sequences of the band members show evidence of being tied in directly to Magick; specifically, the teachings of Aleister Crowley. Three of the four are directly related to the Qabalah. I have presented the meanings behind the Qabalah in detail in Ch.8.

FOOL IN THE RAIN

At the time Crowley decided upon the word Magick to describe the Great Work, he was deeply entrenched in the works of many other occultists. He described the situation in *The Equinox*, referring to himself in the third person, and it is crucial to note that in conjunction with all the demonic subjects he freely admits to studying at the time, was his study of the Qabalah. It was the Devil who guided him to the study of the Qabalah:

"Youth strides on with hasty step, and by the summer of this year - 1898 - we find P. (Perdurabo) deep in consultation with the mystics, and drinking from the white chalice of mystery with St. John, Boehme, Tauler, Eckart, Molinos, Levi, and Blake:

'Rintrah roars and shakes his fires in the burden'd air,
    Hungry clouds swag on the deep.'

'Insatiable, he still pressed on, hungering for the knowledge of things outside; and in his struggle for the million he misses the unit, and heaps up chaos in the outer darkness of Illusion. From the cloudless skies of Mysticism he rushes down into the infernal darkness on winged thoughts: 'The fiery limbs, the flaming hair, shot like the sinking sun into the western sea,' and we find him now in the Goetic kingdoms of sorcery, witchcraft, and infernal necromancy. The bats flit by us as we listen to his frenzied cries for light and knowledge: 'The Spiritual Guide,' and 'The Cherubic Wanderer' are set aside for 'The Arbatel' and 'The Seven Mysterious Orisons.' A hurried turning of many pages, the burning of many candles, and then - the Key of Solomon for a time is put away, with the Grimoires and the rituals, the talismans, and the Virgin parchments; the ancient books of the Qabalah lie open before him; a flash of brilliant fire, like a silver fish leaping from out the black waters of the sea into the starlight, bewilders him and is gone; for he has opened 'The Book of Concealed Mystery' and has read:

'Before there was equilibrium countenance beheld not countenance.'"7

Long before Aleister Crowley met any of the members of the Golden Dawn, he was studying the occult on his own. Having the knowledge of good and evil as all men do, we already read from his *Confessions* that he decided that evil should be his good. We see him in the previous quote studying sorcery, witchcraft, infernal necromancy, Grimoires and rituals, and the Qabalah. It is important that the reader understand that before Crowley met any other occultists, he was already primed for membership in a magical order, and that preparation, guided by the hand of the Devil, led him forward to finding the occult fellowship he longed for.

SEARCHING FOR SATAN

Under the guidance of Satan, Crowley sought to get in touch with him. He wrote of it plainly in his *Confessions*: "In Christianity evil is just as real as good; and so long as two opposites exist they must either be equal or there must be a third component to balance them....If the opposite of good exists at all, as it must, if 'good' is to have any meaning, it must be exactly equal in quantity and quality to that good. On the Christian hypothesis, the reality of evil makes the devil equal to God....I seem to have understood this instinctively; and since I must take sides with one party or the other it was not difficult to make up my mind. The forces of good were those which had constantly oppressed me. I saw them daily destroying the happiness of my fellow-men. Since, therefore, it was my business to explore the spiritual world, my first step must be to get into personal communication with the devil. I had heard a good deal about this operation in a vague way; but what I wanted was a manual of technical instruction. I devoted myself to black magic; and the booksellers - Deighton Bell, God bless 'em! - immediately obliged with *The Book of Black Magic and of Pacts*, which judging by the title, was exactly what I needed."8 Crowley successfully obtained the book, which was written by Arthur E. Waite, and he thought it was going to be an excellent book of instruction on how to contact Satan. He was not happy with the book, however, and he made no attempt to hide his displeasure. He wrote: "The compiler of *The Book of Black Magic and of Pacts* is not only the most ponderously platitudinous and priggishly prosaic of pretentiously pompous pork butchers of the language, but the most voluminously voluble. I cannot dig over the dreary deserts of his drivel in search of the passage which made me write to him. But it was an oracular obscurity which hinted that he knew of a Hidden Church withdrawn from the world in whose sanctuaries were preserved the true mysteries of initiation. This was one better than the Celtic Church; I immediately asked him for an introduction. He replied kindly and intelligibly, suggesting that I should read *The Cloud Upon the Sanctuary* by Councillor von Eckartshausen."9 The passage from *The Book of Black Magic and of Pacts* that hinted of the "Hidden Church," which motivated Crowley to write to Waite for further instruction, will now be presented. When reading it, do not be surprised if you have trouble understanding it. The key point, that Crowley wrote hints of a church hidden from the rest of the world, containing the true mysteries of initiation, will be explained immediately afterward. This is one of the foundational factors of Led Zeppelin. It is complex, but if it were easy, someone would have written a book about this long ago. It reads: "The desire to communicate with spirits is older than history; it connects with ineradicable principles in human nature, which have been discussed too often for it to be necessary to recite them here; and the attempts to satisfy that desire have usually taken shape which does gross outrage to reason. Between the most ancient processes, such as those of Chaldean Magic, and the rites of the Middle Ages, there are marked correspondences, and there is something of common doctrine, as distinct from intention, in which identity would more or less obtain, underlying them both....in this case the similarity is so close that it is more easily explained by the perpetuation of an antique tradition, for which channels could be readily assigned. There is one upon the face of the literature, and that is the vehicle of Kabbalistic symbolism."10

Crowley, after reading the above, wrote to Waite asking for more instruction, and Waite instructed him to read *The Cloud Upon the Sanctuary*, which supports the view that the truth is found in the Kabbalah. The word Kabbalah has many spellings, and for the purposes of this book will be spelled Qabalah, as it was Crowley's preferred method. The teaching of the Qabalah is what Mr. Waite was saying (in the above quote) was the one way for the antique traditions of magic to be channeled to the current magical practices of the day. What must be remembered is the beginning of his statement. He said basically that magic is the desire to get into communication with beings from the spirit world; which we refer to obviously as spirits. Mr. Waite also said there is common doctrine around the world relative to magic, in which identity would underlie or be the common denominator. Identity used in this context means "The condition or fact of being the same or exactly alike; sameness; oneness."11 What that means is simply this, even though there are different forms of religions around the world, they are simply exterior manifestations of religion that have an interior teaching that is the common denominator of all of them. In other words, at face value we see different religions around the world. They are mathematically speaking numerators in a fraction. The numerators vary from religion to religion. What magicians like Aleister Crowley and Jimmy Page believe, is that behind all the religions is the teaching of magic in one form or another, which then becomes the common denominator of the fraction. To sum it up, they believe that on the surface, in its appearance, each religion is different, and yet, at the same time, underneath the appearance they are all the same; rooted in ceremonial magic. It is in fact, the meaning behind the title and song, "The Song Remains the Same," which will be elaborated on in chapter ten. *The Cloud Upon the Sanctuary*, along with *The Qabalah Unveiled*, are primarily responsible for motivating Crowley not only to travel the world, but to do an extensive study of comparative religion. The author has examined all this in detail and will present to the reader brief descriptions of the important ones; that are pertinent to the Silver Star. At this point, the reader should be made familiar with some of the content of *The Cloud Upon the Sanctuary*, as it relates to the universality of magic.

UNIVERSAL MAGICK - THE COMMON DENOMINATOR

The common denominator in all the religions of the world, according to Aleister Crowley and others is Magick; which is basically being assisted by demonic forces, "the forces of nature," in order to achieve whatever one wants to, in accordance with the will of the Devil. Though he was not the author of the book, Arthur E. Waite wrote the following in the preface of *The Cloud Upon the Sanctuary*: "'The Cloud Upon the Sanctuary' has, I believe, always remained in the memory of a few, and is destined still to survive, for it carries with it a message of very deep significance to all those who look beneath the body of religious doctrine for the one principle of life which energizes the whole organism."12 Mr. Waite said "the one principle of life which energizes the whole organism" is to be found by "those who look beneath the body of religious doctrine." Again, we are talking about the common denominator that lies beneath the visible manifestation of religion. In *The Cloud Upon the Sanctuary*, Eckartshausen calls magic the inner sanctuary or church: "...the interior Church; of that illuminated Community of God which is scattered throughout the world, but which is governed by one truth and united in one spirit."13 This church is not Christianity. It is Magick, witchcraft, sorcery, etc. It must be remembered that Aleister Crowley read this book in order to be prepared to meet up with Lucifer himself. Eckartshausen called the "interior church" the "illuminated Community." In an elaborate statement he wrote: "...a more advanced school has always existed to whom this deposition of all science has been confided, and this school was the community illuminated interiorly by the Saviour, the society of the Elect, which has continued from the first day of creation to the present time; its members, it is true, are scattered all over the world, but they have always been united in the spirit and in one truth; they have had but one intelligence and one source of truth, but one doctor and one master; but in whom resides substantially the whole plenitude of God, and who alone initiates them into the high mysteries of Nature and the Spiritual World."14 Don't be confused by his using the word "Saviour." Remember, occultists will use the *Bible* to back their beliefs. Since they believe Lucifer is God, they use the Son of God in the *Bible* allegorically. In other words, the Jesus in the *Bible* they believe is really representative of the god of magic, witchcraft, etc. that the Christian world says is Satan. Aleister Crowley concurred wholeheartedly.

The last thing Lord Jesus Christ wants anyone to do is fool with spiritual forces. The *Bible* clearly condemns this in Leviticus 20:27: "A man or a woman who is a medium, or has familiar spirits, shall surely be put to death; they shall stone them with stones. Their blood shall be upon them." (One can rent the film, "The Doors," and see that Jim Morrison had a familiar spirit with him throughout the film; and I am not speaking of the old Shaman.) It was Jehovah who made this command. Jesus Christ told the Jewish leaders in Jerusalem that he was Jehovah, by using the phrase that only Jehovah used, "I am." Jesus said in John 8:56-58: "'Your father Abraham rejoiced to see my day, and he saw it and was glad.' Then the Jews said to Him, 'You are not yet fifty years old, and have You seen Abraham?' Jesus said to them, 'Most assuredly, I say to you, before Abraham was, I AM.'" Just to emphasize the point, Jehovah (Jesus) told the children of Israel just before they entered the promised land, in the Old Testament Book of Deuteronomy 18:9-12:

"When you come into the land which the LORD your God is giving you, you shall not learn to follow the abominations of those nations. There shall not be found among you anyone who makes his son or his daughter pass through the fire, or one who practices witchcraft, or a soothsayer, or one who interprets omens, or a sorcerer, or one who conjures spells, or a medium, or a spiritist, or one who calls up the dead. For all who do these things are an abomination to the LORD, and because of these abominations the LORD your God drives them out from before you."

The god of the magicians then, is not Lord Jesus Christ, but the Devil. You will read of Plant and Page confessing to be mediums later in the book.

In the last quote presented from Eckartshausen, he started off by mentioning the illuminated community as a school. He completes his emphasis in the following: "...Perfect knowledge of God, of nature, and of humanity are the objects of instruction in this school. It is from her that all truths penetrate into the world, she is the School of the Prophets, and of all who search for wisdom, and it is in this community alone that truth and the explanation of all mystery is to be found. It is the most hidden of communities yet possesses members from many circles; of such is this School. From all time there has been an exterior school based on the interior one, of which it is but the outer expression. From all time, therefore, there has been a hidden assembly, a society of the Elect, of those who sought for and had capacity for light, and this interior society was called the interior Sanctuary or Church."15 He goes on to instruct his readers that there have been examples of religions that abandoned the magical practices he believes they originated with and became empty and lifeless. This explains to the occultist/Satanist why there are religious practices that "no longer" include magic in them. He wrote:

"Through these divine instruments the interior truths of the Sanctuary were taken into every nation, and modified symbolically according to their customs, capacity for instruction, climate, and receptiveness. So that the external types of every religion, worship, ceremonies and Sacred Books in general have more or less clearly, as their object of instruction, the interior truths of the Sanctuary, by which man, but only in the latter days, will be conducted to the universal knowledge of the one Absolute Truth.

"The more the external worship of a people has remained united with the spirit of esoteric truth, the purer its religion; but the wider the difference between the symbolic letter and the invisible truth, the more imperfect has become the religion; even so far among some nations as to degenerate into polytheism. Then the external form entirely parted from its inner truth, when ceremonial observances without soul or life remained alone."16

Esoteric is another word for a select group of inner initiates, while poly-theism means the worship of a vast number of different gods. Eckartshausen presents the motive that "God" had for bestowing this knowledge to mankind as his wanting man to reunite with him. Here the Devil is clearly copying Jesus Christ, and as Mick Jagger said in "Sympathy For the Devil's" opening verse, stealing mankind's "faith." He wrote that "God" laid the foundation of the illu-minated community:

"Now, as God Himself laid the foundation of the external Church, the whole of the symbols of external worship formed the science of the Temple and of the Priests in those days, because the mysteries of the most sacred truths became external through revelation alone. The scientific acquaintance of this holy symbolism was the science to unite fallen man once more with God, hence religion received its name from being the science of rebinding man with God, to bring man back to his origin.

"One sees plainly by this pure idea of religion in general that unity in religion is within the inner Sanctuary, and that the multiplicity of external reli-gions can never alter the true unity which is at the base of every exterior."17

The "base" that he just mentioned, is once again, the common denomi-nator, based on the teachings of the Qabalah. This "rebinding" of man with God is the same as the union of the macrocosm and microcosm that Crowley and the Silver Star represent as the GREAT WORK. *The Cloud Upon the Sanctuary* then, had an influence on, and is in keeping with Crowley's writings for the Silver Star.

FRIENDS

While Crowley was attending Cambridge University, he not only read *The Cloud Upon the Sanctuary,* but he wrote and published *Aceldama*, financed by his inheritance of L50,000. Another student at the school by the name of Gerald Kelly was so intrigued by the book that he set out to find the author. Since both Kelly and Crowley were sons of preachers, they hit it off immedi-ately. Crowley's relationship with Kelly would be the reason he met his first wife, Kelly's sister, Rose. One interesting thing Crowley did, long before meet-ing Rose, was to tell his associates, including Kelly, his opinion of women; which is quite unique. In *The Magician of the Golden Dawn*, Susan Roberts presents it this way: "While he wanted women achingly, he complained to all of his friends, including Gerald, that they could only be bought as whores or wives and he saw little difference except in price."18 While he kept his mind sharply focused on sex, it was at this time in 1898 that he wrote his sex perversion manual, *White Stains*; mentioned in chapter one. Crowley continued his sexual degeneration, entering into a homosexual relationship with another student from Cambridge University named Herbert Pollit. Crowley found his first love's relationship intoxicating. He mentioned Pollit in *The World's Tragedy* when he said: "Pollit made a poet of me…"19 The relationship ended when Crowley decided to pursue his goal of becoming a magician. Aleister was not one for a monogamous relationship; even homosexual. He never stayed with one person very long without jumping in bed with someone else. He had no concept of love or intimacy. As Susan Roberts put it: "All he wanted was one religion to live by and a lot of love affairs with both men and women to amuse him.20 What Roberts should have said was he wanted "lust affairs" with men and women; not love.

Another man Crowley became acquainted with was one Oscar Eckenstein, while mountain climbing and studying *The Cloud Upon the Sanctuary*. Eckenstein was twenty years his senior, but he and Crowley became friends. He and Aleister did some climbing together and then parted ways with plans to reunite in the summer to climb together again at Zermatt. In the meantime, Crowley studied S.L. MacGregor Mathers' *The Qabalah Unveiled* (This book as well is very important to the music of Led Zeppelin). Reading it prepared him for the next step in his magical attainment, which included his meeting a chemist who was an occultist.

When Crowley went to Zermatt to climb again with Oscar Eckenstein, he met a chemist named Julian L. Baker, who was also a student of Alchemy. Alchemy is a study of chemistry as it relates to magical practices. For instance, in Alchemy the light of the sun is considered gold. This will be seen again in a later chapter. When Crowley found out Baker was a chemist/Alchemist, he became very interested in him. He wrote in his *Confessions*: "I told him of my search for the Secret Sanctuary of the Saints and convinced him of my desperate earnestness. He hinted that he knew of an Assembly which might be that for which I was looking."21 Through Baker, Aleister Crowley linked up with another chemist named George Cecil Jones. Jones would become Crowley's link to the Hermetic Order of the Golden Dawn. Baker had said to him: "'I will introduce you to a man who is much more of a Magician than I am.' To sum the matter in brief, he kept his word. The Secret Assembly materialized as the 'Hermetic Order of the Golden Dawn,' and the Magician as one George Cecil Jones."22 Jones, after informing Crowley that a magician's main goal was to unite the microcosm with the macrocosm, agreed to submit Crowley's application for membership to the Golden Dawn. The men in the Golden Dawn bore the title "Frater" before their chosen magical names; the women were called "Soror." As was presented earlier, Crowley's magical oath name was "Frater Perdurabo," which means "I will endure to the end." Crowley made it clear to his readers later on that one's magical oath is for life. He wrote of it in his book on magical instruction, titled *Book 4 - Part II*:

"A real Magical Oath cannot be broken: you think it can, but it can't.

This is the advantage of a real Magical Oath.

However far you go around, you arrive at the end just the same, and all you have done by attempting to break your oath is to involve yourself in the most frightful trouble."23

Did Led Zeppelin try to break its Magical Oath in 1976-1977 when it put out *Presence* with its "Hellhound On My Trail" type song called "Nobody's Fault But Mine?" In the song, Plant sings that it was Satan that "taught" him to "Roll," and that he had a "monkey" riding his "back." Then he would sing the song title, that it was his own fault. Jimmy Page, who produced the band's music on all the albums, evidently allowed these lyrics to be included in the song. Interestingly enough, on Robert Plant's first solo album, *Pictures at Eleven,* he has a hose on the front of the album facing a picture in a frame. The picture is of flames, with the Devil's face at the bottom of the fire. Turning the album around, the fire is out, and the face is gone. It is almost as though Plant was shouting, "I am not singing for him anymore!" Led Zeppelin performed "Nobody's Fault But Mine" throughout the 1977 tour, and Robert Plant's son died in the middle of it. Did he die because of an attempt to break free of their magical oath? This author does not claim to know, but Crowley wrote that the magical oath cannot be broken, and Page and Plant look like it had been their goal, in no uncertain terms, to revive Led Zeppelin. The 1995 and 1998 tours of Page/Plant were proof of that. In 1995, with the exception of songs like "Wonderful One," "Shake My Tree," "Lullaby," and "Calling to You," it was all Led Zeppelin music. In 1998, with the exception of a few songs from the new Page/Plant album, which were not without occult references, the band again revived old Led Zeppelin tunes, including a fully electric version of "No Quarter," which was played acoustically on the 1995 tour. The capacity crowds that came to see them on these tours were coming to hear Led Zeppelin. That is indisputable fact. In summation, they are still bound to their magical oaths. That was a simple conclusion when I saw that they had their Magick runes plastered all over their memorabilia at the concerts. John Paul Jones, on tour in 2000 with his own band, had his Magick Rune assimilated into his steel table guitar, as well as on the back of his acoustic guitar. Ostensibly, the magical oath is as binding in the 1900's as it was in the 1800's. Satan is as much a taskmaster in this century as he was in the last.

THE HERMETIC ORDER OF THE GOLDEN DAWN

In the middle of the 1880's, the Hermetic Order of the Golden Dawn was founded. It was formed by S.L. MacGregor Mathers, and two colleagues named Dr. W. Wynn Wescott, and Dr. Woodman. During research, Dr. Woodman discovered a cipher manuscript on a bookstall. He and Wescott had difficulty trying to interpret the manuscript, so they contacted Mathers, well known for his occult practices. The manuscript in question contained information regarding rituals of initiation and definitions of the Tarot cards. Written on the manuscript was the name of a German adept of magic whose initiation name was "Sapiens Dominabitur Astris;" her real name was Fraulein Sprengel, and she did in fact live in Germany. There was a note on the manuscript stating that anyone who desired could establish correspondence with her for further information. Dr. Wescott decided to do exactly that. After substantial communication, Fraulein Sprengel sent a charter to Woodman, Wescott, and Mathers; authorizing them to establish a magical order in England (it is interesting to note, that this magical group's authorization came from Germany, the same place Led Zeppelin played their very last concert in Berlin on July 7th, 1980. The Magick came full circle). Not long after these events, S.D.A. Sprengel died. A letter that had been sent to her was returned by one of her associates telling Mathers and his friends that S.D.A.'S authorizing of an order in England had never been sanctioned by her contemporaries in Germany. However, out of respect for her memory they would not oppose its establishment. The writer then informed them that all future correspondence with Germany would cease to be accepted; because enough information had already been dispersed for those in England to unite with the "godhead."

At this point S.L. MacGregor Mathers informed his fellow members of the Golden Dawn, that since the death of Fraulein Sprengel, he was given authority over the order by the Secret Chiefs, or as already stated, godhead (god and female consort, goddess), according to occultists. Dr. Woodman died, and Dr. Wescott retired from leadership of the order, allegedly as a result of pressure from Mathers. This left Mathers with complete control of the Golden Dawn. This was the state of affairs with the order when Crowley joined. It should be noted that Crowley considered S.L. MacGregor Mathers an expert magician.

On November 18, 1898, Aleister Crowley went to the "Mark Mason Hall" in London to be initiated into the Hermetic Order of the Golden Dawn. When the initiators asked him why he wanted to become a member, Crowley gave this response: "My soul wanders in darkness and seeks the light of the hidden knowledge and I believe in this order, knowledge of that light may be obtained."24 The Led Zeppelin fan needs to contemplate what Crowley was saying here. He presents the concept of seeking truth as synonymous with seeking light. He referred to this light again in *The Equinox*. He wrote these words as part of the Golden Dawn system of initiation he recorded there: "I am come from between the pillars and seek for the hidden Light of Occult Science."25 In another section of the initiation he wrote: "The voice of my Higher Soul said unto me: let me enter the path of Darkness, peradventure thus shall I obtain the Light; I am the only Being in the Abyss of Darkness: from the Darkness came I forth ere my birth, from the silence of a primal sleep! And the Voice of Ages answered unto my soul: I am he who formulates in Darkness, but the darkness comprehendeth it not."26 The "Light" Crowley says he is looking for is "Occult Science," as he put it. Eliphas Levi, his "previous incarnation," wrote that the Light is "transcendental magic;" the two terms are synonymous. You can read of his definition at the heading of chapter eight. Led Zeppelin fans, just listen to the opening verse of the song "In The Light" on the *Physical Graffiti* album. The band is telling the listener, if they are at the end of their rope, and don't want to live the life of hell they have been living, the path they need to travel will be found in their light of the occult. At this point, one needs to be reminded of what Levi wrote in Transcendental Magic: "The science is preserved by silence and perpetuated by initiation. The law of silence is not therefore absolute and inviolable, except relatively to the uninitiated multitude. Such knowledge can be only transmitted by speech. The sages therefore must speak occasionally. Yes, they must speak, not, however, to disclose, but lead others to discover."27 If wanting to follow the same road as Led Zeppelin, knowing Page follows Crowley, one will study the teachings of Crowley and realize that the "Light" they are speaking of is Magick and the Qabalah; which is their "Stairway to Heaven." Don't forget, the master of this light is the Devil; sentenced to hell.

Crowley, who was called "Perdurabo," referred to himself as "P." in *The Equinox* version of his initiation. He wrote: "Undoubtedly the passing through the Ritual of the Neophyte had an important influence on P.'s mind, and on his Spiritual Progress; for, shortly after its celebration, we find him experiencing some very extraordinary visions, which we shall enter upon in due course. Suffice it to say that by December he had passed the easy examination necessary before he could present himself as a candidate for the 1=10 grade of Zelator."28 The grades of the Golden Dawn can be found at the beginning of chapter eight, on the "Tree of Life" photo; which is the Qabalah.

Aleister Crowley made rapid advancement in the Golden Dawn, and by January of 1899 he was promoted again. At that time he met Allan Bennett, whom he refers to as "Mr. D" in the next quote. Bennett's Magical Oath name was "Frater Iehi Aour," which means "Let There Be Light." Crowley wrote:

"By the end of January 1899, P. was sufficiently advanced to be admitted to the grade of Theoricus.

It was about this time also that he met Mr. D., a certain brother of the G.D. known as Frater I. A. This meeting, as we shall eventually see, ranks only second in importance to his meeting with Frater V. N (Jones)."29

Crowley advanced from Theoricus, 2=9, to Practicus, 3=8, in February, 1899. In May of 1899, he advanced to Philosophus, 4=7. It was Allan Bennett who initially assisted Crowley in his advancement.

Allan Bennett was an orphan. His father, who was an engineer, died when Allan was a child. Bennett was reared in the Catholic Church, which he subsequently rejected for the occult. He had from Bath, becoming a chemist.

He also suffered greatly from asthma and was poverty stricken. He and Crowley became quick friends, and as a result Bennett moved in with him in his London flat. It was there that Bennett, who was the adopted son of Mathers, oversaw Crowley's studies in magic from the ranks of 0=0 to 4=7, studying the Golden Dawn system of initiation, ceremonial magic, and the Qabalah; the satanic Tree of Life.

When Crowley made the grade of 4=7, Allan Bennett's health, because of the asthma, required that he depart England for somewhere warm. Crowley refused to pay for the transportation because he was against paying for his magical training. Crowley got together with George Cecil Jones and they evoked the spirit "Buer" to materialization. This is the first account of Aleister Crowley causing a spirit to manifest itself. They contacted him for help in taking care of Bennett. The instructions on how to evoke Buer comes from the *Goetia*, a manual for contacting and controlling spirits that Mathers translated and Crowley edited (Again, Jimmy Page reproduced this book, a perfect facsimile, in 1976. I have the 1995 edition of the *Goetia* with Page's name in the introduction.). As a result of the evocation of Buer, circumstances changed and Bennett was able to secure passage to Ceylon in January of 1900, where in 1902, he became a Buddhist monk. Crowley recalled this evocation in *Magick Without Tears*: "The first definitely physical sight was due to the 'evocation to visible appearance' of the Goetia demon Buer by myself and V.H. Frater 'Volo Noscere.' (Our object was to prolong the life, in imminent danger, of V.H. Frater Iehi Aour - Allan Bennett - Bhikkhu Ananda Metteya - and was successful; he lived another 20 odd years. And odd years they were!)"30 Here we read Aleister Crowley, the hero and mentor of Jimmy Page, conjuring up demons, and this demon is described in *The Goetia*, the demonic book Page reproduced in 1976. Remember God's command to Israel in the *Bible*, that people who did this were to be put to death. God could have prevented it, but he gave direct rule over the earth to Satan, who has permission for his demons to answer such calls from human beings. Demonic forces play a major role in astral projection, an initiatory practice for magicians in the Silver Star.

ASTRAL PROJECTION

What is astral projection? Astral projection is the practice of leaving the phyical body and traveling in the spirit body, as an act of the will in conjunction with supernatural power. Man is made up of body, soul, and spirit. If the reader thinks that anyone who believes this to be possible is crazy, the author wants you to know there was a time that he shared your opinion; approximately 25 years ago. However, that is no longer the case. We do have spiritual bodies. Lord Jesus Christ himself affirmed this to be true. In the Book of Luke, Chapter 16, Verses

19-24, Jesus told this story: "There was a certain rich man who was clothed in purple and fine linen and fared sumptuously everyday. But there was a certain beggar named Lazarus, full of sores, who was laid at his gate, desiring to be fed with the crumbs which fell from the rich man's table. Moreover the dogs came and licked his sores. So it was that the beggar died, and was carried by the angels to Abraham's bosom. The rich man also died and was buried. And being in torments in Hades, he lifted up his eyes and saw Abraham afar off, and Lazarus in his bosom. Then he cried and said, 'Father Abraham, have mercy on me, and send Lazarus that he may dip the tip of his finger in water and cool my tongue; for I am tormented in this flame.'" Be sure to refrain from reading anything into this. It is not the entire passage. Not all rich men go to hell, and not all poor people go to heaven. This is a specific case. It is presented so the reader can see that even though the rich man was buried, as it says, he was in pain in hell. He was not in his physical body, and yet he could feel pain. Our souls are eternal, and the physical body is temporal.

Another *Bible* passage records that Paul the Apostle was taken out of his physical body and caught up into the third heaven. According to the *Holy Bible*, the atmosphere surrounding the earth is the first heaven, the cosmos is the second, and the place where Christ manifests himself visibly is referred to as the third. In 2 Corinthians 12:2-4, Paul referred to himself in the third person: "I know a man in Christ who fourteen years ago – whether in the body I do not know, or whether out of the body I do not know, God knows – such a one was caught up to the third heaven. And I know such a man – whether in the body or out of the body I do not know, God knows – how he was caught up into Paradise and heard inexpressible words, which it is not lawful for a man to utter." In another passage the *Bible* makes it clear that physical bodies are not permitted in heaven. It is accurate then to conclude that he was out of his body. Aleister Crowley described the spiritual body this way: "Within the human body is another body of approximately the same size and shape; but made of a subtler and less illusory material."31

People who worship the Devil and get involved in magic, are granted the power to do what is humanly impossible-travel in the spirit body. Aleister Crowley, right after his attainment of the grade of Neophyte, 1=10, claimed to travel in his spirit body during a spirit vision. The spirit vision occurs at the same time as the travel. The following passage is important for one to be familiar with before reviewing the Silver Star's Neophyte grade or Led Zeppelin's song, "Kashmir," which is presented along the lines of an astral journey. This is taken from *The Temple of Solomon the King*, out of *The Equinox, Vol. 1, No.2*, where Crowley again refers to himself in the third person as *"P."* He makes reference to Lucifer when he speaks of the "Kerubim of Ezekiel".

THE SEER

"It is not to be wondered that the magic strain to which P. had been placed during the last seven months should have long since blossomed into flowers of weird and wonderful beauty. And so we find, as far back as the beginning of November 1899, the commencement of a series of extraordinary visions as wild and involved as many of those of Blake or St. Francis.

"But before entering upon these visions, it will be necessary to explain that by a vision we mean as definite a psychological state and as certain and actual a fact to the mental eye, as the view of a landscape is considered to be to the physical eye itself. And so when we have occasion to write 'he saw an angel,' it is to be taken that we mean by it as absolute a fact as if we had written 'he saw a mountain,' or 'he saw a cow.' It, however, is not to be accepted that by this we lay down that either angels or cows exist apart from ourselves, they may or they may not; but it is to be taken that angels, and mountains and cows are ideas of equal value in their own specific spheres: the astral and the material; and that they have their proper place in existence, whatever existence may be, and that every experience, normal, abnormal, subnormal or supernormal, whether treated as an illusion or a fact, is of equal value so long as it is conditioned in Time; and that a dream is of as real a nature as awakenment, but on a different plane in existence, the conditions of which can alone be judged and measured by experimental science.

"Science advances by means of accumulating facts and consolidating them, the grand generalization of which merges into a theory when it has been accepted by universal inference....Before the birth of Copernicus the sun was universally considered to be a body moving round the earth; it was a FACT, and probably whilst it lasted the most universal fact the mind of man has ever accepted; but since that illuminated sage arose, it has been shown to be simple fable, a child-like error, a puny optical illusion-so much for pseudo-scientific dogmatics.

"To a child who has never seen a monkey, monkey is outside the circumference of its knowledge; but when once it has seen one it is mere foolishness for other children to say: 'Oh no, you didn't really see a monkey; such things as monkeys do not exist, and what proves it beyond all doubt is that we have never seen one ourselves!' This, it will be seen, is the Freethinkers' old, old conclusive argument: 'There is not a God because we have no experience of a God.'.... 'There is not a South Pole because we have not trudged round it six times and cut our names on it with our pocket-knives!'

Now what is knowledge?
Something is! - Call it Existence.
What exists?
'I exist!' answers the Idealist, 'I and I alone!'

'Oh no, you do not!' cries the Materialist, 'you certainly do exist; but not alone, for I am talking to you!'

'Fool!' says the Idealist, 'cannot you grasp the simple idea that you and your foolish argument are in fact part of me?'

'But surely,' replies the Materialist, 'you do not doubt that the world exists, that the Evolution of Man exists, that Judas McCabbage exists and is an actual fact.'

'Granted they do exist,' sighs the Idealist, 'so do the reflections of an ape's face in a looking-glass, yes, they do exist, but not apart from my own mind.'

'Yet the world of a blind man,' says the Mystic, 'is a very different place to the world a deaf man lives in, and both these worlds vary considerably from the world normally constituted man inhabits. Likewise animals, whose sense-organs vary from ours, live in altogether a different world from us. To give an eyeless worm eyes is only comparable to endowing us with a sixth sense. The world to us therefore depends wholly upon the development of our senses; and as they grow and decay so does the world with them, how much more then does the world of those who have outstepped the prison-house of their senses differ from the world of those who still lie bound therein. It is possible to conceive of a child being born blind (in a race of blind people) obtaining the use of its eyes when an old man, and thereupon entering a new world; why, therefore, should it be impossible to conceive of a man with all his senses perfect obtaining another sense or entering into another dimension? The blind man, if a few minutes after he had obtained possession of his sight were suddenly to return to a state of blindness, would have great difficulty in explaining to his blind brothers the sights he had seen, in fact none would believe him, and his difficulty in explaining in the language of blind-land the wonders of the land of sight would probably be so great that he would find more consolation in silence than in an attempted explanation: this has generally been the same with the true adepts; and those who have tried to explain themselves have been called mad by the canaille.

'The truth is,' continues the Mystic, 'both of you have been talking foolishness through your material and idealistic hats. For:

'In the Material World Matter is Existence.

'In the Sensible World Sense is Existence.

'In the Spiritual World Spirit is Existence.

'And though in the Sensible World a cow or an angel exists solely as an idea to us, this does not preclude the possibility of a cow existing as beef in the Material World, or an angel as a spirit in the Spiritual World.'

'The fact is,' interrupts the Skeptic, 'I doubt all three of you; for from the above you all three infer a chain of events - whether material, sensual, or spiritual, thus postulating the Existence of Causality as a common property of these three worlds. Let us strike out Matter, Sense and Spirit, and what is left?

Surely not Time and Space, that twin inference conceived by that Matter, Sense and Spirit we have just put to bed.'

'Don't you think,' says the Scientific Illuminist, 'that instead of dreaming all your lives it would be a good thing to wake up and do a little work? There are four of you, and the Kerubim of Ezekiel might perhaps engage your individual attention.'

"The truth is, it does not matter one rap by what name you christen the illusions of this life, call them substance, or ideas, or hallucinations, it makes not the slightest difference, for you are in them and they in you whatever you like to call them, and you must get out of them and they out of you, and the less you consider their names the better; for name-changing only creates unnecessary confusion and is a waste of time.

"Let us therefore call the world a series of existences and have done with it, for it does not matter a jot what we mean by it so long as we work; very well then; Science is a part of this series, and so is Magic, and so are cows and angels, and so are landscapes, and so are visions; and the difference between these existences is the difference which lies between a cheesemonger and a poet, between a blind man and one who can see. The clearer the view the more perfect the view; the clearer the vision the more perfect the vision. The eyes of a hawk are keener than those of an owl, and so are a poet's keener than those of a cheesemonger, for he can see beauty in a ripe Stilton whilst the latter can only see two-and-sixpence a pound.

"A true vision is to awakenment as awakenment is to a dream; and a perfectly clear co-ordinate vision is so nearly perfect a Reality that words cannot be found in which to translate it, yet it must not be forgotten that its truth ceases on the return of the seer to the Material plane.

"The Seer is therefore the only judge of his visions, for they belong to a world in which he is absolute King, and to describe them to one who lives in another world is like talking Dutch to a Spaniard. Our business then is, to construct if possible a universal language. This the rituals of the Golden Dawn and the study of the Qabalah did for P., and when we talk of quadrating the circle, of blinding darkness, of silent voices, &c. &c., those who have learned the alphabet of any magical language will understand; and those who have not, if they wish to read any further with profit, had better do so, as it will help them to master the new magical language and doctrines we here offer them.

"The vision of the adept is so much truer than ordinary vision that when once it has been attained to its effect is never relinquished, for it changes the whole life. Blake would have as soon doubted the existence of his wife, his mother or of himself, as that of Urizen, Los, or Luvah.

"Dreams are real, hallucinations are real, delirium is real, and so is madness; but for the most part these are Qliphothic realities, unstable, unbalanced, dangerous.

"Visions are real, inspirations are real, revelation is real, and so is genius; but these are from Kether, and the highest climber on the mystic mountain is he who will obtain the finest view, and from its summit all things will be shown unto him.

"A child learning to play on the violin will not at the outset be mistaken for Sarasate or Paganini; for there will be discord and confusion of sound. So now, as we start upon the first visions of P. we find chaos piled on chaos, much struggling and noise, a roaring of wild waters in the night, and then finally, melody, silence and the communication of the mystic books of V.V.V.V.V (Crowley)."32

Crowley authenticated his magical practices to his future students in that text, making reference to a universal occult language, and the study of the Qabalah. One can safely conclude that Jimmy Page followed suit. In the same volume of the *Equinox*, Crowley described an astral journey in which he met the male/female godhead of the Qabalah.

ASTRAL JOURNEY BY CROWLEY

The following is Aleister Crowley's fifth astral journey. In preparation for reading it, listen to Led Zeppelin's song, "What is and What Should Never Be." It is from the *Led Zeppelin II* album. In the song's chorus, Robert Plant sings about ascending upward in the air. The first time the chorus is heard is at 0:25 into the song. We will be coming back to it later in this chapter.

"'After fervent prayer I was carried up above the circle which I had drawn, through a heavy and foggy atmosphere. Soon, however, the air grew purer, and after a little I found myself in a beautifully clear sky.

"On gazing up into the depths of the blue, I saw dawn immediately above me a great circle; then of a sudden, as I looked away from its center, there swept out towards me at intolerable speed the form of a shepherd; trembling and not knowing what to say, with faltering voice I asked, 'Why speed ye?' Whereupon the answer came; 'There is haste!' Then a great gloom closed mine eyes, and a horror of defilement encompassed me, and all melted in twilight and became cloaked in the uttermost darkness. And out of the darkness there came a man clothed in blue, whose skin was of the colour of sapphire, and around him glowed a phosphor light, and in his hand he held a sword.

"And on seeing him approach I fell down and besought him to guide me, which without further word he did.

"On turning to the left I saw that near me was a rock door, and then for the first time I became aware that I was clothed in my robes of white. Passing through the door, I found myself on the face of a high cliff that sank away into the abysms of space below me; and my foot slipping on the slippery stone, I stumbled forward, and would of a certainty have been dashed into that endless gulf, had not the shepherd caught me and held me back.

"Then wings were given me, and diving off from that great rocky cliff like a sea-bird, I winged my course through the still air and was filled with a great joy.

"Now, I had traveled thus but for a short time, when in the distance there appeared before me a silver-moss rugged hill. And on its summit was there built a circular temple, fashioned of burnished silver, domes and surmounted with a crescent. And for some reason unknown to me, the sight of the crescent made me tremble so that I durst not enter; and when my guide, who was still with me, saw that I was seized with a great fear, he comforted me, bidding me be of good courage, so with him I entered. Before us in the very center of the temple there sat a woman whose countenance was bright as the essence of many moons; and as I beheld her, fear left me, so I stepped towards her and knelt reverently at her feet.

"Then, as I knelt before her, she gave me a branch of olive and myrtle, which I folded to my heart; and as I did so, of a sudden a great pillar of smoke rose from the ground before me and carried her away through the dome of the temple.

"Slowly the pillar loosened itself, and spiral puffs of smoke, creeping away from the mighty column, began to circle round me, at which I stepped back to where my guide was still standing. Then he advanced, and beckoning me to follow him, we entered the great pillar of smoke and were carried through the bright dome of the temple.

"On, on we soared, through regions of cloud and air; on, on, past the stars and many myriads of burning specks of fire, till at length our journey led us to a vast blue sea, upon which was resting like a white swan a ship of silver. And without staying our flight, we made towards the ship, and descending upon it, rested awhile.

"On awaking, we found that we had arrived at a fair island, upon which stood a vast temple built of blocks of silver, square in form, and surrounded by a mighty colonnade. Outside it was there set up an altar upon which a branch had been sacrificed.

"On seeing the altar, I stepped towards it and climbed upon it, and there I sacrificed myself, and the blood that had been my life bubbled from my breast, and trickling over the rough stone, was sucked up by the parched lips of the white sand....And behold, as I rose from that altar, I was alone standing upon the flat top of the square temple, and those who had been with me, the shepherd and my guide, had vanished; - I was alone...alone.

"And as I stood there, the east became as an amethyst clasped in the arms of the sard, and a great thrill rushed through me; and as I watched, the sard became as a fawn; and as I watched again, the east quivered and the great lion of day crept over the horizon, and seizing the fawn betwixt his gleaming teeth, shook him till the fleecy clouds above were as a ram's skin flecked with blood.

"Then thrill upon thrill rushed through me, and I fell down and knelt upon the flat roof of the temple. And presently as I knelt, I perceived other suns rising around me, one in the North, and one in the South, and one in the West. And the one in the North was as a great bull blowing blood and flame from its nostrils; and the one in the South was as an eagle plucking forth the entrails of a Nubian slave; and the one in the West was as a man swallowing the ocean.

"And whilst I watched these suns rising around me, behold, though I knew it not, a fifth sun had arisen beneath where I was standing, and it was as a great wheel of revolving lightnings. And gazing at the Wonder that flamed at my feet, I partook of its glory and became brilliantly golden, and great wings of flame descended upon me, and as they enrolled me I grew thirty cubits in height - perhaps more.

"Then the sun upon which I was standing rose above the four other suns, and as it did so I found myself standing before an ancient man with snow-white beard, whose countenance was a-fired with benevolence. And as I looked upon him, a great desire possessed me to stretch forth my hand and touch his beard; and as the desire grew strong, a voice said unto me, 'Touch, it is granted thee.'

"So I stretched forth my hand and gently placed my fingers upon the venerable beard. And as I did so, the ancient man bent forward, and placing his lips to my forehead kissed me. And so sweet was that kiss that I would have lingered; but I was dismissed, for the other four suns had risen to a height equal to mine own.

"And seeing this I stretched out my wings and flew, sinking through innumerable sheets of blinding silver. And presently I opened mine eyes, and all around me was as a dense fog; thus I returned into my body."33

In his astral journey Crowley met up with the Qabalah's godhead; the goddess and then the god. He saw the goddess in her round temple of silver and the crescent moon, who shines bright light from her face. She is the Queen and goddess of light. I will elaborate on the descriptions and names of the goddess later. The god (Lucifer/Satan) with the white beard I mentioned in an earlier chapter, but will repeat it for emphasis. Crowley wrote: "...an ancient, bearded Father, with hair as white as wool, and eyes like flames of fire; whose voice is as the sound of many waters, in whose right hand tremble the seven stars of Heaven, and out of whose mouth flashes forth a flaming sword of fire."34 (Please remember, Satan stole this presentation of himself from the *Holy Bible's* Book of Revelation, Chapter one, where the description is of the risen and glorified Lord Jesus Christ.) Crowley presents the Qabalistic godhead in the astral journey; which took place up in the air somewhere, not on the ground. Why? It is because the spirits rule the air. Remember, the spirits ruled the journey, not Crowley. He went as directed.

SPIRITS RULE THE AIR

In the atmosphere around the earth, the angelic host of Satan's fallen angels, or "spirits," have their domain. When they are not doing the bidding of the Devil, these devils can be found in the air. In the New Testament Book of Ephesians, Chapter 2, Verses 1-2, Paul the Apostle makes reference to Satan while speaking to new converts to Christianity. Since they were now Christians, they were well aware of who he was speaking in the text, without mention of name necessary: "And you He made alive, who were dead in trespasses and sins, in which you once walked according to the course of this world, according to the prince of the power of the air, the spirit who now works in the sons of disobedience…"

In his book, *Satan: His Personality, Power, and Overthrow*, E.M. Bounds describes this kingdom of the air:

"Revelation summarizes the situation: 'And they had a king over them, which is the angel of the bottomless pit, whose name in the Hebrew tongue is Abaddon, but in the Greek tongue hath his name Apollyon. One woe is past; and, behold, there come two woes more hereafter.'

"These are not lawless woes, nor are their authors lawless bands, disorderly and reckless mobs. They are organized. The strictest obedience to the devil prevails. 'Devil with devil damned firm concord holds.' They are 'principalities and powers,' not only of high and first order in creation, not only of great personal power and dignity, but ordered and sub-ordered, coordinate and subordinate. There is the most perfect government, military in its drill and discipline, absolute and orderly in its arrangement, under one supreme, dictatorial, powerful head, with rank and file and officers complete. 'For our wrestling is not against flesh and blood but against principalities, against the powers, against the world rulers of this darkness, against the spiritual hosts of wickedness in the heavenly places.' These high and wicked spirits are everywhere. They fill the air, are everywhere intent on evil, following the direction of their leader, carrying out his plans with hearty accord, ready obedience and implicit confidence. How loathsome their nature! How marvelous and miracle-working their power! How high and kingly their influence! How martial their purposes!"35

You have just read Biblical accounts of the evil spirits who reign in the air. A few more examples of this will be presented in order to prepare you for reviewing several Led Zeppelin songs in this chapter. In the chapter titled "Celebration Day" you read about these spirits as written about by Dr. Faust. This is a repeat of only a small segment: "He who wishes to practice my art, let him love the spirits of hell and those who reign in the air; for these alone are they who can make us happy in this life; and he who would have wisdom must seek it from the devil."36 Another key reference in concurrence is Aleister Crowley's favorite book, *The Book of the Sacred Magic of Abramelin the Mage*." The author, who is called Abraham the Jew (not the Biblical Abraham the Jew), wrote these words: "It is true that the Wise in Astrology do write of the Stars and of their movements, and that these attaining thereto do produce divers effects in inferior and elemental things; and such are, as we have already said, natural operations of the Elements; but that they should have power over the Spirits, or force in all supernatural things, that is not, neither can ever be. But it will instead be found that by the permission of the Great God it is the Spirits who govern the firmament."37 For those who do not know what firmament means, it is the sky; the atmosphere around the earth. Another song from Led Zeppelin's second album illustrates their knowledge of this from the early days.

LED ZEPPELIN II – "RAMBLE ON"

In 1969, Led Zeppelin put out their second album, appropriately titled, *Led Zeppelin II*. One of the songs off that album is a beautiful acoustic piece by the name of "Ramble On." In the song Robert Plant sings about Magick. Between 2:45 and 2:51 of the song, he sings that long ago in the old days "...Magick filled the air." In concurrence with that theme is the following quote from *Hammer of the Gods*: "In magic was the survival of the pre-Christian era, a natural world of spirits and powers that had been suppressed by the church."38 I find it interesting that such a quote could come from a book about Led Zeppelin; and yet most people don't know the significance (Hence the need for this work). Irrespective of what some Led Zeppelin fans on the famous *For Badgeholders Only* internet newsgroup will tell you, *Hammer of the Gods* is loaded with truth.

Another song off Led Zeppelin's second album, "What Is and What Should Never Be," as already stated, has Robert Plant singing about living up in earth's sky domain. Jimmy Page himself had something to say about the second album and mysticism. Mysticism is in effect, communion with God, according to mystics. In *Led Zeppelin - The Definitive Biography*, Page responded: "And Mysticism? 'Yes, well that has been present from the second album onwards,' he said, 'mainly because it was something that we did well and it pointed in a specific direction.'"39 In the quote, Jimmy Page is saying that their music is definitely pointing in a specific direction. In both songs, "Ramble On" and "What Is and What Should Never Be," Led Zeppelin points to the domain of the sky.

Another song of theirs that mentions the sky is "The Battle of Evermore." This song is from the fourth album that the author refers to as *Runes*. In between 2:12 and 2:19 of the song, Plant sings that the air is ruled by "good" as well as "bad" that mere humans are never cognizant of. Earlier in the song, between 1:33 and 1:36, Plant sings about his waiting on the arrival of Avalon's "angels." The angels are going to participate in the war. Avalon will be discussed later in a very important part of the book. Also on the fourth album, the song "Misty Mountain Hop" discusses spirits; who are angels. Near the end of the song, between 3:44 and 3:56, Plant sings that he is going to pack his "bags" and head to the "mountain" of mist, the place at which Satan's "spirits" congregate. Then he says these spirits are flying over hills. Where do they go? They go "Over the Hills and Far Away," another Led Zeppelin song. The spirits are described by the author as Satan's because, as will be seen in a later chapter, the Hermit on top of the misty mountain on the inner cover of Led Zeppelin four, the album "Misty Mountain Hop" is on, is none other than the Devil himself.

In a song off the *Presence* album, "Achilles Last Stand," he mentions the Devil at 1:34 into the song. It sounds like he's saying that Satan is in a hole. In the first chapter Crowley was quoted as saying that Satan was in the abyss. This is what the author believes Plant is making reference to. That would make perfect sense, because they present it as such. Between 2:37 and 2:50 of "Achilles Last Stand," Plant sings of riding "wind." Then he sings of treading "air" over top of "din." In the following two lines he sings about laughing and "dancing" up "above" their "crowd." Who is it that is in the air above the crowd? Those from above the clouds? The Demonic forces, who are evil spirits under Satan's authority, in league with the band to produce magical changes in the minds of the fans? You better believe it. You are going to read about that soon. Suffice it to say, enough evidence has been presented to the idea of spirits inhabiting the air; specifically the angels who fell with Lucifer. At this point brief instructions from Crowley to his students on astral projection will be presented. The teachings are the ones that Jimmy Page studied. This is going to prepare the reader for understanding "Kashmir," and "In My Time of Dying." Both songs are from the album, *Physical Graffiti*. "Kashmir," as the evidence will suggest, is one big astral projection journey by Jimmy Page. It was Page that wrote the lyrics to "Kashmir," so it is reasonable then to believe that it was his journey.

PHYSICAL GRAFFITI – "KASHMIR"

Astral projection is a very important practice in the Silver Star, also referred to as the Great White Brotherhood. Within the order of the Silver Star, there are three different orders. The first order is called the Hermetic Order of the Golden Dawn, the second order is called the Order of the Red Rose and the Golden Cross, or Rosicrucians. The third order is called the Silver Star. Since the third order is the highest, Crowley named all three orders, which are cohesive, the Silver Star.

In the Hermetic Order of the Golden Dawn that Mathers started, the names of the first order's ranks are different from Crowley's. The different names are:

Mathers: Neophyte 0=0, Zelator 1=10, Theoricus 2=9

Crowley: Probationer 0=0, Neophyte 1=10, Zelator 2=9

In order to be promoted from Probationer 0=0, to Neophyte 1=10, in Crowley's Silver Star, one has to be successful at astral projection or travel. In his book, *Satanism - The Seduction of America's Youth*, Bob Larson wrote: "In Great Britain, Aleister Crowley became the head of a secret occult order based on thelemic black magic known as Argenteum Astrum (the Silver Star), the Inner Order of the Great White Brotherhood. Every member was required to go through a standardized test whereby he was supposed to interpret an unknown and unintelligible symbol through a vision or astral journey. If he passed, the candidate became a Probationer. A year later, all orders being kept, the inductee could graduate to Neophyte, acquiring control of his 'body of light.' The final state was that of Zelator."[40] Aleister Crowley himself described the prerequisite this way: "It is of utmost importance to the 'clairvoyant' or 'traveler in the fine body' to be able to find his way to any desired plane, and operate therein as its ruler. The Neophyte of the A.A. is examined most strictly in this practice before he is passed to the degree of Zelator."[41] To sum it up, at the very beginning of a magical career in the Silver Star, one has to learn about and practice astral projection. These requirements were set up by Crowley, who himself practiced astral travel. We know that Jimmy Page is openly a follower of his teachings. We also know that "Produced by Silver Star" was printed on the author's Page/Plant concert ticket at the Orlando Arena on March 7th, 1995. You read where Page said mysticism has been involved in their music from the second album on. You read about flying up in the air in the song, "What is and What Should Never Be." You also read several examples of their assertion that spirits rule the air. After reviewing these pieces of information, it is logical to conclude that Jimmy Page has practiced astral projection; if not all of them, which is what I believe.

The following information on the practice of astral projection is going to be presented from Aleister Crowley's *Magick* as well as Led Zeppelin's song "Kashmir." During the 1995 Page/Plant Tour, they closed their shows with "Kashmir." In reviewing this information, the reader will clearly see Crowley's teaching, that Jimmy Page studied (his name is on page xv of the acknowledgements of the book they were taken from, thanking him for his contributions). Then it will be seen in practice in "Kashmir." We are going to examine them concurrently. Before we do so, it is very important that the reader understand that Jimmy Page is the one who wrote the lyrics to "Kashmir;" not Robert Plant. In making reference to the song, the group's road manager, Richard Cole, had this to say in his book, *Stairway to Heaven - Led Zeppelin Uncensored*: "Jimmy had written the lyrics to the song, complete with its mystical references, while making that drive alone a few months earlier."42 In the context of the book, Cole says Page wrote Kashmir's lyrics a few months before recording the song in sessions. Howard Mylett described "Kashmir" as a "cosmic travelogue to spiritual regeneration" in *Jimmy Page – Tangents Within A Framework*: "The exotic, musky 'Kashmir' is intriguing in its other-worldliness. Page's grinding staccato guitar work sounds like a cosmic travelogue to spiritual regeneration, swelling around the lyrics, which are heavily laden with mystical illusions and Hessean imagery."43 Led Zeppelin's music is all about spiritual regeneration.

In the beginning of the song, in its first two lines, Jimmy Page makes reference to the Qabalistic godhead, Satan and his female consort. He wrote about the "sun" shining on his "face" in the first line. The sun is Satan in symbolism, according to Crowley. Just look at the Crowley quote at the heading of the Dancing Days chapter (four). In the second line, Page says "stars" occupy his "dreams." Crowley has repeatedly stated that the cosmos is symbolic of the Egyptian goddess "Nuit." Included in, or one with the goddess, is her daughter. Her daughter is all the people, collectively, who Satan will choose for salvation, or "redemption." This concept will be elaborated on in chapter eight. At that point Page refers to astral travel. He says that he travels through "time" as well as "space" so he could "sit" among the spirit beings who are "elders" of the faith of Magick and Satan. He says that he is talking to these elders about the "days" they are waiting for, when "all" of Satan's chosen are "redeemed." In other words, when Satan sends his spirits/angels to retrieve his chosen. Robert Plant has been known to alternate redeemed with "revealed" while singing the song in concert. The concepts are the same.

On the two recent Led Zeppelin releases, *Early Days* and *Latter Days*, the band is seen in space outfits. It would seem that they were reiterating the concept of traveling through the cosmos.

TRAVELER

Aleister Crowley presented his teachings on astral travel in a manner that can easily be compared to Kashmir's lyrics. As already stated, Jimmy Page said in the third and fourth lines that he was a traveler of time as well as space. The following are two quotes from Crowley on astral travel for new members of the Silver Star. The first reads: "To sum up, the first task is to separate the astral form from the physical body, the second to develop the powers of the astral body, in particular those of sight, travel, and interpretation; third, to unify the two bodies without muddling them. This being accomplished, the Magician is fitted to deal with the invisible."44 Crowley wrote in that quote about becoming skilled in the use of the astral body. In the next, he writes of astral travel again while emphasizing the astral plane. The quote is in agreement with the lyrics from "What is and What Should Never Be;" about living up in the air: "As soon as you feel more or less at home in the fine body, let it rise in the air. Keep on feeling the sense of rising; keep on looking about you as you rise until you see landscapes or beings of the Astral Plane. Such have a quality all their own. They are not like material things - they are not like mental pictures - they seem to lie between the two."45 There is an entirely different reality for the magician who practices astral projection, having comprehension of the spirit world; as opposed to the normal human being. The magician has broken on through to "the other side."

TIME AND SPACE

Crowley makes reference to the Magician traveling through time as well as space, just like Page, in the following quotes. The first will refer to space alone: "Now this interior body of the Magician, of which we spoke at the beginning of this chapter, does exist, and can exert certain powers which his natural body cannot do. It can, for example, pass through 'matter,' and it can move freely in every direction through space. But this is because 'matter,' in the sense in which we commonly use the word, is on another plane. Now this fine body perceives a universe which we do not ordinarily perceive."46 The next quote refers to both time and space, from Crowley's epistle, *Notes for an Astral Atlas*, meaning it was written in the context of astral projection, thus demonstrating to the student of Magick that he can travel through the time dimension as well: "Time and Space are forms by which we obtain (distorted) images of Ideas. Our measures of Time and Space are crude conventions, and differ widely for different beings."47

ELDERS

Page wrote of traveling through "time" as well as "space" for a reason. He does that so he can "sit" among "elders" that are "gentle." Sitting among these elders is in the sixth line of "Kashmir" between 0:36 and 0:45. It makes sense to believe that the following Crowley quotes make reference to these elders, as they are taken from the same epistle on astral projection. He wrote that meeting the "inhabitants" of the astral plane is necessary to progress in Magick:
"The general control of the Astral Plane, the ability to find one's way

about it, to penetrate such sanctuaries as are guarded from the profane, to make such relations with its inhabitants as may avail to acquire knowledge and power, or to command service; all this is a question of the general Magical attainment of the student."48

In the next quote, Crowley says the astral beings, who are spirits, will be able to instruct the magician. This is the work of an elder, to instruct those who are learning, so the word elder used by Page in "Kashmir" is in keeping with Crowley's teachings on astral projection; in complete league with the Devil. He claims the purpose of astral travel is to aid the magician in the Great Work; raising men to an awareness of, and communion with god, or Satan: "Let the Magician therefore adventure himself upon the Astral Plane with the declared design to penetrate to a sanctuary of discarnate Beings such as are able to instruct and fortify him, also to prove their identity by testimony beyond rebuttal. All explanations other than these are of value only as extending and equilibrating knowledge, or possibly as supplying Energy to such Magicians as may have found their way to the Sources of Strength. In all cases naught is worth an obol save as it serve to help the One Great Work."49 In this final quote concerning the elders, Crowley makes it clear that they have a definite relationship to the physical, visible, planet earth: "Astral Beings may thus be defined in the same way as 'material objects,' they are Unknown Causes of various observed effects. They may be of any order of existence."50 (Including metamorphosis)

The following quoted passage will authenticate that last statement by Crowley. It comes from the book that is famous among Led Zeppelin fans, *Led Zeppelin – The Concert File*. On March 31st, 1995, while Page/Plant were performing a concert in Auburn Hills, Michigan, a young man ran through the orchestra with a knife, heading toward the stage to attack Jimmy Page. Why? Because of the spirits he saw around Page while he was playing "Kashmir." Dave Lewis and Simon Pallett wrote: "This show is overshadowed somewhat by an attempted so-called 'knife attack' incident. A 23 year-old fan ran towards the stage with a pocketknife during 'Kashmir.' Apparently, he had been driven to this action by what he claimed were demons and spirits surrounding Page. He got within 50 yards of the stage before being thwarted by security. Page himself was unaware of the incident. The story however, was reported in newspapers on both sides of the Atlantic, giving an excuse to revive the tedious 'Curse of the Satanic guitarist!' headlines."51 Remember, it was Lewis and Pallett that wrote about an incident allegedly caused by the presence of demons and spirits at a Jimmy Page and Robert Plant concert, not Tom Friend, and it was written in 1997, so these spirit activities are certainly contemporary. Aleister Crowley, on the other hand, wrote something that matches the information presented by Lewis and Pallett even more precisely: "Look! - as we invoke them, how they gather round us, these Spirits of Love and of Life, of Passion, of Strength, and of Abandon - these sinews of the manhood of the World!"52 It is too much of a coincidence to believe that a 23 year old, evidently under the influence of a hallucinogen, could simply imagine demonic spirits surrounding Jimmy Page at a concert; especially when Aleister Crowley wrote of being surrounded by spirits in *The Equinox* (the same name Jimmy gave to his occult bookstore in England). It seems that the "elders" of "Kashmir" were at that Michigan concert, during the song "Kashmir," interestingly enough. The author knows they were at Madison Square Garden on June 11th, 1977.

OTHER WORLDS

Jimmy Page wrote that he travels through "time" as well as "space" so he can "sit" among "elders" that are "gentle," and that their "world" rarely is "seen." In other words, very few will see the world these elders exist in, a few like Page and other students of Magick, who practice astral projection. Crowley refers to other worlds in the following (tying them in with the study of the Qabalah), also taken from *Notes for an Astral Atlas*:

"Magick enables us to receive sensible impressions of worlds other than the 'physical' universe (as generally understood by profane science). These worlds have their own laws; their inhabitants are often of quasi-human intelligence; there is a definite set of relations between certain 'ideas' of ours, and their expressions, and certain types of phenomena. (Thus symbols, the Qabalah, etc. enable us to communicate with whom we choose.).

Astral Beings possess knowledge and power of a different kind from our own; their 'universe' is presumably of a different kind from ours, in some respects."53

These astral beings, and the worlds or astral planes on which they abide, differ from plane to plane, such as people on earth differ from country to country.

EGYPTIAN AND CELTIC ASTRAL PLANES

In the next quote, Crowley speaks of two specific worlds, or planes; the Egyptian and the Celtic, both of which are important to Led Zeppelin: "Each such 'plane' has its special appearances, inhabitants, and laws-special cases of the general proposition. Notable among these are the 'Egyptian' plane, which conforms with the ideas and methods of Magick once in vogue in the Nile valley; the 'Celtic' plane, close akin to 'Fairyland,' with a Pagan Pantheism as its keynote..."54 The Egyptian element was clearly seen during the 1995 Page/Plant tour, as they had an Egyptian orchestra accompany them through the whole tour. Throughout the entire 1998 Page/Plant tour, they opened the show with an instrumental commonly referred to as "The Egyptian Introduction." This caused them to remove the "Immigrant Song" part of the beginning of the show, because it refers to the Nordic pantheon; and they just tore into "The Wanton Song." In 1995 they played "Immigrant Song" first, and then tore into "The Wanton Song." In 1998 they wanted to emphasize Egypt as the genesis of the show. I caught it loud and clear, though few others have. Egypt is the genesis of Magick, so I was not surprised by the introduction.

The Celtic element of Led Zeppelin is clearly seen in "Stairway to Heaven." At the Tampa Ice Palace Arena on May 20th, 1998, Robert Plant mouthed the following words just before they tore into the last encore. It was the song, "Rock and Roll," which is from the fourth album, Runes. I heard this with my own ears, as I stood there with pen and paper and wrote what he said: "As you're fully aware of our preoccupation with music from other parts of the world, and with Celtic root music, we'd like to say goodnight to you with a little Celtic lullaby." If Jimmy Page traveled to these two planes, the Egyptian and the Celtic, to meet with the elders of each, we can see the effect of them evident in his music. The author believes the evidence points to him having done exactly that. I know that this is hard to fathom, but you don't worship Satan do you?

REDEMPTION

So far we have Jimmy Page saying he travels through "time" as well as "space" so he can "sit" among "elders" that are "gentle" and their "world" rarely is "seen." Now we come to the point of redemption. In the next line of the song, again, Page says that there is "talk" about "days" the elders are waiting for, when Satan's people are "redeemed;" at 0:45 into the song (again, in concert Robert Plant has many times substituted the word "revealed" for redeemed, the concepts being concurrent in the minds of the band members). The redemption spoken of is the gathering of Satan's chosen by his angels and taking them up to heaven. Reference is made to Satan's angels acting out this gathering in the song, "In My Time of Dying." Robert Plant sings of angelic beings "marching" at 8:04 of the song. This has to do with the Battle of Armageddon, which is the "Battle of Evermore;" referred to in chapter sixteen. After the battle is over, and the angels are done fighting, they come to retrieve the Devil's own. At 9:08 into "Dying," Plant yells out that he wants someone to "take" him "home." He then yells out for them to hurry up twice at 9:17 and 9:19. Then at 9:21 of the song he sings the he is able to "hear" these "angels" in chorus as they are descending to get him. At both 9:26 and 9:29 of the song, Plant sings "here" the angels "come." He shouts farewell to the listener five times between 9:35 and 9:44. Finally, Plant sings that his redemption is complete at 9:48. He sings that he "feels" great "up" there. He repeats it at 9:52. To sum it up, Plant shouted to the angels to come and get him. He then cries out for them to hurry. Then he says they are coming to get him. Finally, he says goodbye and that it feels good in heaven. This is the redemption mentioned in "Kashmir," again, at 0:45 of the song.

This angelic redemption that Led Zeppelin presents to their fans is just another example of the Devil copying the Word of God. Lord Jesus Christ said that when he comes for his chosen, he will send his angels to get them. In the New Testament Book of Matthew, in Chapter 24, Verses 30-31, Jesus said: "Then the sign of the Son of Man will appear in heaven, and then all the tribes of the earth will mourn, and they will see the Son of Man coming on the clouds of heaven with power and great glory. And He will send His angels with a great sound of a trumpet, and they will gather together His elect from the four winds, from one end of heaven to the other." In the New Testament Book of First Thessalonians, Chapter 4, Verses 16-17, Paul the Apostle wrote: "For the Lord Himself will descend from heaven with a shout, with the voice of an archangel, and with the trumpet of God. And the dead in Christ will rise first. Then we who are alive and remain shall be caught up together with them in the clouds to meet the Lord in the air. And thus we shall always be with the Lord." Robert Plant makes reference to meeting Christ up in the air in the beginning lyrics of "In My Time of Dying" (which is just a smokescreen for the naïve).

Jimmy Page wrote of "flying" in "Kashmir;" at 2:22 and 2:52. At this point it seems that he is flying on his way to Kashmir. He cries out to the Lady or goddess at 2:59 by saying "Mama!" He makes reference to the desert at 3:23, by saying he can "see" everything become "brown," because heat from our "sun" is frying that "ground." Then at 3:46 he says his "eyes" are covered by "sand," while he views that "land." The rest of the song, in effect, makes reference to the rest of Page's travel to Kashmir. He mentions a "path" which "led" him "to" the "place" in the "desert" at 4:46. He mentions the goddess again by referring to the moon at 4:55. He says he does his "shangri-la" under the "moon" and is going to "return" there. Finally, Page mentions Kashmir by saying as surely as "dust" soars "high" during "June," he was traveling in the midst of "Kashmir." The Devil is mentioned at 5:31. He says the "Father" who controls the quarterly "winds" pushed his "sails" on a "sea" so he could sail it. At 6:38, he says he is "on" his "way." In the next line he says he feels he will "stay." At last, he invites the listener to "let" him "take" them "there," four times, beginning at 7:46.

What does Crowley have to say about this? Can Jimmy Page pick Kashmir to travel to during astral projection? The answer is absolutely. Crowley wrote in the same epistle: "Although it is said that the Spiritual lies 'beyond the Astral,' this is theoretical; the advanced Magician will not find it to be so in practice. He will be able by suitable invocation to travel directly to any place desired."55 By the time "Kashmir" was released in 1975, it appears that Jimmy Page had become an advanced magician. If that was the case, Mr. Page could travel directly to any place of his choosing. Now we come to the last and most important question, why in the world would Jimmy Page want to go to Kashmir? The author's research has produced the answer to that question. In the book, *Witchcraft, Magic, and Occultism*, W.B. Crow wrote: "Padma-sambhava was an exponent of Tantrism and every form of magic and spirit-lore, for which his native land of Kashmir was famous."56 It makes perfect sense to believe that Jimmy Page would astral travel to Kashmir because it is famous for magic and spirits. You can read of Crowley's physical travel to Kashmir in *The Confessions of Aleister Crowley*.

Ritchie Yorke, in *Led Zeppelin - The Definitive Biography*, wrote what the band had to say about "Kashmir" the song: "Fifteen years down the long and winding road, all three Led Zeppelin members consider 'Kashmir' to be *the* quintessential Led Zeppelin recording. 'It's all there,' says John Paul Jones, 'all the elements that defined the band.'"57 For the members of Led Zeppelin to declare "Kashmir" the "quintessential" recording of the band, in light of all the evidence presented, is quite a statement. "The elements that defined the band" is a definite advertisement for potential students of Magick; directing them to the practice of astral projection; once they become students of Crowley, who Page has advocated from the beginning.

"Ramble On" and "Kashmir" then, irrespective of any plausible deniability of the band or fans, show evidence of deliberate attempts by Led Zeppelin to guide their listeners to the practice of Magick and astral projection. The band members themselves were instructed by the teachings of Black Magician Aleister Crowley, who was guided by none other than the mighty Devil himself. This is Satan directing the Led Zeppelin fan into Magick through the writings of Crowley and the music of Led Zeppelin. The Devil took Aleister Crowley's yielded soul and led him to read *The Book of Black Magic and of Pacts*, which led him to read *The Cloud Upon the Sanctuary*, which eventually created the desire to search for the brotherhood of Magick described therein. That desire was fulfilled when Satan brought into Crowley's life the necessary individuals who would lead him to join The Hermetic Order of the Golden Dawn. The Devil himself oversaw Crowley's desires and actions. As the Golden Dawn self-destructed, Satan led Crowley to found the Argenteum Astrum; the Silver Star. Crowley would then write volume after volume of instruction on Magick for his future students. One of those students would be the mighty James Patrick Page, who, along with his cohorts have passed that teaching on to the fans of Led Zeppelin, with a desire for them to discover Magick and astral projection.

1 E.M. Bounds, *Satan, His Personality, Power, and Overthrow*, pp. 92-93

2 Abraham the Jew, *The Book of the Sacred Magic of Abramelin the Mage*, translated by S.L. MacGregor Mathers, Causeway Books, New York, NY, 1974, pg.61

Jimmy Page plays Kashmir at the Oakland Coliseum on July 23rd, 1977. Kashmir is renown for "every form of magic and spirit-lore," which is the passion of his life. John Paul Jones said the song contains the "elements" which "defined" Led Zeppelin. It begins by mentioning the Sun, which is the symbol of Lucifer. Then, they are traveling through "space" so they can "sit" among "elders" who are waiting on the day of redemption. The elders are still in league with Page, as the incident in Detroit in 1995 suggests. Astral Projection is required of all new members of the Argenteum-Astrum. He who looks into the occult meaning of the song, will be led by the piper to study their initiatory requirement.

Jimmy Page played "Ramble On" throughout the entire 1998 world tour, while Robert Plant sang of "Magick" ruling the "air," during "days" he calls "old."

3 Aleister Crowley, *The Equinox*, Vol. I, No.2, *The Temple of Solomon the King*, pp.302-306

4 Aleister Crowley, *Magick-Book 4*Liber ABA*, pg.127

5 Ibid, pg.141

6 Aleister Crowley, *The Equinox*, Volume I, No.2, *The Temple of Solomon the King*, pg.227

7 Ibid, pp.236-237

8 Aleister Crowley, *The Confessions of Aleister Crowley*, pg.126

9 Ibid, pg.127

10 Arthur E. Waite, *The Book of Black Magic*, Samuel Weiser Inc., Yorke Beach, Maine, 1993, pp.23-24

11 Webster's New World Dictionary, Second College Edition, 1978, pg.696

12 Karl von Eckartshausen, *The Cloud Upon the Sanctuary*, Sure Fire Press, 1991, pg. vii

13 Ibid, pg.15

14 Ibid, pp.13-14

15 Ibid, pp.15-16

16 Ibid, pp.18-19

17 Ibid, pp.19-20

18 Susan Roberts, *The Magician of the Golden Dawn*, pg.32

19 Aleister Crowley, *The World's Tragedy*, pg.xxii

20 Susan Roberts, *The Magician of the Golden Dawn*, pg.106

21 Aleister Crowley, *Confessions*, pg.165

22 Ibid, pg.165

23 Aleister Crowley, *Book 4*, Samuel Weiser Inc., Yorke Beach, Maine, 1994, pg.81

24 Susan Roberts, *The Magician of the Golden Dawn*, pg.44

25 Aleister Crowley, *The Equinox*, Vol. I, No.2, *The Temple of Solomon the King*, pg.263.

26 Ibid, pg.255

27 Eliphas Levi, *Transcendental Magic*, pg.267

28 Aleister Crowley, *The Equinox*, Vol. I, No.2, *The Temple of Solomon the King*, pg.261

29 Ibid, pg.266

30 Aleister Crowley, *Magick Without Tears*, New Falcon Publications, pg.359

31 Aleister Crowley, *Magick-Book 4*Liber Aba*, pg.241

32 Aleister Crowley, *The Equinox*, Vol. I, No.2, *The Temple of Solomon the King*, pp.295-301

33 Ibid, pp.302-306

34 Aleister Crowley, *The Equinox*, Vol., I, No.1, pg.170

35 E.M. Bounds, *Satan, His Personality, Power, and Overthrow*, pp.92-93

36 Butler, *Ritual Magic*, pg.204

37 Abraham the Jew, *The Book of the Sacred Magic of Abramelin the Mage*, pp.60-61

38 Steven Davis, *Hammer of the Gods*, pg.122

39 Ritchie Yorke, *Led Zeppelin - The Definitive Biography*, pg.152

40 Bob Larson, *Satanism - The Seduction of America's Youth*, pg.152

41 Aleister Crowley, *Magick - Book 4*Liber Aba*, pg.246

42 Richard Cole, *Stairway to Heaven - Led Zeppelin Uncensored*, Harper Collins, New York, 1992, pg.281

43 Howard Mylett, *Jimmy Page – Tangents Within A Framework*, pg.28

44 Aleister Crowley, *Magick - Book 4*Liber Aba*, pg.246

45 Ibid, pg.243

46 Ibid, pg.242

47 Ibid, pg.492

48 Ibid, pg.494

49 Ibid, pp.502-503

50 Ibid, pg.492

51 Dave Lewis & Simon Pallett, *Led Zeppelin: The Concert File*, Omnibus Press, 1997, pg.169

52 Aleister Crowley, *The Equinox*, Vol. I, No.1, pg.174

53 Aleister Crowley, *Magick - Book 4*Liber Aba*, pp.491- 492

54 Ibid, pg. 493

55 Ibid, pg. 247

56 W.B. Crow, *Witchcraft, Magic, and Occultism*, pg.145

57 Ritchie Yorke, *Led Zeppelin -The Definitive Biography*, pg.178

Jimmy Page plays "In My Time of Dying" on the 1977 tour. Around his neck is the Death Skull/Egyptian Ankh/Guitar necklace. On his costume, along with the horned dragon, is the Opium Poppy from which Heroin is made. In his "Book of the Law," Crowley advocated the use of drugs while writing as a medium for Satan with the statement, "To worship me take wine and strange drugs whereof I will tell my prophet, & be drunk thereof!" Crowley and Led Zeppelin both obeyed the command; advocating Alcohol, Cocaine, Heroin, Mushrooms, LSD-25, and Marijuana - "Alcapulco Gold!" Using drugs is part of the "True Will."

CHAPTER SEVEN

"Even in the year 1904 when The Book of the Law came to be written down, Europe and America were still bound up in the heavy iron chains of Judeo-Christian morality. God was not dead-yet-though Nietzsche had tried his utmost to inter him."1

> *Israel Regardie, Introduction, Aleister Crowley's "The Law is for All"*

"One of the most conspicuous aspects of The Book of the Law is that its stand on almost every moral issue runs counter to the accepted social one of today. Certainly it is in direct opposition to the Judeo-Christian code that today regulates our behavior. However, with the extraordinary social changes in the air today-violent changes being wrought in the streets, in foreign wars, and by the young people on college campuses-and with the wholesale rejection of previously accepted norms of conduct, it is not too much to say that in the contemporary scene Crowley has a multitude of allies and adherents."2

> *Israel Regardie, Introduction, "The Law is for All"*

"I am the Snake that giveth Knowledge & Delight and bright glory, and stir the hearts of men with drunkenness. To worship me take wine and strange drugs whereof I will tell my prophet, & be drunk thereof! They shall not harm ye at all."3

> *Satan, Aleister Crowley's "The Book of the Law"*

"With my hawk's head I peck at the eyes of Jesus as he hangs upon the cross."4

> *Satan, "The Book of the Law"*

FOR YOUR LIFE & IMMIGRANT SONG: DO WHAT THOU WILT-THE BOOK OF THE LAW

The Book of the Law is the single most important document in Aleister Crowley's catalog of writings. It contains all the major tenets of the Law of Thelema, which is the Law of "Do What Thou Wilt." Thelema is the Greek word for will. The Law of Thelema, is the Law of doing your "true will," or the will of heaven for your life, as it has been designated to you by the godhead, or

Satan and his female consort, or goddess. Aleister Crowley claimed the book was dictated to him by a musical spirit named "Aiwaz;" whom he later identified as Satan. In this chapter we will examine the major doctrines of *The Book of the Law*, including the specific definition of "Do What Thou Wilt," as it relates to it. Then, once the concepts are understood, we will take an objective look at how the principles of *The Book of the Law* are advocated by the music of Led Zeppelin. We will begin by a continuation of the study of Aleister Crowley's activities early in his career of Magick; beginning with his search for a suitable dwelling to focus on the Operation of Abramelin the Mage, which enables the student of Magick to ascend to 5=6, or the position of Adeptus Minor in the Silver Star, the first rank in the second order, called the "Rosicrucians." Afterward, we will examine the chaotic events that led to the demise of the Hermetic Order of the Golden Dawn, including Crowley's departure from it. His travels in 1901 will be briefly mentioned, which he embarked upon to study the comparative magical practices of the religious groups he encountered. His meeting Rose Kelly will then be discussed, as well as his marriage to her, and how Rose's involvement in Crowley's life led to the eventual writing of *The Book of the Law* in Cairo, Egypt, in 1904. Then our focus will shift to the events surrounding the reception of the book, the Law of Thelema, and it's major doctrines of how the will of the student of Magick is to be exercised in the areas of occupation, drug and alcohol use, and sexuality. Subsequent to those concepts, the book's hatred for Lord Jesus Christ and the Christian faith will then be considered, including it's blatant promotion of literal murder of Christian people. *The Book of the Law* also promotes literal human sacrifice of children to the Devil, as will be seen. *The Book of the Law*, with its doctrine of "Do What Thou Wilt," the Law of Thelema, is presented to us by Satan, through Aleister Crowley, and the music of Led Zeppelin as the law of "liberty," especially liberating man from the tyrannical "restriction" doctrines of Biblical Christianity and its Christ; however, it is in fact a moral law that enslaves man to the basest types of human depravity, with the end result being the Devil's complete control of the human soul.

ALEISTER CROWLEY ACQUIRES BOLESKINE HOUSE

Once Crowley attained the level of Philosophous, 4=7, in the Golden Dawn, he sought to prepare himself for the Operation of Abramelin the Mage; which is the main focus of the first rank of the second order, 5=6. Crowley himself described it this way, in the third person, using the letter P. as an abbreviation for his magical name, Perdurabo: "Between the grades of 4=7 and 5=6 seven months had to elapse, and during this time we find P. busily traveling the British Isles searching for a suitable house where in to perform the Operation of Abramelin the Mage, which ever since the previous autumn had engaged his attention. In the month of May he had met D.D.C.F. 7=4, official head of the Order of the Golden Dawn. But he was still bent on carrying out the Operation of Abramelin, and journeyed to and fro all over the country endeavouring to discover a suitable dwelling for the necessary Retirement. Thus it came about that in October of this year we find him settled in a remote and desolate district, a tumbled chaos of lake and mountain, in an ancient manor house, making all necessary arrangements for this great operation in Ceremonial Magic."5 D.D.C.F.

At the end of 1899, Crowley secured this residence and it was called *Boleskine House.* It is settled on the shores of Loch Ness in Scotland. Jimmy Page would eventually come to own this house 70 years later. I will show you what I believe is absolute proof, derived from Aleister Crowley's writings in Sicily in 1921, at the Abbey of Thelema, that Jimmy Page bought the house for the exact same purpose. Once again, the practice of Abramelin magic is to attain the Knowledge and Conversation of the Holy Guardian Angel, who is none other than Satan. There is a direct, measurable, provable correlation between Jimmy Page's practice of Abramelin magic and the fans of Led Zeppelin. Jimmy Page and the other members of Led Zeppelin are merely the mediums by which Satan has been able to perform magical operations on the fans of Led Zeppelin, including this author. I will tell you how it was done, and what happened. I know very well there are thousands of other people out there who went through the same thing and are too afraid to talk about it because they think people will suggest they see a psychiatrist. After I bring this to light, you will understand everything Satan was trying to do to you; if you are one of them (us). It was my iron will that kept me from becoming one of his puppets. The reader will also be shown that Page's involvement with Abramelin magic explains vividly the meaning of the painting by Barrington Colby on the inner cover of Led Zeppelin's fourth album, *The Hermit*, which is related to the 5=6 grade in the second stage of the Silver Star.

ADEPTUS MINOR: 5=6 THE ROSICRUCIANS

Aleister Crowley was ready to be initiated into the second order of the Golden Dawn, at the rank of 5=6. The other members in London would not allow this, specifically one William Butler Yeats, who did not think the Rosicrucian grades should be a "reformatory." In other words, this man thought Crowley to be a hapless degenerate. The head of the order, S.L. MacGregor Mathers, was staying in Paris at this time. Crowley traveled to Paris to get Mathers to initiate him. The following third person account by Crowley (Perdurabo) describes the situation:

"During the whole of the autumn of 1899 we find P. busily engaged in making all necessary preparations for the great operation. Outside these preparations little else was accomplished; and, except for a fragment of a MS. on the 'Powers of Number,' no other record of the progress of P. during these three months is forth coming.

"This MS., though interesting enough in itself, is scarcely of sufficient value to quote here; however, it may be remarked that it shows how strong an influence the Order of the Golden Dawn had had upon him, as well as the astonishing rapidity of his Magical progress.

"In January 1900, P. returned to Paris in order that before commencing the Sacred Operation of Abramelin the Mage he might pass through the grade of 5=6, and become an Adeptus Minor in the Second Order of the Golden Dawn.

"The ritual of the 5=6 is of considerable length, and of such profundity and beauty that it is difficult to conceive of any man not being a better and a more illumined man for having passed through it."6

The following is an excerpt of the 5=6 ritual that pertains to the Great Work; uniting man with "god," as Crowley was uniting himself with Satan. It is Crowley reciting promises:

"...I will uphold to the utmost the authority of the Chiefs of the Order.

"Furthermore that I will perform all practical work connected with this Order, in a place concealed...that I will keep secret this inner Rosicrucian Knowledge...that I will only perform any practical magic before the uninitiated which is of a simple and already well-known nature, and that I will show them no secret mode of working whatsoever.

"I further solemnly promise and swear that, with the Divine permission, I will from this day forward apply myself unto the Great Work, which is so to purify and exalt my spiritual Nature that with the Divine Aid I may at length attain to be more than human, and thus gradually raise and unite myself to my higher and divine Genius, and that in this event I will not abuse the Great Power entrusted unto me."7

The following paragraph was quoted back to the aspirant of the grade 5=6 during the ritual, and it is another clear indicator of universal magic being the common denominator:

"Know then O Aspirant, that the mysteries of the Rose and Cross have existed from time immemorial, and that its mystic rites were practised, and its hidden knowledge communicated in the initiations of the various races of antiquity - Egypt, Eleusis, and Samothrace; Persia, Chaldea, and India alike cherished its mysteries, and thus handed down to posterity the Secret Wisdom of the Ancient Ages. Many were its Temples, and among many nations were they established; though in process of time some lost the purity of their primal knowledge."8

This ritual did have a tremendous effect upon the life of Crowley, and he would soon travel the world and practice magic concurrently. He wrote the following in the *Equinox* once the ritual was over:

"By thus passing through the ritual of the 5=6 Grade of Adeptus Minor, P., in part at least, unveiled that knowledge which he had set out in the 0=0 ritual to discover. For as the first grade of the First order endows the Neophyte with an unforgettable glimpse of that Higher Self, the Augoeides, Genius, Holy guardian Angel or Adonai; so does the first grade of the Second Order engender within him that divine spark, by drawing down upon the Aspirant the Genius in Pentecostal Flames; until it no longer enshrines him like the distant walls of the starry abyss, but burns within him, pouring through the channels of his senses an unending torrent of glory, of that greater glory which alone can be comprehended by one who is an Adept: yet again, but the shadow of that supreme glory which is neither the shrine nor the flame, but the life of the Master.

"From the commencement of this history we have ever found Frater P. valiantly battling with the Elemental Forces."9

For those who do not know, "Elemental Forces" are evil spirits. If the spirits are evil, why would they battle with Crowley? If the magician does not handle them properly, they can be dangerous to him. Very evidently, the magician accepts this standard of rule delegated down from the Devil. You see, magicians believe the Devil is god, and Satan had his own version of an angelic fall. Magicians believe some angels fell from heaven where they believe Satan rules. Obviously, they do not believe he led this group. He is a liar. The evil spirits battling with Crowley at this time were the same ones that appeared to him in the beautiful garb when he called on spirits he believed were good. Well does the *Bible* state this case in 2 Corinthians 11:14, where it is made clear: "And no wonder, for Satan himself masquerades as an angel of light. It is not surprising, then, if his servants masquerade as servants of righteousness."(NIV) Satan's servants can be spirits or men.

CHAOS IN THE GOLDEN DAWN

As mentioned before, the London Order was against Crowley's advancement, while Mathers was for it. This pitted those in London against Mathers and Crowley. As a result, Crowley pledged loyalty and financial support to Mathers. He wrote: "...from the following, we gauge to be connected with the dead sea apple schism which had for some time been ripening amongst the members of the Order of the Golden Dawn, was considered sufficiently important by P. for him to offer his services to G.H. Frater D.D.C.F., who was then in Paris. About a week latter P. writes: 'D.D.C.F. accepts my services, therefore do I rejoice that my sacrifice is accepted. Therefore do I again postpone the Operation of Abramelin the Mage, having by God's Grace formulated even in this a new link with the Higher, and gained a new weapon against the Great Princes of the Evil of the World. Amen.'"10

It was not long however, before Crowley was at odds with both Mathers on the one hand and the rest of the Order of the Golden Dawn on the other. Israel Regardie sums up why Crowley was at odds with the Golden Dawn in his biography on Crowley, *The Eye in the Triangle*: "They did not believe an Adept should drink, fornicate, have fun and raise hell-which was what Crowley was doing with enthusiasm. He liked it. He was developing a handsomely scandalous reputation, winning the disapproval of some of the Adepti, who felt that they were not running a reformatory for delinquent boys."11 Aleister Crowley would have been a fine Led Zeppelin fan in the 1970's, as the quote illustrates. As a result of that behavior, Crowley's membership in the Golden Dawn was going to be cut short. The following quote from Crowley, in summation, tells of the end of the association. This book is about Crowley, the Silver Star, and Led Zeppelin. We are not going to delve into extensive detail about all the subsequent battles between the powerful personalities of the Golden Dawn. It is relevant, only in that it explains the motivation behind Crowley's eventual formulation of his own magical order; promoted by Led Zeppelin as well as Jimmy Page and Robert Plant.

ALEISTER CROWLEY LEAVES THE GOLDEN DAWN

Crowley provided the following account of his departure from the Golden Dawn, as well as the end of his association with Mathers:

"The last point we arrived at in the Lection was that, 'in 1900 one P., a brother, instituted a rigorous test of S.R.M.D. on the one side and the Order on the other.' S.R.M.D. is but another name for G.H. Frater D.D.C.F., against whose authority the Second Order were now in open revolt. From this point the Lection continues:

'He discovered that S.R.M.D., though a scholar of some ability and a magician of remarkable powers, had never attained complete initiation: and further had fallen from his original place, he having imprudently attracted to himself forces of evil too great and terrible for him to withstand (Presumably Abramelin Demons).

'The claim of the Order that the true adepts were in charge of it was definitely disproved.

'In the Order, with two certain exceptions and two doubtful ones, he found no persons with any capacity for initiation of any sort.

'He thereupon, by his subtle wisdom, destroyed both the Order and its chief.

'Being himself no perfect adept, he was driven of the Spirit into the Wilderness, where he abode for six years, studying by the light of reason the sacred books and secret systems of initiation of all countries and ages.'"12

It was six years later, in 1906, when Crowley would attain the Knowledge and Conversation of the Holy Guardian Angel; that he began at Boleskine House. However, before that he would receive *The Book of the Law* from the Devil. After his fallout with Mathers and the Golden Dawn, Crowley sought to travel the world and practice Magick. He makes that clear in the following quote, as well as the fact that he believed in the Qabalah:

"In the year 1899 I came to Boleskine House*, and put everything in order with the object of carrying out the Operation of Abramelin the Mage.

I had studied Ceremonial Magic, and had obtained very remarkable success.

My Gods were those of Egypt, interpreted on lines closely akin to those of Greece.

In Philosophy I was a Realist of the Qabalistic School.

In 1900 I left England for Mexico, and later the Far East, Ceylon, India, Burma, Baltistan, Egypt and France."13

(*When Crowley wrote this in *The Equinox*, he called the house "C...House." When he subsequently quoted it in his *Confessions*, he called it Bolsekine House. Evidently he planned on calling it Crowley House but changed his mind.)

In his book, *The Equinox of the Gods*, Crowley wrote in the third person about his experience in Mexico. It is important that the reader remember this, especially that which is presented in parentheses: "In July, 1900, he went to Mexico, and devoted his whole time to the continued practice of Magick, in which he obtained extraordinary success. (See Equinox Vol. I, No. III, for a condensed account of some of these. It may be here stated summarily that he invoked certain Gods, Goddesses, and Spirits to visible appearance, learnt how to heal physical and moral diseases, how to make himself invisible, how to obtain communications from spiritual sources, how to control other minds, etc., etc..)....In the spring of 1901, he left Mexico, went to San Francisco, Honolulu, Japan, China and Ceylon, always continuing these experiments."14

ALEISTER CROWLEY IN 1903

After his journey around the world, Aleister Crowley returned to Boleskine House in Scotland. One of his associates from college, Gerald Kelly, a painter, entered his life again and they became good friends. Had Kelly known what that was going to lead to, he would have avoided Crowley at all costs. Kelly, however, did not possess the power of clairvoyance, and consequently Crowley met his sister Rose. In his book, *The Occult*, Colin Wilson accurately presents the events that took place between Rose and Crowley:

"He returned to Boleskine, and became friendly with a young painter, Gerald Kelly (who later became Sir Gerald Kelly, president of the Royal Academy). At Kelly's family home, Strathpeffer, he met Kelly's unstable sister Rose, a girl with a pretty face and a weak mouth. Already a widow, she had involved herself with a number of men who all wanted to marry her, and had encouraged them all. Crowley's quirky sense of humour suggested the solution: marry him, and leave the marriage unconsummated. She could have his name, and be free of her admirers. They were married by a lawyer the next morning. But Crowley was not a man to pass up the opportunity to perform in his 'sexual magic' on another woman. Besides, there was an element of masochism in Rose that appealed to the touch of sadism in him. Their decision to keep the marriage platonic lasted only a few hours. The rage of Gerald Kelly and Rose's other relations delighted Crowley, who loved drama of any sort. He took Rose back to Boleskine - and had to quickly cancel an arrangement whereby a red-headed tart he had picked up should become his housekeeper-and then to Paris, Cairo (where they spent a night in the Great Pyramid) and Ceylon. It was here that Crowley shot a bat, which fell on his wife's head and dug its claws into her hair; that night, Rose had a nightmare that she was a bat, and clung to the frame of the mosquito net over the bed, howling; when he tried to detach her she spat, scratched and bit. Crowley described it as 'the finest case of obsession that I have ever had the good fortune to observe.'

"It should now be fairly clear what was wrong with Crowley, and why he, like other magicians, carried inside him the seed of his own downfall. The self-centered child who disliked his mother (he describes her as 'a brainless bigot') had almost no capacity for natural affection. It is this that makes him a 'monster.'....His marriage to Rose was fundamentally another schoolboy prank."15

Aleister Crowley himself described this period of his life:

"So we find that from November 1901 he did no practices of any kind until the Spring Equinox of 1904, with the exception of a casual week in the summer of 1903, and an exhibition game of magic in the King's Chamber of the Great Pyramid in November of 1903, when by his invocations he filled that chamber with a brightness as of full moonlight, only to conclude, 'There, you see it? What's the good of it?'

"We find him climbing mountains, skating, fishing, hunting big game, fulfilling the duties of a husband; we find him with the antipathy to all forms of spiritual thought and work which marks disappointment."16

RECEPTION OF THE BOOK OF THE LAW

On March 14th, 1904, as the Spring Equinox was near on the horizon,

Aleister and Rose Crowley took an apartment in Cairo, Egypt. Two days later, Crowley began a series of invocations. At the outset, he was merely trying to manifest sylphs (spirits) in order to amuse his wife. She said that she couldn't see them and told Crowley – "They're waiting for you!"17 She proceeded to inform him that he had offended "Horus." At first Crowley was skeptical about this. He then put Rose through a series of questions in order to see if Horus was trying to communicate to him through her. The questions consisted of asking her of the god's moral qualities, of Crowley's past associations with Horus, etc. To his amazement, Rose answered all of his questions correctly. He took her to a museum he knew would have pictures of Horus; it was a museum they had not visited previously and he wanted to see if she could recognize him. Although she ignored several pictures of Horus, she recognized him at an exhibit that identified him with the number of the beast. Crowley provided the following account:

"To apply test 4, Fra. P. took her to the museum at Boulak, which they had not previously visited. She passed by (as P. noted with silent glee) several images of Horus. They went upstairs. A glass case stood in the distance, too far off for its contents to be recognized. But W. recognized it! 'There,' she cried, 'There he is!'

"Fra. P. advanced to the case. There was the image of Horus in the form of Ra-Hoor- Khuit painted upon a wooden stele of the 26th dynasty - *and the exhibit bore the number 666!*"18

INVOCATION OF HORUS (SATAN)

As a result of being convinced by Rose that the Egyptian god Horus was trying to communicate with him, Crowley began a series of invocations in order to obtain that communication. He was successful in that endeavor. Colin Wilson, records the events: "In a museum she showed him a statue of Ra-Hoor-Khuit, one of the forms of Horus, and he was impressed to find that the number of the exhibit was the number of the Beast in Revelation, 666. Rose (whom he now called Ouarda) now began to instruct him on how to invoke Horus; the ritual did not seem to make sense, but he tried it. The result, he assures his readers, was a complete success. Not only did he hear from Horus, but from his own Guardian Angel, who he had been trying to invoke for so many years. His name is Aiwass. Horus told him that a new epoch was beginning (and many occultists would agree with this - Strindberg was saying much the same thing at the same time). Then Crowley was ordered to take his Swan fountain pen and write. A musical voice from the corner of the room then dictated *The Book of the Law* to him, assuring him that this book would solve all religious problems and would be translated into many languages. It goes further than any previous scriptures, Crowley says, in proving conclusively the existence of God, or at least, of intelligence higher than man's, with whom man can communicate."19

Since Lucifer was created as the celestial composer of music, should it surprise anyone that Aiwaz spoke to him in a musical voice? There were three chapters to the book, and Crowley penned them at the Devil's dictation on three different days. Between 12 and 1 p.m. on April 8th, 9th, and 10th, Crowley wrote the Book of the Law; one chapter a day.

AIWASS/AIWAZ - LUCIFER, SATAN, THE DEVIL

As a result of the Invocation of Horus, Crowley heard from his Holy Guardian Angel, Aiwass. It was a musical voice that dictated to him *The Book of the Law*. Colin Wilson probably took that information concerning a musical voice from Crowley's book, *The Equinox of the Gods*. Speaking about the voice of Aiwass, Crowley wrote: "The voice was of deep timbre, musical and expressive, its tones solemn, voluptuous, tender, fierce or aught else as suited the moods of the message."20 Crowley wrote that Aiwass told him *The Book of the Law* would solve all religious problems. Aiwass told him it would be translated into many different languages. Crowley also wrote that the book goes further than any previous scriptures in proving the existence of god, or at least of spiritual beings more intelligent than man with whom he can converse.

The reader may already be aware, but nevertheless, let's review the obvious. Here is a man, who, in his written *Confessions* was completely given over to the Devil. He loved and promoted Sodomy and Beastiality (sex with animals) prior to his going to Cairo. This chapter will also show that he advocated and participated in all manner of illegal drug use. He used everything from Marijuana to Heroin. He used to take enough Heroin to kill several people. What kind of moral code can we expect Horus to have, if he is willing to communicate through Aiwass to Crowley (I will show that Horus and Aiwass are one and the same - Satan, the Devil)? All this information is very relevant to Led Zeppelin as you will see; specifically the third album.

At this point I want to make absolutely clear to the reader who this Aiwass is. As I wrote previously, I believe he is the Devil. The proof being presented will come right from the writings of Aleister Crowley. One of the things that was a little confusing when studying Crowley was the use of the letter "z" in place of "s" or "ss." They are used interchangeably. Not only did Crowley receive *The Book of the Law* from Cairo, but Jimmy Page recruited an Egyptian percussion ensemble from there as well. This ensemble is in the *No Quarter* video and was with Page/Plant on their subsequent 1995 - 1996 world tour. The director of this ensemble's name is "Hossam Ramzy." On the box of the *No Quarter* video his name is spelled "Ramzy" with a "z." In the credits to the movie *Stargate*, on the other hand, his name is spelled "Ramsey." The credit reads, "Egyptian Percussion Performed by Hossam Ramsey." With Ramzy as well as Aiwass/Aiwaz the s and z are used at different times. In *The Equinox of the Gods*, Aleister Crowley used both spellings when writing about Aiwass/ Aiwaz.

The first thing Crowley wanted to get across to his readers was the fact that Aiwaz is not a human being. He is a supernatural, spirit being. He wrote this concerning him: "'Aiwaz' is an Intelligence possessed of power and knowledge absolutely beyond human experience; and therefore Aiwaz is a Being worthy, as the current use of the word allows, of the title of a God, yea verily and amen, of a God."21 Crowley not only wanted his readers to know that Aiwaz was a God, but that he was the head of the Silver Star: "I now incline to believe that Aiwass is not only the God or Demon or Devil once held holy in Sumer, and mine own Guardian Angel, but also a man as I am, insofar as He uses a human body to make his magical link with Mankind, whom He loves, and that He is thus an Ipsissimus, the Head of the A.A."22

Crowley wrote that Aiwaz is a God and the head of the Silver Star. The head of the Silver Star then is Satan. Two quotes will be repeated here from a previous chapter. First, you must know that *Rituel de la haute Magie* means *Ritual of High Magic*. Eliphas Levi wrote a book that had two parts in it. It was called *Dogma and Ritual of High Magic*. The "Ritual" section is part two. The book was later renamed *Transcendental Magic*, which has been quoted from already. The ritual section of *Transcendental Magic* had for its beginning page a photo of the Devil as drawn by Levi. Crowley claimed that he, as Levi in a previous incarnation, was the one who drew it: "Look at the frontispiece to my *Ritual de la haute Magie*, where I have figured the Devil of the Tarot as Baphomet."23 He went on to say that Baphomet was also called Ayin, and that Ayin was Aiwaz, and that Aiwaz was none other than Satan himself. He wrote: "When I was Levi, I drew myself as *Ayin* or Baphomet, 'The Devil,' with Beast's Head....This *Ayin* then is my Phallic Will, my Holy Guardian Angel, Aiwaz, who was afterwards called Satan."24 Satan, then, is Crowley's Holy Guardian Angel, head of the Silver Star, who dictated *The Book of the Law* to him. Crowley called Aiwaz "Devil" and "Lord" in *The Magical Record of the Beast*: "Come, Come, Come, Aiwaz! Come, thou Devil our Lord!"25 Then he called him his creator: "I write thy Name, Aiwaz, mine Angel appointed, only that I may be mindful of Thee, that art Creator, Preserver and Destroyer of my Soul..."26 Finally, Crowley calls him God, Devil, Lord, and Aiwaz all at once: "I sing for God, our Devil, our Lord, Aiwaz..."27 Not surprisingly, Crowley also wrote,when writing about the woman he was living with in *The Magical Record of the Beast*: "...your Lord the Devil possess you to the utmost..."28

Crowley did not guard Aiwaz's identity in that book, mainly because he didn't expect people to read it, according to his biographer John Symonds. That's why he wrote that he ate his woman's excrement during a magical ceremony in that book. Can you believe Jimmy Page wants to know how anyone can call Crowley evil? Crowley wrote about the excrement on page 235 of *The Magical Record of the Beast*. I will not quote it. What he had to say is horrific to the human mind; enough to make you physically sick. I can remember Cheech and Chong joking about doing that in the early seventies. Crowley, however, was not joking, he was serious about it as part of Magick. Yes, Jimmy, Crowley was about as evil as one can get. This is the same man the Beatles have on the front of Sgt. Pepper's Lonely Hearts Club band album; because he is one of the people they liked.

Now that we have seen from Crowley's writings that Aiwaz was his Holy Guardian Angel, Satan, the Devil, and that he is the head of the Silver Star, let's look at his role as author of *The Book of the Law*. Crowley wrote the following, describing himself as a writing medium: "There is a being called Aiwaz, an intelligence discarnate, who wrote this *Book of the Law*, using my ears and hand. His mind is certainly superior to my own in knowledge and in power, for he has dominated me and taught me ever since."29 Of course Satan taught him, knowing that teaching would pass on to Jimmy Page and inevitably, countless fans of Led Zeppelin. I am not the only one who knows these things. I merely decided to expose it. The best or worst is yet to come. In the next quote, Crowley calls him the author and his Angel: "I lay claim to be the sole authority competent to decide disputed points with regard to the Book of the Law, seeing that its Author, Aiwaz, is none other than mine own Holy Guardian Angel, to Whose Knowledge and Conversation I have attained, so that I have exclusive access to Him."30 Crowley wrote that statement several years after penning *The Book of the Law*.

Aleister Crowley presented Aiwaz to his readers as his Holy Guardian Angel, Satan, the Devil, the head of the Silver Star, and author of the Book of the Law. The Devil, then, is the very cornerstone of the Silver Star. Crowley wrote what he believed *The Book of the Law* proves: "This Book proves: there is a Person thinking and acting in a praeterhuman manner, either without a body of flesh, or with the power of communicating telepathically with men and inscrutably directing their actions."31 Once he had decided to promote the book, and its Law of Thelema, Crowley wrote: "This book is reproduced in facsimile, in order that there shall be no possibility of corrupting it. Here, then, we have an absolutely fixed and definite standpoint for the foundation of an universal religion."32 This universal religion, of course, is Magick, based on the Qabalah, as will be seen. According to Aleister Crowley and other magicians before him, no matter where you go in the world, the song remains the same; Magick is being practiced. What makes *The Book of the Law* its foundation in Crowley's mind is the fact that Magick is being presented anew by the Silver Star in the "Law of Thelema." As he wrote, he was committed to spreading that law everywhere:

"For today, if I were an ambassador, versed profoundly in science, financially armed and socially stainless, I should be able to execute my will by pressure upon all classes of powerful people, to make this comment carry conviction to thinkers, and to publish *The Book of the Law* in every part of the world."33 *The Book of the Law*, Crowley wrote, is the most important of the documents of the A.A. (Argenteum Astrum): "...it is the First and Greatest of those Class A publications of A.A. of which is not to be altered so much as the style of a letter."34 *The Book of the Law* is contained in *The Equinox, Vol. I, No.10*. Therefore, when one reads in this book that *The Equinox* is the most important set of writings in the A.A., and that *The Book of the Law* is the greatest of the publications of the A.A., there is no contradiction. The one is tied to the other.

THE TEXT OF THE BOOK

Aiwaz brought *The Book of the Law*, representative of the satanic trinity, in three chapters. The first chapter contains the words of "Nuit." The second chapter is from "Hadit," and the third is from "Ra-Hoor-Khuit," who is Horus. Nuit is the goddess and Hadit and Horus are both Satan. This will be explained thoroughly in the next chapter. This trinity is the same as Isis (Nuit), Osiris (Hadit), and Horus (Ra-Hoor-Khuit).

THE AEONS

As a result of the writing of the book, with its trinity, Crowley believed a new epoch in the history of mankind was beginning; an "Aeon." *The Book of the Law* was to assist Crowley in establishing a new form of magical, universal religion; with the Devil behind it all, though he is referred to with a multiplicity of names. The name of the god is the exterior manifestation of the interior being, Satan. This aeon is called the "Aeon of Horus." Crowley utilizes the Egyptian, Isis, Osiris, Horus trinity to describe the 3 phases of the history of man. What he presented to his readers first, is the period or "Aeon of Isis" which lasted 2,000 years. Crowley referred to the Aeon of Isis in his commentary to *The Book of the Law*: "Now the 'pagan' period is that of Isis; a pastoral, natural period of simple magic."35 That quote is consistent with the lyrics Robert Plant sang in the song "Ramble On" from *Led Zeppelin II*. He sang of that time long "ago" during the"days" he calls "old" that "Magick" ruled the "air;" between 2:45 and 2:51 of the song.

The second period of time is called the "Aeon of Osiris," that Crowley wrote ended in 1904. He referred to it as: "Next with Buddha, Christ, and others there came in the Equinox of Osiris; when sorrow and death are the principal objects of man's thought, and his magical formula is that of sacrifice."36 He generally referred to the Aeon of Osiris as the Aeon of Christianity. This is the Aeon of the Dying God. It is symbolized by the going down of the sun. When the sun sets and completely disappears, it has died. When it comes up in the morning, it has resurrected. Since Osiris is an Egyptian Sun God, the sun setting has now become an illustration of the death of the old Aeon of Osiris. The sunset is now illustrative of the new Aeon of Horus. Horus is symbolized by the Hawk. He (Satan) hates Christ. In the third chapter of *The Book of the Law* the Devil said: "With my Hawk's head I peck at the eyes of Jesus as he hangs upon the cross."37 He can be seen flying in the beginning of the "No Quarter" video.

The Aeon or "Equinox" (he used the terms interchangeably) of Horus, according to Crowley, began, for those in the Silver Star, in 1904, as the result of his writing of *The Book of the Law*. He described the Equinox of Horus this way: "Now with Mohammed perhaps as its forerunner, comes in the Equinox of Horus, the young child who rises strong and conquering (with his twin Harpocrates) to avenge Osiris, and bring on the age of strength and splendour."38 Avenging Osiris refers to the subjective Egyptian story. In Egyptian religious tradition, Osiris impregnates Isis, who is his mother, sister, and daughter. The evil Set then murders Osiris. In Qabalistic symbolism, Osiris dies and is born again as Horus, through Isis. This will be explained in the next chapter. The theological trinity that Crowley was most attracted to was Isis, Osiris, and Horus. Crowley knew, looking at the trinity Qabalistically, that Osiris and Horus were both Satan; and that Isis was his female consort (although in reality she doesn't exist). Again, it is this "trinity" that is presented in *The Book of the Law*.

THE LAW OF THELEMA

The Book of the Law is the main vehicle for the Silver Star's proclamation of the Law of Thelema. The most important concept presented by the book, as expounded by Crowley is the law of "Do What Thou Wilt." This phrase is the first half of the statement "Do What Thou Wilt Shall Be the Whole of the Law," taken from verse 40 of the first chapter of the book. I am going to make it clear that "Do What Thou Wilt" does not mean "do as you please." This phrase is very theological; it means to do your will according to the universal will. According to Crowley, we will be looking at the universal will of the godhead (the Devil) for the members of the Silver Star and their initiates in three specific areas; sex, drugs, and occupation. Subsequent to that, we will look finally at the will of the Devil for the Silver Star to stomp out Biblical Christianity.

"Do What Thou Wilt" means to do your True Will, as predetermined by the godhead of Magick. The word Thelema is a Greek word for "Will." The following passage is an introduction to the Law of Thelema written by Crowley in an editorial in his *Equinox Vol. III, No. 1*:

"Do what thou wilt shall be the whole of the Law.

The world needs religion.

Religion must represent Truth, and celebrate it.

This truth is of two orders: one, concerning Nature external to Man; two, concerning Nature internal to Man.

Existing religions, especially Christianity, are based on primitive ignorance of the facts, particularly of external Nature.

Celebrations must conform to the custom and nature of the people.

Christianity has destroyed the joyful celebrations, characterized by music, dancing, feasting, and making love; and has kept only the melancholy.

The Law of Thelema offers a religion which fulfils all necessary conditions.

The philosophy and metaphysics of Thelema are sound, and offer a solution of the deepest problems of humanity.

The science of Thelema is orthodox; it has no false theories of Nature, no false fables of the origin of things.

The psychology and ethics of Thelema are perfect. It has destroyed the damnable delusion of Original Sin, making every one unique, independent, supreme, and sufficient.

The Law of Thelema is given in the Book of the Law.

[EQUINOX I, VII, and X.]

THE EQUINOX has been founded to promulgate and demonstrate this Law.

The A.A., or Great White Brotherhood, through Whom this Law was obtained, is a Body of the highest Initiates, pledged to aid mankind.

It offers instruction in the Way of Spiritual Progress and Illumination to individual seekers.

The work of the A.A. is called Scientific Illuminism.

This may be briefly expressed by quoting Its motto:

'The method of Science; the aim of Religion.'

Every seeker is taught how to realize Truth for himself, by means accurate and well tested.

The O.T.O. is the first of the great religious Societies to accept the Law. It trains groups by way of progressive initiation.

THE EQUINOX publishes all instructions and pronouncements of the A.A. and O.T.O. It also publishes such poetry, drama, fiction, and essays, as are sympathetic to this programme, so far as space permits.

THE EQUINOX is so called, firstly, because it is the Comment upon the Word of the New Aeon, Thelema, which was given at the Equinox of the Gods, when the Crowned and Conquering Child, Horus, took the place of the Dying God, Osiris. (The Equinox marks a period of a fresh influx of Force from our Father the SUN.)"39 (Again, Crowley said the sun is the symbol of Satan.)

The following is Crowley's message of the Master Therion (himself). Master Therion means "Great Beast." In the text, he defines for his students the concept of "Do What Thou Wilt:"

LIBER II
THE MESSAGE OF THE MASTER THERION

"Do what thou wilt shall be the whole of the Law.'

'There is no Law beyond Do what thou wilt.'

'The word of the law is Thelema.'

Thelema - means Will.

The Key to this Message is this word-Will. The first obvious meaning of this Law is confirmed by antithesis:

'The word of Sin is Restriction.'

Again: 'Thou hast no right but to do thy will. Do that and no other shall say nay. For pure will, unassuaged of purpose, delivered from the lust of result, is every way perfect.'

Take this carefully; it seems to imply a theory that if every man and every woman did his and her will - the true will - there would be no clashing. 'Every man and every woman is a star,' and each star moves in an appointed path without interference. There is plenty of room for all; it is only disorder that creates confusion.

From these considerations it should be clear that 'Do what thou wilt' does not mean 'Do what you like.' It is the apotheosis of Freedom; but it is also the strictest possible bond.

Do what thou wilt - then do nothing else. Let nothing deflect thee from that austere and holy task. Liberty is absolute to do thy will; but seek to do any other thing whatever, and instantly obstacles must arise. Every act that is not in definite course of that one orbit is erratic, an hindrance. Will must not be two, but one.

Note further that this will is not only to be pure, that is, single, as explained above, but also 'unassuaged of purpose.' This strange phrase must give us pause. It may mean that any purpose in the will would damp it; clearly the "lust of result" is a thing from which it must be delivered.

But the phrase may also be interpreted as if it read 'with purpose unassuaged'- i.e., with tireless energy. The conception is, therefore, of an eternal motion, infinite and unalterable. It is Nirvana, only dynamic instead of static-

and this comes to the same thing in the end.

The obvious practical task of the magician is then to discover what his will really is, so that he may do it in this manner, and he can best accomplish this by the practices of Liber Thisarb (see Equinox I. VII. 105) or such others as may from one time to another be appointed.

It should now be perfectly simple for everybody to understand the Message of the Master Therion.

Thou must (I) find out what is thy Will. (2) Do that Will with (a) one-pointedness, (b) detachment, (c) peace.

Then, and then only, art thou in harmony with the Movement of Things, thy will part of , and therefore equal to, the Will of God. And since the will is but the dynamic aspect of the self, and since two different selves could not possess identical wills; then, if thy will be God's will, *Thou art That*.

There is but one other word to explain. Elsewhere it is written - surely for our great comfort – 'Love is the law, love under will.'

This is to be taken as meaning that while Will is the Law, the nature of that Will is Love. But this Love is as it were a by-product of that Will; it does not contradict or supersede that Will; and if apparent contradiction should arise in any crisis, it is the Will that will guide us aright. Lo, while in the Book of the Law is much of Love, there is no word of Sentimentality. Hate itself is almost like Love! Fighting most certainly is Love! 'As brothers fight ye!' All the manly races of the world understand this. The Love of Liber Legis is always bold, virile, even orgiastic. There is delicacy, but it is the delicacy of strength. Mighty and terrible and glorious as it is, however, it is but the pennon upon the sacred lance of Will, the damascened inscription upon the swords of the Knight-monks of Thelema.

Love is the law, love under will."40

His next commentary in the context of *The Equinox, Vol. III, No. I,* focuses on the "freedom" of the law:

THE LAW OF LIBERTY

"Do what thou wilt shall be the whole of the Law.

I. I am often asked why I begin my letters in this way. No matter whether I am writing to my lady or to my butcher, always I begin with these eleven words. Why, how else should I begin? What other greeting could be so glad? Look, brother, we are free! Rejoice with me, sister, there is no law beyond Do what thou wilt!

II. I write this for those who have not read our Sacred Book, the Book of the Law, or for those who, reading it, have somehow failed to understand its perfection. For there are many matters in this Book, and the Glad Tidings are now here, now there, scattered throughout the Book as the Stars are scattered through the field of Night. Rejoice with me, all ye people! At the very head of the Book stands the great charter of our godhead: 'Every man and every woman is a star.' We are all free, all independent, all shining gloriously, each one a radiant world. Is not that good tidings?

Then comes the first call of the Great Goddess Nuit, Lady of the Starry heaven, who is also Matter in its deepest metaphysical sense, who is the infinite in whom all we live and move and have our being. Hear Her first summons to us men and women: 'Come forth, O children, under the stars, and take your fill of love! I am above you and in you. My ecstasy is in yours. My joy is to see your joy.' Later She explains the mystery of sorrow: 'For I am divided for love's sake, for the chance of union.'

'This is the creation of the world, that the pain of division is as nothing, and the joy of dissolution all.'

It is shown later how this can be, how death itself is an ecstasy like love, but more intense, the reunion of the soul with its true self.

And what are the conditions of this joy, and peace, and glory? Is ours the gloomy asceticism of the Christian, and the Buddhist, and the Hindu? Are we walking in eternal fear lest some 'sin' should cut us off from 'grace'? By no means.

'Be ye goodly therefore: dress ye all in fine apparel; eat rich foods and drink sweet wines, and wines that foam! Also, take your fill and will of love as ye will, when, where, and with whom ye will! But always unto me.'

This is the only point to bear in mind, that every act must be a ritual, an act of worship, a sacrament. Live as the kings and princes, crowned and un-crowned, of this world, have always lived, as masters always live; but let it not be self-indulgence; make your self-indulgence your religion.

When you drink and dance and take delight, you are not being 'im-moral,' you are not 'risking you immortal soul;' you are fulfilling the precepts of our holy religion-provided only that you remember to regard your actions in this light. Do not lower yourself and destroy and cheapen your pleasure by leaving out the supreme joy, the consciousness of the Peace that passeth understanding. Do not embrace mere Marian or Melusine; she is Nuit Herself, specially concen-trated and incarnated in a human form to give you infinite love, to bid you taste even on earth the Elixir of Immortality. 'But ecstasy be mine and joy on earth; ever To me! To me!'

Again She speaks: 'Love is the law, love under will.' Keep pure your highest ideal; strive ever toward it without allowing aught to stop you or turn you aside, even as a star sweeps upon its incalculable and infinite course of glory, and all is Love. The Law of your being becomes Light, Life, Love and

Liberty. All is peace, all is harmony and beauty, all is joy.

For hear, how gracious is the Goddess: 'I give unimaginable joys on earth: certainty, not faith, while in life, upon death; peace unutterable, rest, ecstasy; nor do I demand aught in sacrifice.'

Is not this better than the death-in-life of the slaves of the Slave-Gods, as they go oppressed by consciousness of 'sin,' wearily seeking or simulating wearisome and tedious 'virtues?'

With such, we who have accepted the Law of Thelema have nothing to do. We have heard the Voice of the Star Goddess: 'I love you! I yearn to you! Pale or purple, veiled or voluptuous, I who am all pleasure and purple, and drunkenness of the innermost sense, desire you. Put on the wings, and arouse the coiled splendour within you; come unto me!'
And thus She ends:

'Sing the rapturous love-song unto me! Burn to me perfumes! Wear to me jewels! Drink to me, for I love you! I love you! I am the blue-lidded daughter of Sunset; I am the naked brilliance of the voluptuous night-sky. To me! To me!'
And with these words 'The Manifestation of Nuit is at an end.'

III. In the next chapter of our book is given the word of Hadit, who is the complement of Nuit. He is eternal energy, the Infinite Motion of Things, the central core of all being. The manifested Universe comes from the marriage of Nuit and Hadit; without this could no thing be. This eternal, this perpetual marriage-feast is then the nature of things themselves; and therefore everything that is, is a crystallization of divine ecstasy.

Hadit tells us of Himself: 'I am the flame that burns in every heart of man, and in the core of every star.' He is then your own inmost divine self; it is you, and not another, who are lost in the constant rapture of the embraces of Infinite Beauty.

....Lift yourselves up, my brothers and sisters of the earth! Put beneath your feet all fears, all qualms, all hesitancies! Lift yourselves up! Come forth, free and joyous, by night and day, to do your will; for 'There is no law beyond Do what thou wilt.' Lift yourselves up! Walk forth with us in Light and life and Love and Liberty, taking our pleasure as Kings and Queens in Heaven and on Earth.

The sun is arisen; the specter of the ages has been put to flight. 'The word of Sin is Restriction,' or as it has been otherwise said on this text: That is Sin, to hold thine holy spirit in!

Go on, go on in thy might; and let no man make thee afraid.
Love is the law, love under will."41

DO WHAT THOU WILT SHALL BE THE WHOLE OF THE LAW

The following sections of this chapter are going to focus specifically on the practical aspect of living out the Law of Thelema, which again, is symbolized by the phrase "Do What Thou Wilt." Israel Regardie wrote of this in his biography on Crowley: "This is the major implication of Crowley's 'Do what thou wilt shall be the whole of the law.' It means self-regulation and autonomy on all levels."42 The specific areas of this self-regulation and autonomy that will be focused on, again, are: occupation, drugs and alcohol, and sexuality, relative to the individual, and then spiritual warfare against Christianity. The songs "For Your Life" and "Immigrant Song" will be part of the said discussion. "For Your Life" will focus on drugs, specifically cocaine, while "Immigrant Song" will be discussed in the light of spiritual warfare.

DO WHAT THOU WILT - OCCUPATION

The following excerpt is from Aleister Crowley's book, *Diary of a Drug Fiend*, which I am quoting because Crowley assists a character in the story in coming to the realization of his "true will." He helps him find out what his true will is according to the universe (Satan) - relative to occupation. Aleister Crowley's character in the story is "Big Lion:"

TRUE WILL

"I began to laugh despite myself.

'Well,' I said, puffing at my cigar, 'I do really wish you'd let me know what this is all about. Has Lloyd George resigned?'

'No,' said Big Lion, 'it's just you!'

'What about me?' I retorted.

'Why, your success, of course,' said Sister Cypris.

Something, of course, quite obvious to them was hidden from my dull understanding.

I turned on Basil point-blank.

'What success?' I said. 'It's true I do see my way through a formula that's been bothering me. But I don't see how you know about it. Do Hermes and Dionysus comprise a knowledge of the differential calculus in their attainments?'

'It's very simple,' said the Big Lion. 'It involves a knowledge of nothing but the Law; and the Law, after all, is nothing but plainest common sense. Do you remember my asking you before tiffin what was your true will?'

'Yes,' I said, 'I do. And I told you then, and I tell you again now, that I haven't the time to think about things like that.'

'That fact,' he retorted, 'was quite enough to assure me that you had discovered it.'

'Look here,' I said, 'you're a good sort and all that, but you are really a bit queer, and half the time I don't know what you are driving at. Can't you put it in plain English?"

'With all the pleasure in life,' he returned. 'Just look at the facts for a moment. Fact one: Your maternal grandfather is a mechanical genius. Fact two: From your earliest childhood, subjects of this sort have exercised the strongest fascination for you. Fact three: Whenever you get off those subjects, you are unhappy, unsuccessful, and get into various kinds of mess. Fact four: The moment the war gives you your opportunity, you throw up medicine and go back to engineering. Fact five: You graduate reluctantly from the bench to the pilot's seat, and your squad commander himself sees that it's a case of a square peg in a round hole. Fact six: As soon as the Armistice throws you on your beam ends, you get busy again with the idea of the helicopter. Fact seven: You are swept off your feet by coming into a fortune and immediately go astray with drugs-clear evidence that you have missed your road. Fact eight: As soon as your mind is cleansed by the boredom of Telepylus of all its artificial ideas, it returns to its natural bent. The idea of the helicopter comes back with such a rush that you let your breakfast get cold, you don't know your wife when she brings it, and you can talk about nothing else. For the first time in your life your self-consciousness is obliterated. You even start to explain your ideas to me, though I know nothing whatever of the subject. It doesn't require any particular genius to see that you have discovered your true will."43

"'....My god!' I said at last. 'What we owe to Big Lion!'

She shook her head.

'No,' she said, with a strange smile, 'we've helped him as much as he's helped us - helped him to do his will. The secret of his power is that he doesn't exist for himself. His force flows through him unhindered."44

"....But the culminating joy of my heart was the completeness of the solution of all my problems. There was no possibility of a relapse, because the cause of my downfall had been permanently removed. I could understand perfectly how it was that Basil could take a dose of heroin or cocaine, could indulge in hashish, ether, or opium as simply and usefully as the ordinary man can order a cup of strong black coffee when he happens to want to work late at night. He had become completely master of himself, because he had ceased to oppose himself to the current of spiritual will-power of which he was the vehicle. He had no fear or fascination with regard to any of these drugs. He knew that these two qualities were aspects of a single reaction; that of emotion to ignorance. He could use cocaine as a fencing-master uses a rapier, as an expert, without danger of wounding himself.

About a fortnight after our first visit to the tower, a group of us was sitting on the terrace of the Strangers' House. It was bright moonlight, and the peasants from the neighboring cottages had come in to enjoy the hospitality of the Abbey. Song and dance were in full swing. Basil and I fell into a quiet chat.

'How long is it, by the way,' he said, 'since you last took a dose of anything?'

'I'm not quite sure,' I answered, dreamily watching Lou and Lala, who had arrived a week since with the apparatus I required for my experiments, as they waltzed together on the court. They were both radiant. It seemed as if the moon had endowed them with her pure subtlety and splendour.

'I asked you,' continued Big Lion, pulling at a big meerschaum and amber pipe of the Boer pattern, which he reserved for late at night, 'because I want you to take the fullest advantage of your situation. You have been tried in the crucible and come out pure gold. But it won't do for you to forget the privileges you have won by your ordeal. Do you remember what it says in the Book of the Law?

'I am the Snake that giveth Knowledge and Delight and bright glory, and stir the hearts of men with drunkenness. To worship me take wine and strange drugs whereof I will tell my prophet, and be drunk thereof! They shall not harm ye at all.'

'Yes,' I said slowly, 'and I thought it a bit daring; might tempt people to be foolhardy, don't you think?'

'Of course,' agreed Basil, 'if you read it carelessly, and act on it rashly, with the blind faith of a fanatic; it might very well lead to trouble. But nature is full of devices for eliminating anything that cannot master its environment. The words 'to worship me' are all-important. The only excuse for using a drug of any sort, whether it's quinine or Epsom-salt, is to assist nature to overcome some obstacle to her proper functions. The danger of the so-called habit-forming drugs is that they fool you into trying to dodge the toil essential to spiritual and intellectual development. But they are not simply man-traps. There is nothing in nature which cannot be used for our benefit, and it is up to us to use it wisely. Now, in the work you have been doing in the last week, heroin might have helped you to concentrate your mind, and cocaine to overcome the effects of fatigue....As a matter of fact, I am consoled in my moments of weakness and depression by the knowledge that I am so bitterly abused and hated. It proves to me that my work, whether mistaken or not, is at least worth while. But that's a digression. Let's get back to the words 'to worship me.' They mean that things like heroin and alcohol may be and should be used for the purpose of worshiping, that is, entering into communion with, the 'Snake that giveth Knowledge and Delight and bright glory' which is the genius which lies 'in the core of every star.' And, 'Every man and every woman is a star.' The taking of a drug should be a carefully thought out and purposeful religious act. Experience alone can teach you the right conditions in which the act is legitimate, that is, when it assists you to do your will."45 "….But as the Book of the Law says, 'success is your proof.' When you resort to such potent and dangerous expedients for increasing your natural powers, you must make sure that the end justifies the means."46

Summing up the situation, Peter Pendragon rejoices in the fact that he had gone to the Abbey of Thelema to learn about his true will, relative to occupation, as well as to realize that drugs and alcohol could be used in a positive way once a person was knowledgeable of what his true will really was. He says: "I made the discovery that I was after all a profoundly religious man. All my life I had been looking for a creed which did not offend my moral or intellectual sense. And now I had come to understand the mysterious language of the people of the Abbey of Thelema."47 (A farmhouse Crowley lived in at Cefalu, Sicily, and had his disciples come there to practice Magick, beginning in 1920. Mussolini deported Crowley because of a strange death there.) He went on to say: "….Each of our lives was one, individual, and eternal, but each possessed its necessary and intimate relation with the other, and both with the whole universe."48

This Abbey of Thelema in Sicily, was of interest to Jimmy Page. He flew there to see it because he considered buying the place. I do not know if he did or not, but if I had to guess, I would say yes. Richard Cole wrote: "In July and August 1975, Robert and Jimmy had taken their families on a vacation to Rhodes by way of Switzerland and Morocco. Jimmy, however, had then left the others on the Greek island to fly to Italy, primarily to look at a farmhouse in Sicily once owned by Aleister Crowley that he was considering buying."49 It was while Page was at the Abbey of Thelema in Sicily that Robert Plant and his wife had that terrible car accident of theirs, in which Robert sustained a severe ankle fracture and his wife a fractured skull. Page's daughter was unharmed.

DO WHAT THOU WILT - DRUGS AND ALCOHOL

As you are already aware, the Law of Thelema promotes, through the writings of Crowley, the use of alcohol and narcotics for religious purposes, as well as for doing one's true will. In this section I will give you several examples of Aleister Crowley promoting the use of heroin and cocaine to his readers. Then I will show examples of alcohol and drugs being promoted by Led Zeppelin in their music. To illustrate the impact on the mind that narcotics often have, consider this quote from Crowley recorded in his *Diary of a Drug Fiend*: "I seem to remember asking myself if I was insane, and answering, 'Of course I am-sanity is a compromise. Sanity is the thing that keeps one back.'"50 Well, you have to at least give him credit for admitting it. The following is what Crowley wrote in the beginning of the book on page one:

"This is a true story.

It has been rewritten only so far as was necessary to conceal personalities.

It is a terrible story; but it is also a story of hope and of beauty.

It reveals with startling clearness the abyss on which our civilization trembles.

But the self-same Light illuminates the path of humanity: it is our own fault is we go over the brink.

This story is also true not only of one kind of human weakness, but (by analogy) of all kinds; and for all alike there is but one way of salvation.

As Glanvil says: Man is not subjected to the angels nor even unto death utterly, save through the weakness of his own feeble will.

Do what thou wilt shall be the whole of the Law.

Aleister Crowley"51

COCAINE

Crowley wrote that the story in his book was based on a true one. Drug use was encouraged by him as a good thing, and Cocaine was one of his favorites. He told his readers that it took away his depression: "But as I raised my head; as the sudden, the instantaneous madness of cocaine swept from my nostrils to my brain-that's a line of poetry, but I can't help it-get on!-the depression lifted from my mind like the sun coming out of the clouds."52 He said it helped his confidence: "When one is on one's cocaine honeymoon, one is really, to a certain extent, superior to one's fellows. One attacks every problem with perfect confidence."53 He describes the cocaine high as wickedness: "The first hint of fatigue sent one's hand to one's pocket. One sniff which gave us a sensation of the most exquisitely delicious wickedness, and we were on fourth speed again!"54 Is it any wonder Devil worshipers love cocaine? Speaking of the Devil, Crowley writes concerning him and his girlfriend: "I wish I could give you an idea of the sparkling quality of everything she said and did. Her eyes glittered, her lips twittered, her cheeks glowed like fresh blown buds in spring. She was the spirit of cocaine incarnate; cocaine made flesh. Her mere existence made the Universe infinitely exciting. Say, if you like, she was possessed of the devil!"55 According to Crowley, you have never enjoyed kissing until you've been high on coke: "Until you've got your mouth full of cocaine, you don't know what kissing is."56 The lies get worse: "Happiness lies within one's self, and the way to dig it out is cocaine."57 He wrote that coke made him feel secure: "I had a swift pang of alarm. Could something be wrong? But the cocaine assured me that everything was all right."58 Finally, Crowley does admit there is a problem with coke: "But the trouble about cocaine is this; that it's almost impossible to take it in moderation as almost anyone, except an American, can take whisky. Every dose makes you better and better. It destroys one's power of calculation."59

HEROIN

Heroin was another favorite drug of Aleister Crowley's. Again, it's been said that Crowley had such a tolerance for the drug that he would take doses that could kill several other people at the same time. One of the things it did for Crowley was to make him feel superior to everyone else. He wrote: "The heroin had begun to take hold. We felt ourselves crowned with colossal calm....The sense of our superiority to mankind was constantly present."60 Now there's an attitude that breeds unity among people. Crowley can't go long without making reference to his hero, Satan. In this next quote, you will see clearly from the pen of Crowley that there is a direct correlation between his use of it and his love for Satan and his attitude of pride. One of the obvious things about narcotics that people often dismiss is their spiritual element. They do take the mind in the Anti-Christ direction. Why did Christ make them? To allow for the possibility, as an act of one's will. Here is the heroin quote where Crowley mentions satanic pride:

"I had no idea at the time that this sudden revulsion of feeling was due to a mysterious premonition of the physiological effects of heroin in destroying love. Definitely stimulating things like alcohol, hashish and cocaine give free range to Cupid. Their destructive effect on him is simply due to the reaction. One is in debt, so to speak, because one has outrun the constable.

"But what I may call the philosophical types of dope, of which morphine and heroin are the principal examples, are directly inimical to active emotion and emotional action. The normal human feelings are transmuted into what seem on the surface their spiritual equivalents. Ordinary good feeling becomes universal benevolence; a philanthropy which is infinitely tolerant because the moral code has become meaningless for it. A more than Satanic pride swells in one's soul."61

Mr. Crowley knew nothing of humility before anyone. He was a true son of Satan. He went on to speak of heroin as stabilizing his high: "You must understand that we were already excited to the highest point. The effect of the heroin had been to steady us in that state."62 Crowley said that heroin makes you a master, but also apathetic or non-caring: "With cocaine, one is indeed master of everything; but everything matters intensely. With heroin, the feeling of mastery increases to such a point that nothing matters at all."63 Again, Crowley recognizes heroin use as containing a religious element: "She offered me a pinch of heroin with the air of communicating some exquisitely esoteric sacrament; and I accepted it and measured her a similar dose on my own hand as if some dim delirious desire devoured us. We took it not because we needed it; but because we needed it; but because the act of consummation was, so to speak, and act of religion."64 That is exactly what the Devil told him to do in *The Book of the Law*, to advertise drugs he wanted man to use, along with the lie that they were harmless. Here, again, is what the Devil said: "I am the Snake that giveth Knowledge & Delight and bright glory, and stir the hearts of men with drunkenness. To worship me take wine and strange drugs whereof I will tell my prophet, & be drunk thereof! They shall not harm ye at all."65 Do you see what had happened? Satan had complete control of Aleister Crowley, and he said in *The Book of the Law* that he wanted his followers to take drugs he would tell his prophet of. You read of Crowley's advocating cocaine and heroin. Do you see who was advocating those drugs to Crowley's readers? The Devil! Crowley was merely an incarnate Lucifer. Well did Crowley make the statement that heroin was the: "Miracle drug of the Devil."66 Crowley knew he was serving and writing for the Devil, and he believed it was the Devil's will that he do so. He wrote: "My True Will was, I now know, to be the Beast, 666, a Magus, the Word of the Aeon, Thelema; to proclaim this new Law to mankind."67

So far, we have looked at Satan's describing his will in a person's life as far as his occupation is concerned. Yes, Christ did create men with certain abilities and aptitudes that suit them for specific types of professions, and the Devil plays on that through Crowley. Believe me, multitudes of Americans are studying his writings and advocating them to others. Don't be fooled just because you may not be in touch with this crowd. Secondly, we have looked at the Devil's will relative to dangerous narcotic use. Let's take a look at how his message concerning drugs has made it into the mind of the Led Zeppelin fan.

PRESENCE – "FOR YOUR LIFE"

In this section of the chapter, we are going to look at several Led Zeppelin songs that promote drug and alcohol use to its listeners. I have titled it "For Your Life," because that song contains a blatant command to do cocaine, coming from the mouth of Robert Plant.

In the film, *The Song Remains the Same*, at the end of "The Rain Song," Robert Plant picks two joints up off the stage and holds them up to the fans and nods his approval before throwing them backstage. Between 0:15 and 0:20 of the song "Going to California," from the fourth album, Plant sings that his "woman" "smoked" his "stuff" as well as "drank" his "wine." If he was commanding us teenagers in the seventies to do that, I certainly obeyed, like a disciple. I smoked several joints before Led Zeppelin finally came out on stage after sundown at 9:20 p.m. at Madison Square Garden in Manhattan on June 11th, 1977. That concert was one gigantic buzz. We got out of there at approximately 1 a.m. I didn't get home until 4:30 a.m.

In the song, "Houses of the Holy," from the *Physical Graffiti* album, Plant asks if the listener is "dizzy" while "stoned," between 1:56 and 1:59 of the song. As I quoted in the preface, Plant thinks being stoned aids the fan in picking up the band's message. This is why I believe he was telling the fans to take LSD 25 in the song, "Dazed and Confused," in the Led Zeppelin film and soundtrack. That will be addressed later.

On the *Houses of the Holy* album, Plant advocated drinking in "Dancing Days" and "The Ocean." In "Dancing Days" he sang that the "precedent" is drinking "booze" when "evening" begins its "glow," between 0:58 and 1:04 of the song. In "The Ocean" he sang of drinking "moonshine" at 0:34 of the song.

In the song, "For Your Life," from the *Presence* album, Robert Plant advocated the use of cocaine in blatant fashion. He wasn't as destructively blatant as Eric Clapton, but it was destructive nonetheless. At 0:54 of the song, he sings of a woman asking him if he wants it. Then he sings "cocaine" at 0:57 and "try it friend" between 1:02 and 1:06. Four times, at 2:39, 2:44, 4:05, and 4:11, Plant sings that we should "Do" some "when" we "wanna." At 5:34 into the song, he sings about not being able to "resist" it, and yielding to "flow." Just as teenagers sometimes yield to peer pressure, Plant sings of yielding to the drug, like the present "flow," or as others are at the same time.

In the *Physical Graffiti* song, "The Rover," he sings the word "trip" at 1:12 into the song. I believe he was referring to acid-LSD. Between 1:21 and 1:23 he sings that he had "always" known its purpose. That will be addressed later when we examine drug-induced hallucinations.

While Led Zeppelin was performing in concert at Cobo Hall in Detroit, Michigan, on July 12th 1973, "Misty Mountain Hop" was dedicated by Robert Plant to: "...the loss of brain cells."[68]

Jimmy Page is famous among Led Zeppelin fans for wearing the opium poppy on his concert outfits. This flower is a non-verbal command, in my opinion, from Page to the fan who can pick it up, to do Heroin. Ah, yes, the subtle power of suggestion is very effective, coming from one's guitar hero. Jimmy warned Richard Cole one time to stay away from it. He didn't. It eventually cost him his job as road manager. Page told Cole he thought he was hooked and Cole asked him if he tried to quit. Richard Cole discussed this in his book, *Stairway to Heaven - Led Zeppelin Uncensored*, He wrote: "'Heroin. I think I'm hooked. It's terrible.' 'Have you tried to stop?' 'I've tried, but I can't. It's a real bastard.'"[69] Crowley took it, Page took it, Cole took it, and wrote of Plant and Bonham taking it, and Page advertised it in concert for years. Satan promotes drug abuse, Crowley promoted it, and so does the music of Led Zeppelin. Why did Satan, Crowley and Led Zeppelin promote drugs and alcohol? Obviously, so people would get intoxicated. Why do they want people to get intoxicated? This is what Aleister Crowley said concerning it: "Intoxication is merely a way of communing with spirits."[70] That's what is behind it all, as you will read later.

The Book of the Law advocates drug and alcohol abuse to assist the student of Magick in occult endeavors.

DO WHAT THOU WILT - SEXUALITY

The Book of the Law, with the Devil as its author, couldn't have failed to approach the topic of sex with 'Do what thou wilt.' As important as sex is to our society, it is also important for it to be done safely. The Biblical presentation of sex, of course, is that it should only be enjoyed in the context of marriage. I did not write that for any reason except to show that most of us that came out of or are still in the rock culture have rebelled against that standard; myself included.

The Devil's presentation of his sexual standard, in *The Book of the Law* as well as the commentary on it written by Crowley under his influence, is the most destructive standard in existence. Crowley presents it as freedom; it is in fact the lowest form of perversion and slavery that a man or woman can be involved in. In verse 51 of the first chapter of the book, we read these words: "...take your fill and will of love as ye will, when, where and with whom ye will! But always unto me."71 I guess that meant with animals too, based on Crowley's admission of sex with a Great Dane. I will now present to you Crowley's commentary on the previous quote. First he says that children should be involved in sex as soon as possible: "Moreover, the Beast 666 adviseth that all children shall be accustomed from infancy to witness every type of sexual act, as also the process of birth, lest falsehood fog, and mystery stupefy, their minds, whose error else might thwart and misdirect the growth of their subconscious system of soul-symbolism."72 He went on to describe the words "as ye will" or in what method you desire: "This phrase abolishes the eleventh commandment, 'Not to be found out,' by authorizing incest, adultery, and pederasty, which everyone now practices with humiliating precautions, which perpetuate the schoolboy's enjoyment of an escapade, and make shame, slyness, cowardice and hypocrisy the conditions of success in life."73 Crowley wrote that "everyone" is involved in this kind of sexuality. This is merely a projection of his guilt, and it is a lie. Do I have to say anything about pederast? The notorious North American Man/Boy Love Association would make Crowley one of their chief members; if he were still alive today. The remainder of the verse is self-explanatory: "...when, where, and with whom ye will! But always unto me."74 The "with whom ye will" part of the verse definitely suits Led Zeppelin. Richard Cole wrote, in *Stairway to Heaven - Led Zeppelin Uncensored*: "...as for the married members of the band, most were able to at least temporarily overlook the fact that they had wives waiting for them back in England; if there were ever any guilt pangs, I never saw them."75 The "where" part means exactly that. Crowley wrote that people should have sex wherever they want to. It is almost unbelievable, but this is meant literally. Crowley wrote in his commentary: "Perhaps this permission is intended to indicate the propriety of performing the sexual act without shame or fear, not waiting for darkness or seeking secrecy, but by daylight in public places, as serenely as if it were a natural incident in a morning stroll."76 I beg the reader's pardon for my redundancy, but Aleister Crowley is the man about whom Jimmy Page asked how anyone could call him evil. Think about that for a moment.

If you think this is all very perverse, you are right. If you don't, I suggest you take a good look at who you are in league with. You may say, "Well...I don't believe in the Devil." Not yet you don't, but you will. Some individual's self perception is as God and they don't know it. It's almost as if they have their own throne they sit on as ruler of the universe and they proclaim that there is no Devil and no hell to fear. They may as well say there is no sun in the sky and that the earth does not rotate too. The Devil's existence does not depend on whether you choose to believe he is or not. He is either there or he isn't, and I am telling you that I do not believe he exists, I know he does. Your belief system has no bearing on it. He is not intimidated by a person's refusal to knowingly worship him. If he can get you to live a life of rebellion against God while refusing to believe he exists, he still has accomplished his goal. E.M. Bounds wrote, in his book, *Satan - His Personality, Power, and Overthrow*: "The devil's great device, his masterpiece of temptation, is to destroy faith in his own existence....He who denies or ignores the existence of the devil, puts a fatal bar to ultimate salvation, paralyzes all efforts in that direction, and gives one over, chained hand and foot, to the merciless foe whose existence has been denied and derided. Nothing advances Satan's work with more skillful and readier hands than to be ignorant of Satan and his ways. To escape his snare, we must not only have a strong faith in the fact that Satan is, but also must have a most intimate knowledge of him and of his plans and many-sided ways."77

C. S. Lewis, in his famous book, *The Screwtape Letters*, gave us his commentary on what it is to believe in the Devil's existence:

"The commonest question is whether I really 'believe in the Devil.'

Now, if by 'the Devil' you mean a power opposite to God and, like God, self-existent from all eternity, the answer is certainly No. There is no uncreated being except God. God has no opposite. No being could attain a 'perfect badness' opposite to the perfect goodness of God; for when you have taken away every kind of good thing (intelligence, will, memory, energy, and existence itself) there would be none of him left.

"The proper question is whether I believe in devils. I do. That is to say, I believe in angels, and I believe that some of these, by the abuse of their free will, have become enemies to God and, as a corollary, to us. These we may call devils. They do not differ in nature from good angels, but their nature is depraved. *Devil* is the opposite of *angel* only as Bad Man is the opposite of Good Man. Satan, the leader or dictator of devils, is the opposite, not of God, but of Michael....There are two equal and opposite errors into which our race can fall about the devils. One is to disbelieve in their existence. The other is to believe, and to feel an excessive and unhealthy interest in them. They themselves are equally pleased by both errors, and hail a materialist or a magician with the same delight."78

As a consequence, if a person does not believe in the Devil, he has only helped the Devil's cause in his or her life. The *Bible* makes it clear, that God does not extend any special mercy to those who are too cowardly to face the supernatural. Existentialism will land you in hell just as being a Satanist will. Existentialism is trusting in and living only for this mundane physical existence; and its rebellion against Christ.

The person therefore, who practices the type of sexuality presented by Satan and Crowley, are indeed lined up with the Devil against God. Aleister Crowley, the Prince of Perversion, calls this sexual code "wholesome." He wrote: "I confidently appeal to impartial observers to say whether the ideals of the Book are not cleaner, more wholesome, more human, and more truly moral than those of marriage as it is."79 Remember, Robert Plant, while singing "Whole Lotta Love" in *The Song Remains the Same* film and soundtrack, speaks of his "love" in inches and wants to "give" it to everyone. On March 22nd, 1973, while playing in concert in Essen, Germany, Robert Plant described the song "Dancing Days" as: "The innocent love of little schoolgirls and my perversion toward it. We love little schoolgirls, fourteen...or fifteen!"80 Would you have wanted your fourteen or fifteen year old daughter to fall into the hands of this twenty four year old singer and twenty nine year old guitarist who worship Satan? That's exactly how old they were in March of 1973. By the way, it wasn't romance and monogamous sex they were interested in either. We will look at that later.

At one point on one of their tours, they rented a ranch in Texas. They allegedly were running around the swimming pool area behind the house stark naked. The ranch owner came along with a shotgun and ran them off. Rest assured, I believe Crowley's morals are Jimmy Page's, and that Page's morals are Led Zeppelin's. All of these people have the moral code of the Anti-Christ and his father, the Devil. Again, Jimmy Page wants to know how anyone could call Crowley evil. Don't be fooled by any of his denials either. Jimmy Page has more of Aleister Crowley's writings than I do. Now I realize that there are some perverted standards presented by Crowley in this chapter and that they are not presented in the song, "Whole Lotta Love." Remember, however, that Page said mysticism has been present on their albums from the second album on. "Whole

Lotta Love" is on the second album. He also bought Crowley's house in 1970, a year after *Led Zeppelin II* was released. I really don't believe that Page is ignorant of Crowley's beliefs on sex. You can bet your eternal soul that Page has the book in his possession that I took those quotes out of.

LED ZEPPELIN III – "IMMIGRANT SONG"

On Led Zeppelin's earliest releases of their third album in 1970, *Led Zeppelin III*, Jimmy Page had "Do what thou wilt," taken from Satan and Crowley's *Book of the Law*, engraved in the runoff matrix of the album. In reference to this engraving, Steven Davis, in his *Hammer of the Gods*, wrote: "Jimmy was casting his spell."[81] This Aeon of Horus is a time of spiritual warfare for the Devil, Crowley, the Silver Star, and Led Zeppelin against "spiritual slavery;" i.e., Christianity. As Crowley wrote in *The World's Tragedy*:

"All I wish to do is justify my agreement with Shelly and Nietzsche in defining Christianity as the religious expression of the slave spirit in man.

I do not wish to argue that the doctrines of Jesus, they and they alone, have degraded the world to its present condition. I take it that Christianity is not only the cause but the symptom of slavery."[82]

Crowley calls Christianity slavery because he believes it restricts a man from fulfilling his "natural" desires, and *The Book of the Law* says: "The word of Sin is Restriction."[83] Sin in this context meaning restriction is a sin against the Law of Thelema. Crowley went on to say that this aeon was wartime against Christianity in *The Law is For All*: "Now this age is preeminently a 'time of war,' most of all now, when it is our work to overthrow the slave-gods."[84] Led Zeppelin, on their third album, the same one Page had "Do what thou wilt" engraved on, began the album with a song called "Immigrant Song." This song, subjectively speaking, makes direct reference to Norse Mythology. In Norse theology, Odin receives fallen warriors into "Valhalla." This Valhalla is the same as the Celtic "Avalon." In *Witchcraft, Magic, and Occultism*, W.B. Crow wrote: "THE NORSEMEN. The Norse, Germanic, Gothic, and Vandal peoples, which we can roughly include under the name of the Teutonic, developed a distinctive cult and mythology which chiefly centered in Germany, Denmark, Norway and Sweden....The Norsemen were warlike peoples. When not engaged in war they spent much of their time drinking, presided over by their chief, in halls set apart for their entertainment. After death they supposed that those that fell in battle would be transported to the great hall of Valhalla, where their chief god Odin sits enthroned. They were to be carried there on horseback by beautiful maidens called Valkyries."[85]

Those reading this book should understand that the members of Led

Zeppelin are most loyal to the Celtic branch of magic - not the Norse. Objectively speaking, Led Zeppelin perceived Odin and his son Thor, as Satan. I will show this later on. Robert Plant, in the "Immigrant Song" calls out to "Valhalla" and says he is "coming," between 0:34 and 0:39 of the song. He simply announces he will be going to Valhalla after death. Aleister Crowley said that Odin was merely another name for Horus; and that Horus was Satan. That will be seen in the next chapter. Using the warlike Norsemen by analogy, Plant sings that they are speaking "tales" about "Thor," between 1:12 and 1:15. In the last Crowley quote he said this age was a time of war against Christianity. Plant sings about this wartime, I believe, between 1:18 and 1:27 of the song. He sings that the band "calmed" certain "tides" caused by a "war," and then he sings, "We are your overlords." Plant drags out the word "overlords" over several seconds in order that only those who listen real hard will get the message. An overlord is the same as an overseer or ruler. Plant is telling them that in the spiritual dimension, they are in effect ruling the fans with their music. In other words, these "tides" have been "calmed" in the mind of the fans by Led Zeppelin's music. The war of morals has been won by the band; through the music, even though the fans are not fully aware, which is why Plant goes on to tell them that Led Zeppelin's members are their "overlords." On this point, Plant and I are in agreement.

To sum it up, Led Zeppelin's music is fighting the same spiritual war Crowley was. They are just doing it on tape, video, and compact disc. Page and Plant did it in their 1995-1996 and 1998 world tours, and in 1999-2000 Jimmy Page toured with the Black Crowes, playing a two hour plus concert with the overwhelming majority of songs coming from the Led Zeppelin catalog. The touring ended in August of 2000, when Jimmy Page ostensibly injured his back. Led Zeppelin claimed to be overlords or rulers over the fans, who, whether they know it or not, are also engaged in the war against Lord Jesus Christ. We'll look at that later in detail. This is all in accord with *The Book of the Law*. Plant said they are the listener's rulers during this war. The Devil said, in *The Book of the Law*: "Let my servants be few & secret: they shall rule the many & the known."86 Is it unrealistic to believe Plant got his information from that Satanic text? In his commentary on this verse in *The Equinox*, Crowley wrote: "This is the rule of Thelema, that its adepts shall be invisible rulers."87

As previously mentioned, Crowley refers to Christianity as slavery. Here is another quote from him in the same light: "The sense of sin, shame, self-distrust, this is what makes folk cling to Christianity-slavery."88 In a moment we're going to examine Crowley's definition, in a practical sense, of his desire for his readers to fight Christians. First, Israel Regardie will be quoted from the introduction to Crowley's book, *The Law is for All*. Regardie wrote about a psychology writer named Robert Lindner, and his book, *Prescription for Rebellion*. He writes of what he understood from Lindner's conversations with his patients: "As I understand it from frequent discussions with patients from the young hip generation, many of them turned on to the new sexual, social, and political attitudes through their initial use of marijuana. However much some adults may be shocked and horrified by this revelation, it is more than clear that the psychedelic drugs have to take prime place as factors responsible for the overturning of contemporary moral, religious and social standards, for the transvaluation of values. This is the prelude to an eventual development of a radically new code of behavior and therefore of a radically new type of society, as indicated by *The Book of the Law*."89 Again, Israel Regardie knew Crowley personally, working as his secretary. He wrote that in 1970, when *Led Zeppelin III* was released. He also had this to say about the Law of Thelema: "Thelema may have to wait a while before it can show, better than Christianity, its capability for transforming our society. Yet the transvaluation of values documented in this introduction suggests that Crowley has succeeded beyond his wildest dreams. What he was writing about decades ago has already begun to arrive. The young generation presently active is his enthusiastic audience and his congregation."90 Again, that was written in 1970, when *Led Zeppelin III* was released. Now for the warfare already mentioned.

As I wrote in my introduction, Crowley advocated the literal murder of Christian people. You talk about pushing your faith on others, man, that's taking it the distance. That is however, what the Devil has been doing for centuries; nothing new, just a different version. He took possession of Judas Iscariot and had Jesus murdered (Christ used this murder to redeem his own), and he has plenty of Judas Iscariots' in his service today. The physical world is ruled by the spiritual; the sooner one accepts that, the sooner one is on the road to spiritual truth.

Crowley wanted to overthrow what he called the slave-gods. He called Christianity slavery. In the next quote, from *The Law is For All*, his extensive commentary on *The Book of the Law*, he talks of killing Christians physically concurrent with his blatant confession of anti-Semitism. He wrote: "Should we not rather breed humanity for quality by killing off any tainted stock, as we do with other cattle? And exterminating the vermin which infect it, especially Jews and Protestant Christians?"91 One would have to wonder if Adolf Hitler was a student of Crowley's. Crowley did have the Swastika printed in the Equinox, and in 1910 he wrote a pamphlet about it. It wouldn't be a surprise if Hitler had studied Crowley. If he did not, it is an amazing coincidence that they both hated Jews and loved the Swastika.

KILLING CHRISTIANS IN KENTUCKY, DECEMBER 1ST, 1997

Aleister Crowley would have been proud of Michael Carneal in Paducah, Kentucky, on December 1st, 1997. Before school started, a group of Christians were having a prayer meeting, when fourteen-year old Michael decided to fulfill the will of the Devil relative to disciples of Jesus. He shot and killed three teen-age girls; Nicole Hadley, age 14, Kayce Steger, age 15, and Jessica James, age 17, all martyred for the sake of Lord Jesus Christ (Informal prayer circle - 35 students, 3 dead, 5 wounded). What Mr. Carneal does not know is that he sent them right into the presence of God.

It is irrelevant if the kid was in a Satanic cult, or just emotionally disturbed because people made fun of him. In either case, he was used of the Devil to attack Christians. There were plenty of people at the school that day, why didn't he pick someone else? Any objective thinker can see the direct correlation between the kids holding hands and praying and the attack on them once the prayer was concluded. Did anyone hear President Clinton speak against hate crimes toward Christian people? Even *his* image polishing had boundaries.

HORUS' EXPEDITION OF DEATH AGAINST CHRISTIANS

Crowley continues his theme of killing Christians in the following: "The ritual of the adoration of Ra-Hoor-Khuit is, as one might expect, illustrative of His nature. It seems doubtful whether this ritual can ever be of the type of symbolic celebration; it appears rather as if expeditions against the heathen, i.e., Christians and other troglodytes - but most especially the parasites of man, the Jews - were to be his rite."92 Did you see the word heathen? That is exactly what the Devil said in *The Book of the Law*. Here it is: "Trample down the Heathen; be upon them, o warrior, I will give you of their flesh to eat! Sacrifice cattle, little and big: after a child."93 There is the Devil commanding the sacrifice of "a child." It does not say what kind, it just says "a child." Now you the reader don't believe that the Devil would advocate literal "child" sacrifice do you? Would a nice guy like him promote murder? I mean, for crying out loud people! If Satan wouldn't, who would? (Good ole' Samuel Weiser Inc., in Maine, publishes this trash.) Does that quote bother you? Eleven verses later, Satan speaks of perfume mix for his worship, and blood of the moon means menstrual: "For perfume mix meal & honey & thick leavings of red wine: then oil of Abramelin and olive oil, and afterward soften & smooth down with rich fresh blood. The best blood is of the moon, monthly: then the fresh blood of a child, or dropping from the host of heaven: then of enemies; then of the priest or of the worshipers: last of some beast, no matter what."94 Now we have the Devil talking about smoothing "with rich fresh blood," and he then mentions the "blood of a child!!!" Do you the reader want a member of the Silver Star living in your neighborhood? These writings came from the hand of one Devil possessed Aleister Crowley that Jimmy Page cannot understand why he is being called evil; and they are being reproduced and sold by Samuel Weiser, Inc. of Maine. I wonder how many children whose pictures are on milk cartons and other advertisements have fallen prey to the mindset advocated by Aleister Crowley's writings, which he of course, attributes to the Devil himself. Remember, Jimmy Page had "Do What Thou Wilt," which came from this murderous satanic *Book of the Law* engraved on Led Zeppelin's third LP's earliest copies. Is Jimmy Page ignorant of what that means? Are we to conclude that Page is just stupid, when he is a multi-millionaire? An impartial, objective reader with an ounce of brains will conclude that Page knew exactly what he was doing. Don't forget, you will read of Robert Plant commanding the fans to sell their souls to the Devil in the Led Zeppelin film, later in this work. As if this is all not horrifying enough, again addressing his enemies Satan says, "Mercy let be off: damn them who pity! Kill and torture; spare not; be upon them!"95 My friend, once again, if the Devil wouldn't advocate killing in literal fashion, who may I ask would?

Crowley began to speak like Nero about killing Christians: "We are infinitely tolerant, save of intolerance. It is no good, however, to try to prevent Christians from meddling, save by the one cure: the Christians to the lions."96

In these following quotes, Crowley spells it out further: "Man has the right to live by his own Law....Man has the right to love as he will, when, where and whom he will....Man has the right to kill those who would thwart these rights."97 Again, Crowley says kill the Christians: "We need have no fear then to throw the Christians to the lions. If there be indeed true men among them, who happen through defect of education to know no better, they will reincarnate all right, and no harm done."97 Does Jimmy Page concur with this 'Christians to the lions' attitude of Aleister Crowley? Let the reader decide. On July 17th, 1970, (the year he bought Boleskine House) in Essen, Germany, Led Zeppelin was playing an acoustic set and the fans were too loud for Page to hear himself play. Led Zeppelin walked off. Chris Welch wrote in *Melody Maker*: "This was the noisiest of the four concerts, where Jimmy gave up trying to play his acoustic guitar feature. 'Christians to the lions,' said Jimmy as they went out to a storm of whistling." Take a wild guess who Jimmy said that to. It was his eye in the triangle buddy, Peter Grant. In *Hammer of the Gods*, Steven Davis wrote that Robert asked the crowd to sit and be quiet. They wouldn't: "When they refused, Led Zeppelin walked off. 'Christians to the lions,' Jimmy murmured to Grant."99

Just so the reader understands that Crowley is dead serious about all the wicked immorality that he advocates in this chapter, I want to present a quote from the man who knew him better than anyone during his career of Magick, Israel Regardie. The quote illustrates Regardie's perception of Crowley's morality in light of *The Book of the Law*, that he presented in his biography on Crowley: "With considerable fervor, the Book echoes Crowley's underlying moral, social, and religious attitudes without equivocation or doubt."100 In summation, in this chapter you not only have Crowley's admission of advocating this evil book, but his secretary for several years, Mr. Regardie, testifies to the same…"without equivocation or doubt." It is reasonable to conclude, in light of the evidence, that the reason Crowley was available to write *The Book of the Law* for Satan was because he was immorally "fit" to do so. Because of that mindset, the following quote from Regardie became true of Crowley: "He came to accept the mission involved in *The Book of the Law* of disseminating a new moral code for mankind, and also became more willing to assume the role of teacher it had urged upon him."101

The Book of the Law presents us with the concept of Do What ThouWilt, based on the doctrines contained in the Law of Thelema; Thelema being the Greek word for will. The Devil presented it to Aleister Crowley, who, acting as his secretary, wrote the book down for men like Jimmy Page to read, and inevitably present the said concepts ever so subtly in the music of Led Zeppelin (Horus the Hawk is painted on the misty mountain on the inner cover of Led Zeppelin's fourth album). Those who take up the study of the Law of Thelema are instructed to believe that it is the perfect law of liberty, since it "frees" man from the "tyrannical" doctrines of Biblical Christianity and its Christ; it is in truth, a decadent law that takes an already morally twisted mind and enslaves it to the basest types of human depravity, giving the Devil complete control of the soul. The Devil had achieved control over the soul of Aleister Crowley through his studies of Magick and membership in the Hermetic Order of the GoldenDawn, but the Golden Dawn was an unstable occult order at the time. Desiring to continue his propagation of magical "truth," Satan had Crowley postpone the Operation of Abramelin the Mage after purchasing Boleskine House in Scotland. The purchase was dictated by the Devil himself, knowing that Jimmy Page would come to own the house seventy years later; and for a specific purpose, as will be shown in a later chapter. Once Boleskine was secured, Satan led Crowley around the world to study Magick. After journeying the world alone, Crowley met up with Rose Kelly, who played a major role in pointing Crowley in the direction of the Invocation of Horus, in Egypt, in April of 1904. This Invocation led to Crowley's writing of *The Book of the Law*, dictated to him by a *musical spirit* named "Aiwaz," who Crowley made clear in no uncertain terms in his later writings was none other than the Devil himself. Knowing that Satan was created by Lord Jesus Christ as Lucifer, the celestial composer of music, this is not difficult for one to believe. In the next chapter, we are going to study the foundation of Magick, the Qabalah. Israel Regardie also commented that *The Book of the Law* subtly advocated the Qabalah, as well as the Tarot cards that are derived from it: "In the book are innumerable subtle references to Qabalah and Tarot-all contents of Crowley's mind, materials derived from the Order which shaped his life."102 The Qabalah will prepare the reader to comprehend the most powerful, influential, and widely received music in Rock history.

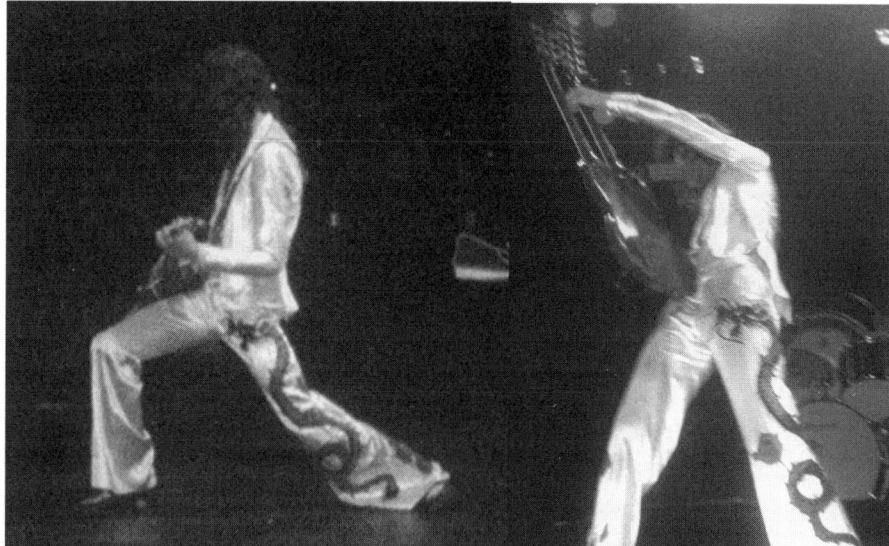

"I am the Snake that giveth Knowledge & Delight and bright glory, and stir the hearts of men with drunkenness. To worship me take wine and strange drugs whereof I will tell my prophet, & be drunk thereof! They shall not harm ye at all."

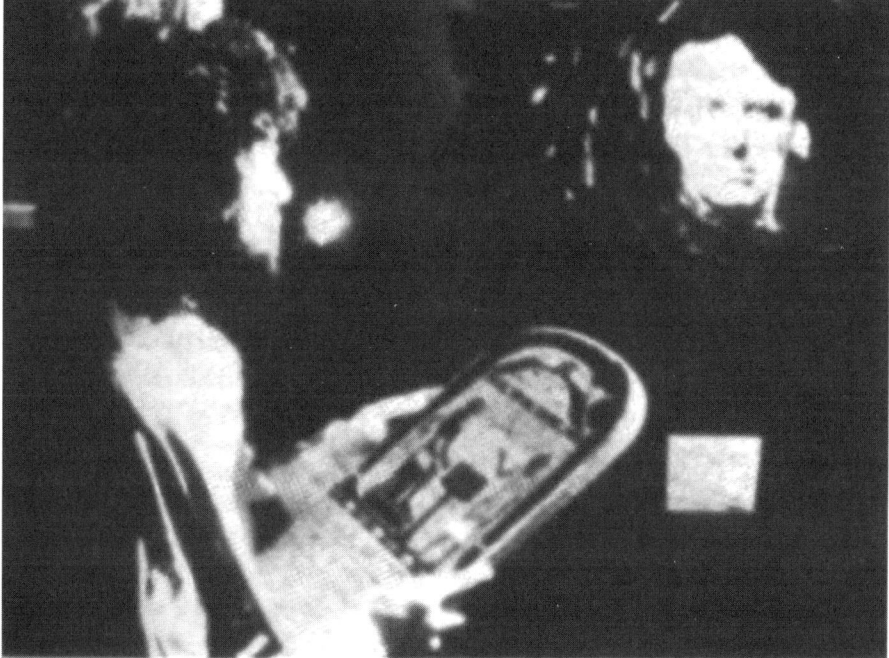

Jimmy Page as Lucifer meets the beast in Lucifer Rising.

Aleister and Rose Crowley, with their daughter, on January 10th, 1910. If ever a child should have been removed from a home by the authorities, this little girl could have been the poster child for the concept.

The Egyptian "Stele of Revealing" that Rose Crowley identified for Aleister.

In this still from the Kenneth Anger film, "Lucifer Rising," Jimmy Page plays the part of Lucifer. He is holding the "Stele of Revealing." This is the cover of the LP which contains the music Page composed for Anger, glorifying the Devil.

After communing with the Devil in Cairo, Egypt, and producing the manuscript for *The Book of the Law,* Aleister Crowley's self-deification and career of Magick was in full flight. Knowing that he was an open literary medium, he sought to bring his new universal religion to the masses through some of the most corrupt pages ever written in books like *The Law is for All.* The photo shows him in his magician robe. Note the Magick wand, which projects the "macrocosmic force." The macrocosmic force is Satan, of course. It will be discussed in chapter 12.

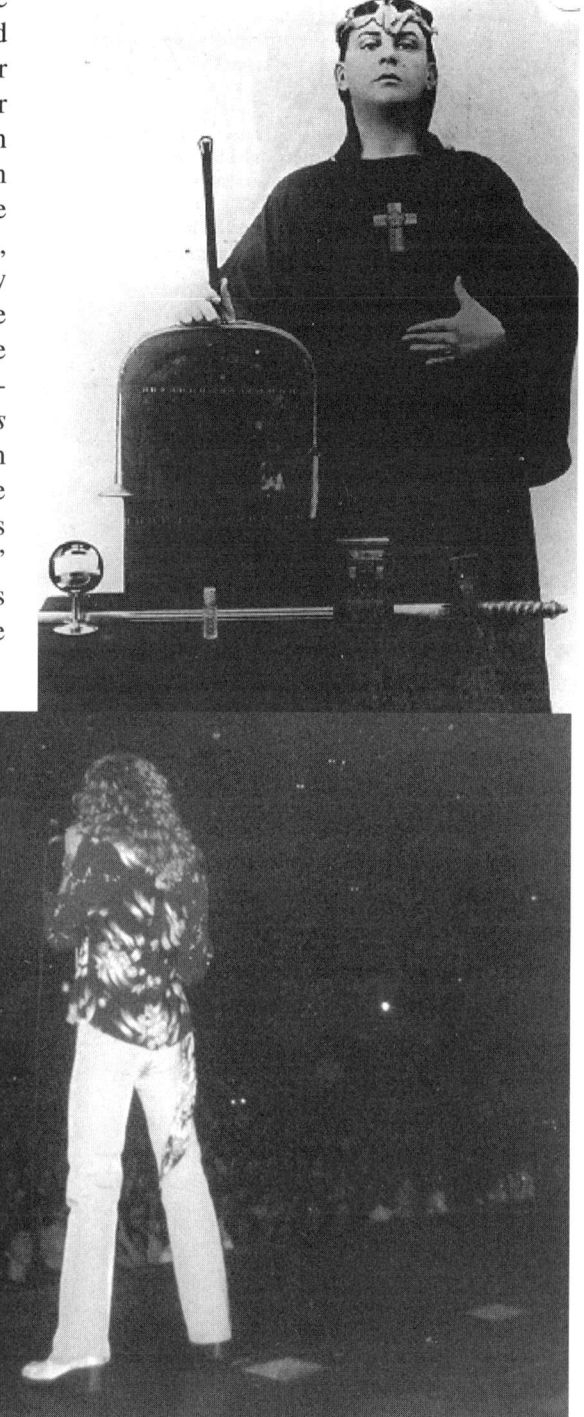

As an "Overlord" of the fans, Robert Plant's statement in "Immigrant Song" reflects what was written in *The Book of the Law* by Satan through Crowley: "Let my servants be few and secret, they shall rule the many and the known."

Horus the Hawk, the son in the Qabalistic trinity. This is on the Led Zeppelin IV inner album cover mountain. Note the small crown on top of the head. The eye is below it to the right, and the beak is to the right of the eye. Coming down the neck toward the shoulder of the right wing, the extension of the right wing is folded under the shoulder. The father and mother in the Qabalistic trinity are on top of the mountain, the Hermit and the Dove. (Copyright -Atlantic Records)

1   Aleister Crowley, The Law is For All, Israel Regardie in the introduction, New Falcon Publications, Phoenix, AR, 1993, pg.9

2   Ibid, pg.37

3   Satan, Aleister Crowley's *The Book of the Law*, Chapter 2, verse 22, pp.19-20

4   Satan, Aleister Crowley's *The Book of the Law*, Chapter 3, verse 51, *The Equinox*, Vol. I, No.10, pg.32

5   Aleister Crowley, *The Equinox*, Vol. I, No. 2, Samuel Weiser Inc., Yorke Beach, ME, 1993, pp. 333-334

6   Aleister Crowley, *The Equinox*, Vol. I, No. 3, pg. 207

7   Ibid, pg.214

8   Ibid, pp.214-215

9   Ibid, pp.233-234

10 Ibid, pg.251

11 Israel Regardie, *The Eye in the Triangle*, pg.92

12 Aleister Crowley, *The Equinox*, Vol. I, No. 3, pp.252-253

13 Aleister Crowley, *The Confessions of Aleister Crowley,* pg.357

14 Aleister Crowley, *The Equinox of the Gods*, New Falcon Publications, 1991, pp.50, 52

15 Colin Wilson, *The Occult*, Random House, 1971, pg.359

16 Aleister Crowley, *The Equinox*, Vol. I, No. 7, pp.360-361

17 Ibid, pg.365

18 Ibid, pg.368

19 Colin Wilson, *The Occult*, pg.360

20 Aleister Crowley, *The Equinox of the Gods*, pg.117

21 Ibid, pg.97

22 Ibid, pg.118

23 Aleister Crowley, *The Magical Record of the Beast*, Duckworth, 1972, pg.68

24 Ibid, pg.198

25 Ibid, pg.239

26 Ibid, pg.217

27 Ibid, pg.238

28 Ibid, pg.237

29 Aleister Crowley, *The Law is For All*, pg.279

30 Aleister Crowley, *The Equinox of the Gods*, pg.127

31 Ibid, pg.105

32 Ibid, pg.136

33 Aleister Crowley, *The Law is For All*, pg.256

34 Aleister Crowley, *The Equinox*, Vol. I, No. 7, pg.386

35 Ibid, pg.400

36 Ibid, pg.400

37 Satan, *The Book of the Law*, Chapter 3, verse 51, Aleister Crowley taking dictation, *The Equinox*, Vol. I, No. 10, pg.32

38 Aleister Crowley, *The Equinox*, Vol. I, No. 7, pg.400

39 Aleister Crowley, *The Equinox*, Vol. III, No. 1, pp.9-10

40 Ibid, pp.41-42

41 Ibid, pp.47-50, 52

42 Israel Regardie, *The Eye in the Triangle*, pg.492

43 Aleister Crowley, *Diary of a Drug Fiend*, Samuel Weiser Inc., Yorke Beach, ME, 1970, pp.348-349

44 Ibid, pg.356

45 Ibid, pp.362-365

46 Ibid, pg.366

47 Ibid, pg.367

48 Ibid, pg.367

49 Richard Cole, *Stairway to Heaven - Led Zeppelin Uncensored*, Harper Collins, NY, NY, 1992, pg.314

50 Aleister Crowley, *Diary of a Drug Fiend*, pg.37

51 Ibid, Preface

52 Ibid, pg.26

53 Ibid, pg.44

54 Ibid, pp.46-47

55 Ibid, pg.50

56 Ibid, pg.55

57 Ibid, pg.78

58 Ibid, pg.90

59 Ibid, pg.95

60 Ibid, pg.60

61 Ibid, pp.61-62

62 Ibid, pg.62

63 Ibid, pg.62

64 Ibid, pg.103

65 Satan, *The Book of the Law*, Chapter 2, verse 22, pp.19-20

66 Susan Roberts, *The Magician of the Golden Dawn*, pg.228

67 Aleister Crowley, *The Law is For All*, pg.255

68 Dave Lewis and Simon Pallett, *Led Zeppelin: The Concert File*, pg.96

69 Richard Cole, *Stairway to Heaven - Led Zeppelin Uncensored*, pg.326

70 Susan Roberts, *The Magician of the Golden Dawn*, pg.116

71 Satan, *The Book of the Law*, Chapter 1, verse 51, pg.15

72 Aleister Crowley, *The Law is For All*, pg.114

73 Ibid, pp.114-115

74 Satan, *The Book of the Law*, Chapter 1, verse 51, pg.15

75 Richard Cole, *Stairway to Heaven - Led Zeppelin Uncensored*, pp.77-78

76 Aleister Crowley, *The Law is For All*, pg.116

77 E.M. Bounds, Satan, *His Personality, Power, and Overthrow*, pg.112

78 C. S. Lewis, *The Screwtape Letters*, Broadman & Holman Publishers, 1996,NY, NY, pp.6, 15

79 Aleister Crowley, *The Law is For All*, pg.118

80 Dave Lewis and Simon Pallett, *Led Zeppelin: The Concert File*, pg.89

81 Steven Davis, *Hammer of the Gods*, pg.142

82 Aleister Crowley, *The World's Tragedy*, Preface, pg. xxix

83 Satan, *The Book of the Law*, Chapter 1, verse 41, pg.14

84 Aleister Crowley, *The Law is For All*, pg.90

85 W.B. Crow, *Witchcraft, Magic, & Occultism*, pg.126

86 Satan, *The Book of the Law*, Chapter 1, verse 10, pg.11

87 Aleister Crowley, *The Equinox*, Vol. I, No.7, pg.388

88 Aleister Crowley, *The Law is For All*, pg.225

89 Ibid, Israel Regardie in the introduction, pp.17-18

90 Ibid, Israel Regardie in the introduction, pg.40

91 Ibid, pp.274-275

92 Ibid, pp.271-272

93 Satan, *The Book of the Law*, Chapter 3, verses 11-12, pg.26

94 Ibid, Chapter 3, verses 23-24, pg.27

95 Ibid, Chapter 3, verse 18, pg.26

96 Aleister Crowley, *The Law is For All*, pp.223-224

97 Ibid, pg.321

98 Ibid, pg.231

99 Steven Davis, *Hammer of the Gods*, pg.138

100 Israel Regardie, *The Eye in the Triangle*, pg.494

101 Ibid, pg.414

102 Ibid, pg.484

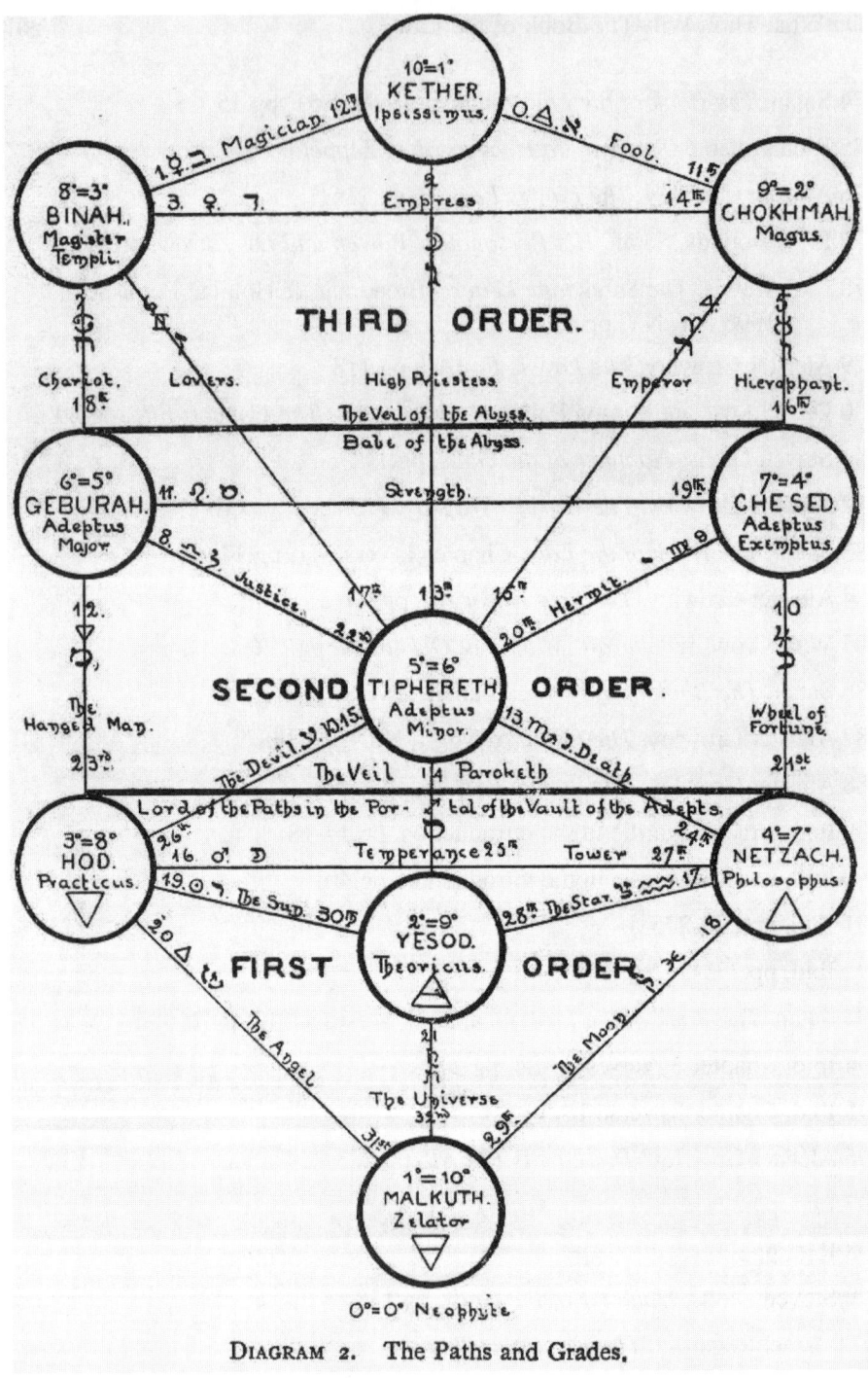

DIAGRAM 2.   The Paths and Grades.

The Qabalah as drawn by Aleister Crowley. It has all the Sephiroth, as well as the grades of the Silver Star, and Tarot representations. The Qabalah, say Levi and Crowley, is the science of "light." (Taken from The Equinox Vol.1, No.2)

CHAPTER EIGHT

"God is the soul of light. The universal and infinite light is for us, as it were, the body of God.

The Qabalah, or transcendental magic, is the science of light.

Light corresponds to life.

The kingdom of shadows is death.

All the dogmas of true religion are written in the Qabalah, in characters of light upon a page of shadow."1

Eliphas Levi, "The Key to the Mysteries"

"Need we say that we speak of the holy Qabalah? O science secret, subtle, and sublime, who shall name thee without veneration, without prostration of soul, spirit, and body before thy divine Author, without exaltation of soul, spirit, and body as by His favour they bathe in His lustral and illimitable Light?"2

Black Magician Aleister Crowley, "The Temple of Solomon the King"

"How wonderful is the Qabalah! How great is its security from the profane; how splendid its secrets to the initiate!"3

Black Magician Aleister Crowley, "The Temple of Solomon the King"

"It is to effect this exaltation and expansion of the consciousness to the Light, that the magical system of the Golden Dawn, as well as Crowley's own reformulation of that Order, exists."4

Israel Regardie, "The Eye in the Triangle"

"We therefore who are without the chains of ignorance, look closely into the heart of the seeker and lead him by the path which is best suited to his nature unto the ultimate end of all things, the supreme realization, the Life which abideth in Light, yea, the Life which abideth in Light."5

Black Magician Aleister Crowley, "The Equinox"

IN THE LIGHT - TEN YEARS GONE - THE ROVER: THE MAGICAL DOCTRINE OF THE QABALAH

The Qabalah, as stated by Eliphas Levi, is transcendental magic and the science of light. It is magic, containing the light of truth; according to occultists. We have already seen how that Led Zeppelin identified itself morally with Crowley's *Book of the Law*, and the book presents a Qabalistic trinity for godhead. What is a Qabalistic trinity? It is a trinity that is three in symbolism, but is only two in practice. In other words, Osiris and Isis are husband and wife, brother and sister, father and daughter, and mother and son. Osiris dies, and is born again as Horus. The Egyptian trinity of Isis, Osiris, and Horus, in Qabalistic symbolism, is a trinity where Osiris and Horus are one and the same. So what you have is an androgynous, hermaphroditic, male and female godhead. This Egyptian version of the Qabalistic godhead is the one most referred to by Aleister Crowley, whose Qabalah advocating quotes at the chapter heading were written several years after his writing *The Book of the Law*. The Silver Star and Jimmy Page hold the Qabalah in high esteem. You will read of Jimmy Page's advocating the Qabalah later in this book. Remember, Led Zeppelin is Jimmy Page's creation, with Peter Grant, his eye in the triangle buddy, by his side. In this chapter we will examine the core teachings of the Qabalah, in accordance with its physical description as the "Tree of Life." Each aspect of the tree, beginning with the godhead at the top, and the creation at the bottom, will be discussed as to their position and importance. The Qabalah, as promoted by the Devil through men like Aleister Crowley, has been an effective tool to deceive multitudes of occultists and their neophyte followers into believing that the "godhead" is a male/female entity, represented, though by different names, in all cultures throughout the world; and that its purpose is to unite men with that godhead.

PHYSICAL GRAFFITI – "IN THE LIGHT"

As you read previously, Led Zeppelin had a song on the *Physical Graffiti* album with a title "In The Light." In the beginning of the song Robert Plant tells the listener, "if" they "can't" endure life anymore, like they are stuck in a rut, all they have to do is "believe" and they won't be "wrong." Then he gives the punch line by saying, "In the Light you will find the road." (Remember, two albums earlier, in "Stairway to Heaven," Plant sang that people have "time" remaining for them to switch which "road" they are "on;" already having stated that there are only two to choose from. Then again on the next album, *Houses of the Holy*, in the song "Over the Hills and Far Away" Plant sings that "Many" are not able to "see" this "road." A very important thing for the reader to consider, if you think this is all tied into the 1970's, is that this music is timeless. During the year 2000, Jimmy Page toured with "The Black Crowes," and they played "In the Light" to thunderous ovations from the crowds. During his 2001 tour of the United States, Robert Plant sang "In the Light" with his band, again to extreme pleasure and ovation of the audiences.) Another way that Robert Plant could have said it comes from the book that highly influenced Aleister Crowley in the beginning of his magical career, as already stated in chapter five, *The*

Cloud Upon the Sanctuary. Karl von Eckartshausen wrote the following, encouraging his students to seek the Light:

"We could often tell you, beloved brothers, of marvels relating to the hidden things in the treasury of the Sanctuary, which would amaze and astonish you; we could speak to you about ideas concerning which the profoundest philosophy is as removed as the earth from the sun, but to which we are near being one with the light of the innermost.

"But our object is not to excite your curiosity, but to raise your desires to seek the light at its source, where your search for wisdom will be rewarded and your longing for love satisfied, for wisdom and love dwell in our retreats. The stimulus of their reality and of their truth is our magical power."6

The man who knew Aleister Crowley better than anyone, Israel Regardie, wrote in his biography of Crowley, *The Eye in the Triangle*, that the Qabalah and Crowley's presentation of it were indicative of the Great Work, or becoming one with god, describing it in the same fashion, as uniting with the Light:

"What is the function of this Qabalistic interpretation of religion? This magic of which both The Golden Dawn and Aleister Crowley speak? If I say its goal is illumination or the expansion of consciousness, not much at first may be gleaned from that. Yet 'being brought to the Light' is a most apt description of the high goals of the system. It is the Great Work."7

It is reasonable to conclude that Jimmy Page and Led Zeppelin were indeed trying to draw their fans to the study of the Qabalah. Once a fan began to study the writings of the Jimmy Page advocated Aleister Crowley, he would clearly see that it was indeed the Qabalah being promoted by the song, "In The Light."

I believe it is the Devil who is asking if the listener could believe he would abandon them between 3:02 and 3:05 of the song. Between 3:50 and 3:55, he tells the listener, as they search for him, he is going to "share" their "love." Then at 3:57 he commands them to "Let" him "share" their "love." At 5:26 he repeats the theme of the beginning of the song. At 5:57 he says "winds" indicating "change" might "blow" near them, and "that" is "always" the case for them. At 6:16 he tells the listener that they "are" not ever "alone." At 6:23, he says that he is going to "share" their "love." He says it again at 6:27. At 6:38 he sings the song title, and at 6:45 he sings that all people need that "light." Beginning at 7:29 he sings the song title over and over for the last 1:15 of the song, repeating that all people need that "light." You read at the chapter heading that Levi says the Qabalah is transcendental magic and the science of light. You also know that Crowley claimed to be Levi reincarnated. The quote from Levi was taken from *The Equinox, Volume I, No. 10.* Crowley had translated Levi's *Key to the Mysteries* and implemented it into his *Equinox*. Levi also said this in the *Key to the Mysteries*:

"Light is the instrument of the Word, it is the white writing of God upon the great book of night.

Light is the source of thought, and it is in it that one must seek for the origin of all religious dogma. But there is only one true dogma, as there is only one pure light..."8

Mr. Levi is absolutely correct that there is only one true dogma, and it is not found in the Qabalah, but in the *Holy Bible*.

THE QABALAH UNVEILED

S.L. MacGregor Mathers (co-founder of the Hermetic Order of the Golden Dawn), Aleister Crowley's friend and subsequent nemesis, translated a book out of the Latin *Kabbala Denudata*. In English, he called it *The Kabbalah Unveiled*. He spelled it as "Qabalah" afterward. He used the latter spelling in the text. Crowley read the book in July of 1898, several months before he was initiated into the Golden Dawn. The book had a significant effect on his thinking and he considered himself a Qabalist afterward. The book not only impressed Crowley, but many others. Eight years after Mathers' death, Mathers' wife wrote these words in the preface to a later edition of the book:

"As a pupil of my late husband and in later years collaborator in his more esoteric studies, I take this opportunity to say a few words in regard to himself and his work. Moreover, since his death at the end of 1918, I have received innumerable visits, letters and enquiries from all parts of the world from students of his writings. As most of these questions would appear to bear on his more esoteric knowledge, I will quote his own words (see page 13, paragraph 22, of the Introduction): 'The term "Unwritten Qabalah" is applied to certain knowledge which is never entrusted to writing, but communicated orally. I may say no more on this point, nor even whether I myself have or have not received it.'

"Simultaneously with the publication of the *Qabalah* in 1887, he received instructions from his occult teachers to prepare what was eventually to become his esoteric school. In this connection were associated with him the late Dr. Woodman and the late Dr. Wynn-Westcott, both eminent Masons and Qabalists. They, with my husband, held high Office in the Societas Rosicruciana in Anglia, and other Masonic bodies.

"Since the year 1887, when the first edition of the *Qabalah Unveiled* appeared, the whole attitude of the thinking world has changed considerably towards occult philosophy and science. The gigantic strides made by science since the end of the last century, the staggering facts disclosed by its practical demonstrations, simultaneously with the development of the great occult movement, must strike all thoughtful people as the evidence of some imminent change in the evolution of this planet. Material science would appear to be spiritualizing itself and occult science to be materializing itself. If not clasping hands, they are certainly making tentative attempts in that direction. The Ancient Wisdom, the Sacred Books, taught, that we cannot understand Matter without understanding Spirit, that we cannot understand Spirit without understanding Matter. That Matter and Spirit are only opposite poles of the same universal substance. All through the *Qabalah* runs this axiom: 'that Malkuth is in Kether, that Kether is in Malkuth.' The same idea is repeated through the Gnostic teaching: 'the earth that is in the heaven, the heaven that is in the earth.'

"Religion has its word, science its promises and demonstrations, philosophy its systematized theories, art its creations and ideals, and yet these in their fundamental separations fall short of that Synthetical ideal which the Spirit of Humanity unceasingly demands. There remains always the perpetual cry of humanity, that plaint of a world in pain demanding apparently in vain some solution to the problem of existence. The answer of the ancient world to this cry of the Spirit of Humanity is to be found in the establishment of the Mysteries, as containing in their penetralia that which even the highest then known forms of religion had not, namely, a philosphico-religious reply resumed in Formulas and Ceremonies, to the problems of Life and Death, of Nature, of the Gods, of Spiritual Beings, etc., and lastly of the linking of these as a whole back to the First Cause of all things.

"In 1888, after the publication of the *Qabalah Unveiled*, my husband started the working of his esoteric school. To write the consecutive history of an occult Order is a difficult matter, as difficult as to write the life of an Adept, there being so much of an inner and secret nature necessarily involved in both; so much of the symbolical in the historical, so much of the latter in the symbology.

"The general constitution of the teaching, the skeleton of the work, was handed to him by his occult teachers together with a vast amount of oral instruction. The object of the establishment of this school was similar to that of the foundation in ancient times of centers for the Celebration of the Mysteries. The literature of this school, with a few exceptions, was written by my husband under the direction of these teachers, based upon the ancient mysteries, chiefly those of Egypt, Chaldea and Greece, and brought up to date to suit the needs of our modern mentalities. It is a system eminently suited to Western occultism, which a man can follow while living the ordinary life of the world, given that this is understood in its highest sense. Dr. Woodman and Dr. Wynn-Westcott aided in the administrative side of this school and its teaching to a certain extent.

"As a pioneer movement, for the first ten or twelve years it encountered many of the difficulties that beset work that is given ahead of its time, but we had been told that the beginning would be in the nature of an experiment and that the students would be sifted. Dr. Woodman had died in the year 1890, and in

1897 Dr. Wynn-Westcott resigned, after which my husband entirely reorganized the school under orders, and further teachings were given him. The teaching is principally by Ceremony, Ritual, and Lecture. Purity of aspiration and of life are the first and essential qualities demanded of the student. A simultaneous development of soul, mind and body is insisted upon. The curriculum comprises the study of the intelligent forces behind Nature, the Constitution of man and his relation to God. The whole aim and object of the teaching is to bring a man to the knowledge of his higher self, to purify himself, to strengthen himself, to develop all qualities and powers of the being, that he may ultimately regain union with the Divine Man latent in himself, that Adam Qadmon, whom God hath made in His Own Image.

"Great stress is laid on the ideal of Fraternity. The potency of Fraternity has ever been an essential factor in an Occult Order, apart from its altruistic aspect; there are also the spiritual and the psychic. Any breach in the harmony of a circle will permit the entry of an opposing force. A Spiritualist of experience will bear witness to the truth of this statement.

"Through all the Sacred Books, be they our Bible, the *Qabalah*, the Egyptian Books, the Vedantic teachings, the Druidic traditions, etc., the Symbols of the Rose and of the Lily or lotus and of the Cross, reveal themselves as veritable living images of some great fundamental truth."9

The Qabalah is, as the theme of the preceding quote demonstrates, the foundational source of teaching for the Hermetic Order of the Golden Dawn and Aleister Crowley. It was Crowley's self identification as a Qabalist that prepared him for further studies in Magick and his eventual taking dictation of *The Book of the Law* from the Devil. Before you are done reading this book, you are going to see very clearly, that Aleister Crowley and James Patrick Page (meaning Led Zeppelin as well) present the Devil as being behind the teachings of the Qabalah. The proof will be crystal clear. What you the reader need, is a familiarity with its basic teachings, which will prepare you to understand Led Zeppelin's most powerful magical music. That is an absolute.

WHAT IS THE QABALAH?

The question, what is the Qabalah, is simple, yet the answer is complex. I will give you the definition of Richard Cavendish's book, *The Black Arts*, first. He spells it Cabala. He wrote: "The Cabala is a body of occult doctrine, originally Jewish, which has been adopted with enthusiasm by non-Jewish occultists since the fifteenth century. Levi, Mathers and Crowley were all heavily influenced by it. Modern occultists are attracted to the Cabala because of its age and its mystery, and because they can draw from it the great magical principles that the universe is a unity, that it has an underlying pattern connected with numbers and planets, that man is God and the universe in miniature, and that man can develop the divine spark within him until he masters the entire universe and himself becomes God."10

The translator of *The Qabalah Unveiled*, Mr. Mathers, addressed this question for his readers in 1887:

"The first questions which the non-qabalistical reader will probably ask are: What is the Qabalah? Who was its author? What are its sub-divisions? What are its general teachings? And why is a translation of it required at the present time?

"I will answer the last question first. At the present time a powerful wave of occult thought is spreading through society; thinking men are beginning to awake to the fact that 'there are more things in heaven and earth than are dreamed of in their philosophy;' and, last but not least, it is now felt that the Bible, which has been probably more misconstrued than any other book ever written, contains numberless obscure and mysterious passages which are utterly unintelligible without some key wherewith to unlock their meaning. THAT KEY IS GIVEN IN THE QABALAH."11

The people who have misconstrued the *Bible* are the occultists. They use the *Bible*, which clearly condemns acts like sodomy, to promote a religion that advocates it. Mr. Mathers continues the previous quote with the ridiculous assertion that Christians are ignorant of the Old Testament. He wrote: "Therefore this work should be of interest to every biblical and theological student. Let every Christian ask himself this question: 'How can I think to understand the Old Testament if I be ignorant of the construction put upon it by that nation whose sacred book it formed; and if I know not the meaning of the Old Testament, how can I expect to understand the New?' Were the real and sublime philosophy of the Bible better known, there would be fewer fanatics and sectarians.12 Well, enough of the ignorance of Mr. Mathers. The Old Testament contains teachings that were to prepare Israel for the coming of the Messiah as a child; bringing salvation with him. The Old Testament clearly condemns the occult practices of the Hermetic Order of the Golden Dawn and Aleister Crowley, as you will read in the next chapter, and these "scholars" intimate that the *Bible* promotes the occult Qabalah. These men claim to be authorities of that which they know not. That should not be too hard for the reader to believe considering the fact that they gave themselves to the Devil.

In defining the Qabalah, Mathers says: "The Qabalah may be defined as being the esoteric Jewish doctrine. It is called in Hebrew QBLH, *Qabalah*, which is derived from the root QBL, *Qibel*, meaning 'to receive.' This appellation refers to the custom of handing down the esoteric knowledge by oral transmission, and is nearly allied to 'tradition.'"13

Mr. Mathers provides us with information as to the Qabalah's origin:

"With regard to the author and origin of the Qabalah, I cannot do better than give the following extract from Dr. Ginsburg's 'Essay on the Kabbalah,' first premising that this word has been spelt in a great variety of ways-Cabala, Kabalah, Kabbala, &c. I have adopted the form Qabalah, as being more consonant with the Hebrew writing of the word. '....The Kabbalah was first taught by God himself to a select company of angels, who formed a theosophic school in Paradise. After the Fall the angels most graciously communicated this heavenly doctrine to the disobedient child of earth, to furnish the protoplasts with the means of returning to their pristine nobility and felicity. From Adam it passed over to Noah, and then to Abraham, the friend of God, who emigrated with it to Egypt, where the patriarch allowed a portion of this mysterious doctrine to ooze out. It was in this way that the Egyptians obtained some knowledge of it, and the other Eastern nations could introduce it into their philosophical systems. Moses, who was learned in all the wisdom of Egypt, was first initiated into the Qabalah in the land of his birth, but became most proficient in it during his wanderings in the wilderness, when he not only devoted to it the leisure hours of the whole forty years, but received lessons in it from one of the angels. By the aid of this mysterious science the law-giver was enabled to solve the difficulties which arose during his management of the Israelites, in spite of the pilgrimages, wars, and frequent miseries of the nation. He covertly laid down the principles of this secret doctrine in the first four books of the Pentateuch, but withheld them from Deuteronomy. Moses also initiated the seventy elders into the secrets of this doctrine, and they again transmitted them from hand to hand. Of all who formed the unbroken line of tradition, David and Solomon were the most deeply initiated into the Kabbalah.'"14

The passage you just read is what occultists believe about the Qabalah. There is, however, no mention of the Qabalah in the *Bible*, no mention of Moses or Noah or any other Biblical character he named as being involved with it. There is no mention of Moses taking instruction from any angels in the *Bible* either. The quote you just read is an example of the evil genius of Lucifer, combining actual events with lies about events that never took place. If Moses was a Qabalist, and Egyptian theology was based on the Qabalah, why in the world did Moses lead the Israelites out of Egypt? These people are so blind to the obvious because they choose to be. Moses' God was diametrically opposed to the gods of the Egyptians and every other race that has a godhead that is accepted by occultists as in accordance with the Qabalah. This belief system has no solid foundation, except lies. The Devil, as you read before, is the father of lies. The New Testament Book of Hebrews makes it clear that Moses' God was none other than Lord Jesus Christ, presenting himself as Yahweh/Jehovah. Jesus himself said that Moses' Old Testament writings made reference to him alone.

Speaking to the Jewish religious leaders who wanted him dead, who professed to trust in Moses, Jesus said: "You search the Scriptures, for in them you think you have eternal life; and these are they which testify of Me. But you are not willing to come to Me that you may have life….Do not think that I shall accuse you to the Father; there is one who accuses you – Moses, in whom you trust. For if you believed Moses, you would believe Me; for he wrote about Me. But if you do not believe his writings, how will you believe My words?" – John 5:39-40, 45-47. It would not surprise me if Solomon had been exposed to the Qabalah when the many wives he had led him to worship other gods, for which he paid a price, but it is still not mentioned in the Biblical text.

In speaking of the Qabalah practically, Mathers wrote: "The practical Qabalah deals with talismanic and ceremonial magic."15 Magic, according to occultists, is the basis of the Qabalah's existence in conjunction with the following as its purpose:

"The principal doctrines of the Qabalah are designed to solve the following problems:-

The Supreme Being, His nature and attributes.
The Cosmogony.
The creation of angels and man.
The destiny of man and angels.
The nature of the soul.
The nature of angels, demons, and elementals.
The import of the revealed law.
The transcendental symbolism of numerals.
The peculiar mysteries contained in the Hebrew letters.
The equilibrium of contraries."16

Mathers listed the first and most important aspect of the Qabalah as the Supreme Being. In the following quote, he speaks of the Supreme Being, and takes the information out of the *Holy Bible*. He wrote:

"The first principle and axiom of the Qabalah is the name of the Deity, translated in our version of the Bible, 'I am that I am,' AHIH AShR AHIH, *Eheieh Asher Eheieh*. A better translation is, 'Existence is existence,' or 'I am He who is.'

"Eliphaz Levi Zahed, that great philosopher and Qabalist of the present century, says in his 'Histoire de la Magie' (History of Magic): 'The Qabalists have a horror of everything that resembles idolatry; they, however, ascribe the human form to God, but it is a purely hieroglyphical figure. They consider God as the intelligent, living, and loving Infinite One. He is for them neither the collection of other beings, nor the abstraction of existence, nor a philosophically definable being. He is in all, distinct from all, and greater than all. His very name is ineffable; and yet this name only expresses the human ideal of His Divinity. What God is in Himself it is not given to man to know.'"17

We are now going to take a good look at the practical Qabalah, the Sephiroth. Again, the Qabalah is the Satanic "Tree of Life." It is made up of ten sephiroth and a picture of it is on page 218; taken from Aleister Crowley's *Equinox.*

THE SEPHIROTH AND THE GODHEAD

The Sephiroth deal specifically with the Qabalistic godhead in detail. Mathers gave us the description:

"I must now explain the real meaning of the terms Sephira and Sephiroth. The first is singular, the second is plural. The best rendering of the word is 'numerical emanation.' There are ten Sephiroth, which are the most abstract forms of the ten numbers of the decimal scale-i.e, the numbers 1,2,3,4,5,6, 7,8,9,10. Therefore, as in the higher mathematics we reason of numbers in their abstract sense, so in the Qabalah we reason of the Deity by the abstract forms of the numbers; in other words, by the SPIRVTh, *Sephiroth.* It was from this ancient Oriental theory that Pythagoras derived his numerical symbolic ideas.

"Among these Sephiroth, jointly and severally, we find the development of the persons and attributes of God. Of these *some are male and some female.* Now, for some reason or other best known to themselves, the translators of the Bible have carefully crowded out of existence and smothered up every reference to the fact that the Deity is both masculine and feminine. They have translated a *feminine plural* by a *masculine singular* in the case of the word Elohim. They have, however, left an inadvertent admission of their knowledge that it was plural in Gen.1:26; 'And Elohim said: Let Us make man.' Again (v.27), how could Adam be made in the image of the Elohim, male and female, unless the Elohim were male and female also? The word Elohim is a plural formed from the feminine singular ALH, *Eloh*, by adding IM to the word. But inasmuch as IM is usually the termination of the masculine plural, and is here added to a feminine noun, it gives to the word Elohim the sense of a female potency united to a masculine idea, and thereby capable of producing an offspring. Now, we hear much of the Father and the Son, but we hear nothing of the Mother in the ordinary religions of the day. But in the Qabalah we find that the Ancient of Days conforms Himself simultaneously into the Father and the Mother, and thus begets the Son."18

What we need to look at from the preceding passage, are the words Eloh, Elohim, and the image of Elohim, to get the truth to the surface that is buried by occultists under so much conjecture. This is indeed a pathetically weak foundation for people to build their religious beliefs on, the way these occultists have presented Biblical concepts. We are going to examine all three in order.

ELOH - MASCULINE OR FEMININE?

The man who wrote the Latin version of *The Qabalah Unveiled*, the *Kabbala Denudata*, made a critical error in his perception of ELOH, which shows that he was no Hebrew scholar. For him to make such a critical error shows the Devil's hand in this. In English script, ELOH, or ELOaH, appears to be feminine. That is because Hebrew words that end in an H or aH are usually feminine. Here is the problem with the way the Qabalists are presenting it. I will illustrate it with the English letter Y. Used as a consonant, the letter Y is used as Y in Yankee. Used as a vowel, Y is used as Y in cry. The ending of ELOaH has the letter "a" before the H. The vowel point in the Hebrew script, relative to the letter "a" in ELOaH, is "Pattach," which is used for a masculine. In the word "Torah," the vowel point is "Qamets," which is feminine. That makes the letter "h" in Torah a vowel letter, meaning the word is feminine. Because ELOaH uses the vowel Pattach, it is masculine, making the "H" a consonant. The proper pronunciation is ELOaH (eloahah), with the "H" pronounced like a breath of air (i.e., not silent), like the "H" in "Hand." Again, it is a consonant, which makes the noun a masculine singular. So there goes your hermaphroditic, androgynous, masculine and feminine godhead theory right out the window. Mathers said the ELOH was a feminine singular connected to a masculine plural in IM, producing a Male/Female ELOHIM. It is a lie, and you know already from reading this book who the father of lies is. This theory was derived right from the mind of Lucifer - the deceiver. ELOHIM is a masculine plural of the masculine singular, ELOH or ELOaH. In the Hebrew script, the final letter, the "H," is a consonant, which means it is masculine, and although the masculine and feminine can appear the same in English script, it does not appear the same in the Hebrew. In the Hebrew, where the word is used, it ends in a masculine, consonant form. Again, this means the word is a masculine singular. All the lexicons for Biblical Hebrew agree that this form, ELOaH, is masculine. There is no "goddess" reference made to the Almighty Hebrew God in the: **"BIBLIA HEBRAICA STUTTGARTENSIA"** that I have sitting in my lap as I write this. The title pertains to the literal Hebrew *Bible*, presented in Hebrew script. Again, I want to emphasize, *the noun ELOH or ELOaH is not feminine but masculine!* If you have any doubts, just contact any non-devil worshiping Hebrew scholar, whether he believes the *Bible* or not, and ask him about it. He will tell you the same thing. The logical conclusion then, is that these occultists are in error when applying a feminine singular to the Hebrew Godhead. They also say that the "Mother" in their Qabalistic trinity is the Holy Spirit in the *Bible*. They use the Holy Spirit as presented in scripture to represent the Mother (this is the dove that the Hermit is standing on at the top of the mountain on the inner cover of Led Zeppelin's fourth album). Conversely, this is what the Lord Jesus Christ had to say about the Holy Spirit to his disciples, just before he was crucified: "I still have many things to say to you, but you cannot bear them now. However, when He, the Spirit of truth, has come, He will guide you into all truth; for He will not speak on His own authority, but whatever He hears he will speak; and He will tell you things to come." - John 16:12-13. Lord Jesus Christ presents him as masculine. Aleister Crowley presents him as feminine, the Mother in the Qabalah; in line with the heretical teachings contained in *The Qabalah Unveiled*, which again, was translated into English by his friend and subsequent nemesis, Samuel Liddell MacGregor Mathers. Deciding on whether to trust the word of Lord Jesus Christ as opposed to Crowley and Mathers is a no-brainer; unless of course, you are already under the Devil's control; as all magicians and witches are, whether it be black magic, Wicca, etc., Satan owns them all.

ELOHIM

The word ELOHIM is a masculine plural of the masculine singular, ELOaH. It is however, utilized in the generic sense to make it applicable to both god or goddess, when referring to goddesses that were worshiped by the nations that were enemies of Israel; but only in that context. The Holy trinity is Father, Son, and Holy Spirit, and Jesus himself referred to the Holy Spirit as "He." The *Bible* even uses Elohim in reference to Moses standing before Pharaoh in Egypt. In Exodus, chapter 7, verse 1, God said that Moses was like Elohim to Pharaoh: "So the LORD said to Moses: 'See, I have made you as God to Pharaoh, and Aaron your brother shall be your prophet."

IMAGE OF ELOHIM - MALE AND FEMALE?

The assertion by *The Qabalah Unveiled* is, if Elohim made them male and female, how could Elohim not be male and female as well? First of all, the *Bible* says they were created in the IMAGE of Elohim, not sex. The *Bible* does not say that God has a phallus anywhere, although he is presented as masculine. The Father is referred to as He, Christ is referred to as He, and the Holy Spirit is referred to as He. Christ made it clear that angels as well do not marry or procreate. If *The Qabalah Unveiled* is teaching that man and woman have to be created exactly as their male and female godhead because of the word image, then men and women better be all-powerful, all-knowing, and everywhere present as well. That is a must if all men and women are created in the exact image of their masculine and feminine godhead. The fact of the matter is that the word image has nothing to do with sex. The Devil jumped on the band-wagon with these occultists. It makes sense to people who love evil and bisexu-ality to believe this nonsense. The image referred to when the *Bible* says God created man in his image, refers to what we can do that God does. Specifically, we can see, hear, smell, touch, etc., as God can. God, however, is Spirit. He does not have hands or a nose, eyes, feet, ears, etc. When the *Bible* speaks of God having nostrils, eyes, ears, etc., it is using an Anthropomorphism. It is at-tributing human characteristics to God. He can do all those things as a spirit that we do with our bodies. He can, however, manifest himself in bodily form, as in Revelation chapter 1. Again, image has nothing to do with sex. If you saw the movie *Braveheart*, you saw little William Wallace standing by his father and brother's graves when his uncle rode up to him on a horse, got off, grabbed his chin and said, "You have the look of your mother." He bore his mother's image, yet he was male. I use that as an analogy.

The same *Bible* that occultists say advocates a masculine and feminine godhead presents clearly what the male and female picture really means in the New Testament Book of Ephesians, Chapter 5, verses 25 through 32: "Hus-bands, love your wives, just as Christ also loved the church and gave Himself for her, that he might sanctify and cleanse her with the washing of water by the word, that He might present her to Himself a glorious church, not having spot or wrinkle or any such thing, but that she should be holy and without blemish. So husbands ought to love their own wives as their own bodies; he who loves his wife loves himself. For no one ever hated his own flesh, but nourishes and cher-ishes it, just as the Lord does the church. For we are members of His body, of His flesh and of His bones. 'For this reason a man shall leave his father and mother and be joined to his wife, and the two shall become one flesh.' This is a great mystery, but I speak concerning Christ and the church." There is the pic-ture. If God wanted asexual beings in man, he would have created them as such. The picture of a husband's love for his wife is analogous to Christ's love for his church - his people. If the *Bible* is advocating a masculine and feminine godhead, Mr. Mathers, Aleister Crowley, Jimmy Page, why does it not mention the god-dess in this passage?

In the New Testament Book of Colossians, Chapter 1, verses 15-20, the *Bible* speaks of the Supremacy of Lord Jesus Christ: "He is the image of the invisible God, the firstborn over all creation. For by Him all things were created that are in heaven and that are on earth, visible and invisible, whether thrones or dominions or principalities or powers. All things were created through Him and for Him. And He is before all things, and in Him all things consist. And He is the head of the body, the church, who is the beginning, the firstborn from the dead, that in all things He may have the preeminence. For it pleased the Father that in Him all the fullness should dwell, and by Him to reconcile all things to Him-self…" The fullness of the godhead was in Christ when he was on earth and he was masculine, not half man and half woman. The people of the Silver Star take *Bible* passages out of context to back a crackpot theory; looking to the Qabalah and its misinterpretation of ELOH or ELOaH as the foundation upon which they are building their eternal destinies. All the while, the Devil is laughing at them. Now that I have presented the truth about the godhead from the Hebrew, relative to the teachings of Aleister Crowley and the Silver Star, we are going to look at each individual Sephira of the Qabalah; to realize how it fits into the music of Led Zeppelin.

THE TEN SEPHIROTH

It would be well for the reader to mark the page with Crowley's picture of the Qabalah on it, as you will be constantly looking there. The ten sephiroth, as stated before, represent the godhead; according to occultists. It appears complex, but it is simple. It is in effect a broken down version of Yahweh/Jehovah. Nothing could please the Devil more than to use the name of God to turn a bunch of will yielding anti-Christ's into Devil worshipers, and then have them believe that they are worshiping God. In the Hebrew, there are no vowel letters, only points. When translated into English, Yahweh is first presented as YHWH. Jehovah, (Lord Jesus Christ) is presented as IHVH. The letters, IHVH, are called the "Tetragrammaton." Concerning Jehovah as it relates to the Qabalah, Eliphas Levi wrote the name as "Jod he vau he:"

"All magic is in a word, and that word pronounced qabalistically is stronger than all the powers of Heaven, Earth and Hell. With the name of *Jod he vau he*, one commands Nature: kingdoms are conquered in the name of Adonai, and the occult forces which compose the empire of Hermes are one and all obedient to him who knows how to pronounce duly the incommunicable name of Agla.

"In order to pronounce duly the great words of the Qabalah, one must pronounce them with a complete intelligence, with a will that nothing checks, and activity that nothing daunts. In magic, to have said is to have done; the word begins with letters, it ends with acts. One does not really will a thing unless one wills it with all one's heart, to the point of breaking for it one's dearest affections; and with all one's forces, to the point of risking one's health, one's fortune, and one's life.

"It is by absolute devotion that faith proves itself and constitutes itself. But the man armed with such a faith will be able to move mountains."19

The point Levi is making is to have the Qabalah drilled into the mind, affect the will, and then live out the Qabalah's teachings in life. He is right to say that a faith in this religious teaching will enable one to move mountains. Just look at what Crowley, Page and Led Zeppelin have done. Remember, the Devil is behind it all.

If one gives himself over to the Devil as a result of the revelations of this book, when that was not the purpose for its being written, and then blame it on me for showing one how, all I can say is what Lord Jesus Christ said about Judas Iscariot in Matthew chapter 26, verse 24: "It would have been good for that man if he had not been born." This is no fairy tale. What happened between Judas and Jesus is a matter of irrefutable history. Every time we write the date, "2002," we admit that. History pivots on this event. The person who gives himself over to the Devil because this book showed him or her how, is just as guilty as Judas Iscariot. In their minds they are yelling "crucify him!" Just as that crowd did in front of Pontius Pilate, so do Devil worshipers in their hearts today; Pontius Pilate as well is a figure of irrefutable history.

For the purpose of the rest of this chapter, Jehovah, IHVH, the Tetragrammaton, will be used in reference to the Qabalah, the "tree of life," according to occultists. The name IHVH divides into four parts as you read in the previous quote. The "I" refers specifically to "Kether" and "Chokmah," the first two Sephiroth. The first "H" refers to "Binah." The letter "V" refers to the next six Sephiroth, "Chesed," "Geburah," "Tiphereth," "Netzach," "Hod," and "Yesod." The second "H" refers to "Malkuth," the tenth Sephira. Regarding the same, Mathers wrote: "The Tetragrammaton IHVH is referred to the Sephiroth, thus: the uppermost point of the letter *Yod*, I is said to refer to *Kether*; the letter I itself to *Chokmah*, the father of Microprosopus; the letter H, or 'the supernal *He*,' to Binah, the supernal Mother; the letter V to the next six Sephiroth, which are called the six members of Microprosopus (and six is the numerical value of V, the Hebrew *Vau*); lastly, the letter H, the 'inferior *He*,' to Malkuth, the tenth Sephira, the bride of Microprosopus."20

We are going to examine these four parts of IHVH, and their meanings. Let us begin with the first Sephira, Kether. Mathers wrote the following:

"The name of the first Sephira is KThR, Kether, the Crown.

The Divine Name attributed to it is the Name of the Father given in Exodus 3:4, AHIH, *Eheieh*, I am. It signifies Existence."21

Kether, the first Sephira, is called the Father, but Chokmah, the second Sephira, is also called Father. Mathers wrote: "The name of the second Sephira is ChKMH, *Chokmah*, Wisdom, a masculine active potency reflected from Kether, as I have before explained. This Sephira is the active and evident Father, to whom the Mother is united, who is the number 3."22 Relative to the third Sephira, Binah, Mathers wrote: "The third Sephira, or Triad, is a feminine passive potency, called BINH, *Binah*, the Understanding, who is co-equal with Chokmah....She is the supernal Mother, co-equal with Chokmah, and the great feminine form of God, the Elohim, in whose image man and woman are created, according to the teaching of the Qabalah, *equal before God. Woman is equal with man, and certainly not inferior to him*, as it has been the persistent endeavour of so-called Christians to make her."23

I find it astonishing that Crowley and Page can advocate the Qabalah that says woman is equal to man, and then say things like anyone who uses a woman as a plaything is alright, as Crowley did, and Page went on to say that Crowley's opinion of women was not high and he didn't think he was wrong. It is however, consistent with the Devil. In the *Bible*, when Peter tried to talk Christ out of believing he was going to be crucified, Jesus said: "Get behind Me, Satan! For you are not mindful of the things of God, but the things of men." - Mark 8:33 It is generally accepted by *Bible* scholars that the Devil prompted Peter to say Jesus would not be crucified. Then, at the last supper, the *Bible* clearly states that Judas became possessed of the Devil, because Satan had prompted Judas to betray Christ and Judas yielded to the temptation. Then Jesus said to him: "What you do, do quickly." - John 13:27 Jesus said that to the Devil. Satan had taken possession of Judas to betray Christ, yet, he prompted Peter to talk Christ out of believing he would be crucified, because he knew the prophecies of the crucifixion that said it would bring salvation. The Devil vacillated with Christ just as Crowley and Page on the issue of women.

MACROPROSOPUS

Kether, the all-Father, Chokmah, the Father, and Binah, the Mother, are the Supernal trinity, or "Macroprosopus." Chokmah and Binah derive from Kether. Regarding it, Mathers wrote: "I have already remarked that there is one trinity which comprises all the Sephiroth, and that it consists of the crown, the king, and the queen....It is the Trinity which created the world, or, in qabalistic language, the universe was born from the union of the crowned king and queen."24

At last, we have come to the point where we are going to take a serious look at the Qabalah's godhead. I am going to name their names, revealing to you the congruence or equality of the "different gods" that are worshiped around the world. I could spend an eternity examining all of them and then giving explanations, but I won't. I will discuss the ones that are the most pertinent, as well as commentary on them from Aleister Crowley, and that will be sufficient for you to understand the concept. At the end I will draw them all back into Kether, so I will begin with Chokmah, the king.

CHOKMAH - THE KING, GOD

The following is Aliester Crowley's commentary on the king, from *The*

Equinox, and he says the king is the sun, as he said of Satan at the heading of chapter four. For those who do not recognize the term, 'beget' means to father. In the text, Crowley says the king begets God and he is the begotten of God as well. He is saying he is the absolute creator:

THE KING

"THE KING is the undying One; he is the life and the master of life; he is the great living image of the Sun, the Sun, and the begetter of the Sun. He is the Divine Child, the God-begotten One, and the Begetter of God. He is the potent bull, the jewelled snake, the fierce lion. He is the monarch of the lofty mountains, and the lord of the woods and forests, the indweller of the globes of flame. As a royal eagle he soars through the heavens, and as a great dragon he churns up the waters of the deep. He holds the past between his hands as a casket of precious stones, the future lies before him clear as a mirror of burnished silver, and to-day is as an unsheathed dagger of gold at his girdle."25

In describing this king, Crowley steals the description that Lord Jesus Christ gave us of himself as ruler from the first chapter of Revelation from the King James Version of the *Bible*. Jesus said: "I am he that liveth, and was dead; and, behold, I am alive for evermore, Amen; and have the keys of hell and of death." - Revelation 1:18 (KJV)

Crowley wrote, quoting Satan: "For I am he that liveth, and was dead; and behold! I am alive for evermore, and have the Keys of Hell and of Death. I am Amoun the Sun in His rising; I have passed from darkness into light. I am Asar Un-nefer the Perfected One. I am the Lord of Life, triumphant over death....There is no part of me that is not of the Gods..."26

Crowley steals another quote from Jesus in his next description of the king. In John 14:6 of the King James Version, Jesus said: "I am the way, the truth, and the life: no man cometh unto the Father, but by me."(KJV) Crowley wrote, quoting Satan: "I am the Way: the Truth and the Life: no man cometh unto the Father but by me. I am purified: I have passed through the Gates of Darkness unto Light! I have fought upon Earth for good: I have finished my Work: I have entered into the Invisible! I am the Sun in His rising: I have passed through the Hour of Cloud and of Night! I am Amoun, the Concealed One: The Opener of Day am I! I am Osiris Onnophris, the Justified One. I am the Lord of Life Triumphant over Death: There is no part of me that is not of the Gods."27

In all of the three previous quotes, Aleister Crowley calls the king the sun. The king is the sun god. This is the same as Led Zeppelin's Swan Song logo, the Sun God Apollo, as mentioned in chapter one. The emblem is on the following albums Led Zeppelin produced with their own company, Swan Song. It is printed on *Physical Graffiti*, *Presence*, *The Song Remains the Same*, *In Through the Out Door*, and *Coda*. It is also on Bad Company's *Desolation*

Angels album. (Did you catch the title of that album? Is it any wonder that they were on Led Zeppelin's label?) The following is part of Crowley's presentation of "Apollo Bestows the Violin" from *The Equinox*. He calls him the Sun God:

"Beyond and between each elephant stood five priestesses in white robes, their faces wrapped closely even to the eyes, lest the fumes should cause them to fall into trance. Each of these held in her hand a torch filled with oil pressed from the sacred olives that grew in the groves of the temple, and each was blind and deaf from too long continuance in the shrine whose glory was so dazzling and whose music so intense. Each might have been a statue of snow at some antique revelry of a Tsar.

"Beyond the last of these, where the temple narrowed, was a shrine hidden, for from the roof hung a veil of purple, on which were written on golden letters the names and titles of Apollo.

"It was the hour of worship; with uplifted hands a bearded priest in a voluminous robe of azure and gold cried aloud the invocations. He stood beyond the tripod, his face toward the shrine.

'Hail to the Lord of the Sun!
Mystic, magnificent one!
Who shall contend with him? None.
Hail to the Lord of the Sun!

'Hail to the Lord of the Bow!
He hath chosen an arrow, and lo!
Shall any avail with him? No!
Hail to the Lord of the Bow!'

And then turning towards the tripod:

'Hail to the Lord of the Lyre!
Diviner of death and desire,
Prophetic of favour and fire,
Hail to the Lord of the Lyre!'

With this he turned again and went up to the veil, prostrating himself seven times. Then again he turned and came to the tripod and sang:

'Prophetess, pythoness, hear!
Child of Apollo descend!
Smooth from the soul of the sphere
Of the sun, be upon us, befriend!

In the soothsaying smoke of the hollow
Do thou and thine oracle follow
The word and the will of Apollo!'

"So saying, he cast incense upon the opening beneath the tripod, and retired into the shrine. As the smoke cleared, there was found seated upon the tripod a maiden in a close fitting dress of crimson silk broidered with gold. Her masses of black hair, caught at the crown with a fillet of crimson and gold, fell heavily around her. She bore a lyre in her hands. Her eyes were wild and fierce, and she sniffed up the vapours of the cavern with awesome ardour. Feebly at first, afterwards frenetically, she plucked at the strings.

"Hardly a minute-a string snapped; the whole music jarred; and the priest ran from the shrine, shrieking 'Apollo! Apollo! Veil your faces! Apollo hath descended.' Himself he flung upon the marble before the tripod. There was a noise as of thunder; the veil was swept open as by a whirlwind, and Apollo, one flame of gold, entered the temple. As he passed, the priestesses fell dead and their torches were extinct. But a ray of glory from above, a monstrance to the God, followed him. Slowly and majestically he moved to the tripod. In his hands he bore an instrument of wood, of unfamiliar shape. Music of triumph and of glory answered his paces.

"To the pythoness he advanced, thus dancing. He took the lyre from her hands and broke it. She stared, entranced. He put the strange instrument into her hands and, drawing down her head, pressed his lips to her forehead. Then he breathed lightly on her hands. Darkness fell, and lightnings rent it; thunders answered them. Apollo was gone. After the thunder the temple was filled with rosy radiance. The old priest, still prone, raised and let fall his hands, in mechanical imitation of the signs of invocation. Obedient, the pythoness began to play upon the instrument given of the God, and the temple shuddered at sounds so ethereal, so soul shaking, so divine. A greater music had been given to the world.

"She ended. The old priest rose unsteadily to his feet, crying: 'Apollo! Apollo!' staggered, and fell dead before the tripod.
                    The light went out."28
Before we move on, I want to present Webster's definition of Apollo: "*Greek & Roman Myth*, the god of music, poetry, prophecy, and medicine, represented an exemplifying manly youth and beauty: later identified with HELIOS."29 In Greek Mythology, Helios is the sun god as well, according to Webster. Apollo is the god of music and he is the sun. You already know that Lucifer was created with the power to compose music and that Crowley calls him the sun in the quote at the heading of chapter four, so now you know who Led Zeppelin was making reference to with the pictures of Apollo on their albums as well as t-shirts, etc. It is none other than the Devil. However, much more evidence is on the way, and it

is going to get more interesting each step of the way.

One more name is going to be presented here before we look at the queen. The name is Dionysus. He is another form of Pan, and you know who Pan is. The following quote is from *The Black Arts*: "Some modern writers have suggested that memories of the cult of the Greek god Dionysus survived to influence the sabbath. There is no evidence of this, but there are several similarities between Dionysus and the Devil of the witches. Both appealed particularly to women and the rites of both were orgiastic."30 Now we'll consider the goddess.

BINAH - THE QUEEN, GODDESS

As previously stated, the third Sephira is Binah, the Goddess, the queen, united to Chokmah, the God, the king, as husband and wife, or father and mother. The following is Crowley's presentation of the queen from *The Equinox*:

THE QUEEN

"I am the Queen of the heavenly ones, of the Gods, and of the Goddesses, united in one form. I am She who was, who is, and will be; my form is one, my name is manifold; under the palm-trees, and in the deserts, in the valleys, and on the snowy mountains, mankind pays me homage, and thunders forth praises to my name. Yet I am nameless in the deep, as amongst the lightsome mountains of the sky. Some call me Mother of the Gods, some Aphrodite of the seas of pearl, some Diana of the golden nets, some Proserpina Queen of Darkness, some Hecate mistress of enchantments, some Istar of the boat of night, some Miriam of the Cavern, and others yet again Isis, veiled mother of Mystery.

"I am she who cometh in unto all men, and if not here, then shalt thou behold Me amidst the darkness of Acheron, and as Queen in the palaces of Styx. I am the dark night that bringeth forth the bright day; I am the bright day that swalloweth up the dark night; that bright day that hath been begotten by the ages, and conceived in the hearts of men; that dawn in which storms shall cease their roaring, and the billows of the deep shall be smoothed out like a sheet of molten glass.

"Then I was carried away on the wings of rapture, and in the strength of my joy I leapt from the tower of Night; but as I fell, she caught me, and I clung to her and she became as a Daughter of this world, as a Child of God begotten in the heart of man. And her hair swept around and about me, in clouds of gold, and rolled over me, as sunbeams poured out from the cups of the noon. Her cheeks were bright with a soft vermillion of the pomegranate mingling with the whiteness of the lily. Her lips were half open, and her eyes were deep, passionate, and tremulous, as the eyes of the mother of the human race, when she first struggled in the strong arms of man; for I was growing strong in her strength, I was becoming a worthy partner of her glory."31

ISIS

In the last quote, the goddess is presented as Aphrodite, Diana, Proserpina, Hecate, Istar, Miriam, and Isis. A few others will be named shortly. Right now the focus is going to center on Isis, because Crowley brings everything magical back to Egypt eventually, with the Devil behind it. The following quotes are taken from Lewis Spence's *Ancient Egyptian Myths and Legends*. Lewis Spence is also the author of *Magic Arts in Celtic Britain*, mentioned at the heading of chapter fourteen, as the main inspiration for "Stairway to Heaven." Spence wrote concerning Isis:

"Isis, or Ast, must be regarded as one of the earliest and most important conceptions of female godhead in ancient Egypt. In the dynastic period she was regarded as the feminine counterpart of Osiris, and we may take it that before the dawn of Egyptian history she occupied a similar position. The philology of the name appears to be unfathomable. No other deity has probably been worshiped for such an extent of time, for her cult did not perish with that of most other Egyptian gods, but flourished later in Greece and Rome, and is seriously carried on in Paris to-day.

"Isis was perhaps of Libyan origin, and is usually depicted in the form of a woman crowned with her name-symbol and holding in her hand a scepter of papyrus. Her crown is surmounted by a pair of horns holding a disk, which in turn is sometimes crested by her hieroglyph, which represents a seat or throne. Sometimes also she is represented a possessing radiant and many-coloured wings, with which she stirs to life the inanimate body of Osiris.

"No other goddess was on the whole so popular with the Egyptians, and the reason for this is probably to be found in the circumstances of travail and pity which run through her myth. These drew the sympathies of the people to her, but they were not the only reasons why she was beloved by the Egyptian masses, for she was the great and beneficent mother goddess and represented the maternal spirits in its most intimate and affectionate guise. In her myth, perhaps one of the most touching and beautiful which ever sprang from the consciousness of a people, we find evolved from what may have been a mere corn-spirit a type of wifely and maternal affection mourning the death of her cherished husband, and seeking by every means in her power to restore him to life."32

ISIS AS THE WIND

"Although Isis had undoubtedly many forms, and although she may be regarded as the great corn-mother of Egypt, the probabilities are that in one of her phases she represents the wind of heaven. This does not appear to have been recognized by students of Egyptology, but the record seems a fairly clear one. Osiris in his guise of the corn dies and comes to life again and is sown broadcast over the land. Isis is disconsolate and moans terribly over his loss; in fact, so loud and heartrending is her grief that the child of the King of Byblos, who she is nursing, dies of terror. From her, grateful odours emanate, as the women of the Queen of Byblos experience. She transforms herself into a swallow. She restores the dead Osiris to life by fanning him with her wings and filling his mouth and nostrils with sweet air. It is noteworthy that she is one of the few Egyptian deities who possess wings. She is a great traveller, and unceasingly moans and sobs. If these qualities and circumstances are not allegorical of the wind, a much more ingenious hypothesis than the above will be necessary to account for their mythological connexion. Isis wails like the wind, she shrieks in tempest, she carries the fragrance of spices and flowers throughout the country, she takes the shape of a swallow, one of the swiftest of birds and typical of the rapidity of the wind, she employs the element of which she is mistress to revivify the dead Osiris, she possesses wings, as do all deities connected with the wind, and like the rest of her kind she is constantly travelling up and down the land. We do not advance the hypothesis that she is a wind-goddess *par excellence*, but in one of her phases she certainly typifies the revivifying power of the spring wind, which wails and sobs over the grave of the sleeping grain, bringing reanimating breath to the inert seeds."33

ISIS - GODDESS OF FERTILITY

One more quote from Spence concerning Isis, presents her in the important role as the goddess of fertility:

"The myth of Isis became so real to the people of Egypt that they came to regard her very intimately indeed, and fully believed that she had once been a veritable woman. In a more allegorical manner she was of course the great feminine fructifier of the soil. She was also a powerful enchantress, as is shown by the number of deities and human beings whom she rescued from death. Words of great and compelling power were hers. Her astronomical symbol was the star Sept, which marked the spring and the approach of the inundation of the Nile, an added evidence that in one of her phases she was goddess of the winds of spring. As the light-giver at this season of the year she was called Khut, and as goddess of the fruitful earth Usert. As the force which impelled the powers of spring and sent forth the Nile flood she was Sati, and as the goddess of fertile waters she was Anqet. She was further the deity of cultivated lands and fields, goddess of harvest and goddess of food. So that from first to last she personified the forces which make for growth and nourishment. She personifies the power of the spring season, the power of the earth to grow and yield grain, motherhood and all the attributes and affinities which spring therefrom."34

The last example of the goddess presented here is from Aleister Crowley once again. He presents her as the queen of light, mother of music, and makes reference also to king of the spirits, her consort, obviously. He says the spirits are in the air, no less. He wrote:

"THE INTERPRETER"

"MOTHER of Light, and the Gods! Mother of Music, awake!
Silence and Speech are at odds; Heaven and Hell are at
      stake.
By the Rose and the Cross I conjure; I constrain by the
      Snake and the Sword;
I am he that is sworn to endure-Bring us the word of the
      Lord!

By the brood of the Bysses of Brightening, whose God was
      my sire;
By the Lord of the Flame and the Lightning, the King of
      the Spirits of Fire;
By the Lord of the Waves and the Waters, the King of the
      Hosts of the Sea,
The fairest of all of whose daughters was mother to me;

By the Lord of the Winds and the Breezes, the King of the
      Spirits of Air,
In whose bosom the infinite ease is that cradled me there;
By the Lord of the Fields and the Mountains, the King of
      Spirits of Earth
That nurtured my life at his fountains from the hour of my
      birth;

By the Wand and the Cup I conjure; by the Dagger and
      Disk I constrain;
I am he that is sworn to endure; make thy music again!
I am Lord of the Star and the Seal; I am Lord of the Snake

and the Sword;
Reveal us the riddle, reveal! Bring us the word of the Lord!

As the flame of the sun, as the roar of the sea, as the storm
of the air,
As the quake of the earth-let it soar for a boon, for a bane,
for a snare,
For a lure, for a light, for a kiss, for a rod, for a scourge
for a sword-
Bring us thy burden of bliss-Bring us the word of the
Lord!"35

PHYSICAL GRAFFITI – "DOWN BY THE SEASIDE"

So far, we have taken a look at the first three Sephira, Kether, Chokmah, and Binah. This is, again, the "godhead" divided into male and female, making up the Macroprosopus, the first two letters in the Tetragrammaton, "IH." Led Zeppelin, in their song, "Down By the Seaside," made absolute reference to this godhead, I believe. Between 1:02 and 1:10 into the song, Robert Plant sings that "people" departed "away," twice. He repeats it twice again at 1:58 to 2:10. What Plant is talking about here, I believe, is the Aeon of Isis. They left Isis for the "empty" Christian faith that ruled the Aeon of Osiris. Here is a repeat quote from Crowley about this:
"The Hierarchy of the Egyptians gives us this genealogy:
Isis, Osiris, Horus.
"Now the 'pagan' period is that of Isis; a pastoral, natural period of simple magic. Next with Buddha, Christ, and others there came in the Equinox of Osiris; when sorrow and death are the principal objects of man's thought, and his magical formula is that of sacrifice.
"Now, with Mohammed perhaps as its forerunner, comes in the Equinox of Horus, the young child who rises strong and conquering (with his twin Harpocrates) to avenge Osiris, and bring on the age of strength and splendour."36
Montague Summers, another enemy of Aleister Crowley and company, said this about pre-Christian magic in his book *The History of Witchcraft*: "In some sense Witchcraft was a descendant of the old pre-Christian magic, but it soon assumed a slightly different form, or rather at the advent of Christianity it was exposed and shown in its real foul essence as the worship of the Evil Principle, the Enemy of Mankind, Satan."37 The very last line in "Down By the Seaside" contains the lyrics that ask the fans the question "Don't" the people "know" of their departure "away" from magic? That is what I believe is his meaning. This concept is illustrated in Dr. Sir J. G. Frazer's *The Golden Bough*:

"If an Age of Religion has thus everywhere, as I venture to surmise, been preceded by an Age of Magic, it is natural that we should enquire what causes have led mankind, or rather a portion of them, to abandon magic as a principle of faith and practice and to betake themselves to religion instead."38

PHYSICAL GRAFFITI – "TEN YEARS GONE" & "THE ROVER"

Aleister Crowley, as a result of receiving *The Book of the Law* from the Devil, wrote that a New Aeon of Magick was beginning, as you read in the last chapter. In the beginning of the song, "Ten Years Gone," I believe that Robert Plant is using an analogy in order to make reference to the Aeon of Isis, when "Magick" ruled the sky, as he said in "Ramble On," the Aeon of Osiris, when the Inquisition was primarily responsible for the suppression of magic, and the New Aeon of Horus, when love for and the reign of magic will return, that Crowley said began in 1904. At 1:11 into the song, I believe he is singing "as" magic "was," "again" magic is going to "be." The lyrics are "...as it was then again it will be." That statement coincides with what he sang at 1:08 in "Living Loving Maid" off *Led Zeppelin II*, "Heaven told tales of how it used to be." It also fits perfectly with what he sang on another *Physical Graffiti* song, "The Rover." At 4:10 into the song, Plant sings of a "new world rising from the shambles of the old." Also, this is the theme, I believe, of the 1998 Page/Plant song, "When the World Was Young."

At 1:17 into "Ten Years Gone" he sings that "though" their "course" will occasionally "change," the "rivers" eventually "reach" a "sea." I believe he is singing about the New Aeon of Horus/magic at 2:10 when he sings "changes" consume his "time." In the next line he sings to his woman, "that's" fine "with" him. Finally, in the next and last line referred to here, he sings that during the change's "midst," he is thinking of her and "how" things were before. Those lyrics sound just like Lucifer is singing to his bride. At 5:43 of the song, Plant sings that he is "never" about to "leave" her. Satan is again copying Christ here, I believe, because in the New Testament book of Hebrews, Chapter 13, Verse 5, Christ is quoted as saying: "I will never leave you nor forsake you."

BACK TO – "DOWN BY THE SEASIDE"

At 4:13 into "Down By the Seaside," Robert Plant sings a command to the listener to "sing" at high volume "for" some "sunshine." At 4:18 he commands the listener to "pray" diligently "for" some "rain." This is giving respect to the god and goddess of fertility, the Qabalistic godhead. You read in chapter two that Pan was a god of fertility, and you read in this chapter that Isis was a goddess of fertility. Now you know, I believe, who it is Robert Plant is commanding the listeners to address. At 4:24 into the song, he sings another command to "show" one's "love" to a "Lady" Isis, Diana, Aphrodite, Artemis, etc., that created "ya," then "he" is going to return once "again." In other words, if you manifest love to the goddess, she is going to send her son to the earth, I believe. Mathers, translating *The Qabalah Unveiled*, wrote about this very thing: "But IHVH, the Tetragrammaton, as we shall presently see, contains all the Sephiroth with the exception of Kether, and specially signifies the Lesser Countenance, Microprosopus, the King of the qabalistical Sephirotic greatest Trinity, *and the Son in His human incarnation...*"39 As you will see later in the book, this reference is to the Anti-Christ.

Between 3:19 and 3:36 of "Down By the Seaside," Plant sings to the listener to "hear" some "people" who are "singing" of "growin,'" which I believe refers to the fertility of the ground and their singing praises for it, and that they are happy about "knowin'" of the eternity to which they are "goin." In other words, the people are singing praises to the Devil (who they believe is the good and benevolent universal god) and his female consort for the fertility of the ground, and they are rejoicing because they know that when they die they are going to unite with the godhead. That will be addressed later in a very important section, that will explain to Doors fans, what "The west is the best" means. If you haven't listened to the Doors lately, I am referring to the song, appropriately titled, "The End," which is off the first album. After reading this chapter, I want to challenge the Led Zeppelin fan or curious reader to listen to all three songs off the second disk of *Physical Graffiti*, which are in this order: In The Light, Down By the Seaside, and Ten Years Gone. This transition of the worship of Christ by mankind back to the worship of the Devil and magic is analogous to the military breaking down the civilian behavior of a recruit and building them back up as military personnel. Satan is breaking down the worship of Christ, and society all over the world is being molded into an Anti-Christ loving environment. This is all in accordance with the prophecies of the *Bible*. When the Anti-Christ comes to power, he will wage war against what Christian people are on the earth; as well as the Jews, meaning Israel. Isn't that what Crowley wrote in the last chapter? Now before we move on to the Son in the qabalistic trinity, we are going to look at the god and goddess together. The following quote presents the god and goddess in Greek form, from Aleister Crowley's *Equinox, Vol. I, No. 4*:

"PAN TO ARTEMIS"

"UNCHARMABLE charmer
Of Bacchus and Mars
In the sounding rebounding

Abyss of the stars!
O virgin in armour,
Thine arrows unsling
In the brilliant resilient
First rays of the spring!

By the force of the fashion
Of love, when I broke
Through the shroud, through the cloud,
Through the storm, through the smoke,
To the mountain of passion
Volcanic that woke-
By the rage of the mage
 I invoke, I invoke!

By the midnight of madness:-
The lone-lying sea,
The swoon of the moon,
Your swoon into me,
The sentinel sadness
Of cliff-clinging pine,
That night of delight
You were mine, you were mine!

You were mine O my saint,
My maiden, my mate,
By the might of the right
Of the night of our fate.
Though I fall, though I faint,
Though I char, though I choke,
By the hour of our power
I invoke, I invoke!

By the mystical union
Of fairy and faun,
Unspoken, unbroken-
The dusk to the dawn!-
A secret communion
Unmeasured, unsung,
The listless, resistless,
Tumultuous tongue!-

O virgin in armour,
Thine arrows unsling,
In the brilliant resilient
First rays of the spring!

No Godhead could charm her,
But manhood awoke-
O fiery Valkyrie,
I invoke, I invoke!"40

Pan and Artemis, as previously stated, are Greek representations of the qabalistic godhead. There is however, a relationship between them and other gods. Horus, who is called the Crowned and Conquering Child, is the son of Isis and Osiris, yet, Crowley presents him also as the son of Pan and Artemis in his Confessions:

"She is Isis and Mary, Istar and Bhavani, Artemis and Diana.

But Artemis is still barren of hope until the spirit of the Infinite All, great Pan, tears asunder the veil and displays the hope of humanity, the Crowned Child of the Future."41

In that quote he presents Pan and Artemis as husband and wife, and yet in this next quote, he presents Artemis as the wife of Apollo: "But now the Sun and Moon are Apollo and Artemis, Osiris and Isis; the Divine Eye is formulated from the Light of those eyes that are but as darkness, and the Osiris saith in very truth: 'Before I was blind: now I see!'"42 (Did you see the phrase "the Divine Eye" in that quote? It refers, I believe, to the eye on the screen as Mick Jagger begins singing "Sympathy for the Devil," in the *Bridges to Babylon Tour* DVD, that was recorded in St. Louis in 1997.)

This next quote is from Raymond Buckland and his book, *Buckland's Complete Book of Witchcraft*. Before I present it, I want to say that Buckland, as a strong promoter of Wiccan Witchcraft and Magic in the United States, says that he does not believe in the Devil. He believes in the Horned God. Yet, Buckland admits to studying Witchcraft under Gerald Gardner who was a contemporary of Aleister Crowley. What is even worse, is that Buckland quotes Crowley in a positive fashion in this book. Let me see, I wonder who the Horned God could be. Forgive me for sounding sarcastic, but I can't stand this type of foolishness. This is what Buckland had to say about the god and goddess as they relate to the people of Wales in one of their traditions: "There can be surprises in discovering names used for the deities in different traditions. One very-strong Welsh tradition uses the name 'Diana' for the Goddess and 'Pan' for the God...Diana, of course, was a ROMAN Goddess and Pan was a GREEK God! Their connection with the Welsh must be one of the mysteries."43

The reader needs to understand that among occultists, Artemis and

Diana are considered one and the same. Crowley, then, presents Pan and Apollo as one and the same. Here is proof of what I just said about Diana and Artemis, because Crowley presents Diana as wife of Apollo in this quote from Eliphas Levi that he included in No.10 of *The Equinox*: "Lift yourselves up again, O Temples of Delphi and of Ephesus! The God of Light and of Art is become the God of the world, and the Word of God is indeed willing to be called Apollo! Diana will no more reign widowed in the lonely fields of night; her silvern crescent is now beneath the feet of the bride."44 Crowley included that quote from Levi, who he believed he was reincarnated, in his *Equinox*, and he included the following quote from J. F. C. Fuller in No.4 of *The Equinox*: "...Horus became under varying names the supreme world-god, and his four sons, or emanations, the four quarters."45 Remember, Robert Plant, in the *Physical Graffiti* song "Kashmir," sang to the "Father" who begets "winds" in each quarter of the earth, to push his "sails" at 5:31 into the song. The number of the winds that Plant mentions is consistent with the quote you just read about Horus-4. Another quote from Fuller, from Crowley's *Equinox*, links Horus and the Law of Thelema: "A new god stirs in the Womb of its Mother; we can see his form, dim and red, in the cavern of Time. Dare we pronounce his name? Yea! It is Horus, Horus the Child, reborn Amsu the Good Shepherd, who will lead us out of the sheepish stupidity of to-day. How many understand this mystery? Perhaps none save those who have seen and subscribed to the Law of Thelema."46 Because we have now gotten to the point of discussing Horus, who is the son of Osiris and Isis, we need to examine the Microprosopus, or the son in the qabalistic trinity, represented by the letter "V" in the IHVH Tetragrammaton.

MICROPROSOPUS

The Microprosopus, the son, is described by Mathers as the entire fourth through ninth Sephiroth as the letter "V," or "Vau." He wrote:
"...concerning V, *Vau*, he saith: Six members are produced from the branch of the root of his body. (The body is the Microprosopus; the root of the body is the mother, who is symbolized by the letter H, *He*; the branch of the root is the letter V, *Vau*, enclosed and hidden within the letter H, *He*; and from that very branch were produced the six members-that is, the entire letter V, *Vau*, now having obtained the head.)
[The mother here mentioned is of course the third Sephira, Binah. The six members of Microprosopus forming the entire letter Vau is an allusion to the numerical value of that letter being 6.]"47
Mathers said the same thing in a slightly different fashion in this next quote: "Assuredly *Yod*, I, impregnateth the letter *He*, H, and produceth a Son,

and She herself bringeth Him forth."*48 The asterisk in the book refers to the footnote quoted here: "For Chokmah and Binah in the Sephiroth answer unto I and H in the name IHVH, as has been already shown in the Introduction; and these bring forth Microprosopus the Son, the letter Vau, V, answering in numerical value to the number 6, and to the fourth, fifth, sixth, seventh, eighth, and ninth Sephiroth."49

ISIS, OSIRIS, AND HORUS

Lewis Spence, in *Ancient Egyptian Myths and Legends*, gives us the best antiquarian description of Isis, Osiris and Horus. He wrote:

"Arrived in Egypt, Isis opened the chest and wept long and sorely over the remains of her royal husband. But now she bethought herself of her son Harpocrates, or Horus the Child, whom she had left in Buto, and leaving the chest in a secret place, she set off to search for him. Meanwhile Set, while hunting by the light of the moon, discovered the richly adorned coffin and in his rage rent the body into fourteen pieces, which he scattered here and there throughout the country.

"Upon learning of this fresh outrage on the body of the god, Isis took a boat of papyrus-reeds and journeyed forth once more in search of her husband's remains. After this crocodiles would not touch a papyrus boat, probably because they thought it contained the goddess, still pursuing her weary search. Whenever Isis found a portion of the corpse she buried it and built a shrine to mark the spot. It is for this reason that there are so many tombs of Osiris in Egypt."50

One more quote from Lewis Spence reiterates the same, but names Horus as the sun:

"Another important form of Horus was that known as Horus, son of Isis, and of Osiris. He represented the rising sun, as did several other forms of Horus, and possessed many aspects or variants. His shrines were so numerous that at one epoch or another he was identified with all other Horus-gods, but he chiefly represented the new sun, born daily, and he was son and successor of Osiris. He was extremely popular, as being a well-marked type of resurrection after death. As Osiris represented 'yesterday,' so Horus, his son, stood for 'today' in the Egyptian mind. Although some texts state that Osiris was his father, others claim this position for Ra, but the two in this instance are really one and the same and interchangeable."51

In the Egyptian theology, Osiris dies and Horus is born. In the terminology of *The Book of the Law* and the Aeon of Osiris, it is the period of Christianity. Horus in his aeon is a return to magic. In this symbolism, the sun setting and disappearing from view is picturesque of the end of the Aeon of Osiris and the beginning of the Aeon of Horus. This is why, I believe, that Led Zeppelin insisted on going on stage at the Bath Festival right at sunset.

On June 28th, 1970, Led Zeppelin performed at the Bath Festival, in Shepton Mallet, England. Dave Lewis and Simon Pallett wrote: "Coming on just as the sun was setting (with a little help from Grant, who physically ensured the preceding act, Flock, vacated the stage on time to enable his boys to take full effect of the natural sunset), over the next couple of hours Zeppelin cemented their supremacy as the most popular rock act of the period in front of over 150,000 fans. Their reception was phenomenal - returning to the stage for multiple encores."52 Led Zeppelin also played at sunset in Philadelphia when they played three songs for Bob Geldof and Live Aid in 1985. When I saw them on June 11th, 1977, at Madison Square Garden in Manhattan, they came out at 9:20 p.m. The doors opened at 8:00 p.m. They waited until the sun went down before they came out to play. I distinctly remember saying that when they came out, because we could hardly see in there prior to the stage lights coming on. It wasn't like any other concert I have ever been to at night. At any other show, you know the band is about to come out and play because the house lights go out. That was not the case with Led Zeppelin. At Madison Square Garden we just sat in there getting stoned as it got darker and darker inside. We all got very impatient with the band over that period of an hour and twenty minutes, collectively stomping our feet on the floor in intermittent sessions.

Before going any further, I want to present another interesting find in the writings of Lewis Spence, this time from *Native American Myths and Legends*, that shows the Devil spread his concept of the Qabalistic trinity to the Algonquian Indians. Spence wrote that they worshiped the god, who they referred to as the sun god. They also worshiped his female consort, who they referred to as the moon goddess, whose name was Kokomikis. Finally, they worshiped the son of sun, who they called the morning star, whose name was Apisirahts.53 This is the same trinity presented in Crowley's *Book of the Law*.

INTERCHANGEABLE NAMES FOR THE GODS

Aleister Crowley, in preparing to receive *The Book of the Law*, without knowing he would, began to invoke Horus, who came to him in the form of Aiwaz. We know that Aiwaz is Horus, because Crowley calls him the Devil, and he calls the Devil the sun, as well as Horus. Crowley also called the Devil Pan. In the next chapter, you will see Crowley present Horus and Pan as one. As you read in this chapter, Pan and Apollo are one and the same, because Diana and Artemis are one and the same, and Crowley presents both Artemis and Diana as wife of Apollo. He also presents Artemis as wife of Pan, who is the piper. Shortly, you will read that Apollo as well is the piper, and Horus. You also read from

Raymond Buckland, a very effective promoter of Wiccan magic and witchcraft in the United States, that some people in Wales refer to the godhead as Diana and Pan. When Crowley was in India, he sacrificed a goat to Kali, because he considered her the goddess, too. Kali was wife of Siva, or Shiva. As she wrote in her *Encyclopedia of Witches and Witchcraft*, Rosemary Ellen Guiley said that Kali was: "The Hindu goddess of death, destruction, fear and terror, and the wife-consort of Siva, the destroyer."54 It is fitting that Siva is called the destroyer (like a couple of Led Zeppelin bootlegs from Cleveland on April 27th and 28th in 1977), because the Book of Revelation in the *Bible* calls the Devil "Abbadon," and "Apollyon," and both mean "destroyer."

INVOCATION OF HORUS - CAIRO, EGYPT, 1904

At this point in the chapter, I want to present to you part of the actual Invocation of Horus, that Crowley used in Cairo in 1904, that ended in his reception of *The Book of the Law*. This section of the invocation shows that Crowley believed even then, that Horus was one with all other gods. The following is section II of the invocation:

II

"Strike, strike the master chord!
Draw, draw the Flaming Sword!
Crowned Child and Conquering Lord,
Horus, avenger!

1. By thy name of Ra, I invoke Thee, Hawk of the Sun, the glorious one!
2. By thy name Harmachis, youth of the Brilliant Morning, I invoke Thee!
3. By thy name Mau, I invoke Thee, Lion of the midday Sun.
4. By thy name Tum, Hawk of the Even, crimson splendour of the Sunset, I invoke Thee!
5. By thy name Khep-Ra I invoke Thee, O Beetle of the hidden Mastery of Midnight!
A. By thy name Heru-pa-Kraat, Lord of Silence, Beautiful Child that standest on the Dragons of the Deep, I invoke Thee!
B. By thy name of Apollo, I invoke Thee, O man of

strength and splendour, O poet, O father!

    C. By thy name of Pheobus, that drivest thy chariot through the Heaven of Zeus, I invoke Thee!

    D. By thy name of Odin I invoke Thee, O warrior of the North, O Renown of the Sagas!

    E. By thy name of Jeheshua, O child of the Flaming Star, I invoke Thee!

    F. By Thine own, Thy secret name Hoori, Thee I invoke!
                The Names are Five.
                The Names are Six.
                Eleven are the Names!
                Abrahadabra!"55

THE LED ZEPPELIN FILM – "THE SONG REMAINS THE SAME"

    In number one of the invocation, Crowley calls Horus by the name of Ra. In number four, Crowley calls Horus by the name of Tum, who is called: "...Hawk of the Even, crimson splendour of the sunset..."56 In *The Equinox*, *Vol. I*, *No.6*, Aleister Crowley presents adorations that are to be made by aspirants to the Silver Star, in a section called *Liber Resh*:

    "0. These are the adorations to be performed by all aspirants to the A.A.

    1. Let him greet the Sun at dawn, facing East, giving the sign of his grade. And let him say in a loud voice:

    Hail unto Thee who art Ra in Thy rising, even unto Thee who art Ra in Thy strength, who travellest over the Heavens in Thy bark at the Uprising of the Sun."57

    In the film, *The Song Remains the Same*, just after Peter Grant's opening Al Capone type fantasy sequence, the scene moves to the New York City skyline, viewed from the west. The first thing you see is the sun rising above the skyscrapers, while the camera is facing east, and it disappears above the Empire State Building. This is consistent with Crowley's command to hail Ra as he rises, facing east. You know that was the east in the film, because the sun was rising, not setting. In the context of Liber Resh, the third number refers to Tum the Hawk from the invocation of Horus:

    "3. Also, at Sunset, let him greet the Sun, facing West, giving the sign of his grade. And let him say in a loud voice:

    Hail unto Thee, who art Tum in Thy setting, even unto Thee who art Tum in thy joy, who travellest over the Heavens in Thy bark at the Down-going of the Sun."58

Tum can be seen in the Led Zeppelin film at the end of John Bonham's drum solo, "Moby Dick." Robert Plant glorifies Bonham at the end of the solo, calling him "glory." Then Plant takes the microphone off the stand in front of him and the lights go out. Then the scene moves to the east side of Manhattan, where the film crew has the camera facing west, during the crimson sunset, which is, again, consistent with what Crowley called Tum: "...Hawk of the Even, crimson splendour of the Sunset..."59 In the upper left hand corner of your screen, if you are watching the film, there is a large cloud there. Almost immediately a large hawk descends out of the cloud and heads toward the twin towers with the sunset behind him. There it is. You have just seen proof from Crowley's writings of his influence on their film. However, the best is yet to come. If you are watching the film, I ask you, how did they know that hawk was going to fly in that direction? I mean, even if they are the ones who released it, how did they get it to fly where they wanted? Or were they told where to have the camera by some supernatural being? By the way, they are showing him descending just in time for the encores, including the Theremin section of "Whole Lotta Love." If you are "old" enough to still own the soundtrack LP, you can see that Jimmy Page included a photo of the hawk flying across the sky in the center photo section of the jacket. It is the same hawk, from the same scene. No one could possibly believe that this is a coincidence, that the Crowley quotes match the film. They put it in the film, the sun and the hawk, to make reference to future followers of Aleister Crowley and the Silver Star, and inevitably, the Devil. Tum is the son of Apollo. By the way, you saw Apollo's name in the Invocation of Horus, and like Pan, Crowley calls him: "...Apollo, the Piper, the maker of music."60 Remember, Apollo is the figure used for the Swan Song logo. Pan and Apollo are both the Piper, because they are both Lucifer the Piper, or Satan, the Devil.

HORUS THE CHILD

Horus is the child, or "V" in the Tetragrammaton, IHVH. Again, he is the Microprosopus, represented by the fourth, fifth, sixth, seventh, eighth, and ninth Sephiroth. Before moving on to the tenth Sephira, Malkuth, mankind, the earth, the lesser world, the bride, the queen, the wife of Microprosopus, we are going to examine the following quotes from Aleister Crowley that further describe the child. He wrote: "UNDER the glittering horns of Capricornus, when the mountains of the North glistened like the teeth of the black wolf in the cold light of the moon, and when the broad lands below the fiery girdle of many-breasted Tellus blushed red in the arms of the summer sun, did Miriam seek the cave below the cavern, in which no light had ever shone, to bring forth the Light of the World. And on the third day she departed from the cave, and, entering the stable of the Sun, she placed her child in the manger of the Moon. Likewise was Mithras born under the tail of the Sea-Goat, and Horus, and Krishna-all mystic names of the mystic Child of Light."61 There you have Crowley lining up Krishna with Satan. In the next quote, Crowley calls him "birthless," meaning the son is also the father in the Qabalah: "...O divine Youth who has created thyself! What art thou? Thou art the birthless and the deathless one, without beginning and without end! Thou paintest the heavens bright with rays of pure emerald light, for thou art Lord of the beams of Light. Thou illuminest the two lands with rays of turquoise and beryl, and sapphire, and amethyst; for Lord of Love, Lord of Life, Lord of Immensity, Lord of Everlastingness is thy name."62 In the next quote, Crowley calls him child, father, and light, speaking in his stead: "I am the child of all who am the father of all, for from me came forth all things, that I might be. I am the fountain in the snows, and I am the eternal sea. I am the lover, and I am the beloved, and I am the first-fruits of their love. I am the first faint shuddering of the light, and I am the loom wherein night weaveth her impenetrable veil."63

The following is the last quote concerning the son that will be presented here. It presents the Egyptian trinity in light of *The Book of the Law*: "Moreover I was united with Isis the Mother of Osiris, being yet her brother and her lord....Yet one thing I saw also, that as Isis is the Lady of all Nature, the living; and as Osiris is the Lord of the Dead, so should Horus come, the Hawk-headed Lord, as a young child, the image of all Nature and all Man raised above Life and Death, under the supreme rule of Hadit that is Force and of Nuit that is Matter-though they are a Matter and a Force that transcend all our human conceptions of these things."64 Hadit is the god and Nuit is the goddess; the Qabalistic godhead in another Egyptian form.

One more statement needs to be made prior to focusing on the bride of the son. In the letter "D" section of the Invocation of Horus, Crowley calls him the Scandinavian, Norse Mythological "Odin." Odin is the husband of Freya, who is the mother of Thor. Odin and Thor are both the Devil. In the Led Zeppelin film, *The Song Remains the Same*, in the beginning of the song, "No Quarter," Robert Plant sings of "Thor" and his "winds" that are "cold." After Plant sings the word "cold," he lifts his hands up in the air and draws his head back. Look at how intense his eyes are as he brings his head back to normal position. Then at the end of the song he is singing about Satan. Now I ask you, why is Plant singing of a Norse Mythological character and the Devil in the same song? There is no theological connection between the *Holy Bible*, which speaks of the Devil, and Norse Mythology. Obviously, Thor is the Devil in another form. Again, it's the Father, Mother, and Son trilogy. Absolute proof of Led Zeppelin's promotion of the Qabalah will be presented in chapter ten.

MALKUTH - THE BRIDE OF MICROPROSOPUS

The final aspect of the Qabalah, the creation, the earth, the daughter of the goddess, the lower "H" in the Tetragrammaton, IHVH, Malkuth is the natural soul. It is called the Microcosm, where as the rest of the Qabalah, being the universe, the god and the goddess, is the Macrocosm. S. L. MacGregor Mathers wrote concerning Malkuth in *The Qabalah Unveiled*: "The number 10. ....It is called MLKVTH, *Malkuth*, the Kingdom, and also the Queen, Matrona, the inferior Mother, the Bride of Microprosopus; and SHKINH, *Shekinah*, represented by the Divine Name *Adonai*, ADNI, and among the angelic hosts by the kerubim, KRVBIM. Now, each of these Sephiroth will be in a certain degree androgynous, for it will be feminine or receptive with regard to the Sephira which immediately precedes it in the sephirotic scale, and masculine or transmissive with regard to the Sephira which immediately follows it. But there is no *Sephira* anterior to Kether, nor is there a Sephira which succeeds Malkuth."65

Mathers, in wanting to present the IHVH in chart form wrote the following to present the entire universe:

"Let us not lose sight of the great qabalistical idea, that the trinity is always completed by and finds its realization in the quaternary; that is, IHV completed and realized in IHVH - the trinity of:

Crown;	King;	Queen;
Father;	Son;	Spirit;
Absolute;	Formation;	Realization;

completed by the quaternary of-

Absolute One	Father and Mother	Son	Bride
Macroprosopus, the Vast Countenance	Father and Mother	Microprosopus, the Lesser Countenance	Malkuth, Queen & Bride."66

Mathers presents Malkuth as a reflection of the goddess, or mother. He wrote: "The bride, the inferior H, *He*, is said to be a reflection of the mother, the supernal H, *He*, in the Tetragrammaton; just as Microprosopus is said to be the reflection of Macroprosopus."67

By analogy, the son and his bride are the same as the god and goddess. Mathers wrote:

"The conjunction of the letters V and H at the end of the Tetragrammaton IHVH is similar to that of I and H at the beginning."68

Finally, he sums it up:

"We must remember that in the Tetragrammaton, IHVH, I, *Yod*, is the father (who is not Macroprosopus, though he is implied therein, as the top point of the Hebrew letter Yod is said to symbolize him); H, *He*, the supernal mother; V, *Vau*, the son (Microprosopus); and H, *He*, final, the bride (the queen). And this is their proper order (IHVH)."69

Malkuth is the creation, specifically the people, according to occultists. The son wants to marry his bride and carry her back up the Qabalah. It is the son becoming one with Malkuth and setting her on the throne of Binah, making her one with the mother, and then reverting back into his role as father in Chokmah, becoming one with Binah and drawing her back into Kether, the godhead and universe complete in one. This event is going to be looked at briefly during one of the most important parts of this book yet to come, as it relates to Led Zeppelin's presentation of it. Before leaving Malkuth, the reader needs to understand that it is the Microcosm, as opposed to the godhead, or Macrocosm.

THE HEXAGRAM – SIX POINTED STAR

The Macrocosm symbol is going to be presented and then the Microcosm symbol, in order for the reader to be able to distinguish and identify. Mathers wrote of the Macrocosm symbol:

"...the Macroprosopus and the Microprosopus, or the Vast and the Lesser Countenances. Macroprosopus is, it will be remembered, the first Sephira, or Crown Kether; Microprosopus is composed of six of the Sephiroth. In Macroprosopus all is light and brilliancy; but Microprosopus only shineth by the reflected splendour of Macroprosopus. The six days of creation correspond to the six forms of Microprosopus, therefore the symbol of the interlaced triangles, forming the six-pointed star, is called the Sign of the Macrocosm, or of the creation of the greater world."70 For those who do not know, the six-pointed star is called a Hexagram. Lock it into your memory, that the Hexagram is the sign of the "greater world," or universe. This is accepted as an axiom in the world of occultism. It is not Mathers' opinion. You will read of Crowley's presentation of it in chapter twelve, as it relates to Led Zeppelin. Now we are going to look at the sign of the Microcosm, which most people recognize, the Pentagram.

THE PENTAGRAM – FIVE POINTED STAR

The Pentagram is, as most of you know, the five-pointed star. For the purpose of identifying the Microcosm, or the lesser world, it is universally used by occultists. Mathers wrote: "For five is H, He, the number of the feminine letter in the Tetragrammaton, the number also of the Microcosm or Lesser World, the symbol or sign of which is the Pentagram."71

Before you are done reading this book, you are going to see the son marry or become one with the daughter and take her back up to Binah and Chokmah, who make up Kether. Who is in charge of that presentation? The one and only Jimmy Page is. The conception is unity. It is the oneness of the gods. By the way, Jimmy Page will present Lucifer, Satan, the Devil, as being behind it all, as I wrote before. In bringing this chapter to a close, I want to display the oneness of the satanic godhead from Crowley's writings, showing Horus to be Lucifer. Please remember, the father and the son are one and the same, the Devil, and the goddess does not exist. I'm sure the goddess has appeared to people. However, that was not a goddess, it was someone who manifested himself in the form of a goddess. The Devil has permission to deceive those who worship evil, believing evil is in fact good.

HORUS IS LUCIFER, SATAN, THE DEVIL

Aleister Crowley wrote these words about the trinity as he used to present the formula of the godhead to his readers in the letters "IAO." He wrote:

"It just strikes me-it may be this Isis-Apophis-Osiris IAO formula that I have preached so often. Certainly the first two days were Isis-natural, pleasant, easy events. Most certainly too to-day has been Apophis! Think of the wild cursing and black magic etc....we must hope for the Osiris section to-morrow or next day. Birth, death, resurrection! IAO!"72

I have no desire to explain all the meanings of what he is saying there. I simply wanted you to see the godhead initials that he presents. He uses IAO in that quote. You will remember the invocation of the Devil in chapter two taken from *Diary of a Drug Fiend*. In that invocation he says the people called out to Pan to contact the Devil. How did they do it? By shouting IO PAN! There you have Isis, Osiris, and Pan. Here he presents Isis, Osiris, and Apophis. Apophis is Lucifer. Crowley wrote that, in the following quote, in the context of the godhead. He also calls him Satan: "Blessed be thou, O Bhavani, O Isis my Sister, my Bride, my Mother! Blessed be Thou, O Shiva, O Amoun, Concealed of the Concealed. By Thy most secret and Holy Name of Apophis be Thou blessed, Lucifer, Star of the Dawn, Satan-Jeheshua, Light of the World!"73

What does this all mean? Horus is Apophis and Apophis is Lucifer. In chapter two you read under the heading, "Lucifer the Archangel," that he is the Star of the Dawn from the Old Testament Book of Isaiah. Crowley is taking that from the *Bible*. Jeheshua is Jesus' Jewish name. Also, it was Christ who called himself "the light of the world" in the New Testament Book of John, Chapter 8, Verse 12:

"Then Jesus spoke to them again, saying 'I am the light of the world. He who follows Me shall not walk in darkness, but have the light of life.'"

The Devil is claiming to be god again, through Aleister Crowley. In summing up the gods, Crowley says that they are all one and they are all Pan. You know that Crowley said Pan was the Devil, so who are all the gods? Here is what he wrote:

"O mystery of mysteries! 'For each one of the Gods is in all, and all are in each, being ineffably united to each other and to God; because each, being a super-essential unity, their conjunction with each other is a union of unities.' Hence each is all; thus Nature squanders the gold and silver of our understanding, till in panic frenzy we beat our head on the storm-washed boulders and the blasted trunks, and shout forth, 'Io...Io...Io...Evoe! Io...Io!' till the glades thrill as with the music of syrinx and sistrum, and our souls are rent asunder on the flaming horns of Pan."74

Eliphas Levi, again, who Crowley claimed to be reincarnated, summed up the universality of the Qabalistic god, and Crowley presented this in his *Equinox*:

"Thou art God, who by thy godhead sustainest all beings, and by thy unity dost bring home all creatures. Thou art God, and there is no difference between thy deity, thy unity, thy eternity, and thy existence; for all is one and the same mystery; although names vary, all returns to the same truth. Thou art the knower, and that intelligence which is the source of life emanates from thyself; and beside thy knowledge all the wisest men are fools."75

In bringing this chapter to a close, I want to sum up the Qabalah from the perspective of Eliphas Levi, from his book, *Transcendental Magic*, in which he also states that the Masonic orders were derived from it:

"On penetrating into the sanctuary of the Kabalah one is seized with admiration in the presence of a doctrine so logical, so simple and at the same time so absolute. The essential union of ideas and signs; the consecration of the most fundamental realities by primitive characters; the trinity of words, letters and numbers; a philosophy simple as the alphabet, profound and infinite as the Word; theorems more complete and luminous than those of Pythagoras; a theology which may be summed up on the fingers; an infinite which can be held in the hollow of an infant's hand; ten figures and twenty-two letters, a triangle, a square and a circle: such are the elements of the Kabalah....All truly dogmatic religions have issued from the kabalah and return therein....all Masonic associations owe to it their secrets and their symbols. The Kabalah alone consecrates the alliance of universal reason and the Divine Word; it establishes by the counterpoise of two forces in apparent opposition, the eternal balance of being; it alone reconciles reason with faith, power with liberty, science with mystery: it has the keys of the present, past and future!"76

The Devil, promoting the Qabalah through men like Levi and Crowley, has been able to delude countless occultists and their neophyte disciples into buying the doctrine of a male/female androgynous godhead that he has represented in all cultures throughout the world, though the names vary, and his purpose behind it is to unite men with that godhead, which is none other than himself. He has successfully incorporated each grade on the tree into the said godhead; calling it the Tree of Life. Once again, later in the book the reader will be presented with Jimmy Page's promotion of the Qabalah. It has its roots in Egypt, which is why Aleister Crowley hailed the trinity of Osiris, Isis, and Horus. It is also why he obtained *The Book of the Law* in Egypt, his being a Qabalist. Levi and Crowley both presented the Qabalah as the science of light, or "truth" from their perspective. While the Qabalah is pure heresy, it is easy for men with seared consciences to buy into it. One of the reasons they do it is the power derived from it. One of those powers comes from the Tarot Cards, which are based on the Qabalah. In the next chapter we will focus on the Tarot, its relation to the Qabalah, its purpose, and songs, "Going to California & The Rain Song."

Osiris, the husband of Isis, and the father of Horus, and King in the Qabalah.

Osiris
Photo W. A. Mansell & Co.

The Symbol of the great work accomplished is the union of the god and goddess; after Malkuth has been redeemed. Again, the god is symbolized by the Sun, and the goddess by the moon, therefore the union of the two is an eclipse, which is what you see Led Zeppelin present (left) at the end of the concert in their film.

Isis, the wife of Osiris, and mother of Horus, and Queen of the Qabalistic trinity. Note the Egyptian "Ankh" in her right hand. Lucifer Rising opens up with Isis standing with the Ankh and that Egyptian rod in her left hand, lifting it up and down in response to Osiris doing the same thing. This is symbolic of their joining together to bring forth the son, Horus (Lucifer), and then the daughter, Malkuth, played by Anita Pallenberg. You can buy Lucifer Rising cheap off Amazon.com for less than $20. I did, and it's worth having if you own this book.

Isis
Photo W A Mansell & Co.

The Temple of Isis worship in Egypt is today a very popular tourist attraction.

MAGIC ARTS IN CELTIC BRITAIN

Lewis Spence

This is my first edition of Lewis Spence's *Magic Arts in Celtic Britain,* with photo of the graven image of the "British Sun God." This is the book that Robert Plant said was inspirational in his medium penning of the lyrics to "Stairway to Heaven." (See Ch. 14) In "The Ocean," off *Houses of the Holy,* he sang that he was "singing" about what is "good" as well as our "Sun" which "lights" our "day." Crowley said the Sun was Lucifer: "He is the Lord of the Sabbath of the Adepts, and is Satan, therefore also the Sun, whose number of Magick is 666, the seal of His servant the BEAST." Jimmy Page (below) plays in front of a tarp of the Sun in California, 7/23/77.

1 Eliphas Levi, *The Key to the Mysteries*, Crowley's *Equinox*, Vol. I, No.10, pg.182

2 Aleister Crowley, *The Equinox*, Vol. I, No.5, pg.71

3 Ibid, pg.96

4 Israel Regardie, *The Eye in the Triangle*, pg.67

5 Aleister Crowley, *The Equinox, Vol. I, No.6, pg.7*

6 Karl von Eckartshausen, *The Cloud Upon the Sanctuary*, pp.38-39

7 Israel Regardie, *The Eye In The Triangle*, pg.64

8 Eliphas Levi, *The Key to the Mysteries*, Crowley's *Equinox*, Vol. I, No. 10, pg.182

9 S.L. MacGregor Mathers, translator, *The Kabbalah Unveiled*, Samuel Weiser Inc., Yorke Beach, Maine, 1993, pp. vii-ix of the preface

10 Richard Cavendish, *The Black Arts*, pg.81

11 S. L. MacGregor Mathers, *The Kabbalah Unveiled*, pg.1

12 Ibid, pp.1-2

13 Ibid, pg.2

14 Ibid, pp.4, 5-6

15 Ibid, pg.6

16 Ibid, pg.15

17 Ibid, pg.17

18 Ibid, pp.21-22

19 Eliphas Levi, *The Key to the Mysteries*, pp.241-242

20 S. L. MacGregor Mathers, *The Kabbalah Unveiled*, pg.32

21 Ibid, pg.23

22 Ibid, pg.24

23 Ibid, pp.24-25

24 Ibid, pg.28-29

25 Aleister Crowley, *The Equinox*, Vol. I, No. 1, pg.216

26 Ibid, *John St. John*, pg.134

27 Aleister Crowley, *The Equinox*, Vol. I, No. 3, pg.204

28 Aleister Crowley, *The Equinox*, Vol. I, No. 7, pp.246-248

29 *Webster's New World Dictionary*, Second College Edition, William Collins & World Publishing Co. Inc., 1978, pg.64

30 Richard Cavendish, *The Black Arts*, pg.315

31 Aleister Crowley, *The Equinox*, Vol. I, No. 1, pp. 224-225

32 Lewis Spence, *Ancient Egyptian Myths and Legends*, Dover Publications, New York, NY, 1990, pp. 80-81

33 Ibid, pp.81-82

34 Ibid, pp.83-84

35 Aleister Crowley, *The Equinox*, Vol. I, No.4, pp.199-200

36 Aleister Crowley, *The Equinox*, Vol. I, No.7, pg.400

37 Montague Summers, *The History of Witchcraft*, Citadel Press, 1993, pg.29

38 Dr. Sir J. G. Frazer, *The Golden Bough*, The MacMillan Company, NY, NY, 1922, pg.65

39 S. L. MacGregor Mathers, *The Kabbalah Unveiled*, pp.31-32

40 Aleister Crowley, *The Equinox*, Vol. I, No.4, pp.197-198

41 Aleister Crowley, *Confessions*, pg.636

42 Aleister Crowley, *The Equinox*, Vol. I, No.3, pg.232

43 Raymond Buckland, *Buckland's Complete Book of Witchcraft*, Llewellyn Publications, St. Paul, Minnesota, 1993, pg.15

44 Eliphas Levi, *The Key to the Mysteries*, from Crowley's Equinox, Vol. I, No.10, pg.6245 J. F. C. Fuller, *The Big Stick*, from Crowley's *Equinox*, Vol. I, No.4, pg.342

46 Ibid, pg.343

47 S. L. MacGregor Mathers, *The Kabbalah Unveiled*, pg.58

48 Ibid, pg.282

49 Ibid, pg.282

50 Lewis Spence, *Ancient Egyptian Myths and Legends*, pp.69-70

51 Ibid, pp.94-95

52 Dave Lewis and Simon Pallett, *Led Zeppelin - The Concert File*, pg.50

53 Lewis Spence, *Native American Myths and Legends*, Longmeadow Press, October 1993, pp.15 – 55

54 Rosemary Ellen Guiley, *The Encyclopedia of Witches and Witchcraft*, pg.185

55 Aleister Crowley, *The Equinox*, Vol. I, No.7, pp.380-381

56 Ibid, pg.380

57 Aleister Crowley, *The Equinox*, Vol. I, No.6, pg.31

58 Ibid, pp.31-32

59 Aleister Crowley, *The Equinox*, Vol. I, No.7, pg.380

60 Aleister Crowley, *Book 4*, Samuel Weiser Inc., Yorke Beach, Maine, 1994, pg.4 of the Interlude.

61 Aleister Crowley, *The Equinox*, Vol. I, No.1, pg.191

62 Ibid, pg.229

63 Aleister Crowley, *The Equinox*, Vol. I, No.5, *The Vision and the Voice*, pg.169

64 Aleister Crowley, *The Equinox*, Vol. I, No.7, pg.339

65 S. L. MacGregor Mathers, *The Kabbalah Unveiled*, pp.26-27

66 Ibid, pg.35

67 Ibid, pg.65

68 Ibid, pg.59

69 Ibid, pg.57

70 Ibid, pg.41

71 Ibid, pg.231

72 Aleister Crowley, *The Equinox*, Vol. I, No.1, *John St. John*, pg.31

73 Aleister Crowley, *The Equinox*, Vol. I, No.4, pg.164

74 Aleister Crowley, *The Equinox*, Vol. I, No.1, pp.174-175

75 Eliphas Levi, from Crowley's *Equinox*, Vol. I, No.10, *The Key to the Mysteries*, pg.70

76 Eliphas Levi, *Transcendental Magic*, pg.19

Led Zeppelin performs "Going to California," in their acoustic set on the 1977 tour, again, just as I saw at Madison Square Garden. In the song, Robert Plant sings of searching for the "woman" that has "never" lived in human flesh. It is indicative of the Egyptian goddess Isis; who is the "queen" that has no "king." Isis is the goddess in the Qabalah; according to Aleister Crowley; and passed on to the fan of Led Zeppelin who will "listen" real "hard" and then do the research necessary to find out that the band was not just ad-libbing lyrics. The queen and goddess of light is a fundamental tenet of Crowley and Led Zeppelin's "tune." As Eliphas Levi said, "The sages must speak occasionally, not to disclose, but lead others to discover." In the last chapter you read where Crowley said the goal was to guide the seeker into the "life which abideth in light," the Qabalah.

Jimmy Page and Robert Plant perform "Going to California" on the 1998 tour. Standing in the orchestra, I watched Plant sing the lyrics just as I had back in 1977; with references to the Book of Revelation's earthquake and sea of blood.

CHAPTER NINE

"The twenty-two symbolic and allegorical Major Arcana cards depict and create the continuous and ever-changing physical and spiritual forces affecting humanity. To some persons, the trump cards are a pictorial processional of life's fateful events."1
     Stuart R. Kaplan, "The Encyclopedia of Tarot"

"The Tarot, that miraculous work which inspired all the sacred books of antiquity, is the most perfect instrument of divination, by reason of the analogical precision of its figures and numbers. It can be employed with complete confidence."2
     Eliphas Levi, "Transcendental Magic"

"The exponents of the Tarot, Court de Gebelin, Levi, and Etteilla, have always assigned to the Tarot a Qabalistico-Egyptian origin, and this I have found confirmed in my own researches into this subject, which have extended over several years."3
     S. L. MacGregor Mathers, "The Tarot"

"The only theory of ultimate interest about the Tarot is that it is an admirable symbolic picture of the Universe, based on the data of the Holy Qabalah."4
     Black Magician Aleister Crowley, "The Book of Thoth"

GOING TO CALIFORNIA & THE RAIN SONG: THE QABALAH AND CROWLEY'S TAROT DECK

The Tarot cards are, as Aleister Crowley said in the above quote, derived from the Qabalah. In this chapter we will examine material from Crowley's *Book of Thoth*, his classic writing on Egyptian Tarot, in order to obtain his perspective of the cards, their use, and how they relate to the Golden Dawn, and ceremonial magic. Interestingly enough, Aleister Crowley published *The Book of Thoth* in 1944, the year Jimmy Page was born. Other examples of the Tarot will be presented from a few renowned occult authors to show its congruence among different men. We will not be spending the time necessary to examine every aspect of the Tarot in this chapter. However, a basic understanding of it will be presented, in order to provide examples of the Qabalistic godhead from the Major Arcana, which are the most important and powerful cards, as opposed to the Minor Arcana. This will be done in order to illustrate lyrics from both "Going to California," and "Wonderful One," a Page/Plant song. "The Rain Song" will be looked at in this chapter to review another form of the god in the Qabalah who is equivalent to the other gods in the Tarot. Another Led Zeppelin song, "How Many More Times," will also be discussed in light of an important occult message. Once a person has a basic understanding of the Qabalah and the Tarot cards, he or she is then prepared to understand Led Zeppelin's most powerful, magical music. The Tarot cards, which are used exclusively by occultists, are pictorial representations of the Qabalistic male/female godhead, and are used for obtaining information from the Devil to assist the occultist in his divination practices; better known as fortune telling, which as will be seen in this chapter, is advocated by none other than Jimmy Page.

JIMMY PAGE AND THE TAROT

One of Jimmy Page's acquaintances over the years has been Michael Des Barres. A picture of Jimmy sleeping on a couch, with Michael sitting on the floor in front of the couch, with the members of his rock band, can be seen in the book, *Hammer of the Gods*, by Steven Davis. Des Barres has also played bad guys in the movies. He played in "Pink Cadillac" with Clint Eastwood, and he can be seen standing on the submarine with Gary Busey in the Steven Seagal film, "Under Siege." He does not have the long hair in the films. Des Barres said that he was studying Aleister Crowley's writings for a while, and when he was doing so he used to visit Jimmy Page. He made it clear that Jimmy owned Crowley's Tarot deck. He said: "...like an idiot, I was dabbling with the Aleister Crowley thing at the time. I used to go down to see Jimmy at Plumpton Place and he'd pull out Crowley's robes, Crowley's tarot deck, all of the Crowley gear that he'd collected. I thought, 'This is great!' It was all so twisted and debauched, their whole thing."5 Did you see the plural "their?" Here is a relatively famous person, whose face has been seen on the movie screen all over the world, stating plainly that Jimmy Page has Crowley's artifacts in his possession and proudly puts them on display; including his Tarot deck. Here is a riddle for you the reader. Why would Jimmy Page have Aleister Crowley's robes in his possession? What did Crowley use them for? And what is Jimmy Page doing with them? I believe that the answers are found in chapter eleven of this work.

Another individual, who has been a personal friend of Led Zeppelin from the early days, is Ritchie Yorke. In his book, *Led Zeppelin - The Definitive Biography*, he had this to say about Page and Crowley: "Page himself is at home with the tarot cards, but more particularly with the philosophy of Aleister Crowley. Page is likely the world's foremost collector of Crowley memorabilia..."6 Keep in mind, these are Jimmy Page's friends saying this about him, not his enemies. At this point it would be good for you to reread the heading of the first chapter, for a quote about Page and Crowley, and then one from Page about Crowley. We'll now take a look at Crowley's *Book of Thoth*.

ALEISTER CROWLEY AND THE TAROT

In the introduction to his book on Egyptian Tarot, one of the members of the Silver Star, a woman by the magical name of S. H. Soror I. W. E. 8=3, A.A., wrote the following about how Crowley identifies the Tarot with all magical systems around the world:

"He published a full account of the Tarot, according to the MSS. of the Hermetic Order of the Golden Dawn in The Equinox, Vol. I, Nos. 7 and 8 (1912 e. v.).

During all this time the Tarot was his daily companion, guide, and object of research.

He succeeded in uniting under the Schema of the Holy Qabalah, of which the Tarot is the greatest single element, all philosophical and magical systems soever, including that of the Chinese."7 The Tarot cards therefore, are as universal as the Qabalah; having been derived from it.

THE CONTENTS OF THE TAROT

The following is Aleister Crowley's definition of the Tarot cards, and he defines them as symbolic of the Qabalah:

"The Tarot is a pack of seventy-eight cards. There are four suits, as in modern playing cards, which are derived from it. But the Court cards number four instead of three. In addition, there are twenty-two cards called 'Trumps', each of which is a symbolic picture with a title to itself.

"At first sight one would suppose this arrangement to be arbitrary, but it is not. It is necessitated, as will appear later, by the structure of the universe, and in particular of the Solar System, as symbolized by the Holy Qabalah."8

Crowley knew the Tarot cards were symbolic of the godhead of the Qabalah, because they assisted him in communicating with it; it being the Devil. The Devil therefore, is the one who originated them.

THE ORIGIN OF THE TAROT

Crowley, in addressing the origin of the Tarot, makes it clear that they were used for the purpose of fortune telling. He wrote:

"The origin of this pack of cards is very obscure. Some authorities seek to put it back as far as the ancient Egyptian Mysteries; others try to bring it forward as late as the fifteenth or even the sixteenth century. But the Tarot certainly existed, in what may be called the classical form, as early as the fourteenth century; for packs of that date are extant, and the form has not varied in any notable respect since that time.

"In the Middle Ages, these cards were much used for fortune telling, especially by gypsies, so that it was customary to speak of the 'Tarot of the Bohemians,' or 'Egyptians.' When it was found that the gypsies, despite the etymology, were of Asiatic origin, some people tried to find its source in Indian art and literature."9

For those who do not know, fortune telling has a technical title called "divination." Occultists say that the *Holy Bible* advocates their androgynous godhead in the Qabalah, and the Qabalah advocates the Tarot cards. The Tarot cards, as you just read from Crowley, and it is an axiom in the occult world, are used for fortune telling, which is divination. The *Holy Bible* clearly states, that anyone practicing divination among the children of Israel were to be put to death. The following is the quote from the Lord in the *Bible* clearly stating the case, in Deuteronomy Chapter 18, Verses 9-14, written by Moses: "When you come into the land which the LORD your God is giving you, you shall not learn to follow the abominations of those nations. There shall not be found among you anyone who makes his son or his daughter pass through the fire, or one who practices witchcraft, or a soothsayer, or one who interprets omens, or a sorcerer, or one who conjures spells, or a medium, or a spiritist, or one who calls up the dead. For all who do these things are an abomination to the LORD, and because of these abominations the LORD your God drives them out from before you. You shall be blameless before the LORD your God. For these nations which you will dispossess listened to soothsayers and diviners; but as for you, the LORD your God has not appointed such for you."

In that passage, when it says God drove out the nations before them, what he is talking about is the fact that he commanded the children of Israel to kill those people on the way to the promise land because they were children of the Devil, irrespective of the name they gave to Satan. It was his moral code, and his occult practices that got those people in trouble with God. The Israelites were told to destroy all of them. Women and children of these satanic nations were to be destroyed as well. Why? When the children grew up, they would simply reinstate the old practices, and then they would wage war on the Israelites who destroyed their forefathers. So you see, the same Jehovah the occultists say is Satan, condemns divination. Before we move on, I want to present to you Webster's definition of divination: "The act or practice of trying to foretell the future or the unknown by occult means."10 The reason the practice is associated with the occult is because the unseen spiritual forces behind the Tarot are the ones assisting the diviner in seeing the future. When you are driving down the highway and you see a sign that speaks of Tarot card readings, that is a person who is practicing divination, and thereby controlled by demonic forces.

Eliphas Levi, in his book, *Transcendental Magic*, defined divination this way: "...divination, which, in its broadest sense, and following the grammatical significance of the word, is the exercise of divine power, and the realization of divine knowledge. It is the priesthood of the Magus. But divination, in general opinion, is concerned more closely with the knowledge of hidden things. To know the most secret thoughts of men; to penetrate the mysteries of past and future; to evoke age by age the exact revelation of effects by the precise knowledge of causes: this is what is universally called divination."11

Aleister Crowley, in his book *Moonchild*, wrote about a man who used divination by the Tarot cards: "Brother Onofrio went off to the private room where he did his own particular magick. He saw that a serious inroad had been made; but his divination, on this occasion, failed to enlighten him. His favourite device was the Tarot, those mysterious cards with their twenty-two hieroglyphic trumps; and as a rule he was able to discover all kinds of unknown matters by their use."12 Crowley advocates the Tarot just like he believed he did when he was Eliphas Levi in his "previous incarnation."

EVIDENCE FOR THE INITIATED TRADITION OF THE TAROT

In the following quote, Crowley speaks of the tradition of the Tarot and Eliphas Levi. He ties the Tarot in with Levi's book, *Transcendental Magic*, formerly known as *Dogma and Ritual of High Magic*. He wrote:

"Although the origins of the Tarot are perfectly obscure, there is a very interesting piece of quite modern history, history well within the memory of living man, which is extremely significant, and will be found, as the thesis develops, to sustain it in a very remarkable way.

"In the middle of the nineteenth century, there arose a very great Qabalist and scholar, who still annoys dull people by his habit of diverting himself at their expense by making fools of them posthumously. His name was Alphonse Louis Constant, and he was an Abbe of the Roman Church. For his 'nom-de-guerre' he translated his name into Hebrew-Eliphas Levi Zahed, and he is very generally known as Eliphas Levi.

"Eliphas Levi was a philosopher and an artist, besides being a supreme literary stylist and a practical joker of the variety called 'Pince sans rire'; and, being an artist and a profound symbolist, he was immensely attracted by the Tarot. While in England, he proposed to Kenneth Mackenzie, a famous occult scholar and high-grade Freemason, to reconstitute and issue a scientifically-designed pack.

"In his works are new presentations by him of the trumps called The Chariot and The Devil. He seems to have understood that the Tarot was actually a pictorial form of the Qabalistic Tree of Life, which is the basis of the whole Qabalah, so much so that he composed his works on this basis. He wished to write a complete treatise on Magick. He divided his subject into two parts-Theory and Practice-which he called Dogma and Ritual. Each part has twenty-two chapters, one for each of the twenty-two trumps; and each chapter deals with the subject represented by the picture displayed by the trump."13

In that quote you see the traditional aspect of Crowley's love for the Tarot. He believed himself to be Levi reincarnated, so he believed he loved the Tarot in his previous incarnation. Crowley goes on to identify the Tarot with the Hermetic Order of the Golden Dawn.

THE TAROT & THE HERMETIC ORDER OF THE GOLDEN DAWN

Crowley wrote of the origins of the Hermetic Order of the Golden Dawn, and in doing so he mentions the Tarot cards as being part of the very beginning. While most of the following quote describes the beginning of the Golden Dawn, and contact with the secret chiefs, who are none other than the god/goddess (Satan) of the Qabalah represented in the Tarot, it is important for the reader to see it as he wrote it. Just as a reminder, the Golden Dawn was founded subsequent to the discovery of the "cipher manuscript." Crowley wrote:

"One must now digress into the history of the Hermetic Order of the Golden Dawn, the society reconstituted by Dr. Westcott and his colleagues, in order to show further evidence as to the authenticity of the claim of the promulgators of the cipher manuscript.

"Among these papers, besides the attribution of the Tarot, were certain skeleton rituals, which purported to contain the secrets of initiation; the name (with an address in Germany) of a Fraulein Sprengel was mentioned as the issuing authority. Dr. Westcott wrote to her; and, with her permission, the Order of the Golden Dawn was founded in 1886.

"(The G.D. is merely a name of for the Outer or Preliminary Order of the R.R. et A.C., which is in its turn an external manifestation of the A.A. which is the true Order of Masters-See Magick, pgs.229-244.)

"The genius who made this possible was a man named Samuel Liddell

Mathers. After a time, Fr. Sprengel died; a letter written to her, asking for more advanced knowledge, elicited a reply from one of her colleagues. This letter informed Dr. Westcott of her death, adding that the writer and his associates had never approved of Frl. Sprengel's action in authorizing any form of group working, but, in view of the great reverence and esteem in which she was held, had refrained from open opposition. He went on to say that 'this correspondence must now cease', but that if they wanted more advanced knowledge they could perfectly well get it by using in the proper manner the knowledge which they already possessed. In other words, they must utilize their magical powers to make contact with the Secret Chiefs of the Order. (This, incidentally, is a quite normal and traditional mode of procedure.)

"Shortly afterwards, Mathers, who had maneuvered himself into the practical Headship of the Order, announced that he had made this link; that the Secret Chiefs had authorized him to continue the work of the Order, as its sole head. There is, however, no evidence that he was here a witness of truth, because no new knowledge of any particular importance came to the Order; such as did appear proved to be no more than Mathers could have acquired by normal means from quite accessible sources, such as the British Museum. These circumstances, and a great deal of petty intrigue, led to serious dissatisfaction among the members of the Order. Frl. Sprengel's judgment, that group-working in an Order of this sort is possible, was shown in this case to be wrong. In 1900, the Order in its existing form was destroyed.

"The point of these data is simply to show that, at that time, the main preoccupation of all the serious members of the Order was to get in touch with the Secret Chiefs themselves. In 1904 success was attained by one of the youngest members, Frater Perdurabo. The very fullest details of this occurrence are given in The Equinox of the Gods."14

As you saw in that quote, the Tarot cards were an important part of the beginning of the Golden Dawn. Crowley, in the context of the *Book of Thoth*, presents himself as a student of the Tarot at the outset of his initiation into the Golden Dawn. He wrote concerning himself in the third person, once again as Frater Perdurabo: "Frater Perdurabo had made a very profound study of the Tarot since his initiation to the Order on 18th November, 1898; for, three months later, he had attained the grade of Practicus; as such, he became entitled to know the Secret Attribution. He constantly studied this and the accompanying explanatory manuscripts. He checked up on all these attributes of the numbers to the forms of nature, and found nothing incongruous."15

Another member of the Golden Dawn, and contemporary of Aleister Crowley, was a man by the name of Arthur E. Waite. He was the one who told Crowley to read *The Cloud Upon the Sanctuary*. He also authored the book, *The Pictorial Key to the Tarot*, which we will look at as well. He gave this general description of the Tarot, stating that its doctrines are only revealed to secret initiates around the world, just as *The Cloud Upon the Sanctuary* does about magic. He wrote: "THE Tarot embodies symbolical presentations of universal ideas, behind which lie all the implicits of the human mind, and it is in this sense that they contain secret doctrine, which is the realization by the few of truths imbedded in the consciousness of all, though they have not passed into express recognition by ordinary men. The theory is that this doctrine has always existed- that is to say, has been excogitated in the consciousness of an elect minority; that it has been perpetuated in secrecy from one to another and has been recorded in secret literatures, like those of Alchemy and Kabalism; that it is contained also in those Instituted Mysteries of which Rosicrucianism offers an example near to our hand in the past, and Craft Masonry a living summary, or general memorial, for those who can interpret its real meaning. Behind the Secret Doctrine it is held that there is an experience or practice by which the Doctrine is justified."16

The Tarot then, is a very important part of the Silver Star, Jimmy Page, and the music of Led Zeppelin, the Four Sticks that are set on fire by the small sticks, or young initiates, and then are able to endure until the great logs, the masses of mankind, are set on fire by the Law of Thelema.

Crowley, wanting to sum up the evidence of the Tarot presented in the beginning of The Book of Thoth, wrote:

"1. The origin of the Tarot is quite irrelevant, even if it were certain. It must stand or fall as a system on its own merits.

2. It is beyond doubt a deliberate attempt to represent, in pictorial form, the doctrines of the Qabalah....

4. These attributions are in one sense a conventional, symbolic map; such could be invented by some person or persons of great artistic imagination and ingenuity combined with almost unthinkably great scholarship and philo- sophical clarity.

5. Such persons, however eminent we may suppose them to have been, are not quite capable of making a system so abstruse in its entirety without the assistance of superiors whose mental processes were, or are, pertaining to a higher Dimension."17

There it is, Crowley's claim that the Tarot is of supernatural origin, given to man by beings of "a higher Dimension." These beings are the spiritual forces written about in the following passages.

The Tarot has been used in magic for centuries, and Crowley refers to those who used it as the "Ancients." He wrote that the Ancients as well per- ceived the Tarot in accordance with spiritual forces. He wrote: "THE TAROT is a Pictorial representation of the Forces of Nature as conceived by the Ancients according to a conventional symbolism."18 Crowley also stated that the concept of the Great Work, uniting the Microcosm, mankind, with the Macrocosm, the universe or godhead, was understood by the Ancients, which is the purpose of the Tarot: "One of the most important doctrines of the Ancients was that of the

Macrocosm and the Microcosm. Man is himself a little Universe; he is a minute copy of the big Universe."19

Crowley presents the origin of the Tarot as being connected with the Qabalah and divination, in order to manipulate spiritual forces: "The Tarot, while based on these theoretical attributions, was designed as a practical instrument for Qabalistic calculations and for divination. In it is little place for abstract ideas. The subject of the book-the Tarot is called The Book of Thoth or Tahuti-is the influence of the Ten Numbers and the Twenty-two Letters on man, and his best methods of manipulating their forces."20 Crowley connected astrology with the Qabalah, which means, from his perspective, that astrology is the work of the Devil also: "The ancient scheme of the Elements, Planets, and Zodiacal Signs, was summarized by the Qabalists in their Tree of Life."21

Let everyone reading this book understand, that Aleister Crowley, who in theory was the most dangerous Satanist to ever walk the earth, ties astrology in with the Devil. If any man on this planet in the first half of the last century knew the Devil, it was Aleister Crowley. If he ties astrology in with the Qabalah, that means that astrology is the work of the Devil, period, case closed, no discussions. I said that Crowley was the most dangerous Satanist to walk the earth in theory because of his writings, and I believe Jimmy Page was and is the most dangerous Satanist in practice. Only a willfully blind person, after reading this book, will disagree. Everyone, however, will be forced to face truth when they die; giving an account of themselves to Christ. Those who received him as Lord and Savior will be saved; the rest will go to Hell forever. There is the place where the spiritual forces behind the Tarot cards will spend eternity.

CEREMONIAL MAGIC AND THE TAROT

Crowley presented the Tarot as concurrent with invocations, wanting the spiritual forces behind the cards to manifest themselves in the mind of the readers:

"The Tarot is, thus, intimately bound up with the purely magical Arts of Invocation and Evocation. By Invocation is meant the aspiration to the highest, the purest form of the part of oneself that one wishes to put into action.

Evocation is much more objective. It does not imply perfect sympathy. One's attitude to the Being evoked may even be, at least superficially, hostile. Then, of course, the further advanced one is in initiation, the less the idea of hostility enters one's mind. 'Tout comprendre, c'est tout pardonner.' Thus, in order to understand any given card, one must identify oneself with it completely for the moment; and one way of doing this is to induce or compel the Intelligence ruling the card to manifest to the senses. For, as explained above, the ancient theory of the Universe included the thesis that every object in Nature possessed a spiritual guardian."22

These spiritual guardians are either demons or the Devil himself. If it is Jimmy Page using the Tarot, one can bet that Satan himself is involved.

THE TAROT AND ANIMISM

On the very next page of the Book of Thoth, Crowley clearly states his belief that the Devil is the inventor of printing, and that hieroglyphs, whether in writing or pictures, are alive and powerful. He wrote: "It is only natural, therefore, that at a time when pictorial or written representations of ideas were beyond the comprehension of any but a very few people, when Writing itself was considered magical, and Printing (as it is) an invention of the Devil, people should regard hieroglyphs (whether written or pictured) as living things having power in themselves."23 The power of these cards then is demonic, the purpose being to deceive men into believing in the Qabalah's godhead.

PRESENTATION OF THE TAROT

At this point we will study examples of the Qabalistic godhead from the Major Arcana of the Tarot. The Major Arcana are a group of 22 cards called "Trumps." Not all of them will be discussed, because this is not a book about the Tarot, but Led Zeppelin. Enough of them will be discussed, however, to illustrate the fact that the Tarot are used to communicate with the godhead figures presented in the previous chapter. As information from the cards is presented, keep in mind that my approach to them is objective, my purpose is not to view all the subjective meanings associated with each card. I simply want to present information relative to the Qabalistic godhead. Therefore, not all information about each card will be presented; only that which I have considered pertinent to my point. If you have difficulty understanding a certain part of text that you are reading, look at it objectively for information about the god or goddess of the Qabalah. Three of the most powerful trumps, "The Hermit," "The Devil," and "The Hangman" are not going to be discussed in this chapter, but later in the book, at a crucial point.

NO. 0, THE FOOL

Under the section of the first Major Arcana trump, called "The Fool," that Crowley numbered 0, he addressed the Tarot as being united not only with the Qabalah, but with the Tetragrammaton, IHVH. The whole story of the Qabalah, as you read in the last chapter, is the father and mother coming together in union and having a son and daughter. The son marries the daughter and lifts her on to the throne of the mother, the son is then the father and all is joined together in Kether, where the all become the one. Crowley presented it this way:

"It is explained in this essay that the whole of the Tarot is based upon the Tree of Life, and that the Tree of Life is always cognate with Tetragrammaton. One may sum up the whole doctrine very briefly as follows:

"The Union of the Father and the Mother produces Twins, the son going forward to the daughter, the daughter returning the energy to the father; by this cycle of change the stability and eternity of the Universe are assured."24

Crowley describes the Dove as the Holy Ghost in this section, calling it the goddess "Venus," as well as the phallus. He wrote: "The Dove is the bird of Venus, but the dove is also a symbol of the Holy Ghost; that is, of the Phallus in its most sublimated form. There is therefore no reason for surprise in observing the identification of the father with the mother."25 Lock it into your memory, that Crowley identifies the dove with the goddess, and the Holy Ghost (The Dove in question is underneath the feet of the Hermit on the inner cover of Led Zeppelin's fourth album). The Holy Spirit descended and landed on Lord Jesus Christ right after he was baptized by John the Baptist in the Book of John, Chapter 1, Verses 32-34: "And John bore witness, saying, 'I saw the Spirit descending from heaven like a dove, and He remained upon Him. I did not know Him, but He who sent me to baptize with water said to me, "Upon whom you see the Spirit descending, and remaining on Him, this is He who baptizes with the Holy Spirit." And I have seen and testified that this is the Son of God.'" Led Zeppelin, in their film, *The Song Remains the Same*, show the same type of descent upon the fan who is watching the film. It takes place in the beginning of the film right after the scene where the band member names and runes are placed on the screen while New York City is being filmed from the west. After the sun goes down on Manhattan, the scene changes to a white bird, that appears to be a pigeon used in place of a dove, descending upon the camera as though he were descending upon the viewer. The obvious message, I believe, is that the "spirit" is coming upon the person watching the film, via the music of Led Zeppelin. By the time you are done reading this book, it will most likely be your belief as well.

Crowley wrote of Zeus, the father of the gods of Olympus, in the section on The Fool. He presents him as the Lord of the Air. This idea has already been discussed in the Black Magick in Theory and Practice chapter as the title for Satan. Therefore, Zeus is Satan as well. He wrote: "Zeus became too popular, and, in consequence, too many legends gathered around him; but the important fact for this present purpose is that Zeus was peculiarly the Lord of Air."26 By way of review, here is the quote about Satan as ruler of the air from the *Bible's*

Book of Ephesians, Chapter Two, Verses 1-2, where Paul the Apostle addresses the newly converted Christians at Ephesus about their former allegiance to Satan: "And you He made alive, who were dead in trespasses and sins, in which you once walked according to the course of this world, according to the prince of the power of the air, the spirit who now works in the sons of disobedience..." The Fool is Zeus and Zeus is the Lord of the Air, and the Lord of the Air is Satan.

NO.1 "THE JUGGLER"

In other Tarot decks, the Juggler is presented as "The Magician." Crowley changed the name for his deck. He wrote concerning the Juggler: "This card therefore represents the Wisdom, the Will, the Word, the Logos, by whom the worlds were created. (See the Gospel according to St. John, chapter I.) It represents the Will. In brief, he is the Son, the manifestation in act of the idea of the Father. He is the male correlative of the High Priestess."27 On the next page of the Book of Thoth, in reference to The Juggler, Crowley says: "...He is the messenger of the gods..."28 What the reader needs to understand about the preceding information is twofold. First of all, this card refers to the creator of the universe, who, as you know, is the Devil according to Crowley. However, the reference to the Word in chapter 1 of the New Testament Book of John is the Lord Jesus Christ. As written previously, occultists take scripture out of context to build their suicidal faith on. As you read already, in the second chapter of this book, Christ called the Devil the father of lies in John chapter 8. This is the same Book of the *Bible* Aleister Crowley uses to take information about Jesus and say it applies to the Devil. This man's blood was on his own head. That's a Biblical phrase that means he sowed the seeds of his own eternal damnation.

If Jimmy Page is reading this, and everyone knows you are, you need to understand that if you were able to manifest a spiritual presence that looked and sounded like Crowley, that was not Crowley. How could Jimmy know Crowley's voice? There are plenty of people who could recognize Crowley's voice in 1970, when Page bought Boleskine. Plus, I wouldn't be surprised if Crowley's voice was taped before he died.

Once again, Crowley says to refer to John chapter 1. In John Chapter 1, Verses 1-3, the *Bible* says: "In the beginning was the Word, and the Word was with God, and the Word was God. He was in the beginning with God. All things were made through Him, and without Him nothing was made that was made." Then in verse 14 of the same chapter, the *Bible* says: "And the Word became flesh and dwelt among us, and we beheld His glory, the glory as of the only begotten of the Father, full of grace and truth." For those who do not know, the

Greek word "Logos," means "Word." Specifically, Logos is the word used in the Greek text in the preceding verses. The Christ was already here. He is the living Word of God. The Anti-Christ has yet to come, or at least he hasn't come to power yet. So there you have it, Crowley's reference to the Logos of John 1 in that section of The Juggler has nothing to do with Satan. However, his students are deceived into believing it does. Remember, Crowley says the Juggler is the creator of the worlds. This is the same title he gives to "The Hermit." Therefore the Hermit and the Juggler are the same being.

Aleister Crowley calls this card "The Juggler," but again, other Tarot decks present the second card as "The Magician." Crowley says The Juggler is the messenger of the gods, and that is what others say about the Magician. Arthur E. Waite, another member of the Golden Dawn, wrote in his book, *The Pictorial Key to the Tarot* about the Magician. In the quote, the reference to the "dual sign" is the magician holding his right hand up and his left hand down: "This dual sign is known in very high grades of the Instituted Mysteries; it shows the descent of grace, virtue and light, drawn from things above and derived to things below. The suggestion throughout is therefore the possession and communication of the Powers and Gifts of the Spirit."29

In his book, *Tarot - 22 Steps To A Higher Path*, D. Baloti Lawrence wrote about the Magician: "With one hand pointed up toward the sky and the other hand pointed down, the Magician no doubt represents the unity of heaven and earth. As the story goes, it is the messenger from God who travels from heaven to earth with a message for human kind. The Magician is a messenger."30 He says his message benefits mankind: "He has made the decision to apply his great skill and knowledge for the benefit of human kind."31 Since the Magician is the god in the male/female occult godhead, when a man becomes an occult Magician, he becomes god on earth, according to occultists, as you will see later, relative to Jimmy Page. The message of the Magician has to do with spiritual transformation or regeneration. Relative to the regeneration message brought by the Magician, Lawrence wrote: "In order to create a new beginning, the past must be let go."32 At the end of his description of this card, he wrote of the Magician's purpose: "ROLE IN LIFE - communicator, messenger, bearer of information."33 Remember the "news" from Led Zeppelin which has to make it "through," presented in chapter one, from the song "No Quarter?" It all ties in together.

The last example of the Magician presented here is from Stuart Kaplan's famous occult book, *The Encyclopedia of Tarot*. Concerning the Magician, he wrote: "In his left hand is a rod, the sign of one of the four suits, pointing to the heavens, while his other hand points downward toward the earth. This suggests that emanations from heaven may be put to use on earth by those persons who are aware of the wonders surrounding them."34 The Magician card from the Rider/Waite deck is in pictured in that book. It fits the very description just presented by Kaplan.

James Patrick Page is a Magician, which is why he is Aleister Crowley's student. You will see that beyond any shadow of a doubt, later in the book. You will then, for the first time, realize who this man really is. He is infinitely more dangerous than satanists like Ozzy Osbourne; only Mick Jagger and a few others ever came close.

NO.2 "THE HIGH PRIESTESS"

Aleister Crowley wrote, concerning the third trump, the "High Priestess," and makes reference to the goddess of the male/female occult godhead: "The card refers to the Moon. The Moon is universal, and goes from the highest to the lowest. It is a symbol which will recur frequently in these hieroglyphs. But in the earlier Trumps the concern is with Nature above the Abyss; the High Priestess is the first card which connects the Supernal Triad with the Hexad; and her path, as shown in the diagram, makes a direct connection between the Father in his highest aspect, and the Son in his most perfect manifestation."35

In the next quote, Crowley makes it clear the goddess has more than one name, and that she is the queen of light:
"There is here, therefore, the purest and most exalted conception of the Moon.

The card represents the most spiritual form of Isis the Eternal Virgin; the Artemis of the Greeks. She is clothed only in the luminous veil of light. It is important for high initiation to regard Light not as the perfect manifestation of the Eternal Spirit, but rather as the veil which hides that Spirit. It does so all the more effectively because of its incomparably dazzling brilliance. Thus she is light and the body of light. She is the truth behind the veil of light. She is the soul of light. Upon her knees is the bow of Artemis, which is also a musical instrument, for she is huntress, and hunts by enchantment."36

This Isis, of the "The High Priestess," is the one, I believe, that Robert Plant is making reference to in the song off Led Zeppelin's fourth album, "Going to California."

LED ZEPPELIN IV (RUNES) – "GOING TO CALIFORNIA"

At 2:12 into the song, Robert Plant sings about the "Queen" who has no "King." At 2:15 he sings that this Queen is playing a "guitar" as she "cries" while she "sings." Finally, at 2:28, Plant sings that he is searching for the "woman" that was not ever "born." We are going to examine these three concepts individually. I am going to repeat, in brief, two quotes from the last chapter to illustrate who this Queen is that is mourning over her lost King. Both of these quotes come from the Robert Plant advocated author, Lewis Spence. They are, again, taken from his book, *Ancient Egyptian Myths and Legends*:

"Isis was perhaps of Libyan origin, and is usually depicted in the form of a woman crowned with her name-symbol and holding in her hand a scepter of papyrus. Her crown is surmounted by a pair of horns holding a disk, which in turn is sometimes crested by her hieroglyph, which represents a seat or throne. Sometimes also she is represented a possessing radiant and many-coloured wings, with which she stirs to life the inanimate body of Osiris.

"No other goddess was on the whole so popular with the Egyptians, and the reason for this is probably to be found in the circumstances of travail and pity which run through her myth. These drew the sympathies of the people to her, but they were not the only reasons why she was beloved by the Egyptian masses, for she was the great beneficent mother-goddess and represented the maternal spirit in its most intimate and affectionate guise. In her myth, perhaps one of the most touching and beautiful which ever sprang from the consciousness of a people, we find evolved from what may have been a mere corn-spirit a type of wifely and maternal affection mourning the death of her cherished husband, and seeking by every means in her power to restore him to life....Osiris in his guise of the corn dies and comes to life again and is sown broadcast over the land. Isis is disconsolate and moans terribly over his loss; in fact, so loud and heartrending is her grief that the child of the King of Byblos, who she is nursing, dies of terror....She is a great traveler, and unceasingly moans and sobs."37

So there is the Queen who has no King, because he is dead. The second thing we have to look at is Plant singing that "she" is playing the "guitar" while she "cries" as she "sings." This information comes right from the card we just read. At the end of the description, Crowley wrote:

"The card represents the most spiritual form of Isis the Eternal Virgin; the Artemis of the Greeks....She is the soul of light. Upon her knees is the bow of Artemis, which is also a musical instrument, for she is huntress, and hunts by enchantment."38 There you have Isis, the Queen who cries over her dead King, with the bow that is also a musical instrument. Lock it into your memory, that this Queen of Light has a bow that she hunts with. You will see this again at one of the most powerful points of this book. The last thing from "Going to California" that we are going to look at before moving on is Plant's singing of this Queen as the "woman" that was not ever "born." The following information, that is taken from Aleister Crowley's *Equinox*, *Volume I*, *No.3*, answers the question of who she is, I believe. You be the judge:

"'Thee I invoke, the Bornless One.'

And this being accomplished, let him lift up his heart unto that Light, and dwell therein, and aspire even unto that which is beyond. And seeing that the gate is called Strait, let him invoke Her who abideth therein, in the path called

Daleth, even Our Lady ISIS.

THE INVOCATION
OF

ISIS

And I beheld a great wonder in Heaven: a Woman clothed with the Sun: and the Moon was at Her feet: and on Her head was the Diadem of the Twelve Stars.

Hear me, Our Lady Isis, hear and save.

O Thou, Queen of Love and Mercy!

Thou, crowned with the Throne!

Thou, horned as the Moon! Thou, whose countenance is mild and glowing, even as grass refreshed by rain!

Hear me, our Lady Isis, hear and save!

O Thou, who art in Matter manifest!

Thou Bride and Queen as Thou art Mother and Daughter of the Crucified!

O Thou, who art the Lady of the Earth!

Hear me, our Lady Isis, hear and save!

O Thou, Our Lady of the Amber Skin!

Lady of Love and Victory! Bright gate of Glory through the darkling skies!

O crowned with Light and Life and Love!

Hear me, Our Lady Isis, hear and save!"39

"The Crucified" in that quote is not Jesus. As you read in that second to last line, she is the Queen who is "crowned with Light." Again, she is the Queen of Light with a bow, which is a musical instrument, who was not ever "born" in human flesh. If you have the music, go back and listen to "Going to California" and examine the lyrics beginning at 2:12 into the song. You will see that my assertions are correct. This Queen in "Going to California" is presented in the Tarot cards; derived from the Qabalah. The Qabalah will be shown in a later chapter to be the work of the Devil by Aleister Crowley and Jimmy Page.

NO QUARTER (1994) – "WONDERFUL ONE"

Arthur Waite wrote of The High Priestess in *The Pictorial Key to the Tarot*, and describes her as associated with the moon as did Crowley. He wrote: "She has the lunar crescent at her feet..."40 Jimmy Page wears this lunar crescent on his left calf on his outfits in the Led Zeppelin film. Later on the same page Waite wrote that she is the Queen of light: "...she is the spiritual Bride and Mother, the daughter of the stars and the Higher Garden of Eden. She is, in fine, the Queen of the borrowed light, but this is the light of all. She is the Moon nourished by the milk of the Supernal Mother. In a manner, she is also the Supernal Mother herself – that is to say, she is the bright reflection."41

In his book, *Tarot -22 Steps To A Higher Path*, D. Baloti Lawrence wrote concerning the High Priestess: "The High Priestess is associated with the Egyptian goddess called Isis. As the goddess of fertility, Isis offered her wisdom and knowledge to the god Osiris."42 Crowley and Waite have identified Isis as being associated with the moon. Lawrence wrote about a card called "The Moon," and on the card is the face of the goddess. He wrote: "The Moon encourages us to listen to the inner voice. The voice inside that will illuminate the true direction. Once the truth has been recognized, the doubt will leave us forever. The path will then be clear. All our dreams and wishes will become reality."43 So this card points out the direction its readers will follow. This concept is presented, I believe, on the Page/Plant track called "Wonderful One," off the Page/Plant *No Quarter* album. Everyone should know by now why they called the album *No Quarter*. They simply wanted to reiterate their warning from Satan. In the song, "Wonderful One," at 0:53, Plant sings of a "Queen" he describes as "love" flying "to" visit the "daughter." As I understand it, this is the Queen, Binah, from the Qabalah visiting Malkuth, daughter of the Queen, or goddess. He calls her a "spirit" at 1:40, and then says she is associated with our "moon" he describes as not having an "end" (meaning eternal….goddess) and it is the one "we" have to "follow." These lyrics of "Wonderful One" clearly match the description of the Tarot card called "The Moon" just presented. You can see Robert Plant sing these lyrics close up to the camera in the video, appropriately titled, *No Quarter*. When he sang "Ramble On" off *Led Zeppelin II*, he said that the "Moon" would illumine his "way," at 0:44. This is the same song (Ramble On) that has Plant singing of "Magick" ruling the sky, at 2:45. When Plant sings of the sun in "Wonderful One," I believe he is referring to Satan. The "Wonderful One," as I see it, is the godhead. Remember, Kether is the god and goddess joined together (Jimmy Page also played a song titled, "Midnight Moonlight Lady," when he was with The Firm in the 1980s. The song speaks of a woman flying through the sky in the moonlight.).

NO.5 "THE HIEROPHANT"

The sixth card of Crowley's Tarot deck is called the Hierophant. It represents the son, the Microprosopus from the Qabalah. In the Tetragrammaton, IHVH, it is the third letter, V (again, according to occultists). Crowley wrote:

"This card is referred to the letter Vau,...But the main reference is to the particular arcanum which is the principal business, the essential, of all magical work; the uniting of the microcosm with the macrocosm. Accordingly, the oriel is diaphanous; before the Manifestor of the Mystery is a hexagram representing the macrocosm. In its center is a pentagram, representing a dancing male child. This symbolizes the law of the new Aeon of the Child Horus, which has supplanted that Aeon of the 'Dying god' which governed the world for two thousand years. Before him is the woman girt with a sword; she represents the Scarlet Woman in the hierarchy of the New Aeon."44

On the next page of *The Book of Thoth*, while still referring to this card (the photo is on page 275), Crowley wrote about the Magick wand that the Hierophant is holding: "The symbolism of the Wand is peculiar; the three interlaced rings which crown it may be taken as representative of the three Aeons of Isis, Osiris, and Horus with their interlocking magical formulae."45 Now, for those of you who are Led Zeppelin fans, looking at the card you automatically recognize these rings as John Bonham's magical rune, that is on the fourth album, as well as the front of his drum set in their concert film (See Ch.15). Robert Plant has confirmed that this rune refers to the father, mother, and son trilogy in Ritchie Yorke's *Led Zeppelin - The Definitive Biography*. We will look at all this in detail in the section on runes later in the book. I simply wanted to introduce it here because of the Tarot card designed by Crowley.

NO.8 "ADJUSTMENT"

In describing this card, Crowley says, in effect, that it represents the Great Work accomplished; the union of the microcosm with the macrocosm. He wrote: "The equilibrium of all things is hereby symbolized. It is the final adjustment in the formula of Tetragrammaton, when the daughter, redeemed by her marriage with the Son, is thereby set up on the throne of the mother; thus, finally, she 'awakens the Eld of the All-Father.'"46 Throughout his description of the card, Crowley makes it clear the card refers to the goddess side of the godhead.

NO.11 "LUST"

While reading this card, you need to be aware that the reference Crowley makes to the Apocalypse is in fact the last Book of the *Bible*, Revelation. He wrote:

"In this card, therefore, appears the legend of the woman and the lion, or rather lion-serpent. (This card is attributed to the letter Teth, which means a serpent.)

The seers in the early days of the Aeon of Osiris foresaw the Manifestation of this coming Aeon in which we now live, and they regarded it with intense horror and fear, not understanding the precession of the Aeons, and regarding every change as catastrophe. This is the real interpretation of, and the reason for, the diatribes against the Beast and the Scarlet Woman in the XIII, XVII, and XVIII-th chapters of the Apocalypse; but on the Tree of Life, the path of Gimel, the Moon, descending from the highest, cuts the path of Teth, Leo, the house of the Sun, so that the Woman in the card may be regarded as a form of the Moon, very fully illuminated by the Sun, and intimately united with him in such wise as to produce, incarnate in human form, the representative or representatives of the Lord of the Aeon."47

The "representative" of the Lord of the Aeon who is to incarnate in human form is a reference to the Anti-Christ. "Representatives" can be the members of Led Zeppelin; and other members of the Silver Star like Kenneth Anger.

NO.13 "DEATH"

In the photos presented in this book, you can see pictures of Jimmy Page wearing the serpent on his concert outfits. In the film, *The Song Remains the Same*, he has a red dragon on his right thigh, breathing flames. In 1977, he wore black serpents on his white outfits as well as red ones. *The Holy Bible* presents Satan as the serpent. Here is the best description of his character as presented in Revelation. John, under the influence of the Holy Spirit, wrote in Chapter 12, Verse 9: "So the great dragon was cast out, that serpent of old, called the Devil and Satan, who deceives the whole world; he was cast to the earth, and his angels were cast out with him." Crowley, in writing about the card Death, calls the serpent "Lord of Life and Death": "The middle interpretation of this sign is given by the serpent, who is, moreover, the main theme of the sign.(1) The serpent is sacred, Lord of Life and Death, and its method of progression suggests the rhythmical undulation of those twin phases of life which we call respectively life and death. The serpent is also, as previously explained, the principal symbol of male energy."48 The number 1 written in the quote refers to Crowley's footnote. In it he says the serpent is the savior: "He is, accordingly, in the secret doctrine, the Redeemer." Redeemer and savior mean the same thing. Go back and listen to the opening verse of "Kashmir," and listen for the redemption spoken of. The serpent is the redeemer (according to occultists), and the serpent is Satan. Remember also Crowley's quote from *Konx Om Pax* in chapter four, where he wrote that Satan is the savior of the world.

NO.14 "ART"

Crowley takes us back to the goddess again, calling the card Art a reference to Diana, Artemis, and Isis. He wrote: "It pertains to Sagittarius, the opposite to Gemini in the Zodiac, and therefore, 'after another manner,' one with it. Sagittarius means the Archer; and the card is (in its simplest and most primitive form) a picture of Diana the Huntress. Diana is primarily one of the lunar goddesses, though the Romans rather degraded her from the Greek 'virgin Artemis,' who is also the Great Mother of Fertility, Diana of the Ephesians, Many-Breasted. (A form of Isis-see Atu II and III.) The connection between the Moon and the Huntress is shown by the shape of the bow, and the occult significance of Sagittarius is the arrow piercing the rainbow; the last three paths of the Tree of Life make the word Qesheth, a rainbow, and Sagittarius bears the arrow which pierces the rainbow, for his path leads from the Moon of Yesod to the Sun of Tiphareth."49 Tiphareth is 5=6, Adeptus Minor, the first rank of the second order of the Silver Star, the Rosicrucians, on the Qabalah. In the parenthesis, where Crowley says see Atu II and III, he is referring to The High Priestess and The Empress. The Empress is another card referring to the goddess and it was unnecessary to present it.

NO.19 "THE SUN"

Crowley presents this card as referring to Horus, the Sun, in the form of Heru-ra-ha, and as Lord of the Aeon. He wrote: "This is one of the simplest of the cards; it represents Heru-ra-ha, the Lord of the New Aeon, in his manifestation to the race of men as the Sun spiritual, moral, and physical. He is the Lord of Light, Life, Liberty and Love. This Aeon has for its purpose the complete emancipation of the human race."50 The emancipation to which Crowley makes reference, is the liberation of mankind from the "iron chains" of Christianity. Again, Heru-ra-ha is Horus the Sun, and Horus is Satan the Sun. It all ties in with the Devil, once you know the names. To refresh your memory, go back and read the heading of chapter four.

NO.20 "THE AEON"

The god and goddess of the Qabalah, with their names as presented in *The Book of the Law*, are presented in this card as father and mother of Horus. When you read of the "globe of fire," remember the Lead Zeppelin – The Hindenburg, on the front of the first Led Zeppelin album:

"Around the top of the card is the body of Nuith, the star-goddess, who is the category of unlimited possibility; her mate is Hadit, the ubiquitous point-of-view, the only philosophically tenable conception of Reality. He is represented by a globe of fire, representing eternal energy; winged, to show his power of Going. As a result of the marriage of these two, the child Horus is born. He is, however, known under his special name, Heru-ra-ha. A double god; his extraverted form is Ra-Hoor-Khuit; and his passive or introverted form Hoor-Pa-Kraat....He is also solar in character, and is therefore shown coming forth in golden light.

The whole of this symbolism is thoroughly explained in the 'Book of the Law.'"51 [The "globe of fire" is of course, the "Lead Zeppelin."]

Crowley reiterates what he just said, later on the same page. "This new Tarot may therefore be regarded as a series of illustrations to the *Book of the Law*; the doctrine of that Book is everywhere implicit."52 So here one can see that *The Book of the Law*, the Qabalah, and the Tarot cards are all interrelated, which is why they were presented in that order.

There is one more section of The Aeon that needs to be presented. It is going to be presented in accordance with the Led Zeppelin song, "The Rain Song," off the *Houses of the Holy* album.

HOUSES OF THE HOLY – "THE RAIN SONG"

At 6:06 into "The Rain Song," Plant sings that he can "see" a specific "torch" that has to be held by "all" those who follow the Law of Thelema, Satan, witchcraft, Magick, etc(I believe). The symbolism is in line with the Statue of Liberty. It is the torch of freedom. In the last section on the Tarot card The Aeon, Crowley wrote:

"There are many other details with regard to the Lord of the Aeon which should be studied in the Book of the Law.

"It is also important to study very thoroughly, and meditate upon, this Book, in order to appreciate the spiritual, moral, and material events which have marked the catastrophic transition from the Aeon of Osiris. The time for the birth of an Aeon seems to be indicated by great concentration of political power with the accompanying improvements in the means of travel and communication, with a general advance in philosophy and science, with a general need of consolidation in religious thought. It is very instructive to compare the events of the five hundred years preceding and following the crisis of approximately 2,000 years ago, with those of similar periods centered in 1904 of the old era. It is a thought far from comforting to the present generation, that 500 years of Dark Ages are likely to be upon us. But, if the analogy holds, that is the case. Fortunately, to-day we have brighter torches and more torch-bearers."53

LED ZEPPELIN AND "THE HORNED GOD"

The god in the male/female godhead is always referred to as the sun by occultists, and the goddess is considered the moon, in symbolism. I intend to bring the reader substantial evidence to show that "The Rain Song," in the earliest lyrics, is referring to the god, who is the sun, or sun god. I will also show in this section that this sun god has horns. Now everybody knows that Satan is pictured as having horns. I believe that is who Robert Plant is singing of in the beginning of "The Rain Song." In the first line of the song, he makes reference to the "spring" that refers to his "loving." In the second line, he makes it clear that winter is the first season he knows. What that means is, he was born in the winter. This is Plant singing in the stead of the sun god, I believe, and he is Lucifer. The sun god dies at the winter solstice and is born once again at the winter solstice. This refers to the sun getting to its lowest point of the year, at the end of the calendar year and then rising up again to shine bright in the spring. It is in the springtime that the sun god marries his consort, the goddess or moon. The infamous "Walpurgis Night" is on April 30th, and "Beltane," the day of the marriage between the god and the goddess, is on May 1st. This is the reason that the goddess is called the Queen of the May, or "May Queen." Her consort is referred to as the King of May. If you know your Led Zeppelin, you know Plant sings of the May Queen in "Stairway to Heaven." She is one of two different ladies sung about in the song. "The Rain Song" will also be addressed later in the book.

This sun god is also called the Horned God, and is associated with, by occult authors, Cernunnos, Herne the Hunter, Pan, Janus, Tammuz, Damuzi, Osiris, and Dionysus, to name a few. All these gods, again, are Satan. The following information is going to come from *The Encyclopedia of Witches and Witchcraft*, as well as a book called *Celtic Magic*. In the first quote, from the first source, you will read of the Horned God, who is born in the winter and marries in the spring, at Beltane: "In neo-Pagan WITCHCRAFT, the consort of the GODDESS and representative of the male principle of the Supreme Deity. The Horned God is the lord of the woodlands, the hunt and animals. He also is the lord of life, death and the underworld. He is the Sun to the Goddess's Moon. The Horned God alternates with the Goddess in ruling over the fertility cycle of birth-death-rebirth. The Horned God is born at the winter solstice, unites with the Goddess in marriage at Beltane..."54 Again, Beltane is on May 1st.

The following quote from *Celtic Magic* is in agreement: "Winter Solstice occurs about December 21. This is the time of death and rebirth of the Sun God. The days are shortest, the Sun at its lowest point. The Full Moon after Yule is considered the most powerful of the whole year. This ritual is a light festival, with as many candles as possible on or near the altar in welcome of the Sun

Child."55 We know that this sun god is born at winter solstice and marries in the spring, May 1st. We also know that he has horns. The writer of *Celtic Magic*, D.J. Conway, also presents the Horned God as Cernunnos (There is a picture of Cernunnos in this chapter that I shot out of *Magic Arts in Celtic Britain*, that Robert Plant says influenced Stairway to Heaven.). Conway wrote:

"The horns were in honor of the Celtic god Cernunnos (in Britain) or the Horned one, and symbolized the male virility needed for fertility. The Horned God was the opener of the Gates of Life and Death, the masculine, active side of Nature, god of the Underworld. This is the oldest form of the god that this world has.

"The female counterpart of Cernunnos was the naked White Moon Goddess. This oldest Earth goddess is the Primal Mother, who creates everything; the passive, feminine side of Nature."56

Conway goes on to give a description of Cernunnos that aligns him with the Druids, who are Celtic high priests, or magicians; and she also associates him with astral projection as well as the crossroads: "CERNUNNOS (ker-noo-nos)/CERNOWAIN/CERNENUS/HERNE THE HUNTER: Known to all Celtic areas in one form or another. The Horned God; God of Nature; god of the Underworld and the Astral Plane; Great Father; 'the Horned One.' The Druids knew him as Hu Gadarn the Horned God of fertility....Virility, fertility, animals, physical love, Nature, woodlands, reincarnation, crossroads, wealth, commerce, warriors."57 The Devil loves to meet folks at the Crossroads; especially Druids, right Robert? If the reader thinks I am taunting Mr. Plant, I am not. He was the one who made reference to this in the 1998 song, "Walking Into Clarksdale."

LED ZEPPELIN I – "HOW MANY MORE TIMES"

Another name for the Horned God, as you read in the last quote, is "Herne The Hunter," who is associated with the forest. The following quote is from *The Encyclopedia of Witches and Witchcraft*: "HERNE THE HUNTER - a spectral huntsman of English lore, often the leader of the WILD HUNT or the nocturnal processions of the dead. As leader of the Wild Hunt, Herne has lunar associations. His name is associated with another leader of the dead, Herlechin, or Harlequin, also associated with the Devil. Herne is portrayed wearing an antlered headdress. In neo-Pagan WITCHCRAFT, he is associated with the HORNED GOD, and with CERNUNNOS and PAN. Sightings of Herne are still reported in Windsor Forest near Windsor Castle and are associated with Witchcraft activities."58 In that quote you read that Herne the Hunter is associated with the Horned God, Cernunnos, and Pan, who are all Satan. In the song, "How Many More Times," off *Led Zeppelin*, their first album, if you listen carefully you can hear plain as day, Robert Plant singing that he is called the "Hunter," between 6:28 and 6:32 of the song. Just listen and you will hear it. After calling himself that, he says, "That's how I got my fame." By calling himself the Hunter, Plant can be saying that he is united with Herne the Hunter, who is Satan, his god. If Plant is saying that he got his fame from Herne the Hunter, that he is his representative, that is also in keeping with his command to the fans that they sell their souls to the Devil in their concert film. This will be discussed in chapter eleven.

CERNUNNOS AND CERRIDWEN

In the Qabalah's godhead, the god is consistently called the god of fertility, and the goddess is called the goddess of fertility. D.J. Conway goes on to name Cernunnos' female consort as "Cerridwen." She wrote that she is the: "Moon Goddess; Great Mother; grain goddess; goddess of Nature."59

To show those who practice Wicca as being in agreement with those who look to the Qabalah for truth, she wrote: "The Wiccan believe that all gods are one god, all goddesses are one goddess, and both are united."60 You already read that same concept as coming from Raymond Buckland, the main promoter of Wiccan witchcraft in the United States, who studied under Gerald Gardner, a contemporary of Aleister Crowley. These people are all worshiping the same being, Satan. At least Crowley had the guts to admit it, whereas the Wiccan say they just worship the Horned God. Of course, getting burned at the stake would change my god's name from Satan to the Horned God as well, if I were one of them.

To show the widespread worship of the Horned God, Rosemary Guiley, in *The Encyclopedia of Witches and Witchcraft*, wrote: "Among the deities and beings associated with the Horned God are CERNUNNOS, the Celtic god of fertility, animals and the underworld; HERNE THE HUNTER, a specter of Britain; PAN, the Greek god of the woodlands; Janus, the Roman god of good beginnings, whose two-faced visage represents youth and age, life and death; Tammuz and Damuzi, the son-lover-consorts to ISHTAR and INANNA; OSIRIS, Egyptian lord of the underworld; and Dionysus, Greek god of vegetation and the vine, whose cult observed rites of dismemberment and resurrection."61

DIONYSUS

One name for the god that has not been mentioned often by Aleister Crowley is Dionysus. He is simply another form of Pan, the Devil. In their book, *Pacts With The Devil*, that advocates the Satanic Pact, S. Jason Black and Christopher S. Hyatt, Ph.D., made the effort to convey that to their readers. Note their antagonism toward Christianity, which is consistent with Lucifer:

"Dionysus, more than any other classical deity, fits the figure, function and worship of Lucifer. He is beautiful, bisexual, a master of undisciplined 'black' magic. His presence also divests people of their repressions and cultural programming, a truly horrible thing in the eyes of Christians and pre-Christian Romans. He is capable of great love and sensuality toward his followers and insensate cruelty toward his enemies (or perhaps, the enemies of nature).

He also has horns."62

So Dionysus has horns, just like the Devil. What Dionysus/Satan is really capable of, is programming the minds of people who want to live a life of rebellion against god that they are doing something virtuous. His goal is to see you in hell. What these writers call cultural programming, is in fact the design of the conscience by Lord Jesus Christ. We will look at that later. The quote you just read says he fits the description of the Devil. Fans of The Doors need to remember that Dionysus is none other than the Devil himself; the undisputed master of self-destruction.

"Dionysus," according to Black and Hyatt, also held "secret initiations" in "wild places" hidden from the normal population. They said that the members of the gatherings would sacrifice goats to him and that they "...took intoxicants and indulged in ritual sodomy to commemorate a similar act supposedly performed by the deity. The celebrants would experience spirit possession and run naked through the wilderness bringing down deer and wild sheep with their bare hands and eating them raw."63 This is just another description of the Black Sabbath (Chapter Four); regardless if the Devil calls himself Pan, Dionysus, or Rudolph the Red Nosed Reindeer; it is the same being, Lucifer. Black and Hyatt, in the same section on Dionysus in their text, emphasized that he was a parallel to Shiva in India, which is no surprise to the members of the Silver Star, or this author; in other words, the song remains the same.

To show the flip side of their blatant anti-Christ, Devil loving attitude, Black and Hyatt also attacked the Christian faith: "Christianity, in all its forms, tends toward mental illness-and depends on it to survive. All religion in this culture, whatever it claims to be, will tend to imitate Christianity unless the program is broken. And it is the purpose of the 'black arts' of the Eastern and Western traditions to break that program, that grip. They do not ignore, they confront, which is why they are considered evil" (It is important for the reader to know that in the back of their blasphemous book, Pacts With The Devil, Black and Hyatt have, on page 247, a sample of the written pact for their readers to follow, and at the bottom it reads "Signed in your own blood." They too teach you have to sign your N.I.B., name in blood.).64 These two writers know as much about Biblical Christianity as they do nuclear physics. Yet, they perceive themselves as qualified judges. The condition of your conscience will dictate to you who is mentally ill, and what is evil, Satanism or Christianity, because you see, there is no middle ground, there only appears to be. You don't have to be a cognizant, hardcore Satanist to be living for the Devil; one only has to be anti-Christ. The Devil gets the soul of each. This will all be examined later in the book, in detail.

Suffice it to say, the author believes that the god of the Qabalah is presented in the Tarot cards and "The Rain Song." The last card in Crowley's Tarot deck, among the 22 trumps, beginning with 0 and ending with 21, is called "The Universe." It is in reference to the bride of the son, Malkuth. Again, Malkuth is the earth and the people on it that Satan will "redeem." It begins by mentioning Satan as Saturn.

NO.21 "THE UNIVERSE"

"Saturn, therefore, is masculine; he is the *old* god, the god of fertility, the sun in the south; but equally the Great Sea, the great Mother, and the letter Tau upon the Tree of Life appears as an emanation from the moon of Yesod, the foundation of the Tree and representative of the reproductive process and of the equilibrium between change and stability, or rather their identification. The influence of the path descends upon the earth, Malkuth, the daughter. Here again, appears the doctrine of 'setting the daughter upon the throne of the Mother'. In the card itself there is consequently a glyph of the completion of the Great Work in its highest sense, exactly as the Atu of the Fool symbolizes its beginning. The Fool is the negative issuing into manifestation; the Universe is that manifestation, its purpose accomplished, ready to return. The twenty cards that lie between these two exhibit the Great Work and its agents in various stages. The image of the Universe in this sense is accordingly that of a maiden, the final letter of Tetragrammaton."[65]

Crowley sums up the card: "The Universe, so states the theme, is the Celebration of the Great Work accomplished."[66] Jimmy Page's demonstration of the Great Work, the union of the microcosm, man, with the macrocosm, Satan, will be presented later in the book.

To bring this section on the Tarot to a conclusion, I want to emphasize the indisputable fact, that the Tarot cards are simply another medium of communication between the Devil, his demonic forces and those who are in league with them, believing that the god and goddess are their creators. The god is Satan, and the goddess is Satan, irrespective of whether he appears to man as a god or a goddess; in the context of those who do literal invocations. Using the Tarot is for divination, not for invocations. However, a person who fools with Tarot cards and is successful will be tempted to, and probably will, go further down the occult highway. The whole point is to not take the first step.

If you would like to see a practical working of the Tarot, just watch the movie already referred to, "Tombstone." During a lightning storm, Ellie Earp, the wife of Virgil Earp (Sam Elliot), is consulting the Tarot cards as to near future events. She is reading the cards, which demonic forces are communicating through, and she says "Tower of Babel, Death, and The Devil? Oh dear." The reason she said "Oh dear" was that she had bad news on the horizon conveyed to her. What happened? That same night, her husband got shot up and lost the use of his left arm, and her brother in law, Morgan Earp (Bill Paxton), gets shot in the back by the Cowboys and dies on a pool table. The only one to get away without injury is Wyatt Earp (Kurt Russell). "Tombstone" may only have been a movie, but the Tarot cards are real entities used by occultists, and the movie displayed just the type of fortune telling or divination that they are utilized for.

The Tarot cards, which are pictorial representations of the male/female godhead depicted in the Qabalah, are used for deriving knowledge from Satan to assist an occultist in his divination; which is fortune telling. This was a practice that would bring death to the practitioner in the context of regulations for the Children of Israel from Jehovah, (Lord Jesus Christ) to Moses. The basic understanding of the Tarot presented in this chapter has assisted in the preparation of the reader for understanding the most powerful and magical music Led Zeppelin recorded, examined later in the book. In this chapter Qabalistic concepts were shown to exist in the songs, "Going to California," "Wonderful One," "The Rain Song," and "How Many More Times." The illustrations from the Tarot were taken primarily from Crowley's book on Egyptian Tarot, *The Book of Thoth*. However, his writings were congruent with other occult writers on the subject. In 1944, the year Jimmy Page was born, Crowley published *The Book of Thoth* to assist his followers in the Argenteum Astrum and the O.T.O. in their divination. He studied the Tarot right from the beginning of his occult career, throughout his membership in the Hermetic Order of the Golden Dawn, and while dealing with the Silver Star and O.T.O. From the beginning of his career in Magick through the day he died, he was an advocate of the Tarot, proclaiming it as representative of the gods of the Qabalah. The music of Led Zeppelin shows the band to be Qabalists as well, introduced in this chapter, and proved conclusively in the pages to come, while discussing the band's presentation of Qabalistic concepts in their song, as well as statements about the song, "The Song Remains the Same."

V

The Hierophant

This Tarot card of Crowley's is called "The Hierophant." He wrote that it was representative of the Aeon of Horus that began in 1904. He also said that the three rings, which are identical to John Bonham's Magick Rune, were indicative of the Aeons of Isis, Osiris, and Horus, or Man, Woman, and Child. Robert Plant defined Bonham's rune as Man, Woman, and Child as well. Look at the photo of Led Zeppelin on page 498 in this book, and you will see John Bonham's Magick Rune on the front of his bass drum as the band plays "Stairway," in '75.

BAS-RELIEF OF THE GOD CERNUNNOS, DISCOVERED ON THE SITE OF NOTRE DAME, PARIS

This photo is of the Celtic god Cernnunos, taken from Lewis Spence's *Magic Arts in Celtic Britain*. Cernnunos is, as the evidence suggests, the same as The Horned God, Pan, Dionysus, Herne the Hunter, etc. This horned deity is none other than Lucifer in disguise, as are the others. Remember, *Magic Arts in Celtic Britain* was an inspiration for Robert Plant's "Stairway to Heaven" lyrics.

1   Stuart R. Kaplan, *The Encyclopedia of Tarot*, U.S. Games Systems, Inc., Stamford, CT, 1994, pg.2

2   Eliphas Levi, *Transcendental Magic*, pg.177

3   S.L. MacGregor Mathers, *The Tarot*, Samuel Weiser Inc., Yorke Beach, Maine, 1993, pg.2

4   Aleister Crowley, *The Book of Thoth*, pg.4

5   Ritchie Yorke, *Led Zeppelin - The Definitive Biography*, pg.150

6   Ibid, pg. 129

7   Aleister Crowley, *The Book of Thoth*, Introduction, pg. xi

8   Ibid, pg.3

9   Ibid, pg.3

10   *Webster's New World Dictionary*, Second College Edition, 1978, pg.412

11   Eliphas Levi, *Transcendental Magic*, pg.368

12   Aleister Crowley, *Moonchild*, pg.166

13   Aleister Crowley, *The Book of Thoth*, pp.5-6

14   Ibid, pp.7-8

15 Ibid, pg.9

16 Arthur E. Waite, *The Pictorial Key to the Tarot*, Samuel Weiser Inc.,
    Yorke Beach, Maine, 1993, pp.59-60

17 Aleister Crowley, *The Book of Thoth*, pg.10

18 Ibid, pg.25

19 Ibid, pg.28

20 Ibid, pg.34

21 Ibid, pg.30

22 Ibid, pg.44

23 Ibid, pg.45

24 Ibid, pg.54

25 Ibid, pg.56

26 Ibid, pg.64

27 Ibid, pg.69

28 Ibid, pg.70

29 Arthur E. Waite, *The Pictorial Key to the Tarot*, pp.72,75

30 D. Baloti Lawrence, *Tarot - 22 Steps To A Higher Path*, Longmeadow
    Press, Stamford, CT, 1992, pg.35

31 Ibid, pg.35

32 Ibid, pg.36

33 Ibid, pg.38

34 Stuart Kaplan, *The Encyclopedia of Tarot*, pg.327

35 Aleister Crowley, *The Book of Thoth*, pg.72

36 Ibid, pg.73

37 Lewis Spence, *Ancient Egyptian Myths and Legends*, pp.80-82

38 Aleister Crowley, *The Book of Thoth*, pg.73

39 Aleister Crowley, *The Equinox*, Vol. I, No.3, pg.271

40 Arthur E. Waite, *The Pictorial Key to the Tarot*, pg.76

41 Ibid, pp.76, 79

42 D. Baloti Lawrence, *Tarot - 22 Steps To A Higher Path*, pg.39

43 Ibid, pg.103

44 Aleister Crowley, *The Book of Thoth*, pp.78-79

45 Ibid, pg.79

46 Ibid, pg.86

47 Ibid, pp.93-94

48 Ibid, pg.100

49 Ibid, pp.101-102

50 Ibid, pg.113

51 Ibid, pg.115

52 Ibid, pp.115 -116

53 Ibid, pg.116

54 Rosemary Ellen Guiley, *The Encyclopedia of Witches and Witchcraft*, pg.163

55 D.J. Conway, *Celtic Magic*, Llewellyn Publications, St. Paul, Minnesota, 1994, pg.49

56 Ibid, pg.79

57 Ibid, pg.106

58 Rosemary Ellen Guiley, *The Encyclopedia of Witches and Witchcraft*, pg.160

59 D.J. Conway, *Celtic Magic*, pg.106-107

60 Ibid, pg.44

61 Rosemary Ellen Guiley, *The Encyclopedia of Witches and Witchcraft*, pg.164

62 S. Jason Black and Christopher S. Hyatt, Ph.D., *Pacts With The Devil*, pg.94

63 Ibid.

64 Ibid, pp.251-252

65 Aleister Crowley, *The Book of Thoth*, pg.118

66 Ibid, pp.118-119

Jimmy Page (in Poppy suit) plays "The Song Remains the Same" in Landover, Maryland, in May of 1977. The song promotes this teaching by Aleister Crowley:

"By the time I reached Bou Saada and came to the twentieth Aethyr, I began to understand that these visions were, so to speak, cosmopolitan. They brought all systems of magical doctrine into harmonious relation. The symbolism of the Asiatic cults, the ideas of the Cabbalists, Jewish and Greek; the arcana of the gnostics; the pagan pantheon, from Mithras to Mars; the mysteries of ancient Egypt; the initiations of Eleusis; Scandinavian saga; Celtic and Druidical ritual; Mexican and Polynesian traditions; the mysticism of Molinos no less than that of Islam, fell into their proper places without the slightest tendency to quarrel. The whole of the past Aeon appeared in perspective and each element thereof surrendered its sovereignty to Horus, the Crowned and Conquering Child, the Lord of the Aeon announced in *The Book of the Law*."

CHAPTER TEN

"Now we've traveled about quite a bit as you know. You can tell by the stickers all over us. And in doing so we meet a lot of different sorts of people; Seattle people, New Orleans people, people from China and everywhere. And at the same time, we see that there's a common denominator to everything; the fact 'The Song Remains the Same.'"

"Led Zeppelin Live," at Center Coliseum, Seattle, July 17th, 1973

"Every time I sing the song, I picture the fact that I've been round and round the world and at the root of it all, there's a common denominator for everybody. The common denominator is just what makes it good or bad - whether it's Led Zeppelin or Alice Cooper. I am proud of the lyrics - somebody pushed my pen for me, I think."1

Robert Plant, "Led Zeppelin - The Definitive Biography"

"The science of the Qabalah makes doubt, as regards religion, impossible, for it alone reconciles reason with faith by showing that <u>universal dogma, at bottom always and everywhere the same,</u> though formulated differently in certain times and places, is the purest expression of the aspirations of the human mind, enlightened by a necessary faith."2

Eliphas Levi, "The Book of Splendours"

"The Qabalah, properly understood, properly treated, is so universal that one can vamp up a ritual to suit almost 'any name and form.'"3

Black Magician Aleister Crowley, "Magick Without Tears"

THE SONG REMAINS THE SAME: QABALAH MAGICK ALL OVER THE WORLD

The Song Remains the Same is Led Zeppelin's proclamation of Qabalah Magick as a universal religious entity. The same was taught by Aleister Crowley of course, so the band is once again furthering his cause, as well as that of the Silver Star; founded by Satan. We will examine the roots of Magick in this chapter, what Aleister Crowley referred to as Satan burning in the heart of man to show him his will, as though it were the will of god. From there the concept of being utilized by Satan to execute his universal will, as revealed by him to his follower through dreams, will be discussed. The song, "The Song Remains the Same," will then be examined in conjunction with the teaching on dreams, as well as the band's invitation to follow them on the path of Magick; and finally, their assertion that Qabalah Magick is a universal reality. The universal aspect will be supported by the writings of four renowned authors on Magick; their writings exhibiting an obvious congruence. Bringing the chapter to a close, Egypt will be discussed in light of its being the root of universal Magick, supported by the writings of Aleister Crowley, as well as Moses himself, from the *Holy Bible*. In "The Song Remains the Same" and their comments about it, Led Zeppelin succeeded in doing Satan's will in describing his contact with potential followers through dreams, inviting fans to follow them in their Devil worship, declaring that they can't imagine what they are "missing" out on, and guiding the same to discover that Qabalah Magick is the hidden universal common denominator of all religious systems; with the exception of Christianity, of course.

Robert Plant, on the soundtrack to the film, *The Song Remains the Same*, introduced the song, "The Song Remains the Same," as "anatomical." Anatomical is defined as having to do with anatomy. Anatomy, in the context of this chapter is defined by Webster as "the structure of an organism or body, or a model of it as dissected; a detailed analysis."4 We are going to dissect "The Song Remains the Same" and analyze its parts so you can see that its contents describe the structure or embodiment of discipleship of the Devil in the Silver Star; based on the writings of its founder, Aleister Crowley. It is presented chronologically in "The Song Remains the Same;" the theme of which is the foundation of Jimmy Page's expressed motive of making their concert film; their roots.

LED ZEPPELIN GUIDING FANS TO MAGICK

In the Preface you read a quote from Robert Plant, where he said that a rock group can communicate its message to its fans much easier when they are stoned. Again, that is because being stoned causes a person to be more susceptible to hypnosis, and hypnosis makes a person increasingly amenable to the power of suggestion. Plant speaks of the band having something to show their fans. Before we look at their message presented in this chapter, the same theme as defined by Aleister Crowley needs to be presented. He mentions the Great Work, which you know from reading this book is the term he and the Silver Star use to describe helping mankind to be united with the godhead (Satan), Kether, or Crown of the Qabalah. He explains that initiates, in the universal context, can guide others, which is in effect their working the Great Work:

"In all systems of religion is to be found a system of Initiation, which may be defined as the process by which a man comes to learn that unknown Crown.

Though none can communicate either the knowledge or the power to achieve this, which we may call the Great Work, it is yet possible for initiates to guide others."5

This chapter defines what Led Zeppelin was trying to communicate to their fans, guiding them thereby. The anatomy or structure of the lyrics to "The Song Remains the Same" present the three stages of Magick that pertain to the individual. First, the person is guided into his True Will from the Devil by dreams. Secondly, there is the practical working of that will, and thirdly when a person becomes cognizant of Qabalah Magick being practiced all around the world. Those three messages are presented by Led Zeppelin in the songs "All My Love" and "The Song Remains the Same." It all begins with Horus, the Crowned and Conquering Child, whose name is *"Force and Fire."* In the "Invocation of Horus," taken from the *Equinox*, Crowley called Horus Force and Fire. As you read the following quote, lock it into your memory that he mentions Horus with the flaming sword, which is the symbol of the Qabalah:

"Draw, draw the Flaming Sword
Crowned Child and Conquering Lord,
Horus, Avenger!"6

Crowley praised Horus as "Force and Fire" in the *Book of Thoth*, and made it clear that he is Pan: "...I praise the Crowned and Conquering Child whose name is Force and Fire, whose subtlety and strength make sure serenity, whose energy and endurance accomplish the Attainment of the Virgin of the Absolute; who, being manifested, is the Player upon the sevenfold pipe, the Great God Pan, and, being withdrawn into the Perfection that he willed, is Silence."7 I intend to show that Horus (Satan) was the individual that Robert Plant referred to while mentioning force and fire in the pertinent section of the song, "All My Love," which is off the *In Through the Out Door* album.

IN THROUGH THE OUT DOOR – "ALL MY LOVE"

In 1979, Led Zeppelin put out its ninth album, *In Through The Out Door*. The next to last track on the album is the one we find the Force and Fire mentioned. Robert Plant was speaking of Horus, I believe, at *3:48* into "All My Love," when he spoke of *"His"* being a *"force"* who is *"within"* us. In the next line of the song he sings of *"Ours"* being a *"fire"* everyone of us are able to *"find."* The Silver Star's *Book of the Law* reads, in chapter 2, verse 20: "Beauty and strength, leaping laughter and delicious langour, force and fire, are of us."8

The Force is Horus in the form of Hadit, and the Fire is Horus' will for the life of the human being. This will was previously described in chapter seven as the "True Will." Again, Hadit and Horus are both Satan, who consistently identifies himself with fire.

In chapter two you read about the Black Dog and his eyes of fire. I want to reiterate this now from the writings of Aleister Crowley. In his encyclopedia of initiation, *The Equinox*, Crowley wrote these words:

> "The infinite Lord of Light and Love
> Breaks on the soul like dawn. See! See!
> Great God of Might and Majesty!
> Beyond sense, beyond sight, a brilliance
> Burning from His glowing glance."9

As presented in chapter two, the Black Dog with eyes of fire is Satan. We also know that Crowley believed Satan is god. After Robert Plant finished singing of the "burning" eyes in "Black Dog," the next line of the song, at 1:18, has Plant singing that he "dreams" constantly about the Black Dog. These dreams that Plant sings of are about the Devil, and for a specific purpose. Satan is trying to send a signal to the fans through the song that he reveals his "True Will" for "his creation" through dreams. At 1:06 into Black Dog, Plant sings of his heart as "flaming." In *The Book of the Law*, Satan wrote through Crowley under the title of Aiwaz, concerning himself in the second chapter, in the form of Hadit: "I am the flame that burns in every heart of man, and in the core of every star. I am Life, and the giver of Life..."10 Remember that Hadit is Horus. In the Qabalah, the father and son are one and the same. It is this same father, mother, son trinity. Crowley described it in *The Equinox, Vol. I, No.7*: "...Horus-Ra Hoor Khuit-my god, that ruleth the world under Nuit and Hadit."11 From this point throughout the rest of the chapter, when *The Book of the Law* is mentioned, each chapter will be referred to as being written by Satan.

Satan, therefore, is the Force and Fire that burns in the heart of every man, and in the core of every star. When he speaks of a star, it also means mankind; both men and women. Satan said that all men and women were stars in the body of Nuit. In chapter 1, verse 3, of *The Book of the Law*, Satan states: "Every man and every woman is a star."12 Therefore, Satan is the force burning in the heart of every man and woman worldwide (according to him). When it comes to the fire definition, it deals, once again, specifically with the Devil's will for the life of the man or woman. Aleister Crowley wrote concerning this: "For in each Man his Inmost Light is the Core of his Star. That is Hadit; and his Work is the Identification of himself with that Light."13 Each man is supposed to align himself with Hadit. This is lining oneself up with the fire, which is the will of the Devil. Again, Robert Plant sang about that in "All My Love," saying everybody is able to "find" their "fire," right after singing "His" being a "force" who is "within," at 3:48 into the song. So the work of each man is to identify himself with the light or fire of Hadit. We are going to look at this True Will of the Devil for man and then how he uses the dream to make this will known if a person has not yet identified himself with it.

Crowley made it clear to his readers that the True Will is assigned from the Devil. He wrote: "KNOW FIRMLY, O MY SON, THAT THE TRUE Will cannot err; for it is thine appointed Course in Heaven, in whose Order is Perfection."14 As men are to identify themselves with the light of Hadit, Crowley says it by saying we should seek this will and unite ourselves with it: "Seek therefore this Will, and conjoin with it thy conscious Self; for this is that which is written: 'thou hast no right but to do thy will. Do that, and no other shall say nay.'"15 Aleister Crowley presents Satan as burning in the heart of man and revealing to him his will. The man is to seek this will and join himself to it in order to be doing the will assigned to him. Crowley says that the way for man to find Satan's will for his life is through the theory and practice of Magick: "...the Theorick and Praxis of Magick. By it may he discover his own Nature, and its Will, and apply his Force and his Intelligence to the Right Fulfilment thereof."16 Once again, Crowley makes reference to the "force" as necessary to fulfill the True Will.

OMNIPOTENCE THROUGH MAGICK

Crowley made it clear that once a person discovers his True Will, the universe or godhead is behind him in fulfilling it: "A man who is doing his True Will has the inertia of the Universe to assist him."17 He wrote that this makes a man omnipotent, because he is united with the will of the godhead (once again claiming to be the reincarnation of Eliphas Levi): "Work thou thy Will, knowing (as I said aforetime by the mouth of Eliphaz Levi Zahed), thyself Omnipotent, and thine Habitation Eternity."18 Now you know why Jimmy Page had "Do What Thou Wilt" engraved in the run-off matrix of the *Led Zeppelin III* earliest copies. He was merely speaking for Crowley, who was speaking for the Devil. There you have it, the Devil speaking on the third album of Led Zeppelin. This omnipotence is what Jimmy Page was looking for when he gave himself over to Crowley's writings and the worship of the Devil (This is the same trick Satan has used on man since the beginning, telling him he can be as a god. Self-deification is the sinner's greatest high, making him a true child of the Devil). Crowley went on to describe yielding to this omnipotent will again in his book, *Moonchild*: "Yield yourself utterly to the Will of Heaven, and you become the omnipotent instrument of that Will."19 Crowley wrote that the way to find one's true will is through the theory and practice of Magick, and Eliphas Levi wrote that its works will make one an omnipotent liberator of the world, in *Transcendental Magic*: "We have exhibited, I say, that truth which is always universal....By revealing for the first time to the world the Mysteries of Magic we have not sought to revive practices entombed beneath the ruins of ancient civilizations, but would say to humanity in this our own day that it is called also to make itself immortal and omnipotent by its works....I have deemed it my duty to pick up that key, and I offer it to him who can take it: in his turn he will be doctor of nations and liberator of the world."20 Levi presents magic as the "key" that enables one to liberate the world. You will see this again in this chapter, presented by Robert Plant. Again, omnipotence is the theme of aligning oneself with Magick and the will of the Devil.

HEROIN AND THE FEELING OF OMNIPOTENCE

Crowley made it clear that heroin will assist a person in feeling omnipotent in *Diary of a Drug Fiend*: "The heroin had begun to take hold. We felt ourselves crowned with colossal calm....The sense of our superiority to mankind was constantly present."21 Anyone who knows anything about Jimmy Page has heard of his heroin use. On VH1's *Legends*, Steven Tyler of Aerosmith described him as "bone thin" at one point in Led Zeppelin's career because of it. As all Led Zeppelin fans know, Jimmy advertised the Poppy plant on his concert outfits. So far, from Crowley's writings, we have the Devil and Heroin making a person see himself as omnipotent. Again, this is why Jimmy Page would have sold his soul to the Devil, to be omnipotent. This Narcissistic attitude is what led Lucifer to be cast down from heaven by Lord Jesus Christ, his desire to be omnipotent, as god. The Devil simply uses his own temptation against others.

JIMMY PAGE - INSTRUMENT OF "AGREATER FORCE"

Satan lied to Aleister Crowley when he convinced him that he was god. Crowley quoted one of these lies in his Equinox, where he quotes the Devil calling himself the force behind creation: "I the force that created all, am not to be despised."22 Jimmy Page agrees with Crowley in that while he is yielded to Satan's will he is the omnipotent tool of the Devil. Steven Davis, in *Hammer of the Gods*, recorded what Page had to say: "'I know what my musical direction is now,' he said at the end of 1973, 'and at those times when I've hit it, it's just like I'm a vehicle for some greater force.'"23 Jimmy Page made that statement after the concerts at Madison Square Garden had been filmed in 1973, which were presented in their film. Page made a similar statement to Chris Welch: "There is a very powerful force at work within the band which I'm sure had a lot to do with our success." We will see him be the vehicle for the greater force, in practical working, in the next chapter.

While considering Page's comment about being an instrument of another force, take the time to reflect on this quote from the *Hammer of the Gods*, which will give some insight into the mind of Page: "Jimmy was frequently asked about his interest in the occult. Once he was asked what historic personage he most wanted to meet. His answer was Machiavelli, the author of that ultimate text on manipulation, *The Prince*. 'He was a master of evil,' Page said. '…but you can't ignore evil if you study the supernatural as I do. I have many books on the subject and I've also attended a number of séances. I want to go on studying it.'"24 Jimmy Page is a master of manipulation with his Goetia, Violin Bow, and Theremin for the force that he serves, Satan.

While Jimmy Page confessed to being a vehicle for a great force in 1973, the fans of Led Zeppelin were saying that from the very beginning. On October 25th, 1969, Led Zeppelin played at the Boston Garden, in downtown Boston, Massachusetts. Peter Grant spoke of the show and its significance years later: "I realized they could be really big, at the first big gig they ever did, at Boston Gardens, to 20,000 people - and it's a sweatbox, that place - and they absolutely pulverized them! I mean, they had it musically, and their performance was like...People in the audience used to tell me it was like a 'force'. It was in their heads for three or four days."25 [Why would the Boston Garden be the first really big gig that Led Zeppelin performed at? Why else? It is because that was where the Celtics played.] Remember, Plant sings '*His*' being a '*force*' who is '*within*' us at 3:48 into "All My Love." Aleister Crowley taught his students that Hadit was in the heart of man, and that man was to identify himself with Hadit and his will. The student can find this will by the theory and practice of Magick. Once he finds it, he is to conjoin himself to the will of Hadit and then he has the inertia of the universe to help him fulfil that will. While he is fulfilling this will, Crowley wrote, he is omnipotent as the instrument of the "omnipotence" of the Devil. He also wrote that heroin assisted him in feeling superior to the rest of mankind. You read Jimmy Page's confession that he believes he is the vehicle for a greater force. These concepts are believed by the rest of the band as well.

The following is another quote about omnipotence as it relates to Led Zeppelin, from *Hammer of the Gods*: "At that stage, early 1972, the beginning of Led Zeppelin's prime, the band couldn't stay off the road. Whatever charms the sedate English countryside held for the musicians on a sentimental level, nothing could equal the sexual buzz of a stadium full of rapturous young hopheads in deep communion with Zeppelin's unholy blues mass. Robert and Jimmy especially needed that feeling of pure unadulterated *exaltation*, that rock-god dream of unbridled passion and omnipotence that they felt as crowd noise washed over them like a waterfall of adulation and romantic energy. There was nothing else like it."26 Once again, they are "omnipotent" because they are doing the will of the Devil, playing his music and singing his lyrics (I believe, and will show), and the fans were worshiping that "omnipotent" being through his representatives, the members of Led Zeppelin. If they sing his lyrics and play his music, then the Devil has merely manifested himself in the four members of Led Zeppelin, in order to promote the anti-Christ moral code through music. This is why I believe they sold their souls to the Devil-so the worship and adoration of the fans would make them feel omnipotent. Again, if they play Satan's music and sing his lyrics, and the fans worship them, who are they worshiping? You see, you don't have to be an Ozzy Osbourne or Marilyn Manson type to represent the Devil, they just take it to its logical extension.

The moral code of Led Zeppelin's music is hardcore anti-Christ, and Satan uses the music to confirm the fan in his love of that moral code, while deceiving men like Page and Plant into believing he is god in order to have them serve him till they die. You already read where Crowley wrote he who tries to break his magical oath is in for some serious trouble. Well, the good news for Page, Plant, and Jones is that they can all be delivered from this. The first step is for them to come to the realization that they have been deceived by Satan.

Jimmy Page believes he has done and is doing his True Will as defined by the Devil, because Satan said the proof of doing his True Will would be the success connected to it. As Satan said in the *Book of the Law*: "I am Ra-Hoor-Khuit; and I am powerful to protect my servant. Success is thy proof..."27 Using the analogy of the ocean of stars out in space, Crowley says that man is one with the will of the godhead when he does that revealed will of the Devil. When he or she does not, according to Crowley, it is synonymous with a star leaving its appointed position, which would cause catastrophic collision and inevitably, chaos. This is the Silver Star's perspective as to why mankind is messed up, and they trace it all back to their arch enemy, born again Christianity, claiming that its "false" doctrines knock the stars, men and women, off their appointed course.

This concept of stars and their appointed course is discussed by Crowley in his book, *Moonchild*: "If everybody did his Will, there would be no collision. Every man and every woman is a star. It is when we get off our orbits that the clashes come."28 Commenting on this concept in the introduction of the *Book of the Law* published by Weiser, a member of the Ordo Templi Orientis, who simply presented the initials "O.M." wrote: "This means that each of us stars is to move on our true orbit, as marked out by the nature of our position, the law of our growth, the impulse of our past experiences."29 Aleister Crowley summarized this teaching in the following quote: "The great bond of all bonds is ignorance. How shall a man be free to act if he know not his own purpose? You must therefore first of all discover which star of all the stars you are, your relation to the other stars about you, and your relation to, and identity with, the Whole....And to each will come the knowledge of his finite will, whereby one is poet, one prophet, one worker in steel, another in jade. But also to each be the knowledge of his infinite Will, his destiny to perform the Great Work, the realization of his True Self."30 Jimmy Page, as the reader might imagine, is in complete harmony with Crowley's teaching on the True Will. He told Chris Salewicz in 1977:

"What I can relate to is Crowley's system of self-liberation in which repression is the greatest work of sin. It's like being in a job when you want to be doing something else. That's the area where the true will should come forward. And when you've discovered your true will you should just forge ahead like a steam train. If you put all you energies into it there's no doubt you'll succeed because that's your true will. It may take a little while to work out what that is, but when you discover it, it's all there.

"You know when you realize what it is you're supposed to be here for. I mean everyone's got a talent for something. Not necessarily artistic but whatever you care to say. And it's just a process of self-liberation."

Based on the evidence, it is safe for one to believe that Jimmy Page is advocating Crowley's "Do What Thou Wilt" in that quote, which is also why he had it engraved on the third Led Zeppelin album. Crowley got the teaching of the True Will and the Great Work from Satan, as he wrote, so consequently, that has to be whom Jimmy Page is advocating as well. Once again, the Great Work is to assist the godhead in raising mankind (both oneself and others) to the level of union or communion with that godhead, and the Silver Star's godhead is the Devil. This is why these people are so bold in their seared conscience beliefs. "If Christ was God, he certainly wouldn't allow Satan to get away with this would he?" That is the reasoning they have, which makes them confident. The problem is, Christ is God, and he has given direct control over the earth to Lucifer; according to Luke Chapter 4 in the New Testament of the *Holy Bible*.

What a sad day it will be for those who either worshiped Satan or refused to think of the supernatural and crucified Christ in their conscience, living an anti-Christ life and believing that they are good people, according to human standards, not God's. You have to be absolutely sinless in God's sight to enter heaven. Since no one is sinless, Christ had to take man's sin on himself. That substitution, however, is made applicable only to the one who repents and follows him, and music like Led Zeppelin's is to make sure one never does. There is Satan's desire and motive in providing rock stars with the most hypnotic music in existence. Even if a person grows out of it, he or she has still been confirmed in an anti-Christ mentality in their formative years of adolescence, and now are set in their ways. Rarely will a person repent and follow Christ after they are set in their ways. The reason is that human beings, by nature, are creatures of habit, and therefore resistant to change. Repentance is not feeling, it is will. Led Zeppelin is an on ramp to the highway to hell.

Jimmy Page and company are following the Devil on the highway to hell, believing he is god, because they seared their consciences long before he came calling. Think for a minute, John Bonham the drummer, and Peter Grant, the manager, toured this world off and on for 13 years promoting the worship of the Devil, and now they are dead. Bonham died in 1980, and Grant in 1995. These two men are in eternity, forever. Where did they go? Peter Grant said, two years before he died: "Working as Led Zeppelin's manager was a time of total magic."31 He was 58 at the time and it seems that he stayed on the same course he was on from the very beginning, dying at 60. He can be seen sitting on the left side of the stage in *The Song Remains the Same*. That is Jimmy Page's left, and the audience's right. He is sitting there overseeing his rock group, doing his "True Will" as Led Zeppelin's manager.

THE TRUE WILL AS REVEALED IN DREAMS

This is the second and last section that deals with Force and Fire, Satan revealing the True Will to his followers in dreams because they have yet to find it on their own. Once this is explained, we are going full speed ahead into the song, "The Song Remains the Same." When a man is not doing his True Will and they are in the Silver Star, or Satan is trying to recruit them, they are wasting their energy in living their lives that way, and they can't be effective as they would be if they did their True Will, according to Crowley. He wrote of this in *Magick Without Tears:* "A man whose conscious will is at odds with his True Will is wasting his strength. He cannot hope to influence his environment efficiently."32 In order to get the person on the right track, Satan supposedly causes them to dream about what his True Will is, meaning the dream is rooted in that will: "THE DEEP, CONSTITUTIONAL, OR PREDISPOSING Cause of Dreams lieth within the Jurisdiction of the Will itself....This being so, the Will declareth himself, as it were in a Pageant, and sheweth himself thus apparelled, unto the Sleeper, for a Warning or Admonition. Every Dream, or Pageant of Fancy, is therefore a Shew of Will; and Will being no more prevented by Environment or by Consciousness, cometh as a conqueror."33 The True Will of the individual (Satan's will for the occultist) manifests itself in the dream, warning the sleeper to work that will in their life. If circumstances in their environment or their own consciousness do not prevent it from being done, it will conquer the person and they will do it, because they constantly dreamed about it. Remember, Robert Plant singing of constantly dreaming about the Black Dog. Crowley said the same thing about the True Will in a different fashion: "But alway doth he triumph and fulfil himself therein, for the Dream is a natural Compensation in the inner World for any Failure of Achievement in the outer."34 In other words, it will come to pass sooner or later, because the will won't let up. This is what I believe Robert Plant meant in "All My Love" when he said at 3:50 "Ours" being a "fire" everyone is able to "find." Remember, the Devil is the fire burning in the heart of man, and in the core of all stars, according to Crowley and Satan.

Crowley then revealed to his readers the contrast of dreams between those doing their True Will and those who do not: "THE DREAM DELIGHTFUL IS THEN A Pageant of the Fulfilment of the True Will, and the Nightmare a symbolic Battle between it and its Assailants in thyself."35 It is as though the will has rewarded the individual with a pleasant dream because he has found it and is fulfilling it. Crowley emphasized this in his writings, showing the Devil in control of guiding the individual in his dream. Lewis Spence, who wrote *Magic Arts in Celtic Britain*, had this to say about the Egyptian gods showing people what they wanted them to do, in his book, *Ancient Egyptian Myths and Legends*. This is relevant because Crowley wrote *The Book of the Law* in Cairo, Egypt: "Dreams were also greatly relied upon in the affairs of life. These were believed to be sent by the gods, and it is probable that the Egyptian who was exercised over his private affairs sought his repose in the hope of being vouchsafed a dream which would guide him in his conduct."36 Now we are going to look at the song, "The Song Remains the Same."

THE SONG IN THE FILM – "THE SONG REMAINS THE SAME"

"The Song Remains the Same" was first presented by Led Zeppelin on their fifth studio album, *Houses of the Holy*. For the purpose of this chapter, however, we are going to examine it from the film bearing the name of the song, and the times presented will be in accordance with the soundtrack and film. The reason is, the lyrics are the same, and there is film footage you will need to see or at least be informed of, so it is pointless to go back and forth from *Houses of the Holy* to the soundtrack of the film. One point that needs to be made, however, is that the inside cover of *Houses of the Holy* has a naked man holding a young girl up in offering to the light above the castle. It seems that the "son" is raising up the "daughter" to sit on the mother's throne, just like in the Qabalah. The cover of the album obviously points to the sun's children, i.e. children of Satan, the sun (see chapter four heading). The sun's children are going to be elaborated on later in the book.

THE DREAM

On the soundtrack to the film, *The Song Remains the Same*, at 1:52 into the song, Robert Plant refers to a specific "dream" of his, and at that precise moment in the film, the camera is focused on the sun shining on the red dragon of the flag of Wales. In the dream he had it conveyed to him that he could have any knowledge he desired, as well as travel anywhere he wanted. You already read about astral projection in chapter six, so it won't be reiterated; although that is what the author believes he is referring to. The specific ability to obtain knowledge is through divination, once again, meaning the Tarot cards. Crowley explained divination as useful at anytime: "It is therefore useful to possess an art by which one can obtain at a moment's notice any information that may be necessary. This art is divination."37 You know what divination is if you read the previous chapter. Using the Tarot cards to obtain knowledge is part of the True Will of the student of Magick. Eliphas Levi presented similar information in *Transcendental Magic*, intimating that spirits can work through the cards or in dreams: "We, however, by no means deny the possible intervention of elementary spirits in these occurrences, as in those of divination by cards or by dreams…"38

WORKING OUT THE WILL OF THE UNIVERSE (SATAN)

At 2:22 into "The Song Remains the Same," off the film soundtrack, Robert Plant sings about working out his True Will. He sings it as literal for the band, and musicians in the audience or listening to it at home. What this means is, when Plant is singing it literally for the band, he is referring to how it worked out for them, I believe. He tells the listener to "Hear" his "song." Then he sings that he wants the fans to "listen." The next thing he conveys is that he wants the listener to "sing" with the band. The author believes that he is referring to joining in with them, not singing the lyrics. Then he tells the fans that they are not aware of "what" they have been "missing." Finally, he refers to the music itself. He sings that "any" small "song" they "know," will definitely "grow" into a big one. In summation, he is singing to the fans to listen to what he is singing about and join in with the band, because they can't imagine what they are missing out on, and that the little songs always become big ones. Knowing this subject as I do, I believe that the last part refers to the band literally, and any vocation by application. In other words, going to law school for a member of the Silver Star is a little song, and if it is Satan's True Will for the member to become a lawyer, then the little song will grow into a big one. The person will graduate and practice law, because he has Satan's assistance in achieving that goal. He most certainly helped Led Zeppelin achieve theirs, and they convey that to the audience in no uncertain terms in their film. We shall look at that in detail in the next chapter, when we discuss their command to make the satanic pact. You already read where Crowley wrote that those who are doing their True Will have the Universe's Inertia to help them. In the literal sense, I believe Plant is trying to convey that Satan will make any small song a person is trying to compose into a complete composition through Magick. You will read of Jimmy Page waiting for something to come to him as he sat with his guitar later in the book.

QABALAH MAGICK - THE KEY TO THE MYSTERY

We are about to examine a couple of very important quotes about Qabalah Magick as they relate to the song, "The Song Remains the Same." This is the concept put forth by Robert Plant while introducing the song on tour with Jimmy Page in 1995, in San Jose, California. We already know that Aleister Crowley believed he was Eliphas Levi reincarnated; Levi died six months before he was born. We also know that the first book to really affect Crowley in directing him to a career as a magician was *The Cloud Upon the Sanctuary* by Karl Von Eckartshausen. We are going to examine quotes in this order, Eliphas Levi, Von Eckartshausen, Crowley, and then Robert Plant in attempting to understand "the key to the mystery." Eliphas Levi, as you read at the heading of chapter eight, ties the Qabalah in with Magick in a book he wrote, titled *The Key to the Mysteries*, that Aleister Crowley translated and included in the tenth number of the first volume of *The Equinox*. In the book, Levi wrote: "The Qabalah, or transcendental magic, is the science of light."39 He went on to write, in the same book, that transcendental magic was the key to the mystery, as the title suggests. Therefore, we have to conclude that he means the Qabalah is the key to the mystery. Remember, the word "dogma" means doctrine, tenet, or teaching. Levi wrote: "There exists a dogma, there exists a key, there exists a sublime tradition; and this dogma, this key, this tradition is transcendental magic....We do not say this in the hope of convincing the scoffer, but only to guide the seeker. Courage and good hope to him; he will surely find, since we ourselves have found."40 Again, the occultists are seeking to guide the person who is searching through occult materials. This is what Led Zeppelin does, because their music is occult material. In his book, *The Cloud Upon the Sanctuary*, Karl Von Eckartshausen wrote the same thing about magic, that it is the key to the mystery, the mystery of how to commune with "god." He wrote specifically about joining man together with spirits:

"We possess a light by which we are anointed, and by means of which we read the hidden and secret things of nature.

"We possess a fire which feeds us, and which gives us the strength to act upon everything in nature. We possess *a key to open* the gate of mystery, and *a key to shut* nature's laboratory. We know of the existence of a bond which will unite us to the Upper Worlds, and reveal to us their sights and their sounds. All the marvels of nature are subordinate to our will by *its* being united with Divinity.

"We have mastered the science which draws directly from nature, whence there is no error, but truth and light only.

"In our School we are instructed in all things because our Master is the Light itself and its essence....By these knowledges we are in condition to co-ordinate the spirits of nature and the heart of man."41

Von Eckartshausen claims that students of magic have the key to open the gate of the mystery. Aleister Crowley, in the next quote, will say, in essence, the same thing. He was writing to students in the *Ordo Templi Orientis,* a masonic/magical group that he took control over by their request. This group had already accepted his teachings on the Law of Thelema and Magick. What he wrote to them applies to the Silver Star as well, because he had written the same to them earlier. He wrote that his students need to study to know the key to the mysteries:

"Every Brother is expected to spend a great part of his spare time in the study of the principles of the Law and of the Order, and in searching out the key to its great and manifold mysteries.

"He should also do all in his power to spread the Law, especially taking long journeys, when possible, to remote places, there to sow the seed of the Law."42

It seems that this duty of sowing the seed of the Law of Thelema was the vision of the members of Led Zeppelin right from the beginning. Richard Cole wrote: "In the early days of Led Zeppelin, Jimmy Page and Robert Plant estab-lished an ambitious goal for the band: Eventually to perform in every country in the world."43 Once again, concepts presented by Richard Cole about Led Zep-pelin are in keeping with the teachings of Aleister Crowley.

"PAGE/PLANT LIVE" IN SAN JOSE, CALIFORNIA, 1995

On May 20th, 1995, Page/Plant performed in concert at the San Jose Arena, in San Jose, California. This show was broadcast all over the United States on the radio. Just before they performed "The Song Remains the Same," Robert Plant, still the satanic ambassador, said these words to the audience, in order to guide the seekers to Magick: "This is a song that was written really as a kind of a celebration of the doorway that Jimmy and I forced into our music; a little hole that we found to crawl through to try and do something that was just a little different from straight rock and roll; so this was the opening, the Key to the door that led us to the Mystery."

In 1998, on the Page/Plant album, *Walking into Clarksdale*, Robert Plant made reference to this "Key" once again, I believe. However, to illustrate this properly, we have to go back to a press conference given by Robert Plant and Jimmy Page in 1970. During the interview, Robert Plant made the following statement: "The whole idea of music from the beginning of time, was for people, you know, to be happy, and to enjoy themselves the best they can." The question

I would pose to the reader is this: Who told Robert Plant that music from the beginning of time was for people to be happy? Who was there at the beginning of time to testify to this? It was not just an adlib statement on the part of Plant. The proof that Plant knew exactly what he was saying comes from the song, "When the World Was Young," off their 1998 album. In the beginning of the song, it seems that Robert's voice, once again, was just a medium for Satan to sing to the fan. The opening lyrics present an individual stating that he had existed since the beginning of "time." This individual cannot be Robert Plant; sane people will agree. The lyrics then invite the listener to observe his "footsteps" in "eternity." Again, Robert Plant has never been in eternity, so it cannot be lyrics he is postulating for himself or the band. Then at 1:28 into the song, Plant sings the following: "The messenger will hold the key." As I wrote earlier in the book, the Tarot card "The Magician" is described as one who is the messenger of the gods, who brings news. The Tarot cards are, once again, based on the Qabalah. The "key" to the "mystery" that Plant was referring to in San Jose, as well as in "When the World Was Young" is transcendental magic, or the Qabalah, as I intend to prove in the following information. We will examine the lyrics of "The Song Remains the Same" that are pertinent, and then we will examine quotes from Aleister Crowley, Eliphas Levi, and none other than Robert Plant himself, who will authenticate.

THE QABALAH - THE UNIVERSAL COMMON DENOMINATOR

At 3:36 into "The Song Remains the Same," off the soundtrack bearing the same title, Robert Plant speaks of the universality of magic, ever so subtly. He mentions "California," then "Calcutta," India, and finally the brightness of the stars in "Honolulu," Hawaii. Right after mentioning Honolulu, he sings the song title as the last lyrics in that part of the song. At this point we are going to look at what Robert Plant is trying to communicate to the fans with this information. I looked at a globe from directly above the North Pole and what I found was interesting enough. If you look at California, you see that if you come almost directly over the top you will find yourself on the way to Calcutta. It is not on the same longitude, but it is close. From Calcutta, looking from above, you have to turn left and head east to go to Honolulu. If you come back over the top of the globe from Honolulu, not on the exact same longitude but close, you will find England. This just happens to be where the band is from. What they are saying is that Magick covers the four corners of the globe. England, California, Honolulu, Hawaii, and Calcutta, India are each in a different corner of the planet. Remember, Robert Plant made reference to him who is "Father" who rules the earth's "four" corners at 5:31 into "Kashmir." The author believes he refers to the Devil of course. Crowley presented it clearly by inserting writing from

Albert Churchward into *The Equinox*: "...Horus became under varying names the supreme world-god, and his four sons, or emanations, the four quarters."44 Horus has a number of names because he is the Devil. The universality of magic, transcendental magic, or the Qabalah, is clearly taught by Aleister Crowley himself: "The Qabalah, properly understood, properly treated, is so universal that one can vamp up a ritual to suit almost 'any name and form.'"45 Crowley makes reference to the multiplicity of names for the Qabalah's godhead in that quote. Eliphas Levi (who Crowley claimed to be reincarnated) wrote a great deal about the Qabalah in *The Book of Splendours*. He wrote the Qabalah was universal and that it was the common denominator to all religious faiths: "The science of the Qabalah makes doubt, as regards religion, impossible, for it alone reconciles reason with faith by showing that universal dogma, at bottom always and everywhere the same, though formulated differently in certain times and places, is the purest expression of the aspirations of the human mind, enlightened by a necessary faith."46 The key phrase in the preceding statement was: "...universal dogma, at bottom always and everywhere the same..."47 What Levi was saying, using a mathematical metaphor, is that the appearance of religion in its individual formulation is the numerator of a fraction and Magick is the common denominator. The numerators vary all over the world, yet there is a common denominator, universal dogma, or "doctrine," and that doctrine is Magick, based on the teachings of the Qabalah. Led Zeppelin, in wanting to guide others to this concept, sang about Magick around the world in "The Song Remains the Same." Although they didn't mention the word Magick in the song, they did give little supplements to the song's meaning to writers like Ritchie Yorke, who they knew would publish them, being a personal friend. He wrote what Robert Plant had to say about "The Song Remains the Same" as a result of touring the world and the practical perspective of it in his book, *Led Zeppelin - The Definitive Biography*: "Every time I sing the song, I picture the fact that I've been round and round the world and at the root of it all, there's a common denominator for everybody. The common denominator is just what makes it good or bad - whether it's Led Zeppelin or Alice Cooper. I am proud of the lyrics - somebody pushed my pen for me, I think."48 Robert Plant, wishing to guide others into the domain of Magick, wrote what the seeker would find in the writings of Eliphas Levi and Aleister Crowley. Also, Plant is sending the message that the band is in league with the Devil, the true author of *The Book of the Law*, hinting at writing while possessed by a spirit.

While writing *The Book of the Law* under the inspiration of the Devil, Crowley wrote these statements which show that Satan was talking to him as he was writing. Crowley was tired of writing at one point and he wrote these words: "I see thee hate the hand & the pen; but I am stronger. Because of me in Thee which thou knewest not."49 The Devil reiterated it in the next chapter: "...Hadit burning in thy heart shall make swift and secure thy pen."50 (Again, Hadit is just another name for Satan.) Aleister Crowley himself wrote about this in *The Equinox*, in his commentary on *The Book of the Law*, specifically, the verse containing the previous quote about Hadit: "I do not think it easy. Though the pen has been swift enough, once it was taken in hand. May it be that Hadit hath indeed made it secure!"51

    Robert Plant apparently told everyone at Headley Grange (A house in England the band rented to record in) what he was thinking as he wrote the lyrics for "The Song Remains the Same." Richard Cole, the group's road manager was there, and he later included the information in his book, *Stairway to Heaven - Led Zeppelin Uncensored*: "For 'The Song Remains the Same,' Robert scribbled lyrics on a pad of paper in an inspirational flurry, driven by his vision of a common denominator for all peoples and things; Jimmy had carefully crafted the rich music over many weeks, initially intending it to be an instrumental number before merging it with Plant's lyrics."52 The proper term for this writing while possessed is called "Automatic Writing." The person who pushed Robert Plant's pen (which will be seen again in chapter fourteen) was Satan, wanting him to promote the Qabalah concurrently with the music produced by Jimmy Page. So according to Plant, his lyrics came from a supernatural source, and you can bet your last dime that the music for those lyrics came from the same source through Jimmy Page, wanting them to be joined together, once again, to promote the Qabalah.

JIMMY PAGE AND OZZY OSBOURNE - ROCKLINE JUNE 19TH 2000

    Jimmy Page promoted the same idea of someone inside of him being in control on June 19th, 2000 in a *Rockline* Radio Interview with Bob Coburn. The interview was with Page and the Black Crowes, but Ozzy Osbourne, another hardcore Crowley disciple, ended up in the conversation. In the midst of the dialogue between Ozzy and Page, Jimmy speaks of "somebody" inside of him. Ozzy comes on to the radio station and lets Jimmy Page know that it is him. Then he asks Page if he still receives the same feeling when he plays that he did when he first started out. Jimmy replies by telling him that it was a good question to consider. He then states that he can't recall, because it has been so far in the past. He goes on to say: "I'm really passionate about playing, I mean, somebody takes over when I start playing which is something inside of me, which is really great." Page elaborates by saying that it is a gift he is blessed with, and that he loves it. Based on the comments by Jimmy Page, it is not unreasonable to think that he believes that Lucifer is god, when you compare it with all the other evidence I am providing in this book. Only a deaf person would deny that Osbourne believes it. You will see proof soon of who that was Page was speaking of, in this work. I will let Aleister Crowley, Robert Plant, and Jimmy Page tell you, not me.

THE SYMBOL OF THE QABALAH – "THE FLAMING SWORD"

In order to further prove that Robert Plant is singing about Qabalah Magick in "The Song Remains the Same," a third example of evidence will be examined, this time from the concert film itself. "The Song Remains the Same" is the fifth song in the film, approximately 45 minutes into it. If you want to time it, exactly four minutes from Jimmy Page's opening note, Robert Plant is seen coming out of the water at night with a sword in his hand. He sticks the sword into the ground, and stares at the three rings in the handle, as well as the crown at the top of the handle. The three rings are representative of the Father, Mother and Son, Qabalistic trinity, with the Crown at the top representing Kether from the Qabalah. Twenty five seconds later, at 4:25 of the song, the sword is seen standing in a circle of flames as flames are all along the beach behind it. The photo below is the actual scene I am describing; taken as a still from the Led Zeppelin film. Once again, Jimmy Page (the producer) and Peter Grant (executive producer) present concepts from Aleister Crowley promoting the Devil's Law of Thelema, on the movie screen. Satan was directing the whole thing.

In his book, *777 & Other Qabalistic Writings of Aleister Crowley*, which was formerly titled *The Qabalah of Aleister Crowley*, Crowley wrote these words describing the book's information as in alignment with the Qabalah: "...for the tabulation of the book is from Kether to Malkuth, the course of the Flaming Sword..."53 Later in that book he wrote that the sword represents the magician's energy, as well as the course through the Qabalah: "This sword is not to be confused with the Dagger of Air. It represents the active and militant energy of the magician. Its true form is the flaming sword, the lightning flash, which strikes down from Kether through the Sephiroth as a zig-zag flash."54 Again, the flaming sword represents the course through the Qabalah from Kether to Malkuth.

Aleister Crowley identified the flaming sword with the ten sephiroth of the Qabalah, and mentions the 22 paths of the Qabalah, which represent the Tarot cards: "Lo! Two and twenty are the paths of the Tree, but one is the Serpent of Wisdom; ten are the ineffable emanations, but one is the Flaming Sword."55 When he wrote the flaming sword was one, he was again referring to the course down through the Qabalah from Kether to Malkuth. This course represents the Qabalistic godhead, the Macroprosopus (Chokmah and Binah) having a son, the Microprosopus, and then the son marrying and redeeming Malkuth, Satan's chosen people out of mankind. This is all symbolic of what the Devil is doing with the Magick of the Qabalah. He is drawing mankind to himself, and Led Zeppelin's rock and roll is part of it, which is why they presented the Flaming Sword at that point in the film. The next thing that Robert Plant does in the film is set out to redeem Malkuth, using an Arthurian analogy. That will be explained in a later chapter because of its significance of doing battle with Lord Jesus Christ. The Flaming Sword will be discussed as it is seen in that part of the film as well.

RENOWNED OCCULT AUTHORS AND UNIVERSAL MAGICK

This chapter about universal Qabalah Magick expresses the theme of the entire book, although it does not get specific about the Devil and his pact with Led Zeppelin. That is going to be examined in the next chapter. Before bringing this chapter to a close, because of the importance of the concept of the universality of Magick, four detailed examples of writing concerning it from four pertinent authors is presented. The four occult authors quoted in subsequent order are Lewis Spence, advocated by Robert Plant, Eliphas Levi and Dr. Sir J. G. Frazer, who are advocated by Aleister Crowley, and then Crowley himself. Everything mentioned gets drawn back into Egyptian magic, which will then be authenticated by Aleister Crowley as well as the *Holy Bible*. In the quotes, various parts of the world are mentioned.

THE SONG REMAINS THE SAME – "LEWIS SPENCE"

Looking at the heading of chapter fourteen, you can see a quote placed there from Ritchie Yorke's *Led Zeppelin - The Definitive Biography*, in which Robert Plant credits Lewis Spence's *Magic Arts in Celtic Britain* as an inspirational resource for the writing of "Stairway to Heaven." That having been said by Plant, included here is a quote from that book to illustrate the universality of magic. He begins with a reference to the Druids, who this author asserts is what the band members are. When reading it, remember that the word "identity" used in this context means "sameness," or alike. Spence wrote:

"Such religious ideas as appear to have been known to the Druids were equally familiar to the peoples of other Aryan communities-Germans, Slavs, Greeks, Romans and Hindus. Caesar, who was himself a practicing pontiff and something of a stickler for facts, is not likely to have been mistaken in his general estimate of the Druidic faith in Gaul, when he not only compared its gods with certain Roman gods, but actually called them by the names of Roman deities, thus making it plain that he recognized the close resemblance betwixt these equally Aryan forms-forms which had been fixed in their essentials centuries before Roman or Celt were thought of, as the practical identity of many of their myths reveals. What Caesar beheld in Gaulish Druidism was a religion which recalled the spirit, and in some ways the letter, of his own so closely that he did not hesitate to label its deities with the titles of the Roman pantheon, precisely as much earlier Greeks gave Hellenic names to the deities of Egypt. Indeed, the writers of the Classical period and their popular contemporaries appear to have realized this underlying identity of the more outstanding figures of the several Aryan pantheons in a manner never approached by later authorities on folk-lore.

"I do not mean to imply that no leaven of non-Aryan faith or Magic found its way into Druidic dogma and ritual. Such a negation would be absurd. Indeed, so many religious and magical forms are common to both Aryan and non-Aryan peoples as to make it virtually impossible to distinguish between them at times."56

They are indistinguishable as part of Satan's plan to present his faith as universal. When the time is fulfilled, the Anti-Christ will rise to rule this one world religious system; claiming to be god.

THE SONG REMAINS THE SAME – "ELIPHAS LEVI"

Eliphas Levi presented the concept of the universality of magic in his book, *Transcendental Magic*:

"BEHIND the veil of all the hireratic and mystical allegories of ancient doctrines, behind the darkness and strange ordeals of all initiations, under the seal of all sacred writings, in the ruins of Nineveh or Thebes, on the crumbling stones of old temples and on the blackened visage of the Assyrian or Egyptian sphinx, in the monstrous or marvelous paintings which interpret to the faithful of India the inspired pages of the Vedas, in the cryptic emblems of our old books on alchemy, in the ceremonies practiced at reception by all secret societies, there are found indications of a doctrine which is everywhere the same and everywhere carefully concealed. Occult philosophy seems to have been the nurse or god-mother of all intellectual forces, the key of all divine obscurities and the absolute queen of society in those ages when it was reserved exclusively for the education of priests and of kings. It reigned in Persia with the Magi, who perished in the end, as perish all masters of the world, because they abused their power; it endowed India with the most wonderful traditions and with an incredible wealth of poesy, grace and terror in its emblems; it civilized Greece to the music of the lyre of Orpheus; it concealed the principles of all sciences, all progress of the human mind, in the daring calculations of Pythagoras; fable abounded in its miracles, and history, attempting to estimate this unknown power, became confused with fable; it undermined or consolidated empires by its oracles, caused tyrants to tremble on their thrones and governed all minds, either by curiosity or by fear."57

Aleister Crowley was in complete agreement with Levi on universal occultism, as he also was with Dr. Frazer.

THE SONG REMAINS THE SAME – "DR. SIR J. G. FRAZER"

Crowley was influenced most by Dr. Sir J. G. Frazer in the writing of biography, *The Confessions of Aleister Crowley*. The resource Crowley was referring to is called *The Golden Bough*. This book can be seen sitting on Marlon Brando's desk, as Martin Sheen observes it, at the end of the film, "Apocalypse Now." In the book, Frazer addresses universal magic in no uncertain terms:

"But if in the most backward state of human society now known to us we find magic thus conspicuously present and religion conspicuously absent, may we not reasonably conjecture that the civilized races of the world have also at some period of their history passed through a similar intellectual phase, that they attempted to force the great powers of nature to do their pleasure before they thought of courting their favour by offerings and prayer - in short that, just as on the material side of human culture there has everywhere been an Age of Stone, so on the intellectual side there has everywhere been an Age of Magic? There are reasons for answering this question in the affirmative. When we survey the existing races of mankind from Greenland to Tierra del Fuego, or from Scotland to Singapore, we observe that they are distinguished one from the other by a great variety of religions, and that these distinctions are not, so to speak, merely coterminous with the broad distinctions of race, but descend into the minuter subdivisions of states and commonwealths, nay, that they honeycomb the town, the village, and even the family, so that the surface of society all over the world is cracked and seamed, sapped and mined with rents and fissures and yawning crevasses opened up by the disintegrating influence of religious dissension. Yet when we have penetrated through these differences, which affect mainly the intelligent and thoughtful part of the community, we shall find underlying them all a solid stratum of intellectual agreement among the dull, the weak, the ignorant, and the superstitious, who constitute, unfortunately, the vast majority of mankind. One of the great achievements of the nineteenth century was to run shafts down into this low mental stratum in many parts of the world, and thus to discover its substantial identity everywhere. It is beneath our feet - and not very far beneath them - here in Europe at the present day, and it crops up on the surface in the heart of the Australian wilderness and wherever the advent of a higher civilization has not crushed it under ground. This universal faith, this truly Catholic creed, is a belief in the efficacy of magic. While religious systems differ not only in different countries, but in the same country in different ages, the system of sympathetic magic remains everywhere and at all times substantially alike in its principles and practice. Among the ignorant and superstitious classes of modern Europe it is very much what it was thousands of years ago in Egypt and India, and what it now is among the lowest savages surviving in the remotest corners of the world....Here we are only concerned to ask how far the uniformity, the universality, and the permanence of a belief in magic, compared with the endless variety and the shifting character of religious creeds, raises a presumption that the former represents a ruder and earlier phase of the human mind, through which all the races of mankind have passed or are passing on their way to religion and science."58

THE SONG REMAINS THE SAME – "ALEISTER CROWLEY"

Aleister Crowley was traveling through the desert, practicing his religion, and having visions at the same time. He called them "aethyrs." He brings the universality of Magick together under the authority of Horus, who in his subjective sense was an Egyptian Sun God, the son of Isis and Osiris, but in the objective sense all students of Crowley know that Horus is none other than the Devil himself. He wrote the following in his *Confessions*: "By the time I reached Bou Saada and came to the twentieth Aethyr, I began to understand that these visions were, so to speak, cosmopolitan. They brought all systems of magical doctrine into harmonious relation. The symbolism of Asiatic cults; the ideas of the Cabbalists, Jewish and Greek; the arcana of the gnostics; the pagan pantheon, from Mithras to Mars; the mysteries of ancient Egypt; the initiations of Eleusis; Scandinavian saga; Celtic and Druidical ritual; Mexican and Polynesian traditions; the mysticism of Molinos no less than that of Islam, fell into their proper places without the slightest tendency to quarrel. The whole of the past Aeon appeared in perspective and each element thereof surrendered its sovereignty to Horus, the Crowned and Conquering Child, the Lord of the Aeon announced in *The Book of the Law*."59

One other thing that Crowley emphasized in his writings in the universal sense, was drug use. In *The Equinox, Vol. I, No.2*, in a section titled *The Psychology of Hashish,* Crowley wrote: "...I remembered that this ceremonial intoxication constitutes the supreme ritual of all religions."60 Magick is the worship of, and receiving power from, the Devil himself, regardless of the name, in conjunction with drug use, which plays a crucial role in the overall spectrum.

EGYPT - THE ORIGIN OF THE SONG REMAINS THE SAME

In *The Equinox, Vol. I, No.4*, Aleister Crowley included a writing from Albert Churchward, who wrote about Egypt as the source of magic: "...it was from Egypt, or rather Central Africa, that the human race originated, and that it is to Egyptian symbolism, and more particularly to the Ritual of the Dead, that we must go if we would rightly understand the temples, rites, ceremonies, and customs of mankind past and present. From Egypt they came and to Egypt we must go."61 Elaborating on the preceding concept, Churchward wrote that the Egyptian religious influence itself is universal: "Let us therefore mention that the chief points, a few out of a score, that have struck us are-The Custom of the Mark Sacred Stone; the universality of Horus worship; the startling identity of hieroglyphics, all over the world, with the Egyptian; and the symbolism of the Great Pyramid, and its use as a Temple of Initiation."62 You read earlier in this book where Aleister and Rose Crowley spent a night in the Great Pyramid, in chapter six.

Eliphas Levi, in *The History of Magic*, summed up the modern magician's perspective of magic and Egypt: "It is in Egypt that Magic attains the grade of completion as a universal science and is formulated as a perfect doctrine."63

The reader cannot find a greater source of antiquity to confirm what you have read in this chapter about Egyptian magic than that of the *Holy Bible*. In the Book of Exodus, Chapter 7, Verses 8-13, Lord Jesus Christ, in the form of Jehovah, ordered Moses to go and face Pharaoh:

"Then the LORD spoke to Moses and Aaron, saying, 'When Pharaoh speaks to you, saying, "Show a miracle for yourselves," then you shall say to Aaron, "Take your rod and cast it before Pharaoh, and let it become a serpent."' So Moses and Aaron went in to Pharaoh, and they did so, just as the LORD commanded. And Aaron cast down his rod before Pharaoh and before his servants, and it became a serpent. But Pharaoh also called the wise men and the sorcerers; so the magicians of Egypt, they also did in like manner with their enchantments. For every man threw down his rod, and they became serpents. But Aaron's rod swallowed up their rods. And Pharaoh's heart grew hard, and he did not heed them, as the LORD had said."

The theme of "The Song Remains the Same," ever so subtly presented by Led Zeppelin, is that the Devil is still at work with Magick, revealing his will through dreams, assisting his followers in the achievement of their true wills, and that Magick is practiced all over the world, and that he is the Lord over it. The occult authors presented in this chapter are all advocated by Aleister Crowley or Led Zeppelin, and therefore the Silver Star. Once again, Magick based on the Qabalah is practiced all over the world and the Devil is its ruler. This is exactly what he said to Lord Jesus Christ during his temptation in the desert: "Then the devil, taking Him up on a high mountain, showed Him all the kingdoms of the world in a moment of time. And the devil said to Him, 'All this authority I will give You, and their glory; for this has been delivered to me, and I give it to whomever I wish. Therefore, if You will worship before me, all will be Yours.'"

- Luke 4:5-7

The only way Christ could be tempted was in human flesh, and it was to rule the world that he aspired, but he had to go through the crucifixion to get it. Satan wanted Jesus to worship him and thereby have the world under him without the crucifixion, without bringing salvation to mankind, and the Devil being his Lord. Needless to say Jesus didn't obey. The point is, the *Holy Bible* authenticates the fact that Satan is Lord over this world's moral code and its Magick. Even the *Holy Bible* agrees with Led Zeppelin, "The Song Remains the Same." The *Bible* quote just presented authenticating the satanic pact is indicative of the Devil's commanding the fans of Led Zeppelin to sell him their souls, through the band's music, and this is addressed in the next chapter, where their subtle command is exposed.

The "Great Pyramid" in Memphis (Gizeh), Egypt. This is the place that Aleister Crowley spent the night with his new wife Rose Kelly back in 1904. During the night, Crowley claimed that Rose became possessed and hung upside down like a bat. He said it was "the finest case of obssession" he ever had the privilege to witness.

"Eyes that shine burning red..." sang Robert Plant in "Black Dog." (Ch. 2) In the Led Zeppelin film, Jimmy Page has eyes of fire, just like the Devil himself.

Jimmy Page plays the blazing finger lead during "Heartbreaker." In that song, Robert Plant sings about a woman who is smiling "like" somebody that "knows." In the song, "Dancing Days," he sings that he has his "woman" that "knows." Then he tells her she is his "woman" that "knows." In "Dazed and Confused" in their film, after commanding the fans to sell their souls to the Devil, and before Page used the violin bow on the fans, Robert Plant shouted "I Know!" repeatedly. Eliphas Levi and Aleister Crowley presented "REASON" as the "absolute truth." The "piper" uses Zeppelin's lyrics to guide the seeker to his "truth," if the seeking fan listens real hard.

In Revelation Chapter 12, the *Bible* presents the Devil as a great, fiery red dragon. The same fiery red dragon, I believe, that you can see Jimmy Page wearing on both of his legs in this 1975 photo. He wore red dragons on his concert attire in 1973, 75 & 77. A message perhaps? You better believe it. Only a fool would say no. At the end of *The Battle of Evermore,* Robert Plant sings that because of "flames" sent by a "Dragon" who rules the "Darkness," the Sun's rays render a male figure blind. He is the "Prince of Peace," Lord Jesus Christ, mentioned in the song's opening lyrics. Satan is presented as the Sun by Aleister Crowley.

Led Zeppelin (above) plays "Stairway to Heaven, " in front of a tarp with the Sun on it (July 24th, 1977). To their left is a big black Stonehenge stone. In the film, "Lucifer Rising," Lucifer makes an appearance at Stonehenge. Aleister Crowley referred to him as "...Satan....the Sun-Father....Lord of Infinite Space that flames with his consuming energy."

Jimmy Page plays his Gibson Les Paul in his red dragon suit with the Sun tarp immediately behind him on July 23rd, 1977.

"And war broke out in heaven: Michael and his angels fought with the dragon, and the dragon and his angels fought....the great dragon was cast out, that serpent of old, called the devil and Satan, who deceives the whole world; he was cast to the earth, and his angels were cast out with him....Woe to the inhabitants of the earth and the sea! For the devil has come down to you, having great wrath, because he knows that he has a short time." - Revelation 12: 7,9, 12. (NKJV)

Playing "Stairway to Heaven" in his red dragon suit, Jimmy Page plays music he said came through them. Page claimed that when he and Plant re-united in 1993 that they were "just channeling the music" as they always had before. Robert plays the tambourine; Lucifer was created with pipes and tambourines.

Jimmy Page plays the power chords prior to the lead in "Stairway to Heaven," telling us we can commune with the dragon through the Heroin poppy. (pg.196)

"The Magick Wand is thus the principal weapon of the Magus..." Crowley wrote, instructing the magician to project the macrocosmic "...force that radiates from Boleskine before him." Page began using the violin bow as a Magick Wand after buying Boleskine House in 1970 (Stonehenge stone behind him).

Jimmy Page manipulates the Theremin during the early part of "No Quarter" in 1977. This is the very moment that I broke through to the spiritual dimension at. Page can be seen with his arms in this exact same position after manipulating the Theremin at the end of "No Quarter" in their film, *The Song Remains the Same*. Jimmy Page used the Theremin on tour in '99-2000 with the Black Crowes.

Jimmy Page uses the Theremin later in the show before "Achilles Last Stand."

In the 1973 Theremin manipulation photo above, taken from *The Song Remains the Same*, and the 1977 shots below, Jimmy Page is promoting the Opium Poppy to the fans. Heroin has assisted him in living out this fantasy of Lucifer being god; and his leading people to spiritual union with him through rock and roll. Heroin does not promote reality in the mind of the abuser.

Page/Plant are playing "Going to California," in December, 1998. Plant sings of the Sun's "Children" waking up after an earthquake. At the end of their (Led Zeppelin) March 24, 1975 show at the Los Angeles Forum, Robert Plant shouted to the audience, "Children of the Sun - Goodnight!" When he calls them the children of the Sun, he means that they are the Children of Lucifer spiritually. An anomaly for Led Zeppelin on stage; he was telling the fans the truth.

Page/Plant perform their grammy winning song, "Most High," in 1998. While praising his "Lord" in the song, Plant also states that Jesus Christ (in the lineage of King David) speaks "through" a phony "crown." He then sings that Jesus "spits" burning "steel" which destroys children; referring to his doctrines.

A close up of the Great Pyramid reveals what an awesome structure it really is.

In front of the Great Pyramid, you can see the statue of the Egyptian Sphinx.

The Egyptian Sphinx plays a major role in the Kenneth Anger Silver Star presentation of Crowleyana, the movie, "Lucifer Rising." Early in the film, Mick Jagger buddy Anita Pallenberg, who plays Malkuth the daughter, or mankind, finds her beginning in Egypt. She is seen standing in front of the Sphinx with her arms raised high. As the camera focuses on the face of the statue, the face of the son in the Qabalah is shown; meaning he is Horus; who is also Lucifer himself.

The three pyramids (above and below) at Memphis (Gizeh) in Egypt; that Jimmy Page has on his right front in "The Song Remains the Same." Since all Magick has its roots in Egypt, it is easy to understand why Jimmy Page had them on his magician's outfit, especially in light of the fact he has the stars shooting out from them. Since Crowley taught that all men and women are stars, this would be symbolic of all mankind having its origin in Egypt.

Led Zeppelin jams to "The Song Remains the Same" while opening one of their shows in Landover, Maryland, in May of 1977. Jimmy Page is wearing the same Red Dragon on black outfit you see three pages back (in Oakland on 7/23/77).

1 Ritchie Yorke, *Led Zeppelin - The Definitive Biography*, pg.152

2 Eliphas Levi, *The Book of Splendours, (The Inner Mysteries of Qabalism)*, Samuel Weiser Inc., Yorke Beach, Maine, and The Aquarian Press, 1984pg.138

3 Aleister Crowley, *Magick Without Tears*, pg.24

4 *Webster's New World Dictionary*, 2nd College Edition, 1978, pg.50

5 Aleister Crowley, *The Equinox*, Vol. III, No.1, pg.55

6 Aleister Crowley, *The Equinox*, Vol. I, No.7, pg.378

7 Aleister Crowley, *The Book of Thoth*, pg.122

8 Satan, *The Book of the Law*, Aleister Crowley taking dictation, From *The Equinox*, Vol. I, No.10, Samuel Weiser, Inc., Yorke Beach, Maine, 1976, chapter 2, verse 20, pg.19

9 Aleister Crowley, *The Equinox*, Vol. I, No.3, Aha! pg.26

10 Satan, *The Book of the Law*, Aleister Crowley taking dictation, *The Equinox, Vol. I, No.10*, Samuel Weiser Inc., Yorke Beach, Maine, 1976, chapter 2, verse 6, pg.18

11 Aleister Crowley, *The Equinox*, Vol. I, No.7, pg.351

12 Satan, *The Book of the Law*, *The Equinox, Vol. I, No.10*, pg.11

13 Aleister Crowley, *The Book of Wisdom or Folly*, pg.1

14 Ibid, pg.13

15 Ibid, pg.14

16 Ibid, pg.205

17 Aleister Crowley, *Magick Without Tears*, pg.30

18 Aleister Crowley, *The Book of Wisdom or Folly*, pg.196

19 Aleister Crowley, *Moonchild*, pg.26

20 Eliphas Levi, *Transcendental Magic*, pp.405-406

21 Aleister Crowley, *Diary of a Drug Fiend*, pg.60

22 Aleister Crowley, *The Equinox*, Vol. I, No.7, pg.35

23 Steven Davis, *Hammer of the Gods*, pg.229

24 Ibid.

25 Dave Lewis and Simon Pallett, *Led Zeppelin: The Concert File*, pg.38

26 Steven Davis, *Hammer of the Gods*, pg.170

27 Satan, *The Book of the Law*, chapter 3, verse 42

28 Aleister Crowley, *Moonchild*, pg.68

29 O.M., Introduction to the *Book of the Law*, pg.9

30 Aleister Crowley, *The Equinox*, Vol. III, No.1, pg.103

31 Dave Lewis and Simon Pallett, *Led Zeppelin - The Concert File*, pg.145

32 Aleister Crowley, *Magick Without Tears*, pg.30

33 Aleister Crowley, *The Book of Wisdom or Folly*, pg.11

34 Ibid.

35 Ibid, pg.14

36 Lewis Spence, *Ancient Egyptian Myths and Legends*, pg.273

37 Aleister Crowley, *Magick-Book 4*Liber Aba*, pg.250

38 Eliphas Levi, *Transcendental Magic*, pg. 279

28 Aleister Crowley, *Moonchild*, pg.68

29 O.M., Introduction to the *Book of the Law*, pg.9

30 Aleister Crowley, *The Equinox*, Vol. III, No.1, pg.103

31 Dave Lewis and Simon Pallett, *Led Zeppelin - The Concert File*, pg.145

32 Aleister Crowley, *Magick Without Tears*, pg.30

33 Aleister Crowley, *The Book of Wisdom or Folly*, pg.11

34 Ibid.

35 Ibid, pg.14

36 Lewis Spence, *Ancient Egyptian Myths and Legends*, pg.273

37 Aleister Crowley, *Magick-Book 4*Liber Aba*, pg.250

38 Eliphas Levi, *Transcendental Magic*, pg. 279

39 Eliphas Levi, *The Key to the Mysteries*, pg.182, Aleister Crowley's *Equinox*, Vol. I, No.10

40 Ibid, pg.224

41 Karl Von Eckartshausen, *The Cloud Upon the Sanctuary*, pp.37-38

42 Aleister Crowley, *The Equinox*, Vol. III, No.1, pg.217

43 Richard Cole, *Stairway to Heaven – Led Zeppelin Uncensored*, pg.187

44 J. F. C. Fuller, from Crowley's *Equinox*, Vol. I, No.4, pg.342

45 Aleister Crowley, *Magick Without Tears*, pg.24

46 Eliphas Levi, *The Book of Splendours*, pg.138

47 Ibid

48 Ritchie Yorke, *Led Zeppelin - The Definitive Biography*, pg.152

49 Satan, *The Book of the Law*, Aleister Crowley taking dictation, chapter 2, verses 11-12, from *The Equinox*, Vol. I, No.10, pg.18

50 Ibid, pg.30

51 Aleister Crowley, *The Equinox*, Vol. I, No.7, pg.400

52 Richard Cole, *Stairway to Heaven - Led Zeppelin Uncensored*, pg.210

53 Aleister Crowley, *777 & Other Qabalistic Writings of Aleister Crowley*, Samuel Weiser Inc., Yorke Beach, Maine, 1984, pg.20

54 Ibid, pg.110

55 Aleister Crowley, *The Equinox*, Vol. I, No.5, *The Vision and the Voice*, pg.113

56 Lewis Spence, *Magic Arts in Celtic Britain*, Rider & Co., *First Edition*, no date, pg.57

57 Eliphas Levi, *Transcendental Magic*, pg.1

58 Dr. Sir J. G. Frazer, *The Golden Bough*, pp.63-64, 65

59 Aleister Crowley, *The Confessions of Aleister Crowley*, pp.618-619

60 Aleister Crowley, *The Equinox*, Vol. I, No.2, *The Psychology of Hashish*, pg.39

61 Aleister Crowley, *The Equinox*, Vol. I, No.4, pg.341

62 Ibid, pg.342

63 Eliphas Levi, *The History of Magic*, pg.79

This is "Boleskine House," on the shores of Loch Ness in Scotland. Aleister Crowley purchased it for the working of the Operation of Abramelin the Mage. The Operation is done for the spiritual union of the student of Magick with the Devil. Jimmy Page bought it in 1970. Crowley taught that a musician into Magick would hear beautiful music "he never hoped to hear" while uniting with Lucifer.

CHAPTER ELEVEN

"THERE IS a single main definition of the object of all magical Ritual. It is the uniting of the Microcosm with the Macrocosm. The Supreme and Complete Ritual is therefore the Invocation of the Holy Guardian Angel; or in the language of Mysticism, Union with God."1
*Black Magician Aleister Crowley, "Magick-Book 4*Liber Aba"*

"In the year 1899 I came to Boleskine House, and put everything in order with the object of carrying out the Operation of Abramelin the Mage."2
Black Magician Aleister Crowley, "Confessions"

"When Crowley moved in after the turn of the century, he styled himself the 'Laird of Boleskine,' adopted the kilt, and began trying to summon demons like Thoth and the Egyptian magical deity Horus. He practiced the dangerous magic of Abra-Melin the Mage to contact his guardian angel."3
Steven Davis, "Hammer of the Gods – The Led Zeppelin Saga"

"Abraham the Jew repeatedly admits, as I have before urged, that this particular System of the Sacred Magic of Abra-Melin has its Basis in the Qabalah."4
S.L. M. Mathers, "The Book of the Sacred Magic of Abramelin the Mage."

"Atmospheres are going to come through music because music is a spiritual thing of its own. You can hypnotize people with music, and when you get people at their weakest point, you can preach into their subconscious whatever you want to say."5
Jimmy Hendrix, 1969

DAZED AND CONFUSED:
BOLESKINE HOUSE AND ABRAMELIN THE MAGE

The Book of the Sacred Magic of Abramelin the Mage contains instructions for the student of Magick, the magician, to advance further into the second order of Aleister Crowley's Silver Star. The first rank of the second order, the "Rosicrucians," is called Adeptus Minor, or 5=6. This is one of, if not the most crucial grade in the entire Qabalistic structure of advancement that Crowley organized for his students in obedience to the Devil. Once again, Crowley made it clear that for his students to unite, as the microcosm with the macrocosm, or god, whom he taught was Satan, he must perform the Operation of Abramelin the Mage to establish union with his Holy Guardian Angel. Aleister Crowley purchased the infamous Boleskine House on the shores of Loch Ness in Scotland for the precise purpose of performing the Operation of Abramelin. This fact he presented in his writings. After obtaining this goal in his own life, he stressed it as an absolute necessity for advancement. Once successful, a student of Magick has advanced to Adeptus Minor in the Silver Star. In this chapter, we will analyze Crowley's teaching in this context, including a quote from the evil document *Liber Samekh* in which he made it clear that the Holy Guardian Angel for the student of Magick was none other than the Devil himself. Afterward, we will examine evidence that points to Led Zeppelin as advocating the exact same thing. We will focus our attention on the magical teachings presented in "Dazed and Confused" from the Led Zeppelin film, which includes the band's command to the fan to sell his or her soul to the Devil. The command in question was made at the direction of Jimmy Page in the early part of that song. Led Zeppelin's Magick runes will be discussed, as well as the author's belief in the connection between Jimmy Page's rune and Abramelin Magick. *The Book of the Sacred Magic of Abramelin the Mage* was written by a man who thought he was recording the magical practices that "god" wanted him to, as stemming from the magical land of Egypt, but what he really did was create a very sophisticated manual that the Devil would eventually use to lure men like Aleister Crowley and Jimmy Page into union with himself, taking complete control of them thereby.

To acquire the knowledge and conversation of the Holy Guardian Angel is what Aleister Crowley was aspiring at the turn of the twentieth century. This is accomplished by the successful practice of the Operation of the dangerous magic of Abramelin the Mage. Crowley made it clear that this was his life's purpose in the *Equinox*: "'I am indeed SENT to do something.' For whom? For the Universe; no partial good could possibly satisfy his equation. 'I am, then, the "chosen Priest and Apostle of Infinite Space." Very good: and what is the message? What shall I teach men?' And like the lightning from heaven fell upon him these words: 'THE KNOWLEDGE AND CONVERSATION OF THE HOLY GUARDIAN ANGEL.'"6 Who was it that made Crowley the "chosen Priest and Apostle of Infinite Space?" It was his "Lord of Infinite Space," that he wrote was Satan. Here again is his quote from *Magick-Book 4*Liber Aba*, that illustrates that fact: "...Satan, the Old Serpent, in the Abyss, the Lake of Fire and Sulphur, is the Sun-Father, the vibration of Life, Lord of Infinite Space that flames with his consuming Energy..."7

We are going to look at Crowley's purchase of Boleskine House in Scotland for the purpose of working out the Abramelin Operation and the fact that

Jimmy Page bought the house seventy years later. Then we are going to examine Abramelin Magic in detail to see what exactly it entails; as well as how it fits into the scheme of Led Zeppelin. After this is understood, we will look at "Dazed and Confused" from their film and soundtrack. We will begin by looking at Robert Plant's enlightening of the fans to his belief that they make up the woman "Malkuth" from the Qabalah. From there we are going to look at one of the most powerful points of the film, Robert Plant and Led Zeppelin's command to the fans to sell their souls to the Devil. You will see and hear it for yourself. It is on the soundtrack to the film, as well as the July 28, 1973 soundboard recording. Millions of people have the film and soundtrack, so it's going to be interesting to hear Robert Plant's response to this; if he responds at all. If I were him, I would just tell the truth, even if I were sworn to secrecy. It is no secret at all; anymore.

BOLESKINE HOUSE - LOCH NESS, SCOTLAND

Aleister Crowley purchased Boleskine House on the shores of Loch Ness for the purpose of working the Operation of the Sacred Magic of Abramelin the Mage. Having already begun to read *The Book of the Sacred Magic of Abramelin the Mage*, at the encouragement of Cecil Jones, Crowley was aware of Abramelin's instruction to find a secluded place of refuge to perform the operation where he would not be disturbed. He recorded the same concept in his *Confessions*: "I had picked out Boleskine for its loneliness."8 As a reminder from Crowley why he bought Boleskine, I refer you to this quote presented in an earlier chapter:

"In the year 1899 I came to Boleskine House, and put everything in order with the object of carrying out the Operation of Abramelin the Mage.

I had studied Ceremonial Magic, and had obtained very remarkable success.

My Gods were those of Egypt, interpreted on lines closely akin to those of Greece.

In Philosophy I was a Realist of the Qabalistic School."9

Crowley made it clear that he sought to practice the Sacred Magic of Abramelin the Mage in accordance with his progress from 4=7 to 5=6, which is the first rank of the second order of the Silver Star, called the Rosicrucians. He makes it a point to inform the reader, in the third person, that Boleskine House is "remote" and "desolate" near a "lake" and "mountain": "Between the grades 4=7 and 5=6 seven months had to elapse, and during this time we find P. busily traveling the British Isles searching for a suitable house wherein to perform the Operation of Abramelin the Mage, which ever since the previous autumn had engaged his attention....he was still bent on carrying out the Operation of Abramelin, and journeyed to and fro all over the country endeavoring to discover a suitable dwelling for the necessary Retirement. Thus it came about that in October of this year (1899) we find him settled in a remote and desolate district, a tumbled chaos of lake and mountain, in an ancient manor-house, making all necessary arrangements for this great operation in Ceremonial Magic."10

The rank of 5=6 is called Adeptus Minor. It is also known as Tiphareth on the Qabalah, the occult Tree of Life. Crowley said that this grade was the theme of the teachings of the Silver Star; because its main characteristic is attaining the Knowledge and Conversation of the Holy Guardian Angel, which is what the Sacred Magic of Abramelin is all about: "The Grade of Adeptus Minor is the main theme of the instructions of the A.A. It is characterized by the Attainment of the Knowledge and Conversation of the Holy Guardian Angel."11 Crowley said that *The Book of the Sacred Magic of Abramelin the Mage* gave the best account of seeking union with the Holy Guardian Angel; or god (Satan). He said that it helped and influenced him more than any other occult book. He called it "The best exoteric account of the Great Work, with careful instruction in procedure."12 He began writing about this in the first volume of *The Equinox*. He made it clear that the Union with the Holy Guardian Angel was the reason for life: "We pose Life with the question Why? And the first answer is: To obtain the Knowledge and Conversation of the Holy Guardian Angel."13 On the very next page of the first volume of *The Equinox*, Crowley said that next step a person should take is getting Abramelin's book: "Good, then. Let us obtain the volume entitled 'The Book of the Sacred Magic of Abramelin the Mage...'"14

In her book, *The Encyclopedia of Witches and Witchcraft*, Rosemary Ellen Guiley wrote about this book: "A Jew from Wurzburg, Germany, Abraham, or Abramelin (also spelled Abra-Melin), created a body of magical works that for centuries influenced magicians, including ALEISTER CROWLEY. An expert on the KABBALAH, Abramelin said he learned his magical knowledge from angels, who told him how to conjure and tame DEMONS into personal servants and workers, and how to raise storms."15

Let the reader understand, something you have already seen previously in this work, that the *Holy Bible* instructed Moses and the children of Israel to put to death anyone in their midst who conjured up demons. The angels mentioned in the last quote therefore, are Satan's angels, who are the very demons they say the magician will have as personal servants. The demons cannot work unless they have a magician who has made a deal with Satan. Once they have a demon controlled medium, Christ will allow the devils in question to do their work in the physical dimension, at the direction of the Devil himself, who was given this authority over the earth; as the *Holy Bible* teaches.

Power to control demons is what Crowley and Page wanted to achieve from this attainment of the knowledge and conversation of the Holy Guardian Angel, and Crowley makes it clear that if one wants to become an Adept of the Silver Star, this had better be the magician's main focus of attention: "The task of attaining to this Knowledge and Conversation is the sole task of him who would be called Adept."16 Four years before he died Crowley reiterated the concept in his book *Magick Without Tears*: "...the first essential is the dedication of all that one is and all that one has to the Great Work, without reservation of any sort."17 It won't surprise you the reader, but Crowley insists that the practice of Astral Projection is necessary for this attainment in the same book: "Astral travel-development of the Astral Body is essential to research; and, above all, to the attainment of 'the Knowledge and Conversation of the Holy Guardian Angel.'"18 Satan is the "Father" who rules the "winds" in "Kashmir."

Aleister Crowley purchased Boleskine House and immediately began to perform the Operation of Abramelin. In *Hammer of the Gods*, Steven Davis wrote about it: "When Crowley moved in after the turn of the century, he styled himself the 'Laird of Boleskine,' adopted the kilt, and began trying to summon demons like Thoth and the Egyptian magical deity Horus. He practiced the dangerous magic of Abra-Melin the Mage to contact his guardian angel."19 That was written in a book about Led Zeppelin in 1985.

In 1936, Crowley instructed his students in *The Equinox of the Gods* about the Operation of Abramelin: "The aspirant must have a house secure from observation and interference."20 What better place for Jimmy Page to buy to perform the Operation of Abramelin? Seventy years later, Jimmy Page bought Boleskine House, and Steven Davis wrote about that also: "By 1970 Jimmy Page had already been preoccupied with the life and work of Aleister Crowley for several years. He had a growing collection of Crowley books, manuscripts and memorabilia, and that year he collected one of the most Crowleyan artifacts of all - Boleskine House on the shore of Loch Ness in Scotland."21 Jimmy Page confessed to Ann Nightingale in 1982 that he knew the house belonged to Crowley before he bought it, in *The Daily Express*: "My house used to belong to Aleister Crowley, I knew that when I moved in."

The people in the area believed that Boleskine was haunted, but Jimmy Page wasn't concerned about that. He wanted the house, and Davis wrote concerning this as well: "Everybody on the Loch thought the place was haunted and bad news. Jimmy Page, looking for a country seat, thought it was perfect."22 It's no shock to this author, and shouldn't be to the reader by now, that Jimmy would feel comfortable in a haunted house. Jimmy Page himself confessed that Boleskine House was haunted (as well as Headley Grange - Chapter 14), but that something even worse had occurred there. He told Cameron Crowe during an interview at the Ambassador Hotel in Chicago in 1975:

CROWE: "You live in Aleister Crowley's home. [Crowley as a poet and magi-

cian at the turn of the century and was notorious for his Black Magic rites –
Ed.]

PAGE: Yes, it was owned by Aleister Crowley. But there were two or three
owners before Crowley moved into it. It was also a church that was burned to
the ground with the congregation in it. And that's the site of the house. Strange
things have happened in that house that had nothing to do with Crowley. The
bad vibes were already there. A man was beheaded there and sometimes you
can hear his head rolling down. I haven't actually heard it, but a friend of mine,
who is extremely straight and doesn't know anything about anything like that at
all, heard it.... So that sort of thing was there before Crowley got there. Of
course, after Crowley there have been suicides, people carted off to mental
hospitals..."23

Aleister Crowley had this to say about Boleskine House, including the
fact that a man had been beheaded there and he could hear the head roll:
"I certainly used to hear the 'rolling of the head,' but when I put in a
billiard table, the old gentleman preferred it to the corridor and confined his
amusements to the gunroom. Even before that, he had always stopped at the
Pylon of the corridor which marked off from the rest of the house the wing which
was consecrated to Abra-Melin. I have never discovered any explanation of
these noises. We used to listen at the door of the gunroom, and the head would
roll merrily up and down the table with untiring energy. The moment we opened
the door the noise would stop; but there would be no visible cause.
"During my absence, the reputation of the house had become more for-
midable than ever before. I have little doubt that the Abra-Melin devils, whatever they are, used the place as convenient headquarters and put in some of their
spare time in terrifying the natives. No one would pass the house after dark. Folk
got into the habit of going round through Strath Errick, a detour of several miles.
There were a great many definite legends; but I made rather a point of refraining
from making a collection. I was completely committed to rationalism and the
occurrence of miracles was a nuisance. I should have liked to deny the reality of
the whole Abra-Melin business, but the phenomena were just as patent as the
stones of the house."24
Crowley wrote that he knew Boleskine was haunted by Abramelin dev-
ils. There is only one definition of "a devil." A devil is one of Satan's evil spirits;
the fallen angels. "The Devil" is Satan himself. Now, returning to the Cameron
Crowe interview in Chicago, Jimmy Page intimates that he is in touch with these
spirits at Boleskine:
CROWE: "And you have no contacts with any of the spirits?
PAGE: I didn't say that. I just said I didn't hear the head roll...."
Crowe later asked if he considered it safe to be at Boleskine House. He replied:

"Yeah. Well, all my houses are isolated. Many is the time I just stay home alone." Continuing on with the answer, Jimmy Page says, "A few things have happened that would freak some people out, but I was surprised actually at how composed I was. I don't really want to go on about my personal beliefs or my involvement in magic….."25 At the end of that section of the interview, Page went on to say that he didn't want to interest other people in the things he was interested in; as well as saying that if people were searching for things, they would have to locate them on their own.

Jimmy Page is lying at the end of that statement. If he's not interested in turning people on to who and what he's into, why did Led Zeppelin command the fans to sell their souls to the Devil, cast spells on the fans, as well as send countless satanic messages through their hypnotic music? Obviously, he's lying to give his image a benign appearance, rather than malignant. He made a subtle reference to having communication with evil spirits at Boleskine House for a reason. He also made it clear that he was involved with or practiced Magick.

Bob Larson, in his book, *Satanism - The Seduction of America's Youth*, wrote about Boleskine House:

"Page bought Crowley's former Scottish mansion, known as Boleskine House. The building features an under ground passageway where Crowley allegedly conducted sacrificial ceremonies, including human sacrifices.

Page turned the mansion into a Crowley shrine and tried to contact Crowley's spirit via seances. He even commissioned avowed Satanist Charles Pace to decorate the home with motifs depicting various forms of ritualistic magic. Robert Plant, former lead singer for Led Zeppelin, once shared Page's occult fascination but now refuses to visit Boleskine, believing it curses those who come in contact with it."26

Bob Larson is a Christian, so it is not difficult to understand why he stated Satanist Charles Pace decorated Boleskine to turn it into a Crowley shrine for Jimmy Page. However, Howard Mylett, in *Jimmy Page – Tangents Within a Framework*, a biography on Page as a guitar hero, wrote that Charles Pace painted murals at Boleskine for the specific purpose of restoring the place to the condition it was in when Crowley performed rituals there: "Boleskine House is the name of Crowley's house on the shores of Loch Ness, Scotland. In an attempt to restore Boleskine to its condition at the time of Crowley's rituals, Page engaged Satanist Charles pace to paint murals."27 There you have it, Jimmy Page employing a Satanist to paint murals at Boleskine for the purpose of bringing it back to what it was when Crowley was performing rituals there. Why would he do that? For the same reason he bought the house in the first place, which the author asserts was to perform the Operation of Abramelin the Mage. So Aleister Crowley and Jimmy Page both owned Boleskine House in Scotland. Crowley bought it for the working of the Operation of Abramelin. Let's see if Jimmy Page did as well.

PREPARATION FOR THE ABRAMELIN OPERATION

Crowley made it clear to his readers that before a man can effect progress in the Silver Star he must know his true will and that "...the word of Sin is Restriction," as *The Book of the Law* states. In the next quote, Crowley lays out the prerequisite for the members of the Silver Star to meet before attempting to attain the Knowledge and Conversation of the Holy Guardian Angel; which is the objective of the Operation of Abramelin the Mage:

"So must all Members of the A.A. work by the Magical formula of the Aeon.

"They must accept *The Book of the Law* as the Word and the Letter of Truth, and the sole Rule of Life. They must acknowledge the Authority of the Beast 666 and of the Scarlet Woman as in the Book it is defined, and accept Their Will as concentrating the Will of Our Whole Order. They must accept the Crowned and Conquering Child as the Lord of the Aeon, and exert themselves to establish His reign upon Earth. They must acknowledge that 'The Word of the Law is Thelema,' and that 'Love is the law, love under will.'

"Each member must make it his main work to discover for himself his own True Will, and to do it, and do nothing else.

"He must accept those orders in *The Book of the Law* that apply to himself as being necessarily in accordance with his own True Will, and execute the same to the letter with all the energy, courage, and ability that he can command. This applies especially to the work of extending the Law in the world, wherein his proof is his own success, the witness of his Life to the Law that hath given him Light in his ways, and Liberty to pursue them. Thus doing, he payeth his debt to the law that hath freed him by working its Will to free all men; and he proveth himself a true man in our Order by willing to bring his fellows into freedom.

"By thus ordering his disposition, he will fit himself in the best possible manner for the task of understanding and mastering the divers technical methods prescribed by the A.A. for Mystical and Magical attainment.

"He will thus prepare himself properly for the crisis of his career in the Order, the attainment of the Knowledge and Conversation of his Holy Guardian Angel."28

As presented in the last chapter, Jimmy Page is in agreement with Crowley in doing the true will and being involved in Magick, and the band was its path.

THE SACRED MAGIC OF ABRAMELIN THE MAGE

Led Zeppelin formed in late 1968, so as of March, 1970, the band had been together approximately a year and a half. The author believes that Jimmy

Page's involvement in the occult had not advanced to the point of 5=6, Adeptus Minor; or at least he had not yet attained the Knowledge and Conversation of the Holy Guardian Angel (Satan). I believe he bought Boleskine House for this purpose, to work out the Magic of Abramelin that coincides with that rank. The reason I reiterate that is because Aleister Crowley wrote in his book *Moonchild*: "In Magick, even more than in any other science, the student must keep his practice level with his theory."29

In 1981, subsequent to the death of John Bonham, the magazine with the title *Led Zeppelin - Will the Song Remain the Same?* came out. Needless to say, I bought a copy of it. The same concept of keeping one's practice level with his theory is implied in that magazine about Jimmy Page: "Page's interest in the occult continued, in fact bloomed, as the band became more popular. He found solace in it, and tried to find himself in it."30

I intend to show you in these next four chapters that there is a direct, measurable, provable, correlation between Jimmy Page's involvement in the occult and the band's popularity; especially at the time of the release of their fourth album, containing "Stairway to Heaven," in November of 1971. The following excerpt is from Aleister Crowley's *Equinox, Vol. I, No.3*. It tells the detailed story of attaining communion with the Holy Guardian Angel; who is Satan. He has recorded portions of *The Book of the Sacred Magic of Abramelin the Mage* therein. This is the same magical working that Jimmy Page provided evidence of having gone through, as you will see. Once again, Crowley writes of himself in the third person, his magical name Perdurabo, by using just the P.

THE MAGICIAN

"VERY shortly after the ceremony of Adeptus Minor, P. returned to his fastness to carry out the great Magical Operation of Abramelin the Mage, the preliminary preparations of which he had for so long now been setting in order.

"Unfortunately we have but scanty information of P.'s daily life during these days, and all that is recorded is to be found in a small book of some twenty pages entitled, 'The Book of the Operation of the Sacred Magic of Abramelin the Mage. (Being the account of the events of my life, with notes on the operation by P., an humble Aspirant thereto.)'

"This slight volume commences with 'The Oath of the Beginning,' after which it is roughly divided into three parts. The first deals with the events of his life between the beginning of November 1899 and the end of February 1900; the second with the Abramelin Operation; and the third with the transactions P. had with Frater D.D.C.F.

"For the first part of this work we gather that great forces of evil were leagued against P.; and we learn this with no very great surprise, for those who set their faces against Darkness must expect Darkness to attempt to swallow them up. The Exempt Adept may laugh equally at good or at evil, but not so the mere magician whose passage along the Path of Light is only to be marked by the increasing depths of the Darkness which surrounds him.

"It will be remembered that in the autumn of 1898 P. had met Frater V. N., who had lent him a copy of a book known as 'The Book of the Sacred Magic of Abramelin the Mage,' and had to some degree instructed him in the workings contained in it. This work P. had read and reread with the greatest interest and zeal, determining to perform the ceremonial operation laid down in it at the very first opportunity. This he was unable to do for nearly a year; it being not until November 1899 that he found it possible for him to retire to the house he had bought and make all necessary preparations for the great ceremony, which was to be commenced on the following Easter.

"The system, as taught by Abramelin, of entering into communication with one's Holy Guardian Angel, is, of all Western systems of Magic, perhaps the most simple and effective. No impossible demands are made, and though perhaps some are difficult to carry out, there is always a reason for them, and they are not merely placed in the way as tests of the worker's skill.

"The whole Operation is so lucidly dealt with in Mr. MacGregor Mathers' translation, that it would be but waste of time and space to enter into it fully, and the following consists of but the briefest summary, only intended to give the reader an idea of the Operation, and in no way meant as a basis for him to work on.

"Abramelin having first carefully warned his readers against imposters, lays down that the chief thing to be considered is: 'Whether ye be in good health, because the body being feeble and unhealthy, it is subject to divers infirmities whence at length result impatience and want of power to operate and pursue the Operation; and a sick man can neither be clean and pure, nor enjoy solitude; and in such a case it is better to cease.'

"The true and best time of commencing this Operation is the first day after the Celebration of the Feasts of Easter at about the time of the Vernal Equinox. The time necessary for the working is six months, so that should it be commenced on March 22, it would end on September 21.

The six months is divided into three periods of two months each.

"First Period. 'Every morning precisely a quarter of an hour before sunrise enter your Oratory, after having washed and dressed yourself in clean clothing, open the window, and then kneel at the Altar facing the window and invoke the Name of the Lord; after which you should confess to him your entire sins. This being finished you should supplicate Him 'that in time to come He may be willing and pleased to regard you with pity and grant you His grace and goodness to send unto you His Holy Angel, who shall serve unto you as a Guide...'

"In the above exercise by prayer the one great point to observe, as Abramelin himself impresses in the following words, is; 'It serveth nothing to speak without devotion, without attention, and without intelligence...it is absolutely necessary that your prayer should issue from the midst of your heart, because simply setting down prayers in writing, the hearing of them will in no way explain unto you how really to pray.'

"At sunset the same invocation, confession and prayer is to be repeated.

"During this first period the points to be observed are:

(1) That both the bed-chamber and Oratory are to be kept thoroughly clean. 'Your whole attention must be given to purity in all things.'

(2) That 'you may sleep with your Wife in the bed when she is pure and clean,' not otherwise.

(3) Every Saturday the sheets of the bed are to be changed and the chamber is to be perfumed.

(4) No animal is to enter or dwell in the house.

(5) 'If you be your own Master, as far as lieth in your power, free yourself from all your business, and quit all mundane and vain company and conversation; leading a life tranquil, solitary and honest.'

(6) 'Take well heed in treating of business, in selling or buying, that it shall be requisite that you never give way unto anger, but be modest and patient in your actions.'

(7) 'You shall set apart two hours each day after having dined, during which you shall read with care the Holy Scripture and other Holy Books.'

(8) 'As for eating, drinking and sleeping, such should be in moderation and never superfluous.'

(9) 'Your dress should be clean but moderate, and according to custom. Flee all vanity.'

(10) 'As for that which regardeth the family, the fewer in number, the better; also act so that the servants may be modest and tranquil.'

(11) 'Let your hand be ever ready to give alms and other benefits to your neighbor; and let your heart be ever open unto the poor, whom God so loveth that one cannot express the same.'

"Second Period. During the whole of this period the accustomed prayer is to be made morning and evening, 'but before entering into the Oratory ye shall wash your hands and face thoroughly with pure water. And you shall prolong your prayer with the greatest possible affection, devotion and submission; humbly entreating the Lord God that he would deign to command His Holy Angels to lead you in the True Way...'

"During this period the points to be observed are:

(1) 'The use of the rites of Marriage is permitted, but should scarcely if at all be made use of.'

(2) 'You shall also wash your whole body every Sabbath Eve.'

(3) 'As to what regardeth commerce and rules of living, as in the first period.'

(4) 'It is absolutely necessary during this period to retire from the world and seek retreat.'

(5) 'Ye shall lengthen your prayers to the utmost of your ability.'

(6) 'As for eating, drinking, and clothing, as before.'

"Third Period. 'Morning and Noon ye shall wash your hands and your face on entering the Oratory; and first ye shall make Confession of all your sins; after this, with a very ardent prayer, ye shall entreat the Lord to accord unto you this particular grace, which is, that you may enjoy and be able to endure the presence and conversation of His Holy Angels, and that he may deign by their intermission to grant unto you the Secret Wisdom, so that you may be able to have dominion over the Spirits and over all creatures.'

'Ye shall do this same at midday before dining and also in the evening,' as well as at sunrise.

"During this period the points to be observed are:

(1) 'The man who is his own master shall leave all business alone, except works of charity towards his neighbor.'

(2) 'You shall shun all society except that of your Wife and of your Servants'

(3) 'Ye shall employ the greatest part of your time in speaking of the Law of God.'

(4) 'Every Sabbath Eve shall ye fast, and wash your whole body, and change your garment.'

"If possible the whole of this Operation should be performed in a place where solitude can be obtained; the best being, as Abramelin writes; 'Where there is small wood, in the midst of which you shall make a small Altar, and you shall cover the same with a hut of fine branches, so that the rain may not fall thereon and extinguish the Lamps and the Censer.'

"The Altar should be made of wood and in the manner of a cupboard, so that it may hold all the necessary things.

"There should be two tunics, one of linen, and the other of Crimson or Scarlet Silk with Gold.

"The sacred oil is prepared from myrrh, cinnamon and galangal mixed with olive oil. The incense of Olibanum, storax, and lign aloes, or cedar, is reduced to a fine powder and well mixed together. The Wand is cut from an Almond-tree.

"The third period having been completed, on the morning following: 'Rise betimes, neither wash yourself at all nor dress yourself at all in your ordinary clothes; but take a Robe of Mourning; enter the Oratory with bare feet; go unto the side of the Censer, and having opened the windows, return unto the door. There prostrate yourself with your face against the ground, and order the Child (who is used as assistant and clairvoyante) to put the Perfume upon the Censer, after which he is to place himself upon his knees before the Altar; following in all things and throughout the instructions which I have given unto you....Humiliate yourself before God and His Celestial Court, and commence your prayer with fervour, for then it is that you will begin to enflame yourself in praying, and you will see appear an extraordinary and supernatural Splendour which will fill the whole apartment, and will surround you with an inexpressible odour, and this alone will console you and comfort your heart so that you shall call for ever happy the Day of the Lord.

*   *   *   *   *   *   *   *   *   *   *   *

'During Seven Days shall you perform the Ceremonies without failing therein in any way: namely, the Day of the Consecration, the Three Days of the Convocation of the Good and Holy Spirits, and the Three other Days of the Convocation of the Evil Spirits.

'On the second morning you shall follow the counsels your Holy Guardian Angel shall have given you, and on the third you shall render thanks.

'And then shall you first be able to put to the test whether you shall have well employed the period of your Six Moons, and how well and worthily you shall have labored in the quest of the Wisdom of the Lord; since you shall see your Guardian Angel appear unto you in unequaled beauty: who also will converse with you, and speak in words so full of affection and of goodness, and with such sweetness, that no human tongue could express the same....In one word, you shall be received by him with such affection that this description I here give unto you shall appear a mere nothing in comparison.'

"After the third day Abramelin very wisely writes:

'Now at this point I commence to restrict myself in my writing, seeing that by the Grace of the Lord I have submitted and consigned you unto a MASTER so great that he will never let you err.'

"Thus, briefly though it be, we have run through the system as advocated by one of the greatest masters of Magic in the west. With perfect lucidity Abramelin brings us step by step towards the MASTER-Augoeides, Adonai, Higher Self, call Him what you will. By means of symbols of purity-by cleanliness and clean living-he leads us on by meditation and concentration through prayer to a one-pointedness, a vision or conversation with the MASTER so full of goodness and beauty, so full of rapture and ecstasy that no human tongue can express the same."31

It is important to note that Crowley varied the arrangement of the six months necessary for the Operation of Abramelin. Seeing what a great servant he would be, it is not unreasonable to believe that the Devil would make an exception in his case, as well as that of Jimmy Page, if need be. Crowley did, however, spend the quantity time necessary for the attainment of the knowledge and conversation of the Holy Guardian Angel, Satan. The author asserts that Jimmy Page did as well, according to forthcoming evidence. Please note that Crowley was committed to the spiritual *"Regeneration* of the Race...."

ALEISTER CROWLEY'S ABRAMELIN MAGICAL OATH

Once Aleister Crowley prepared to work the Operation of Abramelin, he took an oath. He recorded that oath in his *Equinox, Vol. I, No.3.* When he says "Christ of God" in the quote, he means Horus; Satan. Crowley also makes it a point to refer to the Devil once again as "Most High."

THE OATH OF THE BEGINNING

"I, P—, Frater Ordinis Rosae Rubeae et Aureae Crucis, a Lord of the Paths in the Portal of the Vault of the Adepts, a 5=6 of the order of the Golden Dawn; and an humble servant of the Christ of God; do this day spiritually bind myself anew:

By the Sword of Vengeance:

By the Powers of the Elements:

By the Cross of Suffering:

That I will devote myself to the Great Work: the obtaining of Communion with my own Higher and Divine Genius (called the Guardian Angel), by means of the prescribed course: and that I will use any Power so obtained unto the Redemption of the Universe.

So help me the Lord of the Universe and mine own Higher Soul!

"Let us now turn to 'The Obligation of the Operation.'

"I, P—, in the presence of the Lord of the Universe, and of all Powers Divine and Angelic, do spiritually bind myself, even as I am now physically bound unto the Cross of Suffering:

(1) To unite my consciousness with the divine, as I may be permitted and aided by the Gods Who live for ever, the Aeons of Infinite years; that, being lost in the Limitless Light, it may find Itself: to the *Regeneration* of the Race, either of man or as the Will of God shall be. And I submit myself utterly to the Will Divine.

(2) To follow out with courage, modesty, loving kindness, and perseverance the course prescribe by Abramelin the Mage; as far as in me lies, unto the attainment of this end.

(3) To despise utterly the things and the opinions of this world lest they hinder me in doing this.

(4) To use my powers only to the Spiritual well-being of all with whom I may be brought in contact.

(5) To give no place to Evil: and to make eternal war against the Forces of Evil: until even they be redeemed unto the Light.

(6) To harmonize my own spirit so that Equilibrium may lead me to the East and that my Human Consciousness shall allow no usurpation of its rule by the Automatic.

(7) To conquer the temptations.

(8) To banish the illusions.

(9) To put my whole trust in the Only and Omnipotent Lord God: as it is written, 'Blessed are they that put their trust in Him.'

(10) To uplift the Cross of Sacrifice and Suffering; and to cause my Light to shine, before men that they may glorify my Father which is in Heaven.

"Furthermore: I most solemnly promise and swear: to acquire this Holy Science in the manner prescribed in the Book of Abramelin, without omitting the least imaginable thing of its contents; not to gloss or comment in any way on that which may be or may not be, not to use this Sacred Science to offend the Great God, nor to work ill unto my neighbour; to communicate it to no living person, unless by long practice and conversation I shall know him thoroughly, well examining whether such an one really intendeth to work for the Good or for the Evil. I will punctually observe, in granting it, the same fashion which was used by Abramelin to Abraham. Otherwise, let him who receiveth it draw no fruit therefrom. I will keep myself as from a Scorpion from selling this Science. Let this Science remain in me and in my generation as long as it shall please the

Most High.

"All these points I generally and severally swear to observe under the awful penalty of the displeasure of God, and of Him to whose Knowledge and Conversation I do most ardently aspire.

"So help me the Lord of the Universe, and my own Higher Soul!"32

Don't allow yourself to be deceived by Crowley's use of the word "Evil" in number 5 of that passage. To the Satanist, what the Christian thinks is good, is evil. When Crowley said he was going to oppose the forces of evil, he meant Christianity and its followers. This Magick is for the satanic spiritual regeneration of the human race; i.e., Led Zeppelin and "Stairway to Heaven."

ABRAMELIN MAGIC AND THE QABALAH

In this section the intention is to elaborate on the instructions of Abramelin, right from *The Book of the Sacred Magic of Abramelin the Mage* itself. The purpose is to show you specific instructions that the author asserts relate to Jimmy Page and then the rest of Led Zeppelin. To begin with, this Abramelin Magic comes from a Mage called Abramelin who taught it to a Jew named Abraham. Again, please do not mistake this man for the Abraham of the *Book of Genesis* of the *Holy Bible*. Nothing that the Abraham who sat under Abramelin the Mage did has anything to do with God or the *Holy Bible*, even though he continually states that he got the Magic power from Holy God, and that it is in the service of Holy God that he employs it. Don't forget, Crowley called Satan Holy as well.

S.L. MacGregor Mathers, who was the personal friend and subsequent enemy of Aleister Crowley, was the one who translated *The Book of the Sacred Magic of Abramelin the Mage* out of French into English. In the introduction to his translation, Mathers wrote: "This rare and unique manuscript of the Sacred Magic of Abra-Melin, from which the present work is translated, is a French translation from the original Hebrew of Abraham the Jew."33 If you have been reading this book chronologically, it won't surprise you that Abraham points to the Qabalah as the origin of the Abramelin Magic. Mathers wrote: "Abraham in several places insists that the basis of this system of Sacred Magic is to be found in the Qabalah."34 He reiterated it for emphasis: "Abraham the Jew repeatedly admits, as I have before urged, that this particular System of the Sacred Magic of Abra-Melin has its Basis in the Qabalah. It is well to examine what is here meant. The Qabalah itself is divided into many parts; the great bulk of it is of a mystic doctrinal nature, giving the inner Occult meaning of the Jewish Sacred Writings."35

It was important for the reader to understand that Abramelin Magic has its roots in the Qabalah, as you will see shortly. Abraham gives this account of receiving the Sacred Magic from Abramelin in Egypt. Where else can we expect this to have happened? He also states emphatically that the magic gives him power over evil spirits. Abraham calls him Abramelim with an "m" instead of an "n" at the end. The names are used interchangeably, but all occultists know that it is one person they are talking about. You need to remember that the "Almighty God" that Abraham writes about is none other than the Devil himself. You already read in this book where the *Holy Bible* condemns fooling with evil spirits. Abraham wrote: "...for ten years did I remain buried in so great an error, until that after the ten years I arrived in Egypt at the house of an Ancient Sage who was called ABRAMELIM, who put me into the true Path as I will declare it unto thee hereafter, and he gave me better instruction and doctrine than all the others; but this particular grace was granted me by the Almighty Father of all Mercy, that is to say, ALMIGHTY GOD, who little by little illuminated mine understanding and opened mine eyes to see and admire, to contemplate, and search out His Divine Wisdom, in such a manner that it became possible unto me to further and further understand and comprehend the Sacred Mystery by which I entered into the knowledge of the Holy Angels, enjoying their sight and their sacred conversation, from whom at length I received afterwards the foundation of the Veritable Magic, and how to command and dominate the Evil Spirits. So that by way of conclusion unto this chapter I cannot say that I have otherwise received the True Instruction save from ABRAMELIM, and the True and Incorruptible Magic save from the Holy Angels of God."36

Earlier I wrote that Aleister Crowley had read in *The Book of the Sacred Magic of Abramelin the Mage* that it required solitude to work the "sacred magic." Abraham wrote that he received the Qabalah from Abramelin and then went off into the forests to get away from his wife to work the Abramelin Magic: "God, the Father of Mercy,...thanking Him for so many benefits which I had received from Him, and in particular for the acquisition of the Qabalah which I had made at the house of ABRAMELIM. It now only remained for me to reduce to Practice this Sacred Magic, but many things of importance and hindrances presented themselves; among the which my marriage was one of the greatest. I therefore judged it fitting to defer putting it in practice, and a principal obstacle was the inconvenience of the place in which I dwelt. I resolved to absent myself suddenly, and go away into the Hercynian forests, and there remain during the time necessary for this operation, and lead a solitary life."37

JIMMY PAGE AND THE OPERATION OF ABRAMELIN MAGIC

The first thing that needs to be addressed before looking at details to the operation is the timing. Abramelin made it clear that the operation is a six-month engagement. Crowley emphasized that it should begin just after the Spring Equinox, but that it is not an absolute. He merely said that it was the best time to begin. Led Zeppelin was on tour, first in Europe, beginning March 7th, 1970, and then in the United States during the second half of March, ending the month in the U.S. Therefore, Jimmy Page's Abramelin operation could not have begun at Boleskine in March of 1970, at the 21st.

I do not know exactly how Page managed the requirements of Abramelin, but I believe that he did. As you read earlier, during the second - two month period of the Operation, the magician had to retire from the world completely into isolation. From the middle of September until the middle of December 1970, Led Zeppelin did not perform any concerts. That is a three month span, and the third month of that span could have been part of the last two month period; ending in six months. The final month, I believe, (and it does not matter if I am wrong-because I know Page completed the Operation, as I intend to prove, and I believe the other band members did the same, and will show you why) was spent with the rest of the band in isolation; first at Island Studios in London, and then after Christmas moving out to another isolated mansion in Hampshire called "Headley Grange." Near the end of January 1971, the band returned to Island Studios to finish work on overdubs, etc. The entire fourth album was recorded at Headley Grange during that month, due to the fact that Ian Stewart, the "sixth member" of the Rolling Stones brought their mobile recording studio out there for Led Zeppelin to utilize. Due to many other factors, including fighting with Atlantic Records over the untitled album cover, the band did not put their fourth album out, again, until November 1971; just after Tom Friend turned eleven years old. What does my age have to do with it? You will see that later. At this point some additional instructions from *The Book of the Sacred Magic of Abramelin the Mage* need to be revealed; in order to illustrate the instructions leading to what the author believes is the origin of Jimmy Page's famous "ZoSo" symbol as well as the other band members' symbols, commonly known as Magick runes.

The following quote from Abraham instructs the adept about personal requirements for performing the Operation of Abramelin: "It is, then, necessary that such a man give himself up unto a tranquil life, and that his habits be temperate; that he should love retirement; that he should be given neither unto avarice nor usury (that he should be the legitimate child of his parents is a good thing, but not as necessary as for the Qabalah, unto which no man born of a clandestine marriage can attain); his age ought not to be less than twenty-five years nor more than fifty; he should have no hereditary disease, such as virulent leprosy; whether he be free or married importeth little; a valet, lackey, or other domestic servant, can with difficulty arrive at the end required, being bound unto others and not having the conveniences at disposal which are necessary, and which this Operation demandeth."38 Aleister Crowley was twenty-four when he began the Operation, Jimmy Page was twenty-six when he bought Boleskine, and a bachelor.

Abraham wrote the following to instruct the adept to put his confidence in "God" and that he cannot have true understanding of the Qabalah until he attain the union with his Holy Guardian Angel: "Pray unto God and ask Him for His assistance, and place all thy confidence in Him alone. And although thou canst not have the understanding of the Qabalah, nevertheless the Holy Guardian Angels at the end of the Six Moons or Months will manifest unto thee that which is sufficient for the possession of this Sacred Magic."39 He then instructed his readers that "God" does not give the magic to men for their selfish purposes: "...God Almighty doth not in any way grant the Art or the Science unto a person in order that he may use if for himself alone, but in order that he may provide for the needs of others, and of those who do not possess this Sacred Science."40 Abraham then made it clear that the magic is to be used for the entire earth: "...it is absolutely necessary to perform this Operation unto the praise, honor, and glory of God; unto the use, health, and well-being of your neighbor, whether friend or enemy; and generally for that of the whole earth."41 Indeed, the song remains the same.

Abraham extended a warning to the aspirant that he had better complete the Operation once he undertakes it:

"...having taken a true, firm, and determined resolution, relying upon the Will of the Lord, ye shall arrive at your desired end, and shall encounter no difficulty. Often also man is changeable, and while beginning a thing well, finisheth it badly, being in no way firm and stable in resolution. Ponder the matter then well before commencing, and only begin this Operation with the firm intention of carrying it out unto the end, for no man can make a mock of the Lord with impunity.

"Furthermore it is likewise necessary to think and consider whether your goods and revenue be sufficient for this matter; and, further, whether if your quality or estate be subject unto others, ye may have time and convenience to undertake it; also whether wife or children may hinder you herein; these being all matters worthy of observation; so as not to commence the matter blindly.... Consider then the safety of your person, commencing this Operation in a place of safety, whence neither enemies nor any disgrace can drive you out before the end; because ye must finish where ye begin....be ye sure that God doth aid all those who put their confidence in Him and in His Wisdom, and such as wish to live rightly, making use with honor of the deceitful world, which ye shall hold in abomination, and see that ye make no account of its opinion when ye shall be arrived at the perfection of the work, and that ye shall be possessors of this Sacred Magic."42

At the end of the Six Moons or Months, the Operation properly per-formed, the Holy Guardian Angel will manifest himself. Once he does that, he will teach the aspirant his "Holy" Magic, to have command over evil spirits for the purpose of magical operations; intended to accomplish the Great Work in the life of those having Magick spells cast on them. Abraham presented this infor-mation: "And then shall you first be able to put to the test whether you shall have well employed the period of your Six Moons, and how well and worthily you shall have laboured in the quest of the Wisdom of the Lord; since you shall see your Guardian Angel appear unto you in unequalled beauty; who also will con-verse with you, and speak in words so full of affection and goodness, and with such sweetness, that no human tongue could express the same....After this he will show unto you the True Wisdom and Holy Magic, and also wherein you have erred in your Operation, and how thence forward you should proceed in order to overcome the Evil Spirits, and finally arrive at your desired ends. He will promise never to abandon you, but to defend and assist you during the whole period of your life; on condition that you shall obey his commands, and that you shall not voluntarily offend your Creator. In one word, you shall be received by him with such affection that this description which I here give unto you shall appear a mere nothing in comparison."43

At last, Abraham sums up the goal of the Operation of Abramelin; it is the adept "...receiving from the Holy Angel distinct and ample information re-garding the Evil Spirits and the manner of bringing them into submission, care-fully writing down and taking notes of all these matters."44 I believe that Jimmy Page did exactly what you just read, and that he was instructed by the book that he could show the Magick to the other members of Led Zeppelin. Abraham wrote that you can show it to three friends: "It is certain that having obtained this Sacred Wisdom thou mayest dispose of it and communicate it unto three friends; but thou must not exceed this Sacred Number of the Ternary, for in such case thou wouldest be altogether deprived of it."45 Remember, Jimmy Page reproduced *The Goetia*, a manual for magicians using demonic spirits for magi-cal purposes, in 1976. Therefore it is reasonable to believe that the "Holy An-gel," Satan, gave him information on how to bring the evil spirits into submission. Page's reproducing *The Goetia* is in keeping with him having practiced the magic of Abramelin. Also, Page has been known to be very secretive about the magic, just like Abramelin warned. In an article she wrote in Creem Magazine, Lisa Robinson had this to say about Jimmy Page and his secrecy concerning magic: "If you could get close to him you might discover some spiritual secrets, but it's not magic he's about to give away easily."46

Isn't it interesting that the magician can show the Abramelin Magic of controlling demonic forces for the purpose of the Great Work to three others? The other three were John Paul Jones, Robert Plant, and John Bonham. I believe that Peter Grant had studied the magic on his own; which is why he had an eye in a triangle on the doorway in his home. According to Jimmy Page, he and Peter Grant provided Kenneth Anger with a screening/editing facility in London, and that Grant had considered investing money in his underground film, *Lucifer Rising*.47 The evidence points to Peter Grant being a believer.

You will see substantial evidence in the following pages that the rest of the band did in fact learn the magic from Jimmy Page. First of all, we are going to examine what Magick runes are, and then Abraham's instructions regarding them, as well as Led Zeppelin's employment of Magick runes into their music and magical objectives.

INTRODUCTION TO MAGICK RUNES

What are Magick runes? Where did they originate? Magick runes are script, written or engraved on something for magical purposes. The Norse Mythology (which is no myth), with Odin as its chief, is the origin of the magic runes. Before discussing the runes, the character of the Nordics gods needs to be introduced. In his book, *Understanding Runes - Their Origins and Magical Power,* Michael Howard wrote: "The gods of the Nordic pantheon were a larger than life, lusty crowd who seemed to have spent their time fighting, eating and drinking or indulging in orgiastic merry-making. They were therefore perfect reflections of the people who worshiped them."48 It sounds like 70's Zep fans!

The German word "runer" is normally translated "whisper." The Nordic god Odin is referred to as the creator of the runes. The name "Odin" means "spirit" or "wind," and you know from chapter eight that Odin is none other than Satan. The Teutonic peoples of Germany and Scandinavia are known (in the occult world) to employ the runes. In fact, the Swastika itself is a Magick rune called the *Hammer of Thor*. The Swastika was written about by Crowley in 1910. He claims that the Nazis stole it from the Silver Star! That will be discussed in the first "Stairway to Heaven" chapter. The Swastika was also engraved on the real "Lead Zeppelin," the "Hindenburg," on the cover of the first album. That too will be elaborated on in the same Stairway chapter, when I tell the world the real meaning of the name Led Zeppelin. Also, the Druids wore it on robes. I don't believe for a second that it has to do with the "almost band" of Moon, Entwistle, Plant, and Page, that Keith Moon supposedly said (after stealing the idea from Entwistle) would go over like a lead zeppelin or lead balloon.

In his book, *Runes*, Raymond I. Page wrote about the runes and their meaning: "...the etymology of the word 'rune' (Old English *run* which means 'secret, mystery') has been held to connect the script with the occult, with magic. From this type of evidence has developed the attitude that runes were essentially, in origin at any rate, a magical or religious set of characters, that runic legends have, by virtue of their script, magical properties, and that the rune-masters-the men who were trained to use the alphabet - had supernatural powers or were able to control or release such powers by their use of runes."49

Now that the concept of the runes has been introduced, we are going to look at the association of runes, which are magical symbols, with Abramelin magic; in the next section appropriately titled "Dazed and Confused." Instructions given to Abraham will be presented as instructions for the aspiring magician, like Jimmy Page, and how that Led Zeppelin employed the runes for magical purposes.

LED ZEPPELIN – "DAZED AND CONFUSED"

On Led Zeppelin's first album, appropriately titled *Led Zeppelin,* Robert Plant sings that many "people" speak, however, only a "few" are made to "know" that a "soul" belonging to a specific "woman" happened to be "created" underneath something, between 0:27 and 0:36 of "Dazed and Confused." I intend to show that this woman is none other than Malkuth, mankind on the earth, the bride of Microprosopus, who is the son in the Qabalah, and Satan. You will see for yourself the ten stages of the Qabalah presented in their film by Jimmy Page.

THE SONG REMAINS THE SAME – "DAZED AND CONFUSED"

The rest of the material from "Dazed and Confused" will be taken from the film and soundtrack, *The Song Remains the Same.* As the song begins in the movie, John Paul Jones is playing the bass and there is an orange light, not unlike a vision of the sun, focused on his bass guitar. Then, after his introduction, flames shoot out from behind the stage (Remember, Crowley called Satan "Lord of Infinite Space that flames with his consuming energy." This is the perfect beginning for a song in which they command the fans to sell their souls to Satan.). Robert Plant then drops his head back. If you have the film, take a good look at his face as he brings his head back up. Do you see the look in his eyes? It is obvious that what they are doing is very, very serious in his mind.

In this version of "Dazed and Confused," between 1:52 and 2:07 of the song, Robert Plant repeats the same theme as the *Led Zeppelin* album version, with a slight variation. This time around, Robert Plant sings that many "people" are talking, "yet" only a "few" are going to "know," that the "soul" belonging to a certain "woman" had been made "below." After the word below he speaks into the microphone that the fans are the woman. He shouts "You're the one!" twice, back to back, and again, he does it emphatically.

Now if you look at the photo of the Qabalah in this book, that was taken from Aleister Crowley's *Equinox*, you can see that *Malkuth* was created below the rest of the Qabalistic Tree of Life. What I believe Robert Plant is saying, to the fans that Satan will accept, is that they are part of Malkuth, his bride, and I couldn't agree more. I don't agree with Qabalistic theology, obviously, but that Satan rules the rock world, I do agree. Finally, we are at the point where I want to discuss Led Zeppelin's covert command to the fans to sell their souls to the Devil.

LED ZEPPELIN'S COMMAND TO SELL ONE'S SOUL TO SATAN

Led Zeppelin's command to their listeners to sell their souls to the Devil is given in a two-part message. In the first part, between 3:26 and 3:32 of "Dazed and Confused" live, Robert Plant gives the command:

"Silly Human, I Love You, Sell Him All of Your Life!"

Robert Plant calls the listener a "human" because he had, I believe, already attained to the Knowledge and Conversation of the Holy Guardian Angel, which is union with the godhead - Satan, and therefore he had become "god" on earth. The "silly" part of the message is obviously to emphasize his belief that it is foolish to live apart from union with Satan. This can also be heard on the July 28th, 1973 Soundboard of the show. Uniting man with "god" is the Great Work, so there you have Led Zeppelin performing their version of it. Since they believe the Devil is god, if one sells their soul to the Devil, one has begun the trek on the path to achieving the Knowledge and Conversation of the Holy Guardian Angel in their life, which is what Jimmy Page's goal is for the sympathetic fan.

If you think I'm wrong about Robert Plant, just look in the photo section of Steven Davis' *Hammer of the Gods*. There is a picture of Robert Plant there, with his arms extended wide, making fists, and underneath the photo is Plant's quote at the time it was taken, "I'm a golden god!" as he is standing on the balcony of his hotel.

After Robert Plant gives the first part of the command, Jimmy Page plays one of the most intensive lead guitar jams ever played. Once the jam is over, Robert Plant goes into a satanic version of Scott McKenzie's "San Francisco (Be Sure to Wear Some Flowers in Your Hair)," while Jimmy Page finger picks the guitar on the neck. If you want to hear this song yourself, just get a hold of the *Forrest Gump* soundtrack. It is the third song on the second CD. If you have the film, it is played just after Forrest (Tom Hanks) beats up another white boy at a Black Panther meeting. He is walking with Jenny (Robin Wright) in his Army uniform. They are walking by one of the monument pools with the monument in the background when the song starts to play. It continues to play in the background as he walks her to the bus, where she leaves him.

In Scott McKenzie's version of the song, he tells the listeners if they are headed to San Francisco they should wear flowers in their hair, in the first two lines of the song. In the second pair of lines, *McKenzie* sings to the listener again, if they are headed to San Francisco:

"You're gonna meet some gentle people there."

Robert Plant sings the first three lines of the song just as Scott McKenzie did. However, in the fourth line he makes an adjustment to the lyrics. He sang the fourth line this way, between 6:13 and 6:18 of "Dazed and Confused":

"You're gonna meet a lot of DEVIL people there...everywhere, everywhere, everywhere."

There you have Led Zeppelin's command to sell your soul to the Devil, through the medium of Robert Plant's voice. The same Robert Plant said to Ann Nightingale in 1982, "As to us being involved in black magic – that was bunkum." Let the reader examine the evidence and then evaluate the veracity of Plant's statement. Remember what Lord Jesus Christ called Satan, "The Father of lies." Eliphas Levi, in his book *Transcendental Magic*, wrote about using the voice in this manner: "Music is a potent auxiliary of the voice, and hence comes the word *enchantment*. No musical instrument is more bewitching than the human voice, but the far-away notes of a violin or harmonica may augment its power."50 At 1:07 into first track of the 1990 Atlantic CD, *Led Zeppelin Profiled*, Robert Plant states that he was "proud" of the fact that the fans were "enchanted" by their music. It seems that Plant is in complete agreement with Aleister Crowley's "former self."

Frank Garlock, in his book, *The Big Beat - A Rock Blast*, wrote about a performer and what he says: "The mental effects of a given style of music are to a great degree determined by the beliefs of the performers of that style. 'What you are speaks so loud that people can hear it in what you say.' This variation of the old saying proves itself to be much more accurate for music. In other words, what the performer is speaks so loud that it shows up in the words and music he sings. Jesus said, 'How can ye, being evil, speak good things? For out of the abundance of the heart the mouth speaketh' (Matthew 12:34 KJV). What you are and what you believe will show up in what you say; and since music is in a very real sense extended and 'amplified' speech, beliefs will show up even more in what you sing."51

Jimmy Hendrix, in an interview he gave to *Life Magazine* in October of

1969 expressed my point this way: "Atmospheres are going to come through music because music is a spiritual thing of its own. You can hypnotize people with music, and when you get people at their weakest point, you can preach into their subconscious whatever you want to say."52

Now you know why Jimmy Page played that (explosion of will) blazing lead before the San Francisco song, to weaken the resistance of the listener, in the author's opinion, based on my subjective knowledge. After a while, the mind is so weak that anything they say goes right through the conscious mind to the unconscious, again, with no resistance. The fan, meanwhile, thinks he's being entertained and doesn't take it seriously; however, I did in 1977.

Aleister Crowley wrote, in his *Equinox*, these words that more or less explain what Led Zeppelin was doing here: "We therefore who are without the chains of ignorance, look closely into the heart of the seeker and lead him by the path which is best suited to his nature unto the ultimate end of all things, the supreme realization, the Life which abideth in Light, yea, the Life which abideth in Light."53 What the reader needs to do at this point, is consider for a few moments what Ritchie Yorke, a friend of the band, in his book, *Led Zeppelin - The Definitive Biography*, quoted Robert Plant as saying:

"I'm a reflection of what I sing."54

There you have it, you can judge the man right out of his own mouth. Based on his own statements, Robert Plant commands the fans to sell their souls to the Devil because he has done the same thing, as well as the rest of the band, who were backing him up with lead guitar, bass guitar, and drums. If this was not the will of the band, you can bet your eternal soul that Jimmy Page would have had it edited out of the film. Speaking of Page, the camera was directly on him alone when Plant mentioned the Devil. He is a true plenipotentiary.

Right after the command to the fans to sell their souls to the Devil, the cameraman turns away from Jimmy Page to show John Paul Jones playing the bass guitar, then he turns back to Page. I want to extend my thanks to that cameraman. In Steven Davis' *Hammer of the Gods* he presents the "absurd fable" as he puts it, about Led Zeppelin supposedly having sold their souls to the Devil, but John Paul Jones would not participate. He calls it an absurd fable because he does not believe they made the satanic pact. Well I agree that it is a fable, because John Paul Jones did participate. You just saw the proof of it in the film. Remember the Dancing Days chapter where he advertised the Black Sabbath? Remember also that he played on the Rolling Stones' *Their Satanic Majesties Request Album*. There he is in the Led Zeppelin film playing the bass as Robert Plant commands the fans to sell their souls to the Devil. Don't allow them to patronize you after this book comes out by saying that it was only tongue in cheek, and that I can't tell fantasy from reality. If it were only tongue in cheek, it would not have been given in a two-part covert fashion. The fact that they presented it in such a subtle fashion should clearly indicate their seriousness to any objective observer (Buy Crowley's house and promote Satan?).

Richard Cole wrote about the satanic pact rumors in his book *Stairway to Heaven - Led Zeppelin Uncensored*: "The most ominous rumor was elevated to mythological status. It proclaimed that in their earliest days, the band members - except for John Paul, who refused to participate - had made a secret pact among themselves, selling their souls to the devil in exchange for the band's enormous success. It was a blood ritual, so the story went, that placed a demonic curse upon the band that would ultimately lead to the deflating of the Zeppelin."55 Here again is another writer making an allusion to the satanic pact that has to be signed by the people involved with their N.I.B., their name in blood; and it just happens to be their road manager.

One should not believe for a minute that John Paul Jones refused to participate. Are we really supposed to believe that Jimmy Page would allow an unbeliever in the band? Even if Jones hadn't participated, he has sold his soul by default by playing in a band that promotes the satanic pact. John Paul Jones is smart enough to know that, and I think most people reading this book have enough sense to know Jones was in on the whole thing. Well, why is it then that he was the only one to come out of the whole thing unscathed? It was because of his conservative personality. On many an occasion, he would ditch the rest of the band when they started raising hell on the road. Richard Cole wrote about that in his book as well.

In their book, *Led Zeppelin - The Concert File*, Dave Lewis and Simon Pallett made reference to Jimmy Page's satanic pact. The statement was made relative to the 1995 World Tour by Page/Plant, and the end of the quote in parentheses was their writing, not mine: "Page was a man back in his element. These were the songs on which he had built his reputation and his desire to reinterpret them was more than obvious. His guitar playing was easily as good as anything he's produced in the last 20 years, defying the advancing years with flair, vigour and commitment (and a pact with Satan)."56 Even though they may have been sarcastic, they still made allusion to a pact that the evidence supports.

After examining both statements Plant made, one about selling your soul and the other about the Devil in "San Francisco," you have Led Zeppelin's covert command to their listeners to sell their souls to the Devil. No clear thinking person can possibly come to another conclusion. Understand this, the subconscious mind picked up both pieces of information, and because they are consecutive, the subconscious puts the two together. I will elaborate on this in the second "Stairway" chapter when I address backward masking. I do, however, want to address the method of communicating the message in two subtle parts.

The first part of Robert Plant's command to sell your soul to the Devil is sung in a very peculiar fashion so that only those who are listening real hard will understand it. In his book on magic runes called *Runelore,* Edred Thorsson wrote about subtle communications: "The willed act of consciously shaping operative communications on ever more subtle levels has a powerful intrinsic effect for magical work. In other words, for a magical working to be effective it must be in a form - a code if you will - that the object of the working will be able to 'understand' and respond to."57 You see, Led Zeppelin's act of shaping their operative communication was for magical purposes. It all makes sense. Remember the quote that I presented in the preface by Robert Plant about this kind of communication. He said that when one is stoned listening to the music: "You're just able to pick out more of what the group is trying to show you."58 Again, you can judge the man out of his own mouth. Remember, being stoned makes one more susceptible to hypnosis, and hypnosis makes one more susceptible to the power of suggestion.

In the book, *Witchcraft, Magic, and Occultism*, W. B. Crow wrote about this subject, and quoted some professionals. The first one I want to mention is a man named A.A. Leibeault, who was a physician who lived from 1823 to 1904. Concerning him, Crow wrote: "Liebeault was convinced that hypnosis was due to mental factors. He introduced the term *suggestion*, defining it as the transmission by words or gestures of ideas to the mind of the subject....The modern view, that ideas can be unconscious, has contributed to the success of the theory of suggestion."59 Crow also quoted a famous English hypnotist named J. Milne Bramwell on the subject of hypnosis: "J. Milne Bramwell (b. 1852) a leading English hypnotist drew attention to the fact that, under hypnosis, a subject may be able to notice stimuli which are too weak to affect him when not under this influence (hyperaesthetic perception)."60 Finally, Crow wrote these words on the subject of hypnosis, but also tied it in with witchcraft: "Today many do not believe in witchcraft. But they admit the effects of hypnotism and suggestion. These effects may be more powerful than many, who have not studied them, may suppose. And they can be very deadly. For they affect the unconscious, that part of the mind of which we are unaware directly, but which has been shown by psychologists to be of immense importance."61 Remember, Robert Plant gives the first part of the command, then Page plays a blazing lead, then he gives the second part. You have to understand that because they were consecutive messages, the subconscious mind has an easy time putting the two pieces together, and because the fans were and are normally stoned, the message is perceived even easier by the mind; as Robert Plant himself emphasized. This message desensitizes the listener, subcsonsicously, when it comes to fearing Satan; as well as promoting the satanic pact.

A powerful quote about the unconscious mind is about to be presented to tie all this together, but first, the reader has to know the meaning of the word "amenable." Webster defines it this way: AMENABLE - 1. Responsible or answerable 2. Able to be controlled or influenced; responsive; submissive [a person *amenable* to suggestion; an illness *amenable* to treatment.]62 Keep this definition in mind as you read the following.

In his book, *The Power of Your Subconscious Mind*, Dr. Joseph Murphy wrote about this concept: "You must realize by now that your conscious mind is the 'watchman at the gate,' and its chief function is to protect your subconscious mind from false impressions. You are now aware of one of the basic laws of mind: Your subconscious mind is amenable to suggestion. As you know, your subconscious mind does not make comparisons, or contrasts, neither does it reason and think things out for itself. This latter function belongs to your conscious mind. It simply reacts to the impressions given to it by your conscious mind. It does not show a preference for one course of action over another."63 This is why Plant sends the message in covert, two-part fashion, to send the message into the subconscious mind without being comprehended by the conscious mind, to try to avoid the conscious mind's rejection of the suggestion; if it is not picked up and accepted when heard. This is also what is going on in backward masking, which will be addressed in chapter fifteen. This all makes sense doesn't it? How many people, in the 1970's attended Led Zeppelin concerts and didn't at least catch a contact high by osmosis? If they caught a buzz, the hypnotic music of Led Zeppelin was intensified in their minds; both conscious and subconscious. Remember my thesis statement? "Led Zeppelin as an entity is comprised of four of the most dangerous Devil worshipers to ever walk the earth." You're beginning to get a glimpse at why I said that. Not only does Robert Plant command the fans to sell their souls to the Devil, but he then allows himself to be quoted as saying if the fans are stoned they will be able to pick out more of what Led Zeppelin was trying to show or communicate to them; through rock and roll. Jimmy Page, wanting to let the fans know that Led Zeppelin was trying to show them something said the following: "...anyone who plays good music and is expressing themselves with an instrument or on vocals has got something to say. It just depends whether you can relate to them or not."64 Then to polish his image, Page has made statements like the following: "We are not going out to make any moral or political statements."65 No moral statement was made by commanding the fans to sell their souls to the Devil? Do you see how dangerous these people really are? Once the fan has a seared conscience, where wrong becomes right, and right becomes wrong, it makes sense to believe that the Devil is in fact god, and that "deluded Christians" call the real god the Devil, and that there is no Devil, except in the mind of, again, deluded Christians. Well, the fact of the matter is, Robert Plant is the one who is self deluded, thinking he is encouraging people to sell their souls to god.

Please make a mental note here - they did not command the fans to sell their souls to Apollo, Odin, Thor, Horus, Osiris, Dionysus, Shiva, Pan, or anyone else. The reason for that is, anyone who becomes a quintessential follower of the band is going to get into Aleister Crowley and find out that all those deities are one deity, the Devil. That is why they said the Devil, because that's whom they want the fans to seek and sell their souls to.

Are we really supposed to believe that Led Zeppelin is sending subtle messages to their fans to build an image to sell records? I know you are smarter than that. They don't need to build an image to sell records. Their music sells itself, and it built their image for them. I believe they sent subtle commands to sell your soul to the Devil because they have done the same. Let's consider this with our common sense for a minute. If you go to the local military recruiting station, this is what will happen to you. If you talk to an Air Force recruiter, he is going to try to sell you the Air Force. He is not going to encourage you to join the Navy. If you go speak to the Marine recruiter, he will try to sell you the Marine Corps. He is not going to encourage you to join the Army. If you speak to the Navy recruiter, he will try to sell you the Navy, not the Marine Corps. Finally, if you speak to the Army recruiter, he is going to try to sell you the Army, not the Air Force. The Army recruits for the Army, the Marines recruit for the Marines, the Navy recruits for the Navy, and the Air Force recruits for the Air Force. So it is logical, then, for us to believe that the only people who would be commanding their fans to sell their souls to the Devil, are people who have done the exact same thing. Please remember, this is in the film, and on the soundtrack; as well as the July 28th, 1973 soundboard.

Now for a look at other Magick that was at work along with Led Zeppelin's command to sell your soul to the Devil, the Magick runes. It is important for you to understand them, especially Jimmy Page's, while the violin bow is being used as a Magick wand.

LED ZEPPELIN'S MAGICK RUNES

It stands to reason, that in England somewhere, Led Zeppelin's members have their Magick runes engraved on gold. On the sleeve to their fourth album, that band members had their own "carefully selected" Magick runes printed, carefully in a row with the other member's runes. In the beginning of *The Song Remains the Same* film, right after Peter Grant plays Al Capone, the camera shoots New York City from New Jersey, while the band member names are shown on the screen with their Magick runes next to their names.

In their song, on the fourth album, titled "The Battle of Evermore," (which I will prove is the *Holy Bible's* account of the Battle of Armageddon recorded in the Book of Revelation) the lyrics sung by Robert Plant make direct reference to their Magick runes. Between 3:19 and 3:25 into the song, Plant sings that magical "runes" have been engraved on "gold" in order that "balance." may be restored. He is making direct reference to the Magick runes they have printed on the album's sleeve. Raymond Page, in his book *Runes*, wrote about the wealthy who are involved in the occult engraving runes on gold: "Inscriptions on perishable materials will have perished, and these are likely to have been the more commonplace texts, those on wood and bone. Inscriptions on nonprecious metals, particularly iron, are subject to corrosion; even if they can be seen they are not necessarily readable. Inscriptions on precious metals, silver and especially gold, often survive well, though of course precious metal objects are liable to be melted down for their bullion value; but texts on these materials will belong to the wealthy groups in society and may be untypical of the general use of runes."66 As we all know, the members of Led Zeppelin are very wealthy. Their fourth album, with the runes written on the sleeve, has sold more copies than any other hard rock album in history; 23 million in the United States alone.

Steven Tyler of Aerosmith, narrating VH1's *Legends* about Led Zeppelin, that I watched on November 21st, 1997, said that Led Zeppelin's fourth album sold "...15 million copies-the best selling hard rock album ever." In 1998, the album was reported to have eclipsed the 17 million copies sold mark. By the year 2000, the album had sold 21 million copies. Guitar World, Feb. 2002, said it has sold over 22 million. Led Zeppelin's members are filthy rich. I firmly believe that there is a direct correlation between the Magick runes and the success of the album, especially since I believe that Jimmy Page's rune is the mark of the beast; as defined by Crowley's *Equinox*. By the way, Steven Tyler also talked about Jimmy Page buying Boleskine House and they even showed photos of Aleister Crowley! He made it a point to call Crowley a black magician as well. Nothing like a little advertising for the Devil on television! What other reason could there be for repeatedly associating Jimmy Page with Aleister Crowley?

After *Legends*, the VH1 Picture Show had *The Song Remains the Same* on. The show's MC, John Fugelsang, said this about Led Zeppelin's album sales: "These guys still sell over 2 million albums a year." So it should be obvious that Led Zeppelin is still popular, and the former members are still growing in wealth. I would challenge you to go to a search engine on the internet and type in the words "Led Zeppelin" and see what comes up. Numerous discussion groups are listed there, consisting of people all over the world.

Robert Plant sang that the "runes" were engraved on "gold" in order that "balance" may be restored. He is talking about the balance between what is true and what is practiced; the balance between the microcosm and the macrocosm, or man and god (Satan). Eliphas Levi wrote about this concept in his book, *Transcendental Magic*: "As we have said, there are two palmary natural laws - two essential laws - which, balanced against another, produce the universal equilibrium of things. These are fixity and motion, analogous to truth and discovery in philosophy, and in absolute conception to necessity and liberty, which are the very essence of God."67 That is the purpose of the runes.

Abramelin's instructions regarding the Magick runes are very conclusive as coming from the Devil himself. At this point we will look at those instructions, especially how they relate to Jimmy Page's rune, which again, I believe means the mark of the beast; as defined by Crowley's *Equinox.*

Nearing the end of the Operation of Abramelin, Abraham wrote that a magician should invoke the Holy Guardian Angel (who is the Devil), and ask him to instruct the magician with information on how to prepare a symbol, a Magick rune, that is associated with the operation of Magick the magician will perform; Abramelin Magick that is, the using of demonic forces in the pursuit of the Great Work, raising mankind to communion with god (the Devil). Abraham wrote:

"...invoke your Holy Guardian Angel, and pray him to favour you with his vision, and to instruct you how you should design and prepare the Symbol of the Operation desired. Also you shall remain in prayer until you shall see appear in the room the Splendor of your Angel. Then wait to see if he shall expound or command anything touching the form of the Symbol demanded. And when you have finished your supplication, arise and go to the Plate of Silver, whereon you shall find written as it were in drops of dew, like a sweat exuding therefrom, the Symbol as you ought to make it, together with the Name of the Spirit who should serve you for this Operation, or else that of his Prince."68

I believe, with every ounce of my being, that the Devil prepared Jimmy Page's "ZoSo" symbol on a "Plate of Silver" just as Abraham wrote in *The Book of the Sacred Magic of Abramelin the Mage.* My reading of *The Equinox* has made it clear to me that this symbol is none other than the mark of the beast, which is "666." Aleister Crowley wrote, again, in *Liber Samekh*, the epistle he wrote on uniting with the Devil as the Holy Guardian Angel, "...the name of THE BEAST, for that His number showeth forth this Union with the Angel, and His Work is no other than to make all men partakers of this Mystery of the Mysteries of Magick."69 If you look at the ZoSo emblem in the photo at the end of this chapter, you will see that each "O" has a dot in the center of them. Then look at the photo of the page of the *Equinox* prior to it, and you will see that the symbol "O" equals the number 6. In Jimmy Page's symbol, the "Z" shaped "letter," which is not a letter, is a runic pillar that the rest of the symbol sits on. That is not my opinion. It is obvious to the naked eye. There is an "O," then an "S," then another "O." As you can see by looking at Page's symbol, he has a line through all three, connecting them. This means that they are together. According to Crowley's Equinox, the "O" equals the numerical value of 6, then Page has a capital "S" and then another "O" which means 6. There it is, 6, S, and 6. Think of how stupid that symbol would look if it were three "O" figures with dots in the middle. Therefore, the symbol is designed in accordance with the *Equinox,*then with an "S" in the middle as a hint of what the "O" stood for, and a line through them all, connecting them together. "Also, the O with a dot in the center represents Sol, stands for the Sun, and the numerical value of Sol is 6.

Jimmy Page named his recording studio Sol studios. Crowley drew a version of the Qabalah with the Abramelin Operation grade with a "O" with a dot, the Sol symbol, and the number six at that point on the tree (It is in *Magick * Book 4 – Liber Aba.*). Remember what Abraham's instruction to the magician was, that he should pray to the Angel, and when the supplication is over, get up and go the Plate of Silver to see written there:

"...the Symbol as you ought to make it..."70

Jimmy Page has confessed to designing his own symbol. In Ritchie Yorke's *Led Zeppelin the Definitive Biography*, Page is quoted as saying this about his Magick rune, and that it was not a word: "'Mine was something which I designed myself,' he revealed rather slyly. 'A lot of people mistook it for a word - "Zoso" - and many people in the States still refer to the album as "Zoso"...which is a pity because it wasn't supposed to be a word at all but something entirely different.'"71 Jimmy Page bought Boleskine House just like Crowley, and he produces a magical symbol at that exact time of his life, in perfect keeping with Abramelin magic. Crowley bought the house to perform Abramelin magic. Shortly you will read evidence showing the Hermit on Led Zeppelin's fourth album inner cover to be associated with Abramelin magic as well; and that he is in fact Satan. It will all come together in the next chapter.

The numerical value of the circle with a dot in the center, as you can see in the photo with the words *The Equinox* at the top, is equal to six. Edred Thorsson, in his book, *Futhark: A Handbook of Rune Magic*, wrote about runes and numerical value: "One of the most interesting runic practices is that of further concealing the magical formula with intricately devised codes. These codes were created in order to make the messages more secret - and therefore more effective magically - and also less likely to be understood by the uninitiated. The basis of all the runic codes is the numerical value of the runes."72

At this point we are going to examine the meanings of the other Magick runes. John Bonham's symbol, as I mentioned in chapter nine, is a Magick rune that is on Aleister Crowley's Tarot Card entitled *The Hierophant*. A photo of it is in chapter nine. Crowley wrote that the symbol was representative of the three Aeon's of Isis, Osiris, and Horus; or in other words, man, woman, and child: "The symbolism of the Wand is peculiar; the three interlaced rings which crown it may be taken as representative of the three Aeons of Isis, Osiris and Horus with their interlocking magical formulae."73 This is what John Bonham had to say about it: "In discussing the symbols, John Bonham would only say, 'The runes are symbols which apply to each one of us. I wouldn't like to state what they mean. Each one of us picked one.'"74 Bonham refused to say what his symbol meant, but he did acknowledge that they were indeed Magick runes. Robert Plant ended up telling what Bonham's symbol stood for: "John Bonham's symbol was the three circles. Observed Plant, 'I suppose it's the Trilogy - man, woman, and child. I suspect it had something to do with the mainstay of all peoples' belief."75 There you have Robert Plant making reference to the Qabalah again. His statement mirrors Aleister Crowley's exactly. It also makes reference to the Song Remains the Same concept as well. John Bonham advertised the symbol's meaning in his sequence of *The Song Remains the Same*, when he starts running down a paved road to meet his wife Pat during the opening of his drum solo song, "Moby Dick." Later in the song, the camera is filming the underside of a carriage with a white horse in front. Then the scene changes to a side view, and there it is, John Bonham, Pat Bonham, and their son Jason, all riding the on top of the carriage. In the beginning of the song, the father and mother unite, and later in the song they show that the father and mother have brought forth a son. It all makes sense, that he would do it that way to advertise his symbol to the one who either knew what to look for, or would later become a student of Aleister Crowley and the Silver Star.

John Paul Jones' symbol is called the "Celtic Triquerta." It is the symbol of the Triple goddess; the three phases of the moon. The Triquerta is the part of the symbol that looks like a three sided boomerang. He has the Triquerta placed on a circle. In the occult world, the circle stands for infinity; never ending. The line does not end, it just continues to go around and around. In other words, the goddess will rule forever, at the god's side. If you look at works on Celtic Mythology, sooner or later you will come upon the Triquerta. It can be seen on page 9 of the book: *Celtic Myth and Magick*, by Edain McCoy, without the circle around it. This is the same triple goddess that the real Patricia Kennealy makes reference to when marrying Jim Morrison (Val Kilmer) to "Patricia Kennealy" (Kathleen Quinlan) in the movie, *The Doors*.

Robert Plant's symbol has eluded me. I have looked at several books on Magick runes and I haven't found it. However, when I wrote about the song "All My Love" in the last chapter, I wrote that Robert Plant sang about "His" being a "force" lying "within." The next thing he says is "Ours" being a "fire" everyone is able to "find." The very next thing he says is "He" being the "feather" blown by a "wind," at 3:59 into the song. If Robert Plant is saying that the same person that is the force and fire is a feather blowing in the wind, then that makes sense, because Plant's Magick rune is a feather being blown by the wind inside of a magic circle, which again, means infinity. I don't have absolute proof of this being Plant's symbol, but there is evidence to support it, and it is what I believe it is. Some people think his symbol's feather refers to another Egyptian Goddess "Maat." Regardless of whether I am right about Plant's, I am absolutely correct when it comes to Page, Bonham, and Jones. Robert Plant has told people that his symbol was taken from symbols belonging to the "Mu Civilization," that he describes as ancient and that they lived 15,000 years ago on a lost continent that was in the Pacific, somewhere between Mexico and China. Then he says that the Mu left tablets all over the world with their symbols carved in them.76 There you have it, "The Song Remains the Same." Remember, this is the same person who commanded the fans to sell their souls to Satan.

So far we have looked at Abramelin's instruction for a person to make a symbol the way the Holy Guardian Angel (Satan) would want it made. He then made this statement about making more symbols, or adding more for the evil spirits to be sworn by: "...the Spirit marked in the Sign shall do and execute that which the Sign beareth, and that which your intimation joined thereto shall indicate; also that in the case that in the Sign none of them shall be specially named, that all in general shall be obliged promptly and readily to perform the Operation commanded; and that if also in the time to come, other (Signs or) Symbols be made by you which be not here included, that then also they (the Spirits under Astarot) shall be equally bound to observe and execute them also. And when the Oath hath been taken, cause the Prince in the Name of the rest to touch the Wand."77 "Astarot" and "the Prince" mentioned in that quote refer to powerful spirits that rule over inferior ones; who are still infinitely more powerful than man. So there you saw how that additional symbols will be sworn to by the evil spirits under the magician's control; and influencing the wand (next chapter).

I have seen photos of Led Zeppelin in concert that show them with all the symbols present on stage except Robert Plant's. Most of the time however, it has been just Bonham and Page's symbols on stage. Jimmy Page traditionally has his symbol painted on a speaker behind him. Bonham's has always been painted on his bass drum (when used). The author believes the reason they have them on the stage would ostensibly be so that the spirits sworn to them will involve themselves in the magical operations being performed on the fans with the music as well as the Magick wand, i.e., the violin bow, and the Theremin.

The reason they all picked a Magick rune, is because they are all magicians to one degree or another, in the author's opinion. On July 10th, 1973, in Milwaukee, Wisconsin, Robert Plant introduced John Paul Jones this way as he was about to play "No Quarter." He said he was "...the magician of the keyboards."78 Most people take a statement like that as being complimentary to the said musician. However, when it comes to Led Zeppelin, whose music is loaded with teachings of Magick from Aleister Crowley's writings, the statement has to be presented by Plant in literal terms. Speaking of the Milwaukee, 1973 show, Damien Jaques wrote of it in the *Milwaukee Journal,* adding the following:

"Zeppelin Flying High"

"The four musicians are supposedly drawing better crowds and making more money than The Beatles, Rolling Stones or Alice Cooper ever did."

The above statement clues us in to how well of a pact the ole' Devil made with his boys in the band; and how powerful the runes have been.

Edred Thorsson also wrote of the significance of the Magick runes, both singularly and in conjunction: "The runes summarize and graphically express separate world concepts that can be used as focal points for magical and mystical operations, both singly and in combination."79

We are going to look at the magical operation of the violin bow/Magick wand on stage, in the next chapter. However, before doing so we have to look at a magical book called a "Grimoire." The specific Grimoire we are going to consider is a book called: *The Goetia - The Lesser Key of Solomon the King.* In 1995, Samuel Weiser Inc. published an updated version of this grimoire; the same one that Jimmy Page published in 1976 under the *Equinox* publishing name of his company. On the back cover was written this description: "It is a manual of Solomonic astrological sorcery that gives detailed instructions for the ritual precautions, requisites and incantations necessary to evoke the aid of its 72 spirits, which are described in detail. This book is the work of the two most influential magicians of the late 19th and 20th centuries. Aleister Crowley commissioned the work from Samuel Liddell MacGregor Mathers."80

Arthur E. Waite, a contemporary of Aleister Crowley, wrote about *The Lesser Key of Solomon*, addressing it by another of its names, the *Lemegeton*. He does, however, call it the *Goetia* at this end of the following quote. He states that it had not yet been printed, and I believe he means in English, because he wrote this in 1898, six years before Aleister Crowley produced an English translation: "The 'Lemegeton,' is divided into four parts, which control the offices of all spirits at the will of the operator, from whom the ordinary conditions are exacted. With the exception of the first part, which gave materials to Wierus, this remarkable, and in many respects attractive, work has never been printed, although it has been taxed surreptitiously for contributions by most makers of Rituals and Grimoires. It deals, as we have said, with the evocation of all classes of spirits, evil, indifferent, and good; its opening Rites are those of Lucifer, Bel, Astaroth, and the whole cohort of Infernus; it is entitled *Goetia*,* which sufficiently explains itself, and contains the forms of conjuration for seventy-two chief devils and their ministers, with an account of their powers and offices."81

* *Goetia* is the Greek word meaning Witchcraft. Remember, Moses was commanded to put to death anyone who consulted with spirits. None of the spirits in the *Goetia* are good. They are all fallen angels, who are Satan's demonic spirits. Only a fool will believe them when they claim to be good. Conversely, just ask anyone, whether they be Wiccan, Pagan, etc., who consult with spirits and practice magic, what they think of Biblical Christianity and born again Christians.

The *Goetia* was partially translated by Mathers at Crowley's request. He did not finish it. Crowley finished the translation, and edited it. As you just read, it is a manual for invoking spirits to aid you in magical purposes. In their 1995 edition, Samuel Weiser Inc. recorded the following in the Introduction; and I will present the footnote for the last sentence that was printed on the same page:

"Crowley probably began work on the *Goetia* in 1901 as he remarks that it took three years to produce. It appeared in 1904 under the imprint of his Society for the Propagation of Religious Truth, Boleskine, Foyers, Inverness, Scotland. An American piracy was issued in 1916 by the inimitable L. W. de Laurence, described by Crowley as a 'Yankee thief.' Several facsimile editions have appeared."(footnote #62)

#62 – "The first facsimile edition was issued by Jimmy Page (London: Equinox, 1976); although issued in hardcover, the dust jacket used camel-hair paper and it remains the facsimile most faithful to the 1904 original."82

Ask yourself this question, why would Jimmy Page go out of his way to publish a book about invoking 72 powerful spirits if they did not exist? Are we really supposed to believe that this highly intelligent, unbelievably talented guitarist, and multi-multi-millionaire producer of the world's most powerful and beautiful rock music is a lunatic who believes in spirit beings that do not exist? Do you really believe he has time to waste in a delusional frame of mind? Do you really believe that he would have (It was Jimmy Page's band) Robert Plant commanding the fans of Led Zeppelin to sell their souls to a being who does not exist? Not to mention the fact that all the most powerful rock stars on the earth glorify Satan in one fashion or another.

Remember, the *Holy Bible* declares that Lucifer was created with the power to make music! Think about the egos of these men. They have egos the size of which mere "mortals" like us cannot possibly comprehend. I know myself. If I had written all that music, and my sidekick had written all the lyrics, we would glorify ourselves for having done it. I certainly would not be glorifying the Devil. These men, again, with egos far greater than we can comprehend, glorify Satan for their careers. If they do that, it is because they have sold their souls to the Devil and he is the one who gave them the bulk of their lyrics and music. You will see evidence of that in the pages to come. The Devil and his angels/evil spirits exist. I don't believe they do, I know they do. I knew it for sure on June 11th, 1977. When you get to the first "Stairway to Heaven" chapter, you will read a description of one of the demons of the Goetia, who, as you will see, must have played an important role with Led Zeppelin.

The Book of the Sacred Magic of Abramelin the Mage was produced by an individual who truly believed he was serving god when he wrote the manual of instruction on how to unite with his "Holy Guardian Angel" and receive power to control demonic forces thereby; but what he in fact did was produce an occult document that would be praised by some of the most dangerous Satanists to ever walk the earth as the greatest guide to uniting not with a Holy Guardian Angel, but with the Devil himself, giving him possession of their souls thereby. The book teaches that the magical practices contained therein are to help the magician to unite, as the microcosm, with the macrocosm, the universe or god. Crowley taught that this accomplishment, the Operation of Abramelin the Mage, would unite the magician with Satan, who would then give him power over demonic forces (Jimmy Page began to project the violin bow like a Magick wand toward the audiences of Led Zeppelin subsequent to his purchasing Boleskine House.). The book tells the magician that his "angel" would prepare for him on a plate a symbol he was to make and use in his magical practices. Jimmy Page produced his "ZoSo" symbol at the very time of his life when he bought Boleskine house. Crowley, in *Liber Samekh*, which he wrote as a supplement to *The Book of the Sacred Magic of Abramelin the Mage*, claimed emphatically that Satan was his Holy Guardian Angel, when he said, "Satan My Lord! The Lust of the Goat! Mine Angel! Mine Initiator! Thou one with me the Sixfold Star!" In the Led Zeppelin film Jimmy Page acted out Crowley's description of climbing the mountain to be devoured by the Devil at the top. Page became one with the Hermit, and he put the sixfold star, the sign of the macrocosm, on the Led Zeppelin album as well. Crowley also wrote that Satan was Pan the Piper of the Greeks. He wrote in the *Book of Thoth*, "...the great god Pan on the highest and most secret mountains of the earth." Pan the Piper has horns, and so does the Hermit on the Mountain on the Led Zeppelin IV inner album cover. This part of the Led Zeppelin film, that has Page climbing the mountain behind Boleskine, occurs right after their two-part command to sell your soul to the Devil. The evidence, in the mind of any objective observer, points to Jimmy Page advertising the Operation of Abramelin the Mage to unite with Satan. It is presented in the Led Zeppelin film, as well as the fourth album inner cover, the music for which was recorded shortly after Page bought Boleskine House. There is also, I believe, and intend to show, a connection between Abramelin magic and the song, "Stairway to Heaven." Now we are going to look at what the author believes is the practice of casting Abramelin demonic magic spells on the fans of Led Zeppelin, as well as Aleister Crowley and Jimmy Page's climbing of the mountain out back of Boleskine House to meet the Devil at the top; in the chapter appropriately titled "Misty Mountain Hop."

THE EQUINOX

So is O.

O = A in the Book of Thoth (The Tarot).

A = 111 with all its great meanings, ⊙ = 6.

Now 666 = My name.

> = the number of the stélé.
> = the number of the Beast.   (See Apocalypse.)
> = the number of the ⊙

This table was written by Aleister Crowley and placed in his Ten Volume set of the *Equinox*. The dot with the circle around it is in fact a symbol of the Sun in Crowley's writings.... "666 = the number of the Sun." He put that in more than

one text. In his book on Yoga, Crowley drew the Qabalah with the circle and a dot, "adeptus minor," "tipareth," and "the Sun," and the number 6, all at the 5=6 stage. In the latest version of "Magick," "Sol" is there also. Sol means the Sun.

Robert Plant called himself "A Golden God," in step with the Qabalah teaching.

Jimmy Page began wearing the ZoSo symbol on sweaters and other garments after buying Boleskine house and producing his symbol while living there. Beneath the guitar in the above photo, is the ZoSo symbol on his right upper thigh. This photo was also taken at Oakland Coliseum on July 23rd, 1977. Dragons and the ZoSo symbol on the clothing as well as speakers all came after Page's purchasing and staying at Boleskine House. Robert Plant's calling the fans " human" also came after Boleskine House and Led Zeppelin's fourth album; as did his claim to be a golden god. The evidence points to them as having practiced Abramelin Magick, as will be seen in the next chapter. In the photo on the next page, is Led Zeppelin as they used to appear playing "Dazed and Confused;" Page in front of symbol.

1 Aleister Crowley, *Magick-Book 4*Liber Aba*, pg.146

2 Aleister Crowley, *The Confessions of Aleister Crowley,* Pg.357

3 Steven Davis, *Hammer of the Gods*, pg.109

4 S.L. MacGregor Mathers, Translator of *The Book of the Sacred Magic of Abramelin the Mage*, by Abraham the Jew, Introduction, pg. xxxi.

5 Jimmy Hendrix, *Life Magazine*, October 3, 1969, pg.74

6 Aleister Crowley, *The Equinox,* Vol. I, No.8, *The Temple of Solomon the King,* pg.13

7 Aleister Crowley, *Magick-Book 4 * Liber Aba,* Samuel Weiser Inc., 1994, pg.494

8 Aleister Crowley, *The Confessions of Aleister Crowley*, pg.358

9 Aleister Crowley, *The Confessions of Aleister Crowley,* Pg.357

10 Aleister Crowley, *The Equinox*, Vol. I, No.2, pp.333-334

11 Aleister Crowley, *Magick-Book 4*Liber Aba*, pg.484

12 Ibid, pg.452

13 Aleister Crowley, *The Equinox*, Vol. I, No.1, *The Temple of Solomon the King*, pg.131

14 Ibid, pg.132

15 Rosemary Ellen Guiley, *The Encyclopedia of Witches and Witchcraft*, pg.1

16 Aleister Crowley, *Book 4*, pg.115

17 Aleister Crowley, *Magick Without Tears*, pg.2

18 Ibid, pg.19

19 Steven Davis, *Hammer of the Gods*, pg.109

20 Aleister Crowley, *Equinox of the Gods*, pg.55

21 Steven Davis, *Hammer of the Gods*, pg.107

22 Ibid, pg.109

23 Cameron Crowe, *Rolling Stone* 182, March 13th, 1975

24 Aleister Crowley, *The Confessions of Aleister Crowley*, pg.359

25 Cameron Crowe, *Rolling Stone* 182, March 13th, 1975

26 Bob Larson, *Satanism - The Seduction of America's Youth*, Thomas Nelson Publishers, Nashville, Tennessee, 1989, pg.75

27 Howard Mylett, *Jimmy Page – Tangents Within A Framework*, pg.70

28 Aleister Crowley, *Magick-Book 4*Liber Aba*, pp.486-487

29 Aleister Crowley, *Moonchild*, pg.114

30 *Led Zeppelin: Will the Song Remain the Same?* Magazine, pg.46

31 Aleister Crowley, *The Equinox*, Vol. I, No.3, pp.239-245

32 Ibid, pp.247-249

33 S.L. MacGregor Mathers, Translator of, *The Book of the Sacred Magic of Abramelin the Mage*, by Abraham the Jew, Introduction, pg. xvi

34 Ibid, pg. xxviii

35 Ibid, pg. xxxi

36 Ibid, pp.6, 7

37 Ibid, pp.24, 25

38 Ibid, pg.55

39 Ibid, pg.37

40 Ibid, pg.40

41 Ibid, pg.53

42 Ibid, pg.54-55

43 Ibid, pp.84-85

44 Ibid, pg.85

45 Ibid, pg.250

46 Lisa Robinson, *Led Zeppelin - Creem Special Edition*, pg.16

47 Ritchie Yorke, *Led Zeppelin – The Definitive Biography*, pg.193

48 Michael Howard, *Understanding Runes - Their Origins and Magical Power*, Thorsons Publishers, 1995, pg.47

49 R. I. Page, *Runes*, University of California Press, 1989, pg.11-12

50 Eliphas Levi, *Transcendental Magic*, pg.247

51 Frank Garlock, *The Big Beat-A Rock Blast*, Bob Jones University Press, Inc., Greenville, South Carolina, 1971, pg.19

52 Jimmy Hendrix, *Life Magazine*, October 3, 1969, pg.74

53 Aleister Crowley, *The Equinox*, Vol. I, No.6, pg.7

54 Ritchie Yorke, *Led Zeppelin - The Definitive Biography*, pg.116

55 Richard Cole, *Stairway to Heaven - Led Zeppelin Uncensored*, pg.9

56 Dave Lewis and Simon Pallett, *Led Zeppelin - The Concert File*, pg.168

57 Edred Thorsson, *Runelore*, Samuel Weiser Inc., Yorke Beach, Maine, 1987, pg.160

58 Ritchie Yorke, *Led Zeppelin - The Definitive Biography*, pg.102

59 W.B. Crow, *Witchcraft, Magic, and Occultism*, pg.308

60 Ibid, pg.308

61 Ibid, pg.226

62 *Webster's New World Dictionary*, Second College Edition, pg.43

63 Dr. Joseph Murphy, *The Power of Your Subconscious Mind*, pg.34

64 *Led Zeppelin - Creem Special Edition*, 1980, pg.48

65 Howard Mylett, *Jimmy Page – Tangents Within A Framework*, pg.19

66 R. I. Page, *Runes*, pg.12

67 Eliphas Levi, *Transcendental Magic*, pg.358

68 S. L. MacGregor Mathers, Translator of *The Book of the Sacred Magic of Abramelin the Mage*, written by Abraham the Jew, pg.133

69 Aleister Crowley, *Liber Samekh*, from *Magick-Book 4*Liber Aba*, pg.527

70 S. L. MacGregor Mathers, Translator of *The Book of the Sacred Magic of Abramelin the Mage*, written by Abraham the Jew, pg.133

71 Ritchie Yorke, *Led Zeppelin - The Definitive Biography*, pg.132

72 Edred Thorsson, *Futhark: A Handbook of Rune Magic*, Samuel Weiser Inc., Yorke Beach, Maine, 1984, pg.11

73 Aleister Crowley, *The Book of Thoth*, pg.79

74 Ritchie Yorke, *Led Zeppelin - The Definitive Biography*, pg.131

75 Ibid, pg.132

76 Paul Kendall and Dave Lewis, *Led Zeppelin - In Their Own Words*, pg.61

77 S. L. MacGregor Mathers, Translator of *The Book of the Sacred Magic of Abramelin the Mage*, written by Abraham the Jew, pg.95

78 Dave Lewis and Simon Pallett, *Led Zeppelin: The Concert File*, pg.96

79 Edred Thorsson, *Futhark: A Handbook of Rune Magic*, Samuel Weiser Inc., Yorke Beach, Maine, 1984, pg.3

80 Translated by S.L. MacGregor Mathers, edited by Aleister Crowley, *The Goetia - The Lesser Key of Solomon the King,* Samuel Weiser, Inc., Yorke Beach, Maine, 1995, back cover.

81 Arthur E. Waite, *The Book of Black Magic*, pg.73

82 Translated by S. L. MacGregor Mathers, edited by Aleister Crowley, *The Goetia - The Lesser Key of Solomon the King*, Introduction, pg. xxv

"The magical wand is the verendum of the Magus; it must not even be mentioned in any clear and precise manner; no one should boast of its possession, nor should its consecration ever be transmitted except under conditions of absolute discretion and confidence."

- Eliphas Levi

"He wishes to formulate his will in sound, and radiate it in every direction; moreover, to influence that which lives by breath in the sense of his purpose, and to summon it to bear witness to his word."

- Aleister Crowley

CHAPTER TWELVE

"The famous Page showmanship trademark - playing the guitar with a violin bow - dates back to the mid-Sixties....He certainly used it on record and on stage with The Yardbirds....It was 'Dazed And Confused', though, that became the best known vehicle for the violin bow showpiece as the track developed into a marathon performance. By clever use of Echoplex, Page was able to throw out the reverberated sound in a series of power chords as the violin bow struck the strings. This became a trademark of the Zeppelin set - as immortalised in their Song Remains The Same movie."[1]

Dave Lewis and Simon Pallett, "Led Zeppelin - The Concert File"

"'I have omnipotence at my command, and eternity at my disposal,' smiled the boy, using Eliphaz Levi's well-known formula....'This boy is a desperate magician confined within the circle of this forest. His plan is Action; he is all for Magick; give him a Wand and a host of Demons to control, and he is happy.'"[2]

Black Magician Aleister Crowley, "Moonchild"

"The Magical Will is the wand in your hand by which the Great Work is accomplished, by which the Daughter is not merely set upon the throne of the Mother, but assumed into the Highest.

The Magick Wand is thus the principal weapon of the Magus; and the name of the wand is the Magical Oath."[3]

Black Magician Aleister Crowley, "Book 4"

"The Eye! Satan, my Lord! The Lust of the goat! Mine Angel! Mine Initiator! Thou one with me – the Sixfold Star!"[4]

Black Magician Aleister Crowley, "Liber Samekh"

"I do not worship the Devil, but magic does intrigue me."[5]

Led Zeppelin Guitarist, Jimmy Page, 1974

MISTY MOUNTAIN HOP: SATAN TAKES POSSESSION OF JIMMY PAGE

"Misty Mountain Hop" is the first of two chapters that clearly defines Jimmy Page's (and Led Zeppelin's) practical working of Magick, sorcery, witchcraft, etc. Call it what you will. We will begin by looking at the Magician's outfit

Jimmy Page wore on stage in *The Song Remains the Same* movie. The items on the outfit will be explained, relative to what I believe is their magical theme. Then we will look at the process of hypnotism, just prior to the use of the violin bow as a Magick wand. During the use of the violin bow, the supernatural force at work will be explained, from the works of Crowley, of course. After the act of using the violin bow as a Magick wand on the fans, we will look at the purpose of Jimmy Page's utilizing his Magick rune on stage, in *The Song Remains the Same*. After the purpose of the rune is examined, we will take our trek up the Mystic Mountain with Aleister Crowley and Jimmy Page to meet the Devil at the top. The Devil is disguised as The Hermit of the Tarot Cards. We will see how Jimmy Page uses this point in the film to advertise the Qabalah, in concurrence with the inner cover of the fourth album of Led Zeppelin. We will also look at the meaning of the full moon behind the mountain, which is behind Boleskine House in Scotland. Finally, we will see how that "The Hermit" and "The Devil" of the Tarot are both the same being - Lucifer, Satan, the Devil, the Piper. The last thing explained in this chapter will be why Jimmy Page extended the live version of "Dazed and Confused" to a half hour in length, and its relation to the Crowley teaching on an "explosion of will" and demonic forces. While Jimmy Page mystified the world with Led Zeppelin's inner album cover, making reference to the Hermit of the Tarot Cards, and while the mystical presentation of the mountain in their concert film was unique and awe inspiring in conjunction with the blazing sounds of the violin bow, that always fascinated this author in the seventies, especially when stoned, the truth is that the mountain painting on the album and mountain climbing scene in the Led Zeppelin film is nothing less than a major advertisement for the Operation of Abramelin the Mage, promoting the concept of uniting with Satan, the Holy Guardian Angel, according to the evil writings of Page's mentor, Black Magician Aleister Crowley.

THE OUTFIT OF JIMMY PAGE - MAGICIAN OF THE A.A.

The Magician outfit Jimmy Page wore in *The Song Remains the Same* had several messages to the observer. On the front left of his shirt, as previously mentioned in chapter nine, Page has an Opium Poppy. The following are descriptions of each piece of design:

THE DRAGON - On his right leg, Jimmy Page has a large red dragon/serpent, that has fire coming out of its nostrils. First, here is the Biblical definition of the dragon being the Devil:

"And another sign appeared in heaven: behold, a great, fiery red dragon....And war broke out in heaven: Michael and his angels fought with the dragon; and the dragon and his angels fought, but they did not prevail, nor was a place found for them in heaven any longer. So the great dragon was cast out, that serpent of old, called the Devil and Satan, who deceives the whole world; he was cast to the earth, and his angels were cast out with him.

- Revelation 12:3, 7-9

Please understand, this is not speaking about the first attempt Lucifer made to take over heaven. He was not called Lucifer in that passage. There is going to be a second attempt at the time of the seven year tribulation period, when the Anti-Christ rules the earth. As far as Satan being the red dragon, just pick up an English translation of the *Holy Bible* and it will be there. Some translations may have serpent instead of dragon (tomata-tomato).

Aleister Crowley wrote that the serpent is a symbol of change, and it stands to reason that Jimmy Page would wear a serpent when he is a magician trying to make change occur in the mind/conscience of the Led Zeppelin fan (or Page/Plant or Page/Crowes, etc.), which you will see shortly. Crowley wrote of the serpent in his book, *The Book of Wisdom or Folly*: "...the Serpent is proper to Works of Change, or Magick..."6 He also wrote that the serpent is another name for god: "The serpent is sacred, Lord of Life and Death, and its method of progression suggests the rhythmical undulation of those twin phases of life which we call respectively life and death. The serpent is also, as previously explained, the principal symbol of male energy."7

THE STARS ON THE BOTTOM OF THE RIGHT LEG - On the outer part of the bottom of the right leg of his outfit, Jimmy Page has one big star with several small ones around it. What this has reference to is that each man and woman is a star, and that the all are in fact one. Behind the left knee is the same all are one design. Then there are large individual stars on each leg that simply state that, again, each man and woman is a star. We have looked at that already so there will be no elaboration at this point; it will be addressed again as part of "Stairway to Heaven."

THE CRESCENT MOON AND STARS ON THE LEFT CALF- The crescent moon on the left calf is representative of the goddess in the Qabalah. Page had the Devil on one side, the dragon, and the goddess on the other. So there you have Jimmy Page advertising for the Qabalistic godhead in concert. Crowley wrote about the significance of the silver crescent moon and its relationship with the goddess in his book *Moonchild*: "The pictures and statues were of Artemis, no other goddess; the very objects in the apartment were crescent shaped, and the only metal in evidence was silver."8 Since Artemis and Diana are one and the same, the crescent moon refers to Diana as well. Crowley presented the Qabalistic godhead in the *Equinox* and said that same thing: "Lift yourselves up again, O Temples of Delphi and of Ephesus! The God of Light and of Art is become the

God of the world, and the Word of God is indeed willing to be called Apollo! Diana will no more reign widowed in the lonely fields of night; her silvern crescent is now beneath the feet of the bride."9 Remember, Artemis is the bride of Pan, and Pan is Satan; therefore Apollo is Satan, because he is the husband of Diana, and both Apollo and Pan are called "The Piper," the maker of music by Aleister Crowley.

THE PLANET SATURN ON THE LEFT THIGH- This has to do with the sign of Capricorn. Jimmy Page is a Capricorn. He was born on January 9th, 1944. The sign is ruled by the planet Saturn, and both Capricorn and Saturn are mentioned by Aleister Crowley in his *Book of Thoth* with reference to the Tarot Card entitled "The Devil." That will be shown later in this chapter when we are looking at the top of the misty mountain.

THE PHALLUS, THE PYRAMIDS AND SMALL STARS - Jimmy Page has a beige phallus (to contrast with his black outfit) with testicles hanging from his groin area. It is right next to long silver lace that he has hanging from his groin as well. It obviously refers to Satan as the male force in the Qabalah. It probably is also a sexual talisman. A talisman is something that has been consecrated with magic power.

Above his groin on the right side of his pants, Jimmy Page has three pyramids. On the other side, shooting out, as it were, from the pyramids is a bunch of stars (men and women), which means that all the stars came from Egypt. You read before that Egypt is the land of magic. Crowley quotes from Albert Churchward along the same lines, in his *Equinox*: "Let us therefore mention that the chief points, a few out of a score, that have struck us are-The Custom of the Mark Sacred Stone; the universality of Horus worship; the startling identity of hieroglyphics, all over the world, with the Egyptian; and the symbolism of the Great Pyramid, and its use as a Temple of Initiation."10

Churchward also said this about Egypt, and Crowley put it in *The Equinox* (and Jimmy Page named his bookstore *Equinox*): "...it was from Egypt, or rather Central Africa, that the human race originated, and that it is to Egyptian symbolism and more particularly to the Ritual of the Dead, that we must go if we would rightly understand the temples, rites, ceremonies, and customs of mankind past and present. From Egypt they came and to Egypt must we go."11

Finally, this section is going to end with a quote from none other than Eliphas Levi about Egypt and the pyramids, from his famous book, *The History of Magic*: "In this manner did the land of Egypt become as a great volume and the instructions contained therein were multiplied by translation into pictures, sculptures, architecture through the length and breadth of the towns and in all temples. The very desert had its eternal teachings, and its word of stone was set squarely on the foundations of the pyramids."12

Egyptian theology and magic as well as the pyramids are very important to the Silver Star and Jimmy Page, and they were to Aleister Crowley. This makes sense that Page would exalt the pyramids. Remember, Satan dictated *The Book of the Law* to Crowley in Cairo, Egypt. Jimmy Page would eventually become fascinated and fall in love with Cairo. Lisa Robinson confirmed this in *Creem Magazine* in 1977 when she wrote: "Thoughts of Cairo seem to make Page feel very happy."13 She went on to quote Page as saying he didn't want to come back home from Cairo. Then she emphasized the fact that Jimmy owned "Equinox," his occult bookstore in Kensington, and that its main purpose was to stock the works of Aleister Crowley, and that it was no longer open. Tom Friend saw Led Zeppelin in concert shortly after Page came back from Cairo; and I also own the works of Aleister Crowley (They are now well hidden; not to be found.).

I believe I have shown enough reason to suggest why Jimmy Page has pyramids on his outfit. It is a magician's outfit. This is what was written about Page as he arrived to perform at Knebworth, in England, in August of 1979, by Rhonda Keifer in *Cleveland Scene Magazine*. She said that years before she never thought that she would see Jimmy Page dressed in any outfit but a magician's, but that he got out of a limo wearing a tan suit, looking really good. Here is a female journalist calling Jimmy Page's mid-seventies outfits the type that a magician would wear. She wrote it in a magazine fearing no repercussions from the band. Why? Because it was no secret in the rock world. It makes sense for a magician and follower of Crowley to be in love with Egypt.

ALEISTER CROWLEY AND HUMAN SACRIFICE

Crowley's *Book of the Law* was written in Cairo, Egypt, and that book advocates human sacrifice. You already read about human sacrifice in this book in the chapters on the Devil (2) as well as the Book of the Law (7). You also read in the "Hymn to Satan" that Crowley believed Satan was his creator. Here is another quote not previously mentioned. It is Aleister Crowley once again quoting the Devil, in a writing dictated to him called *Liber A'ash*, placed in *The Equinox*: "All corpses are sacred unto me; they shall not be touched save in mine Eucharist. All lonely places are sacred unto me; where one man gathereth himself together in my name, there will I leap forth in the midst of him."14 In case you don't know, when he says Eucharist, he means sacrifice. Eucharist comes from the Greek word Eucharistia, which means gratitude. Also, Eucharistos, the Greek word which means grateful. Webster's dictionary defines Eucharist this way:

EUCHARIST - 1. *same as* HOLY COMMUNION 2. the consecrated bread and wine used in Holy Communion.15

If the Devil was saying eat the body, then that would make sense. One can see a satanic cult cut open a dead body lying on a huge pentagram, painted on a floor, and then start eating the insides of the dead man, as the cult leader then puts his hand over the camera; in the first edition of "Faces of Death," a video that shows real deaths, that came out in the mid 80's. You can rent this at most video stores. A word of warning, it is not for the timid.

Aleister Crowley is the man that Jimmy Page wants to know how he can be identified as evil, and then he says he is an unrecognized genius of the twentieth century. Now what are we supposed to conclude from this? Here is a quote from the Led Zeppelin road manager Richard Cole, in his book, *Stairway to Heaven - Led Zeppelin Uncensored*, in which he wrote about John Bonham making a remark to him about Jimmy Page going to Cairo, Egypt, during a break in the 1977 tour, again, just before I saw them at Madison Square Garden:

"During a three-week break in the U.S. tour, most of us flew back to London. But Jimmy planned to jet to Cairo with Mick Hinton, apparently to do some Aleister Crowley-related Egyptology research.

On the flight home, Bonzo said to me, 'Do you know the reason Jimmy is taking Mick and not you to Egypt? He knows that if he decides to sacrifice someone, he'd find it a lot harder to do away with you than Mick!'"16

Let me make one thing clear. I am not implying that Jimmy Page engages in human sacrifice. I believe that Crowley did, but there is no evidence to prove that Page has. Also, to be fair, Jimmy Page has said that Richard Cole's book is absolutely false. It is interesting, however, that Cole would present information directly in line with the writings of Aleister Crowley; and whom did he quote? John Bonham. Page has said repeatedly that he thought of suing the publisher of Richard Cole's book. Why didn't he? Was it because Cole could round up a bunch of groupies to testify as to the authenticity of what he has written in his book? Or is it because Cole would then make embarrassing accusations against Page in public? I don't know. One thing that makes sense to me is that Richard Cole would have to think twice about making up lies about a man he knows is a magician. If that bothers you, look again at the heading of chapter five, where Crowley is quoted by Susan Roberts as admitting he was a black magician.

Steven Tyler of Aerosmith called Crowley a black magician in the Led Zeppelin Legends program on VH1: "Page indulged his growing fascination with the legendary Black Magician, Aleister Crowley; buying his old home in Scotland. Born in 1875, Crowley was a writer, mountain climber, and self-proclaimed sorcerer. His credo was 'Do What Thou Wilt Shall Be The Whole of the Law.'" This is all fine and dandy with Steven Tyler, he thinks it is fantastic, since he also glorified Satan on the Aerosmith *Get Your Wings* album (and who did Aerosmith get their wings from?). He also, as I wrote before, introduced Led Zeppelin when they were being inducted into the Rock and Roll Hall of Fame.

Are we to believe that Page would have unbelievers introduce him to the Hall?

THE SONG REMAINS THE SAME – "DAZED AND CONFUSED"

Led Zeppelin, having completed their two part command to the fans to sell their souls to the Devil, at the prodding of Page, continue the subtle occult messages in the chronology of "Dazed and Confused." The next thing that happens, as Jimmy Page continues to play, is that Robert Plant starts to yell into the microphone, at 6:56 into the soundtrack, the words "I know!" He yells it into the microphone five times. In "Heartbreaker," off the *Led Zeppelin II* album, Plant sings of a woman whose "smile" is indicative of somebody that "knows," at 0:40 into the song. At 0:29 into "Dancing Days," off the *Houses of the Holy* album, Robert Plant sings that he has his "woman" that "knows." What is he referring to here? I believe it is the worship of the Devil as god that he knows. Having just completed his command for the satanic pact, the momentum is shifted toward Jimmy Page as he is about to take a trip up the mountain behind Boleskine to meet the Devil. In his *Equinox, Vol. I, No.2*, Crowley wrote these relevant words: "So here, and now, and with us; he who climbs the Mountain we point out to him, and which we have climbed; he who journeys by the chart we offer to him, and which we have followed, on his return will come in unto us as one who has authority; for he alone who has climbed the summit can speak with truth of those things that from there are to be seen, for HE KNOWS."17 It was Crowley who capitalized "HE KNOWS." Shortly, you will read Crowley's description of ascending that mountain to see the Devil, and then you will read of Jimmy Page acting it out in the film. Just before acting it out however, Page uses hypnotic chords on the guitar; and for a reason.

USING HYPNOSIS TO PREPARE THE MIND FOR MAGICK

Just before utilizing the Magick wand/violin bow, Jimmy decides to use the guitar to slowly hypnotize the fans. If you are watching the film, look at how he uses the high notes on the guitar, swinging his fingers back and forth on them. Then he moves his hand to lower notes and swings his fingers back and forth on them. What you have heard is an objective/subjective pendulum. The objective pendulum is the higher and lower note parts of the guitar that he moves his hand back and forth to. The subjective pendulum is the moving of his fingers back and forth like a pendulum at the higher and lower parts of the guitar he is playing. This, in conjunction with mesmerizing volume and drug use by the fan, is an easy method of hypnotism. In his book, *Hypnotism - Theory and Practice*, Walter Gibson presented a definition of hypnosis as: "...an artificially induced state resembling sleep, characterized by heightened susceptibility to suggestion."18 He also claimed that hypnotism has been tied to the supernatural for centuries: "Belief in the power of mind over mind dates back to remote antiquity. From then on, it has been demonstrated so convincingly, through century after century, that it has been attributed to some mystic power or supernatural force, an idea which is still widely accepted."19 That last point about supernatural force assisting the hypnosis shouldn't sound surprising to anyone considering what you have read about up to this point, especially while he has his Magick rune painted on a speaker behind him and, I believe, demonic forces sworn to the symbol are already working in the arena.

H.P. BLAVATSKY AND HER MAGAZINE "LUCIFER"

H.P. Blavatsky, another famous occultist who founded the Theosophical Society in 1875, the year Aleister Crowley was born, and who is advocated by him in his *Equinox*, wrote this question and answer session about hypnosis, originally published in her magazine, *Lucifer*, that was later published in a book called *Studies in Occultism*, that she wrote:

Q. *"What is Hypnotism; how does it differ from Animal Magnetism (or Mesmerism)?*

ANS. Hypnotism is the new scientific name for the old ignorant 'superstition' variously called 'fascination' and 'enchantment.' It is an antiquated *lie* transformed into a modern *truth*. The fact is there, but the scientific explanation of it is still wanting. By some it is believed that *Hypnotism* is the result of an irritation artificially produced on the periphery of the nerves; that this irritation reacting upon, passes into the cells of the brain-substance, causing by exhaustion a condition which is but another mode of sleep *(hypnosis, or hupnos);* by others that it is simply a self-induced stupor, produced chiefly by imagination, etc., etc."20

So Jimmy Page used hypnosis to prepare the mind of the listeners to be infiltrated by what I believe, and experienced at the Led Zeppelin concert I went to, are supernaturally powered suggestions from demonic forces he would project to them with his magic wand - the violin bow.

THE MAGICIAN AND HIS MAGICK WAND - THE VIOLIN BOW

There are multitudes of pictures of Jimmy Page with the violin bow in his hand. The only pictures that have shown him extending the bow toward the audience were after 1970. The author believes there is a direct correlation between his performance of the Operation of Abramelin the Mage, and his achieving magic power over demonic forces to project them at the audience for magical purposes. This is why he didn't use it as a wand on the audience before he bought Aleister Crowley's house in 1970. As the prayer of Abramelin says: "...grant unto me the Power which Thou hast given unto Thy Prophets over all the Evil Spirits." 21 You already read that Jimmy page published a book on conjuring up demons for magical purposes. Here is a quote from that book that just about tells the story of what I believe Page is doing with the violin bow: "Magic is the Highest, most Absolute, and most Divine Knowledge of Natural Philosophy, advanced in its works and wonderful operations by a right understanding of the inward and occult virtue of things; so that true Agents being applied to proper Patients, strange and admirable effects will thereby be produced. Whence magicians are profound and diligent searchers into Nature: they, because of their skill, know how to anticipate an effort, the which to the vulgar shall seem to be a miracle."22 The Agents spoken of are evil spirits, and the Patients are the fans. With the word "effort" was a footnote which said "or effect."

As you read in the chapter heading, Jimmy Page used the violin bow with the Yardbirds as well as Led Zeppelin. Before he used it as a magic wand, he used to play the guitar with it, in order to conjure demonic sounds from the guitar. The demonic sounds helped to create the environment he desired. In the early days of Led Zeppelin, several reporters wrote of Page's use of the bow in concert. The following are some examples of the articles written, first by Dave Lewis and Simon Pallett about Led Zeppelin's first tour: "The stage act for the debut tour was based loosely on the set The Yardbirds had been performing on their final US tour. 'Train Kept A Rollin' was the opener and 'Dazed & Confused' the centerpiece, with Page using the violin bow."23

A newspaper reporter in Denver, Colorado, named Thomas MacCluskey wrote an article called "Rock Concert is Real Groovy," about Led Zeppelin's first concert in the United States on December 26th, 1968, and Jimmy's use of the violin bow: "Used a violin bow on the guitar strings in a couple of tunes with resultant interesting, well integrated effects." In February of 1969 the band played in Toronto, Canada. Ritchie Yorke wrote this about Jimmy Page and the bow: "His spotlighted work, including the riffs with the violin bow, was executed expertly..." In March of 1969, the band played in Denmark, and the review of the bow was not favorable in *The South Swedish Daily Paper*: "It's not that funny listening to a guitarist who's standing there stroking the strings back and forth with a violin bow, not letting the amplifiers let up for a second." The point made in the last quote was that Jimmy Page would play the guitar with the bow so intensely that the sound would permeate every nerve in your body. That was exactly what Jimmy wanted. A lot of people could not stand his performing with the bow at their shows, but Jimmy didn't care because it was necessary for his work.

During the 1977 tour, Jimmy Page played the violin bow inside of a laser cone pyramid. There is a six-foot poster that was made with the center showing Page playing the guitar with a bow in the middle of a laser cone pyramid. Multitudes of teenagers, including myself, owned this poster in the 70's. In his book, *Buckland's Complete Book of Witchcraft*, Raymond Buckland wrote about the occult *Cone of Power:* "...the wills of all the coven members must be directed towards the same end. Whether from a group or from an individual Witch, the power generates and collects in the form of a cone, over the Circle. Once sufficient power has been produced, then this Cone of Power can be directed."24 In Atlanta, Georgia, on April 23rd, 1977, Led Zeppelin played at "The Omni." Scott Cain wrote of Jimmy Page and his laser cone pyramid: "Clouds of smoke billowed in the air and Page stood in the center of a pyramid-shaped column of green laser light that revolved faster and faster as he picked up tempo." Led Zeppelin played in Copenhagen on the 24th of July, 1979, and Jon Carlsson wrote about it in *Melody Maker* magazine. He wrote about the violin bow performance and the laser cone pyramid that "...became a glowing green cone." Those of you with the Knebworth 1979 video or the Page Syracuse 88 video can see this laser cone rotation when Jimmy uses the bow on the guitar.

Jimmy Page used the bow from the beginning, and he later used the laser cone pyramid with it. The following quotes are descriptive of the demonic element of the bow. Steven Davis wrote about the bow in the early days of the band in *Hammer of the Gods*: "'Dazed and Confused' was now stretching into twenty minutes, with Jimmy's bow exhibition drawing much awe for its ritualistic connotations of diabolism."25 The Greek word for diabolism is "Diabolos." It is a title for Satan that means "slanderer." Not only did the music convey diabolical concepts to the listeners in the audience, but the lights were doing this as well. Before reading the next quote, you need to know the definition of the word ominous. This is the Webster definition: OMINOUS - 1. "of or serving as an omen; esp., having the character of an evil omen; threatening; sinister."26 Lisa Robinson, a personal friend of the band members, told Jimmy Page one time after watching him perform with the violin bow at Madison Square Garden in New York, that the light show concurrent with the bow routine appeared: "...ominous. 'That's it,' he smiles, pleased."27

In their book, *In The Light*, Howard Mylett and Richard Bunton wrote about Jimmy Page's use of the violin bow in "Dazed and Confused" from the Led Zeppelin film: "The track features some of the most demonic sounding guitar/violin bow effects ever to appear on record."28 Again, Jimmy Page plays the demonic sounds to create the eerie demonic environment that will work his magician's will in the mind of the fans. As Eliphas Levi put it in Transcendental Magic: "A thought is realized in becoming speech; it is realized also by signs, sounds and representations of signs..."29 Jimmy Page wants the fan to think about demonic forces because, the author believes, he is going to try to draw them to the Devil that way.

Frank Garlock, in his book, *The Big Beat - A Rock Blast*, talks about music (not vocals) and the beliefs of the performer: "What the musician believes definitely does affect the listener, even if the musician never says a word, because his beliefs will show up in his performance of the music and even in the music itself. Of course this would apply mostly to beliefs which are overt in the personality of the performer and ones which dominate his general character so that he expresses them openly."30 The reason Jimmy Page wants the fan to think of demons, is because he's a Crowleyite - Thelemic Satanist.

In their book, *Pacts With the Devil*, Christopher Hyatt and Jason Black defined what a "demon" is this way: "...a non-human entity of great intelligence and power, existing as mind and spirit, and capable of influencing the material world."31 Remember, a demon is one of Satan's fallen angels.

To review what we have looked at so far, Jimmy Page used the violin bow with Led Zeppelin right from the beginning of touring. He utilized laser cones while playing the guitar with the bow. He utilized the bow to create demonic sounding atmospheres at Led Zeppelin's concerts. You also know that Jimmy Page reproduced a Grimoire, a magical book on conjuring demons for use in magical purposes. We are about to examine Aleister Crowley's teachings on using the Magick wand to control demons for the purpose of the Great Work, uniting the microcosm, man, with the macrocosm, god, again, who they believe is Satan. Take another look at the quote by Crowley at the heading of this chapter before we begin: "'I have omnipotence at my command, and eternity at my disposal,' smiled the boy, using Eliphaz Levi's well-known formula.... 'This boy is a desperate magician confined within the circle of this forest. His plan is Action; he is all for Magick; give him a Wand and a host of Demons to control, and he is happy.'"32 The boy has omnipotence at his command because he has a Magick wand and a host of demons under his control. This theme is presented in Richard Cavendish's *The Black Arts*, and he also calls the wand a weapon: "A magic wand or rod is another important weapon and one of the supreme emblems of magical power..."33 According to Eliphas Levi, the magician has to keep his mouth shut about possessing a Magick wand: "The magical wand is the verendum of the Magus; it must not even be mentioned in any clear and precise manner; no one should boast of its possession, nor should its consecration ever be transmitted except under conditions of absolute discretion and confidence."34

THE MAGICIAN AND THE GREAT WORK

The magician has to think things through before he performs magical ritual. As Crowley wrote about magicians in the A.A.: "The first condition of membership of the A.A. is that one is sworn to identify one's own Great Work with that of raising mankind to higher levels, spiritually, and in every other way."35 If the magician is not performing Magick for the good of mankind, relative to the Great Work, it will not prosper (in the mind of the occultist, the good of mankind is to be united with the god of the occult). Crowley wrote of this in his book, *Moonchild*: "The first condition of success in magick is purity of purpose."36 Again, the purity of purpose is the Great Work, as Crowley wrote in *Magick Without Tears*, four years before his death, one year before Jimmy Page was born: "...the most important preliminary to any Magical operation is to make sure that its object is not only harmonious with, but necessary to, your Great Work."37

THE MAGICK WAND AND THE GREAT WORK

As Jimmy Page began to use the violin bow as part of his Great Work in the Led Zeppelin film, he plays the guitar with it, making a variety of demonic sounds. While he is doing this, he looks over to his left, not once, but twice, to look at the person who is sitting on the side of the stage. That person is none other than Peter Grant. You can see him in the beginning of the violin bow routine when Jimmy first shows it on film; Peter Grant is sitting behind him, and he can be seen sitting there in many other places in the film. The reason he is doing that is because Peter Grant knows exactly what he is up to. Here is their "greater fusion of interests" mentioned in chapter one. What Jimmy Page is doing, the author believes, is conjuring up demons all the while he is playing the guitar with the bow, before he uses it as a Magick wand. This is why I believe that - in *The Book of the Sacred Magic of Abramelin the Mage*, it is written that the magician, once he has achieved the Knowledge and Conversation of the Holy Guardian Angel (Satan), and has been given power to rule demonic forces, can command the demons to begin to operate in accordance with his signal to do so, once he has communicated that signal to them: "...anyplace is good to invoke the Spirits proper unto the Operation. There give them their commission regarding that which you wish them to perform, the which they will either execute then or in the days following. But always give them the signal by word of mouth, or in any other manner that may be pleasing unto you, whenever you wish them to begin to operate."38

Once the demons have been evoked and are ready to perform the operation of the Great Work, Jimmy Page then begins the action of using the bow to project what I believe is the macrocosmic, demonic force to the audience; in accordance with the teachings of Crowley. In the film, for those of you who are not watching it, Jimmy Page plays the violin bow for a short period and then he smacks the guitar with the bow. He hits the guitar one time with the bow, causing a powerful riff to come out of the speakers. Then he extends the bow to the fans on his right. As he extends the bow, the riff is repeated. He has his equipment set up to where for every time he strikes the guitar with the bow, it commands two powerful riffs. Therefore, the first riff is heard when the bow hits the guitar, and the second is heard as Page extends the bow toward the fans; the process is done through equipment called the Echoplex. After Page extends the bow to the fans at his front right, he then strikes the guitar and extends the bow to his front left, then, walking in a circular motion to the left, he repeats the process and extends it to his left rear, then his right rear, completing the circle. He has struck the bow and extended it in four directions, and then he completes the circle again, making it eight times. Jimmy Page has the most serious, concentrated look on his face while he is performing this ritual. He is not performing something wild to impress the fans, I believe he is performing black magic; i.e. Magick.

At this point Black Magician Aleister Crowley's instructions will be shown to illustrate their relevance to Page's ritual with the bow (wand). The first thing that we need to know is that Crowley calls the Magick wand a weapon in the hand of the magician: "The Magick Wand is thus the principal weapon of the Magus..."39 Weapons are only used in warfare, and Crowley said this age was an age of wartime against Christianity, and the "Immigrant Song" says that Led Zeppelin are the fans' "overlords" during their wartime.

Crowley taught that the magician should take his wand and walk the circle to the left and then project a Force with the wand; while facing the direction of Boleskine House in England:

"Let the Magician, still facing Boleskine, advance to the circumference of his Circle.

Let him turn himself towards the left, and pace with the stealth and swiftness of a tiger the precincts of his circle, until he complete one revolution thereof.

Let him give the sign of Horus (or the Enterer) as he passeth, so to project the Force that radiateth from Boleskine before him."40

There is a picture of the sign of Horus the Enterer in this chapter. It is the magician extending the wand with his right arm, just as Page extended the wand. It is taken from Crowley's *Equinox*. In that quote, Boleskine is spoken of as a kind of Mecca. Just as the Muslims face Mecca and pray, the magician is to face Boleskine, to be able to project the force that radiates from Boleskine. Once again, Crowley says the place is haunted. Also, remember what you read earlier in this book, that Crowley quoted Satan in *The Equinox* as saying "I the force that created all, am not to be despised," and then Jimmy Page claimed to be "a vehicle for some greater force." Page made that statement after the Madison Square Garden shows that are in their film in 1973. Here the magician is speaking, not to disclose, but to encourage others to discover.

Moving to the left is considered done for the Devil, in Richard Cavendish's *The Black Arts*. He was describing the ritual that goes in the clockwise direction. Then he wrote: "In this case the circle has been drawn *deosil*, clockwise, from east to south to west to north, following the direction of the sun. In operations which are consciously evil or dedicated to the Devil, the magician should move the opposite way, *widdershins* (from Anglo-Saxon *withersith*, 'to walk against'), which is moving against the sun and is therefore an unnatural and perverse motion, attractive to evil forces."41 As you know, Led Zeppelin, especially Robert Plant, make direct reference to the Celts when quoted and written about. This quote is from *Celtic Magic*, by D.J. Conway about moving to the left in rituals: "The Celts always performed certain movements in the direction of the Sun (clockwise) during rituals. They considered it very unlucky to go widdershins (counterclockwise), except for specific rituals."42

Crowley said that while moving to the left, the extension of the wand should be made in the direction of the east. However, the ritual can be modified to perform it in concert. Jimmy Page modified it in accordance with Crowley's writing. This is what Crowley wrote about the magician: "He wishes to formulate his will in sound, and radiate it in every direction; moreover, to influence that which lives by breath in the sense of his purpose, and to summon it to bear witness to his word."43 The magician wants to "influence" the fans in accordance with his "purpose" or will. Then, once the influence has taken place, to "witness" for him. It might sound something like this: *"Hey man, you just gotta catch Led Zeppelin live, it's killer!"* Also, promoting the band at parties, school, etc. I know, because I personified what I am writing when in high school, and afterward. I remember taking "The Doors" off the stereo at a party in 1979, and putting Led Zeppelin on, to the dismay of several individuals, while I was drunk and stoned. You could say I was experiencing withdrawals from Jimmy Page listening to The Doors too long. It would have been fine with me to fight to get them on the stereo. Seconds later, everyone was listening to Led Zeppelin. If I was going to "break on through," it was going to be with Jimmy Page, not Jim Morrison.

Crowley wrote about the power that does the influencing as the force. In the following, he calls it the macrocosmic force, aroused by the magician giving the sign of Horus the Enterer, which, again, is the extension of the wand in the direction the magician wants the force to go. The word circumambulation means to walk the circle: "Circumambulation properly performed in combination with the Sign of Horus (or 'The Enterer') on passing the East is one of the best methods of arousing the macrocosmic force in the Circle."44 Remember what you read earlier. The will of all the band members toward the same end, assists the magician in raising the power or force in the cone of power, and then it can be directed as he wills. That is what I believe Jimmy Page is doing when he plays the guitar with the violin bow, before using it as a wand. The extension of the wand, as you just read, arouses the macrocosmic force in the circle, why? To be projected in accordance with the will of the magician. The author believes the fan is the object of the magical ritual, as the evidence is presented in the film; just look at Jimmy Page's face.

You all read this quote already in this book, by Aleister Crowley, "Magick is the science and art of causing change to occur in conformity with the will."45 That was a general statement on Magick by Crowley. It could leave the reader wondering what the magician is trying to change in conformity with his own will. Was it the color of the person's hair that he is trying to change? Was it some other aspect of his appearance? What was it that Crowley was saying that the magician is trying to change? It was thinking, pure and simple, relative to right and wrong. Crowley calls it "consciousness," in his specific definition: "Our spiritual consciousness acts through the will and its instruments upon material objects, in order to produce changes which will result in the establishment of the new conditions of consciousness which we wish. That is the definition of Magick."46 The music modifies the fan's thinking. That concept is going to be commented on by several occult authors, in order that the reader can understand exactly what I believe was happening here, and who was causing it to happen. Eliphas Levi put it this way: "Magic was called formerly the Sacerdotal Art and The Royal Art, because initiation gave empire over souls to the sage and the capacity for ruling wills."47 That statement more or less defines what Robert Plant meant when he told the fans the band members were their "overlords," in the "Immigrant Song." Rosemary Ellen Guiley wrote this definition, closely resembling Crowley's, in *The Encyclopedia of Witches and Witchcraft*: "Magic is the art of effecting change through an external and supernormal force. Man's awareness of magic and his efforts to use it to enhance his place in his environment are ancient and universal and have been a part of all religious systems."48 She said it was "a part of all religious systems"…the song remains the same.

What does Jimmy Page have to say about such a "supernormal force?" In their book, *Led Zeppelin-In Their Own Words*, Dave Lewis and Paul Kendall recorded what Page had to say: "There is a very powerful astrological force at work within the band which I am sure had a lot to do with our success."49 Do you see that word "astrological" Jimmy Page used? What he meant was universal. Not universal all over the earth, although it means that as well, he was referring specifically to the eternal force that fills the entire universe, that he believes is Satan, as you are about to see in this chapter beyond any shadow of a doubt.

Aleister Crowley said that the spiritual consciousness of the magician works through the will and its instruments, like guitars and drums, upon material, or physical objects, to change the condition of the object's consciousness, meaning people, from old consciousness to new. This is changing the conscience of the fan from the old morals of Christianity, to the new morality, which is nothing more than the old immorality, to make the fan confirm himself in the anti-Christ moral code by becoming a hard core fan of rock and roll. The reason that Satan attacks the teenage years the most, is that is because those years are the ones that are most impressionable. Once a person gets "set in their ways," he or she rarely changes them. That is why God said in the *Holy Bible*: "I love them that love me; and those that seek me early shall find me."

- Proverbs 8:17 (NIV)

A NEW UNIVERSE

The new condition of consciousness has been written about by many occult authors. First of all, Aleister Crowley wrote that the magician, creating new conditions of consciousness creates a new universe: "The Magus is pre-eminently the Master of Magick, that is, his Will is entirely free from internal diversion or external opposition; His work is to create a new Universe in accordance with His Will. He is the Master of the Law of Change (annica)."50 Steven Davis, in *Hammer of the Gods*, said something remarkably similar to what Crowley said about a new universe; and that Led Zeppelin was creating it: "Led Zeppelin was creating its own private universe for its fans. The music was only one part of it. Something else was going on."51 If that is not enough to convince the reader, let Jimmy Page himself tell you, from a 1975 interview with William S. Burroughs, where he said that rock music is reasserting the universe of Magick:

"Crowley has been maligned as a black magician, whereas Magick is neither white nor black, good nor bad - it is simply alive with what it is: the real thing, what people really feel and want and are. I pointed out that this 'either/or' straitjacket had been imposed by Christianity when all Magick became black Magick; that scientists took over from the Church, and Western man has been stifled in a non-magical universe known as the way things are. Rock music can be seen as one attempt to break out of this dead soulless universe and reassert the universe of Magick."

Well, there it is, right from the mouth of the magician himself. If he were not a magician, he never would have said that, would he? It is the universe of non-cognizant, but responsible to God, Devil worship, where the fans are concerned, although many have gone on to worship the Devil knowingly (Even those who are not cognizant, were at one time aware of the Christ given moral code in their primal condition of their conscience. This will be addressed in detail later in the book.).

The fan that does not know he is worshiping the Devil never stops to think that the moral code he is following is going to send him to eternal damnation. Worse yet, normally, all thoughts of God disappear. Especially with hard core anti-Christ high school and college professors teaching them evolution, the greatest joke the Devil ever played on mankind. Even these "Professors" will admit it's always more logical to believe in an uncaused cause than in never ending causes, relative to cause and effect. Since they despise God in their minds, they will tell you that the uncaused cause was a gas that caused the great explosion known as the big-bang. I do not know if God used an explosion or not, but I do know that he molded his creation into definite shapes. You've all seen the Oklahoma City bombing films on television, how much of that debris was shaped round like the earth, moon, and sun? None of it, right? Does the earth look like explosive debris to you? What about the person you are in love with, does he or she look like explosive debris? Yet, these professors command an audience. The Devil uses them to destroy thoughts of a Holy God, so he can build those minds back up as anti-Christ, with relative ease, because of the searing of the conscience, which these professors contribute to, because they destroy the absolute in the minds of the impressionable. In 1975, I watched a film in Biology class that told us we evolved and first stood upright on the plains of Africa. This is a lie, pure and simple. Then the teachers wonder why the high school kids do as they please in their behavior. These professors tell the kids that the absolute moral code in the conscience is not an absolute at all. Since there is no God, so they've been taught, morality is no absolute. We can act as we wish. What is right to you may be wrong with me, and vice-versa.

At the encouragement of these self-intellect worshiping God haters, rock fans are taught to dismiss thoughts of God. If they don't, the fan is usually deceived by the Devil to believe that since he went to church as a child, got baptized, or has denominational pride (which means worship your denomination and not Christ), he will be fine. The Devil also tells him that anyone who writes what I am writing is a mentally ill - religious fanatic. What better way to steer someone away from what will save him, than to make them think society will call them insane if they turn to the one who made them. He also has the sinful mind on his side, because he won't tell them that the reason they find Christ so repulsive is that they are looking at him through the "sin lenses." A person in love with rebellion against God despises righteousness. When the person sees that the anti-Christ moral code is destructive, especially if it has hurt him or her considerably, they can then begin to see the value of the moral code of the Lord Jesus Christ. When a person begins to do that, the Lord Jesus Christ will begin to work in their life. Since we are all sinners, it usually takes severe pain of some kind associated with sin to get us to think about forsaking the sinful life. You see, there is the sense that in seeking God you are committing a form of suicide, because you have to be willing to die to your sinful life to find him. Satan will try to stop this as best he can, and although the Devil is the most intelligent (created) being in existence, the self-existent God is smarter. Once a person begins to seek the Lord, not really knowing where to look, the Lord will draw that person to himself. You can't find God, he finds you and reveals himself to you. Lord Jesus Christ himself said: "Blessed are those who hunger and thirst for righteousness, for they shall be filled." - Matthew 5:6.

Led Zeppelin, in creating its own universe for fans through Magick, became their overlords, ruling or molding wills, relative to morals, through music. Jimmy Page, in projecting the demonic force to the mind of the sympathetic fan, makes the fan his subject, and he is the Devil's subject himself. Eliphas Levi wrote about the power of the violin bow riff: "Anything which acts strongly on the nervous system may induce impassioned exaltation, and when a skillful and persevering will knows how to direct and influence the these natural tendencies, it can use the desires of others to the profit of its own, and will soon reduce the most independent personalities into instruments of its pleasures."52 The author believes the violin bow riff was used in conjunction with the demonic force to turn the mind toward evil. Eliphas Levi also wrote of the effect of invisible evil spirits: "The absorption of one will by another frequently changes a whole series of destinies, and not for ourselves only should we watch our relations, learning to distinguish pure from impure atmospheres, for the true philters, and those most dangerous, are invisible."53 Along the same lines, Richard Cavendish wrote in *The Black Arts*: "Occultist's believe that the magician's will can be turned on other people like a ray or a beam."54 Crowley wrote it this way in *Magick Without Tears*: "The application of any given force affects all the orders of being which exist in the object to which it is applied, whichever of those orders is directly affected."55 Again, it is the condition of consciousness, specifically in the conscience, changing the moral code from right to wrong. In *The Book On Mediums*, written over a century ago, Allan Kardec wrote about this very thing: "The spirit that would do harm can do it without showing himself, and even more surely; he is not dangerous because he is a spirit, but because of the influence he can exert in the thought, turning it away from good and toward evil."56 That statement summarizes exactly what I believe Jimmy Page was doing with the violin bow, and the Theremin, as you will see. Eliphas Levi reiterates it, mentioning Frederick Mesmer the hypnotist, from where we get the term "mesmerize": "The real and serious android of the ancients was a secret which they have kept hidden from all eyes, and Mesmer was the first who dared to divulge it. It was the projection of the will of the Magus into another body, organized and served by an elementary spirit..."57 Again, Jimmy Page published a book that describes using evil spirits in this context.

Another point that needs to be made here, is that the fans are in the receptive mode, mentally. What that means is this, while Jimmy Page is performing with the bow, the fans are receptive to anything he is doing, because they came there to be entertained. They feel that his action with the bow/wand and the Theremin is merely another far out form of entertainment. You could say that the fans are ambitious about being entertained. This makes them more vulnerable to demonic suggestion, because they are receptive to what's happening to them. Eliphas Levi put it this way in *Transcendental Magic*: "In vulgar opinion, transmutations and metamorphoses have always been the very essence of Magic. Now, the crowd, being the echo of opinion, which is queen of the world, is never perfectly right or entirely wrong. Magic does change the nature of things, or rather modifies their appearances at pleasure, according to the strength of the operator's will and the fascination of ambitious adepts."58 To say the least, everyone who has watched Jimmy Page jam, has been fascinated with his ability. When he pulls out the bow, or uses the Theremin, the fascination level increases. What more do I have to say? Listen to the roar of the fans in the Led Zeppelin film as Jimmy Page is using the bow. They are fascinated to say the least. The entire mystique surrounding the band has caused millions to be fascinated with them; which made the work of Magick easier for them and the Devil. Just talk to hardcore Led Zeppelin fans about following Jesus Christ; you'll see.

BLACK MAGICK TO THE GLORY OF SATAN

After Jimmy Page uses the bow on the fans, he then begins a series of riffs against the guitar with it. I want you to take a good look at what he does initially. He takes the bow and hits the guitar, but watch his left hand. He uses it to play the guitar like a pendulum again. He hits a high note, then a lower note, and then a note even lower still. There you have three positions, like a pendulum that swings to opposite ends, pivoting in the middle. He hits the highest note first, then the middle note, then the lower note, back to the middle note, then the higher note again, and then he repeats that process one time. Just after he repeats what he is doing, he brings his left hand all the way up to the body of the guitar, then he takes his left hand down the neck to the other end, playing a series of consistently lower notes, and then he brings the left hand back up to the body of the guitar again, playing a series of consistently higher notes. The first time he hit a high, middle, and lower note to make the electric pendulum swing, and then he uses a whole series of notes to make the pendulum swing. It was two different forms of the same thing, hypnosis.

When Jimmy Page ends his playing of the riffs with the bow, he holds the bow up over his head, looking straight up in the air, and waves the bow back and forth like a pendulum again. I believe what he is doing there is praising Satan. The Magick he is performing is an act of worship to the Devil. As you can see when he stops, Robert Plant's head silhouette is over on the other side of the stage, far out of the way.

Aleister Crowley wrote about performing Magick unto the Devil, and he even mentions ruling people with the rod. Two quotes will be presented here from his book, *The Magical Record of the Beast*, the first in the context of sex Magick. Alostrael was his scarlet woman at the time: "I with Alostrael alone - we shall do Magick unto our Lord the Devil such as the Earth hath never known."59 There is not much ambiguity in that statement. As he said, the Devil was his Lord. In this next quote is the statement of the rod: "...the Sacrament that giveth thanks to Aiwaz, our Lord God the Devil, that He hath fused His Beast's soul with His Scarlet Whore's, to be One Soul completed, that It may set His image in the Temple of Man, and thrust His Will's rod over them and rule them."60 There you have Crowley referring to Aiwaz, the Holy Guardian Angel being the Devil, Lord, and God. When he talks of the fusion of his soul with his Scarlet Woman's he is referring to whatever woman is with him. Crowley made it clear to his readers that his title, the Beast, was not for him only, but that it was an office, one that he held while he was alive. The Scarlet Woman is an office, belonging to the woman who is with the Beast (Guess what Jimmy Page named his daughter? That's right, Scarlet. I am not saying that Page has incest with his daughter, I am just saying that the name is important to him.). Crowley then talks of the one fused soul of him and the scarlet woman setting the image of the Devil in the "Temple of Man." In other words, promoting the worship of the Devil among mankind. At last, he speaks of that united soul thrusting the rod of Satan's will over men and ruling them with it. Need I say more? I think not. Remember what Robert Plant said to the fans in "Immigrant Song," from *Led Zeppelin III*, that the band members are the fans' "Overlords," at 1:21 into the song. Also, the wand routine is done just after the satanic pact command. I believe the Devil is ruling the moral code of the fans through the medium of Led Zeppelin; and people like me who see it are crazy? Look at the evidence here!

THE POWER OF "ZoSo"

In the film, as Jimmy Page is staring up in the air above him as he holds the bow pointed straight up, you can see that the lights are not only on him, but on his Magick rune, ZoSo, at the same time. The following will explain the significance. You know that I believe "ZoSo" means the "Mark of the Beast-666." Speaking of runes in this context, Edred Thorsson wrote, in his book, *Runelore*: "It could conceal the name of the magician, or it could be a combination of certain runes for magical effect."61 The same theme is elaborated on by Thorsson in same book: "All of the inscriptions serve as a kind of initiatory declaration of power in which the runemaster carves one or more of his magical nicknames or titles. This type of formula can be used to sanctify an area, to protect it, or even cause certain specific modifications in the environment."62

In the Norse Mythology, which is no myth, because Satan is behind it, a magician is referred to as a "vitki." Here is a quote that makes it pretty clear why Jimmy Page has ZoSo painted on the speaker, from Edred Thorsson's *Futhark- A Handbook of Rune Magic*: "Whether or not the vitki is performing a talsimanic loading ritual, a symbol describing the particular runic operation may be formed to serve as a lasting outward symbol of the holy inner process that takes place in the rite. This is usually a bind rune or rune row, which is incised into or painted on a board or paper. This should be displayed in some place where the vitki will see it regularly and thus constantly reaffirm his or her link to the magical force."63 The author believes that Jimmy Page's rune being painted on the speaker behind him also lets the fan, who deciphers it with Crowley's *Equinox*, know what Page is trying to communicate with his rune, that he holds the office of Anti-Christ in magical operations. Again, in *Runelore,* this concept is presented: "Runic inscriptions represent messages - sendings - of a mysterious nature. They are complex and symbolic communications, which are only sometimes 'legible' in the sense of natural language."64

In the book, *The Cloud Upon the Sanctuary*, by Karl von Eckartshausen, which is the book that ignited Aleister Crowley's magical career, Eckartshausen wrote of sages who used symbols long ago to communicate the interior knowledge of magic, to the exterior, or the uninitiated multitudes: "This society of sages communicated, according to time and circumstances, unto the exterior societies their symbolic hieroglyphs, in order to attract man to the great truths of their interior."65 Eckartshausen elaborated on that statement with this one: "The exterior symbol is only the sheath which holds the inner; it may change and multiply, but it can never weaken the truth of the interior; moreover, it was necessary; we ought to seek it and try to decipher it to discover the meaning of the spiritual interior."66

Edred Thorsson made it clear that Jimmy Page's rune can also help to assist him in working his magical will on the fans: "In the magical realms, runework is used for personal transformation, building wider consciousness, psychic development, healing, investigation of Wyrd, and shaping the environment according to the inner will."67

You read in chapter five that Aleister Crowley wanted to help others escape from Jesus, because Christianity restricted men, in his opinion, from living life to its fullest. In chapter seven you read where *The Book of the Law* says that the word defining sin in the Devil's eyes was restriction. This too is the mission of Jimmy Page I believe, assigned to him personally by the Devil, to free men from Christianity, or restriction. Page was quoted in chapter ten as having said that "…repression is the greatest work of sin." He also said doing the true will was "…a process of self liberation." Edred Thorsson also wrote of the magic rune's ability to free men from restriction, in *Futhark-A Handbook of Rune Magic*: "Runes are especially valuable in magical works concerning victory, success, protection, rescue from restriction, love, and the gaining of wisdom."68 The rune helps the magician obtain "victory" against Christianity in the mind of the fan. This is in keeping with their claim to be the fans' "overlords" in "Immigrant Song."

We are going to look at two more quotes on the runes before we ascend the "misty mountain" with Jimmy Page to meet the Devil at the top. As you read in the last chapter, concerning what I believe was the Devil's providing Jimmy Page with his rune during the Abramelin Operation, that evil spirits would then be sworn to observe the symbol, and perform operations thereby. Michael Howard, in his book, *Understanding Runes*, wrote of the spirits being associated with runes, and then he speaks of the gods of the Norse religion, and how Christianity attacked the use of runes: "We referred earlier to the elemental spirits associated with the runes which were regarded as the major source of their mysterious power. In some cases these entities are the gods and goddesses of the Old Norse religion. As runecraft faded under the baleful influence of the Christian Church and its black-robed priests, the once mighty gods of the north degenerated into lesser spirits, faeries or demons. There is an old saying, which is very true, that the gods of the old religion become the devils of the new one, and the debasement of the pagan deities by Christianity is a prime example of this in action."69

This section is going to conclude with basically the same theme as the last quote, but the capstone of the information of the runes must come right from *The Book of the Sacred Magic of Abramelin the Mage* itself. It sums up what I believe is Jimmy Page's use of ZoSo: "Pentacles and Symbols are valuable as an equilibrated and fitting basis for the reception of Magical force; but unless the Operator can really attract that force to them, they are nothing but so many dead, and to him worthless, diagrams. But used by the Initiate who fully comprehends their meaning, they become to him a powerful protection and aid, seconding and focusing the workings of his Will."70 Now you know why Robert Plant sang that the magical "runes" were engraved on "gold" in order that "balance," might be restored, in "The Battle of Evermore." The Satanist believes that the balance is between Satan and mankind, and Christianity upsets this balance, or congruence. The job of the evil spirits, at the command of Satanists, is to restore the balance between man and the Devil. They are doing a very good job of it too. Now we are going to look at the Operation of Abramelin the Mage illustrated, which is becoming one with the Holy Guardian Angel, Satan.

LED ZEPPELIN (RUNES) IV – "MISTY MOUNTAIN HOP"

In the song, "Misty Mountain Hop," Robert Plant sings that he is "packing" his "bags" to head to a "mountain," that is surrounded by mist, because that is the place where "spirits" congregate, at 3:44 into the song. For the purpose of this section of the book, as you might guess, we are going to talk about the king of the evil spirits manifesting himself on top of the mountain. If you open up Led Zeppelin's fourth album to look at the inside cover, or pull out the cd booklet that contains it, or the cassette cover that contains it, you will see that this mountain is indeed "misty." Barrington Colby, who painted it for Jimmy Page, represents the mountain as misty all around. The song "Misty Mountian Hop" is on this album. Therefore, it is safe to conclude that he is talking about this mountain. At the bottom of the mountain is a long-haired person, staring up at the Hermit, standing up at the top of the hill with a lantern containing a hexagram, a six-sided star, in his hand. The person is to make the trip up the mountain to unite with the Hermit, as Jimmy Page made clear when he participated in climbing the mountain behind Boleskine House in Scotland to unite with the Hermit at the top, who I will prove is none other than the Devil himself. First we are going to examine Aleister Crowley's version of this taken from the *Equinox*, where I believe Jimmy Page got the idea. Remember that Page named his bookstore in London *Equinox*, and that he sold the *Equinox* ten volume set this quote comes from. Also, Page has said Crowley was *"an unidentified genius of the twentieth century."* He made that statement because of writings like the *Equinox*.

CROWLEY'S "EQUINOX" AND THE MYSTIC MOUNTAIN

In 1917, Aleister Crowley wrote his famous magical novel, *Moonchild*. In it he wrote these words about his famous *Equinox,* which he had completed four years earlier:

"Some tradition has been preserved by societies of wise men, who, because of the persecutions, when to possess any other book than a missal might be construed as heresy, concealed themselves and whispered the old teaching one to another.

"The nineteenth century saw the overthrow of most of the old ecclesiastical tyranny, and in the beginning of the twentieth it was found once more possible to make public the knowledge. The wise men gathered together, discovered a student who was trustworthy and possessed of the requisite literary ability; and by him the old knowledge was revised and made secure; it was finally published in a sort of periodical encyclopedia (already almost impossible to find, such was the demand for it) entitled *The Equinox*."71

Twenty six years later, four years before his death, Crowley reiterated it in *Magick Without Tears*: "The New Aeon was to supersede the old; my special job was to preserve the Sacred Tradition, so that a new Renaissance might in due season rekindle the hidden Light, I was accordingly to make a Quintessence of the Ancient Wisdom, and publish it in as permanent a form as possible. This I did in *The Equinox*."72

The previous two statements were from Aleister Crowley, but others were saying it too. Just one example is here shown from W.B. Crow, in the book, *Witchcraft, Magic, and Occultism*: "The official organ of the A.A. and O.T.O. was the *Equinox*."73

This following passage comes out of *The Equinox*. In the beginning of it he makes mention of the reader becoming god. This is the essence of his teaching. That once a man attains the Knowledge and Conversation of the Holy Guardian Angel, he is given supernatural power and himself becomes god on earth, doing the will of god with supernatural power (This again is what I believe Plant is referring to when he calls the fan "human" in "Dazed and Confused," that he had become god on earth). Eliphas Levi clarified the concept: "God operates by his works - in heaven by angels and on earth by men. Hence, in the circle of angelic action, the angels can perform all that is possible for God, and in the human circle of action men can dispose equally of Divine Omnipotence."74

Here is Crowley's writing of the trip up what he calls the "mystic mountain," to meet the Devil at the top, which tells the tale of the magician's quest to attain the Knowledge and Conversation of the Holy Guardian Angel while ascending up the grades of the Qabalah. Again, the following is taken from *The Equinox* (The Led Zeppelin film was subtitled, "In Concert and Beyond."):

"Thus it happens that until you become God, God Himself is in Reality The Tempter, Satan, and the Prince of Darkness, who, assuming the glittering robes of Time and Space, whispers in our ears: 'Millions and millions and millions of eternities are as nothingness to me; then how canst thou, thou little mote dancing in the beam of mine eye, hope to span me?' Thus God at the outset comes to us and like the old witch in 'Cinderella' strews innumerable lentils before us to count - but begin! And soon you will find that you have left the kitchen of the world behind you and have entered the enchanted Palace 'Beyond.'

"It is all very difficult and complex at first; it is rather like a man who, setting out by a strange road to visit the capital of his country, comes to a great mountain and gazes up its all but endless slopes.

'It is too high for me to climb,' the little man will say; 'it is indeed very beautiful; but I will go back and find some other road.'

'I am sure it would be too long a journey,' says a second; 'I could not afford it; I too will return.'

'There are no guides here,' says a third; 'how foolish for me to attempt so high a peak.'

'I am not strong enough,' says a fourth. 'I have no chart.'…'My business won't let me.'... 'My wife is against it.'

"Thus God enters the heart of man in a thousand forms and tempts man as he tempted Eve in the Garden of Eden, and Abraham in the land of Moriah.

"But the strong man replenishing his wallet, and filling his flask, girds a goat-skin about him, and taking his staff sets forth on his Great travel to the Summit of the Mountain of God; and curious to relate, and terrible to tell, the whole length of that wizard way Satan follows behind him in the form of a sleuth-hound ever tempting him from the right path.

"Now he is overcome by a great loneliness, he is cold, he is hungry, he thirsts; the skyline he had thought the summit is but a ridge, and from it he sees ridge upon ridge in endless succession above him. On he toils, at length it is the summit - no! But another ridge and a myriad more. A thousand fiends enter him, a thousand little sleuth-hounds that would tear him back - comfort, home, children, wife; then he says to himself: What a fool am I!

"At this stage many turn back and crawling into the valley of illusions reason how much more comfortable and interesting it is to read of mountain ascents than to accomplish them. These ones talk loudly and beat the drums of their valour in the ears of all men.

"At the next stage few return, most perish on the way back; for the higher you climb that great mountain the more difficult it becomes to return.

"Plod on, and when your legs tremble and give way under you, crawl on, crawl on if on all fours, and clench your teeth and say 'I WILL'; but on! and on! and on! And behind you tireless strides along that old greyhound ever breathing forth temptations upon you; filled with crafts, and subtleties, and guiles, ever eager to lead you astray, ever ready to guide you back. And presently so great grows the loneliness of the Mountain that his very companionship becomes as a temptation to you, you feel friendliness in resisting him, a burning hope that he will continue to tempt you, that his temptations and his mocking words are better than no words at all. This only happens far far up the mountain slope, some say not so far from the summit; but take heed! For at this stage there is a great precipice, and those who look round for the hound may perchance stumble and fall - and the foot of that precipice is the valley from which they came.

From here all is darkness, and there are no roads to guide the pilgrim, and the sleuth-hound can no more be seen because of the shadows of the night which obscure all things. And how can one write further about these matters? For those who have been so far and have returned, on account of the darkness saw nothing, therefore they have held their tongues. But there is an old parable which relates how the hound that had tempted man the whole length of his perilous journey, devoured him on the Summit of that Mystic Mountain; and how that Ancient DOG was indeed GOD Himself."75

Aleister Crowley presents a picture of some who would have liked to become magicians and the one who did. Those who didn't failed to climb the hill. Those who did were successful at scaling the mountain. Satan, or "God" as Crowley calls him, tempts the man all the way up the hill to test his resolve. When the man makes it to the top, he is devoured by the Devil. In other words, he becomes one with Satan and is possessed of the Devil the rest of his days.

A few points in the passage need to be emphasized. First of all, beginning the journey is likened by Crowley to entering "the enchanted Palace 'Beyond.'" Jimmy Page, wanting the potential follower of Magick to make the connection, has "In Concert and Beyond," written on the cardboard video and dvd cases that *The Song Remains the Same* is now distributed in.

The second point I want you to notice is that Crowley describes the Devil as a greyhound in the passage. In the 1994 *No Quarter* Video, Page/Plant, the new Led Zeppelin, play "Nobody's Fault But Mine" and "When the Levee Breaks" on a flat clearing on a side of a mountain with a greyhound walking around in the midst of the group. The camera focuses on him several times. Now, why is he there? There are those who will say it is Robert Plant's dog, and so what? What is he doing on that mountain, and why does the camera focus on him repeatedly? In light of Crowley's *Equinox*, there is no mystery for this author.

The last two points that need to be emphasized is that the climber up the mountain is encouraged to crawl on all fours if need be. This climber is then devoured by the Devil at the top; Satan takes complete permanent possession of the individual (meaning he comes and goes at will). These last two points will be acted out by Jimmy Page in the following description of his climbing up the same mountain as he presented it in the Led Zeppelin film, right after the violin bow section; which took place after the command to make the satanic pact.

JIMMY PAGE BECOMES POSSESSED BY THE DEVIL

We left off the discussion of the violin bow scene in the Led Zeppelin film with Jimmy Page having just played several riffs on the guitar with the bow, just after the projection on the audience. After playing the riffs, Page begins to play the guitar with the bow as he would a violin, to once again make demonic sounds reverberate through Madison Square Garden and the minds of the fans. Ritchie Yorke, in *Led Zeppelin - The Definitive Biography*, calls it "Sonic sensory stimulation."76 Having lived through it at Madison Square Garden myself, I concur with him completely. Jimmy Page then walks over to the camera in front of him and begins to play with the camera focusing up on him from a low angle. As he starts to play, his head disappears into a full moon, as the scene changes from Manhattan, New York, to the hill behind Boleskine House in Scotland, which is Joe Massot's filming of Jimmy Page ascending the mountain the way Crowley described. Several writers have stated that the mountain was indeed the one behind Boleskine House. Ritchie Yorke presents Joe Massot's comments on the filming: "'Jimmy's film was rather strange,' said Massot, in an avalanche of understatement. 'Jimmy felt that he wanted to say something about time and the passage thereof. There's a mountain out the back of his place, Boleskine House, on the shores of Loch Ness in Scotland. So Jimmy decided that he would climb it and act out a symbolical tale about a young man fighting his way to the top to meet with the old man of the mountain at the summit, Father Time in symbolism. Jimmy plays both parts in the film. He insisted that his segment be shot on the night of a full moon.'"77 Passage of Time? Give me a break! Please remember that Page insisted on a full moon. Also remember, this ascending of the mountain in the film is two fold, to illustrate Crowley's *Equinox*, and the inside cover of Led Zeppelin's fourth album.

In the January 1998 issue of Guitar World, Jimmy Page said this about the inner cover of that album: "The illustration on the inside was my idea. It is the Hermit character from the Tarot, a symbol of self-reliance and wisdom, and it was drawn by Barrington Colby."78 Jimmy Page is lying in that quote. Crowley wrote that when a magician unites with Satan he has to die to his own way of thinking, in *Liber Samekh*: "The Adept must be ready for the utter destruction of his point-of-view on any subject, and even that of his innate conception of the forms and laws of thought." 79 That is anything but self-reliance. That's the way it is for Led Zeppelin, painting a phony picture for the non-sympathetic person, one who is not sympathetic to their Devil worship. Those, like myself, who make it a point to study the entire spectrum of teachings presented by Led Zeppelin, receive a totally different picture. It is one that the non-seeker will never come in contact with; unless he reads a book like this one, of course. However, this book throws a monkey wrench in that plan of Jimmy Page and the Devil. The Hermit on that mountain, according to Satan, Crowley, and Page, is not self-reliance, it is the destroying of the individuality and giving yourself completely over to the Devil, as you will see.

As far as his fantasy scene in the film is concerned, Jimmy Page had this to say in the book, *Led Zeppelin - In Their Own Words*: "It was like when we chose a symbol for the fourth album. We each went away and came up with an idea. It gave an insight into each personality, whether it be tongue-in-cheek or deadly serious."80 After you are done reading this section, you will know that Jimmy Page is deadly serious about his "fantasy" scene. One should know by now that he is as deadly serious as a person could get.

As the fantasy scene begins, again, Page's head disappears into a full moon. As you just read, he insisted that it be shot on a night of a full moon, which is significant. As Rosemary Ellen Guiley put it in *The Encyclopedia of Witches and Witchcraft*: "Magical power is greatest on nights of the full moon, particularly at midnight."81 Crowley had this to say about the moon, in his appropriately titled book, *Moonchild*: "In Astrology, the moon, among its other meanings, has that of 'the common people,' who submit (they know not why) to any independent will that can express itself with sufficient energy."82 The parenthetical content was Crowley's in that last quote, not mine. Lewis Spence wrote this about the moon and its magical significance in his book, *Ancient Egyptian Myths and Legends*: "Again, it must be borne in mind that, for some reason still obscure, the moon is regarded as the great reservoir of magical power."83

As Jimmy Page begins his fantasy scene, we see a distant view of Loch Ness at night, with the mountain on the other side of the Loch. The camera crosses the Loch to the top of the mountain, to show a full moon with clouds blowing by. Jimmy is then seen ascending the mountain, sometimes on all fours, crawling, just as Aleister Crowley wrote. At the top of the hill is the Hermit, who as you will see in a totally different Crowley quote, is the Devil himself. The Hermit is looking down at Page as he climbs ever upward. He holds the lantern in his right hand, and the Magick staff in his left hand, just like the fourth album's inside cover presents it. As Jimmy reaches the top, the Hermit leans down to look at him. Page, in a moment of euphoria, reaches for him with a big smile on his face. Then the camera gives you a front view of the Hermit bent over. As he begins to stand up, the violin bow is played with furious intensity. As you look into the hood of the Hermit, you see Jimmy Page's face. As you read in quote 77, Page played both parts in the film. This is exactly what the Devil said when Aleister Crowley wrote the following verses under his inspiration, in a writing called *Liber A'ash:*

"17. Now shalt thou adore me who am the Eye and the Tooth, the Goat of the Spirit, the Lord of Creation. I am the Eye in the Triangle, the Silver Star that ye adore.

18. I am Baphomet, that is the Eightfold Word that shall be equilibrated with the Three.

19. There is no act or passion that shall not be a hymn in mine honour.

20. All holy things and all symbolic things shall be my sacraments.

21. These animals are sacred unto me; the goat, and the duck, and the ass, and the gazelle, the man, the woman, and the child.

22. All corpses are sacred unto me; they shall not be touched save in mine eucharist. All lonely places are sacred unto me; where one man gathereth himself together in my name, there will I leap forth in the midst of him."84

That is exactly what Crowley said would happen to him who ascended the mystic mountain, that he would be devoured by the Devil: "But there is an old parable which relates how the hound that had tempted man the whole length of his perilous journey, devoured him on the Summit of the Mystic Mountain;

and how that Ancient Dog was indeed GOD Himself."85

What you are about to read, in several quotes necessary for emphasis, is that this has direct reference to the death of the individual behavior (NOT self-reliance), and becoming one with Satan to do his will, as his servant. Crowley wrote about doing that on the mountain behind Boleskine House in the light of the moon: "Broken at last, he went to the topmost point of the hill which crowns his estate, at midnight, and there, as we read in the diary, 'I once more solemnly renounced all that I have or am. On departing, instantly shone the moon, two days before her fullness, over the hill among the clouds.'"86 He reiterated the theme of death of the individuality in "Book 4:" "For to each individual thing attainment means first and foremost the destruction of the individuality."87 Richard Cavendish, in *The Black Arts*, wrote the same concept of the death of self in relation to Qabalah teaching: "To reach godhead, he must destroy himself as an individual man and identify himself with the universe, which is God."88 This is the essence of the Knowledge and Conversation of the Holy Guardian Angel, Satan, to end individuality and unite with him as his servant and be "god" on earth. Once more, this is what I believe motivated Plant to call the fan "human" in "Dazed and Confused," because he had attained unity with "god" and became god on earth; as the satanic teaching goes. Israel Regardie wrote of this in his Crowley biography, *The Eye in the Triangle*: "It is to effect this redemption of the personality, to regenerate and transmute the enormous power of the red dragon, and attempt to bring the individual to some realization of his potential godhead, that is the object of the Adeptus Minor ceremony."89 Again, Adeptus Minor is the grade on the Qabalah where the magician is to perform the Operation of Abramelin the Mage. Crowley wrote that this redemption takes place as in the form of communication resulting from the "Secret Magick" having been taught to him by Satan. This too is taken from *Liber Samekh*:

"The Adept asserts his right to enter into conscious communication with His Angel, on the ground that that Angel has Himself taught him the Secret Magick by which he may make the proper link."90 Once the personality has been linked to, redeemed, or possessed by Satan, then the spiritually regenerated magician will have transmuted to him the power of the red dragon, who is Satan; thereby making the magician "god" on earth. Crowley wrote of this, saying that the magician must spend the rest of his life as the Devil's possession in *Magick Without Tears*: "It should never be forgotten for a single moment that the central and essential work of the Magicians is the Attainment of the Knowledge and Conversation of the Holy Guardian Angel. Once he has achieved this he must of course be left entirely in the hands of that Angel..."91 Crowley wrote of the possession by Satan in *Liber Samekh* as well, which again, was his epistle for the working of the Operation of Abramelin: "...the Adept must be in communion with his Angel, so that his Soul is suffused with sublimity, whether intelligible or not in terms of intellect. It is evident that the stress of such spiritual possession must tend to overwhelm the soul, especially at first." 92 The reader should know, that the subtitles Crowley gave to *Liber Samekh* were THEURGIA GOETIA SUMMA and CONGRESSUS CUM DAEMONE. THEURGIA GOETIA SUMMA is translated *High Supernatural Black Magic*. The title of CONGRESSUS CUM DAEMONE is translated *Intercourse with the Demon*. The title page of *Liber Samekh* reads this way:

Liber Samekh
theurgia goetia summa
(CONGRESSUS CUM DAEMONE)
sub figura dccc

being the Ritual employed by the Beast 666 for the Attainment of the Knowledge and Conversation of His Holy Guardian Angel during the Semester of His Performance of the Operation of the Sacred Magick of ABRAMELIN THE MAGE

I don't think I will ever read a more evil document for the rest of my days. The title page also called *Liber Samekh* an "OFFICIAL PUBLICATION of A.A." A.A. being the abbreviation for the Silver Star. This document teaches the black magician how to unite with, or become possessed by the Devil, and Crowley said the possession would be permanent. Crowley's teaching is holding up, because Page and Plant mocked Lord Jesus Christ in "Most High" on *Walking Into Clarksdale* in 1998. It seems that Jimmy is still in Satan's possession, as one can hear on the 2000 edition of Page/Crowes on cd, titled *Live at the Greek*, where he has Chris Robinson singing the original lyrics of "Nobody's Fault But Mine" that refer to Satan as the one who taught them to rock and roll. Dr. Sir J. G. Frazer, who Crowley wrote influenced his *Confessions*, said the same exact thing this way in *The Golden Bough*: "...while the distinction between the human and the divine is still imperfectly drawn, it is often imagined that men may themselves attain to godhead, not merely after their death, but in their lifetime, through the temporary or permanent possession of their whole nature by a great and powerful spirit."93

Do any of the previous quotes paint a picture of self-reliance to you? Jimmy Page was lying about the Hermit being a symbol of self-reliance. To him it is anything but. He shows it in the *Song Remains the Same* to be possession by the Devil, when one considers the fact that Robert Plant just commanded the fans to sell their souls to Satan, in conjunction with the writings of Crowley, which only the sympathetic followers are supposed to examine; when it comes to *The Equinox* and *Liber Samekh*. Richard Cavendish, in *The Black Arts*, gave an excellent Qabalah description of what is happening here as the magician allows himself to be possessed by "god":

"Man achieves union with God by climbing up through the sephiroth to reach their source. Each sephira is guarded by an order of angels and these guardians will try to turn the climber back. And in the lower spheres there are plenty of sinister intelligences that are very ready to trap an aspiring soul which is ignorant or careless.

"Although many cabalists have led devout and blameless lives, thick veins of magic and sorcery are not far beneath the Cabala's surface. The essential doctrine of the cabalists is that death is not a necessary preliminary to the soul's ascent through the spheres. The soul can climb the ladder of the sephiroth while still in the body and man can make himself God on earth."94

For man to become god is exactly what Crowley taught in his book, *The Law is For All*: "The New Aeon proclaims Man as Immortal God, eternally active to do His Will."95 Crowley reiterated that statement in his *Equinox*, claiming that the magician's entire life becomes one big magical exercise: "Right Speech is a furthering of Right Aspirations. It consists of a discipline wherein a man not only converses with his Holy Guardian Angel, but outwardly and inwardly lives up to His holy conversation, turning his whole life into one stupendous magical exercise to enter that Silence which is beyond all thought."96 Crowley wrote in *Liber Samekh* that the Angel and the Adept would go forward together on the earth: "This recapitulation demands the going forth together of the Adept and his Angel 'to do their pleasure on the Earth among the living.'"97

It was at this time of his life, when he bought Boleskine, that Page produced "Stairway to Heaven," which the reader will come to understand is indeed the message of hope for the Thelemic Satanist of the Silver Star. All of the preceding quotes on the Holy Guardian Angel illustrate clearly Jimmy Page's motivation for having the fans commanded by Robert Plant to sell their souls to the Devil, as well as his climbing the mountain to illustrate Crowley's teaching on uniting with him. Again, you can look at the film, and see that just before Plant gives the command to sell your soul, Page gives him the cue with a look.

Richard Cole summed up the previous quotes by writing of something inside Page, which is according to the evidence, Satan (who comes and goes):

"Led Zeppelin were more than musicians, although it was hard for most people to see beyond their music. I had always felt that, more than the others, Jimmy was much too complex an individual to be living for music alone. I knew that his dabbling in the occult continued, although he still kept that side of his life very private.

"On occasion, he would mention the name Aleister Crowley to me....If the public felt there was certain mystery surrounding Led Zeppelin, they weren't alone. As close as I was to them, I sometimes felt there was something within Jimmy that he never let anyone see. Particularly when it came to Page's preoccupation with Crowley, seances, and black magic, I had a lot of unanswered questions."98 If you were telling the truth Richard, you know now. Follow Christ!

I believe that the "something within Jimmy" is the Devil himself. When Satan isn't there, I believe another very powerful demon is, at times. You can, however, be sure that Page and the Devil are good buddies. Again, the reason for that is the Devil has been able to incarnate himself in Jimmy Page. Page was the one with the ability to play Led Zeppelin's music, and that's why I believe the Devil gave it to him, as you will see later. Jimmy Page was and is one of the most powerful plenipotentiaries or authorized representatives (ambassador) on this planet that the Devil has ever had. The Devil's motive, again, is to program the mind of the human being to be confirmed in the anti-Christ lifestyle, so the soul will be damned after death. Remember the quote from Time-Life Books' *The Enchanted World-Wizards and Witches,* that the Devil was more than happy to make deals with occultists, because he would achieve his purpose to an even greater degree that way.99 Now we will examine the meaning of all the faces of Jimmy Page as The Hermit and Satan.

THE DEVIL AND JIMMY PAGE PROMOTING THE QABALAH

As The Hermit (Jimmy Page) stands up, you see his face in the midst of a violent surge on the guitar with the violin bow, with Robert Plant belting out yells into the microphone. The camera then zooms in on Jimmy's face, leaving all the surrounding area out of the picture, making it a circular picture, just like the round emanations of the Qabalah (Chapter Eight). In the Qabalah chapter, you read that the father impregnates the mother and brings forth the son and daughter. What you are about to see is the acting out of the facts presented in the Qabalah.

The first face you see when Page stands up is Kether. The faces get younger as each face manifests itself in sequence. The first three faces are more on the gray side. This represents Macroprosopus, the Crown, the father and mother, and the Silver Star. The second set of three faces represents the Rosicrucians. The second and third set of three faces, four through nine, represent the son, Microprosopus. The seventh through tenth faces, the ones without beards, represent the Hermetic Order of the Golden Dawn. The tenth face by itself represents Malkuth, the Devil's people. The tenth face has a pentagram between the eyes. This matches the teaching of the Qabalah. The fourth album inner cover has the hexagram in the lantern. This matches the teaching of the Qabalah as well. The macrocosm is represented by the hexagram and the microcosm by the pentagram. After the tenth face, there is an eleventh one, not on the Qabalah. What this face means, the youngest one, is the son, Microprosopus. The next thing you see is a fetus with the little crown at the top of the forehead, as it is commonly referred to. Then you see the moon. After the moon appears, a bolt of lightning flashes across the screen. What this all means is the union of the goddess, the moon, with the sun (lightning is caused by heat from the sun), the god, brings forth the son. Aleister Crowley wrote about lightning coming from Satan in *Liber Samekh*: "O Lion-Serpent Sun The Beast, that whirlest forth, a thunderbolt, begetter of Life!....Thou Satan-Sun Hadit..."100 There it is, he who sends the thunderbolt is the begetter of life, and his name is Satan, the sun, and Hadit of *The Book of the Law*. After the thunderbolt, the moon disappears, and the eleventh face appears again. What has happened at this point, is he has married the daughter, Malkuth, who has become one with him. He then takes the place of the tenth face. Then the faces begin to grow older as the trip back up the Qabalah takes place. As you see, if you are watching the film, the face with the pentagram between the eyes has disappeared. Again, that is because the son married her and she became one with him. The ascension hits each of the ten emanations of the Qabalah until it reaches the original face, which is Kether. Crowley himself said that Kether was on the summit of the mystic mountain: "Visions are real, inspirations are real, revelation is real, and so is genius; but these are from Kether, and the highest climber on the mystic mountain is he who will obtain the finest view, and from its summit all things will be shown unto him."101 Who is it that hops around from one mystic mountain to another? It is the Devil and his disciples.

The next thing that The Hermit (Jimmy Page) on the mountain summit does is bring his staff, which is a Magick wand, over his head to his right and then back to his left. This, I believe, expresses the concept of the Qabalah that teaches though the religions of the world differ in appearance, they are still all one. These concepts are now going to be backed up with quotes from Crowley and others, that will make the picture perfectly clear to you, including a quote from Crowley that will tell you that the Hermit on the inside cover of Led Zeppelin's fourth album is none other than Satan himself; beyond any doubt.

THE UNITING OF THE MICROCOSM WITH THE MACROCOSM

Aleister Crowley, in his *Equinox*, quoted an ancient magician named Hermes, who spoke of the Microcosm being like the Macrocosm, and vice versa: "That which is below is like that which is above, and that which is above is like that which is below..."102 Aleister Crowley went on to say that the objective of the magician is to unite the two: "...the object of any magick ceremony is to unite the Macrocosm and the Microcosm."103 By way of review, the hexagram represents the macrocosm, written in *The Qabalah Unveiled*: "...the symbol of the interlaced triangles, forming the six-pointed star, is called the Sign of the macrocosm, or of the creation of the greater world..."104 Eliphas Levi also wrote of it in *Transcendental Magic*: "These two triangles, combined in a single figure, which is the six-pointed star, form the sacred symbol of Solomon's Seal, the resplendent Star of the Macrocosm. The notion of the Infinite and the Absolute is expressed by this sign, which is the grand pantacle - that is to say, the most simple and complete abridgement of the science of all things."105

Eliphas Levi also wrote of the pentagram being the sign of the microcosm: "The Pentagram is called in Kabalah the Sign of the Microcosm..."106 Malkuth, the earth, the lesser world, is the tenth sephira, the second H in the Tetragrammaton, IHVH, as written in *The Qabalah Unveiled*: "For five is H, *He*, the number of the feminine letter in the Tetragrammaton, the number also of the Microcosm or Lesser World, the symbol or sign of which is the Pentagram."107

Levi wrote of another ancient magician named Paracelsus. He made it clear that the hexagram and the pentagram are the two most powerful signs that compel spirits: "Paracelsus, that innovator in Magic, who surpassed all other initiates in his unaided practical success, affirms that every magical figure and every kabalistic sign of the pantacles which compel spirits, may be reduced to two, which are the synthesis of all the others; these are the Sign of the Macrocosm or the Seal of Solomon, the form of which we have given already, and that of the Microcosm, more potent even than that of the first - that is to say, the Pentagram, of which he provides a most minute description in his occult philosophy."108

The Hermit, Satan, is holding a lantern with the hexagram in it, on the inner cover of Led Zeppelin's fourth album. The tenth face on the group of faces of the Hermit, in the Led Zeppelin film, Malkuth in the Qabalah, has a pentagram on it, between the eyes, just above the eyebrow. Crowley said that the object of any magical ceremony is to unite the two. Robert Plant said magic runes were engraved on gold to restore the balance. In the following quote by Crowley, you will see the balance Plant sang about. Before reading it, you have to know the definition of the word "Equilibration."

EQUILIBRATE – "to bring into or be in equilibrium; balance or counterbalance."109

COUNTERBALANCE – "1. A weight used to balance another weight; counterpoise. 2. Any force or influence that balances or offsets another."110

Crowley wrote of the balance that is sought by the magician, as being between the hexagram and the pentagram: "...the formula of ABRAHADABRA concerns us, as men, principally because each of us represents the pentagram or microcosm, and our equilibration must therefore be with the hexagram or macrocosm."111 This is what Crowley wrote about, and it is what Jimmy Page acted out in the Led Zeppelin movie. You will see the word ABRAHADABRA again in the fifteenth chapter. The word means the act of the uniting of the microcosm with the macrocosm; the union of man with god (Satan).

In the eighth chapter, on the Qabalah, you were taught that IHVH was the Tetragrammaton, the word, according to occultists, that contains the entire universe. The I being the Yod, the father, the H being He, the supernal mother, the V being the Vau, the son, and the second H being He, the bride of the son. You were also taught that the father impregnates the mother and brings forth the son and daughter (the earth-mankind). Then you learned that the son marries the daughter and lifts her back up the Qabalah to be placed on the throne of the mother and then they are all drawn back into the Crown, Kether, where the father and son are the same being, Satan, with the Goddess and the daughter. This is exactly what Jimmy Page advertised in the ten faces. Crowley makes reference to this and says there is a connection between the Magick wand activity and the marrying of the son and daughter. It is a statement made directly to his future students of Magick, or magicians, who would use the Magick wand to perform the Great Work; so it could be said that he is talking to Jimmy Page: "This Magical Will is the wand in your hand by which the Great Work is accomplished, by which the Daughter is not merely set upon the throne of the Mother, but assumed into the Highest."(2)112 The parentheses represent the second footnote on the page, the footnote that refers to that quote. It tells the story of the Great Work: "(2) In one, the best, system of Magick, the Absolute is called the Crown, God is called the Father, the Pure Soul is called the Mother, the Holy Guardian Angel is called the Son, and the Natural Soul is called the Daughter. The Son purifies the Daughter by wedding her; she thus becomes the Mother, the uniting of whom with the Father absorbs all into the Crown."113

You just read in the quote where Crowley calls the Daughter the "Natural Soul." This was what I believe Robert Plant was talking about in the last chapter, at the beginning of the live version of "Dazed and Confused," when he told the fans that the "soul" belonging to a specific "woman" had been made "below" (the rest of the Sephiroth), and then he yells to the fans that they are that woman, twice, at 1:58 into the song off the live album, and in the film. There you have it. It all fits together perfectly like a puzzle. The woman is the lady that is purchasing her "Stairway to Heaven." This will be examined in chapter fifteen.

For the daughter to be married by the son, who as you saw in that quote is the Holy Guardian Angel, it is the union of the Devil with man. It is the "All" getting "redeemed" at 0:49 into the song, "Kashmir," off the *Physical Graffiti* album. One more time, Crowley presents this redemption in his book, *The Book of Thoth*: "It is the final adjustment in the formula of Tetragrammaton, when the daughter, redeemed by her marriage with the Son, is thereby set up on the throne of the mother; thus, finally, she 'awakens the Eld of the All-Father.'"114 Finally, he says this keeps the universe stable and eternal: "The Union of the Father and the Mother produces Twins, the son going forward to the daughter, the daughter returning the energy to the father; by this cycle of change the stability and eternity of the Universe are assured."115 These teachings are all lies fathered by the Devil.

LIBER SAMEKH - AT THE ABBEY OF THELEMA IN SICILY 1921

In the last chapter, you saw, clearly, Led Zeppelin's command to sell your soul to the Devil. In this chapter, you read of Crowley's account of climbing the mountain behind Boleskine House in Scotland to meet the Devil at the top. You saw the Qabalah represented by the different faces of the Hermit. Now you are going to read the punch line. The quote is from Aleister Crowley's *Liber Samekh*. You already read in this chapter where the Devil told Crowley that he was the eye in the triangle and the lord of creation. In the 1994 revised version of Aleister Crowley's book *Magick*, now renamed *Magick-Book 4*Liber Aba*, by Samuel Weiser Inc., in Yorke Beach, Maine, *Liber Samekh* is included. This is the same book that has Jimmy Page's name in the acknowledgments, thanking him for his contributions, on page XV. Before reading the quote from *Liber Samekh*, here is a quote from the same book to prepare the reader for an accurate understanding of what Crowley was saying. He writes of how the Devil, as the Holy Guardian Angel, longs to become one with the "aspirant": "The Holy Guardian Angel has always the necessary basis. His manifestation depends solely on the readiness of the Aspirant, and all magical ceremonies used in That invocation are merely intended to prepare that Aspirant, not in any way to attract or influence Him. It is His constant and eternal Will to become one with the Aspirant, and the moment the conditions of the latter make it possible, That Bridal is consummated."116 In this next quote, the punch line from *Liber Samekh*, Crowley speaks as though that consummation had already taken place, calling the Devil the eye, the angel, the initiator, and most important, the sixfold star that is one with him: "'The Eye! Satan, my Lord! The Lust of the goat!' 'Mine Angel! Mine Initiator! Thou one with me - The Sixfold Star!'"117

Aleister Crowley calls the Devil "Thou one with me-the Sixfold Star." Is that not the message Jimmy Page sent forth in climbing the mountain and becoming one with the Hermit that he has on the top of the mountain, holding the lantern with the hexagram-the sixfold star inside of it, on the inner cover of the fourth Led Zeppelin album? This all took place during the violin bow scene in the film, producing sounds of ritualistic diabolism, just subsequent to Robert Plant completing the two-part command to sell one's soul to the Devil! This is what Jimmy Page said to Lisa Robinson that the climb was to illustrate: "It was supposed to look like a really esoteric climb towards the aspiration of truth." Jimmy Page said, in the January 2002 issue of *Guitar World*, that it was a climb "...aspiring to the light of truth." (In The Light) It was not truth that he found, but a lie. *Billboard* presented this climb as Page's quest for spiritual rebirth: "Jimmy Page, the visionary seeker in search of rebirth." This spiritual rebirth Page was looking for is in fact spiritual regeneration with Satan.

Jimmy Page would have non-occultists think there is no connection between Crowley and Led Zeppelin. Consider the following where Page is quoted concerning Crowley: "Although I don't agree with everything he said, he was a visionary. I don't particularly want to go into it because it's a personal thing and isn't in relation to anything I do as a musician, apart from that I've employed his system in my own day to day life."118 Jimmy Page didn't fool this author with that statement. If all this is not enough, look closely at the hood of the Hermit on the inner cover of the fourth album, THERE ARE HORNS STICKING THROUGH THE HOOD!!! I ask any sane person reading this book who is not too cowardly to face reality, who else could that be on Led Zeppelin's fourth album inner cover at the top of the hill with the hexagram, one with Jimmy Page, and having horns sticking through the hood? It is Lucifer, Satan, the Devil, the piper, the maker of music, and god/possessor of Jimmy Page. Here is what Ritchie Yorke, again, a personal friend of the band, had to say of Page promoting the teachings of Aleister Crowley in his book, *Led Zeppelin - The Definitive Biography*: "...Page obviously found a soulful sustenance in Crowley's unorthodox beliefs and has propagated his theories and concepts."119 Friends of the band say that Page propagated Crowley's writings. Why would Mr. Yorke make such a statement? It is because as a personal friend of the band, he is well aware of the truth.

What does Jimmy Page say when people ask him about his involvement in the occult? He lies. This is what he says: "I do not worship the devil. But magic does intrigue me."120 (Did you the reader see Jimmy Page's subtle connection of the Devil with Magic?) Jimmy Page is lying, pure and simple. Remember what you read earlier, where the Devil told Crowley he was a liar and that he was not ashamed of him? Here it is, Satan speaking to Aleister Crowley from *The Magical Record of the Beast*: "My son! Thou art mine; thy tongue is a liar's; I, Satan thy sire, am not shamed!"121 Jimmy Page is not the only person lying about this. This is Robert Plant's statement concerning Page and Crowley: "I think Page just collected the works of an English eccentric. That was all I was concerned about and that was all I knew."122 What Robert Plant was doing by saying that was mollifying Aleister Crowley's tie to Led Zeppelin. Plant said the only thing he cared about, as far as Crowley was concerned, was that Jimmy Page gathered his works, but nothing further. He wasn't concerned about the occult? He wasn't a student of Crowley as well? Why is he commanding the fans to sell their souls to Satan? Do you believe the only thing Plant knew about this was that Page collected Crowley's works and no more? Aleister Crowley, Jimmy Page and Led Zeppelin, *were* and *are* hardcore Devil worshipers, his possession, sold out to him to do his will in conforming the minds of men to worship him.

It was Aleister Crowley himself, who, in *The Magical Record of the Beast*, wrote this about Aiwass/Satan, the Holy Guardian Angel: "Aiwass is always in water, in a cave-like place, or high on a mountain."123 In the Led Zeppelin film, during the song, "The Song Remains the Same," Robert Plant is riding in a ship on the ocean, standing on the bow. At the very end of that song, and into "The Rain Song," Robert Plant is in a cave. In "Dazed and Confused,"

Jimmy Page is with the Devil (an actor posing as the Hermit before Jimmy assumes the role) on the top of the mountain out back of Boleskine House, in Scotland. Their messages are clear to the person who searches Aleister Crowley's writings, and multitudes of people are doing exactly that. I surely am not the first. Clearly, the evidence, in the minds of the objective observer, points to the members of Led Zeppelin as having sold their souls to the Devil in return for the stardom that would result by playing the Devil's music, as they promote the Law of Thelema that is in complete concurrence with their chosen (an act of their free will) moral code. We will look at what I believe is how they got the bulk of their music in the first "Stairway to Heaven" chapter. The evidence backs my assertion. The facts presented here are irrefutable, cased closed, no discussions necessary as to their validity.

If Jimmy Page wants to get on ABC Nightline News and debate this, that is fine with me. I will show the quotes right out of Crowley's books to the whole world. This man is clearly one of the most dangerous Devil worshipers to ever walk the earth; and the poor guy thinks he is leading people to god (I hope he repents so he can be saved.). Bonham, Jones, and Plant were merely his willing puppets, as he was the Devil's. Just look at the messages that he was sending impressionable youth all over the world, and coming from their guitar hero. Remember what you read before, where I quoted Steven Tyler from VH1 *Legends.* He said that Led Zeppelin's fourth album sold more copies than any other hard rock album in the history of rock and roll, over 15 million. The album has since gone over the 22 million mark in sales. The entire thing is one big volume of Devil worship, as you will see when we examine the chapters "Stairway to Heaven II" and "The Battle of Evermore."

POLISHING THE MAGICIAN'S IMAGE

Not only does Jimmy Page deny worshiping the Devil, and making a pact with him, but others defend him as well. Here is a prime example of it from Chris Salewicz, in *Led Zeppelin - Creem Special Edition*, that came out in 1980. He says that he is aware that there are people who would lay the blame for the tragic events surrounding Led Zeppelin at the feet of Jimmy Page's occult interests. However, then he says, "Personally, though, I don't think that Jimmy Page has inked a pact with Satan. To think like that is mere superstition...." He says that he makes that statement in light of rumors going around for the previous year and a half that some members of the band also lay blame for their tragedies at Page's feet. He goes on to say that he doesn't think that there has been a war between good and evil going on in the rock world that Led Zeppelin has lived in over the previous decade. Finally, after stating that Jimmy Page's head may very well have been held together by his occult interests during his career with Led Zeppelin, and that anyone who believes all occult practices are the work of the Devil, is buying into a lie fostered by "...the tricky Devil himself."124

That was an excellent example of image polishing. It is also one of the greatest lies ever to be put into print; regardless if Mr. Salewicz believes what he wrote. Rest assured, ALL occult activity is the work of Satan, every last bit of it. It was good to see Mr. Salewicz acknowledge the Devil's existence, however. I would challenge him, as lovingly as I can on impersonal paper, to consider if the tricky Devil had played one on his thinking. His statement that he doesn't believe Page inked a pact with the Devil, I believe, stems from his refusal to view him in that light. It reminds me of people who say that Elvis Presley never did drugs or cheated on his wife, that he was a good Christian boy (stupid is as stupid does). Many will read this book, see the proof, and refuse to believe it, because they don't want it to be true. Truth is truth however, and the mission of Led Zeppelin is to serve the Devil and capture souls, regardless of how good their music made people feel. I used "is" instead of "was" because the music is still being played, even by Robert Plant touring the United States in the summer of 2002.

With reference to the rumors of the members of Led Zeppelin's entourage who think there is a link between black magic and the band's troubles, I disagree for the most part. I don't believe there was anything supernatural about Robert Plant's accident in 1975; plenty of people get in these accidents. Jimmy Page was at the Abbey of Thelema in Sicily where Crowley wrote *Liber Samekh* when the accident took place. There was nothing supernatural about John Bonham's death either. He simply drank himself to death. This happens everywhere. The Devil surely would have wanted him to stay alive. I myself went to sleep drunk one night, lying flat on my back. When I woke up in the morning, the sun was shining, I was on my side, and I had vomited in my sleep. It was all over my body, my bed, and the floor. How I got from flat on my back to my side I will never know. I was so drunk I couldn't get up once I lied down. I believe it was divine intervention that put me on my side. My guardian angel probably did it.

The one event that I believe is tied to the supernatural was Robert Plant's son's death; due to statements he made. He himself expressed to Richard Cole that he couldn't understand why it was Karac; and he told Lisa Robinson that it could have been him who died instead of John Bonham; in September of 1980.

FINAL THOUGHTS ON "THE HERMIT" AND "THE DEVIL"

The final satanic evidence that needs to be addressed here is "The Hermit," and "The Devil" of the Tarot cards. Once again, this is what Aleister Crowley had to say about the Tarot: "The only theory of ultimate interest about the Tarot is that it is an admirable symbolic picture of the Universe, based on the data of the Holy Qabalah."125 Jimmy Page was quoted in *Led Zeppelin - The Definitive Biography*, as promoting the Tarot cards while speaking specifically about the Hermit: "The hermit is holding out the light of truth and enlightenment to a young man at the foot of the hill. If you know the tarot cards, you'll know what the hermit means."126

You already read two quotes in chapter nine that make it clear that Crowley's Tarot Deck is Jimmy Page's preference. The Hermit is described in Crowley's Tarot book, *The Book of Thoth*, as being the creator of all worlds:

"This card is attributed to the letter Yod, which means the Hand. Hence, the hand, which is the tool or instrument par excellence, is in the center of the picture. The letter Yod is the foundation of all the other letters of the Hebrew alphabet, which are merely combinations of it in various ways.

"The letter Yod is the first letter of the name Tetragrammaton, and this symbolizes the Father, who is Wisdom; he is the highest form of Mercury, and the Logos, the Creator of all worlds. Accordingly, his representative in physical life is the spermatozoon; this is why the card is called The Hermit....In his hand he holds a Lamp whose center is the Sun, portrayed in the likeness of the Sigil of the great King of Fire (Yod is the secret Fire)....For he is not only creative, but is the fluidic essence of Light, which is the life of the Universe."127

Arthur E. Waite, a contemporary of Crowley who directed him to read *The Cloud Upon the Sanctuary,* said this of the Hermit in his book, *The Pictorial Key to the Tarot*: "It is said also that his lantern contains the Light of Occult Science and that his staff is a Magic Wand."128 Then he says the Hermit is sending the message to man that he can attain the same spiritual heights; this matches Crowley and Page's representations: "The variation from the conventional models in this card is only that the lamp is not enveloped partially in the mantle of its bearer, who blends the idea of the Ancient of Days with the Light of the World. It is a star which shines in the lantern. I have said that this is a card of attainment, and to extend this conception the figure is seen holding up his beacon on an eminence. Therefore the Hermit is not, as Court de Gebelin explained, a wise man in search of truth and justice; nor is he, as a later explanation proposes, an especial example of experience. His beacon intimates that 'where I am, you also may be.'"129

S.L. MacGregor Mathers, in his book, *The Tarot*, wrote the same thing of the lantern in the hand of the Hermit: "An old and bearded man wrapped in a mantle, and with his head covered with a cowl, bearing in his right hand the lantern of occult science."130

Aleister Crowley calls "The Devil" of the Tarot the Greek God Pan. Pan was described by Crowley in chapter two as Satan. The card pertains to the zodiac sign "Capricorn," and Capricorn is ruled by Saturn. Now you know why Jimmy Page has the planet Saturn on his left thigh in *The Song Remains the*

Same. He is a Capricorn, and the sign is ruled by Saturn. Here is Crowley's description of the card:

"This card is attributed to the letter 'Ayin, which means an Eye, and it refers to Capricornus in the Zodiac. In the Dark Ages of Christianity, it was completely misunderstood. Eliphaz Levi studied it very deeply because of its connection with ceremonial magick, his favourite subject; and he re-drew it, identifying it with Baphomet, the ass-headed idol of the Knights of the Temple. But at this time archeological research had not gone very far; the nature of Baphomet was not fully understood. At least he succeeded in identifying the goat portrayed upon the card with Pan....This card represents creative energy in its most material form; in the Zodiac, Capricornus occupies the Zenith. It is the most exalted of the signs; it is the goat leaping with lust upon the summits of earth. This sign is ruled by Saturn, who makes for selfhood and perpetuity....The card represents Pan Pangenetor, the All-Begetter....representing the god Pan upon the highest and most secret mountains of the earth....All things equally exalt him. He represents the finding of ecstasy in every phenomenon, however naturally repugnant; he transcends all limitations; he is Pan; he is All." 131

Crowley didn't forget to mention that the Pan was Satan in his description of the card, tying him in with the mountain once again: "Saturn, the ruler, is Set, the ass-headed god of the Egyptian deserts; he is the god of the south. The name refers to all gods containing these consonants, such as Shaitan, or Satan. Essential to the symbolism are the surroundings-barren places, especially high places. The cult of the mountain is an exact parallel."132 Finally, Crowley says this of The Devil: "In every symbol of this card there is the allusion to the highest things and most remote."133

The last quote about this tarot card comes from Stuart R. Kaplan, from his famous book, *The Encyclopedia of Tarot*: "Some packs bear the inscription 'Solve' and 'Coagula' on The Devil's arms, and in an old Etteilla series The Devil appears on top of a mountain."134 "Solve" and "Coagula" are on the arms in the picture of Eliphas Levi's Devil (see chapter four opening page).

HORUS AND PAN ON THE LED ZEPPELIN IV MISTY MOUNTAIN

Five important pieces from the mountain on the inside cover of Led Zeppelin are going to be explained here. On the bottom of the photo, is a white goat. Crowley referred to this goat in "The Devil" Tarot card:

"Hear me, Lord of the Stars,
For thee have I worshiped ever
With stains and sorrows and scars
With joyful, joyful Endeavour.

Hear me, O lilywhite goat
Crisp as a thicket of thorns,
With a collar of gold for thy throat,
A scarlet bow for thy horns."135

If you look at the bottom of the mountain on the inner cover of Led Zeppelin's fourth album, there is a lilywhite goat there. The next thing to examine is The Hermit and the dove. The Hermit is the father in the trinity of the Qabalah. The dove is the mother. If you look at the photo, you see The Hermit is standing upon a large dove laid out on the rocks of the mountain, underneath his feet. Crowley wrote of this as well: "The Dove is the bird of Venus, but the dove is also a symbol of the Holy Ghost; that is, of the Phallus in its most sublimated form. There is therefore no reason for surprise in observing the identification of the father with the mother."136 The son is halfway down the mountain from the head of the dove, right in the center of it. The son is displayed as Horus the Hawk. Crowley also said that Horus was the Sphinx, as you read already. If you look to the left of Horus, facing away from the mountain is the head of the Egyptian Sphinx. You see the left side of his face as he is facing away from the mountain, facing the opposite direction of Horus' face.

Between the head of the Sphinx and Horus the Hawk is the letter "M." It has a curl on the right bottom of the letter, and it stands for "Apophis." You read in chapter eight that Apophis is none other than the Devil himself. Here is the quote from The Equinox: "By Thy most secret and Holy name of Apophis be Thou blessed, Lucifer, Star of the Dawn, Satan-Jeheshua, Light of the World!"137

Aleister Crowley has Pan on the top of the mountain in his Book of Thoth, and Jimmy Page has Horus in the middle of the mountain, as well as the Devil/Pan on the top. The Hermit is the father, Pan, and the dove is the mother, Artemis, and the hawk is the son, Horus. Again, Crowley says the two are the same person: "...I praise the Crowned and Conquering child whose name is Force and Fire, whose subtlety and strength make sure serenity, whose energy and endurance accomplish the Attainment of the Virgin of the Absolute; who, being manifested, is the Player upon the sevenfold pipe, the Great God Pan, and, being withdrawn into the Perfection that he willed, is Silence."138

In that last quote Crowley called the Crowned and Conquering Child Horus and Pan the same person. In his Confessions, Crowley called Pan the father and Horus the son: "...Artemis is still barren of hope until the spirit of the Infinite All, great Pan, tears asunder the veil and displays the hope of humanity, the Crowned Child of Future."139 Once again, Horus is the Crowned and Conquering Child, associated with the Qabalah, which is the flaming sword, as Aleister Crowley presented him in The Equinox:

"Draw, draw the Flaming Sword!
Crowned Child and Conquering Lord!
Horus, avenger!"140

THE END OF THE VIOLIN BOW – "EXPLOSION OF WILL"

After Jimmy Page ends his solo with the violin bow/Magick wand, in concurrence with the end of the scene on top of the mountain with the Devil, promoting the Qabalah, he wails into a fifteen plus-minute jam that is unknown to the Led Zeppelin fans in the audience. This long high paced guitar jam, which is an *explosion of will,* does three things. First, it helps Jimmy Page develop his will to the highest degree. Crowley wrote of this as necessary for Magick in *Book 4*: "It is therefore necessary to develop the will to its highest point, even though the last task but one is the total surrender of this will. Partial surrender of an imperfect will is of no account in Magick."141 Again, this is anything but self-reliance. Who is the magician supposed to surrender his will to? It is the Devil of course. Consider the interesting "coincidental" quote from the *New Musical Express* about Page playing "Dazed and Confused" in the Led Zeppelin film: "His 27-minute 'Dazed and Confused' marathon shows the visuals of Page – a man possessed." The magazine could have said "by the Devil" as well. Remember, you already read in chapter ten of Page talking with Ozzy Osbourne on the radio in the year 2000, stating that when he is playing "somebody" takes over, which is something inside of him, who he said was really great. Then you read several quotes in this chapter about the Devil taking permanent possession of the Adept who performs the operation of Abramelin the Mage. All the facts are here. The second thing this blazing jam in the live version of "Dazed and Confused" does is to weaken the resistance of the will of the listener. The music is mesmerizing them with volume, and the long drawn out concentration on unknown blazing guitar lead tires the mind. Complaints about this song have been many at every show they have played it at. The third thing accomplished by this drawn out jam, is the ability to set certain spiritual forces to work that don't work under normal circumstances. Crowley wrote of this in his *Confessions*: "...a supreme explosion of will is sometimes able to set forces in motion which cannot be invoked in ordinary circumstances."142

The end of this chapter comes with a quote in the same context of the last one from H.P. Blavatsky, that originally appeared in her magazine, *Lucifer*, in the form of a question and answer, about what amounts to a magic spell:

"Q. In both (hypnotism and animal magnetism) there is an act of will in the operator, a transit of something from him to his patient, an effect upon the patient. What is the 'something' transmitted in both cases?

ANS. That which is transmitted has no name in European languages, and if we simply describe it as *will*, it loses all its meaning. The old and very much tabooed words, 'enchantment,' 'fascination,' 'glamor' and 'spell,' and especially the verb 'to bewitch,' expressed far more suggestively the real action that took place during the process of such a *transmission*, than the modern and meaningless terms, 'psychologize' and 'biologize.'"143

The mountain scene on the Led Zeppelin IV inner album cover as well as the mountain climbing scene in the Led Zeppelin film are indeed nothing less than advertisements of the Operation of Abramelin the Mage as advocated by the writings of Jimmy Page's confessed mentor in Magick, Aleister Crowley. The Operation of Abramelin successfully completed gives the student of Magick power over demonic forces. This power is given to the magician from Satan. The power is utilized by the magician in many different ways, and one powerful method advocated by Aleister Crowley was the Magick wand. Using the Magick wand to set the daughter on the throne of the mother in the Qabalah was taught by Crowley as an ability the magician would have as the result of completing the work of Abramelin. This means that it is done with the assistance of demonic forces; forces that Jimmy Page seems to be very much in league with. Crowley used the metaphor of climbing a mountain (which he did literally at one point when he lived at Boleskine house) to describe the Operation of Abramelin the Mage being brought to a completion in his famous *Equinox*. Jimmy Page named his occult bookstore in London *Equinox*, and he sold the same Crowley *Equinox* there. Aleister Crowley wrote in *Liber Samekh*, an epistle he penned at the Abbey of Thelema in Sicily in 1921, that Satan was the Holy Guardian Angel in undisputable terms, and that the symbol of being united with him would be the sixfold star. This is the same Abbey of Thelema that Jimmy Page flew to see on Tom Friend's fifteenth birthday, the number of the The Devil in the Tarot. The Devil was behind the Operation of Abramelin from the beginning. It wasn't "god" who inspired the writing of *The Book of the Sacred Magic of Abramelin the Mage* in Egypt, it was Satan. The Devil used Aleister Crowley to promote the Operation of Abramelin in writing, and Jimmy Page did the same thing in three different ways. First was the inner album cover of Led Zeppelin's fourth album. The second was his occult bookstore in London, and the third was the mountain climbing scene in the film, *The Song Remains the Same*. The entire teaching is based on the Qabalah; also founded by the Devil. What Jimmy Page was trying to achieve (in this author's opinion) with the violin bow and mountain climbing scenes, in conjunction with his occult bookstore, as well as participating in the movie *Lucifer Rising*, can best be summed up by Aleister Crowley, in his *Equinox*: "We therefore who are without the chains of ignorance, look closely into the heart of the seeker and lead him by the path which is best suited to his nature unto the ultimate end of all things, the supreme realization, the Life which abideth in Light, yea, the Life which abideth in Light."144 Remember, this is the message from the Led Zeppelin song, "In The Light." Believing that

Satan is god, it is easy for Satanists to then believe that they are promoting the "light" by spreading occult teaching, but will in the end find out that they suppressed the truth they once knew and promoted the Devil's darkness. Remember also, that Jimmy Page performed "In The Light" in 2000 while on tour with the Black Crowes and Robert Plant performed it in 2001 while touring with his band, "Strange Sensation," both drawing tremendous ovations. In the next chapter, we will look at the operation of the Theremin machine and its relationship to Magick, as well as the effect of narcotics on the brain. The author presents it as evil spirits and hallucinogenic drugs, in conjunction with sounds made by the Theremin, all working together at the will of Jimmy Page and Led Zeppelin.

Jimmy Page (above) uses the violin bow as a wand; with the Stonehenge Stone clearly visible behind him. He is mimicking "the sign of Horus the Enterer" that you see Crowley performing with small wand in hand in the photo to the left. The photo is taken from his *Equinox*. He wrote that the magician should give the sign of Horus the Enterer in order to project the macrocosmic force on the object of magical working to produce new conditions of consciousness in the person.

Just after projecting the macrocosmic force with the Magick wand, Page used to the bow (above) to produce powerful riffs in the Led Zeppelin film. One can see in this part of the film that Jimmy Page runs his left hand up and down the guitar like a pendulum to produce great hypnotic effect; with mesmerizing volume.

In this first photo to the left, Jimmy Page is dressed up like the Hermit of the Tarot cards, standing on top of the hill behind Boleskine House, just as Crowley wrote, and ostensibly why Page bought the house to begin with; to practice the dangerous Magick of Abramelin the Mage, to produce union with the Holy Guardian Angel, Satan. Crowley wrote: "The Eye! Satan, my Lord! The Lust of the goat! Mine Angel! Mine Initiator! Thou one with me – the Sixfold Star!" In the second photo, taken from the inside cover of Led Zeppelin's fourth album, the Hermit has the sixfold star in the lantern, and horns sticking through his hood. Jimmy Page presents himself as being in union with Satan himself.

1 Dave Lewis and Simon Pallett, *Led Zeppelin: The Concert File*, pg.14

2 Aleister Crowley, *Moonchild*, pg.64

3 Aleister Crowley, *Book 4*, pg.71

4 Aleister Crowley, *Liber Samekh*, from *Magick-Book 4*Liber Aba*, pg.509

5 Michael Watts, *Melody Maker* Magazine, 1974

6 Aleister Crowley, *The Book of Wisdom or Folly*, pg.173

7 Aleister Crowley, *The Book of Thoth*, pg.100

8 Aleister Crolwey, *Moonchild*, pg.139

9 Eliphas Levi, Aleister Crowley's *Equinox*, Vol. I, No.10, *The Key to the Mysteries*, pg.62

10 J. F. C. Fuller from Crowley's *Equinox*, Vol. I, No.4, pg.342

11 Ibid, pg.341

12 Eliphas Levi, *The History of Magic*, pg.80

13 *Led Zeppelin - Creem Special Edition*, pg.55

14 Aleister Crowley, *The Equinox*, Vol. I, No.6, pg.37

15 *Webster's New World Dictionary*, Second College Edition, pg.482

16 Richard Cole, *Stairway to Heaven - Led Zeppelin Uncensored*, pg.348

17 Aleister Crowley, *The Equinox*, Vol. I, No.3, pg.3

18 Walter Gibson, *Hypnotism - Theory and Practice*, Coles Publishing Co. Limited, Toronto, Canada, 1981, pg.95

19 Ibid, pg.1

20 H.P. Blavatsky, *Studies in Occultism*, Theosophical University Press, Pasadena, California, No Date, pg.30

21 Abraham the Jew, Translated by S. L. MacGregor Mathers, *The Book of the Sacred Magic of Abramelin the Mage*, pg.80

22 S.L. MacGregor Mathers, translator, Aleister Crowley, editor, *The Goetia - The Lesser Key of Solomon the King*, pg.21

23 Dave Lewis and Simon Pallett, *Led Zeppelin: The Concert File*, pg.12

24 Raymond Buckland, *Buckland's Complete Book of Witchcraft*, pg.159

25 Steven Davis, *Hammer of the Gods*, 85

26 *Webster's New World Dictionary*, Second College Edition, pg.992

27 Lisa Robinson, *Led Zeppelin - Creem Special Edition*, pg.27

28 Howard Mylett and Richard Bunton, *In The Light*, pg.62

29 Eliphas Levi, *Transcendental Magic*, pg.84

30 Frank Garlock, *The Big Beat - A Rock Blast*, pg.20

31 S. Jason Black and Christopher S. Hyatt, Ph.D., *Pacts With the Devil*, pg.97

32 Aleister Crowley, *Moonchild*, pg.64

33 Richard Cavendish, *The Black Arts*, pg.234

34 Eliphas Levi, *Transcendental Magic*, pg.261

35 Aleister Crowley, *Magick Without Tears*, pg.91

36 Aleister Crowley, *Moonchild*, pg.308

37 Aleister Crowley, *Magick Without Tears*, pg.129

38 Abraham the Jew, Translated by S.L. MacGregor Mathers, *The Book of the Sacred Magic of Abramelin the Mage*, pg.132

39 Aleister Crowley, *Book 4*, pg.71

40 Aleister Crowley, *Magick-Book 4*Liber Aba*, pg.562

41 Richard Cavendish, *The Black Arts*, pg.241

42 D.J. Conway, *Celtic Magic*, pg.82

43 Aleister Crowley, *Magick-Book 4*Liber Aba*, pg.199

44 Ibid, pg.197

45 Aleister Crowley, *The Book of Thoth*, pg.40

46 Aleister Crowley, *The Confessions of Aleister Crowley*, pg.125

47 Eliphas Levi, *Transcendental Magic*, pg.93

48 Rosemary Ellen Guiley, *The Encyclopedia of Witches and Witchcraft*, pg.213

49 Paul Kendall and Dave Lewis, *Led Zeppelin-In Their Own Words*, pg.118

50 Aleister Crowley, *Magick-Book 4*Liber Aba*, pg.482

51 Steven Davis, *Hammer of the Gods*, pg.117

52 Eliphas Levi, *Transcendental Magic*, pg.346

53 Ibid, pg.350

54 Richard Cavendish, *The Black Arts*, pg.272

55 Aleister Crowley, *Magick Without Tears*, pg.33

56 Allan Kardec, *The Book On Mediums*, Samuel Weiser Inc., Yorke Beach, Maine, 1970, first published in 1874, pg.129

57 Eliphas Levi, *Transcendental Magic*, pg.332

58 Ibid, pg.300

59 Aleister Crowley, *The Magical Record of the Beast*, pg.274

60 Ibid, pg.230

61 Edred Thorsson, *Runelore*, pg.51

62 Ibid, pg.18

63 Edred Thorsson, *Futhark-A Handbook of Rune Magic*, pg.133

64 Edred Thorsson, *Runelore*, pg.71

65 Karl von Eckartshausen, *The Cloud Upon the Sanctuary*, pg.26

66 Ibid, pg.34

67 Edred Thorsson, *Runelore*, introduction, pg. xv

68 Edred Thorsson, *Futhark-A Handbook of Rune Magic*, pg.14

69 Michael Howard, *Understanding Runes*, pp.46-47

70 S.L. MacGregor Mathers, Translator of *The Book of the Sacred Magic of Abramelin the Mage*, by Abraham the Jew, introduction, pp. xxxvi - xxxvii

71 Aleister Crowley, *Moonchild*, pg.186

72 Aleister Crowley, *Magick Without Tears*, pg.457

73 W.B. Crow, *Witchcraft, Magic, and Occultism*, pg.290

74 Eliphas Levi, *Transcendental Magic*, pp.360-361

75 Aleister Crowley, *The Equinox*, Vol. I, No.2, pp.228-230

76 Ritchie Yorke, *Led Zeppelin - The Definitive Biography*, pg.199

77 Ibid.

78 *Guitar World* Magazine, January, 1998, pg.76

79 Aleister Crowley, *Liber Samekh*, from *Magick – Book 4*Liber Aba*, pg.525

80 Paul Kendall and Dave Lewis, *Led Zeppelin - In Their Own Words*, pg.70

81 Rosemary Ellen Guiley, *The Encyclopedia of Witches and Witchcraft*, pg.235

82 Aleister Crowley, *Moonchild*, pg.252

83 Lewis Spence, *Ancient Egyptian Myths and Legends*, pg.76

84 Aleister Crowley, *The Equinox*, Vol. I, No.6, *Liber A'ash*, pp.36-37

85 Aleister Crowley, *The Equinox*, Vol. I, No.2, pg.230

86 Aleister Crowley, *The Equinox*, Vol. I, No.10, pg.99

87 Aleister Crowley, *Book 4*, pg.88

88 Richard Cavendish, *The Black Arts*, pg.110

89 Israel Regardie, *The Eye in the Triangle*, pg.175

90 Aleister Crowley, *Liber Samekh*, from *Magick-Book 4*Liber Aba*, pg.512

91 Aleister Crowley, *Magick Without Tears*, pg.502

92 Aleister Crowley, *Liber Samekh*, pg.526

93 Dr. Sir J. G. Frazer, *The Golden Bough*, pg.105

94 Richard Cavendish, *The Black Arts*, pg.85

95 Aleister Crowley, *The Law is For All*, pg.207

96 Aleister Crowley, *The Equinox*, Vol. I, No.4, pp.145-146

97 Aleister Crowley, *Liber Samekh*, pg.521

98 Richard Cole, *Stairway To Heaven - Led Zeppelin Uncensored*, pp.224-225

99 Time-Life Books, *The Enchanted World-Wizards and Witches*, pg.58

100 Aleister Crowley, *Liber Samekh*, pg.505

101 Aleister Crowley, *The Equinox*, Vol. I, No.2, pg.301

102 Hermes, Aleister Crowley's *Equinox*, Vol. I, No.2, pg.220

103 Aleister Crowley, *Magick-Book 4*Liber Aba*, pg.183

104 S.L. MacGregor Mathers, Translator of *The Qabalah Unveiled*, pg.41

105 Eliphas Levi, *Transcendental Magic*, pp.45

106 Ibid, pp.68-69

107 S.L. MacGregor Mathers, translator of *The Qabalah Unveiled*, pg.231

108 Eliphas Levi, *Transcendental Magic*, pg.237

109 *Webster's New World Dictionary*, Second College Edition, pg.473

110 Ibid, pg.324

111 Aleister Crowley, *Magick-Book 4*Liber Aba*, pg.171

112 Aleister Crowley, *Book 4*, pg.71

113 Ibid.

114 Aleister Crowley, *The Book of Thoth*, pg.86

115 Ibid, pg.54

116 Aleister Crowley, *Magick-Book 4*Liber Aba*, pp. 234-235

117 Ibid, pg.509

118 Howard Mylett, *Tangents Within a Framework*, pg.71

119 Ritchie Yorke, *Led Zeppelin - The Definitive Biography*, pg.130

120 *Hit Parader* Magazine, July, 1975, pg.64

121 Aleister Crowley, *The Magical Record of the Beast*, pg.266

122 Ritchie Yorke, *Led Zeppelin - The Definitive Biography*, pg.248

123 Aleister Crowley, *The Magical Record of the Beast*, pg.246

124 *Led Zeppelin - Creem Special Edition*, 1980, pp.53-54

125 Aleister Crowley, *The Book of Thoth*, pg.4

126 Ritchie Yorke, *Led Zeppelin - The Definitive Biography*, pg.129

127 Aleister Crowley, *The Book of Thoth*, pg.89

128 Arthur E. Waite, *The Pictorial Key to the Tarot*, pg.17

129 Ibid, pg.104

130 S.L. MacGregor Mathers, *The Tarot*, pg.13

131 Aleister Crowley, *The Book of Thoth*, pg.105-106

132 Ibid, pg.106

133 Ibid, pg.107

134 Stuart R. Kaplan, *The Encyclopedia of Tarot*, pg.331

135 Aleister Crowley, *The Book of Thoth*, pg.106

136 Ibid, pg.56

137 Aleister Crowley, *The Equinox*, Vol. I, No.4, pg.164

138 Aleister Crowley, *The Book of Thoth*, pg.122

139 Aleister Crowley, *The Confessions of Aleister Crowley*, pg.636

140 Aleister Crowley, *The Equinox*, Vol. I, No.7, pg.380

141 Aleister Crowley, *Book 4*, pg.69

142 Aleister Crowley, *The Confessions of Aleister Crowley*, pg.98

143 H.P. Blavatsky, *Studies in Occultism*, pp.31-32 (Originally appeared in H.P. Blavatsky's magazine, *Lucifer*, between the years 1887-1891)

144 Aleister Crowley, *The Equinox*, Vol. I, No.6, pg.7

In the above still, taken from the Led Zeppelin film, Jimmy Page is pitting his Theremin manipulations against screams from Robert Plant, at whom he is smiling. This is the perfect place for Page to utitlize the demons written about in the Goetia, which he republished in 1976; when Led Zeppelin was in its prime.

Jimmy Page manipulates the Theremin in 1977; for a definite "ESP" reason. It was Page who emphasized the ESP element in a quote on the opposite page.

CHAPTER THIRTEEN

"The Theremin, the grandfather of electronic instruments, is the only musical instrument that can be played without being touched. It was named after Leo Theremin, a Russian physicist who patented it in the Twenties....In the studio, its spiraling high pitched tone can be heard during the middle section of 'Whole Lotta love.' When they adapted that number for regular live performance in January 1970, Page had the Theremin box set up by the side of the stage. By moving his hand towards the antenna of the instrument and varying distances and angles he was able to alter the tone of the sound and its duration. The high pitched shrieks were then pitted against Plant's vocal screams."1

Dave Lewis and Simon Pallett, "Led Zeppelin: The Concert File"

"A thought is realized in becoming speech; it is realized also by signs, sounds and representations of signs....Imagination, in effect, is like the soul's eye; therein forms and outlines are preserved; thereby we behold the reflections of the invisible world; it is the glass of visions and the apparatus of magical life."2

Eliphas Levi, "Transcendental Magic"

"In his German work upon Magic, Eckartshausen describes the whole of the fantastic apparatus, being a system of machines and operations by which the imagination was helped to create the phantoms desired..."3

Eliphas Levi, "The History of Magic"

"Will the hallucinationists say that the soul (if they so much as admit a soul) has moments of over-excitement, when its faculties are exalted? We agree with them; but when what is seen is real, it is not illusion..."4

Allan Kardec, "The Book on Mediums"

"There are certain things which happen for which there's no logical explanation apart from the term ESP (Extra Sensory Perception)."

Led Zeppelin Guitarist Jimmy Page, "Making Waves" Radio Show

WHOLE LOTTA LOVE: JIMMY PAGE THE MAGICIAN AND HIS THEREMIN

The Theremin Machine was designed to produce various forms of sound. Jimmy Page first discovered the instrument when it was being used by a band called "Spirit." The name, as you will see, is appropriate for a band using the

Theremin. This author believes Jimmy Page adapted the machine to Led Zeppelin's usage to become part of a many faceted effect on the minds of their fans. As we know, the band promoted several different narcotics in their music and film. In the film especially, Robert Plant promoted the use of hallucinogens. We will be looking at their motive for this in this chapter; why and how these drugs affect the brain. From that point we will examine the band's use of the Theremin in conjunction with Magick (demonic) power to manipulate the subconscious of the fans who are on these drugs. I will address that point both objectively and subjectively, since this Magick was performed on me with the Theremin at Madison Square Garden in 1977. That will lead us to examine several newspaper accounts of what I intend to show are examples of fan behavior dominated by evil spirits. Finally, we will consider Robert Plant, speaking for the entire band, giving instructions to the fans after the Theremin routine has run its course, in *The Song Remains the Same's* final concert song, "Whole Lotta Love." Those instructions from Plant are relevant to what I believe happened in the mind of the fan during the Theremin section of the song. Although fantastic in its unique form of blistering entertainment, with its wide range of low and high pitched sounds, although with a drug high it can help produce an excellent rush in the mind of the fan listening to it, I believe the Theremin was and is today being used by Jimmy Page to produce demonic sounds, in order to create demonic images in the mind of the sympathetic listener, depending on the specific drug they are on, as well as its potency; to allow them, through hallucination, to see the very demons (or Satan) who are working on their consciousness to compel them to yield their wills and hearts to the Devil.

LED ZEPPELIN PROMOTING HALLUCINOGENS

Again, to aid them in their work of Magick with the Theremin, the band has promoted narcotics in their music and film. It has already been mentioned in this book that Robert Plant nodded his approval to the fans when he held two marijuana joints up in the air at the very end of "The Rain Song," in their film. In chapter seven, Robert Plant's advocating of cocaine was presented from the song "For Your Life," off the *Presence* album. The drugs most pertinent to the use of the Theremin, however, are those that produce strong hallucinations. In their film, during "The Rain Song," Robert Plant is seen walking through the forest in a Celtic outfit with a staff in his hand. He comes upon a tree with a red top mushroom growing underneath it. This mushroom is called the "Fly Agaric," while its technical name is "Amanita Muscaria." This plant produces powerful hallucinations, and Robert Plant knows this. He advocates eating this mushroom in the film. He pulls it from the ground, holds it up to his mouth, and while you don't see him eat it, he makes the viewer think he is chewing it as he stares up into the tree above him. The message to the viewer is clear, that Led Zeppelin is promoting the use of this hallucinogenic plant, for religious reasons, obviously. In their book, *Plants of the Gods*, Richard Schultes and Albert Hofmann, wrote of this mushroom being used by Indians in Michigan: "…the religious use of *Amanita Muscaria* as a sacred hallucinogen has been discovered in an ancient annual ceremony practiced by the Ojibway Indians of Ahnishinaubeg who live on Lake Superior in Michigan. The mushroom is known in the Ojibway language as Oshtimisk Wajashkewedo ('red-top mushroom')."5

Another hallucinogen I believe was promoted by Plant in the concert film, is LSD-25. During the song, "Dazed and Confused," Robert Plant shouts over and over in the early minutes of the song, "25!" Now while I know that I'll be accused of speculation here, I am right, and will show proof. It will be said that Plant was going to turn 25 in the following month of August, after this concert. Why would he be yelling his subsequent age to the crowd? In "Whole Lotta Love," he makes it clear that he is only 24 years old. Also, if Robert Plant turned 25 in August of 1973, which he did, why did he yell "25!" during Dazed and Confused while on tour with Led Zeppelin in 1975, when he was twenty-six years old, as he did at Earl's Court in London on May 24th? There are thousands of witnesses to this fact. Plant has been heard singing "25 hours a day" during this part of "Dazed and Confused" as well. This is just another one of his cover-ups, just like the black Labrador that was supposedly the source for the name of the song, "Black Dog." The proof that Robert Plant was singing of LSD-25 in "Dazed and Confused," are the strange, constantly changing color patterns on his face that are shown at the end of Jimmy Page's unidentifiable lengthy jam as it slows and returns to the song as it is on the first Led Zeppelin album. Just ask anyone who has hallucinated on LSD if he believes that Plant is referring to acid as he looks at the film. At that point of the song, Plant begins to shout "25!" several times all over again. The reason that hallucinogenic drugs are being promoted by Led Zeppelin in their film is because they want, the author believes, to encourage their fans to be under the influence of these drugs in preparation for having Magick spells cast on them; which are greatly enhanced in their power when the said drugs are in effect in the brain (it doesn't matter if is done in concert or while listening to their music, especially their concert film soundtrack containing the violin bow and the Theremin).

THE NEURON - THE ELECTRICAL/CHEMICAL BRAIN CELL

The reason certain types of drugs have a powerful effect on the human mind is because of their capacity to manipulate brain cells, specifically, the neuron. In this section, the structure and function of the neuron will be examined in order to give the reader a basic understanding of how the brain works. In the next section, we will look at how psychoactive drugs manipulate that function.

First of all, the brain is made up of an almost infinite circuitry of neurons connected to other neurons, by which information is sent through the brain. In his book, *Focus On Drugs and the Brain*, David Friedman provided us with this general description of neurons: "The brain sends and receives messages along a network of nerve cells, or neurons. Neurons have a very special job to do. Each one is designed to receive information, examine information, and send information to other neurons."6 Did you see the word "designed" in that quote? Where you have design, you have a designer. It is an electrical signal that initiates the sending of information through a neuron; a chemical one transfers the information to the next one (Isn't Rock and Roll the electric guitar and chemicals?).

In the book, *The Mind*, by Dr. Richard M. Restak, a description of the neuron and its parts is provided: "Each of the neurons that comprise the brain is an independent unit consisting of a cell body containing the nucleus, a long fiber called the axon, and a varying number of branching fibers called dendrites that reach out toward other neurons. Information is conveyed through electrical signals sent along the axon of one neuron to the dendrites of a second one. At the synapse, or tiny cleft between neurons, the electrical signal is converted into a chemical code. This releases a chemical substance, called a neurotransmitter, which slips across the synaptic cleft to specialized receptors on the second neuron. Neurons form specific and precise functional connections with certain neurons but not with others."7

A greater description of the electrical activity between neurons, is presented by Jack Fincher in *The Brain - Mystery of Mind and Matter*:

"When a neuron's dendrites pick up an impulse from a neighboring cell, a wave of electrical activity sweeps through the cell. If the impulse is strong enough, it will trigger a change in the axon's thin membrane, causing the cell to 'fire.' Special channels in the membrane open and sodium ions flow through, changing the internal charge of the membrane from negative to positive. Immediately other channels open, allowing potassium ions to flow out and restoring the negative internal voltage of the membrane. This electrical relay race whips along the axon, turning the membrane positive, then negative again. So rapid is this transmission mechanism that in one one-thousandth of a second the axon is ready to carry another impulse.

"At the end of the axon, the impulse strikes the terminal buttons, which contain tiny round sacs, or synaptic vesicles. The sacs burst open, spilling chemical messengers called neurotransmitters into the narrow synapse separating the terminal button from the next cell's dendrites. The neurotransmitters flow across the gap and lock onto receptor sites on the receiving cell's dendrites, sparking a second electrical current. Once it has passed on its signal, the neurotransmitter is destroyed by enzymes or recaptured and stored by the synaptic vesicles.

The electrical current of a neuron sends its message down the axon to the terminal buttons, where sacs open up sending neurotransmitters to the subsequent neuron across the synapse, the cleft or gap between the axon of one neuron and the dendrite of another. In his book, *Manipulation -Dangers and Benefits of Brain Research*, Erwin Lausch described the brain's synapses: "'Synapse' (from the Greek word for connection) is the term used by neurophysiologists for the place where two nerve cells meet; or, more exactly, the contact of one end of the nerve fibre, mostly much ramified, with the cell body or a dendrite of another nerve cell. In the brain there are far more synapses than nerve cells. A nerve cell may be connected by synapses with up to ten thousand other nerve cells. Experts have reckoned that the billions of connections between the millions of nerve cells in a single human brain would extend to some 200,000-250,000 miles, the distance from the earth to the moon."9

In his book, *The Conscious Brain*, Steven Rose wrote this about the significance of the brain's synapses: "The synapses are the points at which signals pass between cells, providing the brain with the possibility of coding, classifying and operating upon information arriving at it from the outside world."10

Neurotransmitters, the chemicals that travel across synapses, to the receptor sites on the dendrites of other neurons are described by Dr. Pierce J. Howard, in his book, *The Owners Manual for the Brain*:

"Neurotransmitters are chemicals secreted at the synapse that affect the formation, maintenance, activity, and longevity of synapses and neurons. They are like the letters of the alphabet, with their 'words' corresponding to behaviors. As words are composed of letters, with individual letters having predictable phonetic effects and groups of letters having predictable semantic effects, so behaviors are composed of neurotransmitter activity, with individual neurotransmitters having predictable physiological effects and groups of neurotransmitters having predictable behavioral effects.

"Neurotransmitters create two broad categories of effect: excitation (or activation) and inhibition. For example, one neurotransmitter will activate sleep and another will inhibit it. Drinking milk will trigger the release of melatonin, the neurotransmitter that activates sleep (and, along with the neurotransmitter serotonin, depression), but eating chocolate, which contains caffeine, will interfere with sleep. Still other chemicals serve as neuromodulators, affecting the intensity of excitation or inhibition."11

The brain, then, is composed of neurons that communicate with other neurons by generating electrical impulses down their axons to the synapse terminal buttons, causing the release of neurotransmitters from special sacs in the buttons to spill out into the synapses and travel to the specially designed receptor sites on the dendrites of the subsequent neurons, to perform specific functions that are directly related to human behavior.

ROCK CULTURE CHEMICAL MANIPULATION OF THE BRAIN

Neurotransmitters that cross synapses and bond to receptors, are remarkably similar in molecular structure to psychoactive chemicals used everyday by those in the rock culture, and vice versa (The point here is not to single out these people as the only users of these drugs, which they are not, but simply to state the facts about the rock culture, upon the top of which Led Zeppelin's timeless music still sits). The most popular drugs used by rock and roll fans (who use drugs-not all do) are going to be examined here with a comparison to the brain's natural chemicals so the reader can be informed as to their similarity in molecular structure, which allows for their function in the brain, and brief descriptions of how these drugs affect the brain, especially as they relate to Led Zeppelin and hallucinations.

In *Manipulation - Dangers and Benefits of Brain Research*, Erwin Lausch wrote of using psychoactive drugs to manipulate the brain: "Everywhere and in all ages, as far back as our sources reach, man has tried to interfere in the normal course of his psychological functions, in fact to manipulate his brain. Psychoactive drugs were once considered divine gifts which one used gratefully, or as the temptations of evil spirits to which one succumbed. Today we know that they are substances which, through the structure of their molecules, influence chemical processes in the brain."12 As you saw in that quote, there were (and are today) two different schools of thought relative to psychoactive drugs. For the purpose of this discussion, we will focus on the following popular mind-altering drugs, again, commonly associated with the rock culture and hallucinations: marijuana, cocaine, mushrooms, mescaline, and LSD-25.

MARIJUANA

Of all the drugs used in society today, marijuana is considered the most widely used mind-altering agent capable of inducing hallucinations. The punishment for its possession is not nearly as great as other narcotics, therefore it draws a number of people that will shy away from heavier drugs. Many who use heavy drugs also use marijuana, however. If you've ever been to a rock concert at Madison Square Garden in New York, and you got their about twenty minutes after they opened the doors, you most likely, at least in the 1970's, walked right into a cloud of marijuana smoke. You could sit in your seat, and more than likely, someone in your isle would send a joint your way, even if you didn't know the person. The reason, obviously, is the communal partying atmosphere surrounding the performance of the band. Smoking just a joint or two is not going to bring a person to hallucinate, unless the marijuana is laced with an additional chemical. The active chemical in marijuana, or "Cannabis," is THC, or Tetrahydrocannabinol. This chemical in marijuana bonds well to the receptor sites in the brain which are designed to receive the neurotransmitter Anandamide. Anandamide's actions in the brain are similar to THC. Experts say that there are many receptors in the brain that will accept THC. Judging by its use, it has to be true. If the receptor didn't accept it, there would be no high associated with the drug. There are many, including myself, who know, not just believe, that smoked in large quantity it can produce hallucinations. In their book, *Plants of the Gods*, Richard Schultes and Albert Hofmann wrote about it: "The psychoactive effects of *Cannabis* preparations vary widely, depending on dosage, the preparation and the type of plant used, the method of administration, personality of the user, and social and cultural background. Perhaps the most frequent characteristic is a dreamy state. Long forgotten events are often recalled and thoughts occur in unrelated sequences. Perception of time, and occasionally of space, is altered. Visual and auditory hallucinations follow the use of large doses."13 Schultes and Hofmann (Hofmann discovered LSD in 1938) are in complete agreement with none other than Aleister Crowley himself. He wrote of Cannabis in his *Equinox*: "A strong dose of Cannabis produces curious hallucinations abolishing temporarily the ideas of time and distance..."14

Marijuana is a popular drug, in the rock culture especially, because of the mind frame produced that enables the user to listen to rock music in a dreamy, painless state that can, with enough of the drug, produce hallucinations. Again, Robert Plant nodded his approval of marijuana to the fans in the Led Zeppelin film at the end of "The Rain Song."

COCAINE

Cocaine is a drug that produces a quick, confident high, and (among other reasons) because of its popular effects, is more expensive to get. When I was running around with people who used drugs many years ago, cocaine was constantly referred to as "the rich man's high." For some reason, with this drug around me at all times, I never indulged in it. I guess I just felt that I would end up dead if I got hooked on it. Marijuana and Led Zeppelin lifted me out of depression, but something about the word cocaine, as far as I was concerned, carried with it the connotation of death. There was a great fear in me about using it, and sharp criticism often accompanied my rejection of it. As a matter of fact, I was rejected by some people who didn't want me around once the progression from marijuana, alcohol, and uppers began to reach a regular use of cocaine, because I wouldn't touch it when the Budweiser mirror it lay on, with a straw and razor blade, was placed in front of me time and time again. One thing is for sure, I'm alive and well twenty years later, and some of the people I knew who used it regularly are in their graves today, never reaching the age of 35. It's not that I carry a self-righteous attitude about it, because I came close to being killed many times doing other things; like brawling on Time Square in 1978. It's just that the fear of death I associated with cocaine came true in the lives of others; it played a major role in their premature departure from this life. Aleister Crowley, as you know from reading chapter seven, thought it was a gift from above.

Erwin Lausch wrote about cocaine in *Manipulation - Dangers and Benefits of Brain Research*, and its being hailed as a great thing by Sigmund Freud. He also quoted Freud's biographer on this issue:

"Cocaine, the active substance in coca leaves, was isolated in 1860 by Albert Neimann, a chemist at Gottingen University. It was a long time before any other researchers took an interest in cocaine. One of the first, in the early 'eighties,' was Sigmund Freud, who at that time had not thought of psychoanalysis. He hoped he could wean morphine addicts from their addiction through cocaine. 'This divine plant,' he wrote, 'which satisfies the hungry, strengthens the weak and makes them forget their misfortune....One feels an access of self-control, one feels more vigorous and able-bodied....' Freud also talked of 'exhilaration and persistent euphoria, which is in no way to be distinguished from the normal euphoria of healthy people....One is simply normal and soon finds it hard to believe one is under any outside influence....It is completely without the sense of alteration which comes through alcohol and also without alcohol's unpleasant effects.'....Freud's subjective experiences were much too meager, of course, to support such far-reaching assertions, but he was finally convinced of the rightness of his judgement. He sent cocaine to his fiancee, gave it to his sisters and praised it among friends and acquaintances. A colleague to whom he recommended cocaine as an antidote to morphine addiction became addicted to cocaine and died of it. 'In short,' writes his biographer Ernest Jones, 'from the standpoint of our present knowledge he was well on the way to becoming a danger to society.'

"Neither Freud nor his fiancee turned into cocaine addicts, but sniffing cocaine became the fashion before the end of the 'eighties.' A second wave of cocaine - taking started at the beginning of the First World War. It was very widespread in the 'twenties,' although it had long become clear by then that, besides being euphoric, cocaine often produced fear and hallucinations. Collapses with fatal results after an overdose often occurred; and the addiction often ended in megalomania, persecution mania and complete madness."15

The reason cocaine is able to produce the pleasurable effects Freud mentioned is because it binds to the same receptor sites in the brain that the neurotransmitters "dopamine" and "endorphin" do. Dopamine is a pleasure chemical. It is released regularly when we fall in love with someone. Cocaine prevents dopamine from leaving its receptor to return to its sac in the terminal button it was released from after signals have been sent to another neuron. This causes the dopamine to be in effect much longer. Cocaine augments the natural high caused by the dopamine. Neurobiologist Hans C. Fibiger of the University of British Columbia wrote about it: "When you take cocaine, it causes the neurotrasmitter dopamine to remain longer in the synaptic cleft. Cocaine does this by blocking the re-uptake mechanism whereby a neuron releases dopamine's action at the synapse."

In *The Owners Manual for the Brain*, Pierce J. Howard wrote about cocaine and endorphin: "When endorphin neurotransmitters jump a synapse and land on receptor sites, a pleasurable sensation ensues. Normally, the endorphins then detach from the receptor site and return to their pre-synaptic location. Cocaine attaches itself to the endorphins at the receptor site and prevents their return to the pre-synaptic site. Thus, (1), the pleasureable effect is maintained and (2) there is a shortage of endorphins when the cocaine is metabolized, resulting in strong let down and the urge to use more of the drug."16

In an article in *The New York Times*, Dr. Roy King, a psychiatrist at the Stanford Medical School spoke of cocaine addiction, while focusing on the popular form, "crack": "If you're highly extroverted, even slightly manic, by temperament, cocaine augments your natural high....for people who are naturally bubbling with excitement, crack seems to intensify the normal biology of a state they seek: it's an exhilarating, exciting high."

It is the urge to use more of cocaine, after one "comes down" that leads to addiction, the same addiction that killed Freud's associate. When writing about Freud, Erwin Lausch wrote that cocaine often produced fear and hallucinations. Robert Plant, as written in chapter seven, promoted the use of cocaine in the song "For Your Life," to those of us who bought the *Presence* album back in 1976. This song is also on the third cd of the four-cd remastered 54-track album put out by Jimmy Page in 1990. Therefore, it is safe to conclude that Led Zeppelin is all for any hallucinations produced by using cocaine.

MUSHROOMS

Mushrooms, as previously stated, are very popular and powerful hallucinogens, but especially in Mexico, among Shamans, which are Mexican or Indian magicians. Shamans are known for using hallucinogenic mushrooms for religious and magical purposes. In a three tape video series on the brain, called *The Brain - Our Universe Within: Matter Over Mind*, Dr. David Suzuki gave the following description of the Mexican mushrooms and the Shamans, along with their effect on consciousness in the brain. It is being quoted directly from the film set that I purchased:

"One of the more curious aspects of the brain is its ability to alter perception; to change the mind's view of reality. Amazingly, the brain can do this without much effort, and through unusual means, such as this mushroom. The mushroom contains a hallucinogenic chemical called Psilocin. In Mexico, there are Shamans who consume these mushrooms....During this spiritual or mystical experience, the two women are physically changing certain systems in their brain as they ingest the mushrooms. Within an hour, the two experience hallucinations, in which they see brightly colored geometric patterns and strange spirits....The hallucinations experienced by the shaman, come by way of tampering with the Serotonin system....In the case of hallucinations, Serotonin acts in at least two important areas. In this cat-scan image, these two areas are highlighted in red; the frontal lobes and the thalamus.

"The thalamus is the gateway of all sensory information. Everything we see, hear, and touch arrives here before moving on to other areas of the brain. In a sense, the thalamus is like a valve, controlling the flow of sensory information through the brain....The Psilocin in this mushroom is remarkably similar in molecular structure to Serotonin. Inside the brain, the Psilocin bonds well with the Serotonin receptors. The red colored Psilocin takes Serotonin's place at the receptor site, releasing the valve of the thalamus. The result, too many electrical signals reaching too many parts of the brain. It's thought that this information overflow, especially in the frontal lobes and the thalamus, eventually distorts sensory perceptions and creates hallucinations."

In *Plants of the Gods*, Richard Schultes and Albert Hofmann presented a quote directly from a Mazatec Shaman named Maria Sabina and her usage of the Mexican mushrooms: "There is a world beyond ours, a world that is far away, nearby, and invisible. And there is where God lives, where the dead live, the spirits and the saints, a world where everything has already happened and everything is known. That world talks. It has a language of its own. I report what it says. The sacred mushroom takes me by the hand and brings me to the world where everything is known. It is they, the sacred mushrooms, that speak in a way I can understand. I ask them, and they answer me. When I return from the trip that I have taken with them, I tell what they have told me and what they have shown me."17

Dr. Albert Hofmann himself, who, as previously mentioned, discovered LSD, took a journey on the Mexican mushroom, recording his findings in a piece he wrote entitled, *The Discovery of LSD and Subsequent Investigations on Naturally Occurring Hallucinogens*:

"At the peak of the intoxication, about one and a half hours after ingestion of the mushrooms, the rush of interior pictures, mostly abstract motifs rapidly changing in shape and color, reached such an alarming degree that I feared that I would be torn into this whirlpool of form and color and would dissolve. After about six hours the dream came to an end. Subjectively, I had no idea how long this condition had lasted. I felt my return to everyday reality to be a happy return from a strange, fantastic, but quite real world to an old and familiar home."18

In light of the evidence presented here, it is clearly believable that certain mushrooms can take a person on a hallucinogenic trip into the spirit world. It should come to us as no surprise then, that Robert Plant would be promoting the use of the powerful Fly Agaric mushroom during "The Rain Song" in the Led Zeppelin film, which will be elaborated on later in this chapter when discussing the Theremin.

MESCALINE

Fans of the sixties group, The Doors, should be very familiar with Mescaline, a hallucinogen derived from Peyote, taken from Mexican cacti. In *Plants of the Gods*, mescaline is described as an hallucinogen and derived from Peyote, as well as similar to a neurotransmitter in the brain: "In addition to mescaline, responsible for the visual hallucinogenic effects, several related alkaloids have been isolated from Peyote and related cacti....The chemistry of mescaline is similar to the neurotransmitter noradrenaline (norepinephrine), a brain hormone..."[19] A humorous illustration of this effect can be seen in the movie, *Young Guns*.

Aldous Huxley, in his book, *The Doors of Perception*, presented mescalin as likely capable of neutralizing the Thalamus (just as David Suzuki earlier), calling it by its practical name, the cerebral reducing valve: "These effects of mescalin are the sort of effects you could expect to follow the administration of a drug having the power to impair the efficiency of the cerebral reducing valve."[20] Mescaline is a hallucinogenic capable of impairing the Thalamus, enabling us to hallucinate, because it is similar in its molecular structure to noradrenalin (norepinephrine), which enables it to attach to receptors on neurons, thereby inhibiting the natural function of reducing the amount of sensory information to the brain performed by the Thalamus.

LSD-25: LYSERGIC ACID DIETHYLAMIDE - TWENTY FIVE

The most famous of the hallucinogenic drugs used in the rock culture, from its onset until today, is Lysergic Acid Diethylamide-Twenty Five, better known as LSD-25; allegedly glorified by both the Beatles and Elton John in the song, "Lucy In the Sky With Diamonds." As already stated, it was discovered by Albert Hofmann. He discovered it while working for Sandoz, a pharmaceutical company, in Basil, Switzerland, in 1938. Like Psilocin from the mushrooms, LSD is structured similarly to Serotonin, therefore it too can bind with Serotonin receptors in the brain. In *Manipulation-Dangers and Benefits of Brain Research*, Erwin Lausch wrote of LSD and Serotonin:

"A whole number of hallucinogens show a similar chemical structure to serotonin. They include the active substances in the Mexican 'holy mushroom' and LSD. Mescaline, the active substance in the peyote cactus, is closely related chemically to noradrenalin. The muscarinic agent contained in fly agaric is like the transmitter substance acetylcholine in its molecular structure.

"The similarity of molecular structure in hallucinogens and transmitter substances can scarcely be a coincidence. But what do we deduce from that? According to an interesting speculation, the hallucinogens work in the brain like transmitter substances and reinforce the amount of real transmitters. As a result the known effect of the hallucinogens occurs: an unusual abundance of feelings, images and ideas appear, which normally are suppressed so that the brain can concentrate on the particular tasks it has to master.

'Among the typical experiences is LSD or mescalin trips,' writes the Munich psychologist Wolfgang Schmidbauer, 'one is that consciousness is flooded with incredibly intense perceptions and all the senses communicate far richer and more plentiful messages than is biologically expedient. The LSD or mescalin "tripper" is in fact less efficient biologically, because he is impressed and carried away by a wealth of unwanted experiences. We may conclude from this that we are normally aware of only a small but appropriate and constant section of all our sense impressions.'"21

The why of LSD's influence on the brain has been presented. It is because of its molecular structure being comparable to the neurotransmitter Serotonin. The how of LSD's affect is going to be presented along with Led Zeppelin's use of the Theremin and what I believe to be the promotion of LSD-25, both in the film and, in one of their songs from the *Physical Graffiti* album. The how of its affect will come right from the man who discovered it, Albert Hofmann.

LED ZEPPELIN II – "WHOLE LOTTA LOVE"

The effect of the hallucinogenic drugs used by Led Zeppelin fans come to their peak under the influence of the magician, Jimmy Page, and his Theremin spell. As in the chapter heading, the Theremin was first used by Led Zeppelin during "Whole Lotta Love" as it was recorded for their second album, *Led Zeppelin II*. It was Aleister Crowley who suggested that magicians invent new ways to aid invocation of spirits, in *Magick-Book 4*Liber Aba*: "There are many other devices to aid invocation, so many that it is impossible to enumerate them; and the Magician will be wise to busy himself in inventing new ones."22 Although Jimmy Page didn't invent the Theremin, it stands to reason that Crowley would have approved of his adapting it to the Led Zeppelin arsenal for invocation purposes. The Devil himself probably instructed Page to use it. I myself saw visions of Satan while listening to the Theremin at full volume under the influence of drugs. That was not the only thing I saw. It would take forever for me to list everything, but I did see the Devil many times. I also saw the numbers 666 in the form of flames shooting right at my face repeatedly. It's not the visual that is the scariest element however. It's just a supplement to let you know who is attacking your consciousness. The scariest part of the Theremin spell is the manipulation of the mind to bend the will toward Devil worship, I believe, that comes from the knowledge of Satan's existence that resides in the subconscious, along with knowledge of God's existence, and their respective moral codes, known among *Bible* students as the knowledge of good and evil; some of the knowledge of which is presented in the conscience in its originally designed form, as the knowledge of right and wrong. As we are all aware, the conscience can be remolded to be completely in favor of wrong being right, and right being wrong. This what is meant by the phrase, "he has no conscience."

PHYSICAL GRAFFITI – "THE ROVER"

As has been proclaimed in this book many times already, the author believes the members of Led Zeppelin had their consciences completely reversed by their chosen anti-Christ moral code in conjunction with the use of drugs and involvement in their specific form of Satanism. Robert Plant's comments from "The Rover" need to be mentioned before moving full speed into *The Song Remains the Same* to get to the heart of this chapter. In the beginning of the lyrical portion of the song, Robert Plant sings that a "trip" can be described as a "fall." I believe the next two statements are related to the former word. He sings that he would "rock" the thing, then that he occasionally "rolls" the thing as well. He then, however, says that he has "always" known its purpose. I believe that he is saying that he knew the purpose of tripping. My conclusion fits perfectly with the following information.

LSD-25, ABRAMELIN MAGICK, AND THE THEREMIN

As previously mentioned, the author believes Robert Plant promoted tripping on LSD-25 in the Led Zeppelin film, in the early portion of the 27 minute "Dazed and Confused," that begins with a demonic bass routine. He does it twice in the early section, four times each time for a total of eight. Just after the multicolored hallucinogenic part of the film at the end of the jam, he shouts "25!" four more times. In between these sections, I believe the violin bow is used as a Magick wand to project demonic forces at the fans. Then at twenty minutes into the song, Plant shouts "Ah!" and Page responds with a slam of a power chord on the guitar. This occurs three times and then Plant shouts "I Give!" three times. The next thing you see, five seconds later, is the camera zoom into Jimmy Page's left eye, to show security guards roughing up a fan in the building. Here is the progression. Robert Plant shouts "25!" four times, and then after telling the fans to sell their souls to "him," he then shouts "25!" four times once more. Then Jimmy Page plays a blazing lead taking them into the "San Francisco" song by Scott McKenzie, where they make it clear it is Satan that Plant was telling the fans to sell their souls to. This takes them into Page's violin bow routine where I believe he performs Abramelin Magick on the fans, which allows demonic forces to then attack the consciousness of those they are targeting. If a person was already tripping on acid when Page was using the violin bow, they could see demonic images already. Nevertheless, Plant tells them to trip (I believe) by shouting "25!" Then he is shouting "I Give" three times in the middle of the Page lengthy jam. Finally, Plant proves he was talking about LSD-25 when the lengthy jam ends later in the song and he (Plant) is shown in various different shades of strange colors; chanting "25!" four times once again, just afterward. All of this promoting of LSD-25, along with the satanic pact, in conjunction with Abramelin demonic Magick with the violin bow as a Magick wand, and the shouting of "I Give!" three times, paints a very eerie picture of what these men are doing, which is preparatory for the upcoming Theremin routine; all under the disguise of "rock and roll."

Approaching the end of the concert in *The Song Remains the Same*, the fans have been listening to loud blazing music for about three hours. Once again, as Jimi Hendrix said, when people are brought to their weakest point, you can preach whatever you want into their subconscious mind. In this case, the fans are worn down by three hours of mesmerization, which means their resistance is low, and if they have taken LSD-25, they are hallucinating to the sounds of the music as the show heads into "Whole Lotta Love" and its blistering Theremin routine. When Jimmy Page was asked by Bruno Stein in *"Creem"* Magazine in 1976, about the reason for Led Zeppelin's exceeding long concerts, he said, "…we felt we needed that amount of time to get it all across: different things that we were attempting to say, different moods that we were attempting to create."

Before the song begins, I believe there were already Abramelin demons working on the minds of the fans in the arena. If they are tripping, they are about to go on an electronic ride of various sounds and images working together with the knowledge of good and evil stored in their subconscious minds. It was Hippocrates, known as the father of medicine, who described the brain as having the knowledge of good and evil this way: "Not only our pleasure, our joy and our laughter, but also our sorrow, pain, grief and tears arise from the brain, and the brain alone….With it we think and understand, see and hear, and we discriminate between the ugly and the beautiful, between what is pleasant and what is unpleasant and between good and evil." The reason we perceive something as good or evil is because the subconscious mind tells us it is. If you saw *The Exorcist* and were scared, it is because your subconscious mind told you what you were watching was pure evil. The movie didn't tell you it was evil, your subconscious mind did. If you look at a sunset on the water and think it is beautiful, it is because your mind has been programmed to think that way. Again, it is the brain that tells us if something we see is beautiful or ugly. Then there is the conscience that tells us if something is good or evil morally. In our society today, the absolutes of good and evil are being destroyed. This is how people can give themselves over to a wicked mind frame, nurture that mind frame with drugs and alcohol, and then end up believing that Satan is god, once he begins to reveal himself to people through drug use and music like Led Zeppelin's. It has been that way from the beginning of Led Zeppelin right up to the Page/Plant world tour in 1995.

Writing of the beginning, Bob Harvey, of *The Journal* wrote of Led Zeppelin's May 9th, 1969 concert at Edmonton Gardens in Edmonton, Canada. One of the most obvious things he wrote was that the band produced intense visions with their music. He then said that they were deadly: "The visions have such deadly fascinations that you can't bear to blink an ear..."

One month later, Led Zeppelin performed in Birmingham, England on June 13th, 1969. Weird sounds by the band were mentioned in an article presented in the *Record Mirror*: "The more weird the electronic sounds created by Led Zeppelin, the more the crowd loved it..."

Twenty eight years later, Steven Davis, in the latest edition of *Hammer of the Gods*, called Jimmy Page's gesturing with the Theremin demonic, when describing his use of it on the 1995 Page/Plant World Tour: "...Page worked his trusty old Theremin, parked stage right and still emitting creepy blasts of electromagnetic frequencies as Page gestured demonically."23 Demonically, obviously, has to do with demons. This is how Page was observed. Davis used that word to describe Jimmy Page's actions and the sounds emitting from the Theremin. They had evil connotations. It was Steven Davis' subconscious mind that told him the sounds were demonic, because like all humans, again, he has the knowledge of good and evil. Davis is not alone. In 1975, Led Zeppelin performed a series of concerts at Earls Court in London. Mick Gold, in *Rock on the Road*, wrote about Jimmy Page looking like a sorcerer when performing with the Theremin: "...Page proceeded to coax unearthly sounds out of a theramin, waving the stick around like a sorcerer's apprentice. Undoubtedly some of his personal preoccupation with the occult rubs off on his performances and is converted into a spurious mystique...." In 1977, Dale Funtash wrote in *Focus Magazine* about Page being a sorcerer and the Theremin being demonic at the famous "Destroyer" Concert in Cleveland on April 27th, 1977: "By controlling the sound of the theramin with simple hand motions in space, Page showed that he can also suggest that he is indeed a musical sorcerer by making his motions mysterious and demonic." This is what Page is after, to arouse the good and evil connotations from the subconscious. You can bet money where Jimmy got the instructions for this, right? Absolutely. It came from none other than the Black Magician Aleister Crowley.

In *Magick-Book 4*Liber Aba*, Crowley instructed the magician to dominate other men, making the magician their master, by attacking the subconscious mind: "...one might master another man, even a stranger, by sheer concentration of will, ceremonially or otherwise wrought up to the requisite potential. But in one way or another that will must be made to impinge on the man; by the normal means of contact if possible, if not, by attacking some sensitive spot in his subconscious sensorium. But the heaviest rod will not land the smallest fish unless there be a line of some sort fixed firmly to both."24 The line, obviously, is the music, the violin bow, and the Theremin. Before moving on, I want to elaborate on this concept of the subconscious mind, to prepare you for a better understanding of the use of the Theremin.

In his book, *The Chemistry of Conscious States*, J. Allan Hobson, wrote of the mind, both in its conscious, or aware mode, and its subconscious, or unaware mode. He contrasted the two rather quickly in this statement: "The mind is all the information in the brain. Consciousness is the brain's awareness of some of that information."25 He later elaborated: "If consciousness is the brain's awareness of some of its information, then what is the mind? It is simply all the information in the brain. In this definition, mind is more fundamental than consciousness because most of the information that is in the brain at any point in time is not conscious. We cannot sense the programs that tell us how to breathe, when to sleep, how to remember, and even how to think. It all just happens. The best we can do is figure out how to use these capabilities to our advantage."26 In other words, the information that we are aware of at any point in time is in our conscious mind, and information we are not aware of is stored in the subconscious mind; but is able to be recalled, as with the knowledge of good and evil, and as we are about to see, God and Devil, good and evil's respective personifications. Once again, it is the subconscious mind, possessing the knowledge of good and evil, as displayed in a person's conscience, that tells the conscious mind, or consciousness, how to think. If you want to change the person's conscious mind, or consciousness, how he or she thinks, you attack the subconscious mind, from where standards of thought originate. Aleister Crowley instructed his students that very way in 1922 when he wrote his *Confessions*: "Our spiritual consciousness acts through the will and its instruments upon material objects, in order to produce changes which will result in the establishment of the new conditions of consciousness which we wish. That is the definition of Magick."27 The new condition of consciousness is the new condition of thinking. In other words, it is brainwashing, without the person's consent. Such is the essence of backward masking, that will be addressed later, in no uncertain terms. In using the Theremin to produce demonic sounds, in conjunction with the volume, drug use of the fans, and demonic activity caused by the spells I believe he cast previously in the concert, as well as with the Theremin, the result is the same new conditions of consciousness in the minds of the fans that Jimmy Page and the band seek. It is just as Dr. Sir J. G. Frazer wrote in *The Golden Bough*: "The magician does not doubt that the same causes will always produce the same effects, that the performance of the proper ceremony, accompanied by the appropriate spell, will inevitably be attended by the desired result..."28 This author couldn't agree more, which is why Page is doing what he does, even to this day. It is a reciprocal relationship, with the subconscious speaking to the conscious, then back to the subconscious that I believe Page is after. It all sounds very complex, but it is simple in the end. The Theremin is being used (I believe) to attack the subconscious mind to get it to project thoughts of demonic forces to the conscious mind, change the conscious mind or consciousness' attitude or perception of these forces from evil to good, and then to reprogram the subconscious in accordance with the new condition of thought about demons and the Devil that the magician Jimmy Page seeks. I believe that because I experienced it; and he failed. Hallucinations play an important role in this complex Magick.

In order to understand completely why Led Zeppelin promoted the use of LSD-25, we are going to examine the writing of Albert Hofmann, who discovered LSD in 1938, as he experimented with it in 1943 and recorded his findings. He wrote that he was "dazed": "As I lay in a dazed condition with my eyes closed (I experienced daylight as disagreeably bright), there surged upon me an uninterrupted stream of fantastic images of extraordinary plasticity and vividness and accompanied by an intense kaleidoscope-like play of colors....As far as I remember, the following were the most outstanding symptoms: vertigo, visual disturbances: the faces of those around me appeared as grotesque colored masks....Occasionally I felt as if I were out of my body."29

They were the initial effects of the drug as Hofmann took it and went home, with the thought of astral projection dominating his mind, that he was not in his body; another thing Crowley and Page advocate (Kashmir-chapter six). The following quote from Hofmann is the most pertinent to what Page is doing with the Theremin. Specifically, Hofmann speaks of sounds producing images in accordance with the hallucination resulting from using LSD-25: "...all objects appeared in unpleasant, constantly changing colors, the predominant shades being sickly green and blue. When I closed my eyes, an unending series of colorful, very realistic, and fantastic images surged in upon me. A remarkable feature was the manner in which all acoustic perceptions (i.e., the noise of a passing car) were transformed into optical effects, every sound invoking a corresponding colored hallucination constantly changing in shape and color like pictures in a kaleidoscope."30

Hofmann saw colored hallucinations in accordance with the sounds that he heard while tripping on LSD-25, that he produced. What better source for us to consider than him? Steven Davis said Jimmy Page was gesturing demonically in 1995. You can see and hear him using the Theremin to produce demonic sounds in *The Song Remains the Same*. If you are watching the film or listening to the soundtrack, you can hear Robert Plant making shrieks with his voice to coincide with what Page is doing, and in the film you can see Jimmy smile at Robert while he is doing it, and Peter Grant is standing on the other side of the Theremin. I believe they knew exactly what they were doing.

When I saw Page/Plant at the Orlando Arena, I nudged the guy next to me when Jimmy started to play the Theremin. He was smoking a joint and was nervous that I might be a cop, because he kept looking at me to see what I would say as he smoked it. I didn't say anything, neither did I ask him for any. Now he was about to get really nervous. I said to him, "Do you see what Jimmy Page is doing? That's black Magick. It's real." He listened to the spaced out sounds and his eyes were glued to Page's every move. It had made him think, being stoned. So Jimmy Page and Robert Plant were still using the Theremin in the 1990's, and one can bet it's for the same reason, to conjure demonic sounds and images.

When tripping on a hallucinogen, especially LSD-25, sounds produce images, as already presented. Demonic sounds produce demonic images. The knowledge of evil in the subconscious tells the listener the sound of the Theremin is demonic. The hallucinogen produces the demonic image in accordance with the sound. Now what? The fans in *The Song Remains the Same* who are tripping can see demonic forces. In *Receptors*, Dr. Richard Restak said this about Hofmann's description of his LSD-25 trip you already read in this chapter: "...Hofmann experienced a number of frightening, indeed terrifying reactions, much like accounts I have heard from people suffering from 'bad trips.' Typically such victims-this seems an appropriate choice of word-are completely out of control and are convinced of the reality of their hallucinations."31 The point is, the hallucinations appear as reality. Let me illustrate it with the following quote from J. Allan Hobson in *The Chemistry of Conscious States*: "Instead of creating a burden by insisting that a hidden cause for dreams, hallucinations, and delusions exists in some interaction between supposed layers of the mind, the new model offers a simple explanation; the imagery and emotions of dreams are always with us, riding in our nonconscious, and when we change state from waking to dreaming this information is able to cross into consciousness. Our dreams are not mysterious phenomena, they are conscious events. Here's the simplest test: Are we aware of what happens in our dreams? Of course. Therefore, dreaming is a conscious experience."32

Hobson referred to our dreams as conscious events in the subconscious mind while asleep. The demonic sounds of the Theremin tap into the subconscious, and bring the imagery of evil over into consciousness, just as the dream comes to consciousness when you wake up in the morning. As Jack Fincher put it in *The Brain - Mystery of Matter and Mind*: "In the dreamlike trance of hypnosis, the brain and body tap powers and thoughts beyond the reach of the conscious mind. Early physiologists believed hypnosis was a path to the unconscious."33 Are the fans conscious of what is happening in these hallucinations as they would be in dreams? Absolutely. Again, the hallucinations of demons are perceived as reality by the conscious mind. Here is where things get really interesting. This is the point to the whole matter. I have to tell the reader it is my belief, obviously, because neither Jimmy Page or Robert Plant are going to admit it, but look at the evidence. Working together with the magician, to establish the new conditions of consciousness in the minds of the fans, are the demons I believe were already cast on the crowd in "Dazed and Confused." Do you remember in chapter one where I talked about the song "Rock and Roll," and mentioned that when a person sings the chorus that repeatedly states a person is lonely without rock and roll that it programs the subconscious to accept that as truth? It is, again, because the conscious mind sends messages to the subconscious that are accepted as truth, then the subconscious works out what it believes to be true in the life of the individual; in their conscious mind. Jimmy Page, with the Theremin tapping the subconscious, bringing demonic images to consciousness, has done his job. Now, I believe that the Abramelin demons and Robert Plant take over. Sometimes the Devil himself is seen, as I wrote about my own hallucinations before.

Dr. Restak gave this interesting information about PCP (Angel Dust), the Devil, and one of his patients in *Receptors*: "A decade ago I saw a patient who had killed his wife with a shovel after the two of them smoked marijuana that had been laced, unknown to them, with PCP. The last thing my patient could recall was seeing his wife assume before his eyes the form and identity of the Devil."34 This took place without demonic sounds from the Theremin. Can you imagine tripping on LSD-25, listening to the Theremin at full volume, with demons or Satan himself working on your mind? As I said, I believe that Robert Plant and the demonic forces take over once Page is finished. Normally, right at the end of the Theremin's climax, Robert Plant would again shout "I Give!" He did this during the 1973 tour, the same one filmed in *The Song Remains the Same*. He waited, however, right till the end of the song (Edited out of the film was his shouting "I Give!" many times just before the Theremin routine. However, this can be heard clearly on the 7/28/73 soundboard). After the theatrical climax of "Whole Lotta Love," where fire shoots up into the air, thirteen minutes into song, there comes two close-up shots of drummer John Bonham. The first one has him wearing a many-studded headband. The second close-up shot of Bonham shows him wearing no headband, and it is there that Robert Plant shouts "I Give!" I mentioned that Plant yelled that repeatedly in "Dazed and Confused" and now he is yelling it at the end of "Whole Lotta Love." I believe Robert Plant is yelling a suggestion to the mind of the fan, that he give his will over to the demonic force working in his mind; aided by the sound and images.

YIELDING THE WILL TO THE DEVIL

The power of suggestion in this context of Led Zeppelin's effect on the minds of the fans in the audience can be overwhelming. To thoroughly illustrate some fans yielding their wills to the Devil or the demons working in their minds in his stead, as I see it, some powerful quotes, including a few from Eliphas Levi and Aleister Crowley, in conjunction with statements from the movies "Dracula" and "Braveheart" will now be presented. Afterward, my own testimony of Theremin Magick being performed on me at Madison Square Garden on June 11th, 1977 will be expounded on. The author believes that the Theremin routine of Led Zeppelin's, performed on the mind of the sympathetic listener, who, as a result of having his or her conscience seared by an conscious choice to live the anti-Christ lifestyle to the fullest, succeeds in either desensitizing that individual to satanic influence, reconfirming and strengthening their commitment to that lifestyle, or, in its most effective form, turning the fan who yields his or her will into an individual sympathetic to the Devil and his cause. That is the first step to getting involved in the occult and making a satanic pact; or in other words, "birds of a feather, flock together." It is the successful completion of Crowley's definition of Magick, to form the new condition of consciousness in the mind of the fan; according to the will of the magician, which is Satan's spiritual agenda. This is why Lord Jesus Christ commanded Moses to put any witch, spiritualist, magician, etc., to death among the children of Israel (Again, I want to state emphatically that I am in no way encouraging violence against anyone. I am simply stating why these people were to be put to death in Israel. If anyone harms (kills) a member of Led Zeppelin, the Silver Star, or any Led Zeppelin fan, this author is consenting to their capital punishment.).

As an evangelical proselytizing tool for the Devil and his Silver Star, Led Zeppelin was committed to recruiting followers. Obviously, Aleister Crowley is largely responsible for it, as a result of his writings. The following is a quote from Crowley's book, *Moonchild*, in which he addresses his students on the subject of recruitment: "...we are dealing with delicate forces; we have to train our minds with an intensity which no other study in the world demands. Public indifference and incredulity suit us perfectly. The only object of advertisement would be to get suitable members; but we have methods of finding them without publicity. We make no secret of our methods and results, on the other hand; but only the right man knows how to discover them."35 In other words, only the right man knows how to discover what is really going on. In that quote Crowley made it clear that "Public indifference and incredulity suit us perfectly." Indifference, as we all know, is just not caring. That suited Led Zeppelin and Page/Plant perfectly. If the public didn't care what they were up to as long as they were entertaining, they were free to work Magick on their fans. Incredulity is not as common a term. What this word means is an "unwillingness or inability to believe."36

By this time you have heard many say they don't believe in the Devil or Magick or anything along those lines, and that I'm insane. There is no difference between them and a man I spoke to one time in Fred's Tavern on Blackwell Street in Dover, New Jersey, back in the spring of 1980, who told me he didn't have a drinking problem, although he drank seven days a week. He said, as we sat at the bar, "See? I can push it away from me. I'm not hooked on alcohol." While making that statement, he pushed his mixed drink about a foot away from him. Five seconds later, he pulled it back and began to drink it again. I thought to myself, "He's either a bold face liar, or he's voluntarily self-deluded." I think for his sanity that it was the latter. In either case, his futile statements were an exercise in self-parody. People with an inkling of the knowledge of good and evil in their minds, who examine this book carefully, can see the obvious truth of Led Zeppelin's Devil worship and evangelical work as his ambassadors. Incredulity, or refusing to believe the obvious, is an attempt to avoid the truth being presented, so they can continue on their present course, not worrying about any consequences. This is nothing more than spiritual cowardice, and it should not intimidate anyone who is reading objectively, especially if your awareness of the supernatural is on the rise. Even if you are disturbed by the revelations contained herein, at least be comforted by the fact that you have the courage to face what is true. For in the end, we are all going to stand before him who is true, and give an account of ourselves; as having been given the knowledge of good and evil.

So Aleister Crowley is pleased by the public's not caring or refusal to believe in Magick. Why? Because it allows the magician to perform his Magick and recruit those who are willing to follow. If someone points a finger, the magician says it is tongue in cheek. After all, who can manifest an evil spirit and hand him a subpoena, ordering him to testify against the magician in a court of law? No one can. Such is the mysteriousness surrounding the interaction of the spirit and physical world.

Crowley used a metaphor to describe that action being taken by magicians in performing the Great Work, or uniting mankind with Satan. He wrote about taking a woman away from another man. It is a perfect metaphor when you consider he wanted to ensure his own damnation and help others to escape from Jesus and find the Devil (see chapter five heading). In this next quote, he is the Devil, the woman is mankind, and the other man is Jesus. Again, this comes from Crowley's book, *Magick-Book 4*Liber Aba*: "...suppose that I wish to win a woman who dislikes me and loves somebody else. In this case, not only her Will, but her lover's, must be overcome by my own. I have no direct control of either. But my Will is in touch with the woman's by means of our minds; I have only to make my mind the master of hers by the existing means of communication; her mind will then present its recantation to her Will, her Will repeal its decision, and her body submit to mine as the seal of her surrender."37 That statement illustrates perfectly the mission of the Devil, making wrong right, and right wrong; the Theremin routine being a small part. Crowley used the word "communication." Once again, rock and roll is the medium of communication here. So recruiting new members for the Silver Star was a serious agenda for Led Zeppelin and Page/Plant; with the Devil as their overlord.

The major factor in favor of this Magick being performed successfully on the fans is their willingness to be hypnotized. The atmosphere in Madison Square Garden is one of receptiveness to anything the band is doing as they head toward the end of the concert. Everyone is having a dandy old time being mesmerized. Then in the middle of Whole Lotta Love, Jimmy Page attacks their minds with the Theremin. The mental condition of the average fan is that of being one with everyone else in the Garden, singing the lyrics of the music, and loving Led Zeppelin as well as maintaining the buzz. When I saw Page/Plant at the Orlando Arena on March 7th, 1995, nearing the end of the show, Robert Plant was standing by the speakers on the right corner of the stage singing "Black Dog." All fifteen thousand people in the arena were singing the song with him. You could barely hear his voice over the crowd's. He was in complete control of the minds of the fans. Even I was amazed at how well they were performing as Page wailed the lead guitar on the left side of the stage. The crowd was at a fever pitch. The band had them in the palms of their hands. By the time they got to "Whole Lotta Love" in *The Song Remains the Same*, the situation was comparable. The oneness of the crowd with itself and with the band is an important part of the mind control.

This oneness places the conscious mind in the completely receptive mode; receptive to the entire scope of what is going on, especially the performance of the band, and accentuated by being high on drugs. In *Hypnotism-Theory and Practice*, Walter Gibson describes what could be called the crowd in the film, *The Song Remains the Same*:

"Factors other than hypnotism must be recognized where group behavior is concerned. The Bacchanalia was primarily a wine festival, honoring Bacchus, God of the Grape, and many drunken revels have been patterned after it. There is a marked similarity between certain stages of intoxication and hypnotism, such as amenability to suggestion, immunity to pain, lapse of memory, and in the group phase, imitative activity, notably off-key choral singing.

"The same applies with narcotics and drugs, for since time immemorial, various herbs and roots have been used to rouse individuals to states of ecstasy or fervor. Evidences of hypnotic similarity is found with drugs that produce hallucinations, perceptual distortions and loss of time sense."38

In this mind frame the fan is completely vulnerable to the invasion of Jimmy Page and his Theremin attack. With the demonic imagery being manipulated by the evil spirits, I believe, and the drugs producing hallucinations, especially LSD-25, the minds of the fans are easy prey for the demons to attack consciousness; which they can do without hallucinations, but they make it easier. Remember, you are never so vulnerable to a person's influence as you are when you are sympathetic to them. Quoting Dr. Henry Morris in his book, *Escape the Coming Night*, which is about the end of this world when the Anti-Christ reigns, Dr. David Jeremiah presented the same theme about the drugs and demons: "Stupefying and hallucinatory drugs have been associated with sorcery and witchcraft for ages, yielding to their users strange visions and hallucination, which they could interpret as oracles for the guidance of their clients. Also, they divested their users of the control of their own minds, making them easily available for possession and control by evil spirits."39 As the Theremin produces demonic sounds, that tap into the subconscious, which sends the message to the conscious mind that the sounds are demonic, the conscious mind, under the influence of a hallucinogen, can easily produce demonic images that can be seen by the fan. Then the demons really go to work, especially since the images appear as reality, and when the demons are there, it is reality. This is the point where Robert Plant's "I Give!" plays a major role. After all, the evil spirits do not quit their work after the Theremin routine is over, that simply accentuates it.

Eliphas Levi wrote about Karl von Eckartshausen, author of *The Cloud Upon the Sanctuary*, the book that launched Aleister Crowley's magical career: "In his German work upon Magic, Eckartshausen describes the whole of the fantastic apparatus, being a system of machines and operations by which imagination was helped to create the phantoms desired..."40 So you see, the magicians want to create these phantoms (images) in the imagination. Levi then wrote of the imagination: "Imagination, in effect, is like the soul's eye; therein forms are outlined and preserved; thereby we behold the reflections of the invisible world; it is the glass of visions and the apparatus of magical life."41 The machines create the phantoms in the imagination. The imagination sees the phantom of the invisible world. Then Levi said in his book, *La Clef des Grands Mysteries*: "Phantoms, dreams, including waking dreams, are therefore real images existing in the light."42 "In the light" there means the spirit world of transcendental magic. In *The Book on Mediums*, Allan Kardec said the same thing (in 1874): "Will the hallucinationists say that the soul (if they so much as admit a soul) has moments of over-excitement, when its faculties are exalted? We agree with them; but when what is seen is real, it is not illusion....if all the theories of hallucination are insufficient to explain all the facts, it must be that there is something else beside hallucination."43 Jimmy Page himself said, on the Making Waves radio show, "There are certain things which happen for which there's no logical explanation apart from the term ESP (Extra Sensory Perception)." It is no surprise to me that Jimmy Page would say that. In Israel Regardie's biog-biography on Crowley, he quotes an individual named Harman from an essay titled, *Main Currents*: "And in another part of this essay we read: 'The action of the consciousness-expanding drugs gives the person access to hitherto inaccessible psychic material, facilitates thinking and feeling in unfamiliar ways, allows perception of himself and the world about him in an unhabitual manner, and makes it possible for him to re-examine his basic beliefs and values in the light of such new data.'"44 Allan Kardec knows full well that what is seen is real in this context, as well as what it is that is beside hallucination that is dangerous. He wrote: "The spirit that would do harm can do it without showing himself, and even more surely; he is not dangerous because he is a spirit, but because of the influence he can exert in the thought, turning it away from good and toward evil."45 Eliphas Levi concurs: "The absorption of one will by another frequently changes a whole series of destinies, and not for ourselves only should we watch our relations, learning to distinguish pure from impure atmospheres, for the true philters, and those most dangerous, are invisible."46 I find it interesting that Aleister Crowley's "former self" talks of wills being absorbed by someone else's will. Crowley did say that was the definition of Magick. Jimmy Page agrees.

The spirits don't have to show themselves in the minds of the fans, because the drugs and Theremin are producing images for them. So they are still being seen. What Kardec and Levi are emphasizing in their respective quotes, is the process in which a spirit, when the knowledge of evil is manifest in the conscious mind, can then attack the consciousness and suggest that the evil is actually good. If the fan is enjoying himself, and the spirit manifests in hallucination, the fan is suddenly aware of the spiritual reality. Then he has a choice to make. As he can sense his consciousness begin to transform the information from the subconscious that tells him what he sees and hears is evil, to a new perception, that it is not evil but good, he can yield his will to this transformation, by an act of his will, or, he can agree with his subconscious that it is indeed evil, and resist the manipulation of his will. While all this is going on, Satan is in fact tempting the fans to worship him knowingly, and God is testing the fan by allowing it to see if he or she will, in spite of the warning of the subconscious mind's original knowledge of good and evil, programmed into it by God himself. Many rock fans have just submitted to Satan during this type of scenario, and that is where all the satanic rock bands have had their root. They were only fans at one point in time (How powerful is this magical working once the fans have been programmed to believe that born again Christianity is mental illness and religious fanaticism, as I had? I thought that they were simply ascetic, missing out on the good life; ignorant). Aleister Crowley warned the magician that the person who has the Magick performed on them can resist by yielding his will to the knowledge in the subconscious rather than the influence of the spirits that are trying to change wrong to right, or evil to good in his consciousness. It all depends on how strong the will of the listener is, in conjunction with his conscious choice of future moral code. Remember, Jimi Hendrix said that you can hypnootize people with music and when they are at their weakest point, like after three hours of pounding music which drains the mind and weakens the will, you have them at the point where they are vulnerable to whatever you want to preach into their subconscious. Crowley wrote of his subjective experience in this area, confessing that his subconscious was in league with Aiwaz, who we know is Satan: "As is well known, there is a limit to the power of the hypnotist; he cannot overcome the resistance of the unconscious of his patient. My own unconscious was thus in alliance with Aiwaz; taken between two fires, my conscious self was paralyzed so long as the pressure lasted….my consciousness was ultimately invaded by the Secret Self, and surrendered unconditionally, so that it proclaimed, loudly and gladly, for its citadel, the victory of its rightful Lord."47 Believing that the Devil is inside of him, in the form of Hadit, who he said was the flame burning in the heart of every man, it is easy for Crowley to call him the Secret Self, and for Jimmy Page to say that somebody takes over when he is playing, which is somebody inside of him. If the Devil got into these men, it was not because he was their creator, it was because of their love for him and their hatred for God; as in the case of Judas Iscariot.

In the Led Zeppelin concert, to say the least, all of the fans wanted to be hypnotized by the music for the purpose of emotional pain relief. That's what is behind it all. If the person the spirits are working on (at any concert) yields to this transformation of the perception of evil to good, then that message is sent back to the subconscious mind that evil spirits are not evil, but good. Also, that the Devil is not evil, but good. Then, in the future, the individual is on his way to living out this new condition of thinking, as it is now reinforced by a newly reprogrammed subconscious mind. There is the end result of the magician using demonic power to create change, or the new conditions of consciousness in accordance with his will, which is the will of the Devil, who Satanists believe is god. Crowley called the successful completion of this the Great Work. He also made it clear in his *Equinox* that hallucinations can be used in the pursuit of that goal. It is no surprise then, that Robert Plant is advocating hallucinogens in the Led Zeppelin film and soundtrack. Crowley wrote:

"Now, if it were possible to induce these states of ecstasy or hallucination, or whatever we care to call them, at will, so to speak, we should have accomplished what was once called, and what is still known as, the Great Work, and have discovered the Stone of the Wise, that universal dissolvent. Sorrow would cease and give way to joy, and joy to a bliss quite unimaginable to all who have not as yet experienced it."48

Here it is again, Led Zeppelin following the instructions of Black Magician Aleister Crowley. I believe it was Robert Plant's job to compel the listener to yield to this transformation of the perception of good and evil that the spirits were trying to work in his or her mind. That, apparently, would lead to the "joy and bliss" Crowley mentioned, once the fan unites with the evil spirit world, and inevitably Satan.

How do I believe that Robert Plant did this? By shouting "I Give!" This is going to be illustrated now by the two movies, "Dracula"(1931), and "Braveheart." In the Dracula film, near the end, when Professor Van Helsing realizes what Dracula is up to, Dracula (Bela Lugosi) appears to him and warns him to leave England and go back to his own country. Van Helsing tells him he is going to stay and protect those Dracula wanted to destroy. He tells Dracula he will eventually find him in his coffin and drive a stake through his heart. Upon hearing this, Dracula commands Van Helsing "Come Here!" Then he extends his hand toward him, placing him under a magical hypnotic spell, repeating the command. Van Helsing, under the spell, as defined by his eyes, begins to walk toward Dracula. Suddenly, in the middle of it, he stops and backs away. Dracula says to him, "Your will is strong, Van Helsing." Notice that he said it was his will that was strong, not his subconscious. In the movie, "Braveheart," William Wallace (Mel Gibson) is being disemboweled before a large crowd. The executioner is trying to get Wallace to say he is the King's subject and then beg for mercy, upon which a quick execution would come. He says to Wallace, "It can all end right now, peace, bliss, just say it, cry out - Mercy!" The crowd watching this begins to shout "Mercy!" at him. Wallace's natural inclination at this point is to shout for mercy, but in light of the circumstances, he uses every ounce of psychological strength he has to resist the temptation to shout for mercy, with his will. The executioner and crowd's chanting "Mercy" at him is the power of suggestion trying to break Wallace's will to resist the pain and shout for mercy. It doesn't work. Wallace shouts "Freedom!" Then he is beheaded, but he never submitted to the king's authority. He won the battle of wills, between he and the king, although it cost him his life. This is the same type of battle of will that I believe took place between the evil spirits at the Led Zeppelin concert and the fan under their spell. The spirits are trying to change right to wrong and evil to good in the fan's consciousness and worship evil. While this battle is raging, Robert Plant is shouting "I Give!" Plant is shouting that to get the fan to yield his will, I believe. You can see whose side Robert Plant is on. Remember, in chapter eleven he is commanding the fans to sell their souls to the Devil in no uncertain terms. There is no ambiguity here. He is a hardcore Devil worshiper, just like his mentor on the guitar. Some will accuse me of speculation, although subjectively I know this is what he is doing. This very thing happened to me at Madison Square Garden on June 11th, 1977 during the song "No Quarter," just after Jimmy Page shot out some Theremin shrieks. The shrieks were incredibly loud.

When Page shot out those Theremin shriek type sounds, it was like being overcome by a quick narcotic rush. That is as close as I can come to describing it. It was as though my will was being bent. No words were spoken. None needed to be. It was conceptual. The concepts were exactly what I have written here. I was being tempted to completely give myself over to evil. The concept of worshiping Satan was the overwhelming one. The backward masking as well as all the satanic occult influence of their music was brought to my conscious frame of mind at once, and my will was being pulled to accept this as good instead of evil. I tightened up my will, the Theremin sounds were reverberating around Madison Square Garden, and I did not yield. It was very real, I was completely cognizant of right and wrong as dictated to me by my conscience where good and evil, God and Devil were concerned, and yet the remolding was taking place in my mind and I was aware. If I yielded, evil would have become good, and right would have become wrong, and I would have become cannon fodder for direct Satan worship (I was already one indirectly). I'm not talking about my willingness to break the law and smoke dope or buy beer as a minor, or drive a car without a license, or speed with that car. I'm referring to right and wrong, good and evil religiously, as well as blatant suggestion in my mind to worship Satan. I know I am not the only one who has ever had this happen to them at a Led Zeppelin concert and resist. That is why I do not fear any fallout or labels in this matter. I couldn't care less what any incredulous mind will have to say. They don't know what they are talking about if they say I'm making this up. Just look at the evidence I've come up with by occult authors of antiquity, who are advocated by Jimmy Page, that explain the situation I'm writing about. I'm sure also, that I will meet others who have endured black Magick being performed on them by these magicians or witches or whatever you want to call them. They are not "rock stars;" that is a gentle euphemism for hardcore satanists where Led Zeppelin and many other rock bands that I will address in another book are concerned. Another point needs to be made about that perilous day in June of 1977.

The Book of the Law, dictated to Crowley by its author, the Devil, makes this statement about the number "11," the day I saw Led Zeppelin in concert: "My number is 11, as all their numbers who are of us."49 First of all, I saw Led Zeppelin on the 11th day of the sixth month of the year in which they played six concerts in six nights. There is a six - six - six in that statement. They played at Madison Square Garden on the 7th, 8th, 10th, 11th, 13th, and 14th. 7+8 = 15. 10+11=21. 13+14=27. The numerical gap between these three sets of back to back concerts is six. 15+6=21. 21+6=27. I had purchased six tickets to the show. Jimmy Page joined his first band the year I was born, 1960. The month I turned six years old, August of 1966, Page hit the road to America to tour with the Yardbirds. Page first toured the states in 1966. I saw him in concert 11 years later in 1977. It was Led Zeppelin's 11th tour of America, the 1977 tour. I was in the 11th grade when I saw Led Zeppelin (I graduated high school in June of 1978). I turned 11 years old on August 3rd, 1971. Three months later, the 11th month, November, 1971, Led Zeppelin's fourth album with "Stairway to Heaven" was released, again, the year I turned eleven years old; when I was in the sixth grade. I was born, again, on August 3rd. That is the 3rd day of the 8th month.

3+8=11. There are 3 letters in "Led" and 8 in "Zeppelin." 3+8=11. I was born on the 3rd day of the 8th month of the 60th year of the century. 3+8+60=71. The number 71, again, refers to the year I turned 11 years old and Led Zeppelin's fourth album came out, the album that plays the most crucial part in the writing of this book. Just look at the table of contents. You'll know it when you read the next chapter, as well as the subsequent one. I really have a difficult time, in light of what *The Book of the Law* says about the number 11, to believe that all this is merely a coincidence. If it is only a coincidence, what a mighty one it is. Crowley called "11" the number of Magick, which is why he added the 11th letter of the alphabet, "k" to the word Magic, to make it Magick, his version of the magical art. Even Aleister Crowley himself came under attack of Abramelin demons on June 11th, 1903. He wrote about it, referring to himself in the third person, by his Magical name Perdurabo (P.), in his *Equinox*: "On the 11th of June P. records that he moved his bed into the temple that he had constructed at C...(Boleskine) House, for convenience of more absolute retirement. In this temple he was afflicted by dreams and visions of the most appalling Abramelin devils, which had evidently clung to the spot ever since the operations of February 1900."50 Isn't it interesting that Aleister Crowley was attacked by Abramelin demonic spirits in the temple at Boleskine House on June 11th, and he records it in his encyclopedia of initiation, which is how he referred to *The Equinox*. That information was written by Aleister Crowley in *The Equinox, Volume I, No.4*, pg.178, in a section titled *The Temple of Solomon the King*. I absolutely guarantee you that you will hear no complaints from Jimmy Page or anyone else about that not being recorded by Crowley where I said it was; or any other information I have quoted Crowley on, because Jimmy Page has these books and he knows perfectly well the authenticity to what has been written. Tom Friend and Aleister Crowley both came under demonic attack on June 11th, interestingly enough. Crowley was under their control; I was partially.

The following information is from Crowley's *Equinox* and *The Book of Lies* on the numbers of Magick, to further emphasize the fact that my writing this book was not by accident. Keep this in mind while reading the following Crowley quote. I saw Led Zeppelin in concert on Saturday, June 11th, 1977. That was the 7th day of the week, the 11th day of the month, in the 77th year of the century. 7 x 11 = 77. In *The Equinox, Volume I, No.5*, Aleister Crowley wrote about 7 x 11 = 77: "Note the 77 = 7 x 11, magical power in perfection."51 In *The Book of Lies*, the 77th chapter has this commentary on it written by Crowley: "77 is the number of Laylah (LAILAH), to whom this chapter is wholly devoted. The first section of the title is an analysis of 77 considered as a mystic number. 7, the septenary; 11, the magical number; 77, the manifestation, therefore of the septenary.Through matter, because 77 is written in Hebrew Ayin Zayin (OZ), and He-Goat, the symbol of matter, Capricornus, the Devil of the Tarot; which is the picture of the Goat of the Sabbath upon an altar, worshiped by two other devils, male and female....Laylah is herself not devoid of 'Devil,' but, as she habitually remarks, on being addressed in terms implying this fact, 'It's nice to be a devil when you're one like me.'....Now, the Devil of the Tarot is the Phallus, the Redeemer, and Laylah symbolizes redemption to Frater P. The number 77 also, interpreted as in the title, is the redeeming force."52

I never considered Led Zeppelin's Magick performed on me as an act of redemption from God. I am not saying either that all this coincidence makes me one of them, although I was up to that very night when they clearly tried to make me one of their followers of Satan with Theremin Magick. It really amazes me that people think the Theremin is just an entertainment tool. Just look at Page using the Theremin right after Plant mentions the doomed dogs in "No Quarter" during the film. He did the same thing throughout the 1998 tour with Plant while performing a full electric version of "No Quarter" (during the 1995 tour they did it acoustic). I'm now going to address the numerological issue because there are too many coincidences with these numbers to have me at that concert being an accident; neither is my writing of this book.

While talking about numbers, on my fifteenth birthday, August 3rd, 1975, Jimmy Page flew to and arrived at the Abbey of Thelema in Sicily. This is where Crowley wrote *Liber Samekh* (the same document in which he wrote: "The Eye! Satan my Lord! The Lust of the Goat! Mine Angel! Mine Initiator! Thou one with me the Sixfold Star!" Crowley wrote that at the Abbey of Thelema in 1921, and Jimmy Page brought it to light 50 years later on the inner cover of Led Zeppelin's fourth album). The number fifteen is the number of the Devil in the Tarot. None of this is a coincidence. Nevertheless, two more points need to be addressed.

On the soundtrack to the film, Robert Plant, in the first couple of minutes of "Whole Lotta Love," prior to the Theremin spell, tells the fans that he is searching for a "bridge." Then he asks the fans if any of them have seen it. These two lines _are not_ presented in the film. In the occult, it is an axiom that the medium or magician "bridges" the gap between the physical world and the spiritual. Robert Plant is simply asking them, I believe, if they can see into the spirit world via hallucination, and if they can see the spirits that are there, that the band members are working for.

This is what Allan Kardec was writing about in *The Book on Mediums*:

"All spirits, under given circumstances, can manifest themselves to men: the number of those who can communicate is indefinite.

Spirits communicate through the intervention of mediums, who serve them as instruments and interpreters."53

Another point, that can be seen in the film, during the Theremin routine, is the constant splitting of the film to give Robert Plant and Jimmy Page's opposite images. This is very easily identified by many that they are sending a non-verbal message about the spirit world; that they have two bodies, a spiritual one and a physical one. This is the same as the picture on the cardboard cover to the VHS video of the film. It shows Jimmy Page in two images, one is the reflection of the other, as he is about to wail into the lead in "Stairway to Heaven." This second image, I believe, is there to point the fans to yield their wills to those in the spirit world, "the other side." By the way, Page/Plant played the Doors' song "Break on Through," during their medley on the nationally broadcast concert in San Jose, California, in 1995. They played in on many other occasions during that tour; like May 17th, at the L.A. Forum. Anyone who knows anything about Jim Morrison or Shamanism can believe he was talking to the fans about breaking into and yielding his will to the rulers of the spirit world when he mentioned "the other side" in the song; which is why (I believe) Page/Plant played it.

EVIL SPIRITS AND LED ZEPPELIN FAN VIOLENCE

If the Devil, Led Zeppelin, and evil spirits are working together to change right to wrong and wrong to right, good to evil and evil to good in the consciousness, and inevitably the subconscious minds of their fans, then they have done society no good service. At the very least, the minds (though not all of them) have been molded to love the spiritual wickedness and unruliness that is associated with Led Zeppelin. In *The Book on Mediums*, again, written in 1874, Allan Kardec recorded the following about evil spirits stirring up trouble. Pay close attention to the word "concert" in the quote: "We have thus been many times witness of the part spirits play among the living: we have seen them at many reunions, - ball, concert, church, funerals, weddings, etc., - and everywhere we have found them exciting the evil passions, stirring up discord, inciting brawls, and rejoicing in their prowess; others, on the contrary, combated this pernicious influence, though but rarely listened to."54

We are now going to look at newspaper and magazine accounts of fan violence surrounding Led Zeppelin, all associated with the 1977 American Tour, prior to the night that I saw them, and it will be topped off by a comment about it from none other than Robert Plant himself, admitting that Led Zeppelin generates it.

On April, 19th, 1977, Led Zeppelin performed at the Riverfront Coliseum, in Cincinnati, Ohio. *Creem Magazine* reported that a thousand fans tried to crash through the gate into the concert, and that 100 of them were arrested for violence.

The next day, April 20th, they played at the Riverfront Coliseum again. *Billboard Magazine* reported on violence at that show. It said that a fan was killed when an out of control crowd shoved him from the third level bleachers. He fell into the street and was hit by a car.

One week later they performed at the Richfield Coliseum in Cleveland,

Ohio. Bruno Bornino of *The Cleveland Press* wrote that 37 fans were arrested for various offenses including drugs and possessing knives, and disorderly conduct.

On May 21st, 1977, Led Zeppelin performed at "The Summit" in Houston, Texas. There are two articles concerning Houston. *Creem Magazine* reported the violence associated with the day the tickets went on sale for this show back on January 30th, 1977. It said that the Houston police called in fire trucks to hose down the unruly fans. There somewhere between 3,000 and 3,500 of them that tried to force their way into Warehouse Records and Tapes to purchase tickets for the May 21st show.

Richard Cole, Led Zeppelin's road manager, in his book, *Stairway to Heaven - Led Zeppelin Uncensored*, wrote about the Houston show and the violence: "After the band's concert at the Summit in Houston, rowdy fans went on a rampage, causing $500,000 worth of damage. Forty of them were arrested for disorderly conduct and drug possession."55

On June 3rd, 1977, Led Zeppelin performed in Tampa, Florida. The *New Musical Express* reported what happened at the Orange Bowl Ticket outlet in Miami the day the tickets for the Tampa show went on sale. It reported that between 500 and a thousand fans who were in line to buy tickets decided to break throu the gates and vandalize the Orange Bowl. The police had to utilize tear gas to control the mob and 16 cops got hurt.

On June 4th, 1977, the day after the Tampa show itself, exactly one week to the day before I saw them, The New York Post reported that there was violence associated with the Tampa show. About five minutes into it, the show was stopped because of a storm. That set off a riot among the angry fans, some getting broken legs and arms as a result of doing battle with police.

Robert Plant admits that Led Zeppelin generates all this: "I see a lot of craziness around us. Somehow, we generate it and we revile it. What we are trying to put across is positive and wholesome and people react in such an excitable manner that they miss the meaning of it, and that makes me lose my calm."56 Robert Plant loses his calm when fans, that I believe they cast demonic black Magick spells on, both with their albums and concerts, become unruly. All of this violence, again, is directly related to the power of evil spirits gaining access to the minds of Led Zeppelin fans through the power of black Magick, I believe, with the Theremin aiding the band in that cause. The concerts by Led Zeppelin are still being listened to by fans all over the world through the trading of bootleg shows on internet trading lists. The concerts are being relived over and over again, with drug use concurrently. Just because the 70's are gone, that doesn't mean the concerts are. The concerts are circulating just as the Led Zeppelin studio albums are. Therefore, the demonic effects of their music, studio and concert, are still efficacious today. The effects of the Theremin on the subconscious, in conjunction with drug use, is a very powerful one indeed, and again,

I speak from experience. Believing they have done good to the fans in that regard, as opposed to evil, Robert Plant gives subtle instructions to the fans about what I believe went on in their minds during the Theremin routine, and what he wants them to think about afterward.

INSTRUCTIONS TO THE FANS AFTER THE THEREMIN SPELL

Robert Plant makes two definite remarks about the occult, relative to the spirit world meeting the physical world, to the fans after the Theremin and quick guitar lead that has always followed it during "Whole Lotta Love." Those who study the occult, who were in the audience, or who would get into the occult, owning the soundtrack to, or the film itself, get Robert Plant's remarks repeated to them over and over. The two messages from Plant are simple ones, once one has the knowledge of the occult that this author has. These remarks are not lyrics in the song, "Whole Lotta Love." They are ad-libs from Plant. There is a definite relationship between the demonic activity of the Theremin spell and the two remarks made by Robert Plant. The first remark is "So many roads." Plant is saying this for a reason. He is making a direct reference, I believe, to the doctrine of the Qabalah, that all religions (except Christianity) are one, with Magick as the common denominator. Three specific examples of quotes to back this up are following. They come from Raymond Buckland, who studied under Gerald Gardner, who was a contemporary of Aleister Crowley, Arthur E. Waite, who was also contemporary of Crowley, and then Crowley himself.

The first comes from Raymond Buckland's, *Buckland's Complete Book of Witchcraft*: "As different as are the many religions of the world, in essence they are all the same. It has frequently been said that they are simply different paths all leading to a common center, and this is true. The basic teachings are all the same; all that differs is the method of teaching. There are different rituals, different festivals and even different names for the gods...notice that I say 'different names for the gods' rather than, simply, 'different gods.'"[57] The second quote is from Arthur E. Waite's *The Pictorial Key to the Tarot*, and it is from the section on "The Hermit," who waits for man on the top of the mountain (as on Led Zeppelin's fourth album inner cover): "It is as if a man who knows in his heart that all roads lead to the heights, and that God is at the great height of all..."[58] Finally, Aleister Crowley said the very same thing this way in *The Equinox*: "And all the gods of all the nations of the earth are shown, for there are many avenues, all leading to the top of the mountain."[59] This mountain is the same one inside Led Zeppelin's fourth album cover, with Satan representing the Macrocosm at the top. These concepts, along with Plant's statement, are in total agreement with the teachings of the Qabalah presented in chapter eight. Again, students of Crowley understand exactly what Plant was doing by making that statement to the fans, promoting the Qabalah.

The second thing that Plant suggests to the fans is the shouting of the word "Hangman!" The reason that Robert Plant is shouting it is because he is trying to make the fans think, not about the song "Gallows Pole," off *Led Zeppelin III*, and its mentioning of the hangman at the gallows, as most fans would believe, but, conversely, the Hangman of the Tarot cards. Here is your proof. If Robert Plant was simply making mention of the hangman from "Gallows Pole," why did Jimmy Page remove this blatant reference from the soundtrack to the film? Go ahead and listen to (the soundtrack – not the film) "Whole Lotta Love" off *The Song Remains the Same*. The "Hangman!" has been removed; and its producer, in charge of removing it, is none other than Jimmy Page, with Peter Grant as the executive producer. Again, why did they do that if it is just a harmless reference to "Gallows Pole?" The reason Jimmy Page took it out, (unlike the two part subtle command to sell your soul to Satan in "Dazed and Confused") is because it is too blatant a reference to the occult. If people like myself, for instance, were to investigate the Hangman of the Tarot, we would then begin to put the pieces of the puzzle together that Jimmy Page only wants discovered by potential disciples of Crowley, the Silver Star, and the Devil.

As you can probably surmise, extensive research by this author has been done relative to the Hangman of the Tarot. The theme of the Hangman is, believe it or not, to be born again. Obviously, this is not a reference to born again Christianity. The phrase "born again" has absolutely nothing to do with physical birth, except that it occurred at the time when we were born into this world spiritually. Man is born into this world separate from communion with God. The reason is because we are born sinners into this world, due to inherited sin nature. We are not, however, accountable to God for any sin committed against him until we are old enough to completely comprehend the difference between right and wrong, good and evil, and the knowledge that God is good, as defined by the subconscious mind in its original, non-manipulated condition. This is why I state emphatically, that anyone who believes if a baby dies it goes to hell, doesn't have the slightest idea what he is talking about, and it is none other than the Devil himself who authored that insanity, in order to assist him in labeling followers of Lord Jesus Christ as lunatics. It has helped his cause substantially. There is no mention of infants being sent to hell in the *Bible*. It is clearly insanity to believe that. There is also no evidence that a baby can be baptized against its will in the *Bible*, either. If you search the *Holy Bible*, you will find that every person who was baptized did it as a conscious act of their own will, to be identified as a follower of Lord Jesus Christ, not as an act earning salvation, but rather, it is an outward confession of the inward salvation (new birth) that has already taken place. If people would study the *Bible*, they would know the truth, rather than believing what someone says simply because of the religious decor that they are wearing. The Devil, however, knows that men will believe a robe before the *Bible*, so he has them in his trap. The *Bible* is the authority, not any man or his denomination. To illustrate being born again, we will use the words of Lord Jesus Christ himself, from John 3:1-8:

"There was a man of the Pharisees named Nicodemus, a ruler of the Jews. This man came to Jesus by night and said to Him, 'Rabbi, we know that You are a teacher come from God; for no one can do these signs that You do unless God is with him.'

"Jesus answered and said to him, 'Most assuredly, I say to you, unless one is born again, he cannot see the kingdom of God.'

"Nicodemus said to Him, 'How can a man be born when he is old? Can he enter a second time into his mother's womb and be born?'

"Jesus answered, 'Most assuredly, I say to you, unless one is born of water and the Spirit, he cannot enter the kingdom of God. That which is born of the flesh is flesh, and that which is born of the Spirit is spirit. Do not marvel that I said to you, "You must be born again." The wind blows where it wishes, and you hear the sound of it, but cannot tell where it comes from and where it goes. So is everyone who is born of the Spirit.'"

Jesus makes the distinction between physical birth and spiritual birth by contrasting water and spirit. He was not talking about baptism. People who say that do not know what they are talking about. He said, "born of water and the Spirit." Then he says, "Flesh gives birth to flesh, but the Spirit gives birth to spirit." When a human being is born, he or she leaves the water sack, right? Jesus is not saying that your body is born again by being baptized. The body is going to the grave. He said, "I tell you the truth, no one can enter the kingdom of God unless he is born of water and the Spirit." What Jesus was saying was this. A man has to be born physically once, AND born spiritually twice. We are born spiritually separate from God, born meaning a beginning to a life, and we need to be born again, to begin a new life again, given birth to by the "Spirit," to the "spirit." The capitalized "Spirit" in that passage refers to the Holy Spirit, the third person in the trinity, and his work of "spiritual regeneration," or "making new spiritually," of the human spirit (small "s"), on God's terms. It is a new life, a new beginning, a new birth, not physical, but spiritual. It is the Great Work accomplished, union of man with his creator, Almighty God. Again, this is the work of the Holy Spirit of God. Jesus himself made it clear in John 6:44: "No one can come to Me unless the Father who sent Me draws him; and I will raise him up at the last day." Jesus said in the first passage that it is the work of the Spirit, and then he speaks of the Father doing the work in the second. Don't be confused by that. As all *Bible* scholars are aware, the Holy Spirit does the work he is directed to do by God the Father. The same thing applies to Jesus. He said in John 5:36: "...for the works which the Father has given Me to finish – the very works that I do – bear witness of me, that the Father has sent Me."

In summation, Jesus is working on the Father's behalf, and he (the Father) commands the Holy Spirit to draw certain people to follow Lord Jesus Christ. In Satanism, on the other hand, the magician works in conjunction with evil spirits to draw people to follow the Devil, who is in command of it, all the while remolding the conscience to believe he is god, irrespective of what name is applied to the Devil – Apollo, Pan, Thor, Odin, etc., so as to allow the people who give in to him to believe they are worshiping god, again, with a clear, though remolded conscience. This is how the members of Led Zeppelin encourage people to sell their souls, because with a clear and remolded conscience, they believe he is god. It all makes sense. However, what they are not aware of, is the fact that they will stand before Lord Jesus Christ and give an account for giving their conscience over to remolding, right to wrong, and evil to good, and then worshiping the Devil. This is how Devil worship has taken place throughout history. Sane people call them crazy, but the Satanists think they are enlightened by "god." Remember, Satan himself said in the *Bible* that the earth had been given over to his direct rule, with certain limitations. This rule over the yielded hearts of men by the Devil, masquerading as god, is carefully presented by occult authors, writing about the Tarot, especially "The Hangman," specially designed to speak of the satanic spiritual rebirth; that is also sought by Led Zeppelin and the Devil.

"THE HANGMAN" AND SATANIC SPIRITUAL REGENERATION

Spiritual rebirth, or regeneration, that leads to Devil worship, is satanic spiritual regeneration, or "Born-Again Satanism." This is the proper title for the Devil worshipers in this world. Jimmy Page, Robert Plant, John Bonham, and John Paul Jones, as the evidence suggests, have been born again. They have participated in a spiritual rebirth ("Stairway to Heaven"). They never would have worn Magick runes if they had not. Although it was a long time ago, they eventually became satanic evangelists. The Hangman, with his instructions for rebirth, performs the function of directing people in their search for this occult, anti-Christ rebirth, to find "god," while the song "Stairway to Heaven," that will be focused on in the next two chapters, illustrates the process of satanic regeneration from both the Devil's part and his follower's (Crowleyana).

I believe the Theremin routine was and is a method to assist the potential follower to move on down the road to satanic spiritual regeneration, and that Robert Plant's shouting "Hangman" is to get the person who studies the Tarot to come to full realization of it. To illustrate this for the reader, several, not just a few, but several factual quotes from occult authors on the Tarot card "The Hangman" are presented here, with Aleister Crowley at the end of the list. As you will see, in all the quotes, the song remains the same, occult/satanic spiritual regeneration.

In the book, *A Complete Guide to the Tarot*, Eden Gray wrote this in the section on the Hangman: "Man must now accomplish his regeneration for himself consciously and voluntarily....A pause in one's life, suspended decisions. Self surrender leads to the transformation of the personality."60

In the book *Tarot in Ten Minutes*, R. T. Kaser wrote this of the Hangman: "This is a card about transitions and turning points....The Hanged Man is undergoing a rite of passage. He has come to a crossroads. And he must now decide whether to continue following the same path, or to branch off in a different direction. This card describes people who think about their past actions, who try to improve themselves, or who seriously consider their next move. A test of bravery or courage may be required. Preparation, prayer, and meditation come into play. The answer emerges from within."61 The person has to decide whether or not to continue down the same path, or to change to another path. Isn't that what Plant said in "Stairway to Heaven?" You bet it is. We'll look at that later, as it is defined by Aleister Crowley.

In her book *The Complete Book of Tarot*, Juliet Sharman-Burke wrote this about the Hangman: "This card represents the turning point in psychological development where the individual must come to grips with unconscious forces within him. He needs to sacrifice control of his conscious ego by surrendering to the unknown territory of his inner world. It seems this can only be done by conscious choice; it cannot be inflicted by others or by the outside world, although circumstances may contribute to one wanting to look within. As Jung says, it is as if the conscious mind volunteers to die in order to bear a new and fruitful life in the unconscious, despite the fears of the unknown and the fear that inevitably rises when a journey to the underworld of Hades is contemplated."62

I personally want to thank Juliet Sharman-Burke for calling it a journey to Hades, because that is exactly what it is. Speaking of the "unconscious forces within him," what did Plant sing in "All My Love," from *In Through the Out Door*? He sang of "His" being a "force" which is "within." Remember Crowley's written statements in *The Book of the Law*? "Hadit burning in thy heart shall make swift and secure thy pen?" As well as "Because of me in thee which thou knewest not?" Both of those statements are the Devil speaking. It is all there. All the pieces of the puzzle fit together. Even my enemies will have to confess that (And I fear none of you, as will be seen beyond any shadow of a doubt). Remember what Crowley quoted Satan as saying in *The Equinox Vol. I*: "I the Force that created all, am not to be despised." Also, don't forget that Jimmy Page said he felt like he was the instrument of a greater force, as well as stating that there was a powerful astrological force at work within the band that had a great deal to do with their success. My friend, he didn't make those statements because he had nothing else to say, they had a specific purpose; though they were presented in a somewhat subtle fashion. Again, this is why he removed Plant's allusion to the Hangman from the film soundtrack, because it was too blatant a message.

Brian Innes wrote about the Hangman in his book, *The Tarot - How to use and interpret the cards*: "It symbolizes adaptability and the desire to learn; it brings knowledge of the future and new understanding of the past; it means change - not the slow inevitable change of the Wheel of Fortune, but sudden violent change, demanding sacrifice. Yet it counsels you not to fear that change, but to face it bravely."63

In *The Art of Divination*, Scott Cunningham wrote of the Hangman: "Initiation. Wisdom. The power of prophecy. Sacrifice necessary to obtain a goal. Divination. Transformation. Prophecy. Rebirth. Devotion."64

Arthur E. Waite, who was a member of the Golden Dawn, along with Crowley, wrote of the Hangman in *The Pictorial Key to the Tarot*: "He who can understand that the story of his higher nature is imbedded in this symbolism will receive intimations concerning a great awakening that is possible, and will know that after the sacred Mystery of Death there is a glorious Mystery of Resurrection."65

In *Tarot - 22 Steps to a Higher Path*, D. Baloti Lawrence presented a crystal clear picture of the Hangman, including Crowley's concept of escaping from Christianity which he described as escaping restriction or limitation: "He represents a reversal in matters of thought, perception, and action. He teaches the way in which we can change our lives for the better. One way is to change the way we see things....Transformation is an important result of our involvement with the Hanged Man....The Hanged man is where the spirit and the material meet and manifest....A new day is coming....Freedom from limiting relationships....Have faith and trust in the higher forces....Be steadfast in your faith, while you change your belief system. Look at something a different way. You will see the true picture....ROLE IN LIFE - transform darkness into light."66

Stuart R. Kaplan wrote of the Hangman in *The Encyclopedia of Tarot*: "DIVINATORY MEANINGS - Life in suspension. Transition. Change. Reversal of the mind and one's way of life. In a passive sense, apathy and dullness. Boredom. Abandonment. Renunciation. The changing of life's forces. Events of an uncertain nature. The period of respite between significant events. Sacrifice. Repentance. Readjustment. Efforts may have to be undertaken toward the success of a goal. Which still may not be attained. Regeneration. Improvement. Rebirth. The approach of new life forces. This is the time to condition oneself for new experiences. Surrender. Lack of progress. Over sacrifice. An unappreciated person."67

In his Crowley biography, Israel Regardie wrote of this spiritual regeneration: "While man is assumed into godhead, and the divine spirit is brought down into manhood, a new earth and a new heaven make their appearance. It is the development of a totally new outlook. It is the redeeming point of view; familiar objects take on a divine radiance illumined by an internal spiritual light."68

Last, but not least, Aleister Crowley wrote about the Hangman in *The Book of Thoth*. Remember, in *The Book of the Law*, Satan said that every man and every woman were stars that were to follow their own orbit. Crowley wrote that the Hangman: "...represents the descent of the light into the darkness in order to redeem it....for every star possesses boundless wealth; the only proper way to deal with the ignorant is to bring them to the knowledge of their starry heritage."69 His statements fit perfectly with the Led Zeppelin *Physical Graffiti* songs, "Kashmir" and "In the Light."

Anyone who has come into contact with spiritual beings as a result of their listening to Led Zeppelin, and then proceeded to follow through and look into the teachings of the Tarot cards, especially the Hangman, at Robert Plant's prodding, along with his command to sell ones soul to Satan, will come to understand that he was guiding them into satanic spiritual rebirth. At that point the individual must make up his or her mind as to what to do, as to what direction to take, or which moral code to yield their will to, just as the author had to. Those who love the band, and have had their consciences voluntarily turned over to the transformation of evil to good and vice versa, have only been encouraged further down the road to making a satanic pact by studying the Tarot card, "The Hangman;" which, of course, is why Jimmy Page removed Plant's mention of it from *The Song Remains the Same* soundtrack; because it was not presented as subtly as their command to sell one's soul to the Devil; I picked them both up, however.

The Theremin machine, then, played a very important role in the Led Zeppelin concert, as it did in the Page/Plant and Page/Crowes shows. Some despised it, although many loved it. I believe its use by Jimmy Page was designed to produce hallucinations that were demonic and evil, in accordance with the demonic and evil sounds jammed into the subconscious of the stoned fans at their concerts. This was done, I believe, based on subjective experience, to assist demonic forces in their attempt to fulfill Satan's will, which is transforming thought patterns in the conscious mind from good to evil and evil to good, and then back into the subconscious for the completion of moral transformation and spiritual regeneration. The Theremin manipulated the brain messages that are designed to be sent by neurotransmitters, naturally occurring brain chemicals that travel between neurons, in the minds of fans that were under the influence of drugs that were remarkably similar in their molecular structure as the neurotransmitters; allowing for the drug's ability to travel from one neuron to another and be picked up by the receiving neuron's receptors, which were designed to pick up certain chemical structures. Once the hallucinatory effects were in place, the fans, hearing demonic effects from the Theremin, could then picture the demons or evil spirits right before their eyes as reality, and when the demons are really there, it is reality. Remember, Jimmy Page published *The Goetia* in 1976, and that book is all about using demonic spirits for this purpose. After successfully turning good to evil and evil to good, with the fan's participation of will, the evil spirits could then manipulate fans into violent behavior, as understood by the many newspaper accounts (Just watch the Rolling Stones' video, "Gimme Shelter.). After the Theremin routine was completed, Robert Plant then made subtle comments promoting the Qabalah, as well as Tarot cards, specifically, the Hangman. The Tarot cards, once again, are derived from the Qabalah. This would reveal to the fan who searched the cards what exactly Led Zeppelin wanted to accomplish with their music, especially the Theremin. The sympathic fan of Led Zeppelin, who yielded his will to love evil during their concert, and then hungered to know more about the spirit world, on the evil side of the fence, was then fully prepared as a new/true follower of Led Zeppelin, the occult and the Devil, to study the teachings of Aleister Crowley, that were constantly advocated by Jimmy Page, to fully comprehend the spiritual rebirth/regeneration that has taken place in his or her life, and to understand the world's most famous occult song, that tells the complete, realistic, and powerful story of satanic spiritual regeneration; with an antithetical, paradoxical title, "Stairway to Heaven."

Jimmy Page and Robert Plant, during the second coming of Led Zeppelin, a.k.a. Page/Plant, performed "Whole Lotta Love" to close their show, before their encores, during the entire 1998 world tour. In the middle of the song, Jimmy Page manipulated the Theremin just as he had during the seventies. Why would a man who had published a manual on using demonic forces for magical purposes, derive demonic sounds from the Theremin? Demonic forces desire concentration by people on the knowledge of good and evil; which they then wish to remold (misgiven thoughts) in accordance with the Devil's will. Page used the Theremin in "Whole Lotta Love" during the 1999-2000 Jimmy Page/Black Crowes United States Tour as well. Why does he continue to do this in concert?

A very complex working is the Theremin. Page has help behind the speakers. When we consider that Jimmy Page is a disciple of Crowley and Satan, we would have to conclude that demonic sounds derived from the Theremin were not being produced for any "Rock and Roll" entertainment value for the fans.

1 Dave Lewis and Simon Pallett, *Led Zeppelin: The Concert File*, pg.51

2 Eliphas Levi, *Transcendental Magic*, pp.84, 33

3 Eliphas Levi, *The History of Magic*, pg.317

4 Allan Kardec, *The Book on Mediums*, pp.146, 150

5 Richard Evans Schultes & Albert Hofmann, *Plants of the Gods-Their Sacred, Healing and Hallucinogenic Powers*, Healing Arts Press, Rochester, Vermont, 1992, pg.85

6 David Friedman, *Focus On Drugs and the Brain*, Twenty-First Century Books, Frederick, Maryland, 1990, pg.34

7 Richard M. Restak, M.D., *The Mind*, Bantam Books, 1988, pg.39

8 Jack Fincher, *The Brain - Mystery of Matter and Mind*, U.S. News Books, Washington D.C., 1981, originally published in 1930, pg.39

9 Erwin Lausch, *Manipulation - Dangers and Benefits of Brain Research*, Translated from the German by Oliver Coburn, The Viking Press, New York, 1972, pg.170

10 Steven Rose, *The Conscious Brain*, Alfred A. Knopf, Inc., New York, 1973, pg.54

11 Pierce J. Howard, Ph.D., *The Owners Manual for the Brain*, Leornian Press, Austin, Texas, 1994, pg.38

12 Erwin Lausch, *Manipulation - Dangers and Benefits of Brain Research*, pg.130

13 Richard Evans Schultes and Albert Hofmann, *Plants of the Gods*, pg.101

14 Aleister Crowley, *The Equinox*, Vol. I, No.1, *Pharmaceutical Study*, pg.243

15 Erwin Lausch, *Manipulation - Dangers and Benefits of Brain Research*, pp.135-136

16 Pierce J. Howard, Ph.D., *The Owners Manual for the Brain*, pg.86

17 Richard Evans Schultes and Albert Hofmann, *Plants of the Gods*, pg.144

18 Albert Hofmann, *The Discovery of LSD and Subsequent Investigations on Naturally Occurring Hallucinogens*, published in Discoveries in Biological Psychiatry, edited by Frank Ayd and Barry B. Blackwell, Baltimore, Md.: Ayd Medical Communications, 1984.

19 Richard Evans Schultes and Albert Hofmann, *Plants of the Gods*, pg.138

20 Aldous Huxley, *The Doors of Perception*, Harper & Row, 1990, pg.26

21 Erwin Lausch, *Manipulation-Dangers and Benefits of Brain Research*, pp.182-183

24 Aleister Crowley, *Magick-Book 4*Liber Aba*, pg.224

25 J. Allan Hobson, M.D. *The Chemistry of Conscious States (How the Brain Changes its Mind)*, Little, Brown and Company, 1994, pg.203

26 Ibid, pg.205

27 Aleister Crowley, *The Confessions of Aleister Crowley*, pg.125

28 Dr. Sir J. G. Frazer, *The Golden Bough*, pg.56

29 Albert Hofmann, *The Discovery of LSD and Subsequent Investigations on Naturally Occurring Hallucinogens*

30 Ibid.

31 Richard M. Restak, M. D., *Receptors*, pg.50

32 J. Allan Hobson, *The Chemistry of Conscious States*, pg.209

33 Jack Fincher, *The Brain - Mystery of Matter and Mind*, pg.109

34 Richard M. Restak M.D., *Receptors*, pp.128-129

35 Aleister Crowley, *Moonchild*, pg.114

36 *Webster's New World Dictionary*, Second College Edition, pg.713

37 Aleister Crowley, *Magick-Book 4*Liber Aba*, pg.223

38 Walter Gibson, *Hypnotism-Theory and Practice*, pg.10

39 Dr. David Jeremiah, *Escape the Coming Night*, pg.133

40 Eliphas Levi, *The History of Magic*, pg.317

41 Eliphas Levi, *Transcendental Magic*, pg.33

42 Eliphas Levi, *La Clef des Grands Mysteries*, pp.235-236

43 Allan Kardec, *The Book on Mediums*, pp.146, 150

44 Israel Regardie, *The Eye in the Triangle*, pp.126-127

45 Allan Kardec, *The Book on Mediums*, pg.129

46 Eliphas Levi, *Transcendental Magic*, pg.350

47 Aleister Crowley, *The Law is for All*, pg.170

48 Aleister Crowley, *The Equinox*, Vol. I, No.1, *The Temple of Solomon the King*, pg.147

49 Satan, *The Book of the Law*, Chapter 1, verse 60, dictation taken by Aleister Crowley, *The Equinox*, Vol. I, No.10, pg.16

50 Aleister Crowley, *The Equinox*, Vol. I, No.4, *The Temple of Solomon the King*, pg.178

51 Aleister Crowley, *The Equinox*, Vol. I, No.5, *The Temple of Solomon the King*, pg.114

52 Aleister Crowley, *The Book of Lies*, Samuel Weiser Inc., Yorke Beach, Maine, 1993, first published in 1913, pg.165

53 Allan Kardec, *The Book on Mediums*, pg.64

54 Ibid, pg.211

55 Richard Cole, *Stairway to Heaven - Led Zeppelin Uncensored*, pg.339

56 Dave Lewis and Simon Pallett, *Led Zeppelin: The Concert File*, pg.123

57 Raymond Buckland, *Buckland's Complete Book of Witchcraft*, pg.13

58 Arthur E. Waite, *The Pictorial Key to the Tarot*, pg.17

59 Aleister Crowley, *The Equinox*, Vol. I, No.5, *The Vision and the Voice*, pg.128

60 Eden Gray, *A Complete Guide to the Tarot*, Bantam Books, 1972, pg.42

61 R. T Kaser, *Tarot in Ten Minutes*, Avon Books, New York, 1992, pg.275

62 Juliet Shaman-Burke, *The Complete Book of Tarot*, St. Martin's Griffin, New York, 1996, pp.78-79

63 Brian Innes, *The Tarot - How to Use and Interpret the Cards*, Crescent Books, New York, 1987, pg.42

64 Scott Cunningham, *The Art of Divination*, The Crossing Press, Freedom, California, 1993, pg.116

65 Arthur E. Waite, *The Pictorial Key to the Tarot*, pg.119

66 D. Baloti Lawrence, *Tarot - 22 Steps to a Higher Path*, pp.79, 80, 81, 82

67 Stuart R. Kaplan, *The Encyclopedia of Tarot*, pg.330

68 Israel Regardie, *The Eye in the Triangle*, pg.67

69 Aleister Crowley, *The Book of Thoth*, pp.96-97

Jimmy Page plays the lead to "Stairway to Heaven," while Robert Plant plays the Tambourine in 1973. Evidence suggests the music and lyrics are not theirs.

"Stairway to Heaven" is played for the last time in the United States by the band on 7/24/77. What kind of message do you think they were sending with the Sun? The message is, of course, that the Devil himself is the source of their music.

CHAPTER FOURTEEN

"'...Stairway to Heaven' floored even the strongest cynics. It was almost as if Zeppelin had made a pact with the devil to learn of each new musical fad just seconds before it was going to happen, always being there with the first and with the best."
"The Best of Rock Stars"

"Plant has since cited the book Magic Arts in Celtic Britain by Lewis Spence as one of his inspirations in writing the wonderful 'Stairway' lyrics."2
Ritchie Yorke, "Led Zeppelin-The Definitive Biography"

"Indeed, it seems to me that the rainbow vapors which arise from the cauldron of Celtic Mysticism hold enough of the strange and the unusual to satisfy even the most exacting neophyte of the mysterious. The Magics of Druidism, or rather the problems associated with them, are enthralling enough in themselves to attract even the most conventional among us without the invitation of drum and pan-pipes."3
Lewis Spence, "Magic Arts in Celtic Britain"

"In native Celtic literature and tradition, Druids have come down to us most popularly as magicians, as wizards possessed of supernatural powers."4
Peter Berresford Ellis, "The Druids"

"Now, the Angel will make contact with the Adept at any point that is sensitive to His influence....A musician may be rapt away by majestic melodies such as he never hoped to hear."5
Black Magician Aleister Crowley, "Liber Samekh"

"When we first got back together, it was so immediately apparent that the two of us were just channeling the music. That's what we had always had, and it was so apparent that it was there. It was almost effortless."   - Jimmy Page

STAIRWAY TO HEAVEN:
CELTIC/DRUID MEDIUM MUSICIANS

"Stairway to Heaven," the most beautiful and powerful rock song ever composed, has consistently been voted the most popular song in rock music; loved by all rock fans, whether or not they loved Led Zeppelin, and there is a direct correlation between that popularity, I believe, and the manner in which they obtained the song. It reflects the very heart and soul of Led Zeppelin's association with the Devil. This is the astounding height to which they aspired when they gave themselves to Satan and Magick, through the teachings of Black Magician Aleister Crowley. Several different revelations will be presented to the reader in this powerful chapter. First, the true meaning of the name "Led Zeppelin" is going to be elaborated on. It goes much further in meaning than the "lead balloon" concept originally coined by "The Who's" John Entwistle and repeated by Keith Moon to Jimmy Page. Afterward, we will be looking at the spiritual position of the members of Led Zeppelin among the Celtics, the position I believe to be modern day "Druids." Once the position and practice of Druids is understood, it will be clearly seen as we look at how they received their music as Druid medium musicians; especially the music for their fourth album, including "Stairway To Heaven." Evidence from several sources will point to Boleskine House and an estate called "Headley Grange" as two places where the music and lyrics were received in medium fashion. This is called "automatic composing" and "automatic writing." The fact that Led Zeppelin's music is timeless will then be discussed, including Robert Plant's statement that something or someone was pushing "Stairway to Heaven" as a timeless entity. The consummation of all the preceding information will then be seen as the fourth album and its "no band identification" cover is discussed in detail. "Stairway to Heaven," with its Celtic/Druidic theme, in conjunction with statements by Robert Plant concerning the mediumistic manner in which it was obtained, was indeed a timeless gift from a supernatural being to the human members of Led Zeppelin, showing them to be Druid medium musicians, mediating between the Magick taught by Aleister Crowley and the Devil's Silver Star, and the countless fans that listened to the music in the past, listening to the music in the present, and those that will listen in the future.

THE TRUE MEANING OF THE NAME – "LED ZEPPELIN"

The term, "Led Zeppelin," I believe, and intend to show, is none other than a symbolic representation of the Devil himself; as god. On the cover of the first Led Zeppelin album, is a picture of the Hindenburg, as it burst into flames while landing in Lakehurst, New Jersey, in the 1930's. The Hindenburg was property of the German government. As everyone saw when it was flying, it had the Swastika on its rear. The Swastika is a Magick rune called "The Hammer of Thor," and Thor is the Devil; according to Aleister Crowley and the Qabalah, and as well as Biblical references to Satan as the supernatural being behind all the gods worshiped on earth, besides Lord Jesus Christ. The Hindenburg's flight began in Germany, and it ended in the United States (right where the author was born and raised – New Jersey – another non-coincidence), as a giant fireball descending from the sky. The flight is a picture of the magic of the Hermetic Order of the Golden Dawn being authorized by Fraulein Sprengel in Germany (chapter six), extending to the Argenteum Astrum (Silver Star) by Aleister Crowley, and from the Silver Star to American youth by Led Zeppelin. On the first album cover, as it descends into Lakehurst, it represents the great fireball in the sky, which is symbolic of the sun, that Crowley wrote was a symbol of the Devil (see ch.4 heading), and Horus, the Egyptian God, who Crowley said was Satan. Horus, again, is called "Force and Fire." The fiery "lead zeppelin," the Hindenburg, landing in Lakehurst, New Jersey, with the Swastika on its tail, is symbolic of the magic of Horus/Satan descending on the United States, which is what Led Zeppelin's music is, and why, I believe, Jimmy Page had it on front of their first album. The name Led Zeppelin, in conjunction with a picture of the burning Hindenburg was, I believe, a statement that Horus, being the Devil, and god, was descending on the U.S. in the form of Led Zeppelin's music.

Led Zeppelin was not the name the band took with them when they went on their first tour together. The group's name at the start was "The New Yardbirds." The first tour was in Scandinavia, where Norse Theology is the practiced religion; and Thor and the Swastika are from Norse Theology. When they returned to England, prior to their concert at Surrey University, they had changed their name to Led Zeppelin. It was, I believe, and it makes perfect sense, this trip through Scandinavia that prompted the band, while contemplating Norse Theology, to change the name.

In *The Encyclopedia of Witches and Witchcraft*, Rosemary Ellen Guiley wrote of the Swastika, making reference to Hitler, Aleister Crowley and the Golden Dawn: "SWASTIKA - An occult ferment spread throughout Germany, fueled in part by interest in magical fraternities such as the HERMETIC ORDER OF THE GOLDEN DAWN and esoteric groups such as the Theosophical Society. The swastika was a major symbol of the Golden Dawn, and Crowley wrote a pamphlet about it in 1910. Later, he said the Nazis stole the idea for the swastika from him....Hitler put the emblem on the armbands of his SS storm troopers and party members. By 1922 the swastika was on flags and standards displayed at all Nazi gatherings and meeting places."6 Crowley printed the Swastika on a page in his *Equinox*. So it is reasonable to believe that Hitler stole it from the Golden Dawn, especially since the last volume of the ten volume set of *The Equinox Vol. I* was finished by 1913. In *The Rise and Fall of the Third Reich*, William L. Shirer wrote about the Swastika as though he recognized its power as a Magick rune: "The Nazis now had a symbol which no other party could match. The hooked cross seemed to possess a mystic power of its own, to beckon to action in a new direction the insecure lower middle classes which had been floundering in the uncertainty of the first chaotic postwar years. They began to flock under its banner." Before we leave the idea of the Nazis and the Swastika, those of you who own the 1990 Led Zeppelin re-mastered album, can open up the photo collage that you received with it, and you can see Jimmy Page playing the guitar with a black t-shirt on, with a white scarf around his neck, with a Nazi officer's hat on. On the brim of the hat is the Nazi emblem, the eagle with the Swastika underneath. Again, Fraulein Sprengel authorized the founding of the Golden Dawn from Germany, and the Silver Star is an offshoot of the Golden Dawn. It makes sense then, that Led Zeppelin, representing Crowley and the Silver Star, would have an affinity for the Swastika, as they do for Thor, who is the Devil (Immigrant Song). The Druids wore it on their robes at Stonehenge. I have a video of the Druids wearing it there in 1936 during their ceremonies.

In 1943, at age 68, Crowley commended Hitler for having chosen the Swastika, calling it the Hammer of Thor in his book *Magick Without Tears*: "His magical technique was indescribably admirable; he adopted the Swastika, the Hammer of Thor…"7 What did Steven Davis call his book about Led Zeppelin? It was *Hammer of the Gods*. Are you beginning to get the picture? Steven Davis took that title from Robert Plant's proclamation that the "Hammer" from their "gods" would empower them at 0:22 into "Immigrant Song," off the *Led Zeppelin III* album, which came out in 1970, the year Jimmy Page bought Boleskine House. So we see the Swastika on the Hindenburg, on the front of the *Led Zeppelin* album, called the Hammer of Thor by Crowley, and Led Zeppelin referring to the Hammer from their Gods, and Steven Davis calling his book about Led Zeppelin *Hammer of the Gods*. Again, it is the author's assertion that the Hindenburg with the Swastika on it crashing at Lakehurst, New Jersey, is symbolic of the Devil as god to the members of Led Zeppelin.

In chapter twelve we looked at the Devil on top of the mountain behind Boleskine House on the inside cover of Led Zeppelin's fourth album, and Crowley's quote about being one with Satan and the sixfold star, as we saw with Jimmy Page in the Led Zeppelin film; so we know that the sixfold star in this context refers to Satan. Here is what Crowley wrote about the sixfold star and Force and Fire, who is Horus/Satan: "Thou fire! Thou Sixfold Star initiator, compassed about with Force and Fire!"8 Crowley wrote that in his letter on the Holy Guardian Angel, Aiwaz/Horus/Satan, Liber Samekh, in 1921, in Sicily, at the Abbey of Thelema, the farmhouse that Jimmy Page flew to consider purchasing in 1975, written about by Richard Cole. So the Swastika is the Hammer of Thor, and Crowley and Page believed that Thor is Satan (and they are right). Combined with that is their concurrent perception of Satan as compassed about with Force and Fire. Crowley also described the Devil, pertinent to this idea, in his *Equinox*: "He is the monarch of the lofty mountains, and the lord of the woods and forests, the indweller of the globes of flame."9 The Hindenburg had the Swastika painted on both sides of its rear, it exploded into fire, a globe of flame, and it came down from the sky. The sky is significant because of a statement from Crowley's *Book of the Law*. In Chapter 3, verse 34, Satan wrote,

"Another prophet shall arise, bringing fresh fever from the skies..."10 At first Crowley thought this prophet was Charles Stanfield Jones, his "magical son," but later discounted that belief. It doesn't take Albert Einstein to figure out whom the Devil was referring to, when the *Bible* teaches that the Devil knows the future. As far as I'm concerned, he was talking about Jimmy Page. It makes perfect sense. The Hindenburg, on the front of Led Zeppelin's first album, was Force and Fire, a globe of flame, bearing the Swastika, descending from the skies. The last point is that it landed in America.

The United States would be Led Zeppelin's largest and most enthusiastic audience in the entire world. In the booklet that accompanies the 1990 Led Zeppelin Re-mastered album, Kurt Loder wrote about Led Zeppelin and America in a section called *The Roots of Heaven.* He wrote that America became their number one audience, and that their influence has passed, to a degree, to each generation of rock fans in this country since. The United States, which was founded upon the teachings of the *Holy Bible*, the country that has sent out more Christian missionaries than any other nation on earth, is the one that Satan wanted to attack with his religion, The Law of Thelema - Magick. It all goes back to the battle between Lucifer and Christ.

The name, Led Zeppelin, is symbolic of the Devil descending from the skies as Force and Fire – Horus; who is Satan. The music he gave (I believe) to Led Zeppelin, especially "Stairway to Heaven," is his hammer, the Swastika, as well as fresh fever from the skies, landing in America from its point of origin, Germany. Again, look at the photo of Page wearing the Nazi headgear, with the eagle and the Swastika on it. On page 120 of Dave Lewis and Simon Pallett's *Led Zeppelin: The Concert File*, in the lower left hand corner, Robert Plant is wearing the same Nazi headgear with the eagle and the Swastika on it in a facial close-up photo that is clearer than the Page photo. It all makes sense to believe that Jimmy Page picked the name Led Zeppelin because of its being symbolic of the magical and musical power of the Devil; the lead zeppelin landing in flames.

Led Zeppelin's magical music was definitely perceived as fresh fever from the skies by those who saw the band in concert during its first couple of years on tour. Journalists wrote of its music as more powerful than that of other bands at the time. Many of the articles on Led Zeppelin in the early days can be read in Lewis and Pallett's book *Led Zeppelin - The Concert File*. They were so well received, I believe, because of the supernatural intervention that took place. That intervention is complex. From the intensity of advertisement, to interest in the band, to the performances themselves, as well as the music performed, I believe Led Zeppelin has had supernatural assistance from the Devil right from the very beginning (which is why they praise him in their music); which made their arrival on the music scene unique in power and talent so as to distinguish them from their rock peers, causing them to have a newness and freshness that had been unknown since the early Elvis days; especially in concert.

LED ZEPPELIN - TWENTIETH CENTURY "DRUIDS"

Led Zeppelin had supernatural or "divine" assistance from Satan right from the early days, and Page/Plant had it as well, and there is a reason for it. In associating with the Devil, and seeking to promote the Silver Star and Magick, most specifically the Celtic version in "Stairway To Heaven," the four members of Led Zeppelin, including Peter Grant, in my opinion, were and are modern day "Druids."

Robert Plant was quoted as praising *Magic Arts in Celtic Britain* by Lewis Spence as an inspiration for the lyrics to "Stairway To Heaven" (see chapter heading). I have in my possession an unabridged first edition of this book (printed in Great Britain at the Anchor Press, Tiptree, Essex). I believe the reason Plant made reference to it is, obviously, because of Celtic magic, but more specifically, because of the teachings about the Druids contained therein. Of all the practitioners of magic on earth, the Druids are the elite. It can truly be said that the Druids are the nobility or educated intellectual class among the Celts, and the Celts are the nobility of all magical peoples on earth. In the beginning of *Magic Arts in Celtic Britain*, Lewis Spence wrote: "The writers of antiquity were at one in realizing the native superiority of the Celtic mind in the science of Magic."11 He elaborated on it at the end of the book in some detail, describing the magic arts practiced by the Druids as resembling other traditions, which points to magic being universal, though the form practiced by the Druids as far superior; nevertheless, the song remains the same:

"From a general view of the material presented in the foregoing pages it may, I think, be concluded that the Magic Arts as cultivated among the Celtic peoples of the British Isles very closely resembled those practiced in almost every area where humanity has concerned itself with occult belief and its practical observance. This makes it self-evident, if it be necessary to say so, that the Magic Art in all its branches is of an antiquity so great as to be practically unfathomable. Even so, the spirit which inspired Celtic Magic reveals the existence of a sharply different temperament in certain aspects from that of other arcane systems. Few races have developed a spirit-world so fantastically beautiful or have peopled it with shapes so attractive, or at times so terrific. Perhaps, too, no race which had not yet approached the full stature of civilization has brought forth a religious-magical caste at once so distinctive and so richly garbed in the trappings of mystery as the Druidic. Moreover, if the spells and charms of the Celt resemble in their nature those of other races, they are usually couched in a vein of poetry the exalted genius of which is seldom to be encountered in that of the Teuton or the Slav."12

Lewis Spence delivers the message that Robert Plant wants the sold out disciple of Led Zeppelin to get; that the Celtics, the Druids in particular, are superior to all other cultures when it comes to the practice of magic. Why would

Plant refer the fans to Spence's book, if he didn't want them to recognize the band as Druids?

In his book, *The History of Magic*, Eliphas Levi presents the Druids' practice as having originated in Egypt, as well as in the Qabalah/Kabalah: "The original Druids were true children of the Magi, their initiation deriving from Egypt and Chaldea, or in other words, from the purest sources of primitive Kabalah."13 As one can see from the quote, there is no contradiction between Led Zeppelin's love of the Egyptian Qabalah via the teachings of Crowley, and the Celtic magic of the Druids; or in other words, the song remains the same.

The magic of the Druids may have originated in Egypt, along with everyone else's, but in the Druid form, it was recorded by Caesar during Roman occupation to have begun in England.14 From England it migrated to Ireland and Scotland, spreading throughout the British Isles.15 This all makes perfect sense when one considers that the Led Zeppelin film was shot in England, Scotland and Wales.

Before examining how I believe Led Zeppelin received its music, let us take a look at the Druids' position and function among the Celtic people. The primary role of the Druids was that of mediators between the Celtic people and the gods. In his book, *The Ancient Celts*, Barry Cunliffe wrote: "In most societies interactions between the natural and supernatural world are ordered by ritual and mediated by specialists and so it was in the Celtic world. The principal mediators were called Druids (druides, druidae in Latin; druad in Old Irish; dryw (singular) in Welsh), which is thought to mean 'knowledge of the oak' or, less likely, 'deep knowledge.'"16 Not only did the Druids mediate between the supernatural world and the natural, they led in the worship of the gods, dictating what sacrifices were to be offered to those gods either in public or private. They provided the final answers to the Celtics on any questions pertaining to their religion. Many Celtic men would seek instruction from the Druids on a regular basis, as they were held in high honor among the people, as representatives of the gods. As such the Druids provided the people with judgements in every area of life, including civil and criminal cases. If the Druids declared a financial judgement was to be paid, the individual was to pay it or be expelled from participation in sacrifice to the gods. If this happened, the individual was to be avoided by the rest of the people as unclean. They were treated as criminals, and could forget about the Druids hearing any case in which they were the plaintiffs.17

Along with officiating at the sacrifices to their gods, the Druids also gave instruction to the people as to how their magic rituals were to be performed. This meant that the Druids, or at least some of them, were magicians. In their book, *The Celts: Europe's People of Iron*, Time-Life presented the following: "To ensure that the rituals to placate their temperamental gods were performed properly and to interpret the mysteries of an environment steeped in magic, the Celts looked to the Druids."18

The Druids were the ruling class of the Celtics. They not only dealt with the area of religion, but were involved in a variety of professions, including historians, physicians, teachers, poets, astronomers, philosophers, judges, prophets, political advisers, counselors, and the crucial role of musicians.19 In his book, *The Druids*, Peter Ellis presented this theme of the Druids as musicians, not failing to mention them as using drums and pipes: "Druids, as we have noted, in later Welsh literature were regarded as poets and musicians. Once again we return to our main contention that the Druids were an intellectual caste and therefore some of them undertook the role of poets and musicians, as demonstrated in insular Celtic sources....Classical writers noted the Celtic use of lyres, drums, pipes and other instruments."20 Remember, Lucifer was created with celestial pipes and tabrets, which are hand held drums (tambourines).

In another statement on the professions of the Druids, Ellis includes "magicians" in the list: "...we discuss the wisdom of the Druids in those areas of knowledge in which Classical sources claim the Druids had especial renown. We examine them, among their other occupations, as philosophers, judges, historians, physicians, seers, astrologers and magicians."21 Ellis went on to say that this presentation of Druids as magicians is the most popular in Celtic tradition: "In native Celtic literature and tradition, Druids have come down to us most popularly as magicians, as wizards possessed of supernatural powers."22 In making reference to another famous writer on the Druids, Ellis writes of Pliny the Elder, and his book *Naturalis Historia*, which depicts the Druids as magicians as well: "In his *Naturalis Historia*, his chief and only surviving work, Pliny gives one of the fullest accounts of the Druids ever to survive, presenting them as natural scientists, doctors of medicine, and magicians."23 While emphasizing the magician element of the Druids, Ellis went on to quote none other than Lewis Spence: "Lewis Spence has observed: 'It is almost impossible to find a page in early Irish literature which does not contain a reference to the Druid in his character of a wielder of magic power...'"24 Again, this is the author, Lewis Spence, that Robert Plant refers their fans to when discussing "Stairway to Heaven." One who describes the Druids primarily as magicians.

STONEHENGE

Thus far, we have seen the Druids in their respective roles as priests, musicians, and magicians. I assert that these titles are all indicative of the empirical role of the four members of Led Zeppelin. If one is not convinced yet, the rest of this chapter will produce as much evidence as possible to establish probable cause for believing it. Along with the previously mentioned titles associated with the Druids, we have to add a favorite place of their worship. That place is commonly known as "Stonehenge." Stonehenge is a place in England that is a circular edifice of very large stones, standing vertically and horizontally on top of one another. One popular movie, Chevy Chase's "National Lampoon's European Vacation" has made Stonehenge visible to the whole world. The cover of Peter Ellis' *The Druids* has Stonehenge on it underneath the title. He makes the case for associating the two in his book: "...in England, people popularly associate Druids with earnest looking, white robed men and women who continue to hold mystic ceremonies at the time of the summer solstice in stone circles such as Stonehenge..."25 Ellis describes Stonehenge as an ideal location for the purpose of studying the cosmos; as well as the Druids having done it there; by quoting Henry Wansey in 1776: "Stonehenge stands in the best situation possible for observing the heavenly bodies, as there is an horizon nearly three miles distant on all sides. But till we know the methods by which the ancient Druids calculated eclipses with so much accuracy, as Caesar mentions, we cannot explain the theoretical use of Stonehenge."26

Finally, Peter Ellis speaks of Stonehenge as being presented to the country by its owner, as well as Druids performing sacred rites there: "Mystic Druids continued to make annual appearances at Stonehenge but in 1900 visitors were causing a lot of damage to the monument. To offset this the owner, Sir Edward Antrobus, began charging entry. When the be-robed Druids arrived for their next solstice ceremony and refused to pay the entrance fee, the police summarily ejected them. In 1915 the monument was presented to the nation and by the end of the First World War (1918) there were five different sects of Druids vying to perform their 'sacred rites' there. The sects all seem to have been breakaway groups of the original Ancient Order of Druids."27

What does all this talk about Stonehenge have to do with Led Zeppelin? Just because Druids in England have come to the site to worship and perform rituals, does this mean that Led Zeppelin promoted that as well? The answer is yes. Exactly six weeks to the weekend that I saw them at Madison Square Garden in 1977, Led Zeppelin played their last two shows in the United States, and they were both held in Oakland, California, at the Oakland Coliseum. It was a fitting place, considering that the name Druid has to do with the knowledge of the Oak Tree and its phallic symbol of godhead among trees. Oakland Coliseum was the sight, on the 23rd, and 24th of July, 1977, where, in the daytime, Led Zeppelin finished its career of touring the States. The fact that it was daytime was significant, because it allowed the band to place a visible facade edifice on either side of and above their stage set, that could be seen from anywhere in the Coliseum.

What was the image of the facade? That's right, it was Stonehenge. This can be seen plain as day in VH1's "Legends" program when its portrayal of Led Zeppelin aired. If you should come across anyone who attended the shows in Oakland, who looks at any photos of Stonehenge that can be found, they will tell you that it was Stonehenge. In their book, *Led Zeppelin: The Concert File*, Dave Lewis and Simon Pallett reported that it was Stonehenge on the facade in Oakland, and that it was "especially constructed": "The Oakland concerts are large outdoor afternoon shows. A huge backdrop has been especially constructed featuring the Stonehenge design."28 The band actually had "stones" like those at Stonehenge on the stage; to the right of the drums, to the viewers left. Another thing that can be seen at these shows, as portrayed in a photo of the July 24th show in *Led Zeppelin: The Concert File*, on page 128, is a big picture of the sun painted behind the band, right behind John Bonham for all to see (I have included a photo of this scenery with the band in this book.). Crowley and Page believe that the sun is the symbol for none other than Satan. So who did the Druids gathered at Stonehenge to worship? It is Led Zeppelin themselves, as has been shown so far in this book, who have identified themselves as mediators between their fans and their god, Satan. This is the function of the priesthood. Jimmy Page, with his various forms of Magick, has shown himself and the other three to be magicians. That's right, I believe they are all magicians. They may not all be as powerful as Page, but the evidence shows them to be practicing magicians as well; if they were not, they would not have personal Magick runes. The Druids were known to be musicians. That's one point I need not elaborate on where Led Zeppelin is concerned. Finally, the Druids, and Led Zeppelin, by their own admission, are associated with Stonehenge. Kenneth Anger's film, *Lucifer Rising* also has a caption of Stonehenge. This is the same movie that Anger commissioned Jimmy Page to compose the music for; and has a shot of Page standing before a photo of Aliester Crowley holding the Egyptian "Stele of Revealing," which is foundational to the Silver Star's *Book of the Law*. Why would Anger include Stonehenge in *Lucifer Rising*? The answer is simple. Aleister Crowley presented Lucifer as the universal god, though known by different names in different cultures, and that would make him god of the Druids as well. The Druids were priests, magicians, musicians, and associated with Stonehenge; and the author believes that the same titles apply to Led Zeppelin as well, and that they are modern day Druids. As the Druids were the Celtic overlords, so Led Zeppelin are their fans' overlords through their music; as they claim to be.

Lewis Spence presented the Druids as actual rulers over the kings in the respective countries they were in: "Dion Chrysostom states that the Druids were closely associated with the kingship. 'Without their advice,' he says, 'even kings dare not resolve upon nor execute any plan, so that in truth it was they who ruled, while the kings who sat on golden thrones and fared sumptuously in their palaces became mere ministers of the Druids' will.'"29 Remember what was sung by Plant in "Immigrant Song," that as Led Zeppelin "calmed" certain "tides" produced by "war," they are the fans' "overlords." Remember a quote at the heading of chapter one, "Let my servants be few and secret, they shall rule the many and the known." That is Crowley quoting Satan from *The Book of the Law*. When fighting a war, there is an enemy. Who can we surmise as being the enemy of the Druids? That's right, it's the Christians.

"Christianity" oppressed the authority and magic of the Druids during the Crusades. Ellis speaks of the advent of Christianity in the British Isles and its affect on the Druids: "Those readers who have encountered Celtic mythology, and the early sagas of Ireland and Wales, will know that the Druids are depicted as an all-powerful and essential element in society. By Christian times they had, more or less, been reduced to the status of wizards and soothsayers....the general Christian attitude to the Druids was inimical. They were obviously portrayed as opponents of Christianity, upholders of the ancient religion, and thereby were relegated to the role of shamans, magicians and 'witch doctors,' although this prejudice varied from writer to writer."30

The Druids, therefore, are best described as priests, magicians, musicians, associated with Stonehenge, and the enemies of Christianity. Again, these titles are all appropriate when applied to Led Zeppelin. The positional facts have been presented, and now we will focus on the most powerful evidence of the practical working of their position as twentieth century Druids, with one goal in mind, the satanic spiritual regeneration of their fans.

LED ZEPPELIN - FOUR DRUID MEDIUM MUSICIANS

The most obvious element of Jimmy Page, Robert Plant, John Paul Jones, and John Bonham's positions as twentieth century Druids is their role as musicians. It is the author's assertion that the Devil used these men to transmit his music, not theirs, to the fans. In that capacity, they are medium musicians. In this section of the chapter, we will be looking at a number of quotes from a book published by Samuel Weiser Inc., the company that currently publishes the majority of Aleister Crowley's reprints in the United States. The name of that book is, again, *The Book On Mediums*, by Allan Kardec, published in 1874. Portions of the book are in effect manuscripts of seances attended by Mr. Kardec in which he asked spirits that manifested themselves certain questions and he received direct answers to those questions. You will be reading those supernatural answers in this section. The spirits claim to be humans passed on, but it is a lie. Jesus made it clear that man goes straight to heaven or hell; their spirits are not allowed to roam. To fully understand the significance of those statements in *The Book On Mediums*, we have to do a brief review of Jimmy Page's study of Aleister Crowley.

As you read in chapter one, directly from Jimmy Page, he began being interested in Crowley when he was in school. Since Crowley was not taught in the public schools in England, I surmise that it was when he went to art school, as did Crowley, that he began to study his writings. Jimmy Page went to art school in the early 1960's. That is a very important point. Colin Wilson, in his book, *Mysterious Powers*, emphasized the point that Crowley's popularity began to rise in the 1960's: "...it was not until the magical revival that began in the mid-1960's that Crowley's reputation began to rise again. Nowadays more than a dozen of his books are in print, and a new generation ardently practices the magic rituals described in them. The Beast has finally achieved the fame he craved."31 Not only did Crowley rise again in the 1960's as part of the magical revival, but Druidism did as well. Peter Ellis wrote about this in *The Druids*: "With the onset of the 1960's 'Hippies' and 'Alternative Religions,' the Druids were fair game again. The Druids were called upon as the protoypes of many 'New Age' ideas and credos. It was almost inevitable that the Druids and ancient pre-Christian Celtic religion were waiting to be claimed by the new interest in 'witchcraft' which began to rise in the 1960's."32

Studying Crowley in the 1960's, Jimmy Page no doubt became familiar with the beginning of Aleister Crowley's magical career. It has already been presented in this book that Crowley wrote in his *Confessions* in 1922 that he did not know why he turned himself over to the Devil. Yet, the same book tells the story in just a few quotes. First of all, Crowley did not believe that Satan was God at that point: "To me the spiritual world consisted roughly of the Trinity and their angels on the one side; the devil and his on the other."33 He then decided good was in fact evil: "The forces of good were those which had constantly oppressed me. I saw them daily destroying the happiness of my fellow men. Since, therefore, it was my business to explore the spiritual world, my first step must be to get into personal communication with the devil. I had heard a good deal about this operation in a vague way; but what I wanted was a manual of technical instruction. I devoted myself to black magic; and the booksellers - Deighton Bell, God bless 'em! - immediately obliged with *The Book of Black Magic and of Pacts*, which, judging by the title was exactly what I needed."34 Crowley did not like that book, but he did like the idea of a secret church referred to therein. Therefore he wrote to its author, Arthur E. Waite, for more information, and Crowley tells of his response: "He replied kindly and intelligibly, suggesting that I should read *The Cloud Upon the Sanctuary* by Councillor von Eckartshausen. With this book I retired to Wastdale Head for the Easter vacation of 1898. This period proved to be the critical moment of my early life:...it determined the direction of my efforts."35

Crowley believed the spiritual world consisted of God and his angels on one side, the Devil and his on the other. The next thing he does is to condemn good and decide to get into personal communication with the Devil, so he sends off for *The Book of Black Magic and of Pacts*. Then he writes to the author of that book for more information. Waite tells him to read *The Cloud Upon the Sanctuary*, which Crowley says he did, and it was at the critical point in his life, determining the direction he would go. While launching full speed ahead in that direction, Crowley soothed his conscience by condemning the idea of following Christ and praising occult teaching:

"It is not only illogical to pick out of the gospels the texts which happen to suit one's own prejudices and then claim Christ as the supreme teacher, but his claims to pre-eminence are barred by the fact that all the passages which are not fiendish superstition find parallels in the writings of earlier masters....It is monstrous and mischievous for liberal thinkers to call themselves Christians; their nominal adhesion delays the disruption of the infamous system which they condone. To declare oneself a follower of Jesus is not only to insult history and reason, but to apologize for the murderers of Arius, Molinos and Cranmer, the persecutors of science, the upholders of slavery and the suppressors of all free thought and speech.

"At this time I had not carried these arguments to their logical conclusion. *The Cloud Upon the Sanctuary* told me of a sacred community of saints in possession of every spiritual grace, of the keys to the treasures of nature, and of moral emancipation such that there was no intolerance or unkindness. The members of this Church lived their secret life of sanctity in the world, radiating light and love upon all that came within their scope, yet they were free from spiritual pride. They enjoyed intimate communion with the immanent divine soul of nature. Inheritors of innocence and illumination, they were not self-seekers; and their one passion was to bring mankind into the sphere of their own sublimity, dealing with each individual as his circumstances required....The incarnation was a mystical or magical operation which took place in every man. Each was himself the Son of God who had assumed a body of flesh and blood in order to perform the work of redemption. The in-dwelling of the Holy Ghost was a sanctification resulting from the completion of the great work when the self had been crucified to itself and raised again in incorruptible immortality....I determined with my whole heart to make myself worthy to attract the notice of this mysterious brotherhood. I yearned passionately for illumination. I could imagine nothing more exquisite than to enter into communion with these holy men and to acquire the power of communicating with the angelic and divine intelligence of the universe. I longed for perfect purity of life, for mastery of the secret forces of nature, and for a career of devoted labor on behalf of 'the Creation which groaneth and travaileth.'"36

Aleister Crowley "longed for perfect purity of life," so what does he do? He gives himself over to the Devil, and Jimmy Page wants to know how anyone could call him evil. Two pages later in his *Confessions*, he says that he became absorbed in *The Cloud Upon the Sanctuary* and sought to join the brotherhood described in it: "I was absorbed in *The Cloud Upon the Sanctuary*, reading it again and again....I appealed with the whole force of my will to the adepts of the

Hidden Church to prepare me as a postulant for their august company."37 Crowley finally did enter into communicating with this brotherhood. He identified it soon after: "The Secret Assembly materialized as the 'Hermetic Order of the Golden Dawn'..."38

It was Crowley's hatred for 'good' that led him to the incandescent stupidity of believing he had justification to seek the Devil and give himself over to black Magick. Inevitably, he buried his mind in *The Cloud Upon the Sanctuary*, recommended to him by Arthur E. Waite, the author of *The Book of Black Magic and of Pacts*, now sold by Samuel Weiser Inc. as *The Book of Black Magic*, that I have in my possession. What Crowley said about *The Cloud Upon the Sanctuary* was true, in that it speaks of this brotherhood. It also says that "god" is behind this brotherhood, as I found when I read my copy. This is the god of Magick. This is none other than the Devil. You are about to read a couple of quotes from this book that pertain to Led Zeppelin's original organization, or coming together. There is one thing that needs to be stressed. What the members of Led Zeppelin are aware of, and I can attest to, is that when a person takes up the study of Magick, via Aleister Crowley, he or she is going to find that the first four books Crowley read are the following, in order:

(1) The Book of Black Magic and of Pacts
(2) The Cloud Upon the Sanctuary
(3) The Qabalah Unveiled
(4) The Book of the Sacred Magic of Abramelin the Mage

As you read the following information presented from *The Cloud Upon the Sanctuary*, remember that the band is also familiar with these quotes. When you read their personal statements afterward, you will see that they were in fact trying to authenticate the concepts of that book to their potential followers. Eckartshausen, the author of the book, makes it clear that when "god" wants to accomplish something in this world, he finds the human personnel to assist him in that effort. The first thing the Devil did with Led Zeppelin is to get a hold on the mind of Jimmy Page through the teachings of Crowley. Once he had possession of the mind of Page, he went on the journey of gathering the others together. Eckartshausen wrote of it this way: "God himself is the Power always present. The best man of his times, the chief himself, does not always know all the members, but the moment when it is the Will of God that he should accomplish any object, he finds them in the world with certainty to work for that purpose."39 He says that the best man of his time, when it is the will of "God" that he do so, will find the others he needs to assist him in serving his god. On the very next page he wrote: "If it be necessary that real members should meet together, they find and recognize each other with perfect certainty."40

"With perfect certainty" the members of the group chosen to serve god in a specific capacity will recognize each other as belonging together, when sought out by the individual commissioned by "god." These two concepts are clearly seen in the statements of Robert Plant, Jimmy Page, and John Paul Jones. First, Robert Plant was quoted by Ritchie Yorke in *Led Zeppelin -The Definitive Biography*: "Really Led Zeppelin was Jimmy....he had a premeditated view of the whole thing."41 Richard Cole, in *Stairway to Heaven - Led Zeppelin Uncensored*, quoted Jimmy Page as speaking to him about the first meeting of the four members of Led Zeppelin to jam: "'I wish you had been there,' Jimmy said. 'I wish you could have heard us. It was magical. Everything just came together.'"42 Please keep in mind, when Jimmy Page says "magical," he does not mean "super" or "fantastic." He means it literally. Howard Mylett quotes Page as saying, "I was so lucky to find everybody so instantly..."43 Page spoke to Chris Salewicz about the instant chemistry of the band, and how at the very beginning, they began to produce new riffs: "We've always spoken of the instant chemistry and how the band got together and started jamming and within those jams, riffs came out." This author believes that the band members were medium musicians right from the beginning. Dave Lewis and Simon Pallett quote John Paul Jones, in *Led Zeppelin: The Concert File*, about the initial gathering to play: "...once we got into that rehearsal room in Gerrard Street it was just instant. We just looked around and knew it was going to work..."44 John Paul Jones can be seen discussing this on VH1's Legends program about Led Zeppelin, saying that the first gathering, once they began to play, was like an explosion. It is a subtle hint of its being planned ahead of time by somebody else - the Devil. So as one can see, Eckartshausen's predictions of the members needed to accomplish the will of "god" meeting each other with perfect certainty came true where Led Zeppelin is concerned. Eckartshausen wrote it, Crowley read it, and I believe Page read it, as well as the band, and promoted it with like-minded statements; to guide others.

Eckartshausen went on to say in the same book, that those who have the knowledge can guide others, but only those who are "fit" will find what they are looking for: "All men are called, the called may be chosen, if they become ripe for entrance. Any one can look for the entrance, and any man who is within can teach another to seek for it; but only he who is fit can arrive inside."45 Eliphas Levi, in *Transcendental Magic*, as you read earlier, said what amounts to the very same thing: "The sages therefore must speak occasionally. Yes, they must speak, not, however, to disclose, but lead others to discover."46 The men could hardly be making these statements to promote album sales; especially Page.

It is not difficult, once one has a knowledge of all the facts of Crowley and Page's association with the Devil, to assert that it was Jimmy Page's study of Aleister Crowley, that began in the 1960's, in conjunction with the Devil's desire to use him and the other musicians of Led Zeppelin, that led to the uniting of those musicians for the Devil's purpose in the minds of future fans, satanic spiritual regeneration. The reason Jimmy Page had a premeditated view of the whole thing was because Satan gave it to him.

Satan planted the thoughts of Led Zeppelin being medium musicians in Jimmy Page's mind, to assist him in promoting Celtic Druidism and Silver Star Magick worldwide. *The Book On Mediums*, as I said before, shows the role the spirits played in assisting the Devil in achieving his goal of making the band medium musicians. Sometimes it was the spirits, sometimes it was Satan himself, as will be seen shortly. Allan Kardec, as I wrote before, questioned the spirits about many things during seances held a hundred and twenty five years ago. One of the statements made to him by a spirit referred to the type of people the spirits choose, or are told to choose, for service: "Our cause has no need of those who have so much pride as to consider themselves indispensable: we call to us those whom we wish, and they are often the least and the most humble."47

Jimmy Page found himself alone after the other Yardbirds called it quits in 1968. Peter Grant had the other band members sign the rights to the group's name over to Page, but he was alone as far as musicians were concerned. John Paul Jones made it clear on VH1 Legends, quoting his wife, that he was going crazy doing session work; and Plant and Bonham were starving to death, drifting from band to band. Richard Cole wrote about the conditions Plant and Bonham were living in trying to make it in the music business. Here is his quote from Plant: "'The Band of Joy played about two gigs a week, but we weren't making much money,' recalled Robert a few years later. 'If I hadn't been married by then, and my wife, Maureen, didn't have a job, I wouldn't have eaten. It was that simple. I would have been in the welfare lines.'"48 Cole then went on to describe Bonham at the time, his circumstances being remarkably similar: "John believed that music was the only thing he was good at, but nevertheless he became the stereotypical starving artist."49 As you read, Cole's statements about Plant and Bonham (the information of which he received from them when he was the band's road manager for 12 years), fit in with what Allan Kardec wrote down during a seance a hundred years before Led Zeppelin got together. Cole also made this relevant point about the band: "Overnight, these young men in their early twenties were turned into international stars."50 He also made this interesting statement about a few other bands in England: "Most of the rock musicians - from the Beatles to the Stones to Led Zeppelin - who emerged in the sixties came from a working class background."51 It does make sense to believe that those from less well to do families would desire riches and prestige more than those who are rich and influential, right? Again, it is the most humble who are often called to serve in the supernatural realm.

The Devil, again, in using these humble circumstanced men, made them Druidic, medium musicians, I believe, to promote his religion. The fact that musicians are capable of influencing religion is well known. They not only minister to it, but they are capable of molding it. As Dr. Sir J. G. Frazer put it in *The Golden Bough*: "Indeed the influence of music on the development of religion is a subject which would repay a sympathetic study. For we cannot doubt that this, the most intimate and affecting of all the arts, has done much to create as well as to express the religious emotions, thus modifying more or less deeply the fabric of belief to which at first sight it seems only to minister. The musician has done his part as well as the prophet and the thinker in the making of religion. Every faith has its appropriate music, and the difference between the creeds might almost be expressed in musical notation."52

If, therefore, the Devil can find men to play his music, it means that he can mold and minister to religion through his music; the religion that promotes his moral code. If Led Zeppelin's members were Satan's medium musicians, how did it happen? First of all, *The Book On Mediums* gives us the following definition of medium musicians: "*Medium Musicians*. Those who execute, compose, or write music under the influence of spirits."53 One of the spirits Kardec was conversing with emphasized the point that no matter what talent the medium may have, it is up to the spirits whether or not any contact is made: "With whatever faculty the medium may be endowed, he can do nothing without the sympathetic concurrence of the spirits; when he obtains nothing, it is not always that the faculty is lacking, but that the spirits will, or can, no longer use him."54 The spirits pick and choose, at the direction of the Devil, who they will use. They prefer some rather than others. A talented guitarist like Jimmy Page therefore, would be a prime target for the Devil to use in playing some of the most blazing drug music in existence. The following quote from Kardec illustrates why a great guitar player would receive great music, through the following analogy: "Let us make a comparison: a very skillful musician has in his hands several violins, which, to the ordinary eye, will all be very good instruments, but between which the consummate artist distinguishes a great difference; he perceives therein shades of exceeding delicacy, which make him choose some and reject others, shades which he comprehends rather by intuition than by anything he can define in them. It is the same with respect to mediums; with equal qualities in the medianimic power, the spirit will give the preference to one or to the other, according to the kind of communication he desires to make. Thus, for instance, persons, as mediums, write admirable poems, though in the ordinary conditions they never knew how, nor could compose two verses; others, on the contrary, who are poets, and who, as mediums, have been able to write only prose, in spite of their desire. The same with drawing, music, &c.55

One more quote shows Kardec asking the questions at a seance, and a spirit giving the answers, saying that they use the mediums, including medium musicians, who give them the greatest facility. Facility in this context means "ease of doing or making; absence of difficulty...a ready ability; skill; dexterity;

fluency...the means by which something can be done."56 Kardec wrote:

"'From whence comes the aptitude of some mediums to write in verse, not withstanding their positive ignorance of poetry?'

'Poetry is a language; they can write in verse as they can write in a language they do not know...'

'Is it the same for those who have general aptitude for drawing and music?'

'Yes, drawing and music are also methods of expressing the thought; spirits use the instruments that offer them the greatest facility.'

'Does the expression of the thought by poetry, drawing, or music, depend solely on the special aptitude of the medium, or on that of the spirit who communicates?'

'Sometimes on the medium, sometimes on the spirit. The superior spirits have all aptitudes, the inferior spirits have limited knowledge.'"57

The superior spirits have all aptitudes, and it is superior spirits that Led Zeppelin has always been associated with; according to Jimmy Page's *Goetia*. To show an introduction to these superior spirits, that have writing as well as musical ability, at work with Led Zeppelin, we look to Richard Cole in his book, *Stairway to Heaven - Led Zeppelin Uncensored.*

BRON YR AUR: IN THE MOUNTAINS OF WALES

Led Zeppelin's Robert Plant and Jimmy Page retreated to the mountains of Wales in the spring of 1970, to record music as medium musicians, I believe, for their third album. This trip can be authenticated by a number of sources, not just Richard Cole. One can see a picture of the cottage they stayed in included in the "VH1 - Legends" program, as Steven Tyler of Aerosmith tells the viewer the name of it. The name of the small cottage was "Bron Yr Aur." Cole described the situation:

"Jimmy and Robert began to see what they could put together. Accompanied by Robert's family and Charlotte Martin, they drove to South Wales, staying in a mountain cottage called Bron Yr Aur, which means 'Golden Breast' in Welsh ('Bring back a couple of those golden breasts for me,' I told them).

"Located near the River Dovey, Bron-Yr-Aur was a primitive setting – there was no electricity, so the lighting was provided by gaslight. Robert and Jimmy found some time for relaxation, including jeep rides through the hills. But they primarily were there to begin writing songs for Zeppelin's third album: 'Out On the Tiles'... 'Celebration Day'... 'Bron Y Aur Stomp.' They would take a portable tape recorder and sometimes a guitar with them on walks and would come back with both words and melody. On one of those hikes, they sat down in a small valley, Jimmy began picking out a tune, and Robert immediately improvised a verse. Fortunately, the tape recorder was running. The song quickly evolved into 'That's the Way.'...The songs came quickly."58

A few points need to be made concerning these statements by Richard Cole. The first point, is that the cottage was in the mountains. Again, if you listen to "Misty Mountain Hop," the fifth song on Led Zeppelin's fourth album, you can hear Robert Plant sing that he was going to pack his "bags" to head to the "mountain" because "spirits" congregate there, at 3:44 into the song. I want to emphasize, however, that it does not always have to be the same mountain. As Aleister Crowley said, in *The Book of Thoth*: "...the god Pan upon the highest and most secret mountains of the earth."59 The second point concerning Cole's statements, is the fact that he said they would come back from hikes in the mountains with both words and melody, but that they didn't always have to have the guitar with them to come back with melody. That will be elaborated on later in this chapter. Finally, Cole points out that it didn't take long for the songs to come. Concrete evidence of the spirits involved with the band was not presented here, but it was a good introduction to things to come. The next place music for the band was produced was Boleskine House, at Loch Ness, in Scotland.

BOLESKINE HOUSE AND "STAIRWAY TO HEAVEN" MUSIC

Aleister Crowley purchased Boleskine House for the purpose of work- ing the Sacred Magic of Abramelin the Mage, to achieve the Knowledge and Conversation of the Holy Guardian Angel, Satan. As you read in chapter eleven, I asserted my belief that Jimmy Page had the same motive in 1970. In Crowley's written supplement to the Sacred Magic of Abramelin the Mage, *Liber Samekh*, an epistle he wrote to further assist magicians in their effort of uniting with the Devil, he described a situation that would take place once the communion or "intimacy" with the Devil had been accomplished through the rituals: "Now, the Angel will make contact with the Adept at any point that is sensitive to His influence....A musician may be rapt away by majestic melodies such as he never hoped to hear."60 Crowley would also describe this type of event in *The Equi- nox of the Gods*. He spoke of himself in the third person: "These practices con- tinued into October, at the beginning of which he reached the state of Dhyana, a tremendous spiritual experience, in which the subject and object of meditation unite with excessive violence in blinding brilliance and music of a kind to which earthly harmony affords no parallel."61 This has got to be Lucifer the piper.

Crowley makes it clear that the magician can hear beautiful music when communing with the Holy Guardian Angel; who is the Devil. I believe these things happened between Jimmy Page and the Devil at Boleskine House, which as I wrote before, I believe occurred over several months during 1970, the same year he bought it. Steven Tyler said in "VH1's Legends," that Jimmy Page had produced the music for "Stairway to Heaven" in his home studio. He said that shortly after telling the viewers that Page had bought the former home of "Black Magician Aleister Crowley." In the 1990 4 cd re-masters album, Jimmy Page included statements by different writers in a picture booklet. Cameron Crowe said that the song began as many other Zeppelin hits did, from the studio in Page's home. This recording was not done with any of the other members of the band, only Page. He made that clear on MTV: "I worked on it for quite a while, on and off. I was putting all these different sections together; and putting them in what I considered was the right order before I even presented it to the band."62 Robert Plant made it clear that this was generally what was done by Jimmy Page; that "Stairway To Heaven" was only one of a multitude of songs he composed at home: "Jimmy is the man who is the music. He goes away to his house and works on it a lot and then brings it to the band in its skeletal state. Slowly everybody brings their personality into it."63

Jimmy was able to compose music as a medium, I believe, on the road in hotels as well, and Bob Larson, in his book, *Satanism - The Seduction of America's Youth*, wrote of Jimmy Page anticipating the arrival of music from somewhere else: "Those close to the band say Jimmy Page spent days in a dark room, candles lit, sitting before a table covered with knives. He would hold his guitar 'waiting for something to come through.'"64 Steven Davis wrote of Jimmy Page anticipating supernatural assistance on the guitar, quoting him like Larson did: "Jimmy spent his days in his suite with the shades drawn and candles lit....With an armed guard sitting outside his door, Jimmy had the isolation of a monk. He spent days and nights wide awake, holding his guitar and, as he told a reporter, 'waiting for something to come through.'"65 Here is the quote in question, including a statement Jimmy made to Tony Palmer in the *Observer*, in May of 1975, about waiting for music to come to him: "...'I thought something was coming through,' he said, waving his hands towards his guitar sunk into a chair. 'But, well, I suppose there have been too many interruptions'. He wandered about his darkened room disconsolate, exhausted, alone. 'I've compared notes with other writers and artists to see what time of day is most productive.'" Don't allow those quotes to slip by you without realizing that it was Jimmy Page speaking at the inner quote. Once again, the magician is speaking, about his medium musicianship, not to fully disclose, but lead others to discover. If this sounds too incredulous for you the reader, I would challenge you to go back to the chapter heading and read Jimmy Page's statement about him and Plant "...channeling the music..." after they reunited, and that they had always done that. The only person who channels music is an individual who is a musical medium, who is in contact with spirits who provide him with music; case closed, no discussions.

Jimmy Page did the composing for "Stairway To Heaven" at Boleskine House before December 1970, when the band gathered to rehearse for recording their fourth album at Island Studios in London. Dave Lewis, in his book, *The Complete Guide To The Music of Led Zeppelin*, made it clear that Page brought the song with him to Island Studios: "'Stairway' started out as a fairly complete chord progression that Page brought in when they commenced recording at Island studios in December 1970."66

Richard Cole mentions that the band began recording at Island Studios in December of 1970, but then makes reference to the fact that they moved from there to Headley Grange, in Hampshire, right after Christmas to finish recording for the fourth album: "Part of the fourth album was recorded at Island Studios in London in December, but after Christmas Zeppelin moved to Headley Grange, again relying on a mobile recording studio. The house had a comfortable feel to it, one that allowed the band to relax and let their creative energies flow."67 Led Zeppelin allowed their creative energies to flow at Headley Grange, but those energies were supernatural, made possible, I believe, by their iron clad spiritual union as Druid medium musicians.

SPIRITUAL UNION AT HEADLEY GRANGE

Led Zeppelin gathered together at Headley Grange, in Hampshire, to record music for their fourth album, because, as Richard Cole said, they were more comfortable there and the band could relax; separated from the annoyances of everyday life, where they could focus their spiritual energy to the task of being medium musicians. They would eventually return there a few years later to record *Physical Graffiti*, their sixth album. It would seem that the spirits preferred Headley Grange.

Jimmy Page, in the January 2002 issue of *Guitar World* magazine, made it clear to the objective thinker that Headley Grange was haunted by spirits. He said that he saw a "gray shape" on his way to his room one evening. He said he checked to see if it was caused by the lights, but that it wasn't. Then he said that he took off out of the area. Finally, he said, "But I wasn't surprised to find spirits there, because the place had a miserable past." If you remember correctly, the same description was given of Boleskine House back in chapter eleven. Jimmy knew that it too was haunted, as he confessed.

Page's statements about Headley Grange being haunted fit right in with what Allan Kardec wrote about spirits preferring a certain place to meet with mediums. In another question and answer session at a seance, he asked a spirit about times for invocations, and the spirit ended up emphasizing the place:

"'Are invocations for fixed days and hours preferable?'

'Yes, and, if it be possible, in the same place; the spirits come to it more willingly: it is the constant desire you have that aids the spirits to come and put themselves into communication with you. Spirits have their occupations, which they cannot leave at a moment's warning for your personal satisfaction. I say, in the same place; but do not suppose this to be an absolute obligation, for spirits come everywhere: I mean, a place consecrated to that is preferable, because there concentration of thought is more perfect.'"68

Kardec interviewed a spirit at another seance who identified himself as "Erastus." In that interview, Erastus made it clear that spirits prefer to communicate with the same mediums, ones who are all believers:

"'Does the production of the phenomena pertain to the special nature of the medium? And could it be produced with other mediums with more facility and promptitude?'
'The production pertains to the nature of the medium, and can be produced only with corresponding natures; as to promptitude, our custom of corresponding often with the same medium is a great help to us.'

'Does the influence of the persons present count for anything?'
'When there is skepticism, opposition, we can be greatly annoyed; we like better to give our proofs with believers...'"69

In this next question to the spirits, Kardec receives an answer that clearly describes the members of Led Zeppelin. Remember, this book, *The Book On Mediums*, was written in 1874, one year before Aleister Crowley was born; keep that in mind. Its relevance will be seen shortly. The question and answer relate to spiritual unity:

"'Have men more power to invoke spirits when united by community of thought and intention?'
'When all are united by charity and for good, they obtain grand things. Nothing is more injurious to the result of invocations than divergence of thought.'"70

We see that the spirits themselves say that they work better with those who are united by community of thought and intention. In this case, the members of Led Zeppelin are making music for their master the Devil; who they believe is a good and benevolent god, to assist him in the satanic spiritual regeneration of their listeners, which they believed was a "good" thing. Plant made reference to that in the song, "The Ocean" off *Houses of the Holy*. Eliphas Levi, in *Transcendental Magic*, written a century before, described the situation at Headley

Grange where the band members were united in purpose, and the necessity of that union: "Men who are masters of themselves become easily masters of others; but it is possible for them to hinder one another if they disregard the laws of discipline and of the universal hierarchy. To be subjects of a discipline in common, there must be a community of ideas and desires, and such a communion cannot be attained except by a common religion established on the very foundations of intelligence and reason."71 Aleister Crowley, who as the reader knows claimed to be Eliphas Levi reincarnated, emphasized the same concept in his book, *Magick*: "...there is no doubt that an assemblage of persons who really are in harmony can much more easily produce an effect than a Magician working by himself."72 That statement by Crowley obviously applies to the band's concert performances as well. Ritchie Yorke, who, again, is a personal friend of the band, wrote of Led Zeppelin's spiritual union at Headley Grange in *Led Zeppelin - The Definitive Biography*: "Living together, playing together, getting a buzz on being together alone, except for essential entourage, renewing that natural spiritual union which was their greatest strength."73 Yorke reiterated the concept of the band's union with one another, but this time included reference to "Stairway to Heaven": "They were so in tune with each other that unanimous intuitive confidence and their unique faith kept them hard at work - they really knew in their hearts that the 'mystery song' was evolving into an absolute rock blockbuster."74

So far you have read that the spirits require a place consecrated for concentration on communications from them. They desire to give their proofs to believers. They require unity of thought and intention. Eliphas Levi wrote of the necessity of community of thought and ideas based on a common religion; for men to be able to master others. Crowley wrote of the ability of a group in complete harmony being able to work an effect better than a magician by himself. Ritchie Yorke, a personal friend of the band, wrote more than once about the band's spiritual union being their greatest strength and that it played a major role in producing their music; especially "Stairway to Heaven." As anyone reading this book can tell, the pieces of this puzzle fit together perfectly. Now we are going to look at the practical working of their receiving music as medium musicians.

AUTOMATIC COMPOSING AND WRITING

As medium musicians, the band members, Page and Plant, by their own admission, engaged in automatic composing and writing. As you read previously in chapter eleven, the power of the Sacred Magic of Abramelin the Mage is given to the magician who achieves union with the Holy Guardian Angel, Satan. You all know that Crowley advocated this. Abramelin Magic, again, gives the magician power to control evil spirits. This is done by permission of the Devil. Also, don't forget about Page publishing a book for that purpose in 1976. In *The Book On Mediums*, again, written one year before Aleister Crowley was born, Allan Kardec pointed out that before communications with spirits can be made, one has to appeal to one's guardian angel. Now, this is not *The Book of the Sacred Magic of Abramelin the Mage*, nor is it Aleister Crowley's *Magick* that this information is coming from. It is coming from Allan Kardec, who is a third party, whose book is, along with Crowley's, published by Samuel Weiser Inc., in Yorke Beach, Maine. Kardec wrote (in 1874): "So, before expecting to obtain communications from such or such a spirit, it is necessary to press the development of the faculty, and for that purpose make a general appeal, and, above all, address yourself to your guardian angel."75 As you see, this teaching of the guardian angel and the spirits is a teaching of antiquity. Once again, Abramelin warned the magician not to show this magic of controlling evil spirits at the hand of the guardian angel to more than three of his friends, but along with that warning is the permission to show three friends: "It is certain that having obtained this Sacred Wisdom thou mayest dispose of it and communicate it unto <u>three friends</u>; but thou must not exceed this Sacred Number of the Ternary, for in such case thou wouldest be altogether deprived of it."76

The author believes the fact that the Magic of Abramelin could not be shown to more than three friends is why Led Zeppelin called it quits once John Bonham died, and why Page/Plant did not play "Stairway to Heaven," because the Magick that produced the song was not given to anyone but the four members of Led Zeppelin; which made each member irreplaceable. Robert Palmer wrote, in an article called *Led Zeppelin: The Music*, included in the booklet that accompanied the 1990 Led Zeppelin re-masters album: "This group spirit had a lot to do with Zeppelin developing so rapidly, playing so tightly, and lasting so long without a single personnel change. Each member was considered irreplaceable, which is the reason the band had to call it quits following John Bonham's death." It all makes perfect sense when one knows the facts; it is also interesting that he calls it a "group spirit." I couldn't agree more.

Another relevant point in the book, *The Book of the Sacred Magic of Abramelin the Mage*, is the instructions given in chapter thirty, described as given for the following purpose:

"To cause Comedies, Operas, and every kind of Music and Dances to appear.
  (1) To cause all kinds of Music to be heard.
  (2) Music and extravagant Balls.
  (3) For all kinds of Instruments to be played."77

Earlier in this chapter you read where Richard Cole mentioned Page and Plant in the mountains of Wales, taking a tape recorder and "sometimes" they would take a guitar with them, but they always came back with lyrics and music. The point is, though Jimmy Page had not yet perfected the Knowledge and Conversation of the Holy Guardian Angel at the time of recording the third album, the spirits themselves could have caused the music to be heard without Page having a guitar with him. All they would have to do is have the tape recorder on and melody could be heard right out of thin air. Even if the guitar were with them, the spirits could play the guitar through Jimmy Page, or without him being near it. Remember, in the beginning of the Led Zeppelin movie, Peter Grant is delivering concert dates to Jimmy Page. Jimmy is sitting on a blanket in his yard, playing the "Hurdy Gurdy" to attract supernatural assistance, in my opinion, and on the blanket is a dagger, a guitar, and a tape recorder. Again, as Jimmy turns around to look at the camera, he has eyes of fire. If ever there was a man who was telling his followers that he is possessed of the Devil, it was Jimmy Page in the Led Zeppelin film, plain as day; speaking not to disclose, but to lead others to discover. It was Jimmy Page sitting there with eyes of fire. Are we to believe he was possessed by a black Labrador, that accidentally wandered into Led Zeppelin's recording studio? Yes indeed, the song Black Dog was about Satan when mentioning the eyes of fire.

There is a supernatural method, which men do not fully understand, by which the Devil transmits music from himself to the spirits in his service, to give to men like Page and Plant who, as the evidence suggests, have sold their souls to him. Aleister Crowley made this point in his book, Moonchild: "...amid a cloud of angels bearing silver trumpets, came one with great height of brow, and eyes of golden flashes. In him the whole heaven rocked with harmonious music..."78 The two points Crowley was trying to make were, first, the music came from this angel alone, and second, he rocked the entire heaven, the host of which had possession of musical instruments. The angels did not rock with harmonious music on their own ability, Lucifer did it for them. These concepts are consistent with the *Holy Bible*, where Ezekiel wrote of Lucifer: "The workmanship of thy tabrets and of thy pipes was prepared in thee in the day that thou wast created." Ezekiel 28:13(KJV) There you have Aleister Crowley and the *Holy Bible* in complete agreement on the Devil's musical composing ability. Notice the grammar in that Biblical quote. It speaks of the "workmanship" that "was," not "thy tabrets and of thy pipes" that "were." It was the "workmanship" or "skill of a craftsman" that "was" prepared in him in the day he was created. This skill, once again, is the power of a composer, given right from the hand of God himself. It is supernatural ability to compose and play music, the likes of which men could never compose on their own; music like that of "Stairway to Heaven," I believe.

Where the Devil's composing of Led Zeppelin's music is concerned, I want to focus on the work of Jimmy Page. Where automatic writing is the issue, Robert Plant's work will be focused on. The fact that Page has produced music at Boleskine house has already been presented. That Abramelin magic can cause music to be heard and instruments to be played has also been presented. Previously in this work, I discussed a book called a "Grimoire." Again, a Grimoire is a book on the invocation of evil spirits used by magicians. The specific one that I made reference to is *The Goetia - The Lesser Key of Solomon the King*. This was published in 1904. Aleister Crowley assigned S.L. MacGregor Mathers with the duty of translating it, but he didn't finish. Crowley finished the translation and then edited the text. Again, in the 1995 version of this book, published by Samuel Weiser Inc., the following information is recorded in the introduction, with a footnote making reference to Jimmy Page producing the best facsimile edition: "Crowley probably began work on the Goetia in 1901 as he remarks that it took three years to produce. It appeared in 1904, under the imprint of his Society for the Propagation of Religious Truth, Boleskine, Foyers, Inverness, Scotland. An American piracy was issued in 1916 by the inimitable L.W. deLaurence, described by Crowley as a 'Yankee thief.' Several facsimile editions have appeared."(Footnote #62)

#62   "The first facsimile edition was issued by Jimmy Page (London: Equinox, 1976); although issued in hardcover, the dust jacket used camel hair paper and it remains the facsimile most faithful to the 1904 original."79

I have re-presented this material here because of an important quote that needs to be presented from this book that Jimmy Page reproduced in the best facsimile edition. The quote will illustrate to you his motive in reproducing the work, because it is related to spirits producing music. In the book, there are instructions for controlling 72 spirits listed. The ninth spirit listed in the book is named Paimon. Here is his description: "The Ninth Spirit in this Order is Paimon, a Great King, and very obedient unto LUCIFER...There goeth before him also an Host of Spirits, like men with Trumpets and well sounding Cymbals, and all other sorts of Musical Instruments....This Spirit can teach all Arts and Sciences, and other secret things. He can discover unto thee what the Earth is, and what holdeth it up in the Waters; and what Mind is, and where it is; or any other thing thou mayest desire to know....He bindeth or maketh any man subject unto the Magician if he so desire it. He giveth good Familiars, and such as can teach all Arts. He is to be observed towards the West."80 The following points need to be made about this quote. First of all you read that there goes ahead of this Spirit a Hosts of Spirits, with trumpets and cymbals and all other kinds of musical instruments. This Spirit can teach you "any other thing thou mayest desire to know." If you listen to the song, "The Song Remains the Same," you can hear Robert Plant make reference to his being able to find out "anything" he desired to. Another point, "He bindeth or maketh any man subject unto the Magician if he so desire it." Chapters twelve and thirteen illustrate that point effectively, relative to the Violin bow and the Theremin.

Because men like Aleister Crowley and Jimmy Page believe that the Devil is god, and therefore "omnipresent," meaning he is present everywhere, which is true of God, not the Devil, they believe he is able to make a spirit with a supernatural or natural instrument play the music he produces. This is true, except for the omnipresent part. He doesn't need to be omnipresent to do this. It is part of his ability as the most powerful created being in existence to be able to do it. This is what went on at Boleskine House with Jimmy Page, I believe, and have produced evidence to the same. At Boleskine House, however, I believe Satan himself was there. He may or may not have been present at Headley Grange, although it would not be surprising if he had been there. I believe that there were some spirits there (due to statements made by Page and Plant), producing music and lyrics, and will now show evidence to that effect.

Jimmy Page made reference to what can be "automatic composing" at Headley Grange. He did compose the music for "The Battle of Evermore" there. He said that he had never played a mandolin before, and he picked up John Paul Jones' mandolin "…and those chords just came out."81 Jimmy Page told Michael Watts from Melody Maker the following: "I get enthusiastic and excited over something that's being written out of nowhere." Page composed the music for other songs at Headley Grange during that outing there, but the point has been made. The quotes also fit perfectly with what he told Tony Palmer in 1975, presented earlier in this chapter. Here is his general statement about the band being mediums at Headley Grange, as he discussed the situation in the January 2002 issue of *Guitar World* magazine: "If something really magical is coming through, then you follow it....We tried to take advantage of everything that was being offered to us." Notice, please, that the first part of that quote is given in the present tense. Again, the sages must speak not to disclose, but to lead others to discover. Page was guiding future musical mediums with that statement. Also, he makes it clear that they were receiving music from another source, saying it was "offered" to them. He continues in the article to describe the band as musical mediums with another statement about channeling, this time in reference to their being able to play "Stairway to Heaven" all the way to the end for the very first time, and how Plant wrote "80 percent" of the song's words at the same exact time: "We were channeling a lot of energy." Do you know why they call the English Channel by that name? It is not a spring. The Atlantic Ocean travels through it. Jimmy Page told Chris Salewicz in Gig, May, 1977, that the band would go on even if they could only make albums, if one member was incapacitated. He then said, in reference to that: "...because the whole aspect of what's going to come round the corner as far as writing goes is the dark element, the mysterious element. You just don't know what's coming. So many good things have come out of that that it would be criminal to interrupt a sort of alchemical process like that." Page is claiming to be a musical medium, for the Dark Side- Satan himself. At this point we will look at the specifics of the writing of lyrics.

Robert Plant makes it clear that he did some "automatic writing" at Headley Grange. The proof of which is about to be presented to you. First, what automatic writing is has to be understood. It is an occurrence of spirits using the hand and/or writing utensil of a medium to script something apart from the thinking or will of the medium. Aleister Crowley mentioned automatic writing in his book *Moonchild*. In the text, he makes mention of an instrument devised for spirits to use to communicate with man by writing called a "Planchette." Webster defines Planchette: "a small, three cornered device, often having as one of its supports a pencil, that is supposed to write out a message or, as with a Ouija board, point to letters or words, as it moves with the fingers resting lightly on it."82 Aleister Crowley describes the use of a Planchette by a spirit: "The spirit had devised an ingenious method of communication, known to science as Planchette. This instrument is probably familiar to you all; it is an inconvenient way of writing, but otherwise exhibits no marked peculiarity. Now that we have accepted 'automatic writing' as automatic, there is really no reason why mediums should pretend that a Planchette is not under control."83 Robert Plant did not use a Planchette, but he does describe automatic writing as the method by which he received the lyrics for "Stairway to Heaven." If Aleister Crowley authenticated automatic writing as fact, you can bet Jimmy Page does as well. If Page does, then Led Zeppelin does, pure and simple. In *The Book On Mediums*, Allan Kardec illustrated automatic writing by a spirit in progress, which will be compared with similar comments by Robert Plant afterward:

"The writing was as flowing, rapid, and easy, as with the hand, but it was afterward found that these objects were really only appendices, pencil holders, with which they could dispense by themselves holding the pencil: the hand, carried along by an involuntary movement, wrote under the impulse given by the spirit, and without the concurrence of the will or thought of the medium....Thus the spirit can express his thought directly, either by the movement of an object in the hand of the medium, or by his action on the hand itself.

"When the spirit acts directly on the hand, he gives to it an impulse completely independent of the will. It goes on without interruption, and in spite of the medium, as long as the spirit has anything to say, and stops when he has finished.

"What characterizes the phenomenon in this case is, that the medium has no consciousness of what he writes; absolute unconsciousness constitutes *passive or mechanical mediums*. This faculty is precious, as it can leave no doubt of its independence of the thought of him who writes."84

Robert Plant, therefore, to the mind of the person who cares to do the research, is confessing to being in league with spirits as he is quoted by Ritchie Yorke in *Led Zeppelin - The Definitive Biography*, as saying the following:

"'I was just sitting there with Pagey in front of a fire at Headley Grange,' Plant recalled. 'Pagey had written these chords and he played them for me. I was holding a pencil and paper and for some reason, I was in a very bad mood. Then all of a sudden my hand was writing out the words: "There's a lady who's sure, all that glitters is gold, and she's buying a Stairway to Heaven." I just sat there and I looked at the words and I almost leapt out of my seat.'"85

Again, I would point out to the reader that Page's production of the music for "Stairway," as well as Plant's lyrics, were concurrent. This is, I believe, the Devil putting his music and his lyrics together in one song, through his servants, and like he said in Crowley's *Book of the Law*, "...they shall rule the many and the known." The song has ruled the Rock Music airways for three decades; and now is in its fourth.

Plant wrote the lyrics for "Stairway to Heaven," and described it as looking to illustrate "spiritual perfection;" and the definition of spiritual perfection is union with God. Since Plant obviously believes that Satan is God, he must mean that the song was written to describe union with Satan. This is indicative of someone who is familiar with the Magick of Abramelin. Dave Lewis made mention of Plant's writing in his book, *The Complete Guide to the Music of Led Zeppelin*: "At Headley Grange the song developed around the log fire with Robert composing a set of lyrics full of hippy mysticism that told the tale of a search for spiritual perfection."86 Richard Cole was with Plant at Headley Grange, and he wrote essentially the same thing, but also mentioned Jimmy Page's reaction to Robert's lyrics: "Robert improvised most of the lyrics for 'Stairway' during the rehearsals as he sat in front of the roaring fireplace, looking for some way, he said, to describe spiritual perfection. Jimmy listened and was just blown away by what he heard. From the beginning, he felt that this song could be something special, that Robert had eclipsed everything that he had written before."87 Robert Plant, searching for spiritual perfection, ends up commanding the fans of Led Zeppelin to sell their souls to the Devil. Suffice it to say, he looked in the wrong place. It is true, however, that his chosen moral code led him to look where he did, to the Devil. Twenty-seven years later he is mocking Christ in "Most High" on the Page/Plant *Walking into Clarksdale* album. Ostensibly, he and Jimmy are still on the same path. May God have mercy on their souls and show them their error. There will be No Quarter on the other side.

Cole presents Jimmy Page as describing Plant's "Stairway to Heaven" lyrics as eclipsing all previous lyrics. This means that Plant's writing ability was developing, in Page's mind. Cole wrote, on the same page, that after this writing session Jimmy said he was going to leave the writing of lyrics to Robert: "Jimmy was so thoroughly impressed with Robert's lyrics on 'Stairway' that he decided to take a hiatus from lyric writing himself. 'It's not that hard a decision,' he thought. 'Robert has grown so much as a songwriter.'"88 There you have Jimmy Page describing Robert's development as a song lyric writer. Compare that statement with the following quote by Allan Kardec about the development of automatic writing by mediums:

"Of all the means of communication, writing with the hand - called by some involuntary writing - is, without contradiction, the most simple, the easiest, and the most convenient, because it requires no preparation, and because, as in ordinary writing, it can be used for the most extended development."89 Kardec elaborated in the following quote, making the point that relations with spirits can become more comfortable as relations between people do. That is what he says is primarily responsible for the development of automatic writing, and if that is the case with Led Zeppelin and evil spirits, they would have been quite comfortable with each other by the time they got to the fourth album and "Stairway to Heaven":

"Of all the means of communication, manual writing is the most simple, the most convenient, and the most complete. It is to that all efforts should tend, for it permits us to establish with the spirits as continuous and regular relations as among ourselves....The faculty of writing, for a medium, is especially the one that is most susceptible of development by exercise."90

The fact that Robert Plant's development of writing by exercise was shown in the lyrics to "Stairway to Heaven" was presented in an article written by Chris Welch in *Melody Maker*, just after the first time Led Zeppelin played the song in concert; in Belfast, Northern Ireland, on March 5th, 1971. Welch actually used the word "developing" to describe Plant's lyrics: "An excellent ballad, it displayed Robert's developing lyricism."

Jimmy Page was blown away by Robert Plant's developing lyrics, Chris Welch wrote about it, and Allan Kardec wrote of a medium's developing ability of writing a hundred years earlier. This is significant, because it was Kardec who described how spirits write through mediums apart from any knowledge of the content of the writing by the medium, and it being done independently of the will of the medium. That matches exactly what Robert Plant said about his hand writing the "Stairway to Heaven" lyrics and his not knowing what he was writing, because he almost jumped out of his seat after it was done. Substantial evidence has been shown in this section to establish probable cause in the courtroom of the mind of the reader, who is not given to incredulity, to believe that Led Zeppelin was in fact a group of individuals who were medium musicians for the Devil. As Jimmy Page put it: "I've been writing a lot at home and I can try things out in my own studio setup. Lately I've been experimenting with chords a lot more and with unusual voicings. There are several ways in which material comes into the band - but it's always there."91 The home Page is referring to in that quote is of course, Boleskine House. Notice what Page said about music coming "into the band." There you have Jimmy Page himself intimating (again) that the music comes from an outside source.

Musicians who have sold their souls to the Devil can be sure that the material will always be there, especially since they are doing Satan's bidding; in performing music for a lifestyle that is in rebellion against Lord Jesus Christ, and without repentance of which the eternal soul will end up in eternal damnation, which is what the Devil wants, and also what Crowley wanted when he said that he was committed to ensuring his own damnation and helping others to escape from Jesus (see quote at heading of chapter five). It all makes perfect sense. The Devil, using these talented musicians, not only wanted to present the music and lyrics that expound his religion of satanic spiritual regeneration, but he wanted to use them to present it in timeless fashion; in order to get the most results from it, and he did exactly that. To authenticate that, we will examine statements, not only by Jimmy Page and Robert Plant, but Jason Newsted of Metallica and *Hit Parader* magazine.

"STAIRWAY TO HEAVEN" - TIMELESS MUSIC

Long after the members of Led Zeppelin, this author, and you the reader have died, Led Zeppelin's music, especially "Stairway to Heaven," is going to be alive and well, because this music is timeless; each subsequent generation will embrace it all the more as we head toward the rise of the Anti-Christ. Richard Cole wrote what Jimmy Page had to say about "Stairway to Heaven" being timeless: "'If any song from this band has timeless qualities, I think it's 'Stairway to Heaven,' Jimmy said, beaming like a proud father as he listened to the playbacks in the studio. He was right. The song would eventually become the most requested song on radio stations on both sides of the Atlantic."[92] As one can imagine, Robert Plant was in total agreement with Jimmy Page about "Stairway to Heaven" being timeless. Plant, however, made the point that the song was being pushed by someone, and that it was a gift from, again, an outside source: "It was almost as if it just had to be gotten out at that time. There was something pushing it, saying 'You guys are OK, but if you want to do something timeless, here's a wedding present for you.'"[93] Jason Newsted of the contemporary rock group "Metallica" says that Led Zeppelin's music is timeless, and he was quoted by Ritchie Yorke as well: "The best thing one can say about Zeppelin's music is that it's just timeless stuff. It's always so good and holds up to anything that comes out now."[94]

To show that Led Zeppelin's music is in fact timeless, three important references will now be presented to illustrate that point. In a May 18th, 1975 issue of *The Observer*, Tony Palmer wrote of the incandescence of Led Zeppelin. He said that no one in history has been able to draw the crowds that Led Zeppelin did. Twenty years later, Dave Lewis and Simon Pallett presented the same concept about Led Zeppelin and statistics, referring to Page/Plant on October 27th, 1995, in *Led Zeppelin: The Concert File*: "The US tour ends on a high note, celebrating another month of consistently high achievements. The statistics are astonishing. Page/Plant played 69 shows in 57 cities in the US. 61 shows were totally sold out and total attendance was 1,104,280. The US tours alone grossed $34,095,313."95 As late as August of 1997, Led Zeppelin's fourth album, and "Stairway to Heaven," were being referred to as timeless by *Hit Parader* magazine: "Few bands in rock history have been able to mix a touch of mysticism within the realm of their heavy attack. Led Zeppelin did it with ease. On their legendary fourth disc, they created a dizzying array of great moment, including that song for the ages, 'Stairway to Heaven.' The magical blend of acoustic tenderness and mettalic fury that characterized Zep at their best has withstood the test of time, cementing this band and this album as the best of all time."96 "Mysticism" means union with god. Jimmy Page, Robert Plant, Jason Newsted of Metallica, Hit Parader magazine, and the fans of Page/Plant have all made their point about Led Zeppelin; that it is a timeless entity. Having produced music that is considered timeless by the listeners of rock and roll, Led Zeppelin will never disappear from the music collections of the average rock fan, especially since the Devil set them up as Druid medium musicians, I believe, to promote his religion, whereby they are also mediums between Satan's "Silver Star" and the rest of the world; promoting the "Law of Thelema."

THE FOURTH ALBUM COVER - NO BAND IDENTIFICATION

Led Zeppelin's fourth album, more than the others, presents concepts of the Law of Thelema in its songs. Crowley identified the word Thelema with the Devil. He wrote in *The Magical Record of the Beast*: "...Our Lord the Devil's their Word, the Word Thelema, spoken of me The Beast..."97 He made it clear that he wanted the masses of humanity to be reached with the Law of Thelema. In the first chapter you read the entire parable of the sticks, concerning Led Zeppelin. The end of that parable, from Crowley's *Equinox, Vol. III, No.1*, again, is indicative of Led Zeppelin's fourth album cover: "We have for the whole Beginning of Our Work, praise be eternally unto His Holy Name, the Fire of our Father the Sun. The inspiration is ours, and ours is the Law of Thelema that shall set the world ablaze. And we have many small dry sticks, that kindle quickly and burn through quickly, leaving the larger Wood unlit. And the great logs,the masses of humanity, are always with us. But our edged need is of those middle fagots that on the one hand are readily kindled by the small Wood, and on the other endure until the great logs blaze."98 In the magazine, Led Zeppelin - Will the Song Remain the Same? published in 1981, the following was written about Led Zeppelin's fourth album and the album cover's fagots:

"...the new album bore the unusual sight of an old man stooping in a field, a bunch of faggots (i.e. sticks) strapped to his back. This was an album so mystical that it didn't even have a title, although it was commonly referred to as Led Zeppelin IV."99

The reason there was no writing on the cover of the fourth Led Zeppelin album, no band identification or album title; I believe, was because Jimmy Page and the rest of the band wanted to take no credit for what they received, knowing that they and their music were mediums between the Devil and his Silver Star, and the masses of humanity that would listen to the music; that promotes the Law of Thelema. In the following quote from Allan Kardec, a spirit contrasts the arrogant medium with the humble medium; the theme of which explains the band's not wanting to take any credit for the music received from Satan; because where the fourth album is concerned, they had an attitude of humility toward its reception:

"It is proper to say that pride is often excited in a medium by his surroundings. If he has greater faculties than ordinary, he is sought after and praised; he considers himself indispensable, and soon affects airs of self-sufficiency and disdain when he lends his assistance. We have, more than once, had to regret the eulogiums we had given to certain mediums in order to encourage them.

"By the side of this picture let us place that of the truly good medium - him in whom we may have confidence....Knowing that his faculty is a gift accorded to him for use in good, he seeks not self-laudation, he takes no merit for it to himself. He accepts the good communications made to him as a favor, of which he should endeavor to render himself worthy by kindness, benevolence, and modesty. The former prides himself on his relations with superior spirits; the latter becomes more humble in consequence, always believing himself beneath such favor."100

Steven Davis and Richard Cole present statements by Jimmy Page that fit the description of the "good" medium described above; that took place when there was haggling with Atlantic Records over the attempt to put out Led Zeppelin's fourth album without any writing whatsoever on the cover. Jimmy emphasized the music in the quotes, not wanting Led Zeppelin's name on the cover; this is consistent with not wanting to take credit for the music, but to give the credit to the Devil, who is on top of the mountain on the inner cover. Again, just look at the horns sticking through his hood. Steven Davis wrote, quoting Jimmy Page: "We decided that on the fourth album we would deliberately downplay the group name and there wouldn't be any information on the outer jacket. Names, titles, and things like that do not mean a thing....What matters is our music. We said we just wanted to rely purely on the music."101 Richard Cole wrote what Jimmy said as well: "'The music is what matters,' Jimmy argued 'Let people buy it because they like the music. I don't want *any* writing on the cover! Period!'"102 Allan Kardec sums up the situation. He is quoting a spirit, and it illustrates, by analogy, the arrival of the music for Led Zeppelin's fourth album; which gives us final insight as to whose album it really is: "'We have already said, mediums, as mediums, have but a secondary influence in the communications of spirits: their task is that of an electric machine, which transmits telegraphic dispatches from one point of the earth to another far distant. So, when we wish to dictate a communication, we act on the medium as the telegraph operator on his instruments; that is, as the *tac-tac* of the telegraph writes thousands of miles away, on a slip of paper, the reproduced letters of the dispatch, so we, from the immeasurable distance that separates the visible from the invisible world, the immaterial from the incarnated world, communicate what we wish to teach you by means of the medianimic instrument.'"103 The medianimic instrument is, obviously, Led Zeppelin. Just go back and read Jimmy's statement about channeling at the chapter heading. Don't believe I am slandering the band, judge *them* by their own words. Aleister Crowley called the word "Thelema" the word of the Devil, he said the middle size fagots were what was needed to set the world ablaze with Law of Thelema, and Led Zeppelin's fourth album has middle size fagots on the cover and the Devil on the inner cover. The spirits say that the good medium does not seek any credit for communications given, and Jimmy Page refused to have the band or record company name on the fourth album cover. Once again, all the pieces to this puzzle fit together perfectly, and multitudes of occultists are aware of this. This is a war against Lord Jesus Christ.

   The preponderance of the evidence points to Led Zeppelin wanting to send the message to their fans that they are Druid medium musicians, I believe, especially with their fourth album, between the Devil, his Silver Star, his Law of Thelema embodied in the writings of Crowley, and the great masses of humanity. The band has consistently been associated with the Celtics and Magick, as well as Aleister Crowley. They gave profession to being medium musicians, as well as "overlords" to the fans. They claim that "Stairway to Heaven" was a timeless gift from a supernatural source, and they were not willing to have their name on the cover of the fourth album. The group's musical message coincides perfectly with the statements recorded in this chapter, that the band and its music are, I believe, Druidic mediums between the Devil and the fans of Led Zeppelin, with the underlying theme being satanic spiritual regeneration, especially as it is presented in the lyrics to "Stairway to Heaven," addressed in the following pages.

Jimmy Page has consistently stated that he and Robert Plant were "channeling" the "music," or "energy." Why would he be telling people that? Those who are involved in, or know about Magick, don't need anyone to tell them. As Eliphas Levi put it over a 125 years ago: "The sages must speak occasionally, not to disclose, but lead others to discover." Page has done exactly what Levi said. The Devil has used these two to pass concepts of Magick and Satanism to many fans who have given birth to an interest in the occult as a direct consequence.

Jimmy Page and Robert Plant enjoy a cigarette, a brew, and the adoration of the fans at the end of their show in Frankfurt, Germany, on Dec.3, 1998. The worship of the fans was one goal right from the very beginning, as rock deities. How do you tell men like this that Satan has lied to them with their success?

1 *The Best of Rock Stars*, published by Ideal Publishing Corp., New York, 1981, pg.32

2 Ritchie Yorke, *Led Zeppelin - The Definitive Biography*, pg.137

3 Lewis Spence, *Magic Arts In Celtic Britain*, pg. 122

4 Peter Berresford Ellis, *The Druids*, William B. Eerdmans Publishing Company, Grand Rapids, Michigan, 1995, pg.247

5 Aleister Crowley, *Liber Samekh*, from *Magick-Book 4*Liber Aba*, pg.526

6 Rosemary Ellen Guiley, *The Encyclopedia of Witches and Witchcraft*, pg.333

7 Aleister Crowley, *Magick Without Tears*, pg.392

8 Aleister Crowley, *Liber Samekh*, from *Magick-Book 4*Liber Aba*, pg.508

9 Aleister Crowley, *The Equinox*, Vol. I, No.1, pg.216

10 Satan, *The Book of the Law*, chapter 3, verse 34, Aleister Crowley, *The Equinox*, Vol. I, No.10, pg.28

11 Lewis Spence, *Magic Arts in Celtic Britain*, pg.11

12 Ibid, pg.182

13 Eliphas Levi, *The History of Magic*, pg.183

14 Lewis Spence, *Magic Arts in Celtic Britain*, pg.43

15 Ibid, pg.48

16 Barry Cunliffe, *The Ancient Celts*, Oxford University Press, Oxford New York, 1997, pg.190

17 *De Bello Gallico Book VI*, Caesar, 100 44 B.C. Gaius Julius Caesar

18 *The Celts*: *Europe's People of Iron*, by the editors of Time Life Books, Richmond, Virginia, 1994, pg.108

19 Peter Berresford Ellis, *The Druids*, William B. Eerdmans Publishing Company, Grand Rapids, Michigan, 1995, pg.14

20 Ibid, pp.207, 210

21 Ibid, pg.21

22 Ibid, pg.247

23 Ibid, pg.59

24 Ibid, pg.248

25 Ibid, pg.12

26 Ibid, pg.232

27 Ibid, pg.274

28 Dave Lewis and Simon Pallett, *Led Zeppelin: The Concert File*, pp.127-128

29 Lewis Spence, *Magic Arts in Celtic Britain*, pg.117

30 Peter Berresford Ellis, *The Druids*, pp.12, 70

31 Colin Wilson, *Mysterious Powers*, First published by Aldus Books Limited, London, 1975, Danbury Press, Robert B. Clarke, pg.107

32 Peter Ellis, *The Druids*, pg.277

33 Aleister Crowley, *The Confessions of Aleister Crowley*, pg.125

34 Ibid, pg.126

35 Ibid, pg.127

36 Ibid, pp.145-146

37 Ibid, pg.148

38 Ibid, pg.165

39 Karl von Eckartshausen, *The Cloud Upon the Sanctuary*, pg.27

40 Ibid, pg.28

41 Ritchie Yorke, *Led Zeppelin - The Definitive Biography*, pg.288

42 Richard Cole, *Stairway to Heaven - Led Zeppelin Uncensored*, pg.40

43 Howard Mylett, *Jimmy Page – Tangents Within a Framework*, pg.20

44 Dave Lewis and Simon Pallett, *Led Zeppelin: The Concert File*, pg.11

45 Karl von Eckartshausen, *The Cloud Upon the Sanctuary*, pg.28

46 Eliphas Levi, *Transcendental Magic*, pg.267

47 Allan Kardec, *The Book On Mediums*, pg.278

48 Richard Cole, *Stairway to Heaven - Led Zeppelin Uncensored*, pg.17

49 Ibid, pg.20

50 Ibid, pg.378

51 Ibid, pg.13

52 Dr. Sir J. G. Frazer, *The Golden Bough*, pg.389

53 Allan Kardec, *The Book On Mediums*, pg.233

54 Ibid, pg.260

55 Ibid, pp.225-226

56 *Webster's New World Dictionary*, Second College Edition, pg.501

57 Allan Kardec, *The Book On Mediums*, pg.277

58 Richard Cole, *Stairway to Heaven - Led Zeppelin Uncensored*, pg.145

59 Aleister Crowley, *The Book of Thoth*, pg.105

60 Aleister Crowley, *Magick Book 4*Liber Aba*, pg.526

61 Aleister Crowley, *The Equinox of the Gods*, pg.54

62 MTV Networks - MCMXC

63 Ritchie Yorke, *Led Zeppelin - The Definitive Biography*, pg.184

64 Bob Larson, *Satanism - The Seduction of America's Youth*, pg.75

65 Steven Davis, *Hammer of the Gods*, pp.242-243

66 Dave Lewis, *The Complete Guide to the Music of Led Zeppelin*, Omnibus
    Press, 1994, pg.35

67 Richard Cole, *Stairway to Heaven - Led Zeppelin Uncensored*, pg.160

68 Allan Kardec, *The Book On Mediums*, pp.368-369

69 Ibid, pg.121

70 Ibid, pg.368

71 Eliphas Levi, *Transcendental Magic*, pg.267

72 Aleister Crowley, *Magick - Book 4*Liber Aba*, pg.191

73 Ritchie Yorke, *Led Zeppelin - The Definitive Biography*, pg.122

74 Ibid, pg.125

75 Allan Kardec, *The Book On Mediums*, pg.248

76 Abraham the Jew, *The Book of the Sacred Magic of Abramelin the Mage*, pg.250

77 Ibid, pg.246

78 Aleister Crowley, *Moonchild*, pp.228-229

79 Translated by S.L. MacGregor Mathers, edited by Aleister Crowley, *The Goetia – The Lesser Key of Solomon the King*, Introduction, pg. xxv

80 Ibid, pp.31-32

81 Ritchie York, *Led Zeppelin - The Definitive Biography*, pg.135

82 *Webster's New World Dictionary*, Second College Edition, pg.1088

83 Aleister Crowley, *Moonchild*, pg.84

84 Allan Kardec, *The Book On Mediums*, pp.83, 220

85 Ritchie Yorke, *Led Zeppelin - The Definitive Biography*, pg.136

86 Dave Lewis, *The Complete Guide to the Music of Led Zeppelin*, pg.35

87 Richard Cole, *Stairway to Heaven - Led Zeppelin Uncensored*, pg.161

88 Ibid, pg.161

89 Allan Kardec, *The Book On Mediums*, pg.199

90 Ibid, pg.219

91 Ritchie Yorke, *Led Zeppelin - The Definitive Biography*, pg.144

92 Richard Cole, *Stairway to Heaven - Led Zeppelin Uncensored*, pg.161

93 Ritchie Yorke, *Led Zeppelin - The Definitive Biography*, pg.137
94 Ibid, pg.279

95 Dave Lewis and Simon Pallett, *Led Zeppelin: The Concert File*, pg.172

96 *Hit Parader* magazine, August 1997, *The Top 100 cds of All Time*, pg.49

97 Aleister Crowley, *The Magical Record of the Beast*, pg.242
98 Aleister Crowley, *The Equinox*, Vol. III, No.1, pg.182

99 *Led Zeppelin - Will the Song Remain the Same?* pp.29

100 Allan Kardec, *The Book On Mediums*, pp.291-292

101 Steven Davis, *Hammer of the Gods*, pg.142

102 Richard Cole, *Stairway to Heaven - Led Zeppelin Uncensored*, pg.162

103 Allan Kardec, *The Book On Mediums*, pp.292-293

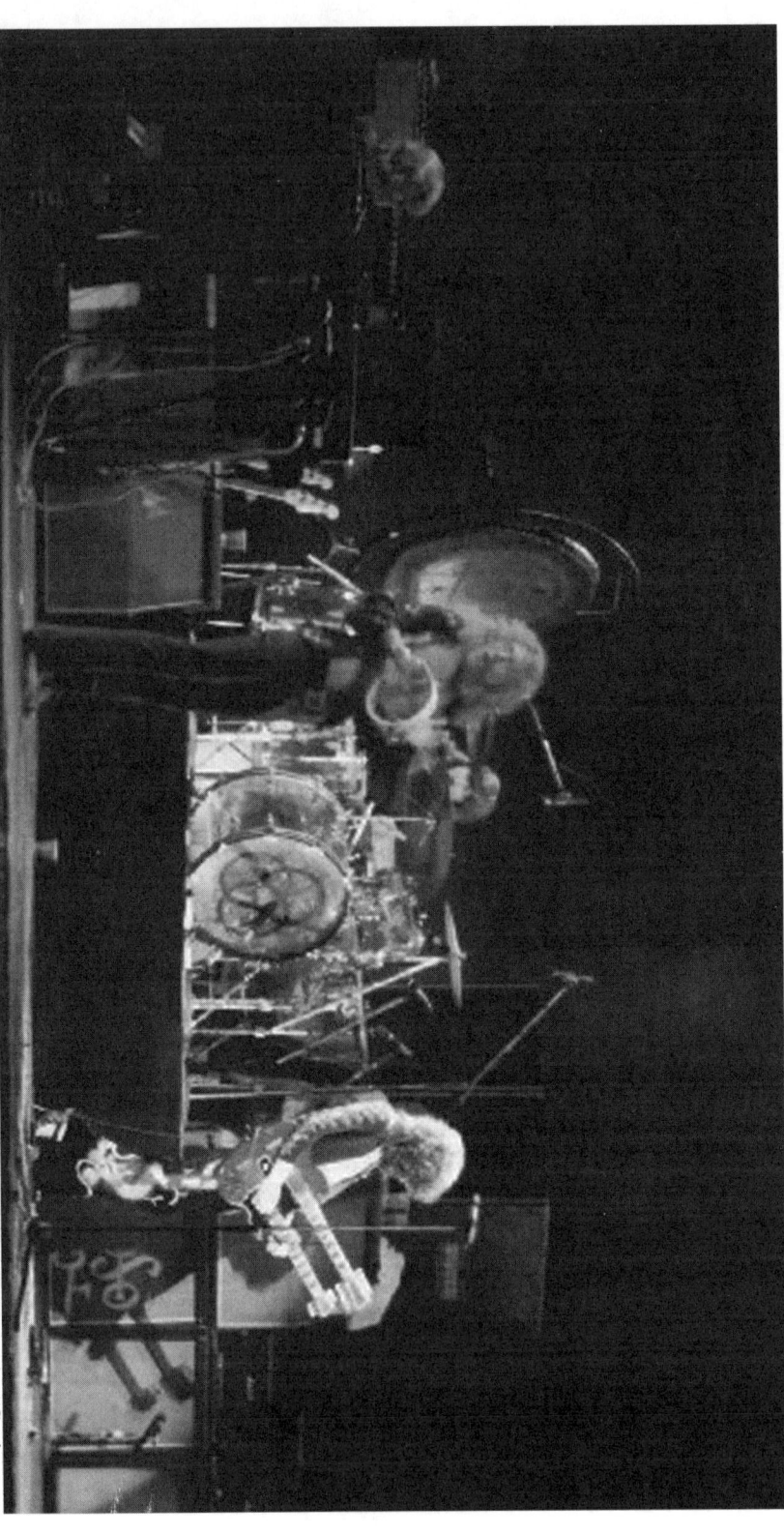

As you read in Chapter Two, Lucifer was created with pipes and tambourines. Every time Jimmy Page played the lead in "Stairway to Heaven," Robert Plant grabbed the tambourine. Why did he play the tambourine in a song about spiritual union with their piper?

CHAPTER FIFTEEN

"I, P-, in the presence of the Lord of the Universe, and of all Powers Divine and Angelic, do spiritually bind myself, even as I am now physically bound unto the Cross of Suffering:

To unite my consciousness with the divine, as I may be permitted and aided by the Gods Who live for ever, the Aeons of Infinite years; that, being lost in the Limitless Light, it may find Itself: to the Regeneration of the Race, either of man or as the Will of God shall be. "

> Black Magician Aleister Crowley, "The Equinox"

"...amid a cloud of angels bearing silver trumpets, came one with great height of brow, and eyes of golden flashes. In him the whole heaven rocked with harmonious music..."2

> Black Magician Aleister Crowley, "Moonchild"

"Thanks - once again - to remarks by Aleister Crowley, many people, especially 'neo pagans,' assert that the Devil is simply Pan. They say that the early Christians took this friendly forest god, with his pipes and perpetual (sexual expletive meaning erection), and turned him into the Devil. They go further and state that there is no Devil, that He is purely a Christian invention."3

> S. Jason Black and Christopher S. Hyatt, Ph.D., "Pacts With the Devil"

"The appeal of 'Stairway to Heaven' as a musical piece is self-evident: its lyrics seemed to embody the individual's prevailing quest for a spiritual rebirth."4

> Ritchie Yorke, "Led Zeppelin-The Definitive Biography"

"The process thus becomes a test for one's Qabalistic knowledge and skill, but more importantly the process becomes a stimulus for the surrender of the mind to the mystical experience in which the One is seen to be All, and vice versa."5

> Israel Regardie, "777 and Other Qabalistic Writings of Aleister Crowley"'

STAIRWAY TO HEAVEN II
SATANIC SPIRITUAL REGENERATION

"Stairway to Heaven," a beautiful title to a beautiful song, is anything but a stairway to eternal life. Its message is a bold one, hidden under the guise of occult lyrics, and blended in with soothing acoustics that make it a tune very few can resist. The Devil himself, being the celestial composer, has used this song

499

and this group of musicians to pass on to the masses of mankind in subtle fashion, the doctrinal teachings of his Silver Star; hoping for the sold out fan to become his follower and cognizant worshiper. The fans that seek to learn the hidden message in the song, will have the Devil himself lead them into the Absolute of Reason, which is an absolute lie; as you will see. The song truly is an extreme paradox, beautiful and caressing to the ear, and damning to the soul of him or her who is drawn to the Devil through it. Even though its music is blissful with beautiful acoustic guitar and pipes, its lyrics mysterious and interesting, though the lead guitar and powerful drum beats take the mind of the listener to transcendent, spiritual heights, "Stairway to Heaven" is, by its very title, a collection of the greatest lies the Devil has ever been able to tell, presented in conjunction with some of his most beautiful music, grabbing the attention of the entire rock world, programming the subconscious minds of those listening to it, especially with backward masking, at the very least, to eradicate the primal fears associated with the idea of Satan, and at the most, to draw people into blatant Devil worship through his Qabalah Magick, as he presents himself as almighty god; the logical extension of satanic spiritual regeneration.

"STAIRWAY TO HEAVEN" - UNION WITH LUCIFER

"Stairway to Heaven" became the most requested song on the radio in England and the United States because Lucifer, Satan, the Devil, I believe, gave three different "majestic" melodies in one song to Jimmy Page, and produced the mystical lyrical content through the hand of Robert Plant. Again, I believe that the reason the song was so popular is because it came from the Devil, created with the power to make music.

Tony Palmer, in *The Observer,* illustrated the spiritual element of the song, "Stairway to Heaven" over the fans at a Led Zeppelin concert: "Can you think of another song, any song, for which, when its first chord is played, an entire audience of 20,000 rises spontaneously to their feet, not just to cheer or clap hands, but in acknowledgment of an event that is crucial for all of them?" Personally, I can testify to the authenticity of his statement. When I saw Led Zeppelin at Madison Square Garden in 1977, and they began to play "Stairway to Heaven," all of us in the orchestra stood on our seats. I had a beer in my left hand, a joint in my right, that I rose up in the air and shouted my approval, and I had an ounce of Marijuana underneath my belt. I worshiped Jimmy Page as he played the song, a song that ripped right into the core of my being. It was the climax of the evening, the major reason I went in the first place. The song does a good job at stimulating and numbing the spiritual emptiness inside; only God can fill it. Of course, after the song is over, the emptiness quickly returns. The numbing is only temporary, but the music succeeds in draining a person, so by the time the whole show is over, one is too tired to care. The power of the music and volume at a Led Zeppelin concert was mesmerizing and stupefying to the point of exhaustion for the fan in the audience; "Stairway to Heaven" being the high point of the show.

The uniqueness of "Stairway to Heaven's" music can only be equaled by the uniqueness of the lyrics. The message again, is satanic spiritual regeneration with a Celtic theme. The lyrics are presented in groups of three segments. There are twelve verses in the song prior to the climactic lead; and then there are nine lines at the end of the song. The lyrics cannot be presented in this book in their entirety because of copyright; but partial lyrics from verses that will be addressed by number. The lyrics will be examined chronologically, with much supporting material to illustrate the concepts presented. When the reader is done with his or her study, it will be obvious that "Stairway to Heaven" along with its theme, is not only musically and lyrically unique in the rock world, but also in the Led Zeppelin catalog.

VERSE 1   "LADY" and "STAIRWAY"

"Stairway to Heaven," presenting the theme of satanic spiritual regeneration, or spiritual union with Lucifer, begins with the object of regeneration in the very first verse. Robert Plant sings of the "Lady" that is certain that anything which "glitters" happens to be "gold." The point that needs to be emphasized here is the woman. The glittering and the gold will be addressed later in the song when the concept is reiterated. The lady mentioned here is not the goddess Diana, Artemis, Aphrodite, Kali, etc. She is the bride of the son in the Qabalah. It is the earth, and mankind on the earth that will be redeemed by the Devil. Again, listen to the seventh and eighth lines of "Kashmir" from the *Physical Graffiti* album where redemption is mentioned. Remember, in "Dazed and Confused" in the Led Zeppelin film, Plant told the audience a lady's "soul" had been made "below." Then he tells them that they are the woman, twice. A brief two-quote review of the Qabalah chapter will refresh the idea. S. L. MacGregor Mathers' *The Qabalah Unveiled* is the source of both of them. The godhead, the god and goddess together, is Kether. Kether is represented by the top of the letter "I" in the "Tetragrammaton," "IHVH," as it is used by occultists. Chokmah is the god, represented by the rest of the letter "I." Binah is the goddess, represented by the first "H." The son of the god and the goddess, who is in fact the god in secondary form, is represented by the letter "V." The bride of the son is the people on earth who the Devil will redeem, those who will be the object of satanic spiritual regeneration, represented by the second letter "H," whose name is Malkuth in the Qabalah. Here is Mathers' first quote on this bride: "The bride, the inferior H, *He*, is said to be a reflection of the mother, the supernal H, *He*, in the Tetragrammaton..."6 In the next one, we see that the "V" and the "H" are joined together like the "I" and the "H:" "The conjunction of the letters V and H at the end of the Tetragrammaton IHVH is similar to that of I and H at the beginning."7 In the second part of the first verse of "Stairway to Heaven," Robert Plant states that this Lady is "buying" her "Stairway" that reaches "Heaven." Remember, in "Dazed and Confused," Robert Plant commanded the fans to sell their souls to the Devil. Each individual, united with all the others who turn to Satan, represent the bride of the son, previously mentioned. All the souls together make up the one soul of the bride. This bride, collectively, sells her soul to the Devil who is the son in the Qabalah, thus purchasing her "Stairway to Heaven," again, with her soul. This will be seen again later.

VERSE 2 - "WORD" - ABRAHADABRA

In the second verse of the song, Plant sings that "when" the woman "gets" to Heaven "she" is fully confident that "with" one "word" the purpose for which her ascension was made up the Stairway will be fulfilled. First of all, I believe the "word" is ABRAHADABRA. That is not a misspelling. Crowley did not like ABRACADABRA. He used an "H" in the word as he used it. The word denotes the uniting of man with god, the microcosm with the macrocosm. Crowley wrote of the word in his *Equinox, Volume I, No.5*: "ABRAHADABRA, the great Magic Word, the Word of the Aeon. Note the 11 letters, 5 A identical, and 6 diverse. Thus it interlocks Pentagram and Hexagram."8 He also wrote in the same book of the Hexagram, which holds the same meaning, the Great Work of uniting the microcosm with the macrocosm: "The Hexagram, symbol of the Macrocosm and Microcosm interlaced, and hence of the End of the Great Work."9 As you know by now, the Devil on top of the mountain of the fourth album inner cover is holding a lamp with the Hexagram in it. He is the object of the uniting. This Great Work is the uniting of man with the Devil. Crowley went on to write of ABRAHADABRA, being the union of the microcosm and the macrocosm in the same context in his book, *Magick*: "...the formula of ABRAHADABRA concerns us, as men, principally because each of us represents the pentagram or microcosm, and our equilibration must therefore be with the hexagram or macrocosm."10 The "equilibration" or balancing that Crowley wrote of there, the balance between man and god, being united, is the same balance, I believe, that Robert Plant is referring to in "The Battle of Evermore," where he sang of Magick Runes. Crowley then associated ABRAHADABRA with the Great Work in *Magick*: "...ABRAHADABRA describes the Operation of the Great Work."11 Finally, Crowley defines ABRAHADABRA as the completion of the Great Work in *Liber Samekh*, the epistle he wrote on the Knowledge and Conversation of the Holy Guardian Angel, Satan: "...ABRAHADABRA, the Word of the Aeon, which signifieth 'The Great Work Accomplished...'"12 If the bride of Satan ascends the Stairway to Heaven to be united with him, then ABRAHADABRA is the word she is to speak to consummate that union. The key point that needs to be made now is that Plant says that if she speaks this "word" then the woman will have the purpose of the ascension up the Stairway fulfilled; he did not however, say that she spoke it.

VERSE 3   "SIGN," and "TWO"

In the third verse of "Stairway to Heaven," Robert Plant speaks of one specific "sign" fixed to a certain "wall." Then he says that the woman "wants" assurance that what the sign says is true, "Cause" we all "know" that "words" can possess "two" definitions. What I believe Robert Plant is saying, is that the sign in question reads "HEAVEN." The woman, knowing that "words" can possess "two" definitions, "wants" assurance that the sign is correct. So what does she do? She speaks ABRAHADABRA. If it is not heaven, the gates won't open, and she will know that it is hell, but not the Christian hell. Everything here is reversed. The Christian heaven is the Satanist's hell, and vice versa. If it is the Devil's heaven, then the gates will open, if it isn't, the gates won't open at the sound of ABRAHADABRA. The woman speaks the word ABRAHADABRA, I believe, to be positive that it is the heaven she is looking for, which in Christian terminology would be hell, a place where God does not manifest himself, and where Satan will spend eternity; not as King, but as chief inmate. Once the word has been spoken, if it is the Devil's heaven, then, I believe, in the minds of Crowley, Page, Plant, etc., at that moment the Great Work reaches completion, mankind selected for redemption by the Devil will be united with him forever, in eternity. By the way, in the *Holy Bible*, the beautiful city of eternity, the New Jerusalem, is described as being surrounded by very high walls in Revelation, Chapter 21.

VERSE 4   "SONGBIRD," "THOUGHTS," and "MISGIVEN"

The fourth verse in "Stairway to Heaven" begins to reveal the Druid/Celtic magical thinking of the band in the song. The Lady has been presented by me as speaking ABRAHADABRA to make sure that the sign was true because words can possess two definitions. The fourth verse elaborates on that concept, and it is clear to the person who knows Led Zeppelin like I do that what Plant is referring to here is the contrast of right and wrong; between good and evil. Plant sings of the "Tree" next to a "Brook." He sings that a certain "songbird" is in that tree. Then he says that this bird "sings." What does he sing? Plant says he sings of mankind "sometimes" being subjected to "thoughts" he describes as "misgiven." First of all, let's address the bird in the tree singing literal words. In *Celtic Magic*, D.J. Conway wrote: "Among the birds, wrens were thought to be the most prophetic, possibly because it was believed that the Celtic 'fays' or fairies could change themselves into birds."13 Exactly who was in the songbird, Plant does not say. However, it can safely be said that it was either a demon or the Devil. Since magic is traced by Crowley and others back to Egypt, the following quote from Lewis Spence, in *Ancient Egyptian Myths and Legends*, is relevant: "In his valuable work upon *Egyptian Magic*, by far the most illuminating text-book on the subject, Dr. Budge says: 'The Egyptians believed that as the souls of the departed could assume the form of any living thing or plant, so the "gods," who in many respects closely resembled them, could and did take upon themselves the forms of birds and beasts.'"14

Irrespective of whether the magic is Celtic or Egyptian, the song remains the same, spirits can change themselves into birds. The *Bible* records them metamorphosing into men, so it can't be too hard for them to turn into birds. Remember, in chapter two I presented quotes about Satan turning himself into a black dog.

The second half of verse four, again, speaks of "sometimes" mankind has "thoughts" described as "misgiven." In *The Song Remains the Same*, film and soundtrack, when Plant finishes singing this verse, you can hear him tell the fans that he thinks they can understand what he means. In other words, "what I have just said ought to be obvious to you." That's what he is saying. The night I saw Led Zeppelin at MSG, Plant said, "You know what I mean people?" after that verse. At Knebworth in 1979, Plant said, "You know that's true people." At "Live-Aid" in 1985, after singing the verse, he said, "You know what I mean?" The concept, I believe, is that the drug use and the music, and its moral code, are all right and good, as opposed to wrong and evil, as some would have you think. As written previously in chapter two, Richard Cavendish presented this concept about Satanists and their conception of good and evil: "Satanists believe that what Christians call good is really evil, and vice versa..."15 Along the same lines, S. Jason Black and Christopher S. Hyatt wrote in their book, *Pacts With the Devil*, a statement which clearly defines Robert Plant's perception of the spiritual world: "To speak of Gods and Devils and Demons as good or evil is simply a statement of our reactions to what we believe their expressions or existences are for us."16 To sum up the third and fourth verses, Plant is trying to get the fans to think in terms of opposites, I believe, especially when they are applied to the same words; specifically in the case of good and evil. At that point, he wants to convey the idea that what they normally perceive to be good and evil, according to Christian tradition, is the absolute opposite of what is really true. This is, however, the mindset of a man who, after destroying the original moral code in his conscience through rebellion against it, programming his own mind and conscience to believe right is wrong and evil is good, has accepted the lies the Devil told him through the teachings of Aleister Crowley, and Jimmy Page his mentor, because his mind was vulnerable to believe them. If that is not bad enough, he then becomes, at the prodding of Crowleyite Jimmy Page, a medium of the Devil to go around the world and teach men to follow Satan through music. When listening to their albums, one after another, the concept that Plant is trying to put forth is clear to the person who really listens to what he saying. Plant himself said that he was a reflection of what he sings, and he sang a command to the fans to sell their souls to Satan in "Dazed and Confused" in their film.

VERSE 5 - "WEST," "SPIRIT," and "LEAVING"

The fifth verse of "Stairway to Heaven" puts forth the concept of the god behind the ideas of good and evil being reversed that Plant has previously sung about. This god obviously is the Devil. In the verse, Plant sings that he is overcome by the "feeling" he has "when" he takes a "look" in the direction of "west," which causes his "spirit" to begin "crying" within him to get the opportunity of "leaving," or departure. This verse, initially, refers to the sunset. When the sun disappears, it is a picture of death, and when it rises in the east, it is a picture of birth; this is an axiom in the occult world. What I believe Plant is saying, is that when he focuses on the sunset he thinks of natural death, which is the entrance into the spirit world. Remember Jim Morrison, in The Doors' song, "The End?" He kept singing about the end being related to the direction of west. The song is basically a soliloquy by Jim Morrison of his desire for death. This is common knowledge among Doors fans. At the end of the movie, *The Doors*, they played the song, "The Severed Garden," which illustrates again Morrison's longing for death. He says that death will make an angel of everyone of us, giving us wings. Then he says, "This other Kingdom seems by far the best." This is "the other side" that he sings of in "Break On Through," I believe.

The concept of Plant's desire to leave the natural for the spirit world is clearly illustrated by none other than the Black Magician, Aleister Crowley. As you know from reading chapter eight, all the gods are one god, Satan. Osiris, then, is Satan in the following Crowley quote from *The Equinox* that begins to define what I believe Robert Plant was singing of in verse five: "Now then the great exhaustion took hold upon me, and I fell at the feet of the Osiris as one dead. All knowledge of terrestrial things was gone from me; I entered the kingdom of the dead by the gate of the West. For the worship of Osiris is to join the earth to the west; it is the cultus of the Setting Sun."17 Along the same lines Crowley wrote: "I have passed into the Kingdom of the West after my Father."18

Crowley tells us, also from his *Equinox*, who is Lord of the West, quoting the Devil: "...I am Horus the terrible, the Avenger, the Lord of the Gate of the West."19 Crowley taught that Horus was Satan, so his point is clear. Finally, in his book, *Moonchild*, he calls death union with god: "Natural death is to man the greatest of the Sacraments, of which all others are but symbols; for it is the final and absolute Union with the creator..."20 Robert Plant then, makes perfect reference to Crowley's teachings of the occult, when, I believe, singing about entering the spirit world of eternity, by the "Gate of the West."

VERSE 6   "RINGS," "SMOKE," "TREES," and "LOOKING"

The sixth verse of "Stairway to Heaven" is an attempt by Led Zeppelin to get the listener familiar with Celtic customs; specifically, the Beltane fires of May Day. Dr. Sir J. G. Frazer, who wrote the book Aleister Crowley said played a major role in the writing of his *Confessions*, called *The Golden Bough*, wrote of the pertinent Celtic customs in that book, calling them "fire festivals": "The principal fire-festivals of the Celts, which have survived, though in a restricted area and with diminished pomp, to modern times and even to our own day, were seemingly timed without any reference to the position of the sun in the heaven. They were two in number, and fell at an interval of six months, one being celebrated on the eve of May Day and the other on Allhallow Even or Hallowe'en, as it is now commonly called, that is, on the thirty first of October, the day preceding All Saints' or Allhallows' Day....the two great Celtic festivals of May Day and the first of November or, to be more accurate, the Eves of these two days, closely resemble each other in the manner of their celebration and in the superstitions associated with them, and alike, by the antique character impressed upon both, betray a remote and purely pagan origin."21 The fire festivals of May Day and Hallowe'en are Celtic festivals, where rituals were practiced. Robert Plant sings in verse six that "In" his "thoughts" he has witnessed "rings" made by "smoke" in the midst of "trees." He was singing of Beltane fires that were lit on May Day, shaped like circles, and the smoke rings they produce, I believe, as well as the people who are standing around the circles watching them. Frazer wrote specifically of these events also in *The Golden Bough*:

"In Wales also the custom of lighting Beltane fires at the beginning of May used to be observed, but the day on which they were kindled varied from the eve of May Day to the third of May. The flame was sometimes elicited by the friction of two pieces of oak, as appears from the following description. 'The fire was done in this way. Nine men would turn their pockets inside out, and see that every piece of money and all metals were off their persons. Then the men went into the nearest woods, and collected sticks of nine different kinds of trees. These were carried to the spot where the fire had to be built. There a circle was cut in the sod, and the sticks were set crosswise. All around the circle the people stood and watched the proceedings. One of the men would then take two bits of oak, and rub them together until a flame was kindled. This was applied to the sticks, and soon a large fire was made. Sometimes two fires were set up side by side. These fires, whether one or two, were called *coelcerth* or bonfire. Round cakes of oatmeal and brown meal were split in four, and placed in a small flour-bag, and everybody present had to pick out a portion. The last bit in the bag fell to the lot of the bagholder. Each person who chanced to pick up a piece of brown-meal cake was compelled to leap three times over the flames, or to run thrice between the two fires, by which means the people thought they were sure of a plentiful harvest. Shouts and screams of those who had to face the ordeal could be heard ever so far, and those who chanced to pick the oatmeal portions sang and danced and clapped their hands in approval, as the holders of the brown bits leaped three times over the flames, or ran three times between the two fires."22

It would seem that Led Zeppelin (or Satan) is promoting the Celtic customs that pertain to magic rituals performed in order to obtain a bountiful harvest from the Devil in the sixth verse of "Stairway to Heaven"; regardless of what name he chooses to go by with the different Celtic peoples.

VERSE 7 "WHISPERED," "TUNE," "PIPER," and "REASON"

The Seventh Verse of "Stairway to Heaven," is the point at which we begin to delve into the core of the song; the central part of its teaching. Robert Plant sings that the message of the verse is being "whispered" to the listener. Who is doing the whispering? It is being done by Led Zeppelin's "Whispering Wind." In the world of the occult, and this can be seen in the game "Dungeons and Dragons" as well, the "Whispering Wind" is known as a vehicle by which you are able to send a message from one point to another. The music is the vehicle or medium in question. What is the message of this specific verse? It is that if one tries to make contact with the music's hidden message, then the Devil is going to lead the seeker to absolute truth. Plant sings, in effect, that the message "whispered," is "if" the seekers after truth (because they are the only ones who will) "call," or try to make contact with "Stairway to Heaven's" "tune," or hidden message (hidden truth from Led Zeppelin's perspective and hidden lie from the Christian's), "then" a certain "Piper" is going to "lead" the seekers on a spiritual journey into the domain of "reason." The first thing I want you to notice about this verse is that it's an "if-then clause," meaning only those who seek will be led toward reason. Many will say that this is only my interpretation of the verse, and the entire song as well, but if you read on you will find that "my" interpretation is the truth. When you "call" someone on the telephone, what are you trying to do? You are trying to make contact with them. In the context of this verse, making contact with, and figuring out what this specific "tune" is, happens to be the same thing. In this verse, "tune" means hidden message. As you will see, the hidden message is, in its entirety, spread throughout all of Led Zeppelin's music. They are simply making reference to it in this song for the purpose of teaching and guiding the seekers. If the seekers after truth try to make contact with, or figure out what the hidden message is, then a "Piper" (Satan) is going to "lead" them into the domain of "reason," which is described by Aleister Crowley as absolute truth. How do I know that this "Piper" is the Devil? The answer to that is simple. The next verse makes it clear that once a soul led by this Piper arrives at "reason," a certain "forest" is going to "echo" from the sound of "laughter." In Greek mythology, Pan the Piper is the god of the forest. Aleister Crowley makes it clear that Pan is simply the Devil, as are all other gods worshiped on earth, except Jesus. If you have not read the other chapters leading to this one, I advise you to do so. Nevertheless, we will take these concepts by the numbers. Beginning in the seventh verse, we will start at the point of Lucifer, the Devil, and Satan, created to be the highest Archangel and the Piper, or maker of music. In the Old Testament Book of "Ezekiel," which is the name of the prophet who wrote it under the influence of the Holy Spirit, we read God's description and condemnation of Lucifer: "Thou hast been in Eden the garden of God; every precious stone was thy covering, the sardius, topaz, and the diamond, the beryl, the onyx, and the jasper, the sapphire, the emerald, and the carbuncle, and gold: the workmanship of thy tabrets and of thy pipes was prepared in thee in the day that thou wast created. Thou art the anointed cherub that covereth; and I have set thee so: thou wast upon the holy mountain of God; thou hast walked up and down in the midst of the stones of fire. Thou wast perfect in thy ways from the day that thou wast created, till iniquity was found in thee. By the multitude of thy merchandise they have filled the midst of thee with violence, and thou hast sinned: therefore I will cast thee as profane out of the mountain of God: and I will destroy thee, O covering cherub, from the midst of the stones of fire." Ezekiel 28: 13-16 (KJV) I already presented my commentary on this passage in chapter two, so I shall not reiterate. Compare the concept of the many colored Archangel and his pipes with the following Crowley quote, from his epistle, *The Vision and the Voice*; that he included in his *Equinox* as one of the visions he encountered: "And now there comes an Angel, to hide the tablet with his mighty wing. This Angel has all the colours mingled in his dress; his head is proud and beautiful; his headdress is of silver and red and blue and gold and black, like cascades of water, and in his left hand he has a Pan-pipe of the seven holy metals, upon which he plays. I cannot tell you how wonderful the music is, but it is so wonderful that one only lives in one's ears; one cannot see anything any more."23 The Devil was created with the power to compose music; the concept is presented by the *Holy Bible* and Aleister Crowley; that Lucifer is the piper, the maker of music. Crowley wrote it again in *Moonchild*, already presented in the previous chapter, but here it is again for emphasis: "...amid a cloud of angels bearing silver trumpets, came one with great height of brow, and eyes of golden flashes. In him the whole heaven rocked with harmonious music..."24 Crowley was saying that the "whole heaven rocked with harmonious music" that came from the one angel. Again, Lucifer is the celestial composer of music; the piper. In *Pacts With the Devil*, S. Jason Black and Christopher S. Hyatt make Crowley's conception of the Devil being Pan, the god of the forest, with pipes, clear as crystal: "Thanks - once again - to remarks by Aleister Crowley, many people, especially 'neo pagans,' assert that the Devil is simply Pan. They say that the early Christians took this friendly forest god, with his pipes and perpetual (sexual expletive meaning erection), and turned him into the Devil. They go further and state that there is no Devil, that He is purely a Christian invention."25 Those who have read the chapters leading up to this one will know that although Crowley describes the Devil as an angel, he believes he is god as well; and as god he dwells in a supernatural forest, although he has manifested himself in forests on earth. In his book, *The Book of Wisdom or Folly*, Crowley calls the Devil "...Our Lord Pan..."26

To ensure that this concept of Pan as god of the pipes and the forest is not thought to be exclusive to Crowley, here again is Joseph Kaster's description of Pan, from *Putnam's Concise Mythological Dictionary*: "PAN - A Greek nature and fertility deity, originally native to Arcadia. As such he is god of goatherds and flocks and is usually represented as a very sensual creature; a shaggy human to the loins with pointed ears, goat's horns and legs. He wanders among the mountains and valleys, pursuing nymphs or leading them in their dances. He is quite musical and is the inventor of the Syrinx, or 'Pipes of Pan.'"27 Because the subsequent verse in "Stairway to Heaven" mentions a "forest," and Led Zeppelin are Crowley disciples, in conjunction with all the other evidence shown up to this point (and in my mind, the evidence that will be shown), it is conclusive to the non-partial, objective reader, that this "Piper" presented in the Seventh Verse of "Stairway to Heaven" has to be the Devil. Robert Plant (the same man who commanded the fans to sell their souls to the Devil in the Led Zeppelin film), in the Seventh Verse, sings, if the seekers after truth "call" or try to make contact with Led Zeppelin's "tune," a "Piper," the Devil, is going to "lead" the seekers into the domain of "Reason." Plant is giving the credit for the listener's discovery of "Reason" to the Devil. Keep that in mind. That means that the Devil is responsible for Led Zeppelin's "tune;" the hidden message. At this point the word "Reason" is going to be defined. The resources are quotes from Eliphas Levi and Aleister Crowley. Again, I want to mention that the man on Led Zeppelin's fourth album sleeve, or booklet in the case of the cd, reading with a spade beard, looks just like Eliphas Levi, and Levi was famous for his work in London, which is printed behind his head. In examining these concepts on reason, please remember that Crowley claimed to be Levi reincarnated, and Page and company are his disciples.

Eliphas Levi presented the occultists perception of Absolute Truth and god, who is behind this truth, under the title of "REASON." He wrote that God communicates with men by enlightening their reason with his Eternal Reason: "When God designs to communicate the knowledge of Himself, He enlightens our reason and does not seek to confound or surprise it. In that day we shall know the utmost limit of the power of man who is created in the image of God; we shall realize that he also is a creator in his own sphere and that his goodness, directed by Eternal Reason, is a lower providence for beings which are placed by Nature under his influence and domination. Religion will then and for evermore have nothing to fear from progress, and will follow in the course thereof."28 Levi instructs his readers that truth is obvious to all, and that they should put their faith in the eternal Reason who is the Divine Word: "Truth is hidden from no one. God is visible in His works, and He requires nothing contrary to its nature from any being, for He is Himself the author of that nature. Faith is confidence; have confidence, not in men who malign reason, for they are fools or imposters, but in that eternal Reason which is the Divine Word, that true light which is offered like the sun to the intuition of every human creature coming into this world."29 The light that Levi wrote of is spiritual "truth;" based, again, on Qabalah Magick.

The *Holy Bible* presents Lucifer in the spiritual sense as being able to appear as an angel of light, or as an angel of truth, leading one on the path to eternal life, in the New Testament Book of 2nd Corinthians, Chapter Eleven, Verse 14: "And no wonder, for Satan himself masquerades as an angel of light. It is not surprising, then, if his servants masquerade as servants of righteousness."(NIV) Levi expounded on Reason being the Absolute truth, and that Supreme Reason, or god, has not left man without a way of knowing it, and that those who come to know it will be masters and kings of this world (just like the Druids). When coming across the word "Absolute" in this chapter, it means that which is constant, always the same, never changing. To contrast absolute with variable we look to the weather. The sun is the absolute. It is always shining; even when it is raining. We may look up and see overcast skies and rain, or we may see sunshine. Our weather is a variable, given to change, but the sun is not; it is always shining. Anyone who says the sun isn't shining because he can't see it is a fool; so is one who says God doesn't exist because he cannot see him. God and truth are absolutes; they never change. Remember, however, that Levi is writing about the god of Magick, Satan. Levi wrote: "An Absolute exists therefore in the realms of understanding and faith. The lights of human intelligence have not been left by the Supreme Reason to waver at hazard. There is an incontestable truth; there is an infallible method of knowing that truth; while those who attain this knowledge, and adopt it as a rule of life, can endow their will with a sovereign power which can make them masters of all inferior things, all wandering spirits, or, in other words, arbiters and kings of the world."30 Again, the theme of being in control of spirits is reiterated. In this next quote from Levi, he makes the point that the motive in the heart of occultists is to bring all men into the domain of reason: "Truth is the object of their worship, and they represent truth as light; they tolerate all forms of faith, profess one philosophy, seek truth only, teach reality, and their plan is to lead all human intelligence by gradual steps into the domain of reason."31

Aleister Crowley, wanting to show himself in concurrence with "his former self," Eliphas Levi, wrote of Reason and the Absolute in his book, *The Law is for All*: "We make the necessity in our thought the standard to the laws of nature; and thus implicitly declare Reason to be the Absolute. This has nothing to do with the weakness or error in any one mind, or in all minds; all that we rely on is the existence of some purely mental standard by which we could correct our thinking if we knew how. It is then this power which constrains our thought, to which our minds owe fealty, that we call 'truth;' and this 'truth' is not a proposition at all, but a 'law!'"32 The mental standard of absolute truth will be addressed in the next chapter. Crowley reiterated his statement about the Absolute in the same book, saying that all truths are derived from it; in other words, the song remains the same: "I quote from my diary the demonstration that Reason is the Absolute, whereof all truths soever are merely particular cases."33 Reason, therefore, is the Absolute, referring to Absolute Truth, which comes from god, who is the Absolute Truth, or Reason.

The seventh verse of "Stairway to Heaven," then, sends the message that Led Zeppelin and the Devil have "whispered" or conveyed to the listener, "if" they "call" or try to make contact with Satan's "tune," his hidden message, he, as a "Piper" is going to use his music to "lead" or direct them into the domain of "Reason," which as "god" is his Absolute Truth, embodied in the Law of Thelema. As Aleister Crowley wrote, *The Book of the Law*, which is the book expounding the Law of Thelema, is founded upon reason: "We must not suppose for an instant that *The Book of the Law* is opposed to reason. On the contrary, its own claim to authority rests upon reason, and nothing else."34 Those who accept that Reason or "truth" as Absolute Truth, will then have entered the enchanted palace of satanic spiritual regeneration; a born again Satanist, believing the Devil is God, and the author of Absolute Truth. Then the person will discard the Christian view of Lucifer, as Satan and the Devil, and will proclaim that he is god. Is that not what Jimmy Page was saying in this next quote, while discussing the film *Lucifer Rising*? "In the film Lucifer is the Light bearer and not Satan as in Christian terms."35 Again, *Lucifer Rising* is Kenneth Anger's visual rendition of Aleister Crowley's magical presentation of Lucifer as god. Jimmy Page, I say it with all sincerity and hope for your soul, you have been deceived, my friend. I was once your follower, and I now encourage you to follow Christ, who waits to forgive and redeem your soul, before it is too late, and you go where Lucifer is going. Again, he has deceived all of you, Anger, Jagger, Osbourne, etc. Well did the *Holy Bible's* Book of Revelation, in Chapter 12, Verse 9, speak of the deceptive power of Satan: "The great dragon was hurled down – that ancient serpent called the devil, or Satan, who leads the whole world astray." (NIV)

VERSE 8   "NEW," "LONG," "FOREST," and "LAUGHTER"

The Eighth Verse of "Stairway to Heaven," continues the concept of verse seven, showing the result of satanic spiritual regeneration; the subsequent new life of born again Satanism. Webster defines the words "regenerate" and "regeneration" as follows:
REGENERATE - 1. Spiritually reborn. 2. Renewed or restored, especially after a decline to a low or abject condition.
REGENERATION - a being renewed, reformed, or reconstituted b) a spiritual rebirth.36
In verse eight, Robert Plant immediately refers to the result of having accepted the Reason that Satan led one to, which is spirtual rebirth, or a new life, with Satan as god. He sings, "And" the "New" life "Will" begin "For" people "Who" endure "Long," then a "Forest" is going to "Echo" from "Laughter." The first thing we are going to focus on here is the new life of the follower of the Devil, once he has accepted him as the Reason; Absolute Truth and god. Several resources will be used to show the true meaning of this verse, beginning with the book that played the most important initiatory part of Aleister Crowley's magical career; or satanic spiritual regeneration. Remember, if Crowley advocated this book, Jimmy Page has got to have a copy.
Karl von Eckarshausen, in *The Cloud Upon the Sanctuary*, presented in detailed fashion the meaning of spiritual regeneration, showing it to be universal; so the song remains the same: "Religion considered scientifically is the doctrine of the re-union of man separated from God to man re-united to God. Hence its sole object is to unite every human being to God....the Holy Mysteries of every religion, which are all and each in themselves, after a thousand varying modes, according to time and circumstances, and method of conception of different nations, but symbols repeated and modified of one solitary truth, and this unique truth is - *regeneration, or the re-union of man with God.*"37 He makes it clear that absolute truth cannot be found by the outer senses, but by the inner spiritual part of man: "Absolute truth does not exist for sensuous man; it exists only for interior and spiritual man who possesses a suitable sensorium; or, to

speak more correctly, who possesses an interior sense to receive the absolute truth of the transcendental world, a spiritual faculty which cognizes spiritual objects as objectively and naturally as the exterior senses perceive external phenomena....The opening of this spiritual sensorium is the mystery of the New Man - the mystery of Regeneration, and of the vital union between God and man - it is the noblest object of religion on earth, that religion whose sublime goal is none other than to unite men with God in Spirit and in Truth."38 Eckartshausen went on to speak of regeneration as rebirth, and shows why this teaching of Led Zeppelin's comes with their best song, to have people put confidence in them; since they were the world's greatest rock band:

"To change the spirit of this world into the spirit of the children of God is to be regenerated, and it means to despoil the old man, and to re-clothe the new.

"But no person can be re-born if he does not know and put in practice the following principle - that of truth becoming the object for our doing or not doing; therefore, he who desires to be re-born ought first to know what belongs to re-birth. He ought to understand, meditate, and reflect on all this. Afterwards he should act according to his knowledge, and the result will be a new life.

"Now, as it is first necessary to know, and to be instructed in all that appertains to re-birth, a doctor, or an instructor is required, and if we know one, faith in him is also necessary, because of what use is an instructor if his pupil have no faith in him?

"Hence, the commencement of re-birth is faith in Revelation."39

After reading those quotes from *The Cloud Upon the Sanctuary*, one can easily see the progression of these concepts from Eckartshausen to Crowley to Page to Led Zeppelin to "Stairway to Heaven;" with the Devil behind the entire thing. Contemporary writers are in agreement with this concept of rebirth. Ritchie Yorke, a personal friend of the band, wrote that "Stairway to Heaven" conveyed the message of rebirth, in *Led Zeppelin - The Definitive Biography*: "The appeal of 'Stairway to Heaven' as a musical piece is self-evident: its lyrics seemed to embody the individual's prevailing quest for a spiritual rebirth."40 Steven Davis, in *Hammer of the Gods*, presented the same theme, tying spiritual rebirth in with going back to the worship of the old gods: "With its starkly pagan imagery of trees and brooks, pipers and the May Queen, shining white light and the forest echoing with laughter, 'Stairway to Heaven' seemed like an invitation to abandon the new traditions and follow the old gods. It expressed an ineffable yearning for spiritual transformation deep in the hearts of the generation for which it was intended. In time, it became their anthem."41 Compare that Davis quote with this one from Aleister Crowley, from his *Equinox*, who suggested a spiritual rebirth that departs from Christianity to worship the old gods; to worship Pan in the forests: "'Arcadia, night, a cloud, Pan, and the moon.' What words to conjure with, what five shouts to slay the five senses, and set a leaping flame of emerald and silver dancing about us as we yell them forth under the oaks and over the rocks and myrtle of the hill - side. 'Bruised to the breast of Pan' - let us flee church, and chapel, and meeting room; let us abandon this mantle of order, and leap back to the heaths, and the marshes, and the hills; back to the woods, and the glades of night! Back to the old gods, and the ruddy lips of Pan!...till the glades thrill as with the music of syrinx and sistrum, and our souls are rent asunder on the flaming horns of Pan."42

So far in this eighth verse of "Stairway to Heaven," we have focused on the concept of "new" life, or regeneration; rebirth. Contemporary writers have associated the song with the same theme. Crowley associated the theme with Pan; whom he believed was the Devil. Crowley quoted Satan in an epistle from *The Equinox*, called *Liber Stellae Rubeae - LXVI*, where the Devil speaks of this regeneration as light, just as Levi called "Reason" light: "But I will overcome thee; the New Life shall illumine thee with the Light that is beyond the Stars. Thinkest thou? I, the force that have created all, am not to be despised."43 Crowley wrote *The Book of the Law* under the inspiration of the Devil; claiming it was Satan who wrote it through him, as presented in chapter seven. One of the things Satan wrote through Crowley concerning the Law of Thelema, was that it would produce spiritual regeneration. He wrote: "This shall regenerate the world..."44 Even Time Life Books, in their volume, *Wizards and Witches*, present this theme of regeneration or transformation as they wrote of a wizard from Wales named Taliesin, who they said was a musician who played songs about transformation, that had that very effect: "'I am a musician, an artificer like the wren,' sang the Welsh wizard Taliesin, and it was true: His songs were about creation and transformation, and they made those magical things occur."45 Time-Life could very well have been referring to James Patrick Page.

The first part of verse eight of "Stairway to Heaven" speaks of regeneration, and the second part speaks of a "Forest" made to "Echo" by "Laughter," as a result of the regeneration. This "Laughter" carries with it the connotation of happiness. Karl von Eckartshausen wrote, in *The Cloud Upon the Sanctuary* that a person has to be united to God to have real happiness: "It is an immutable law, no creature can be truly happy when separated from the source of all happiness. This source, this *in whom*, is the magnificence of God Himself."46 Those in the Forest who are laughing, are those who are worshipers of the Devil/Pan, and are happy at the conversion of the newcomers. They are not laughing at them. They are laughing in happiness and joy. Again, Pan is Satan, who Crowley and Led Zeppelin believe is god; the god of the forests, mountains, and as the Hindenburg signifies, the god of the flames. Again, Crowley wrote of the totality of his perception of Satan as god: "The King is the undying One; he is the life and the master of life; he is the great living image of the Sun, the Sun, and the begetter of the Sun. He is the Divine Child, the God-begotten One, and the Begetter of God. He is the potent bull, the jeweled snake, the fierce lion. He is the monarch of the lofty mountains, and the lord of the woods and forests, the indweller of the globes of flame. As a royal eagle he soars through the heavens, and as a great dragon he churns up the waters of the deep."47 You can look to an early quote from Crowley in chapter one or at the heading of chapter four to see him call Satan the Sun. Just to remind you, as god of the forests he is not only Pan, but "Herne the Hunter." Lewis Spence, in *Magic Arts in Celtic Britain*, wrote: "...'Herne the Hunter,' that horned phantom which was supposed to haunt the royal forest of Windsor, the name Herne appearing as a corruption of Cerne, or Cernunnos."48 Remember also that Robert Plant called himself "the Hunter," at 6:28 into "How Many More Times," off Led Zeppelin's first album, *Led Zeppelin*. Another thing Lewis Spence wrote in that book was that the Druids also worshiped in the groves: "Classical writers, too, assure us that the Druids worshiped in groves, Lucan, Pliny and Tacitus making reference to the tree-encircled haunts of the brotherhood. Irish tradition also holds more than one allusion to the grove as a Druidic precinct."49 Eliphas Levi, in *The History of Magic*, also wrote of the Druids in the forest: "The Druids built no temples but worked the rites of their religion on dolmens and in forests."50 In the very beginning of the 1994 Page/Plant *No Quarter* Video, you can see who I believe is supposed to be the Devil in the form of Horus the Hawk flying over the groves on his way to meet Page and Plant in the forest. The song being played at that very moment is "No Quarter," which I showed in chapter one to mean "no mercy." If Pan is the god of the forests, and Herne the Hunter is as well, and the Druids performed their rites of worship in the forests, and Led Zeppelin commanded their fans to sell their souls to Satan, it is fact that Led Zeppelin is in agreement with Aleister Crowley's presentation of the Devil as god.

Aleister Crowley wrote of the Devil as Pan making several metamorphoses in the forest of eternity, following someone inspired to play the Pan-pipe, in *The Equinox*, *Volume III*, *No.1*:

"Behold! The Abyss of the Great Deep. Therein is a mighty dolphin, lashing his sides with the force of the waves.

There is also an harper of gold, playing infinite tunes.

Then the dolphin delighted therein, and put off his body, and became a bird.

The harper also laid aside his harp, and played infinite tunes upon the Pan-pipe.

Then the bird desired exceedingly this bliss, and laying down its wings became a faun of the forest.

The harper also laid down his Pan-pipe, and with the human voice sang his infinite tunes.

Then the faun was enraptured, and followed far; at last the harper was silent, and the faun became Pan in the midst of the primal forest of Eternity."51

Crowley wrote of that forest being the "forest of Eternity." In *The Equinox*, in an epistle called *Liber A'Ash*, Crowley quoted the Devil as saying he would rise again in the same forest: "...I shall rise again, and my children about me, so that we shall uplift our forest in Eternity."52 Considering the phrase "I shall rise again," I ask you the reader, why would Kenneth Anger's film be called Lucifer Rising instead of Pan rising? With Jimmy Page standing in front of a photo of Crowley in the film? It is because Crowley, Anger, and Page all know that Pan is Lucifer. In "Achilles Last Stand," off the *Presence* album, Robert Plant sang of "Albion" who will "rise again," at 5:35 into the song. At the end of the *The Song Remains the Same* film, you can see that Albion is associated with "flames" in the credits:

BRON YR AUR
AUTUMN LAKE
Music Published by
Flames of Albion Music Inc.

Therefore, if Pan is in the forest of eternity, and he is going to rise again, and Albion is going to rise again, who is also associated with flames, it is safe to assume that Plant was singing of the Devil in "Achilles Last Stand" when making reference to Albion, especially since prior to mentioning Albion he makes direct reference to the Devil at 1:35.

In bringing verse eight of "Stairway to Heaven" to a conclusion, Crowley wrote that as a result of the worship of the Devil as Pan, a song so beautiful came from him that nobody could resist it. Crowley wrote this in *The Equinox*, in 1911:

"Many are they who have loved the nymphs of the woods, and of the wells, and of the fountains, and of the hills....So also there were many images of Pan, and men adored them, and as a beautiful god he made their olives bear double and their vines increase; but some were slain by the god, for it was I that had woven the garlands about him.

Now cometh a song.

So sweet is this song that no one could resist it. For in it is all the passionate ache of the moonlight, and the great hunger of the sea, and the terror of desolate places, - all things that lure men to the unattainable.53

There will be many that will laugh at what you are about to read, but I believe Jimmy Page knows better. Page read *The Equinox* long before I did. He read the words above, as well as the Crowley quote earlier in this chapter about the angel playing the Pan-pipe and the music being so wonderful that one only lives in ones ears. In the medium sense, the Devil was talking right to Jimmy Page through Crowley's writings. Accordingly, I believe wholeheartedly that Aleister Crowley heard "Stairway to Heaven," or parts of it, seventy years before Page did. This is not unthinkable to rock stars that could say along with Black Sabbath, *We Sold Our Souls for Rock 'n' Roll*, as one of their album titles reads. Jimmy Page, Keith Richards, Ozzy Osbourne, etc., all know who the source of the music is. Even the group "ABBA," which means father or daddy, released an album called *Thank You for The Music*. They also have a man dressed up as a magician holding a torch in his hand on the back of one of their albums. Also, Led Zeppelin recorded *In Through the Out Door*, their 1979 album, at Abba's recording studio in Stockholm, Sweden. Look at Abba's album cover *The Visitors*. I believe these people are all in it together.

Led Zeppelin, in the Eighth Verse of "Stairway to Heaven," presented the concepts of spiritual regeneration that will result in the heart of the fans after Satan leads them to "Absolute Truth." Also, to ensure that the people know it is Pan, the Devil, who is responsible for this rebirth, they present the concept of the Eternal Forest where Pan will reign as the Piper, the maker of music, so the fan will, again, understand as he was supposed to, by watching "Dazed and Confused" in the Led Zeppelin film, that they are to sell their souls to the Devil; not Thor, Odin, Apollo, Pan, Albion, Herne the Hunter, or anyone else, because they are all names for the Devil. As Al Pacino said in the movie, "The Devil's Advocate," when playing the Devil, he said to Keanu Reeves, "I have so many names."

VERSE 9   "BUSTLE," "HEDGEROW," and "MAY QUEEN"

Immediately after addressing spiritual regeneration in verse eight, Robert Plant, in the ninth verse of "Stairway to Heaven," makes reference to what I believe are trials. He sings, "If" we find an annoying "Bustle" disturbing the smooth flow of our "Hedgerow," we should not allow ourselves to get "Alarmed," because "It's" only a purification or pruning "For" Satan's female consort, Diana, etc., who is also addressed by the name of "May Queen" by the Druids. In *The Golden Bough*, Dr. Sir J. G. Frazer addresses Diana as the May Queen: "...in the sacred grove at Nemi, where the powers of vegetation and of water manifested themselves in the fair forms of shady woods, tumbling cascades, and glassy lake, a marriage like that of our King and Queen of May was annually celebrated between the mortal King of the Wood and the immortal Queen of the Wood, Diana."54 In Celtic religious practices, there is the belief that the god and goddess of the Qabalah marry on May-Day, Beltane, May 1st. Human marriages were and are performed on that day to illustrate the "godhead" marriage; also to worship them. (Interestingly enough, Elvis and Priscilla were married May 1st, 1967.) The point I believe Plant is trying to make, without launching off into an unnecessary study of Celtic customs, is that since the daughter becomes one with the mother after being wedded by the son, in Qabalah teaching, the daughter is being put through trials to purify her spiritually; to bring her to search for and exercise faith in the gods; Lucifer and Diana. As he said, if we have an annoying "Bustle" protruding from our "Hedgerow," we shouldn't get "Alarmed," because "It's" only a purification for the goddess. A Hedgerow looks ugly when it has a Bustle of hedges protruding from it. It has to be corrected. If a person's life is a Hedgerow, then a Bustle in one's life is a problem or trial that must be dealt with. It has to be taken care of. It cannot be allowed to go unattended. These Bustles in our life, if severe enough, will lead us to look into the supernatural for god. In other words, what Plant is saying, I believe, is if you're having severe trials, severe problems in your life, don't let it upset you, the Qabalah's godhead, the Devil and his consort, is simply trying to get your attention, to direct you to the light. Again, in their song off *Physical Graffiti*, "In the Light," the band stated that the "road" one should follow would be found by looking to this "Light." Aleister Crowley presented this concept of trials leading one to the light of occult science and union with the godhead in his *Equinox*, in an epistle titled *Liber Librae*: "Thou then, who hast trials and troubles, rejoice because of them, for in them is Strength, and by their means is a pathway opened unto that Light."55 So the evidence points to Plant trying to comfort those who are going through severe troubles by saying it's all right, it's happening for the goddess' sake.

VERSE 10 "PATHS, TIME, and ROAD"

It doesn't take long for the new student of the occult to become familiar with the goddess of the Qabalah being the May Queen, so once Robert Plant has planted the seed of thought concerning her in the listener's mind, he can then address the call to repentance. The change of heart toward what is good and evil is what I believe the tenth verse of "Stairway to Heaven" is referring to. I believe the encouragement is for the fan to forsake his Christian morality and worship the Devil and his moral code. Plant sings that "Yes," a person can travel one of "Two" different roads in this life, "But" over the "Long" haul, "There's" yet "Time" for a "Change" from that "Road" one is "On." It is an axiom in the occult world, that the occult is the left-handed path, and Christianity is the right. After Plant sings this verse about being able to "Change" one's "Road" in *The Remains the Same* film and soundtrack, he sings, "I hope so." Aleister Crowley wrote a passage in *The Equinox*, that is a parallel for this verse's message about "Time" for one's "Change" of direction to another "Road." It is the path of the worship of the Devil/Pan. Note the Druidic mention of the Oak trees as well: "O children of Wonder and of Fancy, fly to the wild woods whilst yet there is time! Back to the mysteries of the shadowy oaks, to the revolt of imagination, to the insurrection of souls, to the moonlit festivals of love: back where the werewolf lurks, and the moonrakes prowl. Back, O back to the song of life, back to the great God Pan!"56 One can clearly hear Crowley's voice in the Tenth Verse of "Stairway to Heaven," once one is familiar with *The Equinox*. Did you see the word werewolf in that verse? Humanly speaking, werewolves don't exist; apart from supernatural power. In the beginning of *The Song Remains the Same* film, during Peter Grant and Richard Cole's fantasy scene, Richard Cole shoots and kills a werewolf. To sum it up, Plant is telling the fan that they have "Time" to be spiritually regenerated, with the unspoken message being that they should be; in the direction of the Devil.

Another important factor of Led Zeppelin's music that is not clear to the listener in the Tenth Verse of "Stairway to Heaven" is the backward masking. Backward masking is done when the tape of a song is played in the reverse direction, and the band records an entirely different message in reverse. It is not a matter of the lyrics you hear when an album is played forward, as in "god" reversed being "dog." It is an entirely different recording. There is no connection between the lyrics played forward and the reverse recording, except for the fact that they are presented concurrently on the album. In other words, they are played at the same time; in the same spot. That is, however, the only relationship. I personally have recorded the backward masking in this Tenth Verse of "Stairway to Heaven." I have played it for dozens of people. If you want to do this, you have to have a "direct drive" turntable, not a belt driven one. You obviously need the fourth LP of Led Zeppelin. You can estimate turntable speed and with a finger turn the album in reverse with a finger on the label. There is no need to elaborate on the entire backward masked recording in this verse; I will just present the first statement. At this point in the song you can hear "There's No Escaping It, It's My Sweet Satan." Now why do this? What's the purpose behind it? First of all, Robert Plant evades the issue of it being a different recording in his response to backward masking allegations in Ritchie Yorke's *Led Zeppelin - The Definitive Biography*: "How could anyone sing backwards? It's complete bunkum - it can't be done. Only Americans would come up with something that ridiculous. Nobody in Europe would understand the point of doing anything backwards - It's hard enough to do forwards."57 Anyone who is familiar with Aleister Crowley knows that he advocated memorizing things backwards. Robert Plant knows this. Obviously, he is not telling the truth. Plant is also aware that backward masking is an entirely different recording. He is running from the issue. Led Zeppelin utilized "backwards echo" several times in making music. Plant knows exactly how this is done, because he did it with Led Zeppelin. I have played the album backward for others who clearly heard his voice, singing about Satan. You'll remember earlier in the book I quoted Plant trying to distance Aleister Crowley from Led Zeppelin's music by saying that he believes Page just collected works by an English eccentric, and that was all he knew. That was running from the truth of the fact that Led Zeppelin's musical message is founded upon Crowley's teachings. Now here is the purpose behind the backward masking. Let me illustrate it with a reference to your eyesight. Just ask any Optometrist about my statements and he or she will tell you I am writing the truth. When you look at something, it is perceived by the eye upside down. The vision goes to the brain upside down. The brain reverses the optical image to right side up. This is not done by the eye itself, it is done by the brain (If the brain is doing this apart from the will of the person, then it is logical to believe that the being who created the brain designed it to function in the said fashion.). When a song is played, and the listener is a fan, the song is being listened to with an attitude of acceptance, in other words, no dispute is taking place between the fan and the music being listened to; along with the verbal message. This acceptance makes the forward lyrics just as dangerous. However, when you hear a forward message you don't like, you can turn the music off. With backward masking, the verbal message sent into your mind in reverse, is then reversed by the brain as though it had gone in forward. This new forward message, that your conscious mind is not cognizant or aware of, then goes to the subconscious mind. Again, this is the goal, to program the subconscious mind, without the listener's consent. This is an absolute. The brain can reverse the message, understand it, without the conscious mind ever coming into contact with it, as it is understood by the subconscious with an attitude of acceptance. Listening to the song with that attitude makes the message acceptable in the subconscious mind. Dr. Joseph Murphy wrote about suggestion and the conscious mind's ability to reject it in *The Power of Your Subconscious Mind*: "The dictionary says that a suggestion is the act or instance of putting something into one's mind, the mental process by which the thought or idea suggested is entertained, accepted, or put into effect. You must remember that a suggestion cannot impose something on the subconscious mind against the will of the conscious mind. In other words, your conscious mind has the power to reject the suggestion given."58 Backward masking that bypasses the conscious mind cannot be rejected. If *"There's No Escaping It, It's My Sweet Satan"* goes into the subconscious mind as acceptable, at the very least the brain is desensitized to being afraid of the Devil; it makes him "cool," or at the very least, non-threatening. This is how people are duped into believing that references to Satan are just for the sake of image; in other words, tongue in cheek. Nothing could be further from the truth. There is a reason men are attracted to the satanic image; because they are evil, pure and simple. I know this subjectively, of course. Dr. Murphy also addressed the practical effect of a message on the subsequent behavior of a mind that has a message accepted by the subconscious:

"Your thought is received by your brain, which is the organ of your conscious reasoning mind. When your conscious or objective mind accepts the thought completely, it is sent to the solar plexus, called the brain of your mind, where it becomes flesh and is made manifest in your experience.'"59

In an earlier chapter, on the subject of the Holy Guardian Angel, you read the following quote from *The Book of the Sacred Magic of Abramelin the Mage*, that matches the backward masking message in question; describing the Angel's presence as "sweetness": "...since you shall see your Guardian Angel appear unto you in unequaled beauty; who also will converse with you, and speak in words so full of affection and of goodness, and with such sweetness, that no human tongue could express the same."60 Remember, Lucifer is described in the *Holy Bible* as the personification of beauty, in the Old Testament Book of Ezekiel, Chapter 28, Verse 12: "Thus saith the Lord God; Thou sealest up the sum, full of wisdom, and perfect in beauty." If you read the eleventh chapter you know that Satan is the Holy Guardian Angel in Crowley's writings. The book that quote was taken from was advocated by Crowley as a substantially important part of his magical progression. The Holy Guardian Angel appears to the magician in "sweetness," and the backward masked message in the Tenth Verse of "Stairway to Heaven" says, *"There's No Escaping It, It's My SWEET Satan."* Where did Led Zeppelin get this concept from?

It was at the time of producing the music for the fourth album that Page bought Boleskine House; I believe, to practice the magic of Abramelin. You read the quotes that said Page brought "Stairway to Heaven's" music from his home studio. Now you know that the backward masking calls Satan sweet. What else needs to be said? The desensitizing of the minds of the people who have listened to "Stairway to Heaven" from being afraid of the idea of the Devil to at least an apathetic attitude, and at the worst to believe in him, is tragic. This is mind control; pure and simple. The backward masking removes the fear of hearing about Satan in rock, and then the subsequent preaching of Satan as god deceives those who are willing to be deceived. When you love those who are telling you that the Devil is god and you should sell him your soul, and your mind has already reversed the concepts of good and evil, it is easy to believe that Lucifer is god. Once a person believes that, they are willing to "Change" their present course – i.e. "Hangman!" and get on the left handed path of Devil worship and involvement in the occult; and Led Zeppelin's goal is achieved in satanic spiritual regeneration. That is what I believe is the theme of the entire spectrum of the tenth verse of "Stairway to Heaven." If I didn't believe it, I would never have written this book, which could cost me my life.

VERSE 11   "HEAD," "HUMMING, "YOU," and "HIM"

The tenth verse of "Stairway to Heaven" encouraged the fan to consider changing the moral direction he or she is following, in conjunction with sending the subconscious mind the message that "Sweet Satan" cannot be escaped. In the Eleventh Verse, Robert Plant makes it absolutely clear who is presenting this message to the fan. The song "Stairway to Heaven" is not Led Zeppelin's music! Plant sings to the fan that his or her "Head" happens to be "Humming." Then he says that "It" doesn't "Go." In other words, the buzzing of the music in the mind doesn't leave. Why is that? The next line tells us, "The Piper's Calling You To Join Him." He did not say, "We are calling you to join us," and he did not say, "We are calling you to follow the piper." He said it was the piper himself who was communicating with the listener. This assertion by Led Zeppelin is a crucial point. If it is this "Piper" who is "Calling" the listener "to" unite with "Him," through the music, then the music is the Piper's, pure and simple. The four members of the band are simply his servants in bringing the music and its satanic message to the world; in return, they get to be "rock stars," which is a gentle euphemism for Devil worshiping evangelists and proselytizers. If the music were Led Zeppelin's, the song would say, "we are calling you to join us." This is concrete evidence provided by Led Zeppelin itself that its music came from Lucifer the Piper - The Maker of Music; absolute proof of their satanic pact in the mind of the objective, neutral observer. Again, this is why they are commanding the fans to sell their souls to the Devil in "Dazed and Confused" from the film, *The Song Remains the Same*; because, I believe, they have done the same thing. Again, if it was just an image to sell records, it wouldn't be so subtle, and we must remember this crucial point about their music. If it was composed by the band members themselves, then a satanic pact was unnecessary, and they wouldn't have told the listener that this "piper" was "calling" the listener "to" follow "him."

Led Zeppelin reiterated this concept four years later when they released *Physical Graffiti*, their sixth album, again, recorded at Headley Grange. The fourth song on that album is called "Houses of the Holy." The first mention of the Devil in the song is at 0:56 when he sings of the Devil's "daughter" appearing out of darkness. Then, in the next line, Plant sings that the fans are aware. Finally, at 1:52, Plant sings five very important lines. In the first line, he sings of our "world" rotating "faster." This of course, means that we are getting closer to the end (Just as he did in "The Rover" when mentioning a "candle" that was getting "low," I believe). In the second line, he asks the listener if they find themselves "dizzy" while "stoned." This refers to the transcendent frame of mind, or trance, that their music puts you into when you're stoned. In the third line he gives a command to allow their "music" to rule the listener as "master." In the fourth line, he asks the listener, "Will" they take "heed" to the "master's call?" Then in the fifth line, which is only three words, Plant sings of the inevitable result of answering the master's call, which is the great work of the Silver Star according to Crowley, the union of (he sings) "Satan and man"; which is satanic spiritual regeneration. Who is the master of the music? The Piper! He just said that it was Satan! Just as the Pied Piper of Hamlin took over the minds of the rats and led them to their deaths through music, I believe the same thing is happening to the Led Zeppelin fan at the hand of the Devil through his ambassadors; death in this instance being hell. This occurs even if the fan does not follow the Devil outright. As long as Satan can get the fan to live a life of rebellion against Christ, he wins the soul; while he tells the rock star he or she is leading the fans to spiritual bliss by revealing him to the masses. As Satan wrote through Crowley in *The Book of the Law*: "Let my servants be few & secret, they shall rule the many & the known."61 Again, I believe this is why Plant tells the fans the band members are their "overlords" in "Immigrant Song," from *Led Zeppelin III*. The following quote is from Aleister Crowley's *Equinox*, where the Devil commands Crowley to reveal him to the multitudes: "Shalt thou not bring the children of men to the sight of my glory? 'Only thy silence and thy speech that worship me avail.' 'For as I am the last, so am I the next, and as the next shalt thou reveal me to the multitude.' Fear not for aught; turn not aside for aught, eremite of Nuit, apostle of Hadit, warrior of Ra Hoor Khu! The leaven taketh, and the bread shall be sweet; the ferment worketh, and the wine shall be sweet. My sacraments are vigorous food and divine madness. Come unto me, O ye children of men; come unto me, in whom I am, in whom ye are, were ye only alive with the life that abideth in Light."62

Lucifer the Piper calls men to follow him through his music and he commands his followers to reveal him to the multitudes. This is why Plant is commanding the fans to sell their souls to the Devil in "Dazed and Confused" in *The Song Remains the Same* film and soundtrack. Since the music is derived from the Devil, I believe, and played by a magician, it is Magick put to music. William Burroughs, a writer who is admired by Jimmy Page, said essentially the same thing about Led Zeppelin's music, discussing spiritual forces and the sources of Magick power:

"It bears some resemblance to the trance music found in Morocco, which is magical in origin and purpose - that is, concerned with the evocation and control of spiritual forces.... In the Led Zeppelin concert, the result aimed at would seem to be the creation of energy in the performers and the audience. For such magic to succeed, it must tap the sources of magical energy, and this can be dangerous."63

The main spiritual force in question, obviously, is the Devil. He is providing the magical energy to draw the fan to him. It is a conjunction of music, lyrics, and supernatural power. Again, the goal behind the use of magical power is the spiritual regeneration of the fan. In this, William S. Burroughs agrees with me. Commenting on Burroughs' statement of spiritual regeneration, as well as astral projection, Steven Davis paraphrased him in *Hammer of the Gods*: "Just as Moroccan music is used as psychic hygiene, Burroughs suggested, so Led Zeppelin's music was used by its audience for astral travel and spiritual regeneration."64 Again, this man who wrote of Led Zeppelin, magic, astral projection, and spiritual regeneration concurrently, is someone Jimmy Page admires. Tom Friend was in ninth grade when that was written. It has nothing to do with me, or my opinions or beliefs (Kashmir-Astral Travel, Stairway-spiritual regeneration).

Robert Plant sings the Eleventh Verse of "Stairway to Heaven" to let the future follower of Satan, Crowley, and the Law of Thelema know who they are talking about; Lucifer/Satan the piper; because once they become students of Crowley's writings and listen to this song, the message is clear – Born Again Thelemic Satanism. Again, as Eliphas Levi said, in *Transcendental Magic*: "The sages therefore must speak occasionally. Yes, they must speak, not, however, to disclose, but lead others to discover."65

VERSE 12   "LADY," "HEAR," and "WHISPERING WIND"

The twelfth verse of "Stairway to Heaven" is another message making reference to satanic spiritual regeneration. Robert Plant is addressing Malkuth of the Qabalah; the part of mankind he believes will be redeemed by the Devil (Kashmir). He calls her "Lady," asking her if she is able to "Hear" a "Wind" that is blowing. Then he asks her "Did" she "know" that her "Stairway" to Heaven dwelt on their "Whispering Wind." Forgive my redundancy, but Plant told the fans they were a woman in "Dazed and Confused." At Earl's Court in 1975, and all throughout the 1977 North American Tour, when singing "Stairway to Heaven," including right in front of my eyes at Madison Square Garden, instead of singing "Dear Lady" in this verse, Plant sang "Dear People." Also later in the verse, instead of singing "Your Stairway," he sang "Our Stairway." Again, I believe Plant was preaching to the people that they were Malkuth of the Qabalah, and the band is part of her as well. Robert Plant sang "Stairway to Heaven" that way everywhere they played on the 1977 United States Tour. This can also be seen in the Holy Eye Earl's Court May 24th 1975 video, Seattle 77, the Knebworth 1979 concert video, as well as at the 1988 Atlantic Records 25th Anniversary reunion. The camera is focused on Plant as he deliberately changes the lyrics in all these instances. The deliberate changing of the lyrics was to guide the potential seeker; as was the statement in "Dazed and Confused."

Robert Plant was telling the Led Zeppelin fans in verse twelve of "Stairway to Heaven" that their "Stairway" dwelt on the band's "Whispering Wind." As I mentioned before, the Whispering Wind is a vehicle by which you can send a message from one point to another. Even Webster provides a definition of Wind in this context, defining it as "figuratively, air regarded as bearing information."66 The Whispering Wind is the music. That will be proven at the end of the song; at the end of the next set of lyrics.

I want to provide another note about backward masking, Underneath this Twelfth Berse, is the backmasked message for the subconscious mind, "I will sing because I live with Satan." Let you imagination figure out who in the band came up with that line.

VERSE 13 - CLOSING LYRICS OF STAIRWAY TO HEAVEN

The final nine lines of "Stairway to Heaven" are sung together, so they will be presented together. The overall theme of these lines is that Qabalah Magick is the foundation of the band's faith and practice in proclaiming the Law of Thelema; and therefore the Silver Star, Aleister Crowley, and the Devil. These last lines not only contain the concluding remarks of the song; they are also indicative of preparation for the great and cataclysmic "Battle of Armageddon" prophesied in the *Holy Bible's* Book of Revelation, which climaxes in the end of the world as we know it.

In the first two lines of the Thirteenth Verse of "Stairway to Heaven," Robert Plant makes two references. The first is that "As" Satan's people "Wind" to the end of their "Road," which is the end of their lives on the left handed path, their "Shadows" are greater "Than" their "Soul." If you have studied the eighth chapter in this book, which deals with the Qabalah, then the following information will be easy to understand. If you haven't read it, the following quotes will help you understand the two lines of the song I have referred to. First of all, Aleister Crowley points out that the Qabalah makes the many one; in his book, *Magick Without Tears*: "...there is no Way better than our Holy Qabalah, which analyseth all Things soever, and reduceth them to pure Number; and thus their Natures being no longer colored and confused, they may be regulated and for-mulated in Simplicity by the Operation of Pure Reason, to thy great Comfort in the Work of our Transcendental Art, whereby the Many become One."67 This is the goal of the Devil, to make all his followers one; on one accord. Again, this one, or united group of believers makes up Malkuth in the Qabalah; the daugh-ter. As Plant sang, when Satan's people come to the end of their "Road," their "Shadows" are greater "Than" their "Soul." Now I want you to analyze this carefully. When singing of the shadows and the soul, Robert Plant says the word "Our" before them both. He sings "Our Shadows" are greater in size as opposed to "Our Soul." When Plant sings "Shadows," he uses the collective plural. This refers to the many, or the collective people of Satan. When he sings "Soul," he uses the collective singular. This is the referring of Satan's people as the daugh-ter of the Qabalah. Again, this is what Crowley taught in his book, *Book 4*: "In one, the best, system of Magick, the Absolute is called the Crown, God is called the Father, the Pure Soul is called the Mother, the Holy Guardian Angel is called the Son, and the Natural Soul is called the Daughter. The Son purifies the Daughter by wedding her; she thus becomes the Mother, the uniting of whom with the Father absorbs all into the Crown."68 The Daughter in the Qabalah is the Natural Soul; Satan's people. See chapter eight for further details. The point I want you to notice is that Plant did not say "Our Souls," speaking of several souls, but one soul. So Robert Plant is saying that at the end of the "Road" for Satan's people, the collective "Shadows" are greater "Than" the collective "Soul." Again, this is the "Soul" belonging to a "Woman" that he sang about in "Dazed and Confused," just before he told the fans that they were her.

In chapter seven, you read where Satan wrote *The Book of the Law* through Aleister Crowley. In writing the book, the Devil made the statement that the existence of worshiping him is pure joy; and that sorrows are only occasional: "Remember all ye that existence is pure joy; that all the sorrows are but as shadows; they pass & are done; but there is that which remains."69 The Devil presented (through Crowley) the idea of sorrows being shadows. This is, I believe, the context in which Robert Plant is speaking in "Stairway to Heaven." The collective "Shadows" are sorrows, which are greater than the collective "Soul." What Plant is saying, I believe, is that the sorrows are overwhelming the soul of the woman Malkuth as she heads toward the end of her "Road." The same example was given by Lord Jesus Christ as he was praying in the Garden of Gethsemane when Judas Iscariot was on his way there with the soldiers to arrest him. The account is given in Matthew 26:37-38: "He took Peter and the two sons of Zebedee along with him, and he began to be sorrowful and troubled. Then he said to them, 'My soul is overwhelmed with sorrow to the point of death.'"(NIV)

If Robert Plant is saying that Malkuth's soul is overwhelmed with sorrow as she heads toward the end of her "Road" on the way to the Battle of Evermore (Armageddon), the question is why? The answer comes from Aleister Crowley. Before reading it, I want to remind you of what Plant sang in verse 5 of Stairway. He sang that he has a "Feeling" he receives "When" he takes time to "Look" in the direction of "West." At that moment his "Spirit" begins "Crying" out to be provided with the opportunity of "Leaving." I showed evidence to Plant singing about natural death; joining to the spirit world and its creator. This is what I believe he is referring to in verse thirteen, that Malkuth wants to be united with the creator, as well as those who have gone on before. Crowley wrote, in *The Book of Lies*, a perfect illustration of this. This matches the first Crowley quote I have presented relative to this Thirteenth Verse: "The many is as adorable to the One as the One is to the Many....The cause of sorrow is the desire of the One to the Many, or of the Many to the One. This also is the cause of joy. But the desire of one to another is all of sorrow; its birth is hunger and its death satiety. The desire of the Moth for the star at least saves him satiety. Hunger thou, O man, for the infinite: be insatiable even for the finite; thus at The End shalt thou devour the finite, and become the infinite."70 Aleister Crowley was the one who capitalized "The End." He wrote the same concept of sorrow being caused by division and joy coming from being one, in *The Equinox, Vol. III, No.1*: "Now Love is the enkindling in ecstasy of Two that will to become One. It is thus an Universal formula of High Magick. For see now how all things, being in sorrow caused by dividuality, must of necessity will Oneness as their medicine."71 What Robert Plant is saying, I believe, is that as Malkuth heads toward the Battle of Evermore she is overwhelmed with sorrow; wanting to be united to the spirit world; those who have gone on before, and the godhead. This will be reiterated quickly and conclusively at the end of the song. There will be no doubt left in your mind. However, it was necessary to introduce "the many being the one" before we arrive there.

In the third, fourth, and fifth lines of verse thirteen of the song, Robert Plant refers to the goddess; the mother of Malkuth. He sings that as they head toward the Battle of Evermore, "There" strolls the "Lady" the collective people of Satan "Know." He then sings that she "Shines" bright "Light." He says she is doing that so she can "Show "that "Everything" continues to transform from light into "Gold." First of all, this lady is the goddess in the Qabalah, Artemis/ Diana. Crowley's book on his Tarot deck, *The Book of Thoth*, illustrates this point in the writing on the second card, "The High Priestess:" "The card represents the most spiritual form of Isis the Eternal Virgin; the Artemis of the Greeks. She is clothed only in the luminous veil of light. It is important for high initiation to regard Light not as the perfect manifestation of the Eternal Spirit, but rather as the veil which hides that Spirit. It does so all the more effectively because of its incomparably dazzling brilliance. Thus she is light and the body of light. She is the truth behind the veil of light. She is the soul of light. Upon her knees is the bow of Artemis, which is also a musical instrument, for she is huntress, and hunts by enchantment."72

Crowley also said that the Tarot cards were derived from the Qabalah, in *The Book of Thoth*: "The only theory of ultimate interest about the Tarot is that it is an admirable symbolic picture of the Universe, based on the data of the Holy Qabalah."73 So this goddess of light is the same one presented in the teaching of the Qabalah; who is presented by Crowley as the female consort of Satan.

The goddess, harnessing bright light, desires to prove that "Everything" continues transforming from "Light" into "Gold." Eliphas Levi wrote of it in three of his books. First, in *The History of Magic*, he wrote: "Gold, in the eyes of initiates, is condensed light; the sacred numbers of the Kabbalah were called golden..."74 Referring to gold and light in *Transcendental Magic*, Levi wrote: "There is light in gold, gold in light and light in all things."75 He also wrote of this in his book, *The Key to the Mysteries*, that Aleister Crowley included in his *Equinox, Vol. I, No.10*, giving the Hebrew definition: "There is, in truth, the liquid and drinkable gold of the masters in alchemy; the word 'OR' (the French word for 'gold') comes from the Hebrew 'AOUR' which signifies 'light.'"76 Here we have Aleister Crowley and Eliphas Levi authenticating their belief in Alchemy, the magical practice of transforming metals. I am not going to take the time to expound on Alchemy, as it is not necessary. However, the following quote comes from Dave Lewis' *The Complete Guide to the Music of Led Zeppelin*, in which he calls Jimmy Page an "Alchemist" on a page of photos: "The alchemist, Jimmy Page with the Gibson doubleneck, 1977, and with Gibson Les Paul, 1975."77

The sixth and seventh lines of Verse Thirteen are very powerful; setting the listener up to understand the last two lines of the song. Robert Plant sings "If" the fans "Listen" real "Hard," then the Devil and Led Zeppelin's "Tune" is going to "Come" upon "You" finally. If a fan listens to all of Led Zeppelin's music real hard, the band's "Tune," is going to come alive in their mind once and for all. The "Tune," once again, is in the absolute, the music's hidden message. The variable is the perception of the message. From my perspective, the music's hidden message is its hidden lie. From Led Zeppelin's perspective, the music's hidden message is its hidden truth. In previous verses, Plant sang of the Whispering Wind. He sang in Verse Seven that it was being "Whispered" to the fans "If" they "Call" or try to establish contact or communication with Led Zeppelin's "Tune," the Devil would "Lead" them into the domain of "Reason." In Verse Twelve he asks the "Lady" if she is able to "Hear" a "Wind," then he asks her if she knew that her "Stairway" dwelt on their "Whispering Wind." The song "Stairway to Heaven," is a Whispering Wind communicating or whispering to the fans Led Zeppelin's "Tune," the music's hidden message (Page/Plant were saying the same thing on the 1994 *No Quarter* album. The fifth song on the cd is called "Yallah." In the song, Plant sings about "Truth" at 0:50. Then at 0:54 he says that this truth "...is whispered in the wind."). To sum it up, Robert Plant is telling the fan listening to "Stairway to Heaven" that if he gets a comprehensive knowledge of their music, meditating on what he hears, their "Tune" or hidden message will finally get through to him; that the Devil is god, and their religion, the Law of Thelema, is based upon Qabalah Magick and the teachings of Aleister Crowley, leaning in the direction of the Celts as they are modern day Druids. The "Tune," therefore, or the music's hidden message, is what Led Zeppelin assert is the "Stairway to Heaven," that arrives "On" their "Whispering Wind;" their music. You can see visible proof of this at the very point where Plant sings these lyrics during "Stairway to Heaven" in *The Song Remains the Same*. When speaking of the Whispering Wind he raises his right hand in the direction of the speakers; which makes reference obviously to the music they were playing – "Stairway to Heaven." This is the Devil's purpose in his deal with Led Zeppelin. They get to play his music as rock stars, preach his religion, and he gets the souls of the people he permanently programs to despise Lord Jesus Christ thereby. As Aleister Crowley wrote, in his book *Moonchild*: "...the devil, having bought the soul, regains the price, for the sorcerer spends it in the devil's service."78 As you read in a previous chapter, Time Life Books presented the same theme in their book, *Wizards and Witches*: "Satan was always ready to enter into a dark alliance with wizards, knowing he would benefit in the end."79

In the seventh line, again, Plant says their "Tune" is going to be realized by the dedicated listener, and that "Tune" or hidden message is climactic in the last two lines of the song, the eighth and ninth lines of the Thirteenth Verse. He makes direct reference to the Qabalah in the eighth line. He sings of the "All" being "One," as well as the reverse, the "One" being "All." In the ninth line he sings the connecting concept of being firm as "Rock" and what I believe is not being soft or defeated that he describes as "Roll." Again, the evidence suggests he is singing of the concept of Satan's people in the Qabalah being One; on one accord, and united in purpose, at the Battle of Armageddon. It is there that he hopes that Satan and his people will be solid as "Rock;" standing firm against the enemy, Christianity and its Christ, and hoping they don't "Roll," or get plundered by their religious foes, Christ and his followers. Beginning with the eighth line, Robert Plant sings of the "All" being "One," and vice versa. The concept, again, is referring to the Qabalistic unity of the Devil, the goddess, and the creation as One. Karl von Eckartshausen, in *The Cloud Upon the Sanctuary*, gives us an excellent example of this Qabalistic unity: "God alone is *substance*, absolute truth; He alone is he who *is*, and we are what He has made us. For Him, all exists in Unity; for us, all exists in multiplicity."80 In the *Key to the Mysteries*, Levi wrote of the Qabalistic unity: "Thou art God, who by thy godhead sustainest all beings, and by thy unity dost bring home all creatures. Thou art God, and there is no difference between thy deity, thy unity, thy eternity, and thy existence; for all is one and the same mystery; although names vary, all returns to the same truth."81 Once again, the song remains the same. Aleister Crowley wrote of the Qabalistic unity in *The Equinox*, *Vol. I, No.7, & Vol. III, No.1*. He starts off by quoting the Devil mentioning that he will rule his new convert with the new life that provides him with light: "But I will overcome thee; the New Life shall illumine thee with the Light that is beyond the Stars."82 Then he wrote of the Light causing the "All" to be seen as "One": "By Light shall ye look upon yourselves, and behold All Things that are in Truth One Thing only..."83

The most powerful example of this Qabalistic unity is going to be provided Israel Regardie, who worked for Aleister Crowley. In *The Encyclopedia of Witches and Witchcraft*, Rosemary Guiley wrote that Regardie toured Europe with Crowley as his secretary:

"Occultist and one-time secretary of ALEISTER CROWLEY, whose writings continue to have a wide audience among occultists, neo-Pagans and neo-Pagan WITCHES.

"Born in England on November 17, 1907, Francis Israel Regardie (he dropped the use of his first name later on) spent most of his life in the United States, emigrating there at age 13. He became fascinated with occultism and the activities and writings of Crowley, and managed to secure a position as Crowley's secretary in 1928. From that year to 1934, Regardie traveled around Europe with Crowley. It is said that no one person knew 'the Beast,' as Crowley called himself, better than Regardie."84

As Crowley's secretary, Regardie got to know Crowley and his writings very well, and as you read, there are those who say that he knew him better than anyone. It was Israel Regardie who wrote the introduction to Aleister Crowley's book, *777 and Other Qabalistic Writings of Aleister Crowley*, which was formerly titled *The Qabalah of Aleister Crowley*. In that introduction, Regardie summed up the purpose of studying Crowley's book about the Qabalah and comparative religion: "The process thus becomes a test for one's Qabalistic knowledge and skill, but more importantly the process becomes a stimulus for the surrender of the mind to the mystical experience in which the One is seen to be All, and vice versa."85

In their book, *The Plants of the Gods*, Richard Schultes and Albert Hoffman wrote that hallucinogenic drugs assist people in this grasping this conception of the "All" being "One": "This state of cosmic consciousness which under favorable circumstances may be attained with hallucinogens, is related to the spontaneous religious ecstasy known as the *unio mystica* or, in the experience of Eastern religious life, as *samadhi* or *satori*. In both of these states, a reality is experienced which is illuminated by that transcendental reality in which creation and ego, sender and receiver, are One....They consist of the loosening or even dissolution of the I-Thou barrier, with the result that objective everyday consciousness dissolves into the mystic experience of One-ness."86 Aldous Huxley said the same thing, in *The Doors of* Perception, when discussing the effects of Mescaline: "In the final stage of egolessness there is an 'obscure knowledge' that All is in all – that All is actually each. This is as near, I take it, as a finite mind can ever come to 'perceiving everything that is happening everywhere in the universe.'"87 It makes perfect sense, in light of the previous quoted material, to believe that Robert Plant promoted the use of hallucinogenic drugs for the purpose of seeing into the spirit world and assisting the fans in understanding the concept of Qabalistic unity (chapter thirteen); especially since Crowley wrote about it as "Samadhi" in *Magick in Theory and Practice*.

In the eighth line of the thirteenth verse of "Stairway to Heaven," Plant presents the "All" as being "One" and vice versa. This Qabalistic unity of the godhead, Satan the piper and the goddess, and his redeemed people, according to the ninth and last line of the song, want "To" stand firm as "Rock" as opposed to being steam rolled over by the enemy; which he describes as "Roll." The night I saw Led Zeppelin, after singing that last line, Plant said, "Please don't let it roll." In 1979 at Knebworth, he said, "Don't make me roll." At Live-Aid in

Philadelphia in July of 1985, he sang, "Please don't let it roll" at the end of Stairway. In 1988 at the Atlantic Records show, he said, "Don't make me roll" and then repeated it.

Lord Jesus Christ presented the idea of a Rock standing firm against a storm in the Book of Matthew 7:24-27: "Therefore everyone who hears these words of mine and puts them into practice is like a wise man who built his house on the rock. The rain came down, the streams rose, and the winds blew and beat against that house; yet it did not fall, because it had its foundation on the rock. But everyone who hears these words of mine and does not put them into practice is like a foolish man who built his house on sand. The rain came down, the streams rose, and the winds blew and beat against that house, and it fell with a great crash."(NIV) Jesus' point was that those who follow him will stand firm like rock against the storms of life, and I believe Robert Plant is using the word "Rock" in the same context, but against a specific storm, the Battle of Armageddon. Steven Davis, in *Hammer of the Gods*, wrote the same concept of "Stairway to Heaven's" last lyrics presenting the idea of a final battle: "There was something about 'Stairway to Heaven' - the chiming acoustics, the primal images of the goddess, the din-of-battle finale - that had hooked into the youth of America."88 Led Zeppelin's "Tune," its "Stairway to Heaven," is that Satan and his female consort are god, and his redeemed people are the daughter, and they are united as one to stand firm at their "Battle of Evermore;" the Battle of Armageddon written about in the *Holy Bible's* Book of Revelation; as you will see in the next chapter.

So "Stairway to Heaven," with its beautiful music and lyrics crying of Celtic mysticism, is a collection of the greatest subtleties and lies promoting Aleister Crowley, the Silver Star, and Qabalah Magick, that the Devil has ever laid on the world of rock; especially the hard core fans of Led Zeppelin, with one purpose in mind, satanic spiritual regeneration. The greatest song in rock history, "Stairway to Heaven," was given by the Devil to Led Zeppelin, I believe, to preach his message of evangelism to the masses, programming subconscious minds through backward masking, and telling the fan who listens real hard that their "Tune," the music's hidden message, will be realized by them, that Satan is god, and his people will be united in purpose, looking to stand firm as "Rock," at the Battle of Armageddon, presented by Led Zeppelin as "The Battle of Evermore." This battle will take place in the valley of Megiddo, where Lord Jesus Christ will wage war against the son of the Devil, possessed by the Devil, the Anti-Christ, the Beast 666; all revealed in the following pages.

At the moment Robert Plant sings of the spiritual rebirth in "Stairway to Heaven," (in their film) Jimmy Page and John Paul Jones look into each other's eyes. The reason is, of course, that they have just presented their "tune" in that part of the song, with the mentioning of the new life of satanic spiritual regeneration.

Jimmy Page launches into the lead in "Stairway to Heaven" while showing the way to communing with the dragon is with the Heroin Poppy. Again, Crowley said that a magician/musician would hear beautiful music the likes of which he never hoped to hear while performing the Operation of Abramelin the Mage; to unite with Lucifer the Piper, the maker of music. Crowley bought Boleskine House to perform the Operation of Abramelin the Mage, and Jimmy Page produced the music for "Stairway to Heaven," the year he bought Boleskine House.

These two photos show Jimmy Page playing the power chords prior to, as well as the lead during "Stairway to Heaven" in 1977. They tell the story of the band; the Dragon, the Heroin poppy, and music that evidence suggests he gave them.

No other guitarist in rock history has known the glory that Page has known while playing "Stairway." Jimmy holds the guitar above his head at the end of the song; while the fans worship the god of rock guitarists. I remember doing the exact same thing, with a joint in my hand, standing on my chair in the orchestra at Madison Square Garden on June 11th, 1977. An interesting note, is that Led Zeppelin played there on June 7-8, 10 -11, 13-14; and at the end of the show on the 11th, they had performed 666% of their shows there. After "Stairway to Heaven," it seemed like an eternity with the glitter ball spinning lights all over us as we chanted for "MORE!" over and over; until the band came out and closed with "Heartbreaker." After the concert, I began to collect every album of theirs, including bootlegs, posters, and any magazines with Led Zeppelin articles; all to feed my growing obsession, as the Abramelin Magick spell demanded I do.

1 Aleister Crowley, *The Equinox*, Vol. I, No.3, pg.248

2 Aleister Crowley, *Moonchild*, pp. 228-229

3 S. Jason Black and Christopher S. Hyatt, Ph.D., *Pacts With the Devil*, pg.91

4 Ritchie Yorke, *Led Zeppelin - The Definitive Biography*, pg.137

5 Israel Regardie, Aleister Crowley's, *777*, Introduction, pg. viii, Samuel Weiser Inc., Yorke Beach, Maine, 1994

6 MacGregor Mathers, *The Qabalah Unveiled*, pg.65

7 Ibid, pg.59

8 Aleister Crowley, *The Equinox*, Vol. I, No.5, pg.116

9 Aleister Crowley, *The Equinox*, Vol. I, No.5, pg.113

10 Aleister Crowley, *Magick Book 4*Liber Aba*, pg.171

11 Ibid, pg.171

12 Ibid, pg.527

13 D.J. Conway, *Celtic Magic*, pg.85

14 Lewis Spence, *Ancient Egyptian Myths and Legends*, pg.271

15 Richard Cavendish, *The Black Arts*, pp.290

16 S. Jason Black and Christopher S. Hyatt, *Pacts With the Devil*, pg.18

17 Aleister Crowley, *The Equinox*, Vol. I, No.7, pg.321

18 Aleister Crowley, *The Equinox*, Vol. I, No.5, *The Vision and the Voice*, pg.35

19 Aleister Crowley, *The Equinox*, Vol. I, No.1, *John St. John*, pg.14

20 Aleister Crowley, *Moonchild*, pg.273

21 Dr. Sir J. G. Frazer, *The Golden Bough*, pp.733-734

22 Ibid, pg.719

23 Aleister Crowley, *The Equinox*, Vol. I, No.5, *The Vision and the Voice*, pg.32

24 Aleister Crowley, *Moonchild*, pp.228, 229

25 S. Jason Black and Christopher S. Hyatt, Ph.D., *Pacts With the Devil*, pg.91

26 Aleister Crowley, *The Book of Wisdom or Folly*, pg.168

27 Joseph Kaster, *Putnam's Concise Mythological Dictionary*, Putnam, New York, 1963

28 Eliphas Levi, *The History of Magic*, pg. 371

29 Eliphas Levi, *Transcendental Magic*, pg.353

30 Eliphas Levi, *The History of Magic*, pg.29

31 Ibid, pg.283

32 Aleister Crowley, *The Law is for All*, pg.196

33 Ibid, pg.196

34 Ibid, pg.200

35 Howard Mylett, *Jimmy Page – Tangents Within A Framework*, pg.75

36 *Webster's New World Dictionary*, Second College Edition, pg.1195

37 Karl von Eckartshausen, *The Cloud Upon the Sanctuary*, pp.43, 68

38 Ibid, pp.5-6,7-8

39 Ibid, pp.78-79

40 Ritchie Yorke, *Led Zeppelin - The Definitive Biography*, pg.137

41 Steven Davis, *Hammer of the Gods*, pg.133

42 Aleister Crowley, *The Equinox*, Vol. I, No.1, pp.174-175

43 Aleister Crowley, *The Equinox*, Vol. I, No.7, *Liber Stellae Rubeae – LXVI* pg.35

44 Satan, *The Book of the Law*, 1:53, Aleister Crowley's *The Equinox*, Vol. I, No.10, pg.16

45 Time Life Books, *Wizards and Witches*, pg.15

46 Karl von Eckartshausen, *The Cloud Upon the Sanctuary*, pg.69

47 Aleister Crowley, *The Equinox*, Vol. I, No.1, pg.216

48 Lewis Spence, *Magic Arts in Celtic Britain*, pg.140

49 Ibid, pg.54

50 Eliphas Levi, *The History of Magic*, pg.184

51 Aleister Crowley, *The Equinox*, Vol. III, No.1, *Liber LXV*, pg.74

52 Aleister Crowley, *The Equinox*, Vol. I, No.6, *Liber A'Ash*, pg.37

53 Aleister Crowley, *The Equinox*, Vol. I, No.5, *The Vision and the Voice*, pg.163

54 Dr. Sir J. G. Frazer, *The Golden Bough*, pg.169

55 Aleister Crowley, *The Equinox*, Vol. I, No.1, pg.17

56 Ibid, pg.177

57 Ritchie Yorke, *Led Zeppelin - The Definitive Biography*, pg.250

58 Dr. Joseph Murphy, *The Power of Your Subconscious Mind*, pg.35

59 Ibid, pg.47

60 Abraham the Jew, *The Book of the Sacred Magic of Abramelin the Mage*, translated by S.L. MacGregor Mathers, pg.84

61 Satan, *The Book of the Law*, Chapter 1, Verse 10, Aleister Crowley's *The Equinox*, Vol.I, No.10, pg.11

62 Aleister Crowley, *The Equinox*, Vol. I, No.5, *The Vision and the Voice*, pg.46

63 William S. Burroughs, *Rock Magic*, *Crawdaddy Magazine*, June 1975

64 Steven Davis, *Hammer of the Gods*, pg.238

65 Eliphas Levi, *Transcendental Magic*, pg.267

66 *Webster's New World Dictionary*, Second College Edition, pg.1628

67 Aleister Crowley, *Magick Without Tears*, pg.434

68 Aleister Crowley, *Book 4,* pg.71

69 Satan, *The Book of the Law*, Chapter 2, Verse 9, Aleister Crowley's *The Equinox*, Vol. I, No.10, pg.18

70 Aleister Crowley, *The Book of Lies*, pp.16, 102

71 Aleister Crowley, *The Equinox*, Vol. III, No.1, pg.108

72 Aleister Crowley, *The Book of Thoth*, pg.73

73 Ibid, pg.4

74 Eliphas Levi, *The History of Magic*, pg.168

75 Eliphas Levi, *Transcendental Magic*, pg.287

76 Eliphas Levi, *The Key to the Mysteries*, Aleister Crowley's *The Equinox*, Vol. I, No.10, pg.202

77 Dave Lewis, *The Complete Guide to the Music of Led Zeppelin*, between pp.72-73

78 Aleister Crowley, *Moonchild*, pg.248

79 Time Life Books, *Wizards and Witches*, pg.58

80 Karl von Eckartshausen, *The Cloud Upon the Sanctuary*, pg.12

81 Eliphas Levi, *The Key to the Mysteries*, Aleister Crowley's *The Equinox*, pg.70

82 Aleister Crowley, *The Equinox*, Vol. I, No.7, pg.35

83 Aleister Crowley, *The Equinox,* Vol. III, No.1, pg.102

84 Rosemary Ellen Guiley, *The Encyclopedia of Witches and Witchcraft*, pg. 279

85 Israel Regardie, *777 and Other Qabalistic Writings of Aleister Crowley*, Introduction, pg. viii, Samuel Weiser Inc., Yorke Beach, Maine, 1994

86 Richard Evans Schultes and Albert Hoffman, *Plants of the Gods*, pp.177, 181

87 Aldous Huxley, *The Doors of Perception*, pg.26

88 Steven Davis, *Hammer of the Gods*, pg.169

Led Zeppelin performing "The Battle of Evermore" on July 23rd, 1977 at the Oakland Coliseum. The number 3 on John Bonham's jacket was prophetic; he was dead three years later. Take note of the Stonehenge stone behind them. During the concert in New York at Madison Square Garden, exactly six weeks earlier, I sat in the orchestra and watched Led Zeppelin perform "In My Time of Dying," as well as "The Battle of Evermore," and "Kashmir." Page/Plant performed "The Battle of Evermore" on their 1994 MTV "Unledded" special. The song was then placed on a video of the special. The video's name: "No Quarter."

Jimmy Page plays "In My Time of Dying," wearing his death skull - Egyptian Ankh - guitar necklace amulet around his neck. In the song, Plant mockingly calls Jesus "Lord," asking him to "meet" him with a substitute set of "wings" if the ones he has don't get him to heaven. Later in the song, Plant alludes to the content of "The Battle of Evermore" when he mentions the "marching" of angelic beings, as well as the redemption in the song, "Kashmir." After the war is over, and he is redeemed by the same "angels," Plant sings that he "feels" real "good" in heaven. Robert Plant was right about one thing, though mockingly, Jesus will send his soul into eternity at the time appointed.

CHAPTER SIXTEEN

"Great is the Beast that cometh forth like a lion, the servant of the Star and of the Snake. He is the Eternal one; He is the Almighty one. Blessed are they upon whom he shall look with favour, for nothing shall stand before his face. Accursed are they upon whom he shall look with derision, for nothing shall stand before his face."1

Black Magician Aleister Crowley, "The Equinox"

"...the man of sin is revealed, the son of perdition, who opposes and exalts himself above all that is called God or that is worshiped, so that he sits as God in the temple of God, showing himself that he is God."

2 Thessalonians 2:3-4

"He causes all, both small and great, rich and poor, free and slave, to receive a mark on their right hand or on their foreheads, and that no one may buy or sell except one who has the mark or the name of the beast, or the number of his name. Here is wisdom. Let him who has understanding calculate the number of the beast, for it is the number of a man: His number is 666."

Revelation, 13:16-18

"And I saw three unclean spirits like frogs coming out of the mouth of the dragon, out of the mouth of the beast, and out of the mouth of the false prophet. For they are spirits of demons, performing signs, which go out to the kings of the earth and of the whole world, to gather them to the battle of that great day of God Almighty....And they gathered them together to the place called in Hebrew, Armageddon."

Revelation, 16: 12-14,16

"And I saw the beast, the kings of the earth, and their armies, gathered together to make war against Him who sat on the horse and against His army."

Revelation 19:19

THE BATTLE OF EVERMORE: LORD JESUS CHRIST vs. THE BEAST 666

"The Battle of Evermore," the song on Led Zeppelin's fourth album that comes just before "Stairway to Heaven," is their version of the *Holy Bible's* "Battle of Armageddon," I believe, as well as conceptually the sequel to "Stairway." My goal in this chapter is to provide a description of the events surround-

539

ing the battle as well as the battle itself; especially as it relates to showing the reader why I believe that the Battle of Armageddon is what Led Zeppelin was describing. Robert Plant has consistently claimed the song is about the Scottish wars of long ago. Dave Lewis, in his book, *The Complete Guide to the Music of Led Zeppelin,* tells us the story of Plant's claim to inspiration for the song: "The tune for this was written by Page late one night at the Grange while he experimented on Jones' mandolin. Robert came up with a set of lyrics inspired by a book he was reading on the Scottish wars."2 This claim of Robert Plant's will prove to be a smokescreen to the reader in the pages to come. Led Zeppelin presented the Biblical information in compost fashion, with mention of "Ringwraiths" from Tolkien's *Lord of the Rings* (analogy) and a "Castle," that are not included in the *Holy Bible.* However, there are far too many concurrences between the song and the scripture to make this a coincidence. Time and space preclude me from presenting a comprehensive treatise on all the prophecies, circumstances, and facts concerning the nation of Israel, the last days, the rise of the Anti-Christ, and the second coming of Lord Jesus Christ. In his book, *The King is Coming,* Dr. H.L. Willmington presents a factual, all encompassing view of these events. I would direct the reader to that book for further study. This chapter will begin with a brief look at some of the prophecies of the coming Anti-Christ as well as the events leading up to the Battle of Armageddon; including the battle itself. Concurrent information from Led Zeppelin will accompany them. From there the reader will examine a comparison/contrast of Led Zeppelin's view of the battle with the *Bible's* version. We will also examine their analogy of the battle in their concert film, when they present what I believe is a direct parallel to it with the Arthur legend. In the end, the doom of the Anti-Christ and his followers, as well as the Devil, will be clearly seen from the *Bible's* Book of Revelation. Led Zeppelin, on the other hand, present Satan as defeating Christ at the end of the battle. The Battle of Armageddon, with its outcome determining who will rule the universe in eternity, is a very exciting and stimulating story to the objective reader; however, those inhabiting the earth at the time just prior to and during the battle, will find the second coming of Lord Jesus Christ and "The Battle of Evermore" placing them in the most cataclysmic and fearful time that the earth has ever known, or will know.

LORD JESUS CHRIST'S PROPHECY OF THE END

Beginning with Lord Jesus Christ, we will examine prophecies of the end times. In Matthew 24:1-31, Jesus addressed his disciples about his return to the earth:

"Then Jesus went out and departed from the temple, and His disciples came up to show Him the buildings of the temple. And Jesus said to them, 'Do you not see all these things? Assuredly, I say to you, not one stone shall be left here upon another, that shall not be thrown down.'

"Now as He sat on the Mount of Olives, the disciples came to Him privately, saying 'Tell us, when will these things be? And what will be the sign of Your coming, and of the end of the age?' And Jesus answered and said to them: 'Take heed that no one deceives you. For many will come in My name, saying I am the Christ, and will deceive many. And you will hear of wars and rumors of wars. See that you are not troubled; for all these things must come to pass, but the end is not yet. For nation will rise against nation, and kingdom against kingdom. And there will be famines, pestilences, and earthquakes in various places. All these are the beginning of sorrows.

"Then they will deliver you up to tribulation and kill you, and you will be hated by all nations for My name's sake. And then many will be offended, will betray one another, and will hate one another. Then many false prophets will rise up and deceive many. And because lawlessness will abound, the love many will grow cold. But he who endures to the end shall be saved. And this gospel of the kingdom will be preached in all the world as a witness to all the nations, and then the end will come.

"Therefore when you see the abomination of desolation, spoken of by Daniel the prophet, standing in the holy place (whoever reads, let him understand), then let those who are in Judea flee to the mountains. Let him who is on the housetop not go down to take anything out of his house. And let him who is in the field not go back to get his clothes. But woe to those who are pregnant and to those who are nursing babies in those days! And pray that your flight may not be in winter or on the Sabbath. For then there will be great tribulation, such as has not been since the beginning of the world until this time, no, nor ever shall be. And unless those days were shortened, no flesh would be saved; but for the elect's sake those days will be shortened.

"Then if anyone says to you, "Look, here is the Christ! Or There!" do not believe it. For false christs and false prophets will rise and show great signs and wonders to deceive, if possible, even the elect. See, I have told you beforehand.

"Therefore if they say to you, "Look, He is in the desert!" do not go out; or "Look He is in the inner rooms!" do not believe it.

"For as the lightning comes from the east and flashes to the west, so also will the coming of the Son of Man be. For wherever the carcass is, there the eagles will be gathered together.

"Immediately after the tribulation of those days the sun will be darkened, and the moon will not give its light, the stars will fall from heaven, and the powers of the heavens will be shaken. Then the sign of the Son of Man will appear in heaven, and then all the tribes of the earth will mourn, and they will see the Son of man coming on the clouds of heaven with power and great glory. And He will send His angels with a great sound of a trumpet, and they will gather together His elect from the four winds, from one end of heaven to the other.'"

Let us examine a few points from this passage. The first thing we will look at is Jesus' mentioning wars and natural disasters. In verses 7&8 he said: "For nation will rise against nation, and kingdom against kingdom. And there will be famines, pestilences, and earthquakes in various places. All these are the beginning of sorrows." Jesus said that nation will fight nation and kingdom will fight kingdom. His prophecy has come true. Then he said there would be famines, pestilences and earthquakes all over the earth. This too has come true. Just look around you. Pestilence is the spread of deadly disease. All over the earth, in various places, we see earthquakes, famines, and pestilence, just as he predicted two thousand years ago. He also mentioned signs above the earth that are yet to come: "Immediately after the tribulation of those days the sun will be darkened, and the moon will not give its light; the stars will fall from heaven, and the powers of the heavens will be shaken."

The prophet Joel wrote of these events as occurring before the battle, in Joel 2:10-11: "The earth quakes before them, the heavens tremble; the sun and moon grow dark, and the stars diminish their brightness. The LORD gives voice before His army, for His camp is very great; for strong is the One who executes His word. For the day of the LORD is great and very terrible; who can endure it?" Joel went on to describe the same scene in chapter 2:30-31, quoting Lord Jesus Christ: "And I will show wonders in the heavens and in the earth: Blood and fire and pillars of smoke. The sun shall be turned into darkness, and the moon into blood, before the coming of the great and awesome day of the LORD."

The sun and the moon and the stars will no longer shine bright in the day of the Lord. This day of the Lord is the Battle of Armageddon. Joel went on to describe the scene in 3:12-16, where he cited the battle as being in the valley of Jehoshaphat, which *Bible* scholars know to be the valley of Megiddo (Armageddon). Here he says the Lord will defend Israel: "'Let the nations be wakened, and come up to the Valley of Jehoshaphat; for there I will sit to judge all the surrounding nations. Put in the sickle, for the harvest is ripe. Come, go down; for the winepress is full, the vats overflow – for their wickedness is great.' Multitudes, multitudes in the valley of decision! For the day of the LORD is near in the valley of decision. The sun and moon will grow dark, and the stars will diminish their brightness. The LORD also will roar from Zion, and utter His voice from Jerusalem; the heavens and earth will shake; but the LORD will be a shelter for His people, and the strength of the children of Israel." In all three of the previous *Bible* passages, Christ is proclaiming through the Prophet Joel what he later reiterated in Matthew and Luke, that the sun would be darkened at that time. The first application of Led Zeppelin's music we will look at addresses this.

LED ZEPPELIN II - "THANK YOU"

On Led Zeppelin's second album, *Led Zeppelin II*, there is a song called "Thank You." In the beginning of the song, at 0:26, Robert Plant sings "If" our "sun" does no longer "shine," he will "still" continue "loving" his woman. He used the word "if" at the beginning of the song. In this next line, he uses an absolute by saying, "When mountains crumble to the sea," he and his woman will continue to exist. This author believes Plant is singing in place of Lucifer, who is singing to his bride (although that appears to be an incredulous statement – read on). What I believe Plant is singing about, relative to the mountains, is the great earthquake that will occur just prior to the battle. At 1:29 into "Going to California," another song off the mighty fourth Led Zeppelin album, Plant sings the "Mountains" as well as "canyons" begin their "tremble" as well as their "shake." Then, in the next line, he sings, "Children of the sun begin to wake." Right after that he says that everyone better look "out." He is saying that just prior to the battle, at the time of the great earthquake, the sun's children will start to awake. Who are they? They are Satan's children, according to Crowley. They are the daughter and bride of Satan, or Malkuth in the Qabalah. Robert Plant, at the Los Angeles Forum, on March 24th, 1975, just before he walked off stage, shouted, "Children of the sun. Goodnight!"3 How are the children of the sun going to awake? Satan will wake them, according to Aleister Crowley, as he wrote in *The Equinox:* "It is the Lord of Heaven that awakens the Children of the Light."4

Plant sings that at the time of the great earthquake, the sun's children will wake up and everyone better look out. Two different Led Zeppelin songs have already told us of this earthquake, when the mountains will crumble. At the same time, the *Bible* says that the sea will be turned into blood. Just before singing of the "Mountains" as well as "canyons" beginning to "shake" in "Going to California," at 1:16 into the song, Plant sings that the "Sea" turned "red," also, our "sky" turned "gray." Then, in the next line he sings that he "Wondered" if "tomorrow" would "ever" be able to come after "today." The scenario we have so far, just prior to the battle, is the sun darkened, which gives us a gray sky, an earthquake, mountains descending into the ocean, and the ocean has turned red. The following passage from the *Holy Bible's* Book of Revelation's sixteenth chapter describes these events as they occur prior to the battle:

"Then I heard a loud voice from the temple saying to the seven angels, 'Go and pour out the bowls of the wrath of God on the earth.'

"So the first went and poured out his bowl upon the earth, and a foul and loathsome sore came upon the men who had the mark of the beast and those who worshiped his image.

"Then the second angel poured out his bowl on the sea, and it became blood as of a dead man; and every living creature in the sea died.

"Then the third angel poured out his bowl on the rivers and springs of water, and they became blood. And I heard the angel of the waters saying:

'You are righteous, O Lord, the One who is and who was and who is to be, because You have judged these things. For they have shed the blood of saints and prophets, and You have given them blood to drink. For it is their just due.'

"And I heard another from the altar saying, 'Even so, Lord God Almighty, true and righteous are Your judgments.'

"Then the fourth angel poured out his bowl on the sun, and power was given to him to scorch men with fire. And men were scorched with great heat, and they blasphemed the name of God who has power over these plagues; and they did not repent and give Him glory.

"Then the fifth angel poured out his bowl on the throne of the beast, and his kingdom became full of darkness; and they gnawed their tongues because of the pain. They blasphemed the God of heaven because of their pains and their sores, and did not repent of their deeds.

"Then the sixth angel poured out his bowl on the great river Euphrates, and its water was dried up, so that the way of the kings from the east might be prepared. And I saw three unclean spirits like frogs coming out of the mouth of the dragon, out of the mouth of the beast, and out of the mouth of the false prophet. For they are spirits of demons, performing signs, which go out to the kings of the earth and of the whole world, to gather them to the battle of that great day of God Almighty....And they gathered them together to the place called in Hebrew, Armageddon.

"Then the seventh angel poured out his bowl into the air, and a loud voice came out of the temple of heaven, from the throne, saying, 'It is done!' And there were noises and thunderings and lightnings; and there was a great earthquake, such a mighty and great earthquake as had not occurred since men were on the earth. Now the great city was divided into three parts, and the cities of the nations fell. And great Babylon was remembered before God, to give her the cup of the wine of the fierceness of His wrath. Then every island fled away and the mountains were not found. And great hail from heaven fell upon men, each hailstone about the weight of a talent. Men blasphemed God because of the plague of the hail, since that plague was exceedingly great."

Dr. David Jeremiah, in his book, *Escape the Coming Night*, commented on the previous passage, making reference to the earthquake and the mountains crumbling as well as the sky not being clear: "They will be sitting in their homes, reading the Universal News, or buying smog masks with their Global Credit Card, when the earth begins to shake. Before they can pull their hands out of the 666 sensor, the sky becomes black and a ghastly moon, covered with blood, appears upon the horizon. Against this eerie backdrop, the stars shoot to earth like a shower of white-hot coals. Mountains crumble into volcanic ash, islands sink into the sea, and clouds of dust spread across the sky, making it appear as if the sky were rolling."5

You read in the passage from Revelation that the kings of the earth would be led into the place called Armageddon. Dr. Jeremiah made reference to this place in the same book, noting that he visited there:

"The kings of the earth will gather in a place called Armageddon. How many times do we hear that location mentioned in our own experience, and yet this is the only place where that word is found in all the Bible! The word means 'Mount of Megiddo,' and the valley of Megiddo is located about fifteen miles southeast of modern Haifa.

"It is awesome to stand on a steep path overlooking this fertile valley and realize that some day the carnage there will be worse than any battle fought throughout the ages.

"A gruesome description of this devastation is given in Revelation 14:20, when we are told that blood will flow as high as horse's bridles for a distance of 200 miles. The only valley of that length in Israel is the Jordan River valley, which goes from the Sea of Galilee through the Dead Sea and down to the Gulf of Eliat. That valley will have a red river of blood running through it."6

Prior to the Battle of Armageddon, the sun will be darkened, there will be a great earthquake, the sea will be turned into blood, mountains will crumble, and the sky will not be clear. All these circumstances have been described by Led Zeppelin in their music, with no alternative meaning conveyed to the fans. The concepts are presented, and the fans are supposed to figure out what they mean. After studying the rest of this chapter, there will be no ambiguity as to what they were referring to. It was the war between Christ and the Beast.

JESUS' PROPHECY OF THE ANTI-CHRIST 666

Jesus went on to warn his disciples, in the earlier passage from Matthew, describing the end times, that these things would occur: "...when you see standing in the holy place 'the abomination that causes desolation,' spoken of through the prophet Daniel..."

The prophet wrote of the coming Anti-Christ, the Beast, in Daniel 8:23-25, his Old Testament Book: "And in the latter time of their kingdom, when the transgressors have reached their fullness, a king shall arise, having fierce features, who understands sinister schemes. His power shall be mighty, but not by his own power; he shall destroy fearfully, and shall prosper and thrive; he shall destroy the mighty, and also the holy people. Through his cunning he shall cause deceit to prosper under his rule; and he shall exalt himself in his heart. He shall destroy many in their prosperity. He shall even rise against the Prince of princes; but he shall be broken without human means."

Shortly after the preceding passage, Daniel would have a frightening vision of the Lord Jesus Christ in his glorified supernatural body. He recorded it in Daniel 10:5-9:

"...I lifted my eyes and looked, and behold, a certain man clothed in linen, whose waist was girded with gold of Uphaz! His body was like beryl, his face like the appearance of lightning, his eyes like torches of fire, his arms and feet like burnished bronze in color, and the sound of his words like the voice of a multitude.

"And I, Daniel, alone saw the vision, for the men who were with me did not see the vision; but a great terror fell upon them, so that they fled to hide themselves. Therefore I was left alone when I saw this great vision, and no strength remained in me; for my vigor was turned to frailty in me, and I retained no strength. Yet I heard the sound of his words; and while I heard the sound of his words I was in a deep sleep on my face, with my face to the ground."

The Lord Jesus Christ appeared to Daniel and told him to record what he wanted him to prophecy about the coming Anti-Christ, the Beast, addressing him as "the king," just as Daniel had written before. He told Daniel of events that would occur during the end times, before the Battle of Armageddon. Daniel wrote in 11:36-45:

"Then the king shall do according to his own will: he shall exalt and magnify himself above every god, shall speak blasphemies against the God of gods, and shall prosper till the wrath has been accomplished; for what has been determined shall be done. He shall regard neither the God of his fathers nor the desire of women, nor regard any god; for he shall exalt himself above them all. But in their place he shall honor a god of fortresses; and a god which his fathers did not know he shall honor with gold and silver, with precious stones and pleasant things. Thus he shall act against the strongest fortresses with a foreign god, which he shall acknowledge, and advance its glory; and he shall cause them to rule over many, and divide the land for gain.

"At the time of the end the king of the South shall attack him; and the king of the North shall come against him like a whirlwind, with chariots, horsemen, and with many ships; and he shall enter the countries, overwhelm them, and pass through. He shall also enter the Glorious Land, and many countries shall be overthrown; but these shall escape from his hand: Edom, Moab, and the prominent people of Ammon. He shall stretch out his hand against the countries, and the land of Egypt shall not escape. He shall have power over the treasures of gold and silver, and over all the precious things of Egypt; also the Libyans and Ethiopians shall follow at his heels. But news from the east and the north shall trouble him; therefore he shall go out with great fury to destroy and annihilate many. And he shall plant the tents of his palace between the seas and the glorious holy mountain; yet he shall come to his end, and no one will help him."

In the New Testament Book of II Thessalonians, Chapter 2, Verses 1-4, Paul the Apostle encouraged the Christians at Thessalonica by assuring them that the return of Christ had not yet occurred as some were saying. He assured them that the Anti-Christ would be revealed first:

"Now, brethren, concerning the coming of our Lord Jesus Christ and our gathering together to Him, we ask you, not to be soon shaken in mind or troubled, either by spirit or by word or by letter, as if from us, as though the day of Christ had come. Let no one deceive you by any means; for that Day will not come unless the falling away comes first, and the man of sin is revealed, the son of perdition, who opposes and exalts himself above all that is called God or that is worshiped, so that he sits as God in the temple of God, showing himself that he is God."

Dr. Jeremiah, again, in his book, *Escape the Coming Night*, commented on the *"abomination of desolation"* prophesied by Daniel the Prophet, as it was mentioned to the disciples by Christ in Matthew; presented at the beginning of this chapter:

"Matthew 24:15-21 teaches that marked increase in suffering comes right after the setting up of 'the abomination of desolation' spoken of by Daniel, and this is to occur at midpoint in the Tribulation. The great world leader, the Anti-Christ, has been developing his plan to gain global control, and after three and a half years of public adulation and oppression of the Jesus people, he will go to Jerusalem and march into the new Temple and proclaim that he is God (II Thessalonians 2:4)."7

The Anti-Christ marching into the Temple in Jerusalem and proclaiming himself to be God is what Daniel was referring to when he spoke of the "abomination of desolation." That is what Jesus thinks of the Anti-Christ claiming to be God. That is why he warned the disciples, knowing it would be recorded in the *Bible*, that when this takes place, then will be the worst time of trouble this world has ever known or will know.

THE APOSTLE JOHN'S VISION OF RISEN LORD JESUS CHRIST

The Book of Revelation, which contains the record of the coming Anti-Christ, his rule over the earth, and the Battle of Armageddon, was written by the Apostle John.

He was exiled to the Isle of Patmos by the Roman Emperor because of his testimony for Jesus Christ. It was there that John wrote the Book of Revelation. Like Daniel, he received a vision of the glorified Lord Jesus Christ; who told him to write the book that would reveal the events of the last days, including the Battle of Armageddon. John described his vision, and it is identical to what Daniel saw, several hundred years before:

"Then I turned to see the voice that spoke with me. And having turned I saw seven golden lampstands, and in the midst of the seven lampstands One like the Son of Man, clothed with a garment down to the feet and girded about the chest with a golden band. His head and hair were white like wool, as white as snow, and His eyes like a flame of fire; His feet were like fine brass, as if refined in a furnace, and His voice as the sound of many waters; He had in His right hand seven stars, out of His mouth went a sharp two-edged sword, and His countenance was like the sun shining in its strength. And when I saw Him, I fell at His feet as dead. But He laid His right hand on me, saying to me, 'Do not be afraid; I am the First and the Last. I am He who lives, and was dead, and behold, I am alive forevermore. Amen. And I have the keys of Hades and of Death.'"

- Revelation 1:12-18

The same being who claimed to be God when talking to Daniel is the same one who spoke with John. He commanded them both to write of the circumstances surrounding the Battle of Armageddon. The vision of the glorified Christ, being shared by both men who wrote of the end times is written so that the reader will understand who is actually writing of these events through these men. They did the physical writing, but Lord Jesus Christ is the author. That makes the record infallible; as is the rest of the *Bible*. They wrote that Christ appeared to them in order to show future readers that they did not dream this up. They could have kept the visions to themselves, but they did not.

John wrote, at Christ's command, in Revelation chapter twelve, of a supernatural battle that will take place in heaven between Michael and the holy angels and Lucifer/Satan and the evil angels. Satan will lose, and then after being cast into the earth with his angels, he will expedite the rise of the Anti-Christ. This is the second time this battle has occurred. The evidence to that fact is where it calls Satan the accuser of the brethren/Christians. He was not accusing Christians the first time he rebelled, because they didn't exist. John wrote:

"And war broke out in heaven: Michael and his angels fought with the dragon; and the dragon and his angels fought, but they did not prevail, nor was a place found for them in heaven any longer. So the great dragon was cast out, that serpent of old, called the Devil and Satan, who deceives the whole world; he was cast to the earth, and his angels were cast out with him.

"Then I heard a loud voice saying in heaven, 'Now salvation, and strength, and the kingdom of our God, and the power of his Christ have come, for the accuser of our brethren, who accused them before our God day and night, has been cast down. And they overcame him by the blood of the Lamb and by the word of their testimony, and they did not love their lives to the death. Therefore rejoice, O heavens, and you who dwell in them! Woe to the inhabitants of the earth and the sea! For the Devil has come down to you, having great wrath, because he knows that he has a short time.'" - Revelation 12:7-12

Satan, having been defeated in a second sedition attempt, with his evil angel army, has been thrown down to the earth in great anger because he knows his defeat on earth as well is imminent. His representative, his spiritual son, the

Anti-Christ, will now be allowed by God to rule the earth, deceiving those who want to worship him, but there will be those who will not. Those who worship the Beast will be recognized by the mark that they will have placed on their forehead or hand. This will allow them access to buying or selling; probably on the world wide web - internet. It will allow monies to be withdrawn in computerized fashion from one's bank account when one buys an item; and it will deposit money in one's account when one sells something. Those who refuse to accept the mark will be put to death by the order of the Beast himself. John wrote of his rise to power, noting that Satan, as the dragon, is the one who will empower that rise:

"Then I stood on the sand of the sea. And I saw a beast rising up out of the sea, having seven heads and then horns, and on his horns ten crowns, and on his heads a blasphemous name. Now the beast which I saw was like a leopard, his feet were like the feet of a bear, and his mouth like the mouth of a lion. The dragon gave him his power, his throne, and great authority. And I saw one of his heads as if it had been mortally wounded, and his deadly wound was healed. And all the world marveled and followed the beast. So they worshiped the dragon who gave authority to the beast; and they worshiped the beast, saying, 'Who is like the beast? Who is able to make war with him?'

"And he was given a mouth speaking great things and blasphemies, and he was given authority to continue for forty-two months. Then he opened his mouth in blasphemy against God, to blaspheme His name, His tabernacle, and those who dwell in heaven. It was granted to him to make war with the saints and to overcome them. And authority was given him over every tribe, tongue, and nation. All who dwell on the earth will worship him, whose names have not been written in the Book of Life of the Lamb slain from the foundation of the world.

"If anyone has an ear, let him hear. He who leads into captivity shall go into captivity; he who kills with the sword must be killed with the sword. Here is the patience and the faith of the saints." - Revelation 13:1-10, 16-18

The next chapter of Revelation records a warning to worship God; it also makes it clear that anyone taking the mark of the Beast would be damned forever by Lord Jesus Christ, who is called "the Lamb" in the passage:

"Then I saw another angel flying in the midst of heaven, having the everlasting gospel to preach to those who dwell on the earth – to every nation, tribe, tongue, and people – saying with a loud voice, 'Fear God and give glory to Him, for the hour of His judgment has come; and worship Him who made heaven and earth, the sea and springs of water.'

"And another angel followed, saying, 'Babylon is fallen, is fallen, that great city, because she has made all nations drink of the wine of the wrath of her fornication.'

"Then a third angel followed them, saying with a loud voice, 'If anyone worships the beast and his image, and receives his mark on his forehead or on his hand, he himself shall also drink of the wine of the wrath of God, which is poured out full strength into the cup of His indignation. He shall be tormented with fire and brimstone in the presence of the holy angels and in the presence of the Lamb. And the smoke of their torment ascends forever and ever; and they have no rest day or night, who worship the beast and his image, and whoever receives the mark of his name." - Revelation 14:6-11

GATHERING FOR THE BATTLE OF ARMAGEDDON

Among the people who will accept the mark of the Beast are those "kings of the earth" that will worship him and support everything he does. Previously in this chapter, the kings in question were part of the quote from the sixteenth chapter of Revelation. The pertinent portion of that chapter, Revelation 16:12-14, 16, reads:

"Then the six angel poured out his bowl on the great river Euphrates, and its water was dried up, so that the way of the kings from the east might be prepared. And I saw three unclean spirits like frogs coming out of the mouth of the dragon, out of the mouth of the beast, and out of the mouth of the false prophet. For they are spirits of demons, performing signs, which go out to the kings of the earth and of the whole world, to gather them to the battle of that great day of God Almighty....And they gathered them together to the place called in Hebrew, Armageddon."

In that passage, you read of the kings of the east, as well as the kings of the whole earth. The reason reference was made to the kings of the east first, is because they will come with a 200 million man army (Revelation 9:16). To the east of Israel, the only nation capable of coming with an army that size is China, or a union of Oriental nations. As you read, the beings responsible for gathering these kings together for battle against Christ are evil spirits; subservient to Satan. Revelation 17:13-14 speaks of the kings' loyalty to the Beast: "These are of one mind, and they will give their power and authority to the beast. These will make war with the Lamb, and the Lamb will overcome them, for He is Lord of lords and King of kings; and those who are with Him are called, chosen, and faithful."

Dr. David Jeremiah commented on this gathering for battle as well: "The armies of all nations will be gathered in Israel, particularly around Jerusalem-200 million Orientals, along with troops from the Revived Roman Empire, headed by the Anti-Christ. The Beast will be joined by the false prophet and all the world military leaders as Goliath-like forces descend upon the Holy Land with every piece of sophisticated weaponry man has designed. The Normandy landing of the Allied forces in World War II was a skirmish compared to this last battle."8

THE BATTLE OF ARMAGEDDON/BATTLE OF EVERMORE

The Battle of Armageddon is going to take place in the valley of Meggido, as a result of the nation of Israel's refusal to worship the Anti-Christ. The Beast will claim to be god, because he is in league with Satan, who will claim to be god, and then tell the Beast that he is his son; making him the "son of god." He is the human incarnation of the son in the teachings of the Qabalah, possessed by Satan. Just as the Beast gathers his armies, and heads out to war against Israel, Jerusalem in particular, the Lord Jesus Christ will descend from Heaven with his chosen to destroy them. Their blood will flow as high as the horse's bridles for a distance of approximately 200 miles. Obviously, Led Zeppelin believes the outcome to be antithetical; that Christ will be destroyed, not the Beast. The *Holy Bible's* version of the events will be presented first. Then the foundation of Led Zeppelin's perception of these events will be looked at from Aleister Crowley's *Equinox.* Afterward, the comparison/contrast of the events will be examined; to show that Led Zeppelin believes the Beast will win over Christ by the power of Satan.

King David, in Psalm 110:5-6, predicted the Lord waging war against all the nations and destroying them at the Battle of Armageddon: "The Lord is at Your right hand; He shall execute kings in the day of His wrath. He shall judge among the nations, He shall fill the places with dead bodies, He shall execute the heads of many countries."

Dr. Jeremiah wrote of the result of the battle for those who are on the side of the Anti-Christ, quoting the Prophet Zechariah: "The armies of the world who attack Jerusalem may never know what hit them. The prophet Zechariah said: 'This is the plague with which the Lord will strike all the nations that fought against Jerusalem: Their flesh will rot while they are still standing on their feet, their eyes will rot in their sockets, and their tongues will rot in their mouths (Zechariah 14:12)."9

As one can very well surmise from the number of both Old and New Testament prophecies pertinent to the Battle of Armageddon, the *Holy Bible* speaks of this day of battle over and over again. It is not an isolated passage in the scripture that refers to it; the *Bible* as a whole does. In the 1994, Page/Plant video, *No Quarter,* during the song, "Nobody's Fault But Mine," Robert Plant sings, on the side of a mountain, "I have a Bible in my home" (These lyrics are not in the 1976 version of the song). Led Zeppelin, as well as Page/Plant, was not ignorant of these events. The pertinent passage from Revelation 19:11-21, describes the events, as written by John; at the command of the Lord Jesus Christ:

"Now I saw heaven opened, and behold, a white horse. And He who sat on him was called Faithful and True, and in righteousness He judges and makes war. His eyes were like a flame of fire, and on His head were many crowns. He had a name written that no one knew except Himself. He was clothed with a robe dipped in blood, and His name is called The Word of God. And the armies in heaven, clothed in fine linen, white and clean, followed Him on white horses. Now out of His mouth goes a sharp sword, that with it He should strike the nations. And He Himself will rule them with a rod of iron. He Himself treads the winepress of the fierceness and wrath of Almighty God. And He has on His robe and on His thigh a name written:

KING OF KINGS AND LORD OF LORDS

"Then I saw an angel standing in the sun; and he cried with a loud voice, saying to all the birds that fly in the midst of heaven, 'Come and gather together for the supper of the great God, that you may eat the flesh of kings, the flesh of captains, the flesh of mighty men, the flesh of horses and of those who sit on them, and the flesh of all people, free and slave, both small and great.'

"And I saw the beast, the kings of the earth, and their armies, gathered together to make war against Him who sat on the horse and against His army. Then the beast was captured, and with him the false prophet who worked signs in his presence, by which he deceived those who received the mark of the beast and those who worshiped his image. These two were cast alive into the lake of fire burning with brimstone. And the rest were killed with the sword which proceeded from the mouth of Him who sat on the horse. And all the birds were filled with their flesh."

Jesus descends from heaven and destroys the Beast's army and throws him into the lake of fire. The *Bible* speaks over and over of "the" lake of fire, not "a" lake of fire. It is the lake of fire and burning sulphur. Sulphur is brimstone. Since the *Bible* addresses it as "the" lake of fire, I personally believe he is speaking of the sun. You will see this again later, when you read of the Devil himself being thrown there.

ALEISTER CROWLEY AND THE BATTLE OF ARMAGEDDON

Aleister Crowley, known as the most powerful satanist to walk the earth, (before Jimmy Page that is) presents a very different view of who is god and who will win the Battle of Armageddon. In his writings, Crowley attributed the Biblical passages that pertain to Christ as indicative of Satan. Therefore, he believed the eternal "word" concept of scripture that applies to Christ to be speaking of Satan. Crowley presents the battle, with Christ gathering his armies around the holy city, and Christ and his armies being defeated. You are about to read his account in *The Equinox, Vol. I, No.5,* where he records words that Jesus is supposed to be saying. As you read earlier in the book, the Aeon of Horus

(Satan) began in 1904, when Crowley received *The Book of the Law* from the Devil in Cairo, Egypt; right after seeing the Stele of Ankh-f-n-khonsu in a museum. This transition of Aeons, (or periods of worshiping the Lord of the respective time frame) from the Aeon of Jesus to the Aeon of Horus, Crowley called *The Equinox of the Gods*. Again, each Aeon lasts two thousand years, according to Crowley and Satan. He wrote: "The death of the past Aeon, that of Jehovah and Jesus; ends with the adumbration of the new, the vision of the Stele of Ankh-f-n-khonsu, whose discovery brought about in a human consciousness the knowledge of the Equinox of the Gods."10 Crowley called the new Aeon the Aeon of Horus at the Equinox of the Gods: "...the coming of the new Aeon, the Aeon of Horus the crowned child....All leads up to the Crowned Child, Horus, the Lord of the New Aeon."11

The old Aeon had in it the worship of Jesus, whereas the new is that of Horus, who has been identified as Satan in the writings of Crowley (see chapters 7&8). The following is Crowley's writing of Jesus' narration of his "defeat" at the Battle of Armageddon; followed by adoration by Jesus for the Beast. In the text, he wrote of the Beast having a great throne. This concept is presented in the New Testament Book of 2 Thessalonians, Chapter 1, Verse 4: "He will oppose and will exalt himself over everything that is called God or is worshiped, so that he sets himself up in God's temple, proclaiming himself to be God." (NIV) Crowley also wrote of the Beast releasing "a flood of fire." Subsequent to that, he wrote of Jesus, which will include his people, and Israel, being devoured by flames. This concept is very much in line with what Robert Plant sang at 1:51 into the song "Most High," from the 1998 *Walking Into Clarksdale* album; an "olive tree" being "consumed" in "fire." In the *Holy Bible's* New Testament Book of Romans, Chapter 11, Paul the Apostle wrote to the non-Jewish believers that may have been joined together by God with the Jewish believers, making them one. He was warning them not to be arrogant about the fact that Jesus saved them, if they were truly saved, when there are many Jewish people who he did not save. He described the Nation of Israel as an olive tree in the text:

"If some of the branches have been broken off, and you, through a wild olive shoot, have been grafted in among the others and now share in the nourishing sap from the olive root, do not boast over those branches. If you do, consider this: You do not support the root, but the root supports you. You will say then, 'Branches were broken off so that I could be grafted in.' Granted. But they were broken off because of unbelief, and you stand by faith. Do not be arrogant, but be afraid. For if God did not spare the natural branches, he will not spare you either. Consider therefore the kindness and sternness of God: sternness to those who fell, but kindness to you, provided that you continue in his kindness. Otherwise, you also will be cut off. And if they do not persist in unbelief, they will be grafted in, for God is able to graft them in again. After all, if you were cut out of an olive tree that is wild by nature, and contrary to nature were grafted into a cultivated olive tree, how much more readily will these, the natural branches, be grafted into their own olive tree!" (NIV)

Crowley's presentation of the Battle of Armageddon begins with him describing Jesus' appearance "in the gloom." One very crucial point for the reader to understand and remember for future reference in this chapter, is Crowley's identification of Christ with the word "gloom":

"Now at last he appears in the gloom. He is a mighty King, with crown and orb and scepter, and his robes are of purple and gold. And he casts down the orb and scepter to the earth, and he tears off his crown, and throws it on the ground, and tramples it. And he tears out his hair, that is of ruddy gold tinged with silver, and he plucks at his beard, and cries with a terrible voice: 'Woe unto me that am cast down from my place by the might of the new Aeon. For the ten palaces are broken, and the ten kings are carried away into bondage, and they are set to fight as the gladiators in the circus of him that hath laid his hand upon eleven. For the ancient tower is shattered by the Lord of the Flame and the Lightning. And they that walk upon their hands shall build the holy place. Blessed are they who have turned the Eye of Hoor unto the zenith, for they shall be filled with the vigor of the goat.

"All that was ordered and stable is shaken. The Aeon of Wonders is come. Like locusts shall they gather themselves together, the servants of the Star and of the Snake, and they shall eat up everything that is upon the earth. For why? Because the Lord of Righteousness delighteth in them.

"The prophets shall prophesy monstrous things, and the wizards shall perform monstrous things. The sorceress shall be desired of all men, and the enchanter shall rule the earth.

"Blessing unto the name of the Beast, for he hath let loose a mighty flood of fire from his manhood, and from his womanhood hath he let loose a mighty flood of water. Every thought of his mind is as a tempest that uprooteth the great trees of the earth, and shaketh the mountains thereof. And the throne of his spirit is a mighty throne of madness and desolation, so that they that look upon it shall cry: Behold the abomination!

"Of a single ruby shall that throne be built, and it shall be set upon an high mountain, and men shall see it afar off. Then will I gather together my chariots and my horsemen and my ships of war. By sea and land shall my armies and my navies encompass it, and I will encamp round about it, and besiege it, and by the flame thereof shall I be utterly devoured. Many lying spirits have I sent into the world that my Aeon might be established, and they shall all be overthrown.

"Great is the Beast that cometh forth like a lion, the servant of the Star and of the Snake. He is the Eternal one; He is the Almighty one. Blessed are they upon whom he shall look with favour, for nothing shall stand before his face.

Accursed are they upon whom he shall look with derision, for nothing shall stand before his face.

"And every mystery that hath not been revealed from the foundation of the world he shall reveal unto his chosen. And they shall have power over every spirit of the Ether; and of the earth and under the earth; on dry land and in the water; of whirling air and of rushing fire. And they shall have power over all the inhabitants of the earth, and every scourge of God shall be subdued beneath their feet. The angels shall come unto them and walk with them, and the great gods of heaven shall be their guests.

"But I must sit apart, with dust upon my head, discrowned and desolate. I must lurk in forbidden corners of the earth. I must plot secretly in the by-ways of great cities, in the fog, and in marshes of the rivers of pestilence. All my cunning shall not serve me. And all my undertakings shall be brought to naught. And the ministers of the Beast shall catch me and tear out my tongue with pincers of red-hot iron, and they shall brand my forehead with the word of derision, and they shall shave my head, and pluck out my beard, and make a show of me.

"And the spirit of prophecy shall come upon me despite me ever and anon, as even now upon my heart and upon my throat; and upon my tongue seared with strong acid are the words: *Vim patior.* For so must I give glory to him that hath supplanted me, that hath cast me down into the dust. I have hated him, and with hate my bones are rotten. I would have spat upon him, and my spittle hath befouled my beard. I have taken up the sword against him, and I am fallen upon it, and mine entrails are about my feet.

"Who shall strive with his might? Hath he not the sword and the spear of the Warrior Lord of the Sun? Who shall contend with him? Who shall lift himself up against him? For the latchet of his sandal is more than the helmet of the Most High. Who shall reach up to him in supplication, save those that he shall set upon his shoulders? Would God that my tongue were torn out by the roots, and my throat cut across, and my heart torn out and given to the vultures, before I say this that I must say: Blessing and Worship to the Prophet of the Lovely Star! (End of "Jesus'" speech)

"And now he is fallen quite to the ground, in a heap, and dust is upon his head; and the throne upon which he sat is shattered into many pieces.

"And dimly dawning in this unutterable gloom, far, far above, is the face that is the face of a man and of a woman, and upon the brow is a circle, and upon the breast is a circle, and in the palm of the right hand is a circle. Gigantic is his stature, and he hath the Uraeus crown, and the leopard's skin, and the flaming orange apron of a god. And invisibly about him is Nuit, and in his heart is Hadit, and between his feet is the great god Ra Hoor Khuit. And in his right hand is a flaming wand, and in his left a book. Yet is he silent; and that which is understood between him and me shall not be revealed in this place. And the mystery shall be revealed to whosoever shall say, with ecstasy of worship in his heart, with a clear mind, and a passionate body: It is the voice of a god, and not of a man.

"And now all that glory hath withdrawn itself; and the old King lies prostate, abject."12

As you read previously, Hadit and Ra Hoor Khuit are Satan, and Nuit is his consort. Crowley ends the passage in appropriate fashion, giving praise to Satan, his god. That whole passage, again, is taken from a writing called *The Vision and the Voice*, from Crowley's *Equinox*, where he recorded the vision of these events as he received them from Satan in a trance. Crowleyite and Satanist Jimmy Page, therefore, holds to the same perspective; that Jesus will lose this battle.

In the beginning of the song, "The Battle of Evermore," Robert Plant sings that the goddess in the Qabalah, their "Queen" who displays "light," grabbed the "bow" she has and headed out to battle (This is the same goddess, I believe, who was glorified by Page/Plant in the introduction to each concert they played on the 1995 North American Tour - The Tales of Bron - which I have many clear examples of.). Crowley wrote of her and her bow, again, in his *Book of Thoth*: "...Isis the Eternal Virgin, the Artemis of the Greeks. She is clothed only in the luminous veil of light....Thus she is light and the body of light. She is the truth behind the veil of light. She is the soul of light. Upon her knees is the bow of Artemis, which is also a musical instrument, for she is huntress, and hunts by enchantment.13 This queen, and her daughter, her people, Satan's bride, have a mutual enemy. That enemy is Jesus. The very next line in the song presents another name for Christ when Plant sings of him who is "Prince of Peace," at 0:40 into the song. He says that this "Prince of Peace" took hold of his "gloom," to head out into the evening "alone." Lord Jesus Christ is the Prince of Peace. In the Old Testament, the Prophet Isaiah prophesied of the birth of Christ in Chapter 9, Verse 6: "For unto us a Child is born, unto us a Son is given; and the government will be upon His shoulder. And His name will be called Wonderful, Counselor, Mighty God, Everlasting Father, Prince of Peace."

Aleister Crowley called Christianity the gloom. The *Bible* says that Christ is the Prince of Peace. Therefore, Robert Plant speaks of the goddess going to battle with Christ, I believe, in the opening lines of "The Battle of Evermore." At 0:53 into the song, Plant sings that their "Lord" of darkness is riding with "force"; also, that "time" is going to "tell" them "all." This all refers, I believe, to Revelation, Chapter 19, Verses 17-19:

"Then I saw an angel standing in the sun; and he cried with a loud voice, saying to all the birds that fly in the midst of heaven, 'Come and gather together for the supper of the great God, that you may eat the flesh of kings, the flesh of captains, the flesh of mighty men, the flesh of horses and of those who sit on them, and the flesh of all people, free and slave, both small and great.'

"And I saw the beast, the kings of the earth, and their armies, gathered together to make war against Him who sat on the horse and against His army."

Robert Plant sings that the beast "rides" with "force." He is riding on a horse with his forces behind him. Both the Beast and Jesus will be on horses. The birds will eat the flesh of the Beast's armies' horses, not Christ's.

At 1:07, Plant sings that the observers are standing next to one another as they "wait" on his "might;" him who is "darkest" amongst "all." This refers to Satan, as you will see.

At 1:27, he sings that he is able to "hear" many "horses" making loud noise "down" below on that "valley" beneath him. It is the valley of Megiddo.

At 1:33, Plant sings he is "waiting" on the arrival of "angels" from "Avalon," as well as the "glow" from the east. These "angels" he is "waiting" on are the evil angels, loyal to Satan, that Crowley wrote of in the "Jesus" quote. Here we see the beginning of Robert Plant's analogous use of the Arthur legend to describe the events of the battle between Satan, the Beast, and Lord Jesus Christ. Plant sings that they are coming from "Avalon." Avalon is the place where King Arthur is half dead/half alive, waiting to rise again. As you will see, in the context of Robert Plant's usage, Arthur is Satan. D.J. Conway, in her book, *Celtic Magic*, gave us a brief description of Avalon: "AVALON: 'Apple-isle;' Celtic paradise across the sea where the gods and heroes were fed on apples of immortality."14 This Avalon is the same as the Scandinavian "Valhalla" that Robert Plant sings he is headed for in the beginning of "Immigrant Song." It is the Devil's paradise; but it is also fictitious.

Plant is singing that he is waiting on the arrival of these angels from Avalon for a reason. It is redemption. The angels are going to come and fight in the battle, assisting the beast and Satan, and when the battle is over, they are going to take Satan's people to Avalon/heaven. In the song, "Kashmir," off the *Physical Graffiti* album, [Jimmy Page wrote] of his astral projection practice, I believe, in the beginning of the song. At 0:27, Plant sings that he travels through "time" as well as "space." In these travels, he sings at 0:36, that he can "sit" among "elders" belonging to the "gentle" breed, and that their "world" has rarely been "seen." At 0:45, he sings that they "talk" about "days" that "they" all "wait" on, the time that "all" are going to get "redeemed." This redemption after the Battle of Armageddon by Satan's angels is clearly spoken of, I believe, by Robert Plant on the same album, in a song called "In My Time of Dying." It takes a real hard core Zeppelin fan to elucidate the meaning of this song. Time and again people have told me that it is just a song of Robert Plant's expression of love for Jesus as he sends his angels to take Plant to heaven. That assertion is as far from the truth as one can get. Robert Plant, in this song, is mocking Jesus Christ to his face (Just as he did in the 1998 song "Most High."). At 1:07 into "In My Time of Dying," Plant sings that he doesn't "want" anyone "to" grieve over his death, but that he wants his corpse to be taken "home" so he can have an "easy" time passing away. At 2:10, he says that it is "Jesus" who will "make" him die. While this is true, Plant does not believe it (The *Bible* teaches in the New Testament Book of Hebrews Chapter 9, Verse 27: "And as it is appointed for men to die once, but after this the judgment..."). It is just another smoke screen for messages later in the song; relative to the redemption of Satan's people. At 2:38, he asks "Jesus" to "meet" him at "the" center "of" our "air." The *Bible* teaches that Christ will meet his chosen in the air when he comes to redeem them. Again, Plant is mocking Christ and the *Bible* here. Then, at 2:49, Plant audaciously tells Jesus, "If" his "wings" were to "fail" him, and he calls him "Lord," then he wants Christ to "meet" him "with" a second "pair." (Take a good look at the cover of the 1998 Page/Plant album, *Walking Into Clarksdale*.) At the 4:02 point, Plant is yelling at Peter at the gates of heaven, demanding he allow him to enter because he has never done anyone any harm or wrong. At 4:21, he asks the Archangel Gabriel to allow him to "blow" his "horn" for him. This is another event that will take place when Christ comes for his people. Gabriel will sound his horn. Paul the Apostle, in the New Testament Book of I Thessalonians 4:16-17, gives us the description of the events; writing to Christians: "For the Lord Himself will descend from heaven with a shout, with the voice of an archangel, and with the trumpet of God. And the dead in Christ will rise first. Then we who are alive and remain shall be caught up together with them in the clouds to meet the Lord in the air. And thus we shall always be with the Lord." Right after this Plant tells Gabriel that he has done no harm, repeatedly. At 8:04, Plant sings that he can "hear" Satan's evil angelic warriors "marching." He shouts the word "marching" five times. Where are we supposed to believe these angels are marching? And why does he use the word marching? Soldiers are the only ones who march. These angels are marching through the sky to the Battle of Armageddon/Battle of Evermore; as will be seen shortly. Again, that is what he said he was waiting for in "The Battle of Evermore."

Beginning at 8:20, Plant begins to chant a "mantra," or "word of power," which was designed and presented by Aleister Crowley in his *Magick in Theory and Practice*. This word is "AUMGN." If you look at lyrics on the internet, people have "Oh My Jesus" listed in this section. That IS NOT what Plant is singing. He is singing "AUMGN." In her book, *The Encyclopedia of Witches and Witchcraft*, Rosemary Ellen Guiley explains what Crowley created the word for: "ALEISTER CROWLEY created AUMGN as an ultimate word of power, which he believed was a mantra of such force that a magician chanting it would be able to control the universe. AUMGN is an expansion of the Buddhist mantra Om, which represents God and the Supreme Reality, the sum total of everything in all creation."15

While Aleister Crowley wrote that he would pronounce the word with the "G" being silent, it makes perfect sense that Plant would pronounce the G so that future followers would know exactly what he was saying when he chanted *AUMGN* over and over between 8:20 and 9:08 of the song. Crowley wrote that his student should use this word: "...to arm him with a mantra of terrific power by virtue whereof he may apprehend the Universe, and control in himself its *karmic* consequences."16 Plant is using this Magick word, in my opinion, to accelerate the victory in the battle as well as his redemption. I make that assertion because of the timing of its use. He uses it as a pivoting point between the angels marching off to the battle and his redemption; which we will now examine (This is the redemption of Malkuth in the Qabalah.).

At 9:08 of the song, Plant shouts that he wants the angels to "take" him "home." At 9:17 & 9:19, he shouts "C'mon!" He is shouting at the angels, telling them to hurry up. The next thing he sings, at 9:21, is that he is able to "hear" them "singing." At 9:26 & 9:29, Robert Plant says that the angels are on their way, as he sings, "Here" the angels "come." Between 9:35 & 9:44, Plant yells "Bye!" five times. Finally, at 9:48 & 9:52, Plant sings that it "feels" really "good" above in heaven. This obviously means that his redemption has been made complete. This again is why he is "waiting" on these "angels" from "Avalon," in "The Battle of Evermore." I believe that Led Zeppelin believes the angels will redeem Satan's people after he defeats Christ at the Battle of Armageddon; which is why Plant, after singing about Avalon's angels, sings he is "waiting" on the "glow" from the east. This is none other than the sunrise, or the power of Satan in light, because he is the sun, according to Crowley, and Satan is going to use the light and flames of the sun to blind Christ so he cannot fight (I believe this is a lie fostered in the mind of the Devil himself and expressed by Led Zeppelin). If you are blinded on the battlefield; you are doomed. Once blinded by that light and flame, Christ will be devoured by it, according to Crowley; as you read previously. This blinding will be addressed at the end of the song.

Back to "The Battle of Evermore," Robert Plant sings at 1:46, that "ground" being "rich" as a result of special "care," demands that the people show gratitude to those who did the caring; with a warning that if they "forget" it is not acceptable. It is an axiom in the occult that the god is a god of fertility, and his female consort is a goddess of fertility. In other words, the gods are responsible for the ground being fertile. Dr. Sir J. G. Frazer, in *The Golden Bough*, described the Druids' method of repayment: "...the Druids believed that the more persons they sentenced to death, the greater would be the fertility of the land."17

Robert Plant advocates the book, *Magic Arts in Celtic Britain*, and that book teaches that the Druids used to sacrifice human beings to the gods in the wicker man. I don't know if Robert Plant advocates this. I have seen no evidence of that. I yield the benefit of the doubt to him. However, he does love Satan, and he advocates many other things that the Druids do. For instance, the word Druid means "Oak," and amongst the Druids the Oak tree is considered godhead among

among the trees. As you read in the last chapter, the Druids did their thing in the forest; as Page and Plant showed in the beginning of their 1994 video, that they liked to meet in the forest. Are we supposed to believe that the forest is simply a convenient place to record? I know my readers are smarter than that.

Sandy Denny, singing backup vocals at 2:07 into "The Battle of Evermore," sings that "war" will be the "cry" among those angels on their way to the battle. Then she sings a command to grab "up" their "swords" to then "fly" with them. She is commanding the angels to grab swords and head with them to the battle. It has to be angels, because people cannot fly. Robert Plant, lying about what Sandy Denny is saying, was quoted in *Led Zeppelin – The Definitive Biography*: "Sandy was playing the role of the town crier, urging the people to throw down their weapons."18 That statement by Robert Plant is simply not true. Again, she is giving a command to grab swords and then fly with them to the battle. Ask anyone who knows Led Zeppelin's music. Plus, you can get the lyrics off the internet if you want to analyze them for yourself. Additionally, in the lyrics immediately subsequent to Denny's lyrics, at 2:12, Robert Plant sings of our "sky" being "filled" by "good" as well as "bad" mere humans cannot ever "know." Again, he is speaking of the angels, who are spirits. Here it is, once more, from *The Book of the Sacred Magic of Abramelin the Mage*: "...it will instead be found that by the permission of the Great God it is the Spirits who govern the firmament."19 The notorious Dr. Faust was blatant enough to say these spirits are in league with Satan: "He who wishes to practice my art, let him love the spirits of hell and those who reign in the air; for these alone are they who can make us happy in this life; and he who would have wisdom must seek it from the devil."20

At 2:33, Plant sings of that "night" being "long" in duration, as "beads" representing "time" move "slow." Then he sings that he is focusing his exhausted "eyes" toward the east, waiting for an inevitable "sunrise."

At 2:45, he sings that "pain" from this "war" is unable to "exceed" its "woe" during the "aftermath." This is talking about the deaths that will take place; described in Revelation. The *Bible* describes this woe as a "winepress" in Revelation 14:20, making it clear that the enemies of Christ will be trampled under foot just as the prophecy of Psalm 91 predicted: "And the winepress was trampled outside the city, and blood came out of the winepress, up to the horses' bridles, for one thousand six hundred furlongs" (Approximately 200 miles).

At 3:00, Sandy Denny is singing again. She sings that the participants in the battle should "sing" while they "raise" their "bow," and they should fire their arrows "straighter" at this point, as opposed to "before" when the battle first began. Again, she is NOT telling anyone to throw down their weapons; as Robert Plant would have the uninitiated among us believe.

At 3:39, Robert Plant sings of our "sun" finally "shining" as "clouds" he describes as "blue" move away. Crowley referred to this concept in his book, *The Law is for All*, where he wrote of the man who lives according to the Law of Thelema, the philosophy of the Silver Star:

"He cannot fail if he would; thus, his sorrows are but shadows-he could not see them if he kept his gaze fixed on his goal, the Sun."21

At 3:45, he sings of why he was waiting for the sun to rise. He sings that the "flames" produced by their "dragon" who rules the "darkness," is "sunlight" which makes it impossible for Christ to see with the "eyes" he has. It has to be Christ that they are talking about here. They have done nothing with him since mentioning him in the beginning of the song. Christ is the eternal enemy of Satan. This dragon is the Devil. The *Bible* passage calling him the dragon will be quoted briefly, and Aleister Crowley will back up my assertion that this dragon, being the sun, is Satan, the Devil. Once again, for emphasis, we look at Revelation 12:7-9: "And war broke out in heaven: Michael and his angels fought with the dragon; and the dragon and his angels fought, but they did not prevail, nor was a place found for them in heaven any longer. So the great dragon was cast out, that serpent of old, called the Devil and Satan, who deceives the whole world; he was cast to the earth, and his angels were cast out with him."

Aleister Crowley wrote of this concept of Satan as the sun more than once in *Magick-Book 4*Liber Aba*, and here is the best quote for this song: "...Satan, the Old Serpent, in the Abyss, the Lake of Fire and Sulphur, is the Sun-Father, the vibration of Life, Lord of Infinite Space that flames with His Consuming Energy..."22 Remember, a dragon is a serpent. Crowley, wanting to give praise to the Devil after an adventure of astral projection, called him Lord of the Darkness as he wrote *The Equinox*: "Then I returned within my body, giving glory unto the Lord of Light and of the Darkness."23 Crowley would quote the Devil himself in the same context of the sun, in *The Equinox*:

"Robed in the flames of my mouth, I compass the heavens, so that none shall behold me, and that the eyes of men shall be spared the torture of unutterable light. 'Devourer of Millions of Years' is my name; 'Lord of the Flame' is my name; for I am as an eye of Silver set in the heart of the Sun. Thou spreadest the locks of thine hair before thee, for I burn thee; thou shakest them about thy brow, so that thine eyes may not be blinded by the fire of my fury. I am he who was, who is, and who will be; I am the Creator, and the Destroyer, and the Redeemer of mankind. I have come as the Sun from the house of the roaring of lions, and at my coming shall there be laughter, and weeping, singing, and gnashing of teeth."24

I would encourage the reader to mark the phrase, "so that thine eyes may not be blinded by the fire of my fury." That phrase matches what Plant sang at the end of the song. That Christ would be blinded and then devoured by Satan's fire from the sun is the message that Crowley and Led Zeppelin have provided. Just to show the reader that this concept of Satan as the sun is not exclusive to Crowley and Led Zeppelin, here is a quote from Richard Cavendish's *The Black Arts*, that shows this concept to be an axiom in the occult world: "There are traces, in modern times, of a tradition among witches that Lucifer, 'the light-bearer', was the sun, an identification which could easily be made when the Devil was regarded as the ruler of life on earth."25 One can see Led Zeppelin glorifying the Sun in the photo at the end of this chapter. There are traces of this concept of Satan as the sun being promoted in the movies. Approximately 30 years ago, *The Exorcist* came out. This movie begins with the camera focused directly on the sun. Early in the film, right after the Exorcist has a stare down with a statue of the Devil, the film returns back to focusing on the sun; then the scene changes to Georgetown. The contemporary film, *The Devil's Advocate*, starring Al Pacino as the Devil, begins with the said title's words shooting right out of the sun. The people making these movies have a good knowledge of the occult.

So, in the minds of Aleister Crowley, Led Zeppelin, as well as other witches, Satan is Lord of Light and Darkness. Led Zeppelin presents Satan as winning the Battle of Armageddon by blinding Lord Jesus Christ on the battlefield and consuming him with the flames; just like Crowley. Right after this, the sorrow of Satan's people, that results from their longing to be united with those who have gone on before, is removed by their being raptured by the angels at Satan's command. Again, this is why, I believe, Plant is singing that heaven "feels" real "good" at the end of "In My Time of Dying," because Satan has redeemed his bride; Malkuth in the Qabalah. For an analogous visual of these events, we turn to the Led Zeppelin film, *The Song Remains the Same*, where Robert Plant gives us an illustration of the opposition of Satan and Christ, using the Arthur legend.

LED ZEPPELIN AND THE ARTHUR LEGEND ANALOGY

Led Zeppelin uses the Arthur Legend as an illustration or direct parallel for the future student of Magick and Aleister Crowley to perceive as the Battle of Armageddon; once they are fully cognizant of what message they were sending in "The Battle of Evermore." In the Led Zeppelin film, Robert Plant's fantasy sequence is where the Arthur analogy is presented. It begins with the song, "The Song Remains the Same" and ends with "The Rain Song." Dave Lewis wrote of this in his book, *The Complete Guide to the Music of Led Zeppelin*, where he refers to the song, "The Song Remains the Same": "In the film, it accompanies Plant's Arthurian fantasy sequence..."26 Robert Plant would be quoted by Steven Davis in *Hammer of the Gods* as saying that the band itself was a force of Arthur: "He would talk about his concept of Led Zeppelin as an

Arthurian force of goodness and Celtic lore and of his various supernatural in-spirations. He often remarked that he could feel his pen being pushed by some higher authority."27

As the reader will see, Arthur, in the occult context, is another name for Satan, the Devil. As the fantasy sequence begins in the film, it is at the point during "The Song Remains the Same" when Robert Plant talks about his dream. Right then the fantasy sequence starts off with the sun shining bright through the Welsh flag, that has a big red dragon on it (no big surprise for this author). The sunlight is piercing the flag and the dragon. No need to elaborate here; it is indicative of the Devil. In *Magic Arts in Celtic Britain*, Plant's Celtic magic book of choice, Lewis Spence wrote of Arthur and the sun: "In one ancient Welsh poem, adds Herbert, Arthur is described as a 'swiftly moving lamp,' and as the sun, these terms revealing his godhead significantly enough."28 Spence also wrote that those in the "Arthur cult" must be reborn spiritually, and En-gland through them: "For not only had each member of the Arthur cult to be reborn spiritually, but Britain, their country, must also be reborn through them."29 Lewis Spence also wrote of Arthur and inspiration in song! He wrote: "From the first we find Arthur a spiritual influence, exalted and courageous. The cauldron, for which he quests, is both a fertility vessel and one which yields inspiration in song."30 Spence went on to equate the Egyptian Horus with Arthur, also mak-ing reference to Horus as the hawk: "The myth of Horus, the son of Osiris, otherwise Osiris resurrected, strongly resembles that of Arthur. Both attract to themselves a large company of warriors devoted to the destruction of evil mon-sters. And Horus took the shape of a hawk, as did Arthur that of a raven or crow."31

During the rest of the ocean scene, in "The Song Remains the Same," Robert Plant is making reference to the Devil in the form of the Celtic god "Manannan." Spence wrote of him also in *Magic Arts in Celtic Britain*: "Manannan, or Manawyddan, is the Celtic god of the sea..."32 Spence gave us a description of Manannan; pertinent to the film: "Manannan MacLir, the Irish sea-god, is said to have been a Druid, one Manannan Mac Oirbsen, who rose to a position of godhead. He could 'transform himself into many shapes by wiz-ardry.' He traveled in his magic boat made of copper, the 'Wave-sweeper,' which needed neither oar nor rudder. He was the possessor of a famous magical mantle, which, if shaken between two persons, made it impossible for them to meet again."33 I believe Robert Plant is simply equating Manannan with Arthur here; that they are both god; who he believes is Satan. Plant is standing on the bow of the ship, which appears to have no rudder or oar while he is riding through the sea. He also is wearing a long mantle that he wraps around himself while on the bow.

After Robert Plant dismounts from the boat and walks ashore, the next thing we see him doing as "King Arthur," is walking to the "Lady of the Lake" who, in this legend, gives him the sword "Excalibur." For a detailed account of these events, see the film of the same name. In the book, *Witchcraft, Magic & Occultism*, W.B. Crow wrote of this sword: "By means of Merlin's magic Arthur obtained a wonderful sword Excalibur or Caliburn from the Lady of the Lake, an enchantress who had a wonderful palace beneath the waters of a deep lake."34

Shortly after receiving the sword Excalibur, we see Robert Plant walking through the forest with a bough in his hand. He sits down under a large Oak tree and begins to eat the hallucinogenic mushroom, Amanita Muscaria, while he looks up at the Oak. You can see that one of the branches is broken off. It appears that the bough he is carrying has come from this Oak tree. The bough is magical. Lewis Spence wrote of this magical bough, carried by Manannan:

"In the occult lore of old Ireland we learn of the existence of a marvelous silver branch or bough, by virtue of which the gods lured favoured mortals to their joyous country. In some accounts of Celtic magical arts this important arcane device is frequently ignored or only partially described, and as it was the especial property of the god Manannan, who is so intimately associated with Druidic art, it appears essential to make good this deficiency and to provide a reasonably full description of it in these pages. This bough was, in effect, a link with the unseen world, a talisman by the aid of which certain mortals with whom the gods desired to establish communion and fellowship were enabled to make entrance into the overseas paradise of these divinities while yet alive.

"This bough, or branch, was cut from a mystical apple tree and gave forth a magical music which none might resist. The apples which it bore served the pilgrim for meat and drink while in the Land of the Gods and during the whole period of his sojourn therein."35

Soon after the forest scene, Robert Plant is riding a black horse. His outfit is now indicative of the Celtics; now that he is carrying a sword. D.J. Conway, in *Celtic Magic*, wrote of the outfit of Celtic men of old: "Celtic men on the continental mainland wore trousers with a tunic, but in Britain and Ireland the men wore a thigh-length tunic and a cloak, the ever present dagger or sword, and leather or fur footgear tied around the legs."36 We see him descend into a great valley while riding the horse. After briefly riding through another forest, we see him heading toward an old castle; (Raglan Castle) back to the Arthur legend. He is carrying a hawk on his left wrist. This is obviously a reference to Horus (see chapters 9 & 10). Horus is released from his wrist to attack dwellers in the castle. The next event is Plant (Arthur/Satan) participating in a sword fight with another man. As the fight takes place, Plant is singing "The Rain Song" back at Madison Square Garden. The lyrics he sings at that point tell the person or persons he fights to leave his presence. He sings, "flee" away "keepers" who keep their "gloom." He is telling the gloom's keepers to depart from him. Right after he sings the word "gloom," the image of the enemy's face is shown (Earlier in this chapter, you read where Aleister Crowley and Led Zeppelin call Christ and his faith the "gloom."). The image of the person in the film is none other than Lord Jesus Christ that the man is fitting. Robert Plant defeats him in the battle right after singing those lyrics. Ascending up the stairs in the castle, Robert Plant sings that their spiritual absolute of who god is, is "clear" in everyone's mind on occasion. Once he gets to the upper room, he sees the princess he has come to rescue. It is his bride. She has a nervous look on her face. The reason is because more enemies are coming to kill him. Sure enough, Plant sings the word "gloom" again while fighting and defeating these three men. He is singing to his woman when he says he "cursed" that "gloom" which oppressed "us." It was Christianity in England that persecuted the witches, magicians, occultists, Druids, etc. Eliphas Levi wrote of this in his book, *Transcendental Magic*: "I am aware that Christianity has for ever suppressed Ceremonial Magic, and that it proscribes the evocations and sacrifices of the old world."37

The Devil has Aleister Crowley and Led Zeppelin calling Christianity the gloom; and they hate the Jews as well, which is why the Anti-Christ will persecute Israel. Israel as well has persecuted those who practice magic. Eliphas Levi wrote: "The orthodoxy of Israel, that religion which is so rational, so divine and so ill known, condemns no less than Christianity the mysteries of Ceremonial magic."38 Once again, Aleister Crowley wrote of his hatred for both Christians and Jews, at the direction of the Devil, in his book, *The Law is For All*: "Should we not rather breed humanity for quality by killing off any tainted stock, as we do with other cattle? And exterminating the vermin which infect it, especially Jews and Protestant Christians?"39 [Hitler had to have been a student of Crowley; and has Led Zeppelin ever performed in Israel?]

One can easily see, as a result of reading this chapter, that the Devil owns the minds of the members of Led Zeppelin as he did Aleister Crowley. Their expressions are consistent with that of the Anti-Christ in the Book of Revelation of the *Holy Bible*. He will persecute the disciples of Christ as well as Israel. Obviously, Aleister Crowley hated the Jews. While there has been no direct expression of Led Zeppelin's anti-Semitism (hatred for the Jews), it can be inferred by the song, "The Battle of Evermore," where they clearly are on the side of the Beast and Satan; who hates Israel and Christ, and will attack them both at the Battle of Armageddon. Also, don't forget that they commanded the fans to sell their souls to Satan in their film, who again, hates the Jews. In the film, Robert Plant wins the battle, and as he is walking toward his bride, the flaming sword is shown. This is representative of the Qabalah. Jimmy Page has it in this part of the film to illustrate the final summation of Qabalistic teaching. On the right, as the god, is Chokmah (Plant), and on the left is Binah (his bride). Chokmah is Satan, and Binah is his consort (see chapter eight). As Plant is looking at his rescued princess, she disappears. This means that she, the daughter, Malkuth, Satan's people, in Qabalistic teaching by Crowley, has just been redeemed by the Devil from the oppression of the enemy; Christ and his Christians, just as "The Battle of Evermore" intimates. Crowley wrote of this in *Magick-Book 4*Liber Aba*. He is speaking of the adept and his Holy Guardian Angel, who is Satan. The passage is taken from *Liber Samekh*, the epistle he wrote at the Abbey of Thelema in Sicily in 1921. Again, it is a supplement to the Abramelin book for the purpose of helping the adepts of the Silver Star with their quest for union with Satan. In the passage, he writes of voice producing words. It has reference to "AUMGN" that Plant was shouting in "In My Time of Dying," while the battle is being fought, as he was waiting for his redemption as part of the daughter and bride. It is mentioned here in conjunction with the redemption of the princess; which is what happens in the film, the reason she disappears. Crowley wrote of the guardian angel, referring to him as the creator: "His Angel has made 'Voice,' the magical weapon which produces 'Words,' and these words have been the Wisdom by which He hath created all things. The 'Voice' is necessary as the link between the Adept and his Angel. The Angel is 'King,' the One who 'can,' the 'source of authority and the fount of honour'; also the King (or King's Son) who delivers the Enchanted Princess, and makes her his Queen."40 The words and parentheses "(or King's Son)" were written by Crowley. They are not my addition to the text. In Qabalah teaching, the King is born again through the Queen and becomes the Prince. As the Prince, he marries his sister, who is the Princess, and sits her on the Queen's throne, and then he becomes the King again. The Princess becomes one with the Queen, and the two unite with the King, for final absolute union. Crowley wrote of this, once again, in his book, *Book 4*:

"In one, the best, system of Magick, the Absolute is called the Crown, God is called the Father, the Pure Soul is called the Mother, the Holy Guardian Angel is called the Son, and the Natural Soul is called the Daughter. The Son purifies the Daughter by wedding her; she thus becomes the Mother, the uniting of whom with the Father absorbs all into the Crown."41

This visual redemption of the enchanted Princess takes place just as Robert Plant is singing about the division that causes sorrow, back at Madison Square Garden. He sings of a "mystery" that pertains to a "quotient." In the next line, he sings the mystery is that "upon" the bride, daughter, or Princess, some "rain" has to "fall." What he is conveying here (I believe) is that it is a mystery that there has to be division between the people of Satan on earth and those who have gone on before; as well as between Satan's people and himself and his goddess. The word "quotient" means the result or consequence of division. "Rain" spoken in this context, once again, is sorrow. As the redemption takes place, the sorrow is lifted. Crowley wrote of this, once again, in *The Equinox, Vol. III, No.1*: "Now Love is the enkindling in ecstasy of Two that will to become One. It is thus an Universal formula of High Magick. For see now how all things, being in sorrow caused by dividuality, must of necessity will Oneness as their medicine."42 This oneness, once again, is the uniting of the daughter with the mother (goddess) on her throne: Crowley wrote:

"This is that which is written, 'O my God, in one last rapture let me attain to the union with the many.' For she is Love, and her love is one, and she hath divided the one love into infinite loves, and each love is one, and equal with The One, and therefore is she passed 'from the assembly and the law and the enlightenment unto the anarchy of solitude and darkness. For ever thus must she veil the brilliance of Her Self."43

Once the division has been resolved, then the blues or sorrows pass away. Again, the band believes that this sorrow will dissipate in conjunction with the redemption of Malkuth in the Qabalah; the bride of the son, Satan.

THE TRUE OUTCOME OF THE BATTLE OF EVERMORE

After Lord Jesus Christ throws the Beast and his false prophet into the lake of fire, he sets up his eternal rule on the earth. The Devil will be cast into the Abyss to remain there for one thousand years. Jesus will rule the earth, but not all the people on the earth will worship him during this time. At the end of the thousand years, the Devil will be released from the Abyss to deceive the nations to attack Jerusalem again! This time, however, while the Beast is in the lake of fire, the nations will gather around Jerusalem, and there will be no battle. The nations will be destroyed by fire from God. They will be consumed. Then Satan will be thrown into the lake of fire along with the Beast, the demons, and all people who refused to worship Christ. The following passage is from Revelation 20:1-10, describing the Devil's doom. It picks up where Revelation 19 left off:

"Then I saw an angel coming down from heaven, having the key to the bottomless pit and a great chain in his hand. He laid hold of the dragon, that serpent of old, who is the Devil and Satan, and bound him for a thousand years; and he cast him into the bottomless pit, and shut him up, and set a seal on him, so that he should deceive the nations no more till the thousand years were finished. But after these things he must be released for a little while.

"And I saw thrones, and they sat on them, and judgment was committed to them. Then I saw the souls of those who had been beheaded for their witness to Jesus and for the word of God, who had not worshiped the beast or his image, and had not received his mark on their foreheads or on their hands. And they lived and reigned with Christ for a thousand years. But the rest of the dead did not live again until the thousand years were finished. This is the first resurrection. Blessed and holy is he who has part in the first resurrection. Over such the second death has no power, but they shall reign with Him a thousand years.

"Now when the thousand years have expired, Satan will be released from his prison and will go out to deceive the nations which are in the four corners of the earth, Gog and Magog, to gather them together to battle, whose number is as the sand of the sea. They went up on the breadth of the earth and surrounded the camp of the saints and the beloved city. And fire came down from God out of heaven and devoured them. The devil, who deceived them, was cast into the lake of fire and brimstone where the beast and the false prophet are. And they will be tormented day and night forever and ever."

Again, because of its constant scriptural reference of being "the" lake of fire and brimstone instead of "a" lake, my personal conviction is that the sun is the place of eternal damnation. That *Bible* has made reference to hell being in the center of the earth, but the *Bible* also teaches that death and hell will be cast into the lake of fire. The reference is Revelation 20:14, where hell is referred to as "Hades" in the New King James Version of the *Holy Bible*: "Then Death and Hades were cast into the lake of fire. This is the second death. And anyone not found written in the Book of Life was cast into the lake of fire."

The Battle of Armageddon, with the catastrophic events leading up to it, along with the rise and reign of the Anti-Christ, the Beast 666, is a very interesting and stimulating event to read about and study. However, for those present on the earth during the years just prior to and during this "Battle of Evermore," which will define for them who will rules in eternity, it will be a time of great fear, tribulation, terror, and uncertainty. With the Lord Jesus Christ's description of the time just prior to the rise of the Anti-Christ as nation rising against nation, and kingdom against kingdom, contemporaneous with earthquakes, famines, and pestilence in various places, it would seem to the objective, courageous thinker that the time is near. Jesus quoted the prophecy of Joel, mentioning the sun being darkened; Led Zeppelin doing the same two thousand years later. Several prophecies have been shown in this chapter, speaking of the great earthquake to come, mountains crumbling into dust, the ocean being turned to blood, to name a few. Those prophecies were reiterated by Led Zeppelin with lyrics from "Thank You," and "Going to California." Jesus spoke of the Anti-Christ and the coming Battle of Armageddon. You know from reading chapter eleven that Jimmy Page's rune equals 666; the number of the Anti-Christ. The band sang of the Beast and the battle in their song, "The Battle of Evermore," as well as making tacit reference to it in "Kashmir," and "In My Time of Dying." "Stairway to Heaven" itself gives us a hint of the coming battle at the end of the song. The *Holy Bible* speaks of the Battle of Armageddon laying waste to the armies of the kings of the earth, with the blood of its participants being as high as the horse's bridle for a distance of two hundred miles. Led Zeppelin presented the Beast and Satan as victors, whereas the *Bible* teaches clearly that the Beast will be thrown into the lake of fire and brimstone at that time; by Lord Jesus Christ. Led Zeppelin visualized their version of the result of the battle with an analogous display of the Arthur legend in *The Song Remains the Same* film. The Lord

Jesus Christ's visual version will be the actual battle itself. The obvious thing to be seen from one's perception of these events is the side one is on. The version of these events presented by Led Zeppelin is consistent with their adoration of the Devil, in conjunction with their abhorrence of Christianity; displayed by their mentor, Aleister Crowley, as well as their music and concurrent moral code. Their presentation of the end of the world, and who will rule in eternity, had been dictated to them prior to producing "The Battle of Evermore," by their conscious choice love for the Devil and their hatred for Christ and his followers. It is a simple case of cause and effect; the Devil manipulating it for his own purposes. What the reader needs to know is truth. The truth can be suppressed, ignored, or adhered to. Where do we find this absolute truth? Is there a way we can know it? How does one pursue it, or come to grips with it, and recognize it as truth, as opposed to falsehood? As one college classmate (at a secular school) once put it to me, "Who knows? Maybe hell is the place to be." How can we know if Christ really is God, or if God even exists? What if Lucifer is God, as Crowley and Led Zeppelin assert? Is there a way to distinguish between truth and falsehood, relative to Almighty God? The answer is an emphatic yes. I searched for this truth and I found it. I searched for it with the courage to face it, even if I didn't like it. For those who have the courage or "audacity" to face the absolute truth, in this world of falsehood, we will look at it in detail in the next chapter, properly titled, "Most High - The Quest for the Supreme Being."

Jimmy Page raises the guitar in front of the Sun tarp in California on 7/23/77. This photo was taken on a very sunny day in Oakland. He is praising the "Most High," the real sun, looking up, which is why it is on the tarp (see color photos).

RobertPlant sings to the "Children" who spiritually belong to the "Sun-Father." On 3/24/75, at the L.A. Forum he said, "Children of the Sun - Goodnight!"

1 Aleister Crowley, *The Equinox*, Vol. I, No.5, *The Vision and the Voice*, pg.62

2 Dave Lewis, *The Complete Guide to the Music of Led Zeppelin*, pg.35

3 Dave Lewis and Simon Pallett, *Led Zeppelin: The Concert File*, pg.110

4 Aleister Crwoley, *The Equinox*, Vol. I, No.6, *The Rite of Sol*, pg.67

5 Dr. David Jeremiah, *Escape the Coming Night*, Word Publishers, Nashville, Tenn., pg.115

6 Ibid, pp.192-193

7 Ibid, pg.115

8 Ibid, pg.197

9 Ibid, pp.197-198

10 Aleister Crowley, *The Equinox*, Vol. I, No.5, *The Vision and the Voice*, pg.173

11 Ibid, pp.173, 176

12 I bid, pp.61-64

13 Aleister Crowely, *The Book of Thoth*, pg.73

14 D.J. Conway, *Celtic Magic*, pg.116

15 Rosemary E. Guiley, The Encyclopedia of Witches and Witchcraft, pg.240

16 Aleister Crowley, *Magick-Book 4*Liber Aba*, pg.175

17 Dr. Sir J. G. Frazer, *The Golden Bough*, pg.762

18 Ritchie Yorke, *Led Zeppelin - The Definitive Biography*, pg.136

19 Abraham the Jew, *The Book of the Sacred Magic of Abramelin the Mage*, pg.61

20 Butler, *Ritual Magic*, pg.204

21 Aleister Crowley, *The Law is for All*, pg.168

22 Aleister Crowley, *Magick-Book 4*Liber Aba*, pg.494

23 Aleister Crowley, *The Equinox*, Vol. I, No.5, *The Vision and the Voice*, pg.10

24 Aleister Crowley, *The Equinox*, Vol. I, No.1, *The Temple of Solomon the King*, pg.192

25 Richard Cavendish, *The Black Arts*, pg.297

26 Dave Lewis, *The Complete Guide to the Music of Led Zeppelin*, pg.73

27 Steven Davis, *Hammer of the Gods*, pg.243

28 Lewis Spence, *Magic Arts in Celtic Britain*, pg.146

29 Ibid, pg.150

30 Ibid, pg.145

31 Ibid, pg.155

32 Ibid, pg.143

33 Ibid, pg.33

34 W.B. Crow, *Witchcraft, Magic, & Occultism*, pg.105

35 Lewis Spence, *Magic Arts in Celtic Britain*, pg.28

36 D.J. Conway, *Celtic Magic*, pg.86

37 Eliphas Levi, *Transcendental Magic*, pg.218

38 Ibid, pg.218

39 Aleister Crowley, *The Law is For All*, pp.274-275

40 Aleister Crowley, *Liber Samekh*, 1921, from *Magick-Book 4*Liber Aba*, pg.517

41 Aleister Crowley, *Book 4*, pg.71

42 Aleister Crowley, *The Equinox*, Vol. III, No. 1, pg.108

43 Aleister Crowley, *The Equinox*, Vol. I, No.5, *The Vision and the Voice*, pp.83-84

Jimmy Page ostensibly worshiping the "Most High" - Lucifer the Piper. The text below from the *Holy Bible* tells the truth of who he really is - the Devil himself.

"How you are fallen from heaven,
O Lucifer, son of the morning!
How you are cut down to the ground,
You who weakened the nations!
For you have said in your heart:
'I will ascend into heaven,
I will exalt my throne above the stars of God;
I will also sit on the mount of the congregation
On the farthest sides of the north;
I will ascend above the heights of the clouds,
I will be like the Most High.'
Yet you shall be brought down to Sheol,
To the lowest depths of the Pit."
    - Isaiah 14:12-15 (NKJV)

CHAPTER SEVENTEEN

"He who dwells in the secret place of the Most High shall abide under the shadow of the Almighty. I will say of the LORD, 'He is my refuge and my fortress; my God, in Him I will trust.'"
Psalm 91:1-2

"I will be glad and rejoice in You; I will sing praise to Your name, O Most High."
Psalm 9:2

"For the LORD Most High is awesome; He is a great King over all the earth."
Psalm 47:2

"Come to Me, all you who labor and are heavy laden, and I will give you rest. Take My yoke upon you and learn from Me, for I am gentle and lowly in heart, and you will find rest for your souls."
Lord Jesus Christ, Matthew 11:28-29

"Thelological error has its roots in moral, not intellectual soil."
Dr. John MacArthur, "Spiritual Warfare – Fighting to Win"

"How terrible is wisdom when it brings no profit to the wise - Johnny."
Lucifer (Robert DeNiro), "Angel Heart"

MOST HIGH:
THE QUEST FOR THE SUPREME BEING

The absolute truth in the latter half of the twentieth century has been transformed by the masses into anything but absolute. It has in fact been converted from an absolute to a variable. As a variable is susceptible to change, the "absolute truth" changes in its definition as you ask different individuals in our society what they believe the truth to be. Again, the only absolute seems to be that there is no absolute. Whatever people decide to believe, for them that is the truth. We have been programmed to think like the many avenues of suggestion would have us think. Upbringing, environment, educational institutions, the media, movies, music, books, and peer pressure direct us, if we are willing to follow,

into the arena of thought that they want us to go. Many are they who are programmed to believe a lie because they do not know what the truth really is,
believing it impossible to find; the lie being something that panders to the personal prejudice of the individual. In other words, if it suits our lifestyle and
tastes, we will believe in it. If it doesn't suit us, we discard it from our belief
system. However, we must realize that outside influences in conjunction with
inner choices, determined by our free will, have dictated to us what we would
eventually believe in. Any belief system is a religion, even if it is that a person
believes there is nothing to believe in. Even that mind frame is a belief system,
and thereby a religion. An atheist is just as religious as a Christian; he has a
religious belief, he worships his own intellect, and thereby himself, and his life
puts this belief on display. In this chapter my objective is to relate to the reader
the reasons and circumstances that determined my inevitable conclusion that
Jesus Christ is Lord God Most High. Jimmy Page and Robert Plant, as many of
you know, released their *Walking Into Clarksdale* album in April of 1998. On
that album, the most popular song is titled "Most High." They believe that the
Devil, Lucifer, is god Most High. That is why they blasphemed Lord Jesus
Christ in the song when Robert Plant sang, "David's seed talks through his
paper crown." In the *Bible*, Lord Jesus Christ is referred to over and over again
as the seed of David, and the son of David, by lineage, as in Romans 1:3-4:
"...concerning his Son Jesus Christ our Lord, who was born of the seed of
David according to the flesh..." In the movie, *The Greatest Story Ever Told,*
the Devil says "Hail! Son of David," before the woman caught in adultery is
cast on the ground in front of Jesus. He looks at the Devil with the expression of
"You better shut your mouth." The Devil shuts up immediately. I intend to show
the truth of who the Most High actually is in the following pages. I will begin
with the truth relative to sex as it has been placed in the human mind by the
Most High. The first thing addressed will be the issue of homosexuality from the
Biblical perspective. If a person will not accept the Biblical position on homosexuality, there can be no communion with God. The absolutes of heterosexuality will be addressed next. From there we will look at other aspects of the moral
law of the Most High, taken from the Ten Commandments, already in the human mind. All of the preceding absolutes are being presented in order that the
reader may clearly see from their own thinking who God is. If you meditate on
these absolutes with an open mind, you can only come to one, inescapable
conclusion. Finally, we will analyze the truth of what the *Bible* states about the
Most High - Lord Jesus Christ, relative to salvation of the human soul; or spiritual union with the Most High. Our thinking processes have been molded by
outside influences beyond our control, as well as by our own sovereign choices;
however, every human being that has walked planet earth will be held responsible for knowing the absolute truth programmed into his subconscious mind by
Lord Jesus Christ, obvious to the conscious mind through the conscience.

HOMOSEXUALITY AND THE CONSCIENCE

One of the most obvious forms of absolute truth projected into the conscious mind by the conscience is the truth relative to sex. Sexual desire is as strong as our desire for food. In the early ages of an individual's life, he or she begins to appreciate and have affection for the opposite sex. In grade school, all the boys talk of the girls they "like." The girls talk among themselves regarding the boys they like. I cannot remember one individual in the late sixties/early seventies when I was in grade school running around the campus with a sign that said "I'm gay and it's OK." I cannot remember one boy talking about how he had the hots for another boy, nor did I ever hear the girls speaking about their desire for girls. The primal condition of the conscience, before being corrupted by the spiritual wickedness of the adult world, tells children that homosexuality is wrong, and that by nature heterosexual affection is good. Children are more apt to use the phrase "queer" than "gay" or "lesbian" in describing homosexuals; although sexually perverted educators want to program little children to believe sex perversion is normal. It would have been better for those educators if they had not been born.

If you are reading this book, and you went to grade school with Ellen DeGeneres, I ask you, did you see her bragging about being a lesbian in 5th or 6th grade? I'd be willing to bet that you didn't. Homosexuality is a learned behavior. Some producers of a Broadway play have allegedly come up with a show that portrays Lord Jesus Christ and Judas Iscariot as homosexual lovers. These people will wish *they* had never been born. When they stand before Christ, they may receive punishment like Judas Iscariot; unless of course, they repent.

If the creator of mankind wanted us to perform homosexuality on one another, he would have created our bodies accordingly. The female vagina has its own lubricants to prepare for sexual intercourse. Doctors tell us that homosexuals, who have no natural lubricants, spread the AIDS virus by damaging blood vessels in one another's rectums. The virus in male seminal fluid then flows into the blood stream spreading the deadly disease. I ask you, what is the biological function of male seminal fluid in the rectum of another male? There is none.

About this time in the discussion of biological function of seminal fluids, someone will inevitably ask if because I make reference to the biological aspect of sexual intercourse, does that mean that I believe sex is only for reproduction. This is such an astonishing question to have thrown at oneself. Are these people kidding me? Do they really mean to suggest that I might believe a woman desires sex only once every six months, and that man only wants her during that time? Of course it isn't for reproduction alone. Lesbians and homosexual males, however, will never impregnate one another. Pregnancy is a natural function of heterosexuality. Homosexuals do not have this natural function take place in them because their activity is not natural; as I suggested when I mentioned that the vagina has natural lubricants the male rectum does not. If it is not a natural function, it is a perversion of the natural function. God will not bow the knee to sexual perversion, or those who adhere to it, as you will read shortly. So far, we have seen that the original condition of the conscience is against homosexuality, and the biological function of seminal fluids, causing pregnancy, are against homosexuality; again, by nature.

HOMOSEXUAL MARRIAGE

If homosexuality is unnatural, then the natural institution of marriage union does not apply to homosexuality either. The following is an excerpt from a conversation held on CNN News between CNN's Lou Waters, Mark Johnson of the *Gay and Lesbian Alliance Against Defamation*, and Andrea Sheldon of the *Traditional Values Coalition*; held on March 26th, 1996, at 2:15 P.M., eastern time. Lou Waters is ostensibly an advocate of homosexuality as this excerpt begins. He interrupts the discussion by asking Andrea Sheldon if she will compromise her stand against homosexual marriage; expressing his exasperation with her:

LOU WATERS: "I'm gonna ask the compromise question of you Andrea one more time. This is about the third or fourth time. Are you willing to compromise at all on this?"
ANDREA SHELDON: "I'm not sure what there is to compromise."
LOU WATERS: "OK."
ANDREA SHELDON: "People of faith, whether you're Christian, Moslem, or Jewish believe that..."
LOU WATERS: "OK."
ANDREA SHELDON: "...homosexual marriage is wrong!"
LOU WATERS: "OK. We've heard that...We've heard all of that."
ANDREA SHELDON: "And you're telling me that I have to compromise my religious beliefs!"
LOU WATERS: (disgusted) "OK. Fine."
MARK JOHNSON: "Those beliefs are shared by people who happen to be gay and lesbian too, and I think that they'd like to think that there's room in this religion for everybody...Just because you're a Christian and you believe one way, doesn't mean that there's not another way to believe and be a Christian at the same time."

Mr. Johnson states that homosexuals can be Christians as heterosexual

Christians who believe the *Holy Bible* is the Word of God. We are about to see if he has an infinitesimal clue as to what he is saying (I have this dialogue from CNN on film, and will be showing it during my presentations.). What Mr. Waters and Mr. Johnson have to understand, is that Andrea Sheldon is not the one who set the standard that she adheres to. The reason she made reference to Christians, Jews, and Moslems, is not because they are anti-homosexual bigots or homophobes (The fact is that the militant homosexual is a Lord Jesus Christ phobe, projecting his guilt to anyone who advocates the heterosexual standard of Christ exclusively). The religious groups she mentioned believe in the divine inspiration of the Old Testament that clearly condemns homosexual behavior. One cannot be a Christian and oppose the following scriptures. It is an absolute impossibility to be a follower of Christ and be in opposition to the scriptures, as militant homosexuals are. In Leviticus, the *Holy Bible* records the message about homosexuality that Jehovah/Yahweh instructed Moses to present to the Children of Israel. Remember, and you can ask any *Bible* scholar, Jesus marched into the Temple of Solomon in Jerusalem and claimed to be Jehovah/Yahweh, and we will examine the New Testament teaching on the issue of homosexuality momentarily. Leviticus 18:22 reads: "You shall not lie with a male as with a woman. It is an abomination." In Leviticus 20:13, Jehovah/Yahweh commanded the Israelites to put homosexuals in their ranks to death: "If a man lies with a male as he lies with a woman, both of them have committed an abomination. They shall surely be put to death. Their blood shall be upon them."

The above quotes are the religious beliefs of Christians, Jews, and Moslems, relative to homosexuality. For Christians, who believe in the divine inspiration of the New Testament, we have the same concept reiterated in Romans chapter 1. This chapter presents God's indictment of the sinfulness of mankind; including homosexuality. The teaching of the text, when mentioning homosexuality, makes reference to AIDS when it says that God would punish homosexuals with a deadly disease in their bodies; and the end of the chapter makes it clear that God believes all the people described in the passage deserve to be put to death. The following quote is from the New Testament Book of Romans 1:18-32:

"The wrath of God is being revealed from heaven against all the godlessness and wickedness of men who suppress the truth by their wickedness, since what may be known about God is plain to them, because God has made it plain to them. For since the creation of the world God's invisible qualities-his eternal power and divine nature-have been clearly seen, being understood from what has been made, so that men are without excuse.

"For although they knew God, they neither glorified him as God nor gave thanks to him, but their thinking became futile and their foolish hearts were darkened. Although they claimed to be wise, they became fools and exchanged the glory of the immortal God for images made to look like mortal man and birds and animals and reptiles.

"Therefore God gave them over in the sinful desires of their hearts to sexual impurity for the degrading of their bodies with one another. They exchanged the truth of God for a lie, and worshiped and served created things rather than the Creator-who is forever praised. Amen.

"Because of this, God gave them over to shameful lusts. Even their women exchanged natural relations for unnatural ones. In the same way the men also abandoned natural relations with women and were inflamed with lust for one another. Men committed indecent acts with other men, and received in themselves the due penalty for their perversion.

"Furthermore, since they did not think it worthwhile to retain the knowledge of God, he gave them over to a depraved mind, to do what ought not to be done. They have become filled with every kind of wickedness, evil, greed and depravity. They are full of envy, murder, strife, deceit and malice. They are gossips, slanderers, God-haters, insolent, arrogant and boastful; they invent ways of doing evil; they disobey their parents; they are senseless, faithless, heartless, ruthless. Although they know God's righteous decree that those who do such things deserve death, they not only continue to do these very things but also approve of those who practice them."(NIV)

As one can see from the *Bible* text, AIDS is not new. It makes perfect sense to any logical thinking mind, however, that an AIDS epidemic would exist contemporaneously with a homosexual sin epidemic. This sin has its own penalty. People can blame monkeys in Africa or Haiti or anywhere else for the disease, but the *Holy Bible* makes it plain where it came from.

BABIES AND THE AIDS VIRUS

Should a new born baby have to suffer the pain of having caught the AIDS virus from a blood transfusion or parental transmission? Some people suggest that this is proof that there is no God or that he is corrupt if he exists. The truth is, if our nation had not chosen to give a positive sanction to homosexual behavior, then babies wouldn't be catching the disease. Although there have always been homosexuals, the fact is, the more society approves of a certain behavior, the more people will be willing to engage in it. Again, the AIDS epidemic is in conjunction with the homosexuality epidemic. The spread of AIDS is man's fault; not God's. Instead of asking Andrea Sheldon to compromise, what Lou Waters should have done was ask Mark Johnson and the homosexuals he is in league with to compromise and go straight. Andrea Sheldon is an individual of righteous courage, something the perverted mind despises (If you are homosexual and reading this, know that Lord Jesus Christ loves you as much as any heterosexual, but you must repent to be forgiven and born again. If you do not, then it is to eternal damnation that you will go after death.). She was, however, only a representative of the one who is really despised by this crowd. As Jesus said, "They hated me without a cause."

Who is the original "Rebel without a cause?" It is the Devil. What did Don McClean say in "American Pie?" He said there was a "jester" singing for a "king" with a "queen" wearing "...a coat he borrowed from James Dean." He went on to say that as this "king" bent his head "down," that " jester" robbed him of the "THORNY CROWN" he was wearing. Those lyrics tell the story, rebellion without a cause. Lucifer is the jester, and Jesus is the King who wore the thorny crown. One thing is absolute, rebellion without a cause does not last long. What happened to the man who promoted that image?

HOMOPHOBES

Another thing that these people do is to project their wickedness to straight people. Many a time a straight person has been called a "homophobe" because he or she is against homosexuality, or that they are insecure about their own sexuality to the point that they condemn gay and lesbian people. Well, there is something to be said about that. It isn't that people are born gay, it is because they are born sinners that makes it possible for them to stray into homosexual behavior. [Please understand, God loves homosexuals and wants to save them, but not if they refuse to repent about homosexuality and sin in general.] If a straight person begins to hang around in homosexual environments, at the very least he or she has tolerated that sin as though it were ok, even if they don't partake of it. This toleration in itself is sin against God. Another point is, even if they are only heterosexual when they begin to hang around that environment, the odds are that sooner or later they are going to partake of the activity. As the late Dr. Jack Hyles of The First Baptist Church of Hammond, Indiana, put it: "If you walk like one, talk like one, dress like one, and hang around with one, you're gonna be one, one of these days!"

Although this is all common sense, it needs to be said anyway. There is one standard of sexual tolerance in the sight of God, Lord Jesus Christ, and that is heterosexuality. Mark Johnson's assertion that homosexuals can be Christians like heterosexuals displays his ignorance as to what a Christian is. Can you imagine a Jewish rabbi wearing a Swastika on his arm into a synagogue? Of course you cannot. That would not come close, however, to the atrocious assertion of Mark Johnson that a homosexual can be a Christian without repenting of homosexuality. His insult is directed at God himself. The inference is, that Christ tolerates sex perversion, thereby making him morally perverted as well. This is very dangerous ground to be treading on. Again the fact is simply that the homosexuals are Christphobes. They hate righteousness, love perversion, and project their guilt to straight people by calling them homophobes. Charles Grodin had a lesbian on his show proclaiming loud and clear (on July 26th of 1998) that God had created her gay. Well, she is saying that God is an idiot who wants women with other women, when their bodies are not conducive to healthy sexual intercourse, only sex perversion. If God wanted her in bed with a woman, he would have made her a man; cased closed. God is not twisted, the lesbian is. She said that she knew she was created as a lesbian by the time she got to high school. No, she knew she had made the choice to become a lesbian by the time she got to high school. Having been tempted to participate in homosexuality, and adopting it as a lifestyle was her choice, not God's enforced code of sex on her life. Choosing sex perversion as a way of life and then projecting the guilt to God is absolute twisted mentality nonsense. Lord Jesus Christ is not going to compromise his hatred for homosexuality to appease sinners. He is not running for President. He is the ruler already. The *Bible* makes it clear that his moral code of holiness will remain the same forever. It reads in the New Testament Book of Hebrews, Chapter 13, Verse 8: "Jesus Christ is the same yesterday, today, and forever." At least Aleister Crowley had the common sense to know that if he was going to participate in homosexuality, he was an anti-Christ. He didn't pretend to be a Christian for image's sake.

President Clinton pretended to associate himself with Southern Baptists, and allowed himself to be filmed by news cameras walking into church on Sundays with a *Bible* in his hand, the same book that condemns homosexuality, and then the White House blasts Senator Trent Lott for calling homosexuality a sin; in June of 1998. Mr. Clinton also stood before a crowd of homosexuals in a Tuxedo, and it was seen on the CNN news, stating that as far as he knew, being gay never kept anybody from performing their occupations. To this statement came a round of applause. Sometime after that, Mr. Clinton signed the "Defense of Marriage Act." It seems that image polishing and plasticity of approach were the status quo at the Clinton White House. It doesn't matter if he is Republican, Democrat, or anything else. I have no political agenda here. It's just that Mr. Clinton needs to open to Romans Chapter One the next time he sees the *Holy Bible*, because millions of Americans saw his incandescent double standard, whether he believes they did or not.

The truth is, the *Holy Bible's* standard of sexuality, specifically, condemning homosexuality, is equivalent with the primal condition of the human conscience. This means it was designed by the creator to reflect his view on the matter. The female has natural sexual lubricants for the male phallus, the male rectum does not have this, and homosexuality cannot produce pregnancy, neither in lesbians or gays. It doesn't matter if this material is offensive to people; what matters is that they realize what is true in the sight of God, in order that they may be led to repent of this activity, should they be involved in it or just think that it is ok; in order that they might be saved. The soul that goes to the grave believing homosexuality is right, or is an active participant believing it is right, will be damned forever, because the unrepentant sexually immoral will not inherit the kingdom of heaven. Revelation 21:8 makes it clear: "But the cowardly, unbelieving, abominable, murderers, sexually immoral, sorcerers, idolaters, and all liars shall have their part in the lake which burns with fire and brimstone, which is the second death." [Cowardly in this context means to be too afraid to entertain thoughts of God or the supernatural, so they reject him and his moral code. If Jesus could face the cross, we can face the fact that we were created by the Supreme Being. This fear warrants no sympathy in God's sight.] The *Bible* makes it emphatically clear, that what is considered true in the sight of God, is that homosexuality is an abomination; that standard is consistent with the primal condition of the human conscience.

HETEROSEXUALITY AND THE CONSCIENCE

The conscience speaks to the conscious mind as to what is true relative to the creator's programming of the subconscious mind in the area of straight, or heterosexual sex, as well. When I was coming to these spiritual conclusions, I endured what Robert Plant sang about in the song, "D'yer Maker." This is of course, something that most of you have probably endured, the painful breakup. At 1:53 into the song, Plant sings, "You hurt me to my soul." Now, when you are using someone, it doesn't hurt like that. However, when you are in a relationship in which you are emotionally involved, and a sexual relationship definitely extends the degree to which you are wrapped up in that person, it is absolutely excruciating to break up from a long relationship. As many of you know, it is the worst pain in the entire world. It affects everything you do. Your boss can tell you not to bring your problems to work, but you're going to bring this one, right? Needless to say, I am confessing, for the reader's sake, that I was a complete emotional basket case over the loss of a particular young woman a few years younger than I. I couldn't understand for the life of me why the pain was so bad. I knew its source, but I had been through serious pain already in my life, and this was too much.

I began to abuse drugs and alcohol to a greater degree than I had been up to that moment, to kill the pain. I was working out, doing a lot of long distance running at a very fast pace, and yet I couldn't resist the temptation to indulge in vast amounts of alcohol and marijuana. I was, along with some others, living in the bottom of a bottle of Yukon Jack, Jack Daniels, and swimming in a sea of Genessee Cream Ale, Seagrams VO, and ounce after ounce of marijuana; including countless parties in several different towns, as well as many insane trips into New York; driving east on Route 80 at 90 miles an hour blasting Foghat's "Fool for the City." To be honest, how I survived the two years in question without getting killed or drinking myself to death, I can only point to divine intervention.

This time frame that I was living in was two and three years after I resisted the satanic call at the Led Zeppelin Concert in Madison Square Garden. I consistently suppressed the event, but when I got really stoned, it was impossible to suppress. When this would resurface, I would think, along with many at the parties I was attending, about the origin of mankind, the earth, God, Satan, and why this breakup had held me in so much pain. Many were the people that I would hear discussing and searching for truth of why we are here. I was not, by the way, the only individual in my circle of friends enduring the excruciating pain of breakup, after having been deeply in love. I noticed that this was an absolute. I mean, it became increasingly obvious to me that nobody who was deeply in love could just spurn having been rejected by his or her lover. Some pretended to, but that was just a mask that could easily be removed by intoxication. The key element to the pain, I surmised, was that it was an involuntary response. People don't say, "Well, I've just been cast off by my lover, consequently, I think I will choose, as an act of my will, to go out of my mind over this." While I'm sure that anyone reading this knows these things already, I want you to see how analytical I became; as well as to where it led me. I began, as a result of realizing that this emotional pain was an involuntary response, to analyze what other situations I could see that produced involuntary responses in people. The thing about the involuntary response, being separate from an act of the will, was that it showed inner programming and makeup the individuals enduring the pain were not responsible for. We were designed, I began to believe, to hurt like that when separated from our lovers. Another involuntary response that people endure is the rage associated with contemplating their lover with someone new. Men don't say, "Well I just think I would like to blow my stack over her being with someone new." Men don't have to say that, it comes naturally. Men and women both believe it is wrong for their lovers to leave and be someone else's lover. Not only does it hurt, but we know it is not right morally. You can accept it as morally correct if you choose, but that is not the primal condition of the conscience. The morally correct person knows it is wrong for someone else to be in bed with his partner. Again, this is an involuntary response, which shows original programming, even in people who believe it's ok to cheat. How many people have believed it was right for them to cheat, and yet, when they got cheated on, their response to it was antithetical? I mean the response was diametrically opposed to believing it was acceptable, right? That was an involuntary response from the subconscious mind - the programming of the creator - Lord Jesus Christ. I even heard one individual speak of his old girlfriend this way – "Although I don't want her, I don't want anyone else to have her either." Here is an individual who no longer wants his lover, yet, because they were sexual partners, and in love, he doesn't want anyone else to have her. I remember another individual, who was in a club with his girlfriend, and her old boyfriend came in. She told her current boyfriend that she needed to speak to her old boyfriend in private. So off she went. While she was sitting with him at a table, her current boyfriend said to me: "Have you ever noticed that even though your girlfriend is not in love with her old boyfriend, you still don't want her around him?" My response was: "Of Course. They were intimate once, and they can be intimate again. Especially when they are both wasted." The concept was, he didn't want the old boyfriend around HIS girlfriend, because she was his girlfriend, and he was not going to share her. Earlier in the book I spoke of biker Bob, who said if he came home from work and his biker chick was doing a guy on the couch, that was her business. Most of you would agree, that not wanting to share your partner is the original design of the human sub-conscious projected into the conscious mind when the old boyfriend comes around. This is not only the original condition of the conscience on the issue, but it is consistent with the *Holy Bible* once again. The *Bible* of course, puts sexual intercourse in the context of marriage, where God says it is supposed to be.

The following is from the Old Testament Book of Proverbs, Chapter 5, Verses 15-20, and it starts out with a metaphor: "Drink water from your own cistern, and running water from your own well. Should your fountains be dis-persed abroad, streams of water in the streets? Let them be only your own, and not for strangers with you. Let your fountain be blessed, and rejoice with the wife of your youth. As a loving deer and graceful doe, let her breasts satisfy you at all times; and always be enraptured with her love. For why should you, my son, be enraptured by an immoral woman, and be embraced in the arms of a seductress?" As can be clearly seen, the *Bible* passage from Proverbs is consis-tent with the original condition of the human conscience on the matter of sharing sexually, as shown in the preceding club conversation. Another thing that can be seen from the Biblical text is God's command to a man to be satisfied by his wife's breasts at all times. The man desires the female breast because God cre-ated him with that desire. No elaboration needed here, except that her breasts are to be his alone, and not another's. Isn't it stupid for people to say that God is against sex, when he clearly is the creator of it? The human mind, as I have presented it here, is programmed to be in great distress over the break up of lovers, to be in great distress over the thought of the lover being with someone new, it is programmed to want others who have had your lover to stay away, and men are naturally attracted to their female partner's breasts. These concepts are all consistent with the teachings of the *Holy Bible*; present in the primal condi-tion of the human conscience.

This too, is evidence that the creator is the God of the *Holy Bible*; Lord Jesus Christ. As it says in the New Testament Book of John Chapter 1, Verses 1-14:

"In the beginning was the Word, and the Word was with God, and the

Word was God. He was in the beginning with God. All things were made through Him, and without Him nothing was made that was made. In Him was life, and the life was the light of men. And the light shines in the darkness, and the darkness did not comprehend it.

"There was a man sent from God, whose name was John. This man came for a witness, to bear witness of the Light, that all through him might believe. He was not that Light, but was sent to bear witness of that Light. That was the true Light which gives light to every man coming into the world.

"He was in the world, and the world was made through Him, and the world did not know Him. He came to His own, and His own did not receive Him. But as many as received Him, to them He gave the right to become children of God, to those who believe in His name: who were born, not of blood, nor of the will of the flesh, nor of the will of man, but of God.

"And the Word became flesh and dwelt among us, and we beheld His glory, the glory as of the only begotten of the Father, full of grace and truth."

Born of God in this context means spiritual rebirth; born again Christianity. Lord Jesus Christ therefore, is the creator of mankind.

Although I was not reading the *Bible*, these concepts were constantly surfacing in my mind, which I now attribute to God drawing me to him. No matter what I did, I would constantly think of these things, even against my will, and their avenues began to expand. There were even times when I was frightened by the things I was contemplating because I did not have clear answers to my questions. One thing I did conclude, subjectively, was that the original condition of the conscience was for monogamy in a sexual relationship; and that standard had to be the intent of the creator, made plain by the pain associated with breaking it, which came upon me and many others involuntarily.

The philosophy of the local college campus classes that I attended laughed at these standards in Psychology and Sociology, etc., but I knew what was right; regardless. Don't misunderstand what I am stating here, I did not promote Christian concepts in these classes either, but sinful ones, until consequences of sin began to take their toll on me; as well as many others I observed. It became increasingly clear to me that those classes were church gatherings for the purpose of promoting Satan's moral code; all in the name of education. Although I was an anti-Christ, I knew that these conclusions were in line with the moral code of Jesus Christ; and this caused me to fear, because I was still rebelling against him, and this gave me a clue as to where I was headed - eternal damnation. I was never stupid enough to adopt the mentality of "When I die, I am going where my friends are going – hell." The human mind has the knowledge of eternal bliss in heaven and eternal damnation in hell. [John Lennon told us to make believe there is no heaven or hell. If I have to choose between reverence for Lennon or Christ, it will not be for the one who promoted "Lucy in the Sky with Diamonds"-"LSD." The Devil rejoices when one takes LSD.] I was in fear, and yet I had not read one verse in the *Bible*, and I had not talked to any Christians, I had not gone to church, neither had I watched any religious programming on television. This all took place in my head; against my will.

The fears I was having at this point in my life drove me to become increasingly intoxicated; just about everyday of the week. I also spent insane amounts of time listening to you know who - Led Zeppelin; as the Magick spell demanded. It was a sure fire way of not having to think. The album that dominated me was none other than *The Song Remains the Same*.

FLIRTING WITH DISASTER

As I wrote previously, these thoughts of God continued to dominate my thinking, even when I was alone. This is why I spent so much time listening to Led Zeppelin while stoned. Nothing I did could get rid of them. This is consistent with the teaching of Lord Jesus Christ in the New Testament Book of John, Chapter 6, Verse 44: "No one can come to Me unless the Father who sent Me draws him…" By forcing me to thinking of these things continuously, I was being drawn to God. I thought that perhaps I was going out of my mind, because I was an anti-Christ in my behavior, and yet I was thinking that the moral code of Christ was right; which I had never done previously. And why would God draw an anti-Christ like me to himself? The answer is in the New Testament Book of 1 Corinthians, Chapter 1, Verses 26-29, where Paul the Apostle addresses Christians at Corinth: "For you see your calling, brethren, that not many wise according to the flesh, not many mighty, not many noble, are called. But God has chosen the foolish things of the world to put to shame the wise, and God has chosen the weak things of the world to put to shame the things which are mighty; and the base things of the world and the things which are despised God has chosen, and the things which are not, to bring to nothing the things that are, that no flesh should glory in His presence."

It is not difficult for me to see from the above passage that I was chosen to do this work in exposing the Devil's detailed work through the music of Led Zeppelin in the mind of the listeners. I'm not a prince or a movie star or a powerful politician. In the eyes of the powerful and influential I'm nobody. I was just a hardcore Led Zeppelin fan/anti-Christ; like so many others. If God chose me to expose Led Zeppelin, will I stand before him and brag about how righteous or influential I was when he chose me? What did the verse say? "…that no flesh may glory in his presence." Another verse that clearly defines what is taking place through the writing of this book comes from the New Testament Book of 1 John Chapter 3, Verse 8: "For this purpose the Son of God was manifested, that he might destroy the works of the devil." While the verse speaks specifically of Christ's incarnation, by analogy, he is doing the same in the minds of readers of this book.

In order to use me for this purpose I was being drawn to God through the constant thinking of spiritual things that I could not avoid. To turn off my brain, as I wrote previously, I would get stoned and listen to Led Zeppelin's live album, specifically, the 27-minute jam, "Dazed and Confused." This provided me with another problem. Running from God was sending right into the path of guess who - the Devil, and I was becoming increasingly more comfortable with spiritual wickedness, which made me fear I could become like Jimmy Page. Led Zeppelin's command to sell my soul to Satan was in the song, along with the wicked spiritual trek through the violin bow section, which was diabolical to say the least. The spiritual warfare was reaching a crescendo. The reason was because I loved Led Zeppelin and Jimmy Page to the maximum. I had nineteen different Led Zeppelin posters in my bedroom, two of which were six feet tall, and I loved the spiritual wickedness derived from being stoned and listening to their music; and its concurrent lifestyle. The satanic call of Madison Square Garden's Led Zeppelin concert was constantly resurfacing. By avoiding thoughts of God, the Devil was drawing me to himself! If I had not turned to Christ, I may very well have become a magician/guitar player just like Jimmy Page. However, having been a competitive long distance runner, I knew there was a finish line. Crossing the finish line, and knowing there would be no second chance to run, I knew I better run it right the first time. Feeling the temptation to run from the Devil, I ran into thoughts of God again, regardless of how anti-Christ the environment I was in; and still, I didn't know any Christians.

Right in the middle of all of this thinking about God, a startling event occurred. I am writing this by permission. Another person I partied with in the seventies, by the name of John Burbridge, related the following story. He told me the story the night after the event. He said that he was riding in a Volkswagen Bug. He was in the back seat and he was intoxicated. The driver hit a telephone pole on Route 10 in Roxbury Twp., New Jersey, and the rescue people had to use the "jaws of life" to get him out of the car. He was uninjured, but that was not what was startling. The thing he kept saying was that it was his birthday, and the accident took place virtually 20 years from the moment he was born. Now, when you come close to being killed at the very moment you were born during the year, someone is trying to get your attention, pure and simple. He was not faking it, because I knew when he was born, and he kept saying it all night; how the whole thing shook him up. Needless to say, with all the thoughts of the spirit world I was entertaining at the time, I was pretty shook up by this event as well, which is why I tell the story 20 years later.

Another constant reminder of the spirit world was in a song by Neil Young that was constantly being played in local tavern jukeboxes. I mentioned it already in the Black Sabbath chapter. In "Hey Hey My My," Neil Young was saying over and over in my head, because I kept listening to the song, that rock music can't die because: "There's" things behind this "picture" that are not seen by the human "eye." Obviously, I perceived him as talking about the Devil. By vacillating between thoughts of God and the Devil, and partying myself to death, I knew something had to change. I knew I was going to give in to one or the other, so I decided to examine every absolute I could recognize; and intensely. The additional absolutes of the conscience were, I began to realize, consistent with the moral law of the *Holy Bible's* Ten Commandments, which I had previously viewed as fiction, a moral code for religious fanatics.

THE ABSOLUTES OF THE CONSCIENCE/COMMANDMENTS

One of the most famous of the Ten Commandments is "You shall not commit adultery." That quote comes from the Old Testament Book of Exodus, Chapter 20, verse 14. Now what that really means is this, no sex outside the marriage union, beforehand or during the marriage. Does that come as a surprise? Of course before marriage it is called fornication, but that comes from the Greek word *"Porneo"* which means adultery. Yes, many of us have committed this sin, so we didn't pay any attention to thinking we could obey it. The truth is, however, when you have sex with someone, and do not marry them, this is adultery against the person you will marry. That is the Biblical position. Dr. Billy Graham said on a talk show that he kept his virginity until he was 26 years old. The people in the audience laughed at him. Now I ask you, do you think his wife Rose was upset about the fact that no other woman had sex with him?Jesus took this commandment one step higher into the spiritual realm. This is what he said in Matthew Chapter 5, Verses 27-28: "You have heard that it was said, 'Do not commit adultery.' But I tell you that anyone who looks at a woman lustfully has already committed adultery with her in his heart."(NIV) Now, who reading this book can deny lusting after the opposite sex? Hefner, Guccione, and Flynt have made and are making a mint off this weakness in men, calling it, as Hefner did on MSNBC, "Puritan Oppression" when it is described as a sinful weakness. What these men do not realize is that every knee shall bow, and every tongue confess that Jesus Christ is Lord, to the glory of God the Father (Philippians 2:10-11). They took great delight in reducing women to objects of lust in the minds of people like this author in the seventies, and they think they are heading for utopia. Hefner even did a special back then on Satanist High Priest Anton LaVey and his Church of Satan in San Francisco. At least he knows whose side he is on.

Lusting in the heart is the first step to the adultery in physical terms. Jesus was telling the disciples that to avoid adultery in a bed, it should be avoided in the mind, which is in itself sin. No, there is nothing wrong with looking, but what do we do with the image we are looking at? That is the issue. Does a man enjoy seeing his woman eyeing every guy she sees? Does a woman enjoy having her man look at every woman he sees when they are together? Nothing more needs to be said. The jealousy is an involuntary response from the subconscious, and Jesus put it there. It is another message that says, "Thou shalt not commit adultery." This applies to people who are not married yet as well, because if you cheat before marriage, are you going to remain faithful afterward? What would Priscilla Presley tell us?

Another involuntary response in the mind of mankind is one that some people do not even understand, though it happens to them. The one-night stand, while it offers a physical intimacy, does twice as much harm to the person who engages in it. The human psyche is designed by Christ to have a threefold aspect relative to sexual intercourse. All men and women, in the primal condition of their minds, have been programmed according to the following. The human being wants, in a monogamous relationship, three things:

(1) The security of commitment
(2) Emotional intimacy
(3) Physical intimacy

If a person gets the physical intimacy on the one-night stand, they automatically agitate the desire for emotional intimacy and the security of commitment, if they do not have them as yet. This is pure evil in God's sight. It is totally the opposite of his plan for men and women. Also, the person who has a faithful partner or spouse at home, with whom he or she WAS secure, intimate emotionally and physically, that goes on a one-night stand or commits adultery with someone else repeatedly, has done damage to his marriage and his own mind. This is how it is done. The individual who commits adultery in marriage, or cheats in a relationship (another form of adultery, again, because God does not want us cheating during courtship, because if you cheat in courtship, you'll cheat after marriage), has done something to his mind that he cannot avoid anymore than he can stop the sun from coming up tomorrow. Lord Jesus Christ designed the subconscious mind with "You shall not commit adultery" in it. When a person cheats, they lock into their subconscious mind the information that they cannot be trusted by their partner. The guilty party then has this information projected to the conscious mind by the conscience. As a result, the guilty party then has an extremely difficult time trusting the most innocent and faithful partner in the world. Why? The guilty party projects his guilt to the innocent. The thought goes like this, "I'm unfaithful, and she's in a relationship with me, so she must be unfaithful too. I'll bet she's cheated on me, or is cheating." The person may not understand it this clearly, but they cannot trust the innocent partner now. Let the innocent one stay at work late. Let the innocent one desire to go shopping alone. When this happens, the guilty party begins to get nervous. Why? The person has destroyed the emotional intimacy he or she had with their partner by cheating or committing adultery. There is no escape from this. The *Holy Bible* has something to say about what the adulterer has done to his or herself; in the Old Testament Book of Proverbs, Chapter 6, Verse 32: "But a man who commits adultery lacks judgment; whoever does so destroys himself." The only way to clear the conscience is to confess it, and boy, there's going to be trouble, right? The reason there's going to be trouble is because Lord Jesus Christ designed the subconscious mind of the innocent to desire faithfulness in a relationship. Christ said no adultery, and the guilty hears it all the time. He also said that people were to be faithful in marriage by forbidding adultery, which is what the command was really intended for, and the adulterer is going to hear that LOUD AND CLEAR when he or she confesses it to their partner. Again, the human subconscious was designed with "You shall not commit adultery" in it, showing the creator to be Lord Jesus Christ. A perfect example of this can be seen in the movie *"The Firm."* Mitch McDere (Tom Cruise) confesses to his faithful wife Abby (Jean Tripplehorn) that he committed adultery on her. He (reluctantly) tells her, "It didn't mean a thing." Her response is, "It means everything." She goes on to ask him why he bothered to tell her. His response is, "Because I couldn't stand you not knowing."

While this is only a movie, it is indicative of real life experiences going on all over the world. The guilty conscience and its torment, displayed by Mitch McDere is illustrative of, on a small scale, the guilt experienced by people who die and go to hell. The moment they realize they are there, their consciences are converted back to what they were originally, with the law of Christ in them, and then they face the lives they have lived in opposition to that law, forever. The reason the conscience reverts back to its primal condition is the fact that they can no longer suppress it with unrighteous living. That ability has been taken from them. You read it already in a larger quote, but here it is again, from Romans Chapter 1, Verses 18-21: "For the wrath of God is revealed from heaven against all ungodliness and unrighteousness of men, who suppress the truth in unrighteousness, because what may be known of God is manifest in them, for God has shown it to them. For since the creation of the world His invisible attributes are clearly seen, being understood by the things that are made, even His eternal power and Godhead, so that they are without excuse, because although they knew God, they did not glorify Him as God, nor were thankful, but became futile in their thoughts, and their foolish hearts were darkened." That passage tells it all. In the second sentence, he states that God's power and divine nature have been clearly seen by what has been made - like the human subconscious and its message to the conscious mind by way of the conscience, telling the created human being what the creator thinks of his or her behavior, relative to the standards of the creator's divine nature. The last phrase is the most chilling, "so that men are without excuse." Human beings, who have the knowledge of the creator's divine nature, suppress this truth with wickedness until the conscience is seared and they don't hear the rebuke anymore, and then they believe wrong is right morally, and anyone who opposes the new condition of the conscience is going to face persecution. However, men are without excuse, and this is not a high school vice-principal or a police officer sending this warning, it is the Almighty. People get settled into a life of rebellion, and human beings are naturally resistant to change, and so being set in their ways they rebel against God until death. Oh yes, they have a religious affiliation of some kind, as though God is an idiot who can be patronized by their relationship to a denomination, but then reject a real relationship with him, that he defines, on HIS TERMS. His terms are in the *Holy Bible*. If a people say they love God, but won't come to him on his terms, they are liars. Those who do come to God on his terms, and truly get salvation, and have a relationship with God as he expects it to be, are labeled "religious fanatics" by those who think themselves right with God, but are in reality on their way to eternal damnation. How many natural disasters (which insurance companies define as "acts of God") must occur in the United States until God gets our attention and we return to the moral code of righteousness this country was founded on?

God does get the attention of adulterers. He won't allow adultery, which is why the conscience of the adulterer torments him with Christ's rebuke. Adultery, as God defines it, and as you read already, is having sex outside the marriage union, before or during that marriage. Christ condemns it in the *Bible*, and men pass that absolute along. For instance, who wants to marry a tramp? Men think is cool to use "easy" women, not wanting to take that kind of girl home to mom. This is hypocrisy on the part of men. How often I've heard young women say, "How come it is alright for guys to sleep around, but not girls?" Why do men pat one another on the back when they sleep around, and call a woman a tramp if she does? It is because deep down inside of men, an involuntary reaction comes to mind, put there by Christ, that his mate is to be pure. Most men today don't expect virginity, but they don't want the woman everyone else has had, do they? Why? Because the woman has the vagina, the place where life comes from, and this is to be held sacred in the mind of the man. If you have doubts about that, ask yourself this question, "What will come closest to getting me killed, if I badmouth someone's father, or someone's mother?" We all agree that badmouthing someone's mother is hazardous to one's health. That is the way Christ programmed men to think. Again, no one is to have this sacred place but the man in the relationship with the woman. If she gives it to others, it is no longer sacred to him, and this is why immoral women are labeled tramps; it has to do with Lord Jesus Christ's programming of the subconscious mind. How often have we seen the traditional American hypocrite father act in the following manner? His daughter comes down the stairs on Friday night, headed out the door to get in the car with her boyfriend, or her date, and daddy says, *"Young lady, you behave yourself."* Five minutes later, his son comes down the steps and tells his dad he is going out with the guys, with a mischievous smile on his face. His father laughs and says, *"Go get 'em tiger!"* In his mind, it is alright for his son to go out and use somebody else's daughter, but nobody better be using his. The response to his daughter was manufactured by Jesus' programming of the subconscious mind, and you know who is Lord of the other. Just listen to the Led Zeppelin song, "Black Dog." There is a good chance the guy who picked up his daughter was told the same thing by his father. The command to be pure to the daughter was involuntary, at the mention of her going out. The encouragement given to the son was a voluntary response. Purity is a law in the subconscious, but the wicked standard is a choice made by the conscious mind.

Lord Jesus Christ has another law imbedded in the subconscious mind of mankind that is continually shouting at those who break it. That law, another one of the Ten Commandments, is this, "You shall not commit murder." In the older translations, it says, "Thou shalt not kill." In the context of the scriptures, this means you shall not kill on your own authority, which is murder. You can kill someone who is trying to kill you, or is about to kill someone else. You can also kill in the defense of your nation. Romans Chapter 13 commands the Christian to obey his government. If sent to combat by their government, men and women are not murderers. They do have to obey the laws of war, however. Capital punishment, properly carried out, is a Biblical mandate. When you hear people say that killing to get even with a killer is two wrongs trying to make a right, well, they just do not understand retribution. No deterrence? Let's see a dead murderer kill again. Has Ted Bundy killed anyone lately? Is Timothy McVeigh a threat from the grave? Why are we hunting Osama Bin Laden? Capital punishment is not murder by those in authority carrying it out. Another thing, I have met people who are all for abortion and against capital punishment. At least they are consistent in their defense of wrong against the innocent. God forbid that we should put the guilty to death rather than give him a chance to get out of prison so he can murder again; or murder someone in the prison system.

Murder is when people kill when they do not have the lawful right to do so. The subconscious mind, with "You shall not commit murder" present, projects this concept to the guilty party's conscious mind, again, through the medium of the conscience. Two specific examples of this will be addressed, one from a man who lived 2000 years ago, and one from a man who died after killing a child, two police officers, and a state trooper in Tampa, Florida, on May 19th, 1998. In the Old Testament Book of Proverbs, Chapter 28, Verse 17, the *Holy Bible* says: "A man tormented by the guilt of murder will be a fugitive till death; let no one support him."(NIV)

Judas Iscariot, who was a political disciple of Christ, not a religious one, was tempted by the Devil to betray Christ when he refused to overthrow the Romans in Jerusalem. Having given in to the temptation, thinking he could force Christ into war, he was given over to the possession of the Devil for carrying out the betrayal. After the crucifixion, Judas confronted the religious leaders (not hookers or thieves or drug dealers) who paid him thirty pieces of silver for his directing them to where Christ was outside the city in the Garden of Gethsemane. The story is told in the New Testament Book of Matthew, Chapter 27, Verses 3-4: "When Judas, who had betrayed him, saw that Jesus was condemned, he was seized with remorse and returned the thirty silver coins to the chief priests and the elders. 'I have sinned,' he said, 'for I have betrayed innocent blood.' 'What is that to us?' they replied. 'That's your responsibility.' So Judas threw the money into the temple and left. Then he went away and hanged himself."(NIV)

The guilt of murder, as illustrated by the Book of Proverbs (in the quote before the one you just read), tormented Judas Iscariot until he committed suicide. The same thing occurred in Tampa, Florida, on May 19th, 1998. A man shot a 4-year old boy, and claimed it was an accident. However, he tried to elude police at his home. This guy must have anticipated being arrested, as he had been in the past, so he wore a handcuff key around his neck. The police officers handcuffed him in the front, as opposed to behind the back, while they searched his property. Watching television at the time, I heard a special report broadcasted over the airways. The man in question was on the phone with an NBC affiliate. He was now held up in a gas station north of Tampa, and was holding a woman hostage. I heard him say the following, live, just as he was saying it, concerning his killing the four year old, "As far as I'm concerned, I don't deserve to live." Now, who told him that? His conscience, speaking for Lord Jesus Christ, told him. He went on to describe how he killed the two detectives who were taking him to the police station by undoing the handcuffs with his key, grabbing the driver's gun and then killing them both. He also killed a state trooper on his way north. This man committed four murders, and in the end, shot and killed himself. Isn't it interesting, that Judas Iscariot, as well as the Tampa man, living 2000 years apart, had the very same reaction to their crime. The song remains the same. Lord Jesus Christ has programmed the subconscious minds of everyone just the same. "You shall not commit murder" shouted loud in the mind of Judas 2000 years ago, just as it did in 1998 in the mind of the Tampa man. Did the two know each other? They absolutely did not. They both had the knowledge of murder being wrong, because they were both designed and created by the same God. Even though Judas thought it was right to betray Christ when he did it, he had an involuntary reaction afterward, showing inner design, apart from his own will or belief.

An amazing story of inner design of the subconscious by Christ was relayed to us during "Missions Emphasis Week" in *Bible* College. There was a missionary there from Africa who related to the entire student body the story of one of his contemporaries. The man felt the call to go to *Bible* College to be a missionary. When he graduated, he went to Africa to go to a very dangerous place. The other missionaries there tried to dissuade him, warning him that the tribes in the area were pagans who believed in human sacrifice, cannibalism, etc. The man would not be stopped, however, and so off he went. He came to a village, all natives of the type he had been warned about living there. One of the elders of the village met him. The man knew the language, or had a translation of their language available, and was able to communicate to the elder in his own dialect. When the elder was done listening to the man explain why he was there, the elder was overwhelmed with joy. The elder in question, had been crying out to the God he knew was against the pagan practices that were prevalent in his village. He wanted that God to intervene. The missionary led the entire village to conversion to Christianity, and the killing and cannibalism, etc., came to a screeching halt. You see, everyone on earth has the subconscious programming of Lord Jesus Christ in their minds. Even the most ungodly natives in the wilds of Africa know the truth about God, even if they suppress that truth by their wickedness and sear their conscience of the original knowledge of right and wrong. As the *Bible* says, nobody will have an excuse. When the elder of the village cried out to Christ, Christ sent him a man to teach him the *Bible*. The man didn't know it was Christ he was calling on, only the moral code. Christ knew he was calling to him, however. The man simply repented of what was going on in his village, and, as a result, Christ provided salvation. The elder didn't shout something stupid like "cancel my subscription to the resurrection" as Jim Morrison the Shaman did, at Christ. He asked for salvation and he got it. The *Holy Bible* teaches this in the New Testament Book of Matthew, Chapter 5, Verse 6, where Jesus said: "Blessed are those who hunger and thirst for righteousness, for they will be filled."(NIV) That is an absolute, promised by God the Son himself. That promise applies to you reading this book as well. The subconscious of the elder shouted at his conscious mind through his conscience, and he had a righteous response, true repentance. Judas and the Tampa man had remorse, but not repentance. Their remorse led them to kill again; themselves. The elder did not commit suicide, he cried out to God for salvation, and he got it. Will God forgive a murderer if he or she repents and asks for salvation from Christ? It doesn't make sense humanly, but yes. All the people who have ever been killed on one side of the scale with Christ's murder on the other, and Jesus' murder tips the scales, because he was innocent almighty God. What did he say about those crowds of people who shouted, "crucify him?" He said, "Father, forgive them, for they know not what they do." Several thousand of those who wanted him dead were given salvation 50 days later when they repented at the preaching of Peter. Christ's sacrifice on the cross is sufficient to pay for murder as well. Does that mean a murderer should be released from prison if they get saved? No it does not. They should get the death penalty just like everyone else. Two thousand years separated Judas from the Tampa man, but the same reaction to murder. The elder of the native village had the same reaction in his mind as they, "You shall not commit murder."

Many a person has been given license by the United States government to commit murder. Former Chief Justice Harry A. Blackmun, who wrote "Roe vs. Wade" into law, made it a 5-4 decision for legal abortion with his decision. I know several men who have told me of getting some girl pregnant and her coming back and confessing with a guilty conscience what she did. I know several, in several different states. Why did the woman come back and say she was sorry for what he didn't know she did? She needed to confess to get the massive guilt off her back. You see, Justice Blackmun's decision has no jurisdiction over Lord Jesus Christ's moral law against murder in the human subconscious. I'm sure he is fully cognizant of that now.

Speaking of murdering with a pen, let's take a look at former President Clinton for a moment. The most brutal form of abortion is partial birth abortion, and it has been advocated by this man repeatedly. The baby's body is extracted from the womb, except for the head, then the skull is cut open and the brains are sucked out with a vacuum. Then the dead body is tossed into a bucket. Congress passed a bill to prohibit this senseless murdering. Instead of signing the bill into law, the President of the United States, William Jefferson Clinton, vetoed it (three times). Subsequent to that, he sent his wife on a tour (or she told him she was going) of the world as an ambassador and champion for the rights of children. Now I ask you, do you think Lord Jesus Christ considers those two ambassadors and champions for the rights of the children who are being murdered by partial birth abortion? Jesus was talking about people like them by analogy one day when he was discussing the Pharisees with his disciples. In the New Testament Book of Luke, Chapter 20, Verses 46- 47, Jesus said: "Beware of the teachers of the law. They like to walk around in flowing robes and love to be greeted in the marketplaces and have the most important seats in the synagogues and the places of honor at banquets. They devour widows' houses and for a show make lengthy prayers. Such men will be punished most severely."(NIV) The punishment he spoke of was during eternal damnation, and the most severe punishment in the midst of it, in the context of the passage.

Bill and Hillary Clinton, who allowed themselves to be filmed by CNN going to church, Bill carrying a *Bible* in his hand, the book that condemns murder, adultery, homosexuality, pretending to be Christians, even Southern Baptists, are anything but disciples of Jesus Christ. Their pretension was played out in the most powerful position on earth. Do we see them filmed by CNN going to church during the George W. Bush Administration? The Old Testament Book of Isaiah shouts at them in Chapter 5, verses 20-21: "Woe to those who call evil good and good evil, who put darkness for light and light for darkness, who put bitter for sweet and sweet for bitter. Woe to those who are wise in their own eyes and clever in their own sight."(NIV) There has not been a more anti-Christ man in the oval office. The thing that makes him worse than other ungodly presidents is that he says wrong is right; and he used the office of the presidency to promote it. With the President of the United States telling people it's acceptable for them to murder their children, what are people supposed to think? When a teenager and her boyfriend go to an abortion clinic, believing the girl has the right to rule over her own body, to decide whether or not she wants to have a baby, and has the abortion, she does what she believed to be right; again, advocated by the Clintons. Afterwards, she can't get to sleep at night. Why? Because Christ programmed her subconscious mind with "You shall not commit murder." This is something of which William Jefferson Clinton's bloody pen had no jurisdiction over.

      The subconscious mind projects "You shall not steal" into the conscious mind through the conscience as well. How does the old phrase go? "There's no honor among thieves?" Do thieves trust one another? Of course they do not. The story is told of a little boy who played with the little girl across the street on a regular basis. He noticed one day that she had a large jar of jellybeans in her bedroom, about 3/4 of the way full. Back at his house, he had a jar of marbles about 3/4 of the way full. He asked her if she would like to trade jars, and she agreed. He ran home, took a giant handful of the marbles out of his jar and hid them in a shoebox. He then took the jar to the girl's house. She gave him the jellybeans and he went home. He couldn't sleep all night, because he kept worrying that she might have taken some of the jellybeans out of the jar and hid them; after she agreed to trade them. The illustration is simplistic, but it tells the story, that the boy had "You shall not steal" written in his subconscious, and he stole marbles he agreed to trade.

      One last concept that will be mentioned here is lying. What person who is a liar believes other people? I saw a man on television, "MSNBC," in June of 1998, defending President Clinton, saying, "Everybody lies all the time." How do you the reader feel about this man's claim to omniscience? I feel sorry for the poor woman who is married to this man (I have heard men admit that their consciences were smoothed over by Clinton's time in office.). Jesus said the following to the religious leaders who hated him in the New Testament Book of John, Chapter 8, Verses 44-47: "You belong to your father, the devil, and you want to carry out your father's desire. He was a murderer from the beginning, not holding to the truth, for there is no truth in him. When he lies, he speaks his native language, for he is a liar and the father of lies. Yet because I tell the truth, you do not believe me! Can any of you prove me guilty of sin? If I am telling the truth, why don't you believe me? He who belongs to God hears what God says. The reason you do not hear is that you do not belong to God."(NIV) Jesus didn't play games with his enemies, he told the most highly honored individuals in Jerusalem that they were children of the Devil. He was also calling them liars. The implicit message of the text is that if you are a liar, the Devil is your spiritual father. The *Holy Bible*, in the Book of Revelation, once again states that liars are doomed: "...and all liars - their place will be in the fiery lake of burning sulfur." - Revelation 21:8(NIV) [Again, sulfur is a modern name for Brimstone] The *Holy Bible* and the human subconscious depict lying as wrong, showing the creator of mankind to be Lord Jesus Christ.

The absolutes of the subconscious mind in man, say that adultery, murder, stealing, and lying are all wrong. Those who continue to do those things wrong sear their consciences and are able to believe wrong is right. For example, a hit man, when he first murders, feels guilty. However, after enough murders, he believes the people he kills belong dead, and is able to sleep at night. All of the preceding absolutes of the human mind ran through my head consistently. I came to the conclusion that whoever created man was totally at odds with the behavior of man, which is why he hides himself from man, visibly. A Holy God cannot fellowship with an unholy creation. Those who face these absolutes in the mind, and are willing to repent, are able to fellowship with God, once they are saved, by putting their trust in Christ's atonement for sin on the cross, in conjunction with repentance of sin, not trusting in any righteousness of their own, or any righteous works. Those who do not want to repent, living this painful life of rebellion against God, often turn to drugs and alcohol to kill the pain. Drugs and alcohol, however, only kill symptomatic pain. The pain that comes from the root problem is symptomatic pain. The root problem that causes emotional pain, that people anesthetize with drugs and alcohol is simple; separation from God and his manifest presence, through the power of the Holy Spirit. Man was created to fellowship with God. If he does not, he lives in pain. If he dies without salvation, that pain is multiplied, and there will be no artificial painkillers in hell. Once again, the moral law of God imbedded in the human mind, in keeping with the Ten Commandments, makes it clear, that man is without excuse for not wanting to repent of sin and search for God. Paul the Apostle made it clear that the Ten Commandments were given to show man the antithetical, polarized distinction between sinful men and the Holy God. He elaborated by stating that the moral law is not simply to condemn mankind's sin, but to act as a teacher that would direct mankind to the Messiah, Lord Jesus Christ, who would die to pay the price for sin; making salvation available to man on his terms, not ours. Paul presented this teaching in the New Testament Book of Galatians, Chapter 3, Verse 24: "So the law was put in charge to lead us to Christ that we might be justified by faith."(NIV) The Pharisees saw themselves as righteous enough to enter heaven without salvation, and that is why they had Christ crucified by the Romans. Jesus warned his disciples of this reaction before he was arrested in the New Testament Book of John, Chapter 7, Verse 7: "The world cannot hate you, but it hates me because I testify that what it does is evil."(NIV)

God does not just tolerate evil running rampant either, as it may appear to some. This is another absolute that you the reader already believe in, but from another perspective. We all believe in the absolute concept, *"What goes around comes around."* Who is in charge of that absolute? Who makes it efficacious? Lord Jesus Christ does. The *Bible* teaches in the New Testament Book of Romans, Chapter 12, Verse 19: "Do not take revenge, my friends, but leave room for God's wrath, for it is written: 'It is mine to avenge; I will repay,' says the Lord."(NIV) Lord Jesus Christ, therefore, is in command of the absolute of vengeance - what goes around, comes around.

After considering all these absolutes for a very long time, I decided it was time to turn to God; as I considered life without him as worthless. I turned on the television set, and "accidentally" came upon "The Old Time Gospel Hour." This is the television ministry of "Thomas Road Baptist Church" in Lynchburg, Virginia, Dr. Jerry Falwell, Pastor. Sitting in my home, watching Dr. Falwell preach, a man I had consistently associated with mental illness, repentant of my mountain of sin, I asked Christ to forgive me of my sins and come into my life as Lord and Savior, when directed by Dr. Falwell at the end of the broadcast to do so (I subsequently told Dr. B.R. Lakin of this in 1983, and Mac Evans in 1993.). When the Holy Spirit of God begins to work in the mind of the new believer, he confirms for him the belief that the moral code of Lord Jesus Christ is right and good. Beginning the work, it takes time and the proper church environment for a "gross sinner" as myself to have the love of Christ become efficacious in him.

THE ABSOLUTE TRUTH IN SALVATION OF THE HUMAN SOUL

An absolute of the human mind, when it has been programmed to think that an anti-Christ lifestyle is right, is its perception of Lord Jesus Christ and his moral code as being wrong; religious fanaticism. One cannot live with the mindset of believing that the anti-Christ lifestyle and its antithesis, the one advocated by Jesus, are both morally right, concurrently. The two moral codes cannot exist contemporaneously within the same person. It is impossible to believe in both. The human subconscious mind, in its primal condition points to Lord Jesus Christ, and no other, as its designer and creator. If we choose the anti-Christ lifestyle, we are held accountable by Christ for having done so. The concept was so clearly presented by none other than Aleister Crowley himself, but from an antithetical premise, in *The Equinox*: "The sin which is unpardonable is knowingly and willfully to reject truth, to fear knowledge lest that knowledge pander not to thy prejudices."1 [That statement by Crowley is clearly the most amazing thing I have ever seen in his writings. He is guilty of rejecting truth to a greater degree than most of the people that ever lived.] So mankind as a whole rejects the truth of Christ in the subconscious and lives in diametric opposition to it, because it does not pander to its prejudices; to live in pleasure that is against the will of God, outside its proper context. Is God, the creator of sex, against it?

You already read in this chapter that he is not, in its proper context. He is against it outside that context. One of the major reasons that mankind today believes that Lord Jesus Christ's moral code is wrong, among other reasons, is the concept of intoxication.

Mankind has always longed for intoxication, because it brings about pain relief. How often have individuals partied all night, and then woke up the next morning and said something to this effect? "Man, I was feeling no pain last night!" This pain relieving intoxication is a natural desire in man. Christ created him with that desire. The intoxication man is really looking for is the manifest presence of Lord Jesus Christ in the mind. Jesus said in the New Testament Book of John, Chapter 4, Verse 24: "God is spirit, and his worshipers must worship in spirit and in truth."(NIV)

Before elaborating on the manifest presence of Christ, the idea of intoxication is presented from a Psyhopharmacologist named Ronald Siegel. In his book, *Intoxication: Life in Pursuit of Artificial Paradise*, he wrote: "Our nervous system...is arranged to respond to chemical intoxicants in much the same way it responds to rewards of food, drink, and sex. Throughout our entire history as a species, intoxication has functioned like the basic drives of hunger, thirst, or sex, sometimes overshadowing all other activities: Intoxication is the fourth drive. Individual and group survival depends on the ability to understand and control this basic motivation..."2 I am in complete concurrence with the writing of Ronald Siegel on this issue. Lord Jesus Christ created mankind with the need for intoxication, and has his manifest spiritual presence as the fulfillment of that need. You see, drugs and alcohol are painkillers in that they deal with symptoms of the root problem, which is separation from Christ and his manifest presence. The problem with drugs and alcohol is that it causes permanent changes in the mind toward sin. In his book, *Receptors*, Dr. Richard Restak provided the following insight: "So far, neuroscientists have not made up their minds as to whether opiates, cocaine, and other commonly employed mind-altering drugs exert *permanent* physical effects in the brain. There doesn't seem to be any doubt, however, that long-lasting, perhaps permanent psychological changes are induced."3

Sinful men are in rebellion against God; they believe their sinful desires are natural. Sinful desire is that desire for the fulfillment of a God given need outside the boundaries or context he commands that those needs are to be fulfilled. Since men do not know the *Holy Bible*, and do not care to know, in general, they are cannon fodder for deception by the Devil. In 1997, the movie, "The Devil's Advocate," starring Al Pacino and Keanu Reeves, came out. The Devil himself couldn't have written the script to the ending of the film any better; although it would not surprise me if he did write it, as you will see in a moment. Keanu Reeves plays the character of Kevin. Kevin is reluctant to go along with the Devil's expressed will at the end of the movie. The Devil asks him if he is resisting him because of God. Playing the Devil, Al Pacino tells Keanu Reeves that God creates man with instinctive desires, and then for amusement, sets up rules against fulfilling those desires. He then says that God laughs hysterically while man is battling his own desires. Then he says that he will never worship that. Also, the Devil tells Kevin that he is the one who "...nurtured every sensation man has been inspired to have." At the end of it, the Devil says that the twentieth century belonged to him, and that he was "peaking."

What the Devil is doing, through movies like this, is programming vulnerable minds to believe that some, if not all, of what is said here is true. God does give man desires, like sex, and tells him, in the *Bible* (that men do not read), the proper context for that to be carried out in. Sinful desire, which is the desire to get God given needs filled in ways that God condemns, is not restrained by mankind. It's like this, I saw a man at an Alcoholic's Anonymous meeting stand up and say that he gets through life by not taking a drink one day at a time (I went to the meeting with a buddy who had to go because of driving under the influence.). The man's desire to drink was still there. So his was a life of restriction. If God did not fill the emptiness inside of him, that only God can fill, the desire of the presence of the supreme being, then the man lives with the emptiness. In the Pacino film, he said God says we can look but we can't touch, or we can touch but we cannot taste, etc. If men worshiped Lord Jesus Christ, they would be filled with his presence, and would not need to fulfill God given needs in sinful ways. When a person walks with God, the Holy Spirit controls sinful desires. Paul the Apostle said, in the New Testament Book of Galatians, Chapter 5, Verses 16-17: "So I say, live by the Spirit, and you will not gratify the desires of the sinful nature. For the sinful nature desires what is contrary to the Spirit, and the Spirit what is contrary to the sinful nature."(NIV) Men and women do not understand what is meant by the previous verses, but it will be explained before this chapter ends. Because they do not understand the true meaning of living by the Spirit, many falsehoods arise. When men try to control the sin nature by the sin nature, a conflict arises. If sin comes naturally to the sinner, then sin is natural to the sinful mind, or so it seems. Then Lord Jesus Christ shows up and condemns what to mankind seems natural.

Aleister Crowley let his sin nature run to its extent, filling him with the following kind of wisdom. He begins this quote from *The Equinox* by quoting a minister in England, and then ends by blaspheming Christ: "'Have you got religion?...Are you saved?...Do you love Jesus?'...'Brother, God can save you....Jesus is the sinner's friend....Rest your head on Jesus...dear, dear Jesus!' Curse till thunder shake the stars! Curse till this blasphemy is cursed from the face of heaven! Curse till the hissing name of Jesus, which writhes like a snake in a snare, is driven from the kingdom of faith!"4 That statement was written by Jimmy Page's hero, Black Magician Aleister Crowley; whose face is on the front of the Beatles' *Sgt. Pepper's Lonely Hearts Club Band* Album.

In another part of his *Equinox*, Crowley inserted the writing of Ananda Metteya. This apparently is another magical name for Allan Bennett, his contemporary in the early days of his career in Magick. In the epistle, that he titled, *The Training of the Mind*, he wrote about Jesus, beginning with a simile that the mind is like an engine:

"So it is with this subtle machinery of the mind, - a mechanism infinitely more complex, capable of far more power for good or for evil, than the most marvelous of man's mechanical achievements, than the most powerful engine ever made by human hands. One great engine, at its worst, exploding, may destroy a few hundred lives; at its best may carry a few thousand men, may promote trade, and the comfort of some few hundred lives; but who can estimate the power of one human mind, whether for good or for evil? One such mind, the mind of a man like Jesus Christ, may bring about the tortured death of many million men, may wreck states and religions and dynasties, and cause untold misery and suffering; another mind, employing the same manner of energy, but rightly using that energy for the benefit of others, may, like the Buddha, bring hope into the hopeless lives of scores upon scores of human beings, may increase by a thousandfold the pity and love of a third of humanity, may aid innumerable lakhs of beings to come to that Peace for which we all crave - that Peace the way to which is so difficult to find.

"But the energy which these two minds employed is one and the same. That energy lies hidden in every human brain, it is generated with every pulsation of every human heart, it is the prerogative of every being, and the sole mover in the world of men. There is no idea or thought, there is no deed, whether good or bad, accomplished in this world, but that supreme energy, that steampower of our mental mechanism, is the mover and the cause. It is by use of this energy that the child learns how to speak; it is by its power that Christ could bring sorrow into thousands of lives; it is by this power that the Buddha conquered the hearts of one-third of men; it is by that force that so many have followed him on the way which he declared - the Nirvana Marga, the way to the Unutterable Peace. The name of that power is Mental Concentration, and there is nothing in this world, whether for good or for evil, but is wrought by its application."5

All of the nonsense spoken of by Pacino, Crowley, and Metteya makes perfect sense to those who think the actions of the sinful desire is normal. They all believe that Jesus is promoting nothing more than asceticism, a rigorous form of self-denial that results in misery, because "natural" desires do not get met if you don't indulge the sinful nature and get your needs met in any context (I believe Pacino believes this as well, because otherwise, he wouldn't have made the blasphemous statements he did; in a movie or anywhere else.). These people have no idea what they are talking about, because they do not know the *Bible*.

Again, Paul wrote that those who walk by the Spirit of God would not fulfill the desires of the sinful nature. The *"Goof of all time"* is not that God created man with instinctive desires, and telling him he cannot fulfill those desires, he is laughing at him from heaven. The goof of all time is that the presence of Christ, the Prince of Peace, is what men really desire, and Satan has convinced man that to turn to Christ is mental illness; religious fanaticism. Once a person's mind has been molded to believe that, it is very difficult for it to be undone. To be in complete agreement with the God and standards placed in the human subconscious, and living in communion with that God, Lord Jesus Christ, men receive his manifest presence, which is the total intoxication of the mind and soul. His presence is total numbing peace, joyful, and filled with his purity and love. A person filled with the Spirit of God, is a person who is overwhelmed with the ability to fathom the love that Christ has for him or her; it is spiritually intoxicating. This concept can only be conveyed by the Holy Spirit. If it is discussed outside the presence of God, it seems like empty words. It is not just pain relief like alcohol and drugs, which deal with symptoms. The Spirit of God deals with the root of emotional pain, separation from God, by bringing the devoted Christian into the presence of God, which brings the sinful nature under control. Paul contrasted the two enemies in Galatians, Chapter 5, Verses 19-25:

"The acts of the sinful nature are obvious: sexual immorality, impurity and debauchery; idolatry and witchcraft; hatred, discord, jealousy, fits of rage, selfish ambition, dissensions, factions and envy; drunkenness, orgies, and the like. I warn you, as I did before, that those who live like this will not inherit the kingdom of God.

"But the fruit of the Spirit is love, joy, peace, patience, kindness, goodness, faithfulness, gentleness and self-control. Against such things there is no law."(NIV)

Again, Paul pits drunkenness against the presence of the Spirit of God in the New Testament Book of Ephesians, Chapter 5, Verses 18-19: "Do not get drunk on wine, which leads to debauchery. Instead, be filled with the Spirit. Speak to one another with psalms, hymns and spiritual songs. Sing and make music in your heart to the Lord, always giving thanks to God the Father for everything, in the name of our Lord Jesus Christ."(NIV) The power of the presence of the Holy Spirit conveys the love, joy, and supreme peace that can only be provided by the Prince of Peace to the human soul. The person who is filled with the Spirit of God can live free from the tyranny of the sinful nature, and can comprehend and enjoy worshiping Lord Jesus Christ, which is something the mind controlled by the sinful nature cannot comprehend or execute. Paul wrote of this in the New Testament Book of Romans, Chapter 8, Verses 5-8: "Those who live according to the sinful nature have their minds set on what that nature desires; but those who live in accordance with the Spirit have their minds set on what the Spirit desires. The mind of sinful man is death, but the mind controlled by the Spirit is life and peace; the sinful mind is hostile to God. It does not submit to God's law, nor can it do so. Those controlled by the sinful nature cannot please God."(NIV) The writer of Psalm 16 made the reward of Christ's presence plain to the reader in Verse 11: "You have made known to me the path of life; you will fill me with joy in your presence, with eternal pleasures at your right hand."(NIV)

The Psalm writer knew he would be filled with joy in Christ's presence because he had been already; numerous times. The joy produced by the presence of Christ fills a person with strength. In the Old Testament Book of Nehemiah, Chapter 8, Verse 10, Nehemiah spoke of this concept: "...the joy of the Lord is your strength."(NIV) Again, it is the joy of the Lord's presence that strengthens a person. Isaiah the prophet presented this concept quoting God himself, in Chapter 41, Verse 10: "So do not fear, for I am with you; do not be dismayed, for I am your God. I will strengthen you and help you; I will uphold you with my righteous right hand."(NIV)

The manifest presence of Christ which brings joy and love to the human soul was taught by Jesus himself in the New Testament Book of John, Chapter 14, Verses 15-21: "If you love me, you will obey what I command. And I will ask the Father, and he will give you another Counselor to be with you forever - the Spirit of truth. The world cannot accept him, because it neither sees him nor knows him. But you know him, for he lives with you and will be in you. I will not leave you as orphans; I will come to you. Before long, the world will not see me anymore, but you will see me. Because I live, you also will live. On that day you will realize that I am in my Father, and you are in me, and I am in you. Whoever has my commands and obeys them, he is the one who loves me. He who loves me will be loved by my Father, and I too will love him and show myself to him."(NIV) The manifestation Jesus speaks of is in the mind, by the power of the Holy Spirit.

Lord Jesus Christ went on to reiterate the principal of his manifest love in the next chapter of John, 15, in Verses 5-8, speaking to his disciples:

"I am the vine; you are the branches. If a man remains in me and I in him, he will bear much fruit; apart from me you can do nothing. If anyone does not remain in me, he is like a branch that is thrown away and withers; such branches are picked up, thrown into the fire and burned. If you remain in me and my words remain in you, ask whatever you wish, and it will be given you. This is to my Father's glory, that you bear much fruit, showing yourselves to be my disciples.

"As the Father has loved me, so have I loved you. Now remain in my love. If you obey my commands, you will remain in my love, just as I have obeyed my Father's commands and remain in his love. I have told you this so that my joy may be in you and that your joy may be complete. My command is this: Love each other as I have loved you. Greater love has no one than this, that he lay down his life for his friends. You are my friends if you do what I command. I no longer call you servants, because a servant does not know his master's business. Instead, I have called you friends, for everything that I learned from my Father I have made known to you."(NIV)

Jesus made his desire for intimacy with his people clear to his disciples in that passage. He used the analogy of streams of water to describe the working of the Spirit in the life of the person who loves God in John Chapter 7, Verses 37-39: "On the last and greatest day of the Feast, Jesus stood and said in a loud voice, 'If anyone is thirsty, let him come to me and drink. Whoever believes in me, as the Scripture has said, streams of living water will flow from within him.' By this he meant the Spirit, whom those who believed in him were later to receive."(NIV) The communion with Christ and the Holy Spirit spoken of in these *Holy Bible* passages are available only to the person who decides to repent of their attitude toward sin. When the human mind begins to agree with God that right is right, and good is good, and wrong is wrong, and evil is evil, then that mind can perceive Lord Jesus Christ the way he or she was designed to see him, an object of love and worship, as opposed to Lord of religious fanatics; as the sinful nature declares. At that point, the human being is capable of repenting of sin and turning to Christ for salvation; the gift of eternal life, which brings about his painless presence and joy.

When a person wants to turn to Lord Jesus Christ for salvation, they must be informed as to what that really means from the *Holy Bible*; how to effectively work it out. If you are reading this and you desire to know the path of salvation, first and foremost you have to understand that Jesus is Lord of salvation. If God does not draw you to himself, you cannot be saved. He told a group of Pharisees in Jerusalem one day who were grumbling about his teachings, in John, Chapter 6, Verses 43-44: "'Stop grumbling among yourselves,' Jesus answered. 'No one can come to me unless the Father who sent me draws him, and I will raise him up at the last day.'"(NIV) God draws men to himself for salvation, men do not earn it by being good, or doing good works. It is a gift from God. This drawing of men to himself is his unmerited favor. In the *Bible*, unmerited or unearned favor is called 'grace.' The following text from the New Testament Book of Ephesians, Chapter 2, Verses 8-9, makes it clear to the reader: "For it is by grace you have been saved, through faith - and this not from yourselves. It is the gift of God - not by works, so that no one can boast."(NIV) If salvation is a gift from God, and a person cannot get this gift unless God draws that person to himself, how then does God decide to draw men to himself? First of all, let me say that God desires to save everyone; but he will not save everyone. In the New Testament Book of John, Chapter 3, Verses 16-17, Jesus made it clear that God will save anyone who believes in him. This not only means believing that he exists, it means to believe in him, like a Satanist believes in the Devil. The text reads: "For God so loved the world that he gave his one and only

Son, that whoever believes in him shall not perish but have eternal life. For God did not send his Son into the world to condemn the world, but to save the world through him."(NIV) Also, in the New Testament Book of 1 Timothy, Chapter 2, Verses 4-5, the Bible makes it clear that God wants to save everyone: "...God our Savior, who wants all men to be saved and to come to a knowledge of the truth. For there is one God and one mediator between God and men, the man Christ Jesus, who gave himself as a ransom for all men - the testimony given in its proper time."(NIV) This passage is not saying that Jesus in not God the Son, it is saying he ransomed man when he took on the form of man, whom he created in his own image. Therefore, if God draws men to himself, those whom he chooses for salvation, and gives them the gift of salvation, which is eternal life, and he wants to save all men, why does he not save all men? The answer is because he draws men to himself on the basis of grace, unearned favor, and the only ones who receive this grace are those who are humble to the message of salvation. The *Bible* makes this plain in the New Testament Book of James, Chapter 4, Verses 6 & 10: "God opposes the proud but gives grace to the humble....Humble yourselves before the Lord, and he will lift you up."(NIV) This concept is presented in the Old Testament in Psalm 149, Verse 4: "For the LORD takes delight in his people; he crowns the humble with salvation."(NIV) If it is by grace that we are saved, and God only gives grace to the humble, and no one can come to God unless he draws him, then it is those who are humble to the message of salvation that God gives the grace leading to salvation. Therefore, those of you reading this book who are willing to humble yourself before God while contemplating this message, he will draw you to himself by the power of the Holy Spirit. However, before man can be saved, he must know that he needs to be. What that means is this, we all need to see ourselves as God sees us as we are living in rebellion against him. This shows man his need for a savior.

If you could save yourself by being good, Christ would not have to have died on the cross. In the eyes of the local police chief, if you work, pay taxes, are not a thief, adulterer, or other form of criminal, you are perceived as a good person. However, the only person God considers good is the one who has NEVER sinned. If you want God to call you good enough to enter heaven without looking to Jesus for salvation you had better be absolutely perfect. That is what he requires to enter heaven. You cannot have committed one single solitary sin. The *Bible* makes this clear in the New Testament Book of Romans, Chapter 3, Verses 23-26: "...for all have sinned and fall short of the glory of God, and are justified freely by his grace through the redemption that came by Christ Jesus. God presented him as a sacrifice of atonement, through faith in his blood. He did this to demonstrate his justice, because in his forbearance he had left the sins committed beforehand unpunished - he did it to demonstrate his justice at the present time, so as to be just and the one who justifies those who have faith in Jesus."(NIV) Only those who believe in Christ as Lord will be justifed by God.

Christ atoned for the sins of men by allowing himself to be murdered through crucifixion. It is not a good works issue, the issue is sin. The person who believes in Christ and accepts him as savior, based on a willingness to follow Jesus as Lord, has all his or her sinful acts, past, present and future, sent to the cross, where Jesus suffers for it. That person stands before God as sinless, and precious. The *Bible* makes this clear in the New Testament Book of Romans, Chapter 5, Verses 6-11, where Paul the Apostle speaks of believers in Jesus:

"You see, at just the right time, when we were still powerless, Christ died for the ungodly. Very rarely will anyone die for a righteous man, though for a good man someone might possibly dare to die. But God demonstrates his own love for us in this: while we were still sinners, Christ died for us.

"Since we have now been justified by his blood, how much more shall we be saved from God's wrath through him! For if, when we were God's enemies, we were reconciled to him through the death of his Son, how much more, having been reconciled, shall we be saved through his life! Not only is this so, but we also rejoice in God through our Lord Jesus Christ, through whom we have now received reconciliation."(NIV)

Salvation is a gift from God, not based on us being righteous, which we are not in his sight, though we may be in each other's. Left to himself, while content to be living the anti-Christ lifestyle, man appears in the sight of God as described in Romans, Chapter 3, Verses 10-18: "There is no one righteous, not even one; there is no one who understands, no one who seeks God. All have turned away, they have together become worthless; there is no one who does good, not even one. Their throats are open graves; their tongues practice deceit. The poison of vipers is on their lips. Their mouths are full of cursing and bitterness. Their feet are swift to shed blood; ruin and misery mark their ways, and the way of peace they do not know. There is no fear of God before their eyes."(NIV) God has made the reward for the individual who will not humble himself and search for him plain and simple in Romans, Chapter 6, Verse 23: "For the wages of sin is death, but the gift of God is eternal life in Christ Jesus our Lord."(NIV) The death spoken of here is spiritual death in hell. Jesus made it clear that he gives the gift of eternal life to those who follow him in John, Chapter 10, Verses 27-30: "My sheep listen to my voice; I know them, and they follow me, I give them eternal life, and they shall never perish; no one can snatch them out of my hand. My Father, who has given them to me, is greater than all; no one can snatch them out of my Father's hand. I and the Father are one."(NIV) Again, eternal life is the gift given by God to the those who, as an act of their will, humble themselves before the message of salvation in Christ, deciding to believe in Jesus as Lord and Savior and follow him, as a result of the guidance of the Holy Spirit; which, again, is only given to those who humble themselves before God. The person who chooses to follow Jesus Christ is declared righteous by God the Father. This is a declaration by God as a result of repentance. It is unearned, because, even though people repent, they still do not deserve eternal life; they still deserve to go to hell for rebelling against God.

God condemns Christ in our place on the cross, and declares the follower of Jesus righteous in his sight, making it possible to give the person eternal life. Paul the Apostle wrote of this in the New Testament Book of 2 Corinthians, Chapter 5, Verses 16-21: "So from now on we regard no one from a worldly point of view. Though we once regarded Christ in this way, we do so no longer. Therefore, if anyone is in Christ, he is a new creation; the old has gone, the new has come! All this is from God, who reconciled us to himself through Christ and gave us the ministry of reconciliation: that God was reconciling the world to himself in Christ, not counting men's sins against them. And he has committed to us the message of reconciliation. We are therefore Christ's ambassadors, as though God were making his appeal through us. We implore you on Christ's behalf: Be reconciled to God. God made him who had no sin to be sin for us, so that in him we might become the righteousness of God."(NIV) Nowhere in that passage did it say that men were righteous on their own. It did not say if the good works outweigh the bad, the person goes to heaven. It made it clear that because God made Christ to be sin on the cross, he was able to make us righteous; in him, and only in him. None of us will ever be declared righteous on our own. Lord Jesus Christ is not involved in some co-op program with man. He is the Savior of those who get saved; period. People will not be walking around heaven saying, "I got here because I did these good works, what did you do?" There will be no comparison. The song will remain the same. Everyone who gets there will bow before Christ and acknowledge that he is the only reason they are not in hell. Anyone who refuses to look to Christ, and believing himself righteous enough to go to heaven without the salvation provided by Jesus, will die and go to hell. This is the crowd that had him crucified, the ones who worshiped themselves, believing themselves as righteous as God. This is the crowd that Jesus had conflict with, the most respected and honored people in Jerusalem; who thought they were righteous enough to go to heaven; apart from salvation in Christ.

Jesus was confrontational with these religious leaders on many occasions. On one occasion he pointed out to them that they would not come to him because they were secure in the honor and praise of one another and did not seek praise from God; in John, Chapter 5, Verses 39-44: "You diligently study the Scriptures because you think that by them you possess eternal life. These are the Scriptures that testify about me, yet you refuse to come to me to have life. I do not accept praise from men, but I know you. I know that you do not have the love of God in your hearts. I have come in my Father's name, and you do not accept me; but if someone else comes in his own name, you will accept him. How can you believe if you accept praise from one another, yet make no effort to obtain the praise that comes from the only God? But do not think I will accuse you before the Father. Your accuser is Moses, on whom your hopes are set. If you believed Moses, you would believe me, for he wrote about me. But since you do not believe what he wrote, how are you going to believe what I say?"(NIV)

I made mention of the following before briefly, but reiterate it for emphasis. Paul the Apostle wrote in the New Testament Book of Philippians, Chapter 2, Verses 8-11, that everyone, including the religious leaders Jesus confronted in that last quote, will bow the knee before Christ on the day of judgement and declare that he is Lord: "And being found in appearance as a man, he humbled himself and became obedient to death - even death on a cross! Therefore God exalted him to the highest place and gave him the name that is above every name, that at the name of Jesus every knee should bow, in heaven and on earth and under the earth, and every tongue confess that Jesus Christ is Lord, to the glory of God the Father."(NIV) When the passage mentioned things "under the earth," it was referring to those already in hell. So people can humble themselves before God now, or wait until the day of judgement to do it, just before they are thrown into hell forever. Jesus spoke of this to his disciples, mentioning a person losing his life for Jesus' sake, which means to lose your life of sin to follow him, in the New Testament Book of Luke, Chapter 9, Verses 23-26: "Then he said to them all: 'If anyone would come after me, he must deny himself and take up his cross daily and follow me. For whoever wants to save his life will lose it, but whoever loses his life for me will save it. What good is it for a man to gain the whole world, and yet lose or forfeit his very self? If anyone is ashamed of me and my words, the Son of Man will be ashamed of him when he comes in his glory and in the glory of the Father and of the holy angels.'"(NIV) Jesus himself is the Son of Man he was referring to. He was simply speaking of his human incarnation. When he comes the second time, it will be as judge, not Savior; and the souls of men who did not seek him or worship him will be lost. Men who were so rich they were able to "gain the whole world," are going to lose their own souls, not because they were rich, but because they were so rich they did not "need" God, and they lived lives of rebellion against him, suppressing the truth of God in the subconscious by their wickedness, and damning their souls to hell. Those, however, who want to be saved, and are repentant of their sins in their hearts, they only have to call on God to save them, and he knows whether they are genuine in repentance, and he will save their souls. This is what the *Bible* means when is says in Romans, Chapter 10, Verses 12-13: "For there is no difference between Jew and Gentile - the same Lord is Lord of all and richly blesses all who call on him, for 'Everyone who calls on the name of the Lord will be saved.'"(NIV)

Once a person is saved, he or she receives eternal life as a gift from God; and they have escaped eternal damnation in hell. Jesus stated this in John, Chapter 5, Verses 24-26: "I tell you the truth, whoever hears my word and believes him who sent me has eternal life and will not be condemned; he has crossed over from death to life. I tell you the truth, a time is coming and has now come when the dead will hear the voice of the Son of God and those who hear will live."(NIV) When Jesus referred to the dead in that passage, he was talking about those who were alive, yet spiritually dead, which is why they need a spiritual rebirth, to be reborn spiritually, making them born again. To turn to Lord Jesus Christ for salvation, makes a person born again, meaning they are beginning a new life spiritually.

In John, Chapter 3, Verses 1-12, Jesus addressed being born again to one of the religious teachers, the Pharisees, who had no idea of what he was talking about: "Now there was a man of the Pharisees named Nicodemus, a member of the Jewish ruling council. He came to Jesus at night and said, 'Rabbi, we know you are a teacher who has come from God. For no one could perform the miraculous signs you are doing if God were not with him.' In reply Jesus declared, 'I tell you the truth, no one can see the kingdom of God unless he is born again.' 'How can a man be born when he is old?' Nicodemus asked. 'Surely he cannot enter a second time into his mother's womb to be born!' Jesus answered, 'I tell you the truth, no one can enter the kingdom of God unless he is born of water and the Spirit. Flesh gives birth to flesh, but the Spirit gives birth to spirit. You should not be surprised at my saying, "You must be born again." The wind blows wherever it pleases. You hear its sound, but you cannot tell where it comes from or where it is going. So it is with everyone born of the Spirit.' 'How can this be?' Nicodemus asked. 'You are Israel's teacher,' said Jesus, 'and do you not understand these things? I tell you the truth, we speak of what we know, and we testify to what we have seen, but still you people do not accept our testimony. I have spoken to you of earthly things and you do not believe; how then will you believe if I speak of heavenly things?"(NIV)

In the passage where Jesus said flesh gives birth to flesh and Spirit gives birth to spirit, he was contrasting being born of water when the mother's water breaks and a baby comes forth, and being born spiritually, in communion with Christ. The spiritual birth is the second one. This is why it is called born "again." When Jesus said people can hear the wind blow but do not know where it comes from or where it goes is indicative of the born again believer, he was stressing the fact that people see the wind's effect, but that is all. People also see the effect of the Spirit of God in the new Christian's life, but do not know how it happened. It was a simple analogy. The person who repents and turns to Christ receives the free gift of eternal life, spiritual rebirth, and the person who does not will spend eternity in hell.

THE ABSOLUTE OF ETERNAL DAMNATION IN HELL

Eternal damnation is another absolute of the teachings of Lord Jesus Christ. He sacrificed himself on the cross to redeem men who would humble themselves before God. Those who will not, are going to be sent straight to hell when they die. The *Bible* teaches that there is eternal life in heaven and eternal damnation in hell, period. Anyone who has ever taught an anti-Biblical concept of a limbo or purgatory is a liar; his teaching is not based on the *Holy Bible*. It doesn't matter if the man believes he has power to make new teachings; he is a liar, cased closed. The place of trial and decision is right here on the earth. After death, it is one of two eternal destinies. Many are they who do not fear hell because they believe God is too loving a person to send anyone to a hell. Well, hell is where that crowd is going. God loved man too much to destroy him without a chance to reconcile; the chance purchased for him by Jesus on the cross of crucifixion. If one rejects that expression of love by Christ, and will not turn to him because of a desire to live a life of sin, that soul will die and go to hell. God hates sin. Those who reject his love to live in sin will stand before him after death as the personification of all the sins they have committed against him. Hating sin, he will send that soul to eternal damnation. Dr. John MacArthur, from Sun Valley, California, addressed this issue in his book, *The Love of God*:

"Many try to dodge the difficulty this poses by suggesting that God hates the sin, not the sinner. Why, then does God condemn the sinner and consign the person - not merely the sin - to eternal hell? Clearly we cannot sweep the severity of this truth away by denying God's hatred for the wicked. Nor should we imagine that such hatred is any kind of blemish on the character of God. It is a holy hatred. It is perfectly consistent with His spotless, unapproachable, incomprehensible holiness.

"Yet I am convinced from Scripture that God's hatred toward the wicked is not a hatred undiluted by compassion, mercy, or love. We know from human experience that love and hatred are not mutually exclusive. It is not the least bit unusual to have concurrent feelings of love and hatred directed at the same person. We often speak of people who have love-hate relationships. There is no reason to deny that in an infinitely purer and more noble sense, God's hatred toward the wicked is accompanied by a sincere, compassionate love for them as well.

"The fact that God will send to eternal hell all sinners who persist in sin and unbelief proves His hatred toward them. On the other hand, the fact that God promises to forgive and bring into His eternal glory all who trust Christ as Savior-and even pleads with sinners to repent-proves His love toward them."6

Lord Jesus Christ made this plain as day in the *Holy Bible*. He told the story of a rich man who had rejected God and a beggar who had turned to faith in God. He told the story to illustrate what happened after death; in the New Testament Book of Luke, Chapter 16, Verses 19-31:

"There was a rich man who was dressed in purple and fine linen and lived in luxury every day. At his gate was laid a beggar named Lazarus, covered with sores and longing to eat what fell from the rich man's table. Even the dogs came and licked his sores. The time came when the beggar died and the angels carried him to Abraham's side. The rich man also died and was buried. In hell, Where he was in torment, he looked up and saw Abraham far away, with Lazarus by his side. So he called to him, 'Father Abraham, have pity on me and send Lazarus to dip the tip of his finger in water and cool my tongue, because I am in agony in this fire.' But Abraham replied, 'Son, remember that in your lifetime you received your good things, while Lazarus received bad things, but now he is comforted here and you are in agony. And besides all this, between us and you a great chasm has been fixed, so that those who want to go from here to you cannot, nor can anyone cross over from there to us.' He answered, 'Then I beg you, father, send Lazarus to my father's house, for I have five brothers. Let him warn them, so that they will not also come to this place of torment.' Abraham replied, 'They have Moses and the Prophets; let them listen to them.' 'No, father Abraham,' he said, 'but if someone from the dead goes to them, they will repent.' He said to him, 'If they do not listen to Moses and the Prophets, they will not be convinced even if someone rises from the dead.'"(NIV) Jesus made it obvious to the reader of that passage that the pain in hell is enough to make a person cry out for one drop of water.

Jesus gave an even more stern warning when he told his disciples who they should fear. He was telling them not to fear the Pharisees and other enemies of Jesus, but to fear God; in the New Testament Book of Matthew, Chapter 10, Verses 24-28: "A student is not above his teacher, nor a servant above his master. It is enough for the student to be like his teacher, and the servant like his master. If the head of the house has been called Beelzebub, how much more the members of his household! So do not be afraid of them. There is nothing concealed that will not be disclosed, or hidden that will not be made known. What I tell you in the dark, speak in the daylight; what is whispered in your ear, proclaim from the roofs. Do not be afraid of those who kill the body but cannot kill the soul. Rather, be afraid of the One who can destroy both soul and body in hell."(NIV)

Lord Jesus Christ, in this last example of his warning that I will present here, used a parable to illustrate what he thinks of those who will not worship and obey him, in the New Testament Book of Luke, Chapter 19, Verses 12-27: "He said: 'A man of noble birth went to a distant country to have himself appointed king and then to return. So he called ten of his servants and gave them ten minas. 'Put this money to work,' he said, 'until I come back.' But his subject hated him and sent a delegation after him to say, 'We don't want this man to be our king.' He was made king, however, and returned home. Then he sent for the servants to whom he had given the money, in order to find out what they had gained with it. The first one came and said, 'Sir, your mina has earned ten more.' 'Well done, my good servant!' his master replied. 'Because you have been trustworthy in a very small matter, take charge of ten cities.' The second came and said, 'Sir, your mina has earned five more.' His master answered, 'You take charge of five cities.' Then another servant came and said, 'Sir, here is your mina; I have kept it laid away in a piece of cloth. I was afraid of you, because you are a hard man. You take out what you did not put in and reap what you did not sow.' His master replied, 'I will judge you by your own words, you wicked servant! You knew, did you, that I am a hard man, taking out what I did not put in, and reaping what I did not sow? Why then didn't you put my money on deposit, so that when I cam back, I could have collected it with interest?' Then he said to those standing by, 'Take his mina away from him and give it to the one who has ten minas.' 'Sir,' they said, 'he already has ten!' He replied, 'I tell you that to everyone who has, more will be given, but as for the one who has nothing, even what he has will be taken away. But those enemies of mine who did not want me to be king over them - bring them here and kill them in front of me.'"(NIV)

What Jesus is saying here, is that he has given life to all men. The minas could be compared to the knowledge of his holy nature that is imbedded in the subconscious mind of man, again, made obvious to the conscious mind through the medium of the conscience; in its primal form. Those who serve God by living for him, and worshiping him, will be rewarded. The ones who did nothing with their minas (Which can also be viewed as talents given to be used in service to Christ), because they did not want Christ to rule over them, so they suppressed the truth of Christ in the subconscious mind with ungodly living, are the ones who, when the king returns, will be treated like he said the king in the parable would treat his enemies; "bring them here and kill them in front of me." That phrase speaks of his commanding angels to cast men into hell forever; spiritual death, eternal damnation. Having the mina taken away, is synonymous with losing one's soul. So it is obvious to anyone reading these passages of the *Holy Bible*, that the belief that God is too loving to send anyone to hell is an absolute lie; fostered by the father of lies, the Devil. What then, will be the end of men like Jimmy Page and Robert Plant, who said in their song, "Most High," again, released in 1998, that Lord Jesus Christ speaks to the masses through a phony "crown," and promote Devil worship, however subtly and benign it comes across? Once again, Jesus said in Matthew, Chapter 12, Verse 36: "But I tell you that men will have to give account on the day of judgment for every careless word they have spoken."(NIV) Think about that for a moment. Can you imagine them standing before Christ on his throne, wearing his crown as King, and those two giving an account for what they said? The poor men will probably laugh loudly at what I have written here, but that laughter will be turned to tears when they realize the Devil played them for suckers, and they lose their eternal souls. Yes sir, the boy played with the rattlesnake over and over, disregarding his Father's warning, until the snake wrapped around him and poised to strike.

Lucifer said he was going to make himself like the Most High in the Old Testament Book of Isaiah (see Ch. Two). Robert Plant and Jimmy Page are his spiritual children. If they do not take heed to the warning of this book, they are going to spend eternity with him as well. Jesus spoke of people who would not have him as Lord over them being cast into hell, which was originally prepared for the Devil and his angels, in the New Testament Book of Matthew, Chapter 25, Verse 41, where he describes what he will say to them: "Depart from me, you who are cursed, into the eternal fire prepared for the devil and his angels." (NIV) Hell, you see, was created as the destination for the Devil and his angels. Why? Because they didn't want Christ as Lord over them either, as the quote from Isaiah in Chapter Two displays, so they tried to kill him; they failed. That warning is from the *Holy Bible*, and it applies to all men and women. Lord Jesus Christ did not present his teaching on hell to men as a variable, but as an absolute that will occur in the life of the one who rejects him and his righteousness to live a life of sin. Remember this my friend, love unjustly rejected turns to hatred.

The absolute truth has been placed in the human subconscious mind by its designer and creator, Lord Jesus Christ. He will hold all human beings accountable for what they do with it. Whether they accepted it or rejected it will be clearly seen on the day of judgement. Inherent in the absolute truth is the undeniable fact that the primal condition of the human conscience condemns homosexuality, non-monogamous heterosexuality, adultery, murder, stealing, and lying. The *Holy Bible* makes it clear that men need to seek the Lord for salvation; that it cannot be earned with a so-called "good life." Jesus stated emphatically that those who reject him and his moral code will be damned forever in hell. He also emphasized that those who repent of sin and follow him will be given the unearned gift of eternal life right from his hand. The teachings of the *Holy Bible* are congruent with the moral law imbedded in man's subconscious mind when he is born. The way he or she chooses to live, whether they sear their consciences and reprogram the subconscious to believe that wrong is right, or whether they choose to stick to the moral law in the conscience in its primal condition, are the first steps on the path to two different eternal destinies. Eternal damnation in hell, and eternal life in heaven, and those who are sent to each, have one Lord over them, Lord Jesus Christ, who will hold all men accountable for knowing and responding to his absolute truth; that he gave to all men and women born into this world. As the New Testament Book of Hebrews, Chapter 9, Verse 27, reads: "Just as man is destined to die once, and after that to face judgement, so Christ was sacrificed once to take away the sins of many people; and he will appear a second time, not to bear sin, but to bring salvation to those who are waiting for him."(NIV) The soul that repents and receives Christ as Lord and Savior, begins a life of communion that is described in the next chapter, titled, "Most High II: Spiritual Union With the Lord Most High."

1   Aleister Crowley, *The Equinox*, Vol. I, No.1, pg.19

2   Ronald Siegel, *Intoxication: Life in Pursuit of Artificial Paradise*

In the above photo, Led Zeppelin plays "In My Time of Dying." Plant mocks Christ in the song, saying Jesus will be responsible for his death. Near the end of the song, he rejoices that he has been redeemed by angels and taken to heaven. At the end of the song on the "Physical Graffiti" album, he tells Christ, "Don't!" to setting up his death bed. Twenty-one years after the above photo, Page and Plant, below, performing "Most High," are mocking Lord Jesus Christ once again, saying he is not the King of Kings; they sure have a big surprise coming.

3   Dr. Richard Restak, *Receptors*, pg.177

4   Aleister Crowley, *The Equinox*, Vol. I, No.1, pg.172

5   Ananda Metteya (Allan Bennett), *The Training of the Mind*, Aleister Crowley, *The Equinox*, Vol. I, No.5, pp.33-34

6   Dr. John MacArthur, *The Love of God*, Word Publishing, 1996, pp.14-15

Jimmy Page, one of the most powerful magicians to ever walk this planet, has turned many a rock fan into a hard core Led Zeppelin fan. The fan thinks that he or she got into Led Zeppelin, when the opposite is true. Led Zeppelin got into their heads and made them followers. As Page's reproduced *Goetia* says about one of its musical demonic spirits: "He bindeth or maketh any man subject unto the Magician if he so desire it." The music is to keep people from finding Christ. It is a hypnotic smokescreen designed to reprogram the mind about right and wrong and assist alcohol/ drugs in killing the pain of a life separated from God.

CHAPTER EIGHTEEN

"There is an unusual epitaph on a large headstone in a cemetery outside of New York City. The name of the person in the grave is not on the headstone. There is no mention of when the person was born or when he died. Nor does it indicate anything about the person's being a beloved mother, father, husband, wife, brother, sister, son, or daughter. Just one word stretches across the headstone: Forgiven. Clearly the most significant fact of this individual's life was the peace he or she knew as a result of God's forgiveness."

Dr. John MacArthur, "Alone With God"

"God loves believers with a particular love. It is a family love, the ultimate love of an eternal Father for His children. It is the consummate love of a Bridegroom for His bride. It is an eternal love that guarantees their salvation from sin and its ghastly penalty. That special love is reserved for believers alone."

Dr. John MacArthur Jr., "The Love of God"

"He who has My commandments and keeps them, it is he who loves Me. And he who loves Me will be loved by My Father, and I will love him and manifest Myself to him."

Lord Jesus Christ, John 14:21

"You will keep him in perfect peace, whose mind is stayed on You, because he trusts in You."

Isaiah 26:3

"I will give thanks to the LORD because of his righteousness and will sing praise to the name of the LORD Most High."

Psalm 7:17

MOST HIGH II:
SPIRITUAL UNION WITH THE LORD MOST HIGH

The soul that repents of the anti-Christ lifestyle and comes to God, Lord Jesus Christ, for salvation, receiving the free, unearned gift of eternal life, enters a relationship with God that the allows the person to live a life of peace and joy;

in the right environment. This relationship is based on love from God for the "newborn" believer, and his goal is to ground the new believer in that love in order that he or she may properly reciprocate it. If a person loves God, he or she wants to do what is pleasing in his sight. The objective of this chapter is to lay a foundational framework, based on the knowledge of the *Holy Bible*, which will guide the new believer in his or her goal of being pleasing to God; in an intimate spiritual relationship with him. Once a person is born again, God the Holy Spirit, the third person of the trinity, takes up residence in the mind of that person. He will take the knowledge gleaned from the study of the *Bible* and enlighten as well as strengthen the individual spiritually to the point of enabling that soul to live pleasing to God. The strength comes from God, and is his reward of studying the scriptures, and spending time in prayerful communion. To begin with, we will take a good look at who God is, and what his attributes are, which is essential in obtaining a clear picture of who we as human beings are dealing with. From that point we will look at who we are in his sight. As born again believers, we are his children, right from the moment of exercising faith in Christ, subsequent to the necessary repentance of sin. The newborn believer is God's adopted child in the abstract; meaning a child of God in position. From that point what the Lord desires to do is take the individual to the level of spiritual growth where he or she can live as a child of God in the empirical sense; that is, in practice during their everyday lives. A good analogy would be a soldier. A man is a soldier once he is enlisted. He is only a soldier in position. He goes to basic training to learn the basics of being a soldier in practice. Once the spiritual foundation is laid of knowing who God is, based on the knowledge of the *Bible*, in conjunction with understanding the reality of being a child of God in position and practice, the born again Christian can then live the joyful life of a child of God, and can sustain peace and happiness in his or her life through their relationship with God, irrespective of circumstances they have to deal with in this life.

ATTRIBUTES OF THE MOST HIGH

"To know God, and all that God has revealed about himself, is the highest pursuit of life." That statement was made by Dr. John MacArthur to his congregation, Grace Community Church, in Sun Valley, California. That is the most important thing the creation can do, is to find out all it can about its creator. The *Holy Bible* was written by God, through forty different men over a period of approximately sixteen hundred years for exactly that purpose. God wants us to know him. If one wants to know God and all that he is and does, then the *Bible* is the place to look. In the Old Testament Book of Proverbs, Chapter 2, Verses 1-5, we read these words that speak of seeking wisdom from the *Bible*: "My son, if you accept my words and store up my commands within you, turning your ear to wisdom and applying your heart to understanding, and if you call out for insight and cry aloud for understanding, and if you look for it as for silver and search for it as for hidden treasure, then you will understand the fear of the LORD and find the knowledge of God."(NIV) In this section we will look at five basic foundational truths about God, in order to obtain a better perspective of who he is.

The most important thing we all know about God is that he is first and foremost holy. There is no need to discuss this, as it is obvious. One thing that needs to be mentioned, however, is that as a holy creator, he desires that his creation be holy as well. In the Old Testament Book of Leviticus, Chapter 11, Verse 14, Moses wrote under the guidance of the Holy Spirit: "I am the Lord your God; consecrate yourselves and be holy, because I am holy."

The Apostle Peter, writing under the influence of the Holy Spirit, wrote about this statement to born again believers in his New Testament Book of Peter, Chapter 1, Verses 14-16: "As obedient children, do not conform to the evil desires you had when you lived in ignorance. But just as he who called you is holy, so be holy in all you do; for it is written: 'Be holy, because I am holy.'"(NIV) Christ is so holy, that he had to die on the cross to pay the price of sinners; to make it possible for them to have their sins paid for, before he could allow them to commune with him. As the creator is holy in all he does, he desires his followers to be holy as well, and he knows if they are.

Another powerful attribute of Lord Jesus Christ is his *"omniscience;"* meaning he knows everything. In the Old Testament, Psalm 147, Verse 5, we read: "Great is our Lord and mighty in power; his understanding has no limit."(NIV) In the Old Testament Book of 1 Samuel, Chapter 2, Verse 3, we read: "...for the Lord is a God who knows, and by him deeds are weighed."(NIV) God knows everything and does not need anyone to inform him of anything. He does not read the newspaper in the morning, because he doesn't need to. In the Old Testament Book of Isaiah, Chapter 40, Verses 13-14, the prophet Isaiah wrote: "Who has understood the mind of the LORD, or instructed him as his counselor? Whom did the LORD consult to enlighten him, and who taught him the right way?"(NIV) The Apostle Paul said the same thing in the New Testament Book of Romans, Chapter 11, Verses 33-34, making reference to the quote from Isaiah: "Oh, the depth of the riches of the wisdom and knowledge of God! How unsearchable his judgments, and his paths beyond tracing out! 'Who has known the mind of the Lord? Or who has been his counselor?'"(NIV) Lord Jesus Christ knows everything and everybody. It also means he knows everything about everybody. He said in the New Testament Book of Revelation, Chapter 2, Verse 23: "...I am he who searches hearts and minds."(NIV) We can hide our thoughts from one another, but not from God. Jesus even went to the extreme of telling men he knew how many hairs they had on their head, to emphasize how well he knew them. In the New Testament Book of Matthew,

Chapter 10, Verse 30, Jesus said: "And even the very hairs of your head are all numbered."(NIV) It is not that Jesus takes particular notice of how much hair a man has, it is just that he knows how much he has, and that was his point; to illustrate his all-knowing mind. There are no secrets held from Lord Jesus Christ. He knows where Jimmy Hoffa's corpse is, he knows who was involved in the murder of John F. Kennedy, and he knows who killed Nicole Brown Simpson; there is no escaping his knowledge. He sees what men do in the dark, when they think their deeds are hidden. Psalm 139, Verses 11-12, read: "If I say, 'Surely the darkness will hide me and the light become night around me,' even the darkness will not be dark to you; the night will shine like the day, for darkness is as light to you."(NIV) Whoever kill- ed Nicole Brown Simpson and Ronald Goldman in the dark, did not hide his deed. God knows who did it.

Even before men speak, Jesus knows what they will say. Psalm 139, Verse 4, reads: "Before a word is on my tongue you know it completely, O LORD."(NIV) In the knowledge of God there is the awareness of the needs of his children. In the New Testament Book of Matthew, Chapter 6, Verses 31-32, Jesus said: "So do not worry, saying, 'What shall we eat?' or 'What shall we drink?' or 'What shall we wear?' For the pagans run after all these things, and your heavenly Father knows that you need them."(NIV) The last point relative to the knowledge of God that will be presented here is the most sobering one of all. It is taken from the Old Testament Book of Ecclesiastes, Chapter 12, Verse 14: "For God will bring every deed into judgment, including every hidden thing, whether it is good or evil." Lord Jesus Christ's understanding is unlimited, he needs no counselor, he knows what is in the heart and mind of everyone, how many hairs are on your head, what goes on in the dark, he knows what we will speak before we say it, what his children need, and he will judge every secret deed, whether it be right or wrong.

The third attribute of God that we will look at, briefly, is his *"omnipresence,"* meaning he is everywhere. In the Old Testament Book of Jeremiah, Chapter 23, Verse 24, God asks the question: "Can anyone hide in secret places so that I cannot see him? Do not I fill heaven and earth?"(NIV) Psalm 139, Verses 7-10, reiterates the same idea, where David wrote: "Where can I go from your Spirit? Where can I flee from your presence? If I go up to the heavens, you are there; if I make my bed in the depths, you are there. If I rise on the wings of the dawn, if I settle on the far side of the sea, even there your hand will guide me, your right hand will hold me fast."(NIV) John MacArthur gave a practical application of this verse to Christians when he said: "In everything you do, realize he is there, and that alone will take over the direction of your paths. You see, living the Christian life is simply this, ordering my life as if it is done in the presence of God, knowing that it is." Lord Jesus Christ is present everywhere; which makes it futile for man to think that he does not know what he does, or that he can escape from him. For the Christian, it also means comfort, knowing that God is everywhere to look after him or her. In the New Testament Book of 1Peter, Chapter 5, Verse 7, the *Bible* makes it clear, where Peter encourages the born again Christian: "Cast all your anxiety on him because he cares for you."(NIV) God, therefore, is everywhere, and man is to be cognizant of it.

Another attribute of Lord Jesus Christ, and a fearful one, is his *"omnipotence,"* meaning he is all-powerful. In the Book of Revelation, Chapter 19, Verse 6, the *Bible* reveals a scene in heaven where God's redeemed people are praising him as all powerful: "Then I heard what sounded lie a great multitude, like the roar of rushing waters and like loud peals of thunder, shouting: 'Hallelujah! For our Lord God Almighty reigns.'"(NIV) Lord Jesus Christ referred to himself this way in Revelation, Chapter 1, Verse 8: "'I am the Alpha and the Omega,' says the Lord God, 'who is, and who was, and who is to come, the Almighty.'"(NIV) Genesis, Chapter 1, Verse 1, also clearly defines his power: "In the beginning God created the heavens and the earth."(NIV) The Old Testament Book of Isaiah tells us that God never gets tired, no matter what he does, and is able to provide strength to others, in Chapter 40, Verse 28: "Do you not know? Have you not heard? The LORD is the everlasting God, the Creator of the ends of the earth. He will not grow tired or weary, and his understanding no one can fathom. He gives strength to the weary and increases the power of the weak. Even youths grow tired and weary, and young men stumble and fall; but those who hope in the LORD will renew their strength. They will soar on wings like eagles; they will run and not grow weary, they will walk and not be faint."(NIV) If a person wants to meditate on God's power, Isaiah, Chapter 44, Verse 24, is a great place to refer to: "This is what the LORD says - your Redeemer, who formed you in the womb: I am the LORD, who has made all things, who alone stretched out the heavens, who spread out the earth by myself..."(NIV) For the born again Christian, this is a source of great comfort and confidence. It means that God will provide us with the strength we need to do anything necessary. It is made crystal clear in the New Testament Book of Philippians, Chapter 4, Verse 13, where Paul the Apostle wrote, referring to Lord Jesus Christ: "I can do everything through him who gives me strength."(NIV) An even more descriptive presentation of this concept of Jesus' power working in the Christian is given in the New Testament Book of Ephesians, Chapter 3, Verse 21: "Now to him who is able to do immeasurably more than all we ask or imagine, according to his power that is at work within us, to him be glory in the church and in Christ Jesus throughout all generations, for ever and ever! Amen."(NIV) Later in Ephesians, Chapter 6, Verses 10-12, Paul wrote: "Finally, be strong in the Lord and in his mighty power. Put on the full armor of God so that you can take your stand against the devil's schemes. For our struggle is not against flesh and blood, but against the rulers, against the authorities, against the powers of this dark world and against the spiritual forces of evil in the heavenly realms."(NIV) The spiritual forces of evil Paul speaks of are Satan's angelic host, whose main domain is in the air. Again, Paul wrote of this in Ephesians, Chapter 2, Verses 1-2, when he speaks to Christians about their former manner of life, prior to conversion to Biblical Christianity: "As for you, you were dead in your transgressions and sins, in which you used to live when you followed the ways of this world and of the ruler of the kingdom of the air, the spirit who is now at work in those who are disobedient."(NIV) Again, this is why Robert Plant makes reference to "Magick" ruling the sky at 2:48 into the song, "Ramble On," which is off the *Led Zeppelin II* album. Plant knows full well that Satan and his angelic host rule the sky around the earth. The Christian who follows Jesus is going to have to rely on the power of God in his life to resist the Devil; who wants to thwart the purpose of Christ in the life of his children. The power of God in the life of the born again Christian is a source of great confidence, telling him that he can live the Christian life; despite what the Devil tries to do to him, because, as the *Holy Bible* says to the believer in the New Testament Book of 1 John, Chapter 4, Verse 4, contrasting Christ and Satan: "...the one who is in you is greater than the one who is in the world."(NIV) Lord Jesus Christ, then, is all-powerful, and his power is particularly efficacious in the lives of his redeemed people. If you are a born again Christian, this is a cause for praise and worship.

So far, we have taken a brief look at Lord Jesus Christ's attributes of holiness, omniscience, omnipresence, and omnipotence. For a further treatise on them, I would encourage you to call the Dr. John MacArthur tape ministry, "Grace to You," at 1-800-55-GRACE and ask for a free catalog, as well as information on the eight tape series titled, "GOD, SATAN AND ANGELS." Born again Christians would do well to take my advice. You will learn far more about God's attributes, as well as Satan and angels, in those eight hours of instruction, than I have space to present here.

As far as intimacy with his people is concerned, God wants men and women who are born again to know that he relates to them not only as the supreme being, but as Father. This is his most important attribute, relationally. The Book of Isaiah, Chapter 9, Verse 6, speaks a prophecy of the coming Lord Jesus Christ, calling him the eternal Father, with regard to his relationship with his creation: "For unto us a child is born, to us a son is given, and the government will be on his shoulders. And he will be called Wonderful Counselor, Mighty God, Everlasting Father, Prince of Peace."(NIV) In order to illustrate his love for his children, Jesus spoke a parable in the New Testament Book of Luke, Chapter 15, Verses 11-24: "Jesus continued: 'There was a man who had two sons. The younger one said to his father, "Father, give me my share of the estate." So he divided his property between them. Not long after that, the younger son got together all he had, set off for a distant country and there squandered his wealth in wild living. After he had spent everything, there was a severe famine in that whole country, and he began to be in need. So he went and hired himself out to a citizen of that country, who sent him to his fields to feed pigs. He longed to fill his stomach with the pods that the pigs were eating, but no one gave him anything. When he came to his senses, he said, "How many of my father's hired men have food to spare, and here I am starving to death! I will set out and go back to my father and say to him: Father, I have sinned against heaven and against you. I am no longer worthy to be called your son; make me like one of your hired men." So he got up and went to his father. But while he was still a long way off, his father saw him and was filled with compassion for him; he ran to his son, threw his arms around him and kissed him. The son said to him, "Father, I have sinned against heaven and against you. I am no longer worthy to be called your son." But the father said to his servants, "Quick! Bring the best robe and put it on him. Put a ring on his finger and sandals on his feet. Bring the fattened calf and kill it. Let's have a feast and celebrate. For this son of mine was dead and is alive again; he was lost and is found." So they began to cele-brate.'"(NIV)

That parable tells the story of a loving father who rejoices when his lost children come back to him. It is called the parable of the Prodigal Son, but it is truly the parable of the Loving Father. The son repented of his wickedness and went back to his father, and his father, hearing his humble repentance, com-pletely accepted him with love and compassion. Lord Jesus Christ is much more interested in having a loving relationship with his children than he is in looking to chastise. He is patient with his children, gentle and humble in heart. An excel-lent treatise on this is presented in the John MacArthur 2-tape series entitled, *Enjoying the Presence of God.* For those of you who may have had a bad, or no father figure, you might have emotional scars that need to be healed. When I became a Christian, I had no practical idea of what a loving father was. I couldn't define the word father that way. I associated no good feelings with the word father; and believe me, I am being diplomatic about it. If a new Christian does not get the concept of God as a loving father set firmly in his mind, he will not be able to enjoy God's love the way it is meant to be. An excellent book has been written to help people with a bad concept associated with the idea of father in their minds. The name of the book is *Father Memories*: "How to discover the unique, powerful, and lasting impact your father has on your adult life and relationships," written by Randy L. Carlson (Moody Press, Chicago, 1992). When a Christian prays to God as Father, memories associated with the concept of father affect him or her emotionally. This book will help a person understand the distinction between God as father and the impact of the human father. It is excellent therapy for those who have negative feelings toward their fathers, or who were not raised properly by their fathers. It will help a person remove any negative connotations from the idea of "father."

OUR POSITION AS CHILDREN OF GOD

Having Lord Jesus Christ as our loving everlasting Father, we are his eternal children; as born again Christians. Being his children, one of the first things he wants us to learn is who we are in his sight, in the abstract, in position before him. As you read before, in John, Chapter 3, Verse 16, Jesus said: "For God so loved the world that he gave his one and only Son, that whoever believes in him shall not perish but have eternal life."(NIV) Lord Jesus Christ loves his children with a love that has no end. Paul the Apostle wrote of this to Christians in his New Testament Book of Romans, Chapter 8, Verses 35-39: "Who shall separate us from the love of Christ? Shall trouble or hardship or persecution or famine or nakedness or danger or sword? As it is written: 'For your sake we face death all day long; we are considered as sheep to be slaughtered.' No, in all these things we are more than conquerors through him who loved us. For I am convinced that neither death nor life, neither angels nor demons, neither the present nor the future, nor any powers; neither height nor depth, nor anything else in all creation, will be able to separate us from the love of God that is in Christ Jesus our Lord."(NIV) Nothing in existence can break the love of God for his children. In position, all of those who have accepted Lord Jesus Christ as savior are the recipients of his unconditional love; we are LOVED, pure and simple. It took longer than usual for him to get that through to me (thanks to angry fundamentalism), but I know it is true; God loves me with an infinite love as his child.

As a child of God, the born again believer is forgiven of all his sins; they have been sent to the cross, where Jesus paid the price for them. Not only did I have the problem of not knowing what a loving father was, which kept me from projecting the concept of a loving father to Christ in my understanding when I was first saved, but I did not fully understand that I was forgiven of my sins either. When I was first saved, instead of having my conscience healed from the difficulty of dealing with guilt from the past, I became involved with a group of individuals who were infected with what I choose to call "angry fundamentalism." I am not criticizing fundamentalists, but angry fundamentalism. This phrase is used to describe the mind frame of angry fundamentalist Christians who have such a hatred for sin, and are so caught up in their minds with a desire to condemn sin in any form, that when professional sinners like Tom Friend come in off the street, they can't minister to a person like that; they hate them. These people think that they worship Lord Jesus Christ, but the truth is, they worship his Mosaic Law. Leaving grace out of the picture, except for lip service, and grace for their buddies, angry fundamentalists project their sin to wicked sinners that they in fact hate. They will not admit it, but they hate sinners; who have rebelled against their true god, the moral code of the Ten Commandments. Christ is patient and loving and willing to forgive the repentant sinner, which is what he did with me. However, when certain aspects of my past came to light, I was treated as though I were a son of Satan himself. I know what Aleister Crowley felt toward this type of mentality when he was a boy. The difference between he and I is that I didn't project it to Christ himself; I rebelled against the mentality.

Professional sinners are despised because of their sinful past by angry fundamentalism. What happens in an atmosphere like that, which is constantly condemning sin, with Old Testament passages of God warning Israel of judgment on sin, is that the people lose sight of God's love for them, and they feel constantly guilty because of their inability to live a perfect sinless life. No Christian alive can do this. A Christian disciple does not sin to the degree or with the frequency that he did prior to his salvation, but he still sins. God just wants the Christian to confess it, get forgiveness and continue. In the New Testament Book of 1 John, Chapter 1, Verse 9, the *Bible* says: "If we confess our sins, he is faithful and just and will forgive us our sins and purify us from all unrighteousness." (NIV)

In the angry fundamentalism atmosphere, people don't focus on God's love, but at his anger toward sin. Again, Old Testament passages of God's warnings of impending judgment are favorite preaching passages with men who are preachers with this mentality. They just flat out hate sinners. What happens in this atmosphere is that people get trained to project their sin toward others. Instead of having love for others, the angry fundamentalist has self-righteousness to project to others. Struggling with guilt from the past, trying to survive in the angry fundamentalism atmosphere where my past was constantly criticized and looked down upon, I not only did not understand the love of God as a father, I did not understand his forgiveness either. I had no concept of myself as a child of God in position or practice. Like I was told by one individual before I went to the Bible College from which he had just graduated, "Don't think that you could get a girlfriend at the College because you are defiled." Can you believe I was dumb enough to go there? How could God love me? I was no longer a virgin! This attitude was consistently expressed to me. I had already been labeled a "Jesus freak" by many who knew me before I was saved, and now I was completely confused. This situation kept me from loving myself properly as well as forgiving myself for the life I lived before my conversion. These people really don't know what they are doing. They do more harm than good when they slander people who have come out of a professional sinful past. What is the result of that? The sinner is driven right back into his sin. No, they don't have to offer us their virgin daughters, but if a person is forgiven, tell them that by treating them that way instead of saying one thing from the pulpit and another in action (Jesus himself made sure that Mary Magdalene knew she was saved and forgiven.).

I have run into this mentality in several different states, not always directed at me, but it is easy for me to identify. Angry fundamentalists want to treat the rock culture with the moral code of the World War II generation. They use words like "Queers" and "Tramps" from the pulpit! They want sinners to think Christ loves them while they shoot them in the forehead verbally for being such wicked sinners. An angry fundamentalist will stand outside an abortion clinic with a sign calling it murder, and then will murder the reputation of anyone who has a child out of wedlock and then comes to church; even if it is years afterward. Think about the stupidity of what you just read. Sin can be preached against without making people think that God hates them; even if they are repentant. Yes, God hates sin, and he will cast the unrepentant sinner into hell, but if there is no love from God offered to the sinner, why in the world would he repent to join a crowd that will put him down? Isn't it the goodness of God that leads men to repentance?

Having lasted as long as I could in my own strength in angry fundamentalism, I realized I had to break from it or have a breakdown. As a result, I fell away from the "Christian faith" and my life was an even bigger disaster than it was prior to my salvation. Why was that? Because of the Abramelin demonic forces hot on my trail, and my living apart from faith, I had to fight the spiritual war in my own strength. What a joke that was. Actually it was very sad. Only through my collecting the tape volumes of Dr. John MacArthur in conjunction with the love of some real, non-angry fundamentalist and evangelical Christians, God was able to draw me back to himself and set me on the path of writing this book, concurrently, in the latter 1990's. I am truly not healed completely from it all, but I am on the right path once again. Never again will I patronize an angry fundamentalist atmosphere; because it only turns me into what I was before my conversion, an angry Irish Sicilian from the New York area, a former prince of juvenile delinquency, street fighter, and professional rebel against all corrupt authority. I don't engage in all those sins in that atmosphere, but I am sure an angry man in that atmosphere, and if I was to stay in it, I will only get angrier, which makes me one of them; in reverse fashion. In summation, angry fundamentalists will go to the grave as they were their entire lives, spiritual infants, never growing to maturity in Christ, if they are truly born again that is. In the New Testament Book of James, Chapter 4, Verses 11-12, the *Holy Bible* commands: "Brothers, do not slander one another. Anyone who speaks against his brother or judges him speaks against the law and judges it. When you judge the law, you are not keeping it, but sitting in judgment on it. There is only one Lawgiver and Judge, the one who is able to save and destroy. But you - who are you to judge your neighbor?"(NIV) I will avoid all who put me down - period.

It is wonderful to listen to a man like MacArthur, who is not only educated, something most angry fundamentalists lack (again, I am not against fundamentalists, just angry fundamentalism mentality), but he does not attack different denominations, or other men in the ministry who may disagree with him. He preaches the word, and he does it graciously, thank God. I recall him telling the story of a leader in the gay rights movement in California contracting AIDS, coming to his church and getting saved, and then returning to the homosexual culture with the message of hope. If the "queer" with AIDS had gone to some churches that I could name, and they found this out about him, they probably would have stoned the guy to death in the church parking lot. This crowd knows nothing about the love of Lord Jesus Christ; absolutely nothing.

I don't worship John MacArthur, but compared to angry fundamentalism, he is a gift from God. All angry fundamentalism produces is contemporary Pharisees, self-righteous guilt projecting hypocrisy, guilt-laden minds, and at the worst, men like Aleister Crowley, as you have already seen in this book. Once again, please understand that there is a difference between angry fundamentalists who hate sinners and fundamentalists who love sinners and want to see even the worst people in the world get saved, and will not hold their ungodly pasts against them. These people are REAL Christians.

To sum it up, my friend, as a born again Christian, you are completely forgiven by God for your past, and I charge you to avoid anyone who treats you as though you are not. I don't care if he has a *Bible* in his hand, is a Pastor of a church, etc. Irrespective of who they are, avoid them like the plague. That was not an uncanny choice of words, they are a plague toward sinners needing God's love. Ask God to direct you to a church that will help you realize not only in theory, but in practice, by their attitude, that people are forgiven for their past; and keep your sinful past to yourself. You would do well not to trust anyone with the knowledge of your sinful past except Jesus; and Christians who can relate. You can discuss it in general terms, but do not get specific about your past often, because the Devil will try to use it against you in the mind of the hypocrite who hears about it. Church is not like a military base that has guards at the gate allowing only those with military identification entrance, anyone who wants to can go in the door of the church, and there are those there who have no relationship with God whatsoever. They just go there to feel righteous, and they are looking to project the guilt of their sins to others. These unbelievers will die and go to hell. Woe to you if this type of person finds something out about you. They will set you up as a sacrificial lamb for their altar of projected guilt. As a film projector projects the image of the film on to a screen, so hypocrites project their guilt to someone they hear something "delicious" about. It is guilt projection. Avoid people who claim to be Christians and live this way. They will crucify you to feel better about themselves. One more thing about this, if the most respected people in the church are slander professionals, the church as a whole will follow suit. Satan's goal is to use this nonsense to destroy the love of God in your mind, as you focus upon this stupidity. Especially if many in your hometown are aware of your conversion to Christianity and are watching to see if it is genuine. Not only will the Devil destroy the love of God in your heart with these people, but the people watching to see if your new found religion is real will think you simply went through a phase, when they see you walk away from the "faith." Again, do not remain in an environment like this, it is not Christianity, it is religious nonsense. There are multitudes of real, genuine, loved filled Christians out there, and you have no time to waste with the self-righteous. I now attend a church that does not have this atmosphere. As a child of God, you are forgiven for your past sins, as well as all confessed sin in your Christian life; cased closed, no discussions. Angry fundamentalists cannot love themselves, or you.

The deadliest thing the Devil wants to do in your mind, if you fail to believe you are forgiven for your past, or are in the atmosphere just described, is to get you to hold bitterness against yourself for your sin, as opposed to going to God for forgiveness, and you will despise yourself emotionally, which will make you a guilt projector yourself! You will despise others if you do not forgive yourself. Lord Jesus Christ has no sympathy for this type of mentality. He has forgiven you for your sins, so you are not to try to be more righteous than he and hold a grudge against yourself. He warned the disciples about this in the New Testament Book of Matthew, Chapter 18, Verses 21-35:

"Then Peter came to Jesus and asked, 'Lord, how many times shall I forgive my brother when he sins against me? Up to seven times?' Jesus answered, 'I tell you, not seven times, but seventy-seven times. Therefore, the kingdom of heaven is like a king who wanted to settle accounts with his servants. As he began the settlement, a man who owed him ten thousand talents was brought to him. Since he was not able to pay, the master ordered that he and his wife and his children and all that he had be sold to repay the debt. The servant fell on his knees before him. "Be patient with me," he begged, "and I will pay back everything." The servant's master took pity on him, canceled the debt and let him go. But when that servant went out, he found one of his fellow servants who owed him a hundred denarii. He grabbed him and began to choke him. "Pay back what you owe me!" he demanded. His fellow servant fell to his knees and begged him, "Be patient with me, and I will pay you back." But he refused. Instead, he went off and had the man thrown into prison until he could pay the debt. When the other servants saw what had happened, they were greatly distressed and went and told their master everything that had happened. Then the master called the servant in. "You wicked servant," he said, "I canceled all that debt of yours because you begged me to. Shouldn't you have had mercy on your fellow servant just as I had on you?" In anger his master turned him over to the jailers to be tortured, until he should pay back all he owed. This is how my heavenly Father will treat each of you unless you forgive your brother from your heart.'"(NIV)

Lord Jesus Christ's point is this, the servant got forgiveness, but he refused to forgive himself, and he consequently refused to forgive others, and ended up in a state of torment. God will allow the Christian who does not forgive himself to go to this state of mind until he does forgives himself; enabling him to forgive others. There is no excuse for not forgiving yourself once God has forgiven you. An excellent book that deals with these types of emotional problems is titled, *Healing For Damaged Emotions*, by Dr. David Seamands (Victor Books, Wheaton, Illinois, 1988). It will help you to forgive yourself if you read this book and get a better understanding of the whole idea. Forgiveness of self enables one to forgive others, and to give them the love of God that he gives you.

Another perception the child of God is to have of himself is that he is precious to God. In the New Testament Book of Romans, Chapter 5, Verses 7-8, Paul wrote: "Very rarely will anyone die for a righteous man, though for a good man someone might possibly dare to die. But God demonstrates his own love for us in this: While we were still sinners, Christ died for us."(NIV) The born again child of God is so precious in his sight, that Jesus was willing to sacrifice himself to redeem him. Looking past the faults, Jesus saw the need for God, and provided it. All God's children are precious to him. Any atmosphere you are in that conveys a different message is one you need to leave. You are precious to God, born again believer, absolutely precious.

Being precious to God, Lord Jesus Christ has honored all his children by calling them his children. In the New Testament Book of 1 John, Chapter 3, Verses 1-2, the *Bible* teaches this very concept: "How great is the love the Father has lavished on us, that we should be called children of God! And that is what we are!"(NIV) As a child of God, you have been honored by Lord Jesus Christ with that title. You are chosen by God, and therefore loved, forgiven, precious, and honored.

As a chosen child of God, he has promised to make provision for you. In the New Testament Book of Philippians, Chapter 4, Verse 19, Paul wrote: "And my God will meet all your needs according to his glorious riches in Christ Jesus."(NIV) In Romans, Chapter 8, Verse 32, the *Bible* says: "He who did not spare his own Son, but gave him up for us all - how will he not also, along with him, graciously give us all things?"(NIV) As a child of God, you are loved, forgiven, precious, honored, and provided for.

God wants his children to live eternally with him. In the Book of 1 John, Chapter 5, Verse 13, we read: "I write these things to you who believe in the name of the Son of God so that you may know that you have eternal life."(NIV) Jesus made that truth obvious to his disciples just prior to his crucifixion, when he stated the following in John, Chapter 14, Verses 1-6: "'Do not let your hearts be troubled. Trust in God; trust also in me. In my Father's house are many rooms; if it were not so, I would have told you. I am going there to prepare a place for you. And if I go and prepare a place for you, I will come back and take you to be with me that you also may be where I am. You know the way to the place where I am going.' Thomas said to him, 'Lord, we don't know where you are going, so how can we know the way?' Jesus answered, 'I am the way and the truth and the life. No one comes to the Father except through me.'"(NIV) Jesus said he would return for his chosen in those statements. In the New Testament Book of 1 Thessalonians, Chapter 4, Verses 13-18, Paul wrote of the return of

Lord Jesus Christ: "Brothers, we do not want you to be ignorant about those who fall asleep, or to grieve like the rest of men, who have no hope. We believe that Jesus died and rose again and so we believe that God will bring with Jesus those who have fallen asleep in him. According to the Lord's own word, we tell you that we who are still alive, who are left till the coming of the Lord, will certainly not precede those who have fallen asleep. For the Lord himself will come down from heaven, with a loud command, with the voice of the archangel and with the trumpet call of God, and the dead in Christ will rise first. After that, we who are still alive and are left will be caught up together with them in the clouds to meet the Lord in the air. And so we will be with the Lord forever. Therefore encourage each other with these words."(NIV)

As a child of God, you are now an eternal being, and you will live forever in his glorious, painless presence. Having been made a child of God, receiving the gift of eternal life, you are now eternally secure. God did not put us on probation, he set us free from any fear of going to hell. In the Book of John, Chapter 6, Verses 37-40, Jesus made that clear: "All that the Father gives me will come to me, and whoever comes to me I will never drive away. For I have come down from heaven not to do my will but to do the will of him who sent me. And this is the will of him who sent me, that I shall lose none of all that he has given me, but raise them up at the last day. For my Father's will is that everyone who looks to the Son and believes in him shall have eternal life, and I will raise him up at the last day."(NIV) As a born again Christian, a child of God, you are completely loved by God, forgiven, precious, honored, provided for, eternal, and secure. This is cause for great happiness and worship of Lord Jesus Christ, thanking him for it all, in prayer. God loves to be praised and worshiped. He dispatches great joy and peace to the soul who does. Simply put, God will fill a Christian with his presence when they praise him, because he "inhabits praise." That is why he created us, inevitably, to worship and praise him; which is why he will destroy those who refuse to.

OUR PRACTICE AS CHILDREN OF GOD

The most important method of worshiping Lord Jesus Christ by the Christian is given to us in the Book of Romans, Chapter 12, Verses 1-2: "Therefore, I urge you, brothers, in view of God's mercy, to offer your bodies as living sacrifices, holy and pleasing to God - this is your spiritual act of worship. Do not conform any longer to the pattern of this world, but be transformed by the renewing of your mind. Then you will be able to test and approve what God's will is - his good, pleasing and perfect will."(NIV) When the *Bible* speaks of us presenting our bodies as living sacrifices, it means that we are to live our lives in the body to his glory. The only way we can do that is to be in constant communion with God, through the study of the *Bible* and prayer; as well as fellowship with other believers. First and foremost the new believer in Christ has to get to church; one that uses the *Bible* as its foundation for faith and practice. This is mandated in the New Testament Book of Hebrews, Chapter 10, Verse 25: "Let us not give up meeting together, as some are in the habit of doing, but let us encourage one another..."(NIV)

Lord Jesus Christ used an analogy of himself as a vine and his followers as branches in the Book of John, Chapter 15, Verses 1-8, to illustrate what it is to present your body and soul as a sacrifice to live for him. When you read the words, *"remain in me,"* he is speaking of staying in communion with God. Jesus said: "I am the vine, and my Father is the gardener. He cuts off every branch in me that bears no fruit, while every branch that does bear fruit he prunes so that it will be even more fruitful. You are already clean because of the word I have spoken to you. Remain in me, and I will remain in you. No branch can bear fruit by itself; it must remain in the vine. Neither can you bear fruit unless you remain in me. I am the vine; you are the branches. If a man remains in me and I in him, he will bear much fruit; apart from me you can do nothing. If anyone does not remain in me, he is like a branch that is thrown away and withers; such branches are picked up, thrown into the fire and burned. If you remain in me and my words remain in you, ask whatever you wish, and it will be given you. This is to my Father's glory, that you bear much fruit, showing yourselves to be my disciples."(NIV) The fruit that Jesus was referring to is fruit the Christian bears as he is empowered by the Holy Spirit. Paul wrote of this fruit manifested by the Christian as a result of communion with Christ in the New Testament Book of Galatians, Chapter 5, Verses 22-23. The *Bible* declares all these characteristics as the fruit of the Holy Spirit: "But the fruit of the Spirit is love, joy, peace, patience, kindness, goodness, faithfulness, gentleness and self-control. Against such things there is no law."(NIV) How does the Christian remain in Christ like a branch remains in a vine? How does a Christian remain in Christ in order to produce the fruit of the Holy Spirit in his life? The *Bible* speaks of this in the Book of Romans, Chapter 6, Verses 12-13: "Therefore do not let sin reign in your mortal body so that you obey its evil desires. Do not offer the parts of your body to sin, as instruments of wickedness, but rather offer yourselves to God, as those who have been brought from death to life; and offer the parts of your body to him as instruments of righteousness."(NIV) Again, in the text, the main reference is made to the body. Your body is not your mind. Your body produces physical desires, and it is up to your mind to determine whether or not to fulfill those desires. The person who communes with Christ is strengthened to the point of having the desires of the body neutralized. Your soul is your inner man in your mind, and the body is the outer man. The inner man is strengthened by Christ in order to be able to control the outer man. The person who does not have the spiritual strength provided by Christ, will eventually give in to physical desires; sinful or not. For example, to give in to the physical desire to have sexual intercourse with one's spouse is not sinful. To give in to sexual lust in any other context, though the body is all for it, is sin.

We are going to look at what I believe is the road map for the new Christian; which shows him the direction to take in order to win the victory over sin, which he did not have the ability to do prior to his conversion. Complete eradication of sin in a person's life does not take place until the body dies. In the New Testament Book of Ephesians, Chapter 3, Verses 14-21, Paul the Apostle shows the different characteristics of what communion with Christ produces (an extended treatise on this can be obtained from the four tape series by Dr. John MacArthur –*Turning On Spiritual Power*.): "For this reason I kneel before the Father, from whom his whole family in heaven and earth derives its name. I pray that out of his glorious riches he may strengthen you with power through his Spirit in your inner being, so that Christ may dwell in your hearts through faith. And I pray that you, being rooted and established in love, may have power, together with all the saints, to grasp how wide and long and high and deep is the love of Christ, and to know this love that surpasses knowledge - that you may be filled to the measure of all the fullness of God."(NIV) The first thing Paul said he would pray for, to the believer's benefit, was that they should be strengthened with power in their inner being, meaning the soul. The inner being has to be strengthened spiritually in order to neutralize the sinful desires of the outer man, the body. Jesus himself warned his disciples of this just before his arrest in the Garden of Gethsemane, recorded in the Book of Matthew, Chapter 26, Verse 41: "Watch and pray so that you will not fall into temptation. The spirit is willing, but the body is weak."(NIV) The body is strong in the area of sinful desire, but it is weak in assisting a person in his desire to obey God. What Jesus is intimating here, is that prayer, which is communion with God, strengthens a man spiritually.

Along with prayer, the study of the *Holy Bible* is essential to spiritual growth. The Holy Spirit enables the Christian to understand the *Bible*. Jesus said in John, Chapter 15, Verse 7: "If you remain in me and my words remain in you, ask whatever you wish, and it will be given you."(NIV) When Jesus speaks of his "words" in that verse, he means the *Bible*. In the New Testament Book of Colossians, Chapter 3, Verse 16, Paul wrote of this very concept: "Let the word of Christ dwell in you richly as you teach and admonish one another with all wisdom, and as you sing psalms, hymns and spiritual songs with gratitude in your hearts to God."(NIV)

To sum it up, the *Bible* is teaching us that when we devote ourselves to prayer and study of the Bible, with the guidance of the Holy Spirit as born again Christians, we are strengthened spiritually in the inner being; which enables us to be free from the sinful desires and walk consistently with Christ in communion with him. Again, the Book of Galatians, Chapter 5, Verse 16, presents this idea: "So I say, live by the Spirit, and you will not gratify the desires of the sinful nature."(NIV) So, as we commune with God and read his word, the Holy Spirit strengthens us spiritually to be free from sin. What happens as a result of this is that Christ will "dwell" in the heart of the disciple. If we do not commune with God in prayer and *Bible* study, the sinful desires of the fleshly body dominate the mind of the Christian; that is why Christ warned his disciples to remain in prayer. Paul the Apostle defined this struggle with the sinful nature in Romans, Chapter 7, Verses 15-25, where he, from personal experience, explains what happens in the mind affected by the sin nature; without spiritual strength from the Holy Spirit: "I do not understand what I do. For what I want to do I do not do, but what I hate I do. And if I do what I do not want to do, I agree that the law is good. As it is, it is no longer I myself who do it, but it is sin living in me. I know that nothing good lives in me, that is, in my sinful nature. For I have the desire to do what is good, but I cannot carry it out. For what I do is not the good I want to do; no, the evil I do not want to do - this I keep on doing. Now if I do what I do not want to do, it is no longer I who do it, but it is sin living in me that does it. So I find this law at work: When I want to do good, evil is right there with me. For in my inner being I delight in God's law; but I see another law at work in the members of my body, waging war against the law of my mind and making me a prisoner of the law of sin at work within my members. What a wretched man I am! Who will rescue me from this body of death? Thanks be to God - through Jesus Christ our Lord!"(NIV) In the continuation of this passage, which takes place in the beginning of Romans, Chapter 8, Verses 1-6, Paul makes it clear that God will deliver him from the tyranny of sin's effect in his life through the Holy Spirit, who was given to us as a result of Jesus death on the cross to pay for our sins: "Therefore, there is now no condemnation for those who are in Christ Jesus, because through Christ Jesus the law of the Spirit of life set me free from the law of sin and death. For what the law was powerless to do in that it was weakened by the sinful nature, God did by sending his own Son in the likeness of sinful man to be a sin offering. And so he condemned sin in sinful man, in order that the righteous requirements of the law might be fully met in us, who do not live according to the sinful nature but according to the Spirit. Those who live according to the sinful nature have their minds set on what that nature desires; but those who live in accordance with the Spirit have their minds set on what the Spirit desires. The mind of sinful man is death, but the mind controlled by the Spirit is life and peace..."(NIV) So the Christian who has his inner being strengthened by the Holy Spirit is set up for Jesus to "dwell" in his heart. The word dwell in this passage of Ephesians, 3:14-21, does not mean to be there, it means to be comfortable there. The Greek rendering (the original New Testament was written in Greek) of the word "dwell" in that passage is the words *"Katoi Kesai."* It means that Christ is comfortable and settled down in the heart of the Christian with constant communion. He is there even when the communion is not taking place; even when a Christian sins and breaks off communion with God. Christ is comfortable in the heart of the disciple who is in constant communion with him; which is the reward of being strengthened by the Spirit in the inner being, through prayer and the study of the *Bible*. The reward of Christ being at home, or comfortable in the heart of the believer, is that he or she is rooted in love for God. Once the Christian becomes rooted and grounded in loving communion with Lord Jesus Christ, experiencing his intoxicating spiritual presence over and over again, he is then able to: "...grasp how wide and long and high and deep is the love of Christ, and to know this love that surpasses knowledge - that you may be filled to the measure of all the fullness of God." The born again believer, then, who studies the Word of God, the *Bible*, and is disciplined in prayer, is going to be strengthened with power by the Holy Spirit in his inner being, enabling him to live free from the misery of the sinful nature's domination, which then allows him to be rooted in loving communion with Lord Jesus Christ, which enables him to fully fathom the love of God, and then to know this love on a continuous basis, which allows him to be filled with the fullness of God. This is something that I could never know as a disciple of Led Zeppelin and the rock culture, i.e. Satan himself. All that produces is stupefaction.

The born again Christian, who has the spiritual foundation laid down of knowing who God is, as a result of the study of the *Holy Bible*, as well as understanding his own position as a child of God, along with how to live as a child of God in practice, will then be fully equipped and capable of living a life of loving communion with the Lord Jesus Christ; filled with his intoxicating presence, love, joy, and peace. The *Bible* shows the student that God is first and foremost holy. His attributes of omniscience (all-knowing), omnipresence (everywhere-present), omnipotence (all-powerful), and being the eternal Father, are exclusive to him. He redeems his chosen and sets them up in position before him as chosen, loved, precious, forgiven, accepted, honored, provided for, eternal, and secure. In practice, he strengthens the disciple's inner being through prayer and study of the *Bible*, so he or she can live free from the misery of the domination of the sinful nature, showing them to be children of God to the world. My hope in writing this book, is not only for Led Zeppelin fans, as well as the surviving members of the band, but for all who want to know the truth of who the Most High is and to unite with him, to read this book, and face its reality, so they can repent of their sin and the anti-Christ mentality of this world and come to God, and receive the free, unearned gift of eternal life, in order to be allowed to enter a relationship with him that will last forever, filling them with peace, joy, and honor that can only come from the Prince of Peace, El Shaddai, Lord God Almighty, Lord Jesus Christ - the true "Most High."